THE EVOLUTION OF MANAGEMENT THOUGHT

Sixth Edition

DANIEL A. WREN

The University of Oklahoma

and

ARTHUR G. BEDEIAN

Louisiana State University and A&M College

WILEY

JOHN WILEY & SONS, INC.

PUBLISHER	George Hoffman
EXECUTIVE EDITOR	Lise Johnson
ASSISTANT EDITOR	Carissa Marker Doshi
MARKETING MANAGER	Carly DeCandia
DESIGN DIRECTOR	Harry Nolan
SENIOR DESIGNER	Kevin Murphy
SENIOR PRODUCTION EDITOR	Patricia McFadden
SENIOR MEDIA EDITOR	Daniel Haag
PRODUCTION MANAGEMENT SERVICES	Pine Tree Composition

This book was set in 10 pt. Minon Regular by Laserwords Private Limited, Chennai, India and was printed and bound by Courier/Westford. The cover was printed by Courier/Westford.

This book is printed on acid-free paper. ∞

To order books or for customer service please, call 1-800-CALL WILEY (225-5945).

ISBN-13: 978-0-470-12897-8

Printed in the United States of America

10 9 8 7 6 5 4

Dedication

To Leon, Maude, and Karen
my links with the past;
To Jonathan, Laura, and Lynda;
and to another generation,
Karen Nicole, Tanner Ray, and Ethan Daniel
my links with the future.

To Varsenick and Arthur Bedeian
for reasons lost to history;
To Lynda, Katherine, and TAB
for every reason;
To Anna-Kennon, Kate McGee, and Laura Gabrielle
for making me so very happy.

Brief Contents

Contents

The Railroads: Pioneering in U.S. Management 83

Summary 93

Chapter 6

■ Industrial Growth and Systematic Management 95

The Growth of U.S. Enterprise 95

The Renaissance of Systematic Management 99

Big Business and Its Changing Environment 107

Summary of Part I 115

Chapter 9

THE HUMAN FACTOR:
PREPARING THE WAY 189

About the Authors

D aniel A. Wren, PhD, the University of Illinois, is David Ross Boyd, Professor of Management Emeritus and Curator of the Harry W. Bass Business History Collection at the University of Oklahoma. He has served as president of the Southern Management Association, as chairman of the Management History Division of the Academy of Management, is a Fellow of the Southern Management Association, and a Fellow of the Academy of Management. He has been honored with the Merrick Foundation Award for teaching excellence and the Distinguished Educator Award from the National Academy of Management for his contributions "as the foremost management historian of his generation." His research has appeared in numerous scholarly journals, and he is the author of *White Collar Hobo: The Travels of Whiting Williams* (Iowa State University Press) and, with Ronald Greenwood, coauthor of *Management Innovators: The People and Ideas that have Shaped Modern Business* (Oxford University Press).

Arthur G. Bedeian, DBA, is a Boyd Professor and the Ralph and Kacoo Olinde Distinguished Professor of Management at Louisiana State University and A&M College. A past president of the Academy of Management and former dean of the Academy's Fellows Group, he has also served as president of the Foundation for Administrative Research, the Allied Southern Business Association, the Southern Management Association, and the Southeastern Institute for Decision Sciences. He is a Fellow of both the Southern Management Association and the International Academy of Management. He is a recipient of the Academy of Management's Distinguished Service Award, Ronald G. Greenwood Lifetime Achievement Award, and Richard M. Hodgetts Distinguished Career Award. A former editor of the *Journal of Management*, he has served on the editorial boards of the *Academy of Management Review*, *Journal of Applied Psychology*, *Organizational Research Methods*, *Journal of Management History*, *Management & Organizational History*, and *Academy of Management Learning and Education*, among others.

Preface

O ur interest in the evolution of management thought has persisted throughout our professional careers. Over this time, we have come to more fully appreciate that everything about the management discipline—its language, its theories, its models, and its methodologies, not to mention its implicit values, its professional institutions, and its scholarly ways—comes from its inherited past. Unfortunately, this past sometimes escapes those anxious to take credit for being the first to make a discovery but find instead that others have traveled the same intellectual byways. History may not repeat itself, but it does provide a baseline for evaluating the significance of new theories and techniques, as well as a means for appreciating the evolution of management thought across time and the enduring contributions of our discipline's leading thinkers.

Like its predecessors, *The Evolution of Management Thought*, sixth edition, places the people and ideas that comprise the management discipline's intellectual heritage within a chronological framework. Each of its four major parts can stand alone, if that is desired; substantial cross-referencing provides coherence and a central unifying theme. This format allows considerable latitude in scheduling class assignments, as well as determining course coverage. In preparing this new edition, our purpose was to refresh the old, retaining the valuable lessons it offers, and to incorporate insights from more recent research. The past exists in a reciprocal relationship with the present such that present management applications are quite literally what the past has made them. Writing management history is thus a task that is never complete.

Every chapter in this edition has been thoroughly reviewed and updated to convey an appreciation of the people and ideas underlying the evolution of management theory and practice. Our intent is to get the history right and to place various theories of management in their historical context, showing how they changed as times changed.

As with previous editions, we have tried to make the present volume an unfolding story about the lives and the times of those who are our intellectual predecessors. These men and women have bequeathed us a heritage that management scholars unfamiliar with the past often take for granted, frequently do not acknowledge, and sometimes reject because they do not think yesterday's solutions have any practical value for today's problems. Our predecessors, however, were very much as we are: they were attempting to cope with the manifold problems of managing mass assemblages of human and physical resources; they were trying to develop philosophies and theories about human behavior; they were agents for change; and they were struggling with the age-old problems of allocating scarce resources to meet the goals and desires of organizations and people. Our challenges today are basically the same, only the proposed solutions have changed as we have learned more, as we have sharpened our diagnostic tools, and as cultural values have changed.

The continuing interest of scholars who care about the evolution of management thought and the students who find value in the lessons history provides made this edition possible. The research and presentations of our colleagues in the Management History Division of the Academy of Management, the renaissance of the *Journal of Management History*, and the appearance of the new journal, *Management & Organizational History*, are reassuring signs that this interest is growing. Some of those who pushed management history into the limelight as a scholarly endeavor and from whom we learned so much are deceased, but not forgotten. In particular, we wish to remember Claude George, John Mee, Dick Whiting, Jerry Arnold, Ron Greenwood, Jim Worthy, Dick Hodgetts, and Al Bolton. Their insights and enthusiasm will never be forgotten. Still among us are those who realize the value of understanding management history and who continue to assist in developing new generations of management scholars who appreciate our common intellectual heritage. We are indebted to all of them.

We are especially grateful to Regina Greenwood and Julia Teahen for developing PowerPoint slides to accompany this new edition. Their slides feature photographs, charts, and other visual material that enliven the text material. We would also like to thank Shannon G. Taylor who provided many useful comments and suggestions. Credits for reproduced photographs are attributed to their appropriate sources, but special thanks go to Kerry Magruder for his electronic magic in bringing these images to print.

At John Wiley & Sons we wish to express our appreciation to Carissa Doshi, Assistant Editor, and Trish McFadden, Production Editor, who cheerfully saw this project through its various stages from manuscript to print. Sunitha Arun Bhaskar, at Pine Tree Composition, provided valuable assistance throughout. We thank Karen Slaght for her skillful copy editing.

We particularly appreciate the suggestions and encouragement of the many people who have used previous editions of *The Evolution of Management Thought* in the classroom and in their own research. As a true history is never complete, we would welcome being told of any discrepancies in the following pages, as well as receiving additional information or materials that might be incorporated into a future edition.

Daniel A. Wren

Norman, Oklahoma

August 5, 2008

Arthur G. Bedeian

Baton Rouge, Louisiana

August 5, 2008

Early Management Thought

P art I covers a wide span of time and traces developments in management thought up to the scientific
management era in the United States. After a brief
introduction to the role of management in organizations, this
part examines examples of very early management thought
and then demonstrates how changes in economic, social,
and political environments set the stage for the Industrial
Revolution. This revolution created certain management
problems in the embryonic factory system and led to the
need for a formal study of management. The genesis of
modern management thought is found in the work of early
pioneers who sought to solve the problems created by the
factory system. Part I concludes by tracing this genesis of
management thought to the United States and examining
early experiences with the factory, some early management
writers, and the cultural environment of the United States
before the scientific management era.

CHAPTER

1

A Prologue to the Past

The practice of management is ancient, but formal study of the body of management knowledge is relatively new. Management is essential to organized endeavors. For a broad working definition, let us view management as an activity that performs certain functions to obtain the effective acquisition, allocation, and utilization of human efforts and physical resources to accomplish some goal. Management thought, then, is the existing body of knowledge about the activity of management and its functions, purpose, and scope.

The purpose of this study is to trace the significant periods in the evolution of management thought from its earliest informal days to the present. The study of management, like the study of people and their cultures, is an unfolding story of changing ideas about the nature of work, the nature of human beings, and the functioning of organizations. The methodology of this study of management will be analytic, synthetic, and interdisciplinary. It will be analytic in examining people who made significant contributions, their backgrounds, their ideas, and their influence. It will be synthetic in examining trends, movements, and environmental forces that furnish a conceptual framework for understanding individuals and their approaches to the solution of management problems. It will be interdisciplinary in the sense that it includes—but moves beyond—traditional management writings to draw on economic history, sociology, psychology, social history, political science, and cultural anthropology to place management thought in a cultural and historical perspective. The objective is to place management thought in the context of its cultural environment and thereby to understand not only what management thought was and is, but also to explain why it developed as it did.

We should study the past to illuminate the present, but management history as a separate area of study is generally neglected in most schools of business administration. A smattering of history is taught at various levels, but the area generally lacks depth, direction, and unity. Henry Wadsworth Longfellow said, "Let the dead past bury its dead," but there is much to be said for resurrection. We live and study in an age represented by a diversity of approaches to management. Students are presented with quantitative, behavioral, functional, and other approaches in their various courses. Although such a variety of intellectual inputs may be stimulating, it typically leaves students with a fragmented picture of management and assumes that they have the ability to integrate these various ideas for themselves.

In many cases, this burden is far too great. A study of evolving management thought can present the origins of ideas and approaches, trace their development, grant some perspective in terms of the cultural environment, and thus provide a conceptual framework that will enhance the process of integration. A study of the past contributes to a more logical, coherent picture of the present. Without a knowledge of history, individuals have only their own limited experiences as a basis for thought and action. As one scholar commented, "[History] is the universal experience—definitely longer, wider, and more varied than any individual's experience."[1] History should therefore equip perceptive people with additional alternatives and answers to build into their decision-making models. Lawrence distinguishes between historical research (inquiry into past persons and events) and historical perspective (using history as raw material for understanding the present). The object of historical perspective is to "sharpen one's vision of the present, not the past. . . . It pushes thinking about alternative explanations for phenomena, helps identify more or less stable concepts, and expands research horizons by suggesting new ways of studying old questions."[2] Smith noted, "Reading, exploring, and discussing history can provide students with opportunities to acquire knowledge of their field and its practices, gain wisdom, and develop and use judgment."[3] Present pedagogy can be improved, knowledge expanded, and insights gained by examining the lives and labors of management's intellectual progenitors. Theory, a legitimate goal in any discipline, is based on the warp and woof of individuals' ideas in the fabric of management. By tracing the origin and development of modern management concepts, we can better understand the analytical and conceptual tools of our trade. In understanding the growth and development of large-scale enterprise, the dynamics of technology, the ebb and flow of cultural values, and the changing assumptions about the nature and nurture of people, we can better equip young men and women with the skills and attitudes they need to prepare themselves for future positions of responsibility.

Today is not like yesterday, nor will tomorrow be like today; yet today is a synergism of all our yesterdays, and tomorrow will be the same. Mark Twain said

---

1. B. H. Liddell Hart, *Why Don't We Learn From History?* (London: George Allen and Unwin, 1972), p. 15.

2. Barbara S. Lawrence, "Historical Perspective: Using the Past to Study the Present," *Academy of Management Review* 9 (April 1984), pp. 307, 311.

3. George E. Smith, "Management History and Historical Context: Potential Benefits of Its Inclusion in the Management Curriculum," *Academy of Management Learning & Education*, 6 (December 2007), p. 524.

that history may not repeat itself, "but sometimes it rhymes."[4] There are many lessons in history for management scholars; the important one is the study of the past as prologue.

A CULTURAL FRAMEWORK

How have our concepts of managing organizations evolved throughout history? To understand this evolution, this dynamic process of change and growth, we need to establish a cultural framework of analysis for the evolution of management thought. Management is not a closed-end activity because managers operate organizations and make decisions within a given set of cultural values and institutions. Thus management has open-system characteristics in that managers affect their environment and in turn are affected by it.

Culture is our total community heritage of nonbiological, humanly transmitted traits and includes the economic, social, and political forms of behavior associated with the human race. Culture is a very broad subject, so this study is limited to those specific economic, social, political, and technological ideas that influence the job of managing an organization. Human behavior is a product of past and present cultural forces, and the discipline of management is also a product of the economic, social, political, and technological forces of the past and present. As Bedeian has observed, "past arrangements—institutions, roles, cultural forms—are not simply superseded, but transformed and recombined to produce the present. In this sense, the past repeatedly informs and reinforms the present such that the search for understanding is never finished."[5] Modern individuals examine present organizations and read contemporary authors, yet they have little appreciation of the background of our technology, political bodies, or arrangements for the allocation of resources. Management thought did not develop in a cultural vacuum; managers have always found their jobs affected by the existing culture.

In the study of modern management, the past must be examined to see how our communal heritage was established. The elements of our culture were previously described as economic, social, political, and technological. In practice, these elements are closely interrelated and interact to form the total culture; they are separated here and throughout the following pages only for ease of presentation. Here our attention shall be confined to the portions of our culture that apply most directly to management, omitting other cultural phenomena, such as art, music, and so on.

---

4. Mark Twain, quoted by Thomas K. McGraw, "Why History Matters to Managers," *Harvard Business Review* 64 (January–February 1986), p. 83.

5. Arthur G. Bedeian, "Exploring the Past," *Journal of Management History* 4 (1998), p. 4. See also Arthur G. Bedeian, "The Gift of Professional Maturity," *Academy of Management Learning and Education* 3 (2004), pp. 92–98.

THE ECONOMIC FACET

The economic facet of culture is the relationship of people to resources. Resources may be created by humans or nature; the term denotes as well both tangible objects and intangible efforts that can be utilized to achieve some stated end. Physical resources include land, buildings, raw materials, semifinished products, tools, and equipment or other tangible objects used by people and organizations. Technology, our understanding of the art and applied science of making and using tools and equipment, advances at different rates and influences how resources are used at any given time in history.

Human thought and effort are also resources because they design, assemble, shape, and perform other activities that result in the production of some product or service. Every society has the economic problem of a scarcity of resources and a multiplicity of economic ends. The mobilization of these scarce resources to produce and distribute products, services, and satisfaction has taken a variety of forms throughout history. Heilbroner characterized these methods of allocating resources as by tradition, by command, and by the market.[6] The traditional method operates on past societal precepts; technology is essentially static, occupations are passed down from one generation to the next, agriculture predominates over industry, and the social and economic systems remain essentially closed to change. The command method is the imposition of the will of some central person or agency on the rest of the economy to determine how resources are allocated and utilized. The economic commander-in-chief may be the monarch, the fascist dictator, or the collectivist central planning agency. What is to be produced, what prices and wages will be, and how economic goods and services are to be distributed are decisions made by some central source. The market method, which Heilbroner noted as a relatively recent phenomenon, relies on an impersonal network of forces and decisions to allocate resources. Prices, wages, and interest rates are set by a bargaining process between those who have the product or service and those who want it; all resources flow to their best reward, and no central agency nor prior precepts need to intervene. In actual practice, modern societies display a mixture of the elements of tradition, command, and the market. Much of our total cultural heritage has been influenced by tradition and command as the predominant economic philosophies. However, we will see later that the market philosophy created the need for the formal, systematic development of a body of management thought. In brief, the state of technology and the source of decisions about the societal allocation of resources have a large bearing on how managers go about their jobs. A tradition-directed economy circumscribes the role of the manager with prior precepts; the command orientation makes the manager an executor of central decisions; but the market system opens the way to the innovative utilization of resources to meet a multiplicity of ends.

---

6. Robert L. Heilbroner, *The Making of Economic Society* (Englewood Cliffs, NJ: Prentice Hall, 1962), pp. 10–16.

THE SOCIAL FACET

The social facet refers to the relationship of people to other people in a given culture. Humans do not live alone but find advantages in forming groups for mutual survival or for furthering personal goals. In forming groups, the initial input is a variety of people of differing needs, abilities, and values. Out of this heterogeneity, some homogeneity must evolve or the group will not survive. Thus all participants form a "contract," which encompasses some common rules and agreements about how to behave to preserve the group. The unwritten but nevertheless binding contract defines assumptions about the behavior of others and expectations about the reciprocal treatment of the individual. It includes some agreement about how best to combine and coordinate efforts to accomplish a given task, be it the making of an economic product or achieving the satisfaction of social fellowship.

Values, or cultural standards of conduct defining the propriety of a given type of behavior, are another part of social interactions. Thus ethics in interpersonal relations is an age-old problem. Economic transactions, deeply imbedded in social trust, are an integral part of a societal contract. Values shift from one time period to another and from one culture to another. Managerial efforts are affected by the relationships between individuals and the group and by the social values prevailing in the culture.

THE POLITICAL FACET

The political part of culture is the relation of the individual to the state and includes the legal and political arrangements for the establishment of social order and for the protection of life and property. The absence of state and order is anarchy; unless there is some provision for protection of rational beings from irrational ones, the result is total economic, social, and political chaos. Where order begins, anarchy ends. Political institutions that bring order and stability take a variety of forms, ranging from representative government to a monarchy or dictatorship. Political assumptions about the nature of humankind range from one end of the continuum, self-governing people, to the other extreme position, direction from one person or a ruling body at the top, which imposes its will on others based on the assumption that people cannot, or will not, govern themselves. Provisions for property, contracts, and justice are also key concepts in the political aspect of cultures. In a democracy, people typically have the right of private property, the freedom to enter or not to enter into contracts, and an appeal system for justice. Under a dictatorship or monarchy, the right to hold and use private property is severely restricted, the right to contract is limited, and the system of justice depends on the whims of those in power. The cultural role of management is affected by the form of government, by the power to hold or not hold property, by the ability to engage in contracts for the production and distribution of goods, and by the appeal mechanism available to redress grievances.

THE TECHNOLOGICAL FACET

Technology is the art and applied science of making tools and equipment. Historians refer to past eons such as the Stone Age, the Iron Age, and the Bronze Age when humans made tools of these materials to use for various purposes. Since this primitive past, technology has been advancing for thousands of years, sometimes rapidly, sometimes more slowly, and proceeding at a different pace in various cultures.

Technology is a means to an end, which can produce beneficial as well as detrimental results. Landes has warned

> that the wrestling and exploitation of knowledge are perilous acts, but man must and will know, and once knowing, will not forget ... the marriage of science and technology are the climax of millennia of intellectual advance. They have also been an enormous force of good and evil, and there have been moments when the evil has far outweighed the good. Still, the march of knowledge and technique continues....[7]

It is this progress that has moved us from labor-intensive to capital-intensive to knowledge-intensive possibilities for industry and trade.

Technology often does not advance in tradition-bound or closed societies because it threatens the status quo. Kieser has written of medieval guilds, which kept

> production and selling conditions for all members to be as equal as possible. No [guild] master should be able to gain an advantage at the expense of his co-masters ... the master was only allowed to employ a restricted number of journeymen ... and he was not allowed to choose these men himself.... Wages and working hours were uniformly regulated. The pursuit of customers was strictly forbidden.... Innovations were suppressed.[8]

Clinging to past precepts provides no incentive to seek new knowledge, to explore, nor to experiment. Science and technology cannot advance without education, the freedom of inquiry, and the encouragement of risk taking.

Culture makes a difference, and we will see examples of how technology affects the economic, social, and political facets of human existence. By applying science in an artful manner, we have the potential of influencing all facets of our culture. In his inaugural address in 1790, America's first president, George Washington, said,

---

7. David S. Landes, *The Unbound Prometheus* (Cambridge: The University Press, 1969), p. 555. For a global perspective, see David S. Landes, *The Wealth and Poverty of Nations: Why Some Are So Rich and Some So Poor* (New York: W. W. Norton), 1998.

8. Alfred Kieser, "Organizational, Institutional, and Societal Evolution: Medieval Craft Guilds and the Genesis of Formal Organizations," *Administrative Science Quarterly* 34 (1989), p. 553.

"Knowledge is in every country the surest basis of public happiness." This quest for knowledge is never ending, impelling us to learn, to do better, to live better.

Interacting to form any culture, the economic, social, political, and technological facets are useful tools of analysis for examining the evolution of management thought. Managers are affected by their cultural environment, and the ways in which they allocate and utilize resources have evolved within the changing views about economic, social, and political institutions and values and technological know-how.

PEOPLE, MANAGEMENT, AND ORGANIZATIONS

From this introduction to the cultural environment of management, let us turn more specifically to the basic elements of our study. Even before people began to record their activities, they encountered the necessity of managing their efforts in cooperative endeavors. As an overview, Figure 1-1 begins with the state of nature and traces the quest for needs satisfaction through organizations. Management, an activity essential to organized endeavors, facilitates the operation of organizations to satisfy the needs of people.

FIGURE 1-1	PEOPLE, MANAGEMENT, AND ORGANIZATIONS

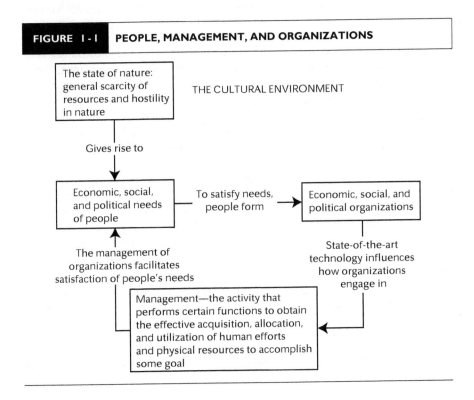

THE HUMAN BEING

The human being is the fundamental unit of analysis in the study of humankind, the study of organizations, and the study of management. Humans have always faced a relatively hostile environment characterized by scarce food supplies, inadequate shelter, and in general, a paucity of other resources with which to satisfy their manifold needs. Humans are not biologically stronger than many other species that exist or have existed on earth. To explain their survival, we must look beyond the physical powers of human beings for other characteristics that have enabled humans to progress to the point of controlling and manipulating their environment within certain natural physical boundaries. Even these boundaries are constantly challenged as we explore outer space and expand our technology.

The solution to the question of why humans have survived is found in their ability to reason. In the long evolutionary process, it was not always the most physically fit who survived, for humans were still physically inferior to many other predators, but it was the most cognitively capable who fashioned tools and weapons, mastered the use of fire, developed the ability to think conceptually, advanced their powers of communication, and engaged in group activities that required a marked degree of planning, cooperation, and coordination. These were the people who fashioned equalizing clubs and spears for defense, who formed implements for tilling the soil, and who developed organizational means that gave humans a differential advantage over their natural enemies.

Paleoanthropologists have constantly pushed our knowledge of humankind further and further into the past.[9] They found *Homo habilis*, "handy man," who fashioned tools; *Homo erectus*, who characterized bipedalism; and *Homo sapiens*, the thinker. Humans are thinkers, doers, and makers; they are active, creative, and ever changing in their quest to better themselves and their species. Their most basic needs are economic ones, those necessary to physical survival in a harsh world in which food, drink, shelter, and other fundamental needs of life must be obtained. With cultural advancement, these economic needs become more complex, but they still form a base of human existence. Beyond these basic needs, which are essential to existence itself, are social needs. These needs for affiliation most probably arose out of physiological drives in the sex act and the selection of a mate. The family became the most elementary unit of human group relationships, an organization that provided satisfaction as well as duties. Survival of the family became a goal, and humans found that they could better protect and enhance their welfare by forming groups or tribes for mutual advantage in food gathering, defense, and family care activities. As Bronowski concluded: "We are joined in families, the families are joined in kinship groups, the kinship groups in clans, the clans in tribes, and the

---

9. For example, see Donald Johanson and Maitland A. Edey, *Lucy: The Beginnings of Humankind* (New York: Simon and Schuster, 1981).

tribes in nations. This is the most primitive revelation of a hierarchy of organization, layer upon layer, that links the present to the past of man's existence."[10]

Early humans found that the knowledge and skills of one generation must be transmitted to the next if the species were to survive. Such were the elementary beginnings of education and the transmission of knowledge. In forming groups and living with their fellow humans to minister to both economic and social needs, they required rules and a means to ensure the viability of the organization. They formed elementary political units with agreed-upon codes governing economic, social, political, and often religious behavior. Out of these common economic, social, and political needs, organized human activity began. People found advantages in participating and cooperating with others to achieve their own goals.

ORGANIZATIONS AND MANAGEMENT

As humans have evolved, so have organizations. People found that they could magnify their own abilities by working with others and could thereby better satisfy their own needs. The inputs of various skills and abilities into the group led to the recognition that some were better at some tasks than others. Group tasks were differentiated; that is, there was a division of labor to take advantage of these varying skills. Once labor was divided, some agreement had to be reached about how to structure and interrelate these various work assignments to accomplish group objectives. Quite logically, the group also stratified tasks and developed a hierarchy of authority or power. Perhaps the assignment of work to others was made by the strongest, the eldest, or the most articulate of the group, who became the earliest leader. In any case, the group had to achieve some unity of agreement about what was to be done, how, and who would be responsible for accomplishment.

This most elementary appearance of the first organization is reflected in essentially the same common elements of organizations throughout history. First, there had to be a goal, a purpose, an objective, or something to be accomplished. Perhaps it was the annual berry picking, the hunt, the sowing of a crop, or the defense of the group from marauding nomads. Second, people had to be attracted to the purpose or the common will to participate. They had to perceive that it was in their best interest to work toward the group goal. The first bonds of organization were in people's attraction to the group as a means of satisfying their own needs. Third, the organizational members needed something with which to work or fight. These were the resources or means to the end and comprised the people themselves, the weapons, the tilling implements, or whatever. Fourth, various activities of the participants had to be structured so that their actions would interact and be interrelated in achieving the common goal. If each proceeded without timing and coordination of effort, the result would be chaos. Finally, the group discovered that results could be better achieved if someone had the assigned task of keeping the whole group on

---

10. Jacob Bronowski, *The Ascent of Man* (Boston: Little, Brown, and Company, 1973), pp. 95–96.

its course toward the goal. Someone had to resolve differences of opinion, decide on strategy and timing, and maintain the structure of activities and relationships toward the objective. This emergence of an activity of managing apart from the activities of doing was to become an essential aspect of all types of cooperative endeavors. Management as an activity has always existed to make people's desires manifest through organized effort. Management facilitates the efforts of people in organized groups and arises when people seek to cooperate to achieve goals.

People have always participated in organizations, and organizations have always existed to serve the ends of people. These ends are manifold and are reflected in organizational arrangements for the satisfaction of economic needs and wants, for the provision for individual and social desires, for the transmission of knowledge from one generation to the next, and for the protection of life and property from internal and external threats. As their conceptual ability has been refined through evolution, people have refined their understanding of the art of arranging physical and human resources toward purposeful ends. We call this art "management," and its evolution is the focal point of our study.

Summary

Our ideas about people, management, and organizations have evolved within the context of various cultural values and institutions throughout history. The development of a body of knowledge about how to manage has also evolved within a framework of the economic, social, political, and technological facets of various cultures. Management thought is both a process in and a product of its cultural environment and must be examined within this cultural framework. People have natural economic, social, and political needs that they seek to satisfy through organized efforts. Management arises as individuals seek to satisfy these needs through group action, and it facilitates the accomplishment of goals for the individual and the group. Various organizations, such as the family, the tribe, the state, and the church, have appeared throughout history as means to people's ends. People create organizations to enlarge on their own specialized talents, to protect themselves, to enrich their lives, and to satisfy a variety of other needs. To reach these ends, organizations are formed of people who have a common purpose and who are attracted to the group to satisfy their needs. These organizations must be managed, and our study will focus on how our ideas about management have evolved over time.

2

Management before Industrialization

Historically, industrialization is a relatively recent phenomenon. Humankind existed for eons before the great advances in power, transportation, communications, and technology that came to be known as the Industrial Revolution. Before industrialization, organizations were primarily the household, tribe, church, military, and government. Some people engaged in economic undertakings, but not on a scale comparable to what emerged as a result of the Industrial Revolution. Nevertheless, there was still a need for management in the conduct of military campaigns, in household affairs, in the administration of government, and in the operation of the church. This chapter examines these first attempts at management in early civilizations and discusses the changing cultural values that led to the Industrial Revolution.

MANAGEMENT IN EARLY CIVILIZATIONS

THE NEAR EAST

As group affiliations evolved from the family to the nation, the question of organizational authority became a problem. In the family, authority rested in the patriarch or the matriarch, but in the nation, there was often a conflict between chiefs and priests, the former claiming secular power and the latter, heavenly dominion. From this struggle and this division of authority came the idea of the priest-ruler, or divine king. A king was not a King until ordained by priests, a tradition that long endured.

One such divine king was the Babylonian Hammurabi (ca. 2123–2071 BCE), who received his right to rule and his code of laws from the sun god. Babylon, near modern Baghdad, rested between the Tigris and the Euphrates rivers in what was once called the cradle of civilization. In 2250 BC, Hammurabi issued a code of 282 laws, which governed business dealings, personal behavior, interpersonal relations, punishments, and a host of other societal matters.

Law 104, for example, was the first historical mention of accounting. It dealt with the handling of receipts and established an agency relationship and accountability between the merchant and the agent. His Code also regulated wages and fees, such as fixing surgeons' fees and wages for "builders, brickmakers, tailors, stonemasons, boatmen, herdsmen, and laborers."[1] In 604 BCE, when Nebuchadnezzar was King of Babylonia, weavers of cloth were paid in food, and the quantity was granted depending on the spinner or weaver's output. This was before, and possibly influenced, the later biblical notion, "If anyone will not work, let him not eat" (2 Thess. 3:10), or, in the words of the prophet Mohammed, "He who neither worketh for himself, nor for others, will not receive the reward of God."[2] In the case of the weavers the motive was clear; in Hammurabi's Code, however, there was no incentive to do more than required because wages were regulated. Here were early examples of authority and differing ideas about wage payments.

THE FAR EAST

The ancient Chinese civilization has opened its doors occasionally to let Westerners peek in. The oldest known military treatise is the product of the Chinese general Sun Tzu (ca. 600 BCE). He wrote of marshaling the army into subdivisions, of establishing gradations of rank among the officers, and of using gongs, flags, and signal fires for communications. He advocated lengthy deliberations and sound plans before going into battle: "Thus do many calculations [plans] lead to victory, and few calculations to defeat." It is possible that General Sun Tzu held a staff officer's position: "The General that hearkens to my counsel and acts upon it, will conquer.... The General that hearkens not to my counsel nor acts upon it, will suffer defeat." It appears that the problems of line and staff relationships are at least 2,500 years old. Sun Tzu also provided strategic decision rules for the leaders:

> This is the art of offensive strategy: when our forces are ten to the enemy's one, to surround him; when five to one, to attack him; if double his strength, to divide him ... if equally matched, you may engage him; if weaker numerically, be capable of withdrawing; if quite unequal in every way, be capable of eluding him.[3]

If the marketplace is a surrogate for war, "competitive strengths" can be compared to "forces" and "competitor" to "enemy," and we can see the historical foundations of modern management strategy.

---

1. Robert F. Harper, ed., *The Code of Hammurabi: King of Babylon* (Chicago: University of Chicago Press, 1904), p. 281.

2. Cited in MOW International Research Team, *The Meaning of Working* (New York: Academic Press, 1987), p. 4.

3. Sun Tzu, *The Art of War*, trans. Samuel B. Griffith (Oxford: Oxford University Press, 1963), pp. 79–80.

Confucius (ca. 552–479 BCE) left his mark on the ages through his moral teachings and only incidentally through his advocacy of a merit system. In his time, the highest respectable goal was service in the government: merchants ranked only slightly above convicts in social esteem. The competition for governmental posts was severe, and Confucius advocated that offices should go to individuals of proven merit and ability. Merit exams, based on Confucian advice, began during the Han dynasty (206 BCE–AD 220). Merit as a basis for selection would in time lead to merit rating (performance appraisal) for promotions. Although the record is spotty, the Sung dynasty started a merit rating system around AD 962. Research indicates that the Chinese had problems with bureaucracy, much as we do today. Selection of officials on the basis of classical scholarship qualities did not always bring the best administrators to office. Corruption and manipulation by officials and lesser functionaries were common, leading to numerous attempts to reform the system.[4]

The Chinese bureaucracy was fully developed into a hierarchy of officials perhaps as early as 1000 BCE, long before Confucius. Indeed, the Confucian philosophy was in contradiction to the legalists of that time. The legalists sought to use rewards and punishments through a system of laws to ensure performance, whereas Confucius advocated cultivating and improving the moral nature of people to secure cooperation. How ancient this struggle between the formalists and the humanists, the system and the individual! There is also evidence that the Chinese were familiar with the division of labor and the departmental form of organization as early as AD 1. An inscription on a rice bowl indicates that it was made in a government workshop in which there was a high degree of specialization of labor among the various artisans. The workshop was divided into three departments: accounting, security, and production.[5] Such artifacts enable us to understand the age-old practice of management.

Chanakya Kautilya (ca. 332–298 BCE) was a noted and feared minister to Chandragupta Maurya, the greatest statesman of Hindu India. Kautilya's *Arthasastra* founded Indian public administration and contained advice on how to establish and maintain economic, social, and political order. Kautilya cautioned that it was difficult to find competent officials because humans "are naturally fickle-minded, and like horses at work, exhibit constant change in their temper." Further, "it is impossible for a government servant not to eat up, at least, a bit of the King's revenue." To keep order, he advised close controls, severe punishment, a network of spies within the government to watch other employees, and techniques to tempt employees to test their loyalty. Kautilya's assumptions about human nature are as modern as they are ancient, as are the prescriptions he provided on maintaining order. Although he was largely unknown in the Western world, we find his ideas again in the words of

---

4. Richard L. A. Sterba, "Clandestine Management in the Imperial Chinese Bureaucracy," *Academy of Management Review* 3, no. 1 (January 1978), pp. 69–78.

5. Rodger D. Collons, "Factory Production—1 A.D.," *Academy of Management Journal* 14, no. 2 (June 1971), pp. 270–273.

others. Kautilya also wrote on the desired traits in administrators ("of high ancestry... blessed with wisdom... eloquent... intelligent, enthusiastic... sociable") and how to select personnel through interviews and checking references. He wrote of the use of staff advisers ("Never listen to just one or two"), established departments with directors, and prepared detailed job descriptions for various offices.[6] Although he worked in public administration, his writings reinforce the idea of how ancient many of our management concepts and assumptions are.

EGYPT

The Egyptians developed extensive irrigation projects as an adjunct to the annual inundation by the Nile, and the engineering feats of the pyramids and canals were marvels superior to anything the Greeks and Romans later developed. Mining and most engineering projects were state monopolies and required the development of an extensive bureaucracy to administer state affairs. The labor supply consisted of both freemen and slaves. Strong cultural traditions bound freemen to occupations, and chains took care of other labor problems.

There is evidence that the Egyptians were aware of limits to the number of people one manager could supervise. In the earliest dynasties, it was the custom to kill and bury workers and servants with the departed pharaoh. With more civilization came the progressive idea of burying carvings or of making engravings to represent or symbolize the presence of servants rather than killing them. Whether this was due to a moral advancement or to a scarcity of labor cannot be determined historically. The interesting thing learned from the excavated engravings of servants (*ushabtis*, or "answerers") was that there was a ratio of about ten servants to each supervisor. Excavations also revealed distinctive dress for managers and workers. The supervisors wore kilts or robes, whereas the ushabtis were dressed to represent their trade or occupation.[7] The "rule of ten" in the span of control was an Egyptian practice that can be found in numerous civilizations, as we shall see shortly.

One of the most ancient terms used to describe a professional managerial role is *vizier*, from this we derive the word *supervisor*. The existence of this office was recorded as early as 1750 BCE, although it is probably more ancient than that. One of the best-known viziers was the Hebrew Joseph, who had been sold into bondage by his brothers. Because of Joseph's ability to forecast, the pharaoh made him vizier. This was delegation, leaving spiritual matters in the hands of the pharaoh and temporal matters in the hands of Joseph. The office of vizier was an ancient office of director, organizer, coordinator, and decision maker. Under the vizier, an elaborate bureaucracy was developed to measure the rise of the Nile River, on which every part of the economy depended, to forecast the grain crop and revenues,

---

6. T. N. Ramaswamy, ed., *Essentials of Indian Statecraft: Kautilya's Arthasastra* (London: Asia Publishing House, 1962).

7. W. M. Flinders Petrie, *Social Life in Ancient Egypt* (London: Constable & Co. Ltd., 1924), pp. 21–22.

to allocate these revenues to the various governmental units, and to supervise all industry and trade. Here were some rather sophisticated (for the times) methods of managing through forecasting, planning work, dividing the work among the various people and departments, and establishing a "professional" full-time administrator to coordinate and control the state enterprise.

THE HEBREWS

The Old Testament is a story of the leadership of a people in quest of a land. The great leaders of the Hebrew people combined spiritual and secular powers; examples include Abraham (ca. 1900 BCE), Joseph (ca. 1750 BCE), Moses (ca. 1300 BCE), and David (ca. 1000 BCE). After the great leaders had passed away, tribal leadership became the task of judges, who led by virtue of their possession of spiritual power, or what has come down to us as "charisma." The Book of Judges tells how twelve judges, in successive reigns amounting to 410 years, held sway over Israel.

It is very likely, however, the Egyptians provided the seeds for the managerial concepts we see reported in the Bible. Joseph was sold into slavery, rose to be the vizier, and gained valuable administrative experience. Moses, while in captivity in Egypt, observed the Egyptian "rule of ten." The Bible tells us that it was on the advice of his father-in-law, Jethro (thus making Jethro the first known management consultant), that Moses "chose able men from all over Israel and made them judges over the people—thousands, hundreds, fifties, and tens. They were constantly available to administer justice. They brought the hard cases to Moses but judged the smaller matters themselves" (Living Bible, Exod. 18:25–26). Thus Moses was able to employ an exception principle in managing, as well as to establish a more orderly organizational structure for tribal management. Other managerial advice can be found in the Bible: "Without deliberation, plans come to nothing; where counselors are many, plans succeed" (Prov. 15:22). This bears a marked resemblance to the advice of Sun Tzu, who was a continent and many years away. For controlling, we are told: "Where there are many hands, lock things up" (Ecclus. 42:6).[8] Leadership, delegation, span of management, planning, organizing, and controlling were managerial practices found among ancient peoples.

GREECE

Will Durant captured the essence of the rise and fall of many civilizations in writing, "a nation is born stoic, and dies epicurean."[9] In the stoic phase of the cycle, adversity breeds cohesion and deprivation fosters initiative. Self-control, thrift,

---

8. For other examples, see Robert L. Hagerman, "Accounting in the Bible," *Accounting Historians Journal* 7 (Fall 1980), pp. 71–76.

9. Will Durant, *The Story of Civilization, Part I: Our Oriental Heritage* (New York: Simon and Schuster, 1935), p. 259.

hard work, and an orderly life bring prosperity. As affluence reigns, self-control becomes self-indulgence, thrift becomes a vice, industry and perseverance yield to opportunism, and social order breaks down. Epicureans take no thought for the morrow, and decline begins; the fall comes not from without, but from internal decay. The cycle was true for Greece and for Rome. America was founded by stoics, the Puritans; does the past foretell the future?

The institutions, art, language, drama, and literature of ancient Greece form a significant part of our own culture. However, Greek economic philosophy was antibusiness, and trade and commerce were considered beneath the dignity of the Greek ideal. Work, considered ignoble by the aristocratic or philosophical Greek, was to be carried out by slaves and less-than-respectable citizens. Manual workers and merchants were excluded from citizenship in the Greek democracy because of the low esteem given to manual and trade occupations. Government administration was based solely on election and participation by all citizens, and the prevailing philosophy discouraged professional experts as administrators.

Socrates (469–399 BCE) observed that managerial skills were transferable: "[the] management of private concerns differs from that of public concerns only in magnitude . . . neither can be carried on without men . . . and those who understand how to employ [others] are successful directors of private and public concerns, and those who do not understand, will err in the management of both."[10] Plato (ca. 428–348 BCE), a pupil of Socrates, remarked on human diversity and how this led to the division of labor:

> I am myself reminded that we are not all alike: there are diversities of natures among us which are adapted to different occupations. . . . And, if so, we must infer that all things are produced more plentifully and easily and of a better quality when one man does one thing which is natural to him and does it at the right time, and leaves other things [duties].[11]

This notion that a division of labor would optimize productivity would persist for nearly 2,000 years, forming the basis for organizing work and determining how to best utilize the diverse abilities of people.

Aristotle (384–322 BCE), a student of Plato, provided numerous insights into management and organization in his *Politics*. Some examples include:

> On the specialization of labor: "Every work is better done which receives the sole, and not the divided attention of the worker"

---

10. Xenophon, [Socrates'] *Memorabilia and Oeconomicus*, trans. E. C. Marchant (Cambridge, MA: Harvard University Press, 1968), p. 189.

11. Plato, *Republic*, trans. Benjamin Jowett, Great Books of the Western World, vol. 7, bk 2 (Chicago: Encyclopedia Britannica, Inc., 1952), p. 317.

On departmentation: "Every office should have a special function [and one question is] should offices be divided according to the subjects with which they deal, or according to the persons with which they deal?"

On centralization, decentralization, and delegation of authority: "We should also know over which matters several local tribunals are to have jurisdiction, and [those] in which authority should be centralized; for example, should one person keep order in the market and another in some other place, or should the same person be responsible everywhere?"

On synergy: "The whole is naturally superior to the part"

On leadership: "He who has never learned to obey cannot be a good commander."[12]

In his *Metaphysics*, Aristotle developed the thesis that reality is knowable through the senses and through reason. By rejecting mysticism, Aristotle became the father of the scientific method and established the intellectual foundation for the Renaissance and the Age of Reason. Eventually this spirit of scientific inquiry would form a basis for scientific management.

Another Greek, Xenophon, described the advantages of the division of labor (ca. 370 BCE):

There are places [workshops] even where one man earns a living by only stitching shoes, another cutting them out, another by sewing the uppers together, while there is another who performs none of these operations but only assembles the parts. It follows...that he who devotes himself to a very highly specialized line of work is bound to do it in the best possible manner.[13]

Greece fell to the Romans, a hardy stock of people from the banks of the Tiber. It destroyed itself by depleting its forests and natural resources, by internal moral decay, by political disorder, and by decimating its leadership through revolts and counterrevolts. Stoicism, like its later Christian counterparts Calvinism and Puritanism, produced the strongest characters of that time. Despite its antitrade philosophy, the age of Greece illustrates the first seeds of democracy, the advent of decentralized participatory government, the first attempts to establish individual liberty, the beginnings of the scientific method for problem solving, and some early insights into the division of labor, departmentation, delegation, and leadership.

---

12. Aristotle, *Politics*, trans. Benjamin Jowett, Great Books of the Western World, vol. 9 (Chicago: Encyclopaedia Britannica, Inc., 1952), pp. 474, 487, 500.

13. Cited by Friedrick Klemm, *A History of Western Technology* (New York: Charles Scribner's Sons, 1959), p. 28.

ROME

Rome was born stoic and conquered the decaying Hellenic civilization. The Romans developed a quasi-factory system to manufacture armaments for the legions, for the pottery makers who produced for a world market, and later for textiles that were sold for export. The famous Roman road system was built to speed the distribution of goods, as well as to speed the movement of troops to dissident colonies. The Romans inherited the Greek disdain for trade and left business activities in the hands of Greek and Asian freemen. A growing external trade required commercial standardization, and the state developed a guaranteed system of measures, weights, and coins. The first resemblance to a corporate organization appeared in the form of joint-stock companies, which sold stocks to the public to carry out government contracts to supply the war effort. There was a highly specialized labor force that, with few exceptions, worked in small shops as independent artisans selling for the market rather than for individual customers. Free workers formed guilds (*collegia*), but these were for social aims and mutual benefits, such as defraying the cost of funerals, rather than for establishing wages, hours, or conditions of employment. The state regulated all aspects of Roman economic life: it levied tariffs on trade, set fines on monopolists, regulated the guilds, and used its revenues to fight a multitude of wars. Large-scale organizations could not exist because the government prohibited joint-stock companies for any purpose other than the execution of government contracts.

The Roman army followed the "rule of ten," although its application varied from time to time. The cavalry had *decuriones*, units of ten horse soldiers, with three decuriones constituting a *turma* and ten turmae (three hundred cavalry) supporting a legion. Centurions led one hundred soldiers (even though actual troop size rarely reached that level), and these centuries were organized into cohorts, with ten cohorts making up a legion. Thus the Roman genius for order and discipline established units to perform certain tasks as well as a hierarchy of authority to ensure performance. Other contributions of Rome to our heritage came chiefly from law and government, which were manifestations of this concern for order. Roman law became a model for later civilizations, and the Roman separation of legislative and executive powers provided a model system of checks and balances for later constitutional governments.

THE CATHOLIC CHURCH

From its seedbed in the Middle East, Christianity faced theological as well as organizational problems. As the faith spread, novel sects grew, and the first blush of a youthful theology threatened to become an adolescence of diversity. Early congregations operated independently, each defining its own doctrine and conditions for membership. Bishops became heads of various local churches, and the roles of presbyters and deacons began to emerge as assistants for the bishop. By the third century AD, an ordered hierarchy was more apparent with the addition of subdeacons and acolytes, who performed personal and secretarial duties, and exorcists and readers, who performed liturgical duties. All these ranks were enumerated by Bishop Cornelius in a message to Fabius of Antioch (AD 251). At the Council of Arles (AD 314) some bishops were made more equal than others, giving rise to a chief bishop, the bishop of Rome. At the Council of Nicaea (AD 325), the bishop of Rome was named to the office of pope. The outcome was centralized doctrine and authority in Rome and the papacy. However, the conflict between centralized and decentralized authority has reappeared throughout history, not only in the Catholic Church but also in other organizations. In modern organizational terms, the Catholic Church leaders perceived a need to institutionalize the organization, that is, to specify policies, procedures, doctrine, and authority. The problem is a recurring one even today: the need for unanimity of purpose, yet discretion for local problems and conditions.

FEUDALISM AND THE MIDDLE AGES

Renaissance writers coined the phrase "Middle Ages" to refer to what occurred from the decline of Rome to the Renaissance period. Slavery became uneconomical in the late Roman period: the upkeep of slaves was costly, and they showed no particular enthusiasm for their work. The abolition of slavery came not with moral progress but with economic change. Development of free people as tenant farmers proved to be more economical. The growth of large estates and the political disorder following the fall of Rome led to economic, social, and political chaos, ripe for the emergence of the feudal system. Feudalism as a cultural system prevailed from about 600 to about 1500. At the base of the feudal system were the serfs, who tilled plots of land owned by the manorial lords, much like modern sharecroppers, and were given military protection in exchange for a portion of the products of their labor. The feudal system tied people to the land, fixed rigid class distinctions, established an age of landed aristocracy that was to endure to the Industrial Revolution, forced education to a standstill, made poverty and ignorance the hallmark of the masses, and completely stifled human progress until the Age of Reformation. It is no wonder that some historians prefer to call this period the Dark Ages.

Although some writers romanticize the Middle Ages for chivalry, the Crusades, the healthy agrarian life, and the dignity of the artisan, the period was really rather bleak. Many of the problems typically associated with the Industrial Revolution actually began during this period. People razed the forests for fire and cooking wood, ignoring any reforestation needs, and overgrazed or tilled carelessly the open lands. As the forests diminished, coal became a more important source of fuel, thus creating air pollution. Eleanor, queen of England, was forced from her castle at Nottingham in 1257 by the coal smoke and fumes from a nearby village. Water pollution resulted from human and animal waste flowing from open sewers into the streams. The situation grew worse until the British parliament passed the first known antipollution legislation in 1388, almost four centuries before the Industrial Revolution.[14] These were nasty, brutish times, but developing events would lead to better days.

THE REVIVAL OF COMMERCE

Feudalism gave birth to the Crusades and, in turn, died as a result of them. Two centuries of religious fervor had left Jerusalem in the hands of the Muslims, and Europe was seething with the potential for change. The Crusades also stimulated commerce by opening new trade routes and exposing parochial, feudal Europe to the wealth of the Middle East. The Crusades weakened Christian belief. Embarking on their journeys with invincible religious conviction, the Crusaders returned with the realization that Middle Eastern culture was superior in manners, morals, trade, industry, and warfare.

Another eye-opener was the return of a Venetian trader, Marco Polo (1254–1324), from the Far Eastern lands of China, Tibet, Burma, and India in 1295. In addition to his fantastic tales of a previously unseen part of the world, he told how the Tartar (actually, Tatar) tribes of Mongolia and Manchuria organized their armies for battle: "[The Chief] puts himself at the head of an army of a hundred thousand horses . . . and appoints an officer to the command of ten men, and others to command a hundred, a thousand, and ten thousand men respectively . . . by this arrangement each officer has only to attend to the management of ten men or ten bodies of men."[15] How did these Far Eastern lands, having never before visited or been visited by the West, arrive at this "rule of ten"? For that matter, how did the Incas, a civilization that flourished from about 1200 to 1532 in what is roughly modern Peru and Chile, have "a decimal system of controls, with overseers of ten, a hundred, a thousand, and up to ten thousand people"?[16] History often reveals more than it resolves.

The results of the cultural confrontations of the Crusades led to a more secular life in Europe through weakening religious bonds. Interest arose in exploration, and a new spirit of trade and commerce filled the land of feudalism. New markets, new ideas, the rise of towns, the first seeds of a new middle class, freer circulation of money and credit instruments, and the resurgence of political order created the base for the Renaissance and the Reformation.

Before the Industrial Revolution, how were goods produced? Many products were made or grown in the home for a family's use. Other products, however, came from two basic methods of industrial organization: the guilds and the domestic

---

14. Jean Gimpel, *The Medieval Machine* (New York: Holt, Rinehart, and Winston, 1976), pp. 75–85.

15. Marco Polo, *The Travels of Marco Polo* (New York: The Modern Library, 1954), p. 92. Written in 1298.

16. John Hemming, "The Lost Cities of the Incas," in J. J. Thorndike, ed., *Discovery of Lost Worlds* (New York: American Heritage, 1979), p. 263.

system. Guilds, as far as we know, existed primarily between 1100 and 1500 and consisted of two types: merchant guilds, which were the buyers and sellers of goods; and craft guilds, which were the makers of the goods. Within the craft guilds there was a hierarchy of authority of masters, journeymen, and apprentices. The master owned the tools and raw materials and the finished product; journeymen were paid workers who had finished their apprenticeship but had not yet established their own shop; and apprentices were those who were learning the trade. Each town or village typically regulated the number of masters to be permitted for any craft, the number of apprentices a master could have, and the *maximum* wages an apprentice could earn. If an apprentice ran away, wanted posters appeared, and law enforcement authorities were sent for the culprit. Each guild was protected from competition by the local officials, who forbade the entry of products from outside the village and, in turn, taxed or licensed the guilds as the price of their protection. As we saw in Chapter 1, the craft guilds also suppressed innovations.

Guilds were regulated as to quality of work and acted to control certain types of work: for example, craft guild rules prohibited shoemakers from tanning hides, which was the job of the tanners, and weavers from dyeing cloth, which was the job of the dyers. Conversely, tanners and dyers had to stick to their own work also. Thus craft guilds used the division of labor to gain greater job control. The modern union practices of controlling job access, defining the jurisdiction of each craft, and restricting encroachment by others is a legacy of the medieval age.

Merchant guilds were numerous and resembled modern trade associations. Merchants of earlier times were intermediaries in trade, buying raw materials to sell to producers or taking finished products for resale. Merchants were thus the cornerstone of what was called the domestic, or "putting out," system of production. A merchant procured raw material and contracted the work out to individual workers or families who, using their own equipment, would complete the product in their homes and then return it to the merchant for a wage. The faults of the domestic system lay in the simple tools and technology, with little incentive to improve them, and in the inefficiencies of small-scale production with a limited division of labor. As the volume of trade grew, the domestic system proved inefficient, and the need for more capital, the benefits of specializing labor, and the economies of scale of a centralized workplace led to the factory system.

In the domestic system, however, we find an early example of what moderns term "transaction cost economics," the idea that, in some instances, a managerial hierarchy may allocate resources more effectively than the market. The domestic system relied on the negotiation of contracts with those who would do the work in their homes, and the price that would be paid for that work would be the ongoing market price. In their homes, workers could work at their own pace, making the completion of the product unpredictable from the point of view of the merchant. There was no monitoring of performance, possibly leading to an uneven quality of the finished product. Payment for performance provided an incentive, however, for the worker to finish the work as contracted with the merchant. At any point in time, the merchant could have numerous contracts in operation, making monitoring of work more difficult. With the emergence of steam power and the factory system, we will see how a central workplace and a managerial hierarchy facilitated monitoring of performance, reduced risk and uncertainty and gave the firm an advantage over the domestic means of production.

Growing trade also required a rationalization of the methods of keeping accounts. Although traders and bankers such as Francesco Datini of Prato and Genoa and the Medicis of Florence were using the essentials of double-entry bookkeeping as early as 1340,[17] a Franciscan monk, Luca Pacioli, first described it in print in his *Summa de Arithmetica, geometrica, proportioni, et proportionalita* in 1494. Pacioli's system was the first information system for management: It provided the entrepreneur with information on cash and inventory position and enabled a check on cash flow. The system did not keep track of costs, however. It was not until the twentieth century that any advancements were made on Pacioli's system.

As trade expanded, the emerging economic order placed more souls in jeopardy with respect to the prevailing church doctrine against charging interest and the profit motive. Saint Thomas Aquinas, a thirteenth-century theologian, had addressed the issue of justice in trade matters with the idea of a "just price," which was the market, or prevailing, price. In 1468, Friar Johannes Nider extended this notion by developing certain trade rules (we might call them a code of ethical conduct), which, if followed, would assure merchants that their transactions were just. For example, the rules declared that the goods should be "lawful, honorable, and useful"; that the price should be just; that the seller should beware (*caveat venditor*) and not engage in "trickery" nor "intimidation" nor sell to "simpletons," who would not be informed buyers; and that those who buy "looking for nothing but a rise in prices [i.e., speculation] sin gravely."[18] Nider's book, written during the Renaissance, was the first to focus on business ethics, and it indicates that an ancient concern for ethical trade practices is woven into our social fabric. As one author summarized Nider's message for today:

> Nider's thoughts are surprisingly modern. . . . Through his eyes we see the moral dilemmas of the past and of the present; the moral choices that must be made in everyday life in business and our personal conduct; and the need for guidelines that provide the ropes to keep us from falling. Nider addressed evergreen issues that ethicists faced in the past and encounter in the present—that laws alone cannot deflect human frailties nor chicanery; that ultimate responsibility

---

17. Morgen Witzel, *Builders and Dreamers: The Making and Meaning of Management* (London: Prentice Hall, 2002).

18. Johannes Nider, *On The Contracts of Merchants*, trans. Charles H. Reeves, ed. Ronald B. Shuman (Norman, OK: University of Oklahoma Press, 1966), pp. 38–45. Originally published in Cologne in 1468 as *De Contractibus Mercatorum*.

for one's actions cannot be avoided; and that virtuous conduct is necessary in exchange relationships.[19]

Feudalism was dead, interred by the expansion of trade, the growth of urbanization, the creation of a merchant class, and the development of strong central governments. But the age of industrialization had not yet arrived. New wine was fermenting, straining the old societal containers. What was needed now was a new spirit, a new sanction for human efforts.

THE CULTURAL REBIRTH

The new wine that was straining the cultural containers was a trinity of forces that would eventually lead to the Industrial Revolution and a new culture for humankind. These forces established the cultural foundations of a new industrial age that brought people from subservience to newfound freedoms in economic arrangements for the allocation of resources, in social relations, and in political institutions. The rediscovery of the classics and renewed interest in reason and science epitomized the Renaissance and broke the ancient hold of theology on people through the Protestant Reformation and the subsequent Protestant ethic. The liberty ethic established new concepts in relations between people and the state through constitutional government. The market ethic brought forth the notion of a market-directed economy. These three ethics, or standards for cultural conduct, interacted in practice to change cultural values toward people, work, and profits. The outcome of this cultural rebirth was the creation of a new environment that would lead to the need for the formal study of management.

THE PROTESTANT ETHIC

During the Middle Ages, the Catholic Church dominated life and provided the hope of an afterlife as the only consolation for this one. With the church as superstate, the admonitions of doctrine against lending for interest, against desiring anything from this world other than subsistence, and against materialistic trade and profits perpetuated the opinion of business as an evil necessity. The complete domination of life by the church led people to think not of this world, but of the other; not of gain, but of salvation. According to the church, the self-interest of trade diverted people's thoughts from God to gain, from obedience to initiative, and from humility to activity.

The loosening of religious bonds by the Crusades and the spread of general prosperity through the revival of commerce was bound sooner or later to lead to a

19. Daniel A. Wren, "Medieval or Modern? A Scholastic's View of Business Ethics, circa 1430," *Journal of Business Ethics* 28 (2000), p. 117.

revolt against the church. Although earlier individuals had protested the practices of the Roman Catholic Church, Martin Luther is generally considered the architect of the Protestant Reformation. He agreed with the church, however, in condemning interest, considered commerce a "nasty business," and spoke out vehemently against the Fuggers, the leading commercial family in Germany.

John Calvin was inspired by the reformation attempts of Luther, and like Luther, he followed the Augustinian creed of predestination and brought to the Reformation a somber view of the smallness and weakness of humans. His view of a combination of church and state as ideal led to his theocracy of Geneva and clearly repudiated the philosophy of the Renaissance. Calvin's concept of the elect, those predestined to be saved, gave a new spirit to his followers. Because everything was predetermined, all people should believe that they were of the elect and, based on this divine election, would have the courage to face the tribulations of any harsh world. Did the stern Protestantism of Luther and Calvin provide the religious sanctions for rational capitalism?

Max Weber would answer in the affirmative by stating the case for Protestantism having created the spirit of capitalism. Weber made a clear distinction between the irrational, unlimited greed for gain and the rational capitalism of the Protestant ethic:

> The impulse to acquisition, pursuit of gain, of money, of the greatest possible amount of money, has in itself nothing to do with capitalism. This impulse [to acquisition] has been common to all sorts and conditions of men at all times and in all countries of the earth, wherever the objective possibility of it is or has been given. It should be taught in the kindergarten of cultural history that this naïve idea of capitalism must be given up once and for all. Unlimited greed for gain is not in the least identical with capitalism, and is still less its spirit. Capitalism *may* even be identical with the restraint, or at least a rational tempering, of this irrational impulse. But capitalism is identical with the pursuit of profit, and forever *renewed* profit, by means of continuous, rational, capitalistic enterprise. For it must be so: in a wholly capitalistic order of society, an individual capitalistic enterprise which did not take advantage of its opportunities for profit-making would be doomed to extinction.[20]

Weber began his search for an explanation of the capitalistic spirit by noting the overwhelming number of Protestants among business leaders, entrepreneurs, and highly skilled laborers, and more highly technically and commercially trained personnel. In Weber's view, Luther developed the idea of a calling in the sense of a task set by God, a life task. This was a new idea brought about during

---

20. Max Weber, *The Protestant Ethic and the Spirit of Capitalism*, trans. Talcott Parsons (New York: Charles Scribner's Sons, 1958), p. 17. Originally published in Germany in 1905 and revised in 1920 to include answers to various critics.

the Reformation, and became a central dogma of Protestant denominations. It discarded Catholic notions of subsistence living and monastic asceticism by urging individuals to fulfill the obligations imposed on them in this world, that is, their calling (German *Beruf*). It placed worldly affairs as the highest form of moral activity for the individual and gave the performance of earthly duties a religious significance and sanction. Every person's occupation was a calling, and all were legitimate in the sight of God. Weber did not say that Luther intended capitalism to follow from his concept of the calling; on the contrary, later connotations led to refinement of this idea into a success-oriented spirit of capitalism. The calling did place a new interpretation on the purpose of life: instead of waiting for the Judgment Day, a person should choose and pursue an occupation, not for the purpose of material gain beyond needs, but because it was divine will. The result of this Protestant dogma was a worldly asceticism that asked people to renounce earthly sensuality to labor in this world for the glorification of God. All people had to consider themselves members of the elect, and if they did not, their lack of confidence was interpreted as a lack of faith. To attain self-confidence, people had to engage in intense worldly activity, for that and that alone could dispel religious doubts and give certainty of grace. In practice, this came to mean that God helps those who help themselves.

Catholic laypersons, in contrast, fulfilled their required religious duties conscientiously. Beyond that minimum, their good works did not need to form a rationalized system of life. They could use their good works to atone for particular sins, to better their chances for salvation, or as a sort of insurance premium for later years. To make a sharper distinction, Weber described the demands of Calvinism:

> The God of Calvinism demanded of his believers not single good works, but a life of good works combined into a unified system. There was no place for the very human Catholic cycle of sin, repentance, atonement, release, followed by a renewed sin. Nor was there any balance of merit for a life as a whole which could be adjusted by temporal punishments or the Churches' [*sic*] means of grace.[21]

The Calvinist was therefore required to live a life of good works, not an inconsistent series of wrongs balanced by repentant rights. Weber saw this as a keystone in developing a spirit of effort and gain; people were no longer able to give free rein to irrational impulses but were required by dogma to exercise self-control over their every action. They proved their faith by worldly activity, acting with zeal and self-discipline.

This new Protestant asceticism, which Weber also characterized as Puritanism, did not condone the pursuit of wealth for its own sake, for wealth would lead to pleasure and to all the temptations of the flesh. Instead, activity became the goal

---

21. Ibid., p. 117.

of the good life. Numerous corollaries developed in practice: (1) wasting time was the deadliest of sins, since every hour wasted was negating the opportunity to labor for the glory of God; (2) willingness to work was essential: "He who will not work shall not eat"; (3) the division and specialization of labor was a result of divine will because it led to the development of a higher degree of skill and improvement in the quality and quantity of production and hence served the good of all; and (4) consumption beyond basic needs was wasteful and therefore sinful: "Waste not, want not."[22] According to Weber, each of these ideas had a significant impact on the motivations of people, leading to a spirit of enterprise.

Intense activity moved people from a contemplative life to one of continuous physical and mental labor. Willingness to work placed the motivational burden on individuals, and their self-directed, self-controlled lives gave them an internal gyroscope. The specialization of labor placed each person in a calling and required a person's best, and the nonspecialized worker demonstrated a lack of grace. The Protestant ethic postulated that God desired profitability, that this was a sign of grace, and that to waste anything and reduce profits or to forgo what might be a profitable venture worked against God's will. By not seeking luxury, people created a surplus or profit from their labors. The created wealth could not be consumed beyond a person's basic needs, and thus the surplus was to be reinvested in other ventures or in the improvement of present ones.

Protestantism resulted in specific guidelines for the creation of a capitalistic spirit. According to Weber, people had a duty to work, a duty to use their wealth wisely, and a duty to live self-denying lives. An unequal distribution of goods in the world was divine providence at work because each person had unequal talents and therefore reaped unequal rewards. Wealth was no assurance of heaven, and the poor did not need to worry as long as they performed their calling properly. For Weber, the spirit of capitalism was created by the Protestant ethic, which equated spiritual worth and temporal success. With no room for self-indulgence and with the tenets of self-control and self- direction, a new age of individualism had been born.

A CRITICISM OF THE WEBERIAN THESIS

Every thesis generates its antithesis, and Weber's Protestant ethic is no exception. R. H. Tawney reversed Weber's thesis and argued that capitalism was the cause and justification of Protestantism, not the effect. Tawney noted that Catholic cities were chief commercial centers, that Catholics were leading bankers, and that the capitalistic spirit was present in many places far in advance of the sixteenth- and seventeenth-century influences that Weber discussed. According to Tawney, "Is it not a little artificial to suggest that capitalist enterprise had to wait, as Weber appears to imply, till religious changes had produced a capitalist spirit? Would it not be

---

22. Ibid., pp. 157–173.

equally plausible, and equally one-sided, to argue that the religious changes were themselves merely the result of economic movements?"[23]

In Tawney's view, the rise of capitalism was action and reaction, molding and in turn being molded by other significant cultural forces. The Renaissance brought a new focus on reason, discovery, exploration, and science; all were challenges to the monolithic authority of the church. The Renaissance contributed the humanist's views that made life on earth more important and brought the promise of a new social order in which there would be mobility for people; it signaled the mastery of people over their environment rather than the reverse case of the Middle Ages.[24] Growing economic life posed new problems for church doctrine, and merchants and artisans engaged in profit-making activities regardless of dogma. Perhaps, then, the Reformation was an attempt to create materialistic loopholes for the emerging merchant class.

With two sets of assumptions two different conclusions could be reached: (1) Weber's notion that the church changed and then the spirit of capitalism abounded; or (2) Tawney's view that economic motivation was steam pushing on the lid of church authority until the safety valve of a change in dogma (i.e., the Reformation and its later proliferation into various sects) could sanction economic efforts.

MODERN SUPPORT FOR WEBER

Despite the criticisms of Weber's thesis, there is modern evidence that Protestants hold different values toward work. In *The Achieving Society*, McClelland began a search for the psychological factors that were generally important for economic development. The factor he isolated was the need for achievement, or the shorthand version, "n achievement." McClelland's study was both historical and cross-cultural, and his findings support Weber's thesis. First, McClelland found that high n achievement was essential to engaging in entrepreneurial activities; second, that high n achievement in a society was significantly correlated to rapid economic development; and third, that certain ethnic, religious, and minority groups showed marked differences in n achievement. He found that children of Protestants had higher n achievement than children of Catholics, and children of Jews had still higher n achievement. McClelland concluded that individualistic religions, for example, the Protestant ones, tended to be associated with a high need for achievement, whereas authoritarian religions, such as traditional Catholicism, tended to have a lower need for achievement. He did concede, however, that there are wide variations among various modern Catholic communities.

---

23. R. H. Tawney, Foreword to Weber's *Protestant Ethic*, p. 8. While Weber and earlier writers addressed traditional Catholicism, Michael Novak has noted changes in Catholicism that challenged the exclusivity of a "Protestant Ethic." See Novak's *The Catholic Ethic and the Spirit of Capitalism* (New York: Free Press, 1993) and *Business as a Calling* (New York: Free Press, 1996).

24. R. H. Tawney, *Religion and the Rise of Capitalism* (London: John Murray, 1926), pp. 61–63.

What was involved in the need for achievement was not so much the need to reach certain goals, such as wealth, status, respect, and so on, but the need to enjoy the satisfactions of success. Wealth was a way of keeping score, not the goal. The entrepreneurial personality was characterized by special attitudes toward risk taking, willingness to expend energy, willingness to innovate, and a readiness to make decisions and accept responsibility. Historically the concern for achievement appeared in a culture some fifty or so years before a rapid rate of economic growth and prosperity. McClelland found this to be true in ancient Greece (before its golden age), in Spain in the Middle Ages (before the age of exploration), and in England during two different periods. The first period was from 1500 to 1625 when Protestantism and Puritanism were growing in strength concurrently with a need for achievement. The second period came in the eighteenth century just prior to the Industrial Revolution. The reasoning that McClelland used to support Weber was basically thus: (1) the Protestant Reformation emphasized self-reliance rather than reliance on others in all facets of life; (2) Protestant parents changed child-rearing practices to teach self-reliance and independence; (3) McClelland and his associates demonstrated empirically that these practices led to a higher need for achievement in sons; and (4) a higher need for achievement led to spurts of economic activity such as that characterized by Weber as the spirit of capitalism.[25] Therefore, McClelland was able to draw a relationship empirically between the influence of Protestantism and Weber's spirit of modern capitalism.

Lenski summarized the criticisms of Weber, evaluated them, and presented the evidence both for and against Weber. On balance, he found the evidence more in favor of Weber than against him. Lenski examined vertical mobility and concomitant characteristics of aspirations, ambition, and attitudes toward work in an attempt to define the relationship between religious affiliation and the ability of people to move upward in the job world. The findings resulted in a ranking of first (most mobile), Jews; second, Protestants; and third (least mobile), Catholics. Lenski's explanation resided in the differences among these three groups with respect to achievement motivation and their attitudes toward work. Jews and Protestants showed a positive attitude toward work and derived satisfaction from work. Catholics held neutral attitudes toward work and indicated that it was done for some purpose other than the satisfaction that came from work itself. In Lenski's view, "Catholics continued to regard work primarily as a necessary evil; a consequence of Adam's fall and a penalty for sin. By contrast, Protestants came to view it as an opportunity for serving God, or, in the Deist version, for building character."[26]

---

25. David C. McClelland, *The Achieving Society* (New York: Van Nostrand Reinhold Co., 1961), pp. 47–53. See also John W. Atkinson, *A Theory of Achievement Motivation* (New York: D. Van Nostrand Co., 1966).

26. Gerhard Lenski, *The Religious Factor: A Sociological Study of Religious Impact on Politics, Economics, and Family Life* (Garden City, NY: Doubleday and Co., 1961), p. 83.

The implications of McClelland's and Lenski's findings can be far reaching for contemporary people. Not only did they find empirical support for Weber, but their work also suggests that achievement values can be taught and instilled in various societies. In underdeveloped nations the problem may be underachievement; if so, an inculcation of achievement values would provide means for self-help programs to speed the progress of or the adjustment to industrialization.

THE LIBERTY ETHIC

Given the postulates of a need for achievement and the sanctions of individual rewards for worldly efforts, the political system must be conducive to individual liberty. The divine right of kings, the aristocracy of the manor lord, the exercise of secular authority by the church, and serfdom as a birthright were not favorable conditions for developing an industrialized society. In the Age of Enlightenment, political philosophers began to stimulate the thoughts of people with such new ideas as equality, justice, the rights of citizens, a rule of reason, and notions of a republic governed by the consent of the governed. These were radical ideas in those times, ideas that threatened the existing order with a profound revolution in the views of the relationship between citizen and state.

Before this facet of the cultural rebirth, political theory called for the domination of the many by the few and found its best proponents in Nicolo Machiavelli and Thomas Hobbes. Machiavelli, an out-of-office administrator and diplomat in the city-state of Florence, wrote *The Prince* in 1513.[27] He was an experienced observer of the intrigues of state and papacy and set forth a how-to book for a ruler or aspiring ruler. *The Prince*, dedicated to Lorenzo di Piero de Medici, was an exposition on how to rule; not how to be good or wise, but how to rule successfully. Machiavelli identified three ways to the top: "fortune," "ability," and "villainy." Those who rose through their good fortune had little trouble in getting to the top spot, but had difficulty maintaining it because they depended on the goodwill of others and were indebted entirely to those who elevated them. Those who gained the crest by ability endured a thousand difficulties getting there, but would be able to maintain their position more easily. Villainy, an oft-chosen path in Machiavelli's Florence, used methods that would gain power, but not glory; afterward their crown would always rest uneasily as they awaited the next villain or revolt.[28]

Machiavelli's basic assumption about the nature of people was indicative of his rationale for the type of leadership he advocated: "Whoever desires to found a state and give it laws must start with the assumption that all men are bad and ever ready to

27. Nicolo Machiavelli, *The Prince*, trans. Luigi Ricci (New York: New American Library, 1952). Written in 1513, but not published until 1532 because of its controversial nature.

28. Daniel A. Wren and Ronald G. Greenwood, *Management Innovators: The People and Ideas That Have Shaped Modern Business* (New York: Oxford University Press, 1998), pp. 191–194.

display their vicious nature, whenever they may find occasion for it."[29] To cope with these brutes, rulers were justified in pursuing any leadership style that suited their purpose. They should be concerned with having a good reputation, but not with being virtuous; should they have to choose between being feared and being loved, it would be better to be feared; and above all, rulers must be both like a lion and like a fox, employing force and deceit. Machiavelli wrote of the ruler, but not of the ruled; of power, but not of rights; and of ends, but not of means. Machiavelli fed the ideas of Lord Acton about power corrupting, and absolute power corrupting absolutely. Machiavellian has come to connote those unscrupulous, crafty, and cunning in policy. For his time, and perhaps for ours, Machiavelli personified the command philosophy of governing people.

Thomas Hobbes's *Leviathan* (1651) was a later argument for a strong central leadership. He began his analysis with humankind in a state of nature, without civil government, and proceeded to the conclusion that some greater power, the Leviathan, must exist to bring order from chaos.[30] This person or body became sovereign; because it was given all rights by the governed, its powers could not be revoked, and it became an absolute sovereign. It made no difference to Hobbes whether the sovereign was civil or ecclesiastical, as long as the central power regulated all overt conduct and expression, both civil and religious. The sovereign ruled all, and the individual was subordinate to those who ruled.

In the history of human liberty, John Locke's essay, *Concerning Civil Government* (1690), must stand as a great contribution to political theory and an effective instigator of political action. It served to state the principles of the English bloodless revolution of 1688, which brought about fundamental changes in the English constitution. It also set the stage for the American Revolution of 1776 by inspiring the authors of the Declaration of Independence and furnished inspiration to Jean Jacques Rousseau's *Social Contract* and the ensuing French Revolution. Perhaps no other one person has had such a profound effect on political theory and action. Locke attacked the divine right of kings, whose proponents traced it to Adam's God-given right to rule his children, and set forth some new concepts of authority: "Who shall be judge whether the prince or legislative body act contrary to their trust?...To this I reply, the people shall be judge."[31]

---

29. Nicolo Machiavelli, *Discourses on Livy*, trans. Alan H. Gilbert, reprinted in *Machiavelli: The Chief Works and Others*, vol. 1 (Durham, NC: Duke University Press, 1956), p. 203.

30. Thomas Hobbes, *Leviathan, or the Matter, Forme, and Power of a Common-Wealth Ecclesiastical and Civill*, (London: printed for Andrew Ckooke, at the Green Dragon in St. Paul's Churchyard, 1651).

31. John Locke, *Second Essay Concerning Civil Government*, Great Books of the Western World, vol. 35 (Chicago: Encyclopaedia Britannica, 1952), p. 81. Originally published in 1690.

This notion found more explicit support in America's Declaration of Independence:

> We hold these truths to be self-evident, that all men are created equal; that they are endowed by their creator with certain inalienable rights; that among these are life, liberty, and the pursuit of happiness. That to secure these rights, governments are instituted among men deriving their just powers from the consent of the governed.

Locke's work is so broad that it is possible here only to sample his main contributions: first, that people are governed by a natural law of reason and not by the arbitrary rules of tradition or the whims of a central authoritarian figure; and second, that civil society is built on private property. The law of nature and reason commands one not to harm another's possessions, and individuals enter into a civil society in order to preserve more perfectly their liberty and property, which are then protected by both natural law and civil law. Because people have a natural right to property, the state cannot take it away, but must protect their right to it.

Locke was a Puritan in the England of Cromwell. His writing must have affected that of Adam Smith and most certainly established the basis for Rousseau's writings. In the emergence of the philosophical Age of Enlightenment, Locke put forth a new civil order: (1) a law based on reason, not arbitrary dictates; (2) a government deriving its powers from the governed; (3) liberty to pursue individual goals as a natural right; and (4) private property and its use in the pursuit of happiness as a natural and legally protected right. These four ideas interwove in practice to form a solid political foundation for industrial growth. It provided a sanction for laissez-faire economics and the pursuit of individual rewards, guaranteed the rights of property, gave protection to contracts, and provided for a system of justice among people.

THE MARKET ETHIC

Economic thinking was basically sterile during the Middle Ages because localized, subsistence-level economies needed no economic theory to explain their workings. Early people perceived the main factors of production as land and labor, and even the latter did not pose much of a problem. Capital as an input factor was scorned and its return damned. Any idea that management was a resource input to the organization was completely lacking in early economic thought.

In the sixteenth and seventeenth centuries, the reemergence of strong national entities began to reshape economic thought. As new lands were discovered through exploration, new trade routes and new products created an international market. This revolution in trade resulted in the economic philosophy of mercantilism and injected the government into a central role of financing and protecting trade to build strong national economies. This economic chauvinism meant that the state intervened in all economic affairs, engaged in state economic planning, and regulated private economic activity to a large degree.[32] Mercantilism eventually fell of its own weight. Much of its planning went awry because it tried to keep alive uneconomic enterprises, curbed private initiative, built elaborate bureaucratic, red-tape controls, and fostered wars and trade rivalries that destroyed the very markets it was trying to create. The mercantilists were a philosophical contradiction to the emerging eighteenth-century Age of Enlightenment. The mercantilists thought only of the state, whereas the philosophy of the enlightenment championed individual rights and viewed all human institutions in terms of the contribution they could make to the happiness of each individual.

In the eighteenth century, the Physiocratic school of economic thought emerged to the challenge of mercantilism. Francois Quesnay, its founder, maintained that wealth did not lie in gold and silver but sprang from agricultural production. He advocated laissez-faire capitalism, meaning that the government should leave alone the mechanisms of the market; for him, economics had a natural order and harmony and government intervention interfered with the natural course of events.

Adam Smith (1723–1790), a Scottish political economist, was not a Physiocrat per se but was influenced by that school's view of a natural harmony in economics. In *Wealth of Nations*, Smith established the classical school and became the founder of liberal economics. Smith thought that the tariff policies of mercantilism were destructive and that, rather than protecting industry, these policies penalized efficiency by a state fiat and consequently misallocated the nation's resources. Smith proposed that only the market and competition be the regulators of economic activity. The "invisible hand" of the market would ensure that resources flowed to their best consumption and their most efficient reward, and the economic self-interest of each person and nation, acting in a fully competitive market, would bring about the greatest prosperity of all. As Smith stated it:

> As every individual, therefore, endeavors as much as he can both to employ his capital in the support of domestik [sic] industry, and so to direct that industry that its produce may be of the greatest value; every individual necessarily labours to render the annual revenue of the society as great as he can. He generally, indeed, neither intends to promote the publick interest, nor knows how much he is promoting it. By preferring the support of domestik [sic] to that of foreign industry, he intends only his own security; and by directing that industry in such a manner as its produce may be of the greatest value, he intends only his own gain, and he is in this, as in many other cases, led by an invisible hand to promote an end which was no part of his intention. Nor is it always the worse for the society that it was no part

---

32. John Fred Bell, *A History of Economic Thought*, 2nd ed. (New York: Ronald Press, 1967), p. 53.

of it. By pursuing his own interest he frequently promotes that of the society more effectually than when he really intends to promote it. I have never known much good done by those who affected to trade for the publick good.[33]

For Adam Smith, the concept of specialization of labor was a pillar of this market mechanism. He cited the example of the pin makers: when each performed a limited operation, they could produce 48,000 pins a day, whereas one unspecialized worker could produce no more than twenty pins per day. He admitted that this was a trifling example, but he found the same principles of division of labor operating successfully in many industries:

This great increase of the quantity of work which, in consequence of the division of labour, the same number of people are capable of performing, is owing to three dif-

Adam Smith. Courtesy of the Warren J. Samuels Portrait Collection at Duke University.

ferent circumstances: first, to the increase of dexterity in every particular workman; secondly, to the saving of the time which is commonly lost in passing from one species of work to another; and lastly, to the invention of a great number of machines which facilitate and abridge labour, and enable one man to do the work of many.[34]

Although Smith saw the benefits of specialized labor, he also foresaw its dysfunctional consequences:

The man whose whole life is spent in performing a few simple operations . . . naturally loses, therefore, the habit of [mental] exertion, and generally becomes stupid and ignorant as it is possible for a human creature to become. . . . His dexterity at his own particular trade seems . . . to be acquired at the expense of his intellectual, social, and martial virtues.[35]

33. Adam Smith, *An Inquiry Into the Nature and Causes of the Wealth of Nations*, (London: W. Strahan and T. Cadell in the Strand, 1776), vol. 2, bk. IV, ch. 2, p. 350. This solitary mention of the "invisible hand" was also used in an economic context in Smith's *The Theory of Moral Sentiments* (London: W. Strahan and T. Cadell, 1759), pt. IV, ch. 1, p. 466.

34. Smith, *Wealth of Nations*, vol. 1, bk. I, ch. 1, pp. 9–11.

35. Ibid., vol. 2, bk. V, ch. 1, pp. 366–367.

Smith argued that it was the province of government, through public education, to overcome the debilitating effects of the division of labor. In his view, the manager, in order to gain productivity, must rely on the division of labor. The concept of division of labor benefited all society and provided an economic rationale for the factory system. When markets were limited, a household or domestic production arrangement could meet market needs. As the population grew and as new trade territories became feasible, a greater division of labor was possible, and the factory system as a productive device began to gain momentum.

The first edition of *The Wealth of Nations* was published in March 1776 and was sold out in six months; the second edition (1778) contained minor changes; but the third edition (1784) contained substantial revision, among them Smith's concern for joint-stock, that is, limited liability firms. In Britain, the joint-stock form of organization had been established previously by royal charter or by an act of Parliament, such as the East India Company, and the Hudson Bay Company. Apparently, individuals were forming other joint-stock companies in preference over "private copartnery," or partnerships, and Smith had doubts about this arrangement:

> The directors of such [joint-stock] companies, however, being the managers rather of other people's money than of their own, it cannot well be expected, that they should watch over it with the same anxious vigilance with which the partners in a private copartnery frequently watch over their own. Like the stewards of a rich man, they are apt to consider attention to small matters as not for their master's honour, and very easily give themselves a dispensation from having it. Negligence and profusion, therefore, must always prevail, more or less, in the management of the affairs of such a company.[36]

During Smith's time, the largest employers were textile firms, and these were not capital intensive. Yet Smith anticipated that the separation of shareholder ownership and management by nonowners had a potential downside. Those who managed "other people's money" incurred less personal risk (except, perhaps, the loss of their jobs) and would be less vigilant and prudent in their duties.

When his writing appeared in the early stages of the Industrial Revolution, Smith found a large number of vocal supporters and fertile soil for his liberal economics. He was in tune with the philosophy of the Enlightenment and the newly emerging group of entrepreneurs who wished to sweep away the restrictions of mercantilism and the controlling power of the landed aristocracy. Great Britain found in the market ethic an economic sanction for private initiative rather than mercantilism, competition rather than protection, innovation rather than economic

---

36. Ibid., 3rd ed. (1784), vol. 2, bk. 5, ch. 1, pp. 123–124. Compare this with the New Testament parable of the hired shepherd, who flees when the flock is endangered. John 10:11–13.

stagnancy, and self-interest rather than state interest as the motivating force. The market ethic was another element in this trinity of forces that created the cultural environment for the flowering of the industrial system.

Summary

Early management thought was dominated by cultural values that were antibusiness, antiachievement, and largely antihuman. Industrialization could not emerge when people were bound to their stations in life, when monarchs ruled by central dictates, and when people were urged to take no thought of individual fulfillment in this world but to wait for a better one. Before the Industrial Revolution, economies and societies were essentially static, and political values involved unilateral decision making by some central authority. Although some early ideas of management appeared, they were largely localized. Organizations could be run on the divine right of the king, on the appeal of dogma to the faithful, and on the rigorous discipline of the military. There was little or no need to develop a formal body of management thought under these nonindustrialized circumstances.

Three forces were interacting and combining to provide for a new age of industrialization. Characterized as ethics, or standards governing human conduct, they illustrate how economic, social, and political attitudes were changing during the cultural rebirth. The ethics discussed were in reality a struggle between the old traditional and the newly emerging society. The Protestant ethic was a challenge to the central authority of the church and a response to the needs of people for achievement in this world; the liberty ethic reflected the ancient struggle between monolithic and representative forms of government and sought to protect individual rights; and the market ethic was a gauntlet flung before the landed aristocracy, who preferred mercantilism. The struggle represented here is an old one: the state versus the individual, human rights and due process versus whimsical autocracy, and centralization versus decentralization. The struggle goes on.

This cultural rebirth would establish the preconditions for industrialization and subsequently the need for a rational, formalized, systematic body of knowledge about how to manage. The emergence and refinement of the market economy required managers to become more creative and to be better informed about how best to manage an organization. Faced with a competitive, changing environment, the manager had to develop a body of knowledge about how best to utilize resources. People began thinking of individual gain and had to be accommodated in some rational managerial framework. The emergence of modern management had to be based on rational ways of making decisions; no longer could the organization be operated on the whims of a few. This change did not come suddenly but evolved over a long period of time as the culture changed. How these changes came about and how they affected the evolution of management thought is the subject of this book. It is an intriguing story.

3

The Industrial Revolution: Problems and Perspective

The Industrial Revolution heralded a new age for civilization. The cultural rebirth had created new social, economic, and political conditions ripe for advances in science and technology. Subsequent improvements in technology made possible large combinations of physical and human resources and ushered in the factory system to replace the domestic system of production. This chapter will examine the salient characteristics of the Industrial Revolution and the managerial problems it created, as well as attempt to achieve some perspective on the consequences of this cultural revolution.

THE INDUSTRIAL REVOLUTION IN GREAT BRITAIN

Industrial progress is always closely tied to advancements in science and technology. In the fifteenth century, Johannes Gutenberg (1400–1468) developed the first metallic movable type for a printing press and opened the door to an information revolution that continues today. While medieval scientists attempted to deduce physical laws from the writings of Plato, Aristotle, Saint Augustine, and the Bible, a new age of scientific inquiry began in the sixteenth and seventeenth centuries as church bonds loosened. This Age of Reason, this revolution in scientific thought, was the product of such individuals as Francis Bacon, Nicolaus Copernicus, Galileo, William Gilbert, William Harvey, Isaac Newton, and others. The scientific revolution emphasized the spirit of observation and inquiry and established the foundation for the technological revolution that was to follow.

Ever since humankind began to improve methods of tilling the soil, making weapons, and weaving cloth, there have been advancements in technology or the art and applied science of making and using tools and equipment. Technology has been evolving and advancing for thousands of years, but a revolution came in late-eighteenth-century England that marked the beginning of an advance in technology more rapid than ever before. The essence of this revolution was the substitution of machine power for human, animal, wind, water, and other natural sources of power. Deane, in pinpointing the emergence of the Industrial Revolution, illustrated the difference between preindustrialized and industrialized societies. Preindustrial societies are characterized by low per capita income, economic stagnation, dependence on agriculture, a low degree of specialization of labor, and very little geographical integration of markets. Industrial societies are characterized by rising or high per capita income, economic growth, low dependence on agriculture, a high degree of specialization of labor, and a widespread geographical integration of markets.[1] Using these factors as indicators, Deane concluded that the shift in Great Britain from a preindustrial to an industrial nation became most evident in 1750 and accelerated thereafter.

THE STEAM ENGINE

In Chapter 2 we saw the two primary methods of production, the domestic system and the craft guilds. In both, the scale of production was small, the market limited, and the work was labor, rather than capital, intensive. Merchants put out materials to homes, where families spun, bleached, dyed, or performed whatever functions were necessary. Thus we find the ancient sources of family names for weavers, dyers, tailors, fullers, and so on. In craft shops, work was passed from one stage to another as, for example, tanners did their work, passed it along to curriers, and in turn came the shoemakers and the saddlers, who turned the prepared leather into finished products. Labor was specialized, capital investment low, and the power source resided in humans, animals, and the forces of nature.

Great Britain's largest industry of this time was textiles. From the colonies came the cotton, wool, and other fibers to be cleaned, combed, spun, and so on into cloth. Mechanical improvements in the textile industry preceded the Industrial Revolution. John Kay began the mechanization of weaving with his flying shuttle in 1733; in 1765, James Hargreaves changed the position of the spinning wheel from vertical to horizontal, stacked the wheels on top of one another, and wove eight threads at once by turning them all with one pulley and belt. He called his gadget the spinning jenny (after his wife) and added more wheels and power until he could weave eighty threads at once. In 1769, Richard Arkwright developed a water frame that stretched the cotton fibers into a tighter, harder yarn. His factories grew with this innovation until by 1776 he employed five thousand workers.

Despite these mechanical improvements, the heart of the Industrial Revolution was really the steam engine. The steam engine was not new: Hero of Alexandria (ca. AD 200) had developed one for the sake of amusement; others had built models but had had mechanical problems. Thomas Newcomen had developed a

---

1. Phyllis Deane, *The First Industrial Revolution* (London: Cambridge University Press, 1965), pp. 5–19.

steam-propelled engine to pump water out of coal mines that were flooding as deeper and deeper shafts went down. It was the task of James Watt, trained as a maker of scientific instruments, to perfect the earlier work of others. Watt developed his first workable steam engine in 1765, but financing and moving from the prototype to an industrial installation took eleven years. During this time he formed a partnership with Matthew Boulton, a leading British ironmaster, to make steam engines. In 1776, Watt's first engine was sold to John Wilkinson for use in his ironworks. To set a price, an agreement was made that the steam engine would be rated at the equivalent of how many horses could do the same amount of work; hence the derivation of the word *horsepower* for mechanical engines.

James Watt. Courtesy of the History of Science Collections, University of Oklahoma.

Until 1782, however, Watt's engines were used only to pump water and blow air for blast furnaces to smelt metals. In 1781, Watt made his greatest technological breakthrough when he was able to transform the up-and-down motion of the drive beam into the rotary motion of an engine. This led to a host of new uses for steam power; for example, lifting coal and ore from mines, supplying power for breweries and oil mills, and eventually powering railway locomotives and steamships. In 1788, Watt patented a fly-ball governor, which adjusted the flow of steam to promote the uniform speed of the engine. This first cybernetic control device operated on a centrifugal principle: As the engine sped up, arms on a rotating shaft rose and the steam intake vents closed, reducing power intake; as the engine slowed, the arms dropped, allowing more power.

The historian Arnold Toynbee noted that two men, Adam Smith and James Watt, were the most responsible for destroying the old Britain, building a new one, and launching the world toward industrialization. Smith brought about the revolution in economic thought; Watt, the revolution in the use of steam power.[2] Harnessed to the wheels of a hundred industries, the steam engine provided more efficient and cheaper power, power for ships, trains, and factories, revolutionizing British commerce and industry. Steam power lowered production costs, lowered prices, and expanded markets. A spirit of innovation led to inventions, inventions led to factories, and factories led to a need for direction and organization. The expanded market called for more workers, more machines, and a larger production scale on a regular basis. Capital was needed to finance these larger undertakings, and the individuals who could command the capital began to bring together workers

---

2. Arnold Toynbee, *The Industrial Revolution* (Boston: Beacon Press, 1956), p. 89. Originally published in 1884.

and machines under one common authority. Instead of being in their homes, for example, weavers were in a workplace with a steam engine to power their looms; similarly, combers, bleachers, dyers, and so on found their efforts shifting from the home to the factory. As these workers came into the central workplace, there was a greater need for monitoring and coordinating their efforts. The factory system proceeded irregularly in various industries, but the new age of industrialization was evident. A new power source was perfected, a greater capital intensity was required, the need for directing and coordinating efforts was paramount, and the fledgling factory system toddled forth to create an abundance such as the world had never seen.

MANAGEMENT: THE FOURTH FACTOR OF PRODUCTION

Before the Industrial Revolution, economic theory focused on two factors of production, land and labor, and recognized capital as an input factor only as church bonds loosened. In addition to these, another began to evolve, the entrepreneur. Richard Cantillon, an Irishman who moved to Paris and made a fortune in currency speculation, appears to have been the first to use the word *entrepreneur* in an economic sense. His pre–Industrial Revolution *Essay on the Nature of Commerce*, published some years after his death, used the word *entrepreneur* very loosely.[3] *Entrepreneur* applied to anyone who bought or made a product at a certain cost to sell at an uncertain price. In Cantillon's description, it described the work of any self-employed persons such as farmers, water-carriers, brewers, hatmakers, chimney-sweeps, and so forth. As one authority has observed, Cantillon's entrepreneur: "May be a merchant or landowner but he equally may be a capitalist employing labour; in all cases, however, the entrepreneurial role remains distinctly that of someone making decisions under uncertainty."[4]

Cantillon's *Essay* influenced the idea of Francois Quesnay, leader of the Physiocrats, who recognized a farmer-entrepreneur, but held that manufacturing and commerce were sterile and unable to produce a surplus. Adam Smith recognized the entrepreneur as a factor, but treated the return or the surplus created as a return to capital. Writing after Adam Smith, Jean Baptiste Say (1767–1832) provided a more definitive explanation of the entrepreneurial role. According to Say, entrepreneurship

> Requires a combination of moral qualities that are not often found together. Judgment, perseverance, and a knowledge of the world as

---

3. Richard Cantillon, *Essai sur la Nature du Commerce au General*, ed. and trans. Henry Higgs (London: Macmillan & Co., 1931). Cantillon wrote this between 1730 and 1734; he died in 1734; and his book was published in 1755. In translation, Higgs took Cantillon's *entrepreneur* literally, that is, "undertaker."

4. Mark Blaug, *Great Economists before Keynes* (Cambridge: Cambridge University Press, 1986), p. 38.

well as of business. [The entrepreneur] is called upon to estimate with tolerable accuracy the importance of the specific product, the probable amount of the demand, and the means of its production: at one time he must employ a great number of hands; at another, buy or order the raw material, collect laborers, find consumers, and give at all times a rigid attention to order and economy; in a word, he must possess the art of superintendence and administration.[5]

Say noted that some entrepreneurs owned the undertaking but more frequently than not they owned only a share, having borrowed from others or having formed a partnership. The entrepreneur thus became a manager for others and assumed an additional risk in combining the factors of land, labor, and capital. For assuming the added risk in combining the traditional three factors of production, the entrepreneur became a fourth factor of production and received a separate reward for managing in addition to a return on the personal capital invested. (A point that Adam Smith failed to see.) As the organization grew, the entrepreneur alone could not direct and control all activities, and it became necessary to delegate some activities to a level of submanagers. These submanagers were the first nonowning, salaried managers who had the responsibility of making decisions within a broader framework of policies established by the entrepreneur. As the entrepreneur expanded the organization and took on an increasing number of lower-level managers, many problems were to arise in the process of delegation.

MANAGEMENT PROBLEMS
IN THE EARLY FACTORY

The emerging factory system posed management problems different from those ever encountered before. The church could organize and manage its properties because of dogma and the devotion of the faithful; the military could control large numbers of personnel through a rigid hierarchy of discipline and authority; and governmental bureaucracies could operate without having to meet competition or show a profit. The managers in the new factory system could not resort to any of these devices to ensure the proper utilization of resources.

The Industrial Revolution spawned a number of industries, and the early 1800s were characterized by the growth of these firms in an increasingly competitive environment. For the firm, the pressure for growth came from the need

---

5. Jean Baptiste Say, *A Treatise on Political Economy*, 2 vols., trans. C. R. Princep (Boston: Wells and Lilly, 1821), vol. 2, p. 72. Originally published as *Traite d'Economie Politique*, 2 vols. (Paris: chez Deterville, 1803). Princep translated *entrepreneur* as "master-agent" or "adventurer"; as neither is very descriptive, the French term has been Anglicized.

for economies of scale to compete more effectively. Some advocated resisting the pressures for growth; for example, a report of the Committee on Woollen Manufacturers of 1806 stated that the development of large factories would not lead to many advantages for the entrepreneur. By continuing the domestic system, the entrepreneur could save much capital investment and would not need to "submit to the constant trouble and solicitude of watching over a numerous body of workmen."[6] Competition still demanded growth, but the retarding factor was the lack of a pool of trained managers who could cope with large-scale factory problems. Hence the size of the early firm was often limited by the number of people the entrepreneur could supervise personally. The result was a dual line of advance for the factory system: on the one hand, technology and capital made a larger scale of production possible and forces of competition made a larger size imperative; on the other hand, the enlargement of operations created a myriad of managerial problems.

THE LABOR PROBLEM

Once an entrepreneur decided to embark on a venture, capital had to be raised to buy the power source, machinery, buildings, tools, and so forth. None of this could become a reality until workers were employed to operate the machinery and perform the necessary duties. Developing a workforce, however, was not an easy task. Broadly conceived, the labor problem had three aspects: recruitment, training, and motivation. The existing labor force consisted largely of unskilled agrarian workers, and the shift from a small workshop, a farm, or a family-operated operation was a drastic one for these people. They had to pull up roots from a long-familiar milieu and go to the brawling, bustling city for employment. Andrew Ure and others complained that factory work was uncongenial to the typical workers, who were accustomed to the domestic or agrarian life and did not look kindly on the monotony of factory jobs, the year-round regularization of hours, and the constant demands of attention to their work. Workers tended to be restless, shiftless, and deviant. The firm of Roebuck and Garrett, for example, moved their factory from Birmingham, England, to Scotland because they found the Scots were more reliable and obedient.[7] A contemporary observer described early textile weavers as fiercely independent and generally insubordinate. For the most part, they were Puritans and were as opposed to factory regimen and the managerial hierarchy of authority as they were to the Church of England.[8]

---

6. Sidney Pollard, *The Genesis of Modern Management: A Study of the Industrial Revolution in Great Britain* (Cambridge, MA: Harvard University Press, 1965), p. 11.

7. Ibid., p. 161.

8. Richard Guest, *A Compendious History of the Cotton Manufacture* (Manchester, England: Joseph Pratt, 1823), pp. 40–43.

Recruitment

The transition from the farm to the factory was eased for some workers, however, by the prospects of a steadier job and wage incentives. Agrarian workers were accustomed to a subsistence living derived from the vagaries of the soil and the seasons. Studies of labor mobility in Great Britain during the period of industrial growth showed that workers were moving toward the north and west where the factories were primarily located. This demonstrated a "sensitivity of labor to wage incentives," as the workers now had the opportunity to improve their standard of life.[9] Of course, not all workers responded to the cash stimulus, preferring their agrarian or craft pursuits.

Particularly vexing to employers, however, was the shortage of skilled labor. Some skilled labor did exist in small, scattered guilds and workshops, but these workers were more resistant to factory life. The Woolcombers Guild, for example, resisted mechanization and factory work, preferring their guild tradition. In the midlands of England, the center of the textile industry, wool combers were in such short supply that this advertisement appeared: "To Woolcombers. Wm. Toplis and Co. have opened a free shop, at Mansfield ... for Combers from any part of the Kingdom. The prices given are equal to any society [i.e. guild] and good steady workmen may make very handsome wages."[10] Employers also had to offer all sorts of inducements to skilled workers and had to make major concessions to keep them on the job. The loss of key workers could shut down an entire factory. James Watt had pressing problems with finding workers who could cut and fit the valves and cylinders to the proper tolerances; indeed, many of his early failures were of execution, not design. Arkwright kept his skilled people working extra hours because they were so scarce. Many iron mills kept their furnaces going even in slack times in order to keep from losing their labor force. Employers used every possible medium to advertise for workers, and one authority reported that children and paupers were employed only after other sources of labor were absorbed.[11] In brief, it was difficult to recruit a workforce that had the necessary skills. Labor mobility was enhanced by wage incentives, but traditions bound some to their trades and others to their agrarian life.

Training

The second major problem was that of training. Once the personnel were recruited, they had to be taught the new skills of an industrial life. Literacy was uncommon,

---

9. R. M. Hartwell, "Business Management in England during the Period of Early Industrialization: Inducements and Obstacles," in C. J. Kennedy, ed., *Papers of the Sixteenth Business History Conference* (Lincoln, Nebr.: 1969), p. 66.

10. Cited in Stanley D. Chapman, *The Early Factory Masters: The Transition to the Factory System in the Midlands Textile Industry* (New York: Augustus M. Kelley, 1967), p. 192.

11. Ibid., p. 168.

and basic educational skills were lacking; drawings, instruction sheets, and procedures for machine operation demanded some ability to read, to figure, and to respond with predictable results. Training was conducted largely by oral instruction, demonstration, and trial and error. The new employee learned from someone else, usually a coworker, how to operate a machine or process a piece of material. Standardized methods were unheard of, and workers blithely followed the precepts of someone else who knew little more than they. The shortage of skilled workers, such as machinists, millwrights, and instrument makers, was a serious problem. An even more serious problem, however, came in the form of the new skills needed in the factory, because no previous jobs had required exactly these same skills. Transferring the workers' existing skills to new situations meant problems of training as well as resistance to the new methods. The traditional prejudices against anything new added to management's discomfort. Finally, workers were not accustomed to abiding by the accuracy and tolerances demanded by the technique of interchangeable parts on which many factories were based. Even the relatively crude measuring tools required instruction for use. The workers, accustomed to individualizing their work, resisted the standardization of parts, methods, and tools required by the interchangeable-parts method of production.

The haphazard acquisition of knowledge from coworkers or inept supervisors, the lack of standard methods of work, and worker resistance to new methods posed serious problems for efficient factory operation. Employers resorted to developing their own schools to teach elementary arithmetic and geometry and other skills needed in the factory and not available in the populace. Jobs were specialized because of the ease of teaching them to the workers. The goal was not only efficiency, but also solving the practical problems of finding and training personnel. In short, industrialization required an educated workforce, something sorely lacking in the early days of the Industrial Revolution. Jobs were limited in scope to ease the training problems, and employers sought to provide opportunities to develop employees' skills.

Discipline and Motivation

The third problem, and by no means the least considerable, was that of discipline and motivation. Accustomed to the craft traditions of independence and the agrarian mores of self-sufficiency, workers had to develop habits of industry, such as punctuality, regular attendance, the acceptance of a new regime of supervision, and the mechanical pacing of work effort. Instead of supervising by the traditional aspects of artisanry and the hallowed master-servant relationship, the factory substituted a different discipline: it demanded regularity rather than spurts of work, and accuracy and standardization rather than individuality in design and methods. Apparently the new habits did not come easily: worker attendance was irregular; feast days, which were common traditions in the domestic system, caused large-scale absenteeism for factory operators; and workers tended to work in spurts by laboring long hours, collecting their money, and then disappearing for countless days of dissipation. As one observer commented, "If a person can get sufficient [income] in four days to support himself for seven days, he will keep holiday the other three; that is, he will live in riot and debauchery."[12] Some workers took a weekly holiday they called Saint Monday, which meant either not working or working very slowly at the beginning of the week. To combat the problem of feast days, some early employers resorted to using the traditional holidays for company-sponsored outings and feasts to build company loyalty, break the monotony of the work year, and cement personal relations. For example, Arkwright held a feast for five hundred employees at his Cromford mill in 1776, and Matthew Boulton hosted seven hundred at his Soho plant.

Machine smashing, although sporadic, was another disciplinary problem. However, much of this behavior antedated the perfection of the steam engine and the growth of large factories. In 1753, John Kay's flying shuttle and other inventions were smashed and his home destroyed by workers protesting the introduction of this laborsaving machinery. James Hargreaves suffered a similar fate at his Blackburn mill in 1768. Operators of the old hand spinners were convinced that the new jenny would put them out of work, so they raided Hargreaves's house and smashed his machines. The machine-breaking era peaked in 1811–1812, and the movement gained a label for the machine smashers, the Luddites, which originated because a youth in Ludlam had smashed his knitting frame when his father had been too harsh with him.

The Luddite movement never had a unified purpose or a single leader. Scattered groups did the smashing, each proclaiming they were following orders from their fictitious general, "Ned Ludd." The name "Luddite" was first used in 1811, when a rash of machine breaking occurred, primarily in the hosiery-knitting trade around Nottingham. However, these protests appeared to be based on grounds other than fear of unemployment resulting from technological advancement. In Nottingham wages were falling, unemployment was rampant, and food prices were rising owing to the government's policy on food imports. Machine smashing was a convenient way to demonstrate dissatisfaction, although it was other latent forces, not technology, that caused the problem.[13] Disciplinary efforts against the Luddites were rather draconian. One Luddite, named Mellor, assassinated a mill owner, and he and his followers were hanged in York (1812). Public fears of further violence led to more hangings of Luddites (Nottinghamshire, Lancaster, and Chester), and the movement soon died for lack of leadership.

Efforts to motivate people fell into three categories and, on close inspection, appear to have changed only in application, not theory, up to the present day. Positive inducements (the carrot), negative sanctions (the stick), and efforts to build a new factory ethos became the methods for providing motivation and discipline. The carrot was the opportunity to earn more money through wage incentives; thus

---

12. J. Powell, *A View of Real Grievances* (1772), quoted in Asa Briggs, ed., *How They Lived*, vol. 3 (Oxford: Basil Blackwell, 1969), p. 184.

13. Malcolm I. Thomis, *The Luddites: Machine Breaking in Regency England* (Hamden, CT: Archer Books, 1970).

the employee's pay was based on output or performance. This notion of wage incentives represented a major break with tradition. Economists of the seventeenth and eighteenth centuries of the mercantilist school of economics believed that income and the supply of labor offered were negatively related, that is, as wages rose, workers would choose to go spend their money, returning only after it had been spent and more was needed. This viewpoint may be illustrated in the conclusion of a wool merchant who worked under the domestic system:

> It is a fact well known . . . that scarcity, to a certain degree, promotes industry . . . a reduction of wages in the woolen manufacture would be a national blessing and advantage, and no real injury to the poor. By this means we might keep our trade, uphold our rents, and reform the people in the bargain.[14]

This pre–Industrial Revolution point of view that the hungriest worker was the best worker justified keeping wages low to ensure an abundant, motivated workforce. In contrast were the writings of Adam Smith:

> The wages of labour are the encouragement of industry, which, like every other human quality, improves in proportion to the encouragement it receives. . . . When wages are high, accordingly, we shall always find the workmen more active, diligent, and expeditious than where they are low. . . . Some workmen, indeed when they can earn in four days what will maintain them through the week, will be idle the other three. This, however, is by no means the case with the greater part. Workmen, on the contrary, when they are liberally paid by the piece, are very apt to over-work themselves, and to ruin their health and constitution in a few years. . . . If masters [employers] would always listen to the dictates of reason and humanity, they have frequent occasion rather to moderate, than to animate the [work] of many of their workmen.[15]

With an appeal to moderation in application, the classical economics of Adam Smith disagreed with the tradition that the worker must be kept at the subsistence level and that the best worker was the hungriest one. Rather, Adam Smith held that monetary incentives brought out the best in people and that they would work harder to get more. Often called the "economic man" assumption, this break with mercantilistic theory brought the opportunity for individual rewards based on initiative.

The factory system continued the domestic system practice of payment based on output. Wage incentives were used more widely in operations that were labor

---

14. J. Smith, *Memoirs of Wool* (1747), quoted in Briggs, p. 213.

15. Adam Smith, *The Wealth of Nations* (1776), vol. 1, bk. I, ch. 8, p. 100.

intensive, that is, where the cost of labor was a large part of total cost and where payment could be tied to individual performance. For example, almost one-half the British cotton-mill workers were on piece rates, as were workers in Boulton and Watt's engine works, but in coal mining, which emphasized teamwork, group piecework plans were tried but were generally ineffective.[16] Performance standards, however, were based on the historically average times for the jobs rather than on a careful study of the jobs themselves and the time that task completion should take.

The stick, negative sanctions, was a practice for which the early industrial system is frequently criticized. Corporal punishment, especially of children, was used, though authors disagree on its frequency and severity. The prevailing attitude toward children, even in respectable homes, was that they should be seen and not heard and that to spare the rod was to spoil the child. In the context of the period, employers treated children as they were accustomed to being treated at home,[17] although that does not condone the treatment.

Graduated fines were more common methods of discipline: one plant fined workers thirty cents for being absent Monday morning and seventy cents for singing, swearing, or being drunk.[18] Because wages often amounted to two or three dollars a week, this was a fairly large portion of a worker's pay. Samuel Oldknow, considered one of the most progressive employers of the period, posted the following rule:

> That when any person, either Man, Woman or Child, is heard to CURSE or SWEAR, the same shall forfeit One Shilling—And when any Hand is absent from Work (unless unavoidably detained by sickness, or Leave being first obtained), the same shall forfeit as many Hours of Work as have been lost; and if by the Job or Piece, after the Rate of 2 [shillings] 6 [pence] per Day—Such Forfeitures to be put into a Box, and distributed to the Sick and Necessitous, at the discretion of their Employer.[19]

The third method of motivation was a general concept oriented toward creating a new factory ethos. The goal was to use religious morals and values to create the proper attitudes toward work. The encouragement of moral education, even on company time and in early company towns, reading of the Good Book, regular attendance at church, and exhortations to avoid the deadly sins of laziness, sloth, and avarice were methods of inculcating in the working population the right habits of industry. A coalition of employers and ministers exhorted the populace to guard against

---

16. E. Brian Peach and Daniel A. Wren, "Pay for Performance from Antiquity to the 1950's," *Journal of Organizational Behavior Management* 12, no. 1 (1992), p. 12.

17. Chapman, *Early Factory Masters*, p. 203.

18. Pollard, *Genesis of Modern Management*, p. 187.

19. The rule was posted December 1, 1797, and is reprinted in B. W. Clapp, ed., *Documents in English Economic History*, vol. 1 (London: G. Bell and Sons, Ltd., 1976), p. 387. Capitalization is from the original.

the moral depravities, which were not only sinful, but also led to a lackadaisical, dissipated workforce. The Quaker Lead Company, for example, punished workers for "tippling [drinking], fighting, and night rambling."[20] Doubtless this moral suasion emanated from more than a concern for the soul of the worker. Pollard presented a succinct statement of these attempts to create a new ethos: "The drive to raise the level of respectability and morality among the working classes was not undertaken for their own sake, but primarily . . . as an aspect of building up a new factory discipline."[21]

THE SEARCH FOR MANAGERIAL TALENT

In addition to the problems of finding, training, and motivating workers, there was also a problem finding qualified managers. As organizations grew, the ability of an owner–manager to supervise the employees was diminished, and an intermediate level of supervision appeared. Judging from early literature, the salaried managers, that is, those in the layer of management below entrepreneur, were usually illiterate workers promoted from the ranks because they evidenced a greater degree of technical skills or had the ability to keep discipline. Typically they were paid only a little more than the other workers and more often than not were attracted to the managerial position because it gave them the power to hire their spouses and children to work in the factory. Untrained in the intricacies of managing, the managers were left on their own to develop a leadership style. Problems were met and solved on an ad hoc basis, and only a few managers could learn from the experiences of others in solving factory problems or handling people. The general view of leadership was that success or failure to produce results depended on the character of the leader, on personal traits and idiosyncrasies, and not on any generalized concepts of leadership. Other sources of management talent provided little enlightenment. Entrepreneurs frequently used relatives in managerial positions, presumably based on the assumption that they were more trustworthy or would act to preserve their potential inheritance. This practice also provided training that would help secure ownership and keep control in the family for the next generation. Another source of talent was the countinghouse; entrepreneurs recruited likely looking bank clerks and tellers, thinking they probably had both business and financial acumen. On-the-job experience was relied on to furnish recruits with the necessary knowledge for managing.

The transformation of Great Britain from an agrarian to an industrial society meant that there was no managerial class, or, in modern terms, no group of professional managers. First, there was no common body of knowledge about how to manage. The training of managers supplemented experience on the job with instruction in techniques of production, sources and characteristics of materials,

---

20. Pollard, *Genesis of Modern Management*, p. 193.

21. Ibid., p. 197.

operations of machines, trade practices, and the legal obligations of the firm. This training was oriented toward a specific industry, cotton, woolen, mining, or whatever, and did not lend itself readily to generalization. A manager, trained in one industry, was bound to that industry; to move to another, the manager would need to learn new skills. Second, there was no common code of management behavior, no universal set of expectations about how a manager should act. Codes were developed for specific industries and gave advice about the manager's responsibility for safety, the security of the plant and equipment, design standards for engineering, and procedures to follow in safeguarding the owner's interests.

James Montgomery of Glasgow, Scotland, prepared what were most probably the first management texts.[22] Montgomery's managerial advice was largely technical in nature; he advised how to discern quality and quantity of work, how to adjust and repair machinery, how to keep costs down, and how to "avoid unnecessary severity" in disciplining subordinates. He noted that a manager must be "just and impartial—firm and decisive—always on the alert to prevent rather than check faults after they have taken place. . . ."[23] This latter comment on controlling was perceptive and indicated an early understanding that the control function is essentially looking forward rather than backward. However, Montgomery's advice was for the cotton industry, and like most other early writers, he did not seek to develop any generalized principles of management.

Montgomery was so highly regarded as a manager that he was brought to the United States in 1836 to become superintendent of the York Mills in Saco, Maine. This gave Montgomery the opportunity to conduct what was probably the first comparative study of management through the analysis of different economies. He found that the United States had higher costs of production, paid higher wages (including wages for women), but had lower costs of materials. British firms had lower costs, paid lower wages, but paid more for raw materials. The relative competitive efficiency resided in Great Britain, in Montgomery's opinion, because the British firms were better managed.[24] Montgomery's study was of cotton mills only, but it gives some idea of the differing states of managerial knowledge in the United States and Great Britain in 1840.

Early managerial salaries left much to be desired. The first-line supervisors, or overlookers, were paid little more than the workers. Often the white-collar salaried managers were paid on the basis of their social class rather than on the

---

22. James Montgomery, *The Carding and Spinning Masters' Assistant; or the Theory and Practice of Cotton Spinning* (Glasgow: J. Niven, Jr., 1832); idem, *The Cotton Spinner's Manual* (Glasgow: J. Niven, Jr., 1835). Montgomery's contributions are discussed and portions of the 1832 work are reproduced in James P. Baughman, ed., "James Montgomery on Factory Management, 1832," *Business History Review* 42, no. 2 (Summer 1968), pp. 219–226.

23. Baughman, quoting Montgomery, in "James Montgomery on Factory Management, 1832," p. 226.

24. James Montgomery, *The Cotton Manufacture of the United States of America Contrasted and Compared with That of Great Britain* (London: John N. Van, 1840), p. 138.

extent of their responsibility. By 1800, however, Pollard noted that the shortage of talent had forced payment based on the job and not the person.[25] By 1830, the salaries of nonowner managers had risen rapidly and compressed the differential between their pay and that of the owner managers. By the mid-nineteenth century, John Stuart Mill observed that those who managed others had to possess a higher "intelligence factor," that is, "something acquired through education, both formal and informal and on the job learning."[26] Those who were superintendents of others faced many nonroutine obligations dealing with complex problems, justifying their higher salaries. Mill disagreed with Adam Smith's concern about the separation of ownership and management. The "zeal" of hired managers could be stimulated by connecting "their pecuniary interest with the interest of their employers, by giving them part of their remuneration in the form of a percentage of the profits."[27] In history we find the seeds of incentives for nonowning salaried managers to tie their efforts more closely to the performance of the firm.

In Great Britain, but not in France or Italy, the status of the entrepreneur was rising, inducing many young people to seek their fortunes in commerce, or at least to become a junior partner in a large firm. The second- and third-generation offspring of the founder–entrepreneur changed their style to give more status to the salaried managers. They tended to delegate more to and depended more on the salaried managers. Perhaps their affluence, built by the success of preceding generations, made them less desirous of becoming personally involved in daily activities, or perhaps the firms had grown to such a size and the fund of managerial talent had reached such a point that finding reliable subordinates was easier than it had been for their predecessors. In the early factory, the problems of finding and developing managerial talent were acute. There were no business schools for recruiting and no systematic programs for developing people into managers, and managerial skill was judged a localized, idiosyncratic matter.

MANAGEMENT FUNCTIONS IN THE EARLY FACTORY

In addition to the difficulties of staffing the factory, the task of acquiring competent submanagers, and the avoidance of the Luddites, early managers faced planning, organizing, and controlling problems similar to those faced by managers today. In planning operations, the early factory required more farsightedness than the domestic system. As the factory system developed, the new industrialist became more rational, more pragmatically interested in laying a foundation for long-term growth rather than short-term speculative gains. Early mines required long-range planning to develop the veins, and early factories required costly equipment. As

---

25. Pollard, *Genesis of Modern Management*, p. 139.

26. P. Bruce Buchan, "John Stuart Mill—Contributions to the Principles of Management: The Intelligence Factor," *British Journal of Management* 4 (1993), p. 71.

27. John Stuart Mill, quoted in Buchan, p. 73.

capital was sunk, business managers had to be more rational and more aware of the long-term implications of their decisions. Examples of planning in industry are few, and those that do exist are largely technically oriented rather than comprehensive in company scope and application. Robert Owen and Richard Arkwright led the way in preplanning factory layout. Their requirements, or principles, emphasized the orderliness of the work flow and factory cleanliness.

Factory technology demanded the planning of power sources and connections, the arrangement of machinery and space for a smooth flow through of work, and the reduction of confusion through bins and well-placed stores of materials. The firm of Boulton and Watt also stressed factory layout and developed detailed systems for controlling stocks of materials and parts. They engaged in rudimentary work study for production planning, work flow, and assembly methods at their Soho factory (the engine works).[28] The use of standardized, interchangeable parts made planning necessary, both in design and execution of the assembly. James Watt, Jr., saw at an early stage that standard parts would lessen the tasks of controlling work and that detailed planning and proper initial execution would ensure that the final product would meet specifications. Standard parts also eased repairs for the customer and reduced both the company's and the customer's inventory of spare parts, thus simplifying the stock control system.

In organizing, managers were limited to a large extent by the caliber of the subordinate managers. Early departmentation, or the grouping of activities, was often based on the number of partners or relatives. With a gesture toward egalitarianism, each one became a department head with one or two salaried managers below to supervise the workers. It has been estimated that in 1820 in the cotton industry there was an average of one first-line supervisor for every twenty-eight workers.[29] Similar ratios were apparent in mining, construction, and other textile firms, suggesting that the organizations were relatively flat, with few levels of management. These small firms were typically family owned and managed, staff personnel were little more than clerks, and the firms were rarely fully integrated; for example, a cotton mill spun cloth, but relied on other firms or agents to finish the process and sell the merchandise.

There is evidence in the textile industry that technology played an important role in how activities and relationships were structured in the emerging factory system.[30] In the beginning, most workshops followed a batch processing technology; that is, there were relatively short runs of manufacturing a quantity of like products at the

---

28. Eric Roll, *An Early Experiment in Industrial Organisation: Being a History of the Firm of Boulton and Watt, 1775–1805* (London: Longmans, Green and Co., 1930). The development of relatively advanced managerial techniques at Boulton and Watt is credited to the founders' sons, Matthew Robinson Boulton and James Watt, Jr. (p. xv).

29. Pollard, *Genesis of Modern Management*, p. 135.

30. Stanley D. Chapman, "The Textile Factory before Arkwright: A Typology of Factory Development," *Business History Review* 48, no. 4 (Winter 1974), pp. 468–473.

same time, followed by another batch of slightly different products, and so on. This description seems to characterize the textile industry until the early 1800s.

As new applications of steam power were made, another technology emerged as more efficient. The new strategy was to arrange the power-driven machines in a line sequence to flow toward completion of the product. This flow technology resembled more the mass production assembly line, with an output of large quantities of standardized products made at a lower per unit cost and intended for a mass market. With this increase in production quantity, it became more economical to specialize labor even further, adding each person's efforts to the flow of work. It was not a moving assembly line as we know it today, but the product was moved from one stage of production to another by carts, workers, chutes, and so on. Departments were established for the various operations necessary to the product flow. With more departments came the need for another level of management to coordinate the work as it flowed from one stage to another. The consequence was scalar organizational growth, creating a taller hierarchy of management and more elaborate procedures and systems so efforts could be integrated. It appears that early textile firms discovered long ago that technology affects the organizational structure. Early batch production methods allowed more informality; however, the application of steam-driven power led to a new factory technology, which required more formality in organizational design.

In controlling performance, entrepreneurs faced numerous problems. Needing to delegate authority to cope with larger enterprises because they could no longer personally oversee all operations, they found that the shortage of trained and trusted submanagers posed problems of accountability. As Adam Smith had observed, it was a rare salaried manager who would exercise the same vigilance over other people's money as over his or her own. Accounting knowledge had not advanced since Pacioli, and its use as an aid to managers was an almost unheard-of phenomenon. Books were kept to account for earnings, wages, material, and sales, but few managers used these accounts as an aid to decision making. Josiah Wedgwood, manufacturer of various pottery products, was one of those few, and he refined his accounts until he was able to use them in setting prices, fixing worker piece rates, determining the percentage of selling expenses to sales, and tracing the embezzlement of certain funds by his head clerk.[31] Unfortunately, it would be more than a century later before better costing techniques were developed.

Through trial-and-error experience, early entrepreneurs attempted to cope with the problems of managing a factory and a workforce. The emphasis on technical rather than managerial problems was probably due to the crude state of the technological art and the pressure to keep abreast of competition and to make the new gadgets work. Management was deemed a localized matter, not subject to generalization, and success was thought to depend on the personal qualities of the managers,

---

31. Neil McKendrick, "Josiah Wedgwood and Cost Accounting in the Industrial Revolution," *Economic History Review*, 2nd ser., 23 (April 1970), pp. 45–67.

not on their grasp of broader principles of management. Management was a personal art, not a discipline; pragmatic, not theoretical; and parochial, not universal.

Some individuals were attempting to fill this void in management knowledge, and their efforts are the subject of Chapter 4. Before turning to them, let us try to gain some perspective on the cultural impact of the Industrial Revolution.

Cultural Consequences of the Industrial Revolution

The revolution was not only technological but also cultural. The new machines, the new factories, and the new cities shook people's tradition-based roots and demanded participation in a new era. In the hearts of many, there is an idealization of the agrarian life before industrialization. Critics have charged that capitalism, together with its offspring—the market and factory systems—robbed people of a golden age of equality and freedom. More specifically, the criticisms have been that people were enslaved to the owners of capital, that they became little more than a commodity in the marketplace of life, that capitalists exploited child and female labor, and that industrialization created poverty, urbanization, pollution, and a host of other societal ills. Let us examine some of these criticisms and attempt to gain a perspective on the cultural consequences of this new age of industrialization and capitalism.

THE CONDITION OF THE WORKER

Economics earned its sobriquet, the dismal science, during the early nineteenth century. Thomas Malthus set out to disprove the optimism of Adam Smith and liberal economics with his famous population argument. Malthus postulated that population increases in geometric proportion whereas the food supply at best increases only arithmetically. The population is limited by the means of subsistence, and the masses tend to reproduce beyond these means, preventing any improvement in their condition. Government relief of the poor only encourages a population increase, food prices go up, and the poor are no better off. The only answer for Malthus (he was not very optimistic about the outcome) was to restrict the supply of labor and to encourage self-restraint in the reproduction of the masses. His was a hopeless view of people as no more than commodities in the marketplace of life, basically powerless to overcome their disadvantage.

David Ricardo did not appear much more optimistic; his "iron law of wages" said that in the long run real wages would tend to stabilize at some minimum level that would provide the worker with just enough means to subsist. The Utopian socialists, such as Robert Owen, saw people as powerless in their environment and wanted to replace the individualism of the market with a communal life. The Utopians did not write of the necessity of revolt but felt they could achieve change through their writings and by example. An opposite view was developed by Karl

Marx and Friedrich Engels, who advocated the need for force as the midwife of history. Because people were powerless in their view, and because they were kept at the subsistence level by the exploitation of the factory masters, they had to unite to break their chains. Although the writings of Marx and Engels were more political essays than economic analyses, they did reflect the economists' dismal view of the world at that time.

Were people powerless and exploited to the poverty level by capitalism? The subsistence level for the masses was not new; they had spent the previous thousand or more years in essentially the same status but as agrarian peasants tied to a feudal landlord. Under mercantilism, the British government regulated wages to keep them low to maintain a favorable balance of trade, and as we saw earlier, it was a common belief that low wages provided an incentive to work. The Industrial Revolution did not create poverty; it inherited it. With Adam Smith came the new market-based philosophy that high wages made people more diligent. The rise of capitalism was creating the means for releasing people from drudgery through laborsaving machines, making people more productive and better paid for less exertion of effort.[32] Furthermore, it is difficult to agree with Marx and Engels that the workers were exploited by the factory owners for basically two reasons: first, the severe shortage of labor would have diminished the managers' power to do as they liked with their labor; and second, workers' real wages were steadily rising from 1790 to 1830 and the workers' lot was improving "well above the level of mere subsistence."[33] For those who were willing to enter the factory and learn its new skills, the new machines and methods made them more productive and raised wages; in turn, added industrial efficiency reduced the prices of goods and raised real wages. The increasing use of incentive payment plans held out a promise of economic betterment for people; no longer tied to remitting a tithe to the feudal lord, workers could, through effort, enhance their own well-being.

Working conditions and the need for time thrift have also been cited by critics as examples of how the agrarian golden life was lost. Hopkins, however, studied a heavily industrialized region of England and concluded "that there was no marked deterioration of working conditions . . . [and to suggest that] the majority of workers . . . were forced to become the slaves of a new time discipline is really a very doubtful proposition, and its unthinking repetition can serve only to perpetuate a historical myth."[34] Any claims of worker exploitation should be considered as being of doubtful validity; through incentives, rising real wages, steady employment, and

---

32. Friedrich A. Hayek, "History and Politics," in F. A. Hayek, ed., *Capitalism and the Historians* (Chicago: University of Chicago Press, 1954), pp. 15–16.

33. T. S. Ashton, "The Standard of Life of the Workers in England: 1790–1830," in Hayek, *Capitalism*, p. 158.

34. Eric Hopkins, "Working Hours and Conditions during the Industrial Revolution: A Re-Appraisal," *Economic History Review* 35 (February 1982), pp. 63, 66.

regular hours, workers were improving their lot when compared with their previous subsistence levels.

CHILD AND FEMALE LABOR

Child and female labor were not inventions of the Industrial Revolution. The domestic system and agricultural life required the participation of all and were built on the family as the basic economic unit. One authority noted that child labor was at its worst in the domestic system long before the factory system.[35] Child and female workers were found primarily in the textile industry, where the technology was simple, and rarely in other industries. Employers would have preferred a mature, stable, adult workforce, but these individuals were scarce and hard to attract. Concern in Great Britain over child labor practices led to two famous parliamentary investigations: the first in 1819 at the behest of Robert Owen, and chaired by Sir Robert Peel, himself an extensive employer of children in his factories, and the second by the Sadler Committee of 1832. Extensive and detailed evidence was given before these committees.[36] Children often began working a twelve-hour day (including meals) at age five and occasionally spent a fourteen-hour day at the factory. This practice was widespread, being found in the cotton, wool, flax, and silk mills, and existing legislation concerning child labor provided no enforcement mechanism. In their testimony, witnesses described the hours (long), wages (low), working conditions (often extremely poor), and the methods of discipline (often harsh). Overall, however, there is evidence that "the Industrial Revolution [did] not increase exploitation [but] gradually improved the situation of children. ... Industrialization, far from being the source of the enslavement of children, was the source of their liberation."[37] Industrialization created more jobs and better jobs; as workers' wages and their real wages rose, child labor declined.

Female workers were attracted to the factory for the wages to build a dowry, for the opportunity of finding a husband, or to supplement the family income. One observer, Mantoux, felt that the entrepreneurs were "tyrannical, hard, sometimes cruel, their passions and greeds were those of upstarts. They had the reputation of being heavy drinkers and of having little regard for the honour of their female employees."[38] Mantoux was guilty of overgeneralization; ample examples

35. R. Whatley Cooke Taylor, *Introduction to a History of the Factory System* (London: Richard Bentley & Sons, 1886), p. 402.

36. For some excerpts, see E. Royston Pike, "Hard Times," *Human Documents of the Industrial Revolution* (New York: Praeger Publishers, 1966), especially pp. 100–218.

37. Clark Nardinelli, "Were Children Exploited during the Industrial Revolution?" in P. J. Uselding, ed., *Research in Economic History*, vol. 11 (1988), p. 268.

38. Paul J. Mantoux, *The Industrial Revolution in the Eighteenth Century*, trans. Marjorie Vernon (New York: Macmillan Co., 1928), p. 397.

can be given, such as Josiah Wedgwood, Matthew Boulton, James Watt, John Wilkinson, Robert Owen, and a host of others, for whom there is no evidence of loose and fancy-free behavior toward their female employees.[39] Only one specific case was cited in parliamentary testimony, and the tenor of the critics' position was that of the "temptations and opportunities" presented by the presence of both males and females in the same workshop.[40] Evidently, if the workers had been segregated by gender, no testimony would have appeared at all. In contrast with the traditional norm of paying what was "suitable" for women's work, Burnette found that, during the Industrial Revolution, "Women seem to have been paid market wages, and the assertion that women were paid customary [i.e., traditional] wages needs to be revised."[41] There was also great concern that unemployed females would be forced by circumstances to prostitution, but a Doctor Hawkins presented evidence for Manchester that of the fifty prostitutes who had been apprehended in the previous four years (1829–1833), only eight came from the factories, while twenty-nine came from the ranks of former household servants.[42]

Evidence concerning child and female labor is contradictory; most testimony hints at the moral degradation of factory life, but the hard statistics are lacking. It appears that emotional and religious overtones were given more credence, isolated instances were ballooned, and no thorough studies compared the past with the conditions at that time. As textile technology advanced and as income rose, child labor decreased dramatically before the passage of legislation regarding the employment of children.[43] What the critics have overlooked is the fact that capitalism was slowly but surely allowing the release of children from the workforce. As better machines were developed to perform the simple jobs, it became uneconomical to employ children. It was an economic force—broadening capitalism—not legislative fiat or a moral rebirth, that freed children from the looms.[44] As for legislation and governmental bodies, it was the Poor Law Authorities, a government office, that sent the paupers into the factories! The paupers were poor or deserted children legally in the care of the state; to relieve the state of the burdens of maintenance, they were sent to whomever would accept their care and feeding.

---

39. See W. O. Henderson, *J. C. Fischer and His Diary of Industrial England 1814–1851* (New York: Augustus M. Kelley, 1966), p. 57. Undoubtedly some of these individuals existed, as they do in all ages, but Fischer maintained that they were not representative of the era.

40. Pike, "Hard Times," p. 285, with the lurid title of "Seduction in the Mills."

41. Joyce Burnette, "An Investigation of the Female-Male Wage Gap during the Industrial Revolution in Britain," *Economic History Review* 50 (1997) p. 278.

42. Pike, "Hard Times," p. 297.

43. Clark Nardinelli, "Child Labor and the Factory Acts," *Journal of Economic History* 40 (December 1980), pp. 739–755.

44. W. H. Hutt, "The Factory System of the Early Nineteenth Century," in Hayek, *Capitalism*, p. 184.

To understand the critics of the factory system, it is necessary to consider the Victorian value system that was in operation. The Victorian period began before Queen Victoria ascended the throne in 1837.[45] The Victorian values of a profound social conscience about employing women and children and a formal adherence to strict standards of personal and social morality began forming around 1800. Economic and social conditions had been worse before the Industrial Revolution, but the Victorian value sets of people like Charles Dickens established the rationale for criticizing the emerging factory system.

There is evidence that the factory system led to a general rise in the standard of living (something lacking in the previous thousand years), to falling urban death rates and decreasing infant mortality. These factors led to a population explosion in Great Britain: its inhabitants increased from six million in 1750 to nine million in 1800 and to twelve million in 1820. Further, infant mortality before the age of five fell from 74.5 percent in 1730–1749 to 31.8 percent in 1810–1829. The absence of significant medical advances during the period suggests the conclusion that people were better able to feed, clothe, and care for themselves.[46] Heilbroner pointed out that factory life, even with urban poverty, represented an improvement over life in an agrarian and domestic system. Poverty was not new; it had just been collected in one place, the city, and made more easily visible to the legislators, intellectuals, and others. Isolated and scattered, agrarian poverty did not shock the sensibilities, but next door and down the street, it became a problem. Heilbroner further answered the critics of the Industrial Revolution in saying that the criticism was based on political and not economic unrest. Great Britain of that period was characterized by a surging interest in rights and justice and in political reform; the populace had "a critical temper of mind before which any economic system would have suffered censure."[47] This criticism was directed at the entrepreneurs, not because they were to blame, but because they were a convenient symbol of change.

One cannot tax capitalism with the unsavory conditions and practices of the Industrial Revolution. The factory system inherited child and female labor, poverty, and long working hours from the past, it did not create them; the new age of industrial capitalism was creating through the factory a method for people to gain leverage for a better life.

---

45. John W. Osbourne, *The Silent Revolution: The Industrial Revolution in England as a Source of Cultural Change* (New York: Charles Scribner's Sons, 1970), pp. ix–xi.

46. Margaret C. Buer, *Health, Wealth and Population in the Early Days of the Industrial Revolution, 1760–1815* (London: George E. Routledge & Sons, 1926), p. 30. Cited by Robert Hessen, "The Effects of the Industrial Revolution on Women and Children," in Ayn Rand, *Capitalism: The Unknown Ideal* (New York: American Library, 1966), p. 104.

47. Robert L. Heilbroner, *The Making of Economic Society* (Englewood Cliffs, NJ: Prentice Hall, 1962), pp. 85–86.

SUMMARY

The Industrial Revolution created a new cultural environment and a revised set of problems for management. People's needs were becoming more complex as they sought to adjust to life in the city and to factory life. Organizations were being reshaped by the demands for heavy infusions of capital, by the division of labor, and by the need for economical, predictable performance. Organizations needed to innovate and compete in a market economy; this created pressures for growth and the economies to be obtained from large-scale production and distribution. Economic theory recognized that the entrepreneur–manager performed a distinct role in combining the traditional three factors of production in the ever-growing factory system. With size came the need for managers, the need for a capable, disciplined, trained, motivated workforce, and the need for rationalizing the planning, organizing, and controlling of operations in the early enterprise. The next chapter examines some early management pioneers who proposed solutions for coping with the growing factory system.

4 Management Pioneers in the Early Factory

A prevailing theme so far has been the relationship of management thought to its cultural environment. The factory system posed new problems for owners, managers, and society at large. This chapter focuses on four individuals who pioneered in proposing solutions to the manifold pressures of coping with the earliest industrial organizations. History leaves a notoriously scanty scent. Records and memorabilia have been lost or destroyed, notable ideas may never be committed to writing, and judgments must be made on perhaps a small part of what actually occurred. Of the early management pioneers, history has provided us with the best records for four men: Robert Owen, Charles Babbage, Andrew Ure, and Charles Dupin.

ROBERT OWEN: THE SEARCH FOR A NEW HARMONY

Robert Owen (1771–1858) was a paradox in the turbulent era of the Industrial Revolution. A successful entrepreneur himself, he attempted to halt the surge of industrialism and the evils he saw in it as he called for a new moral order based on a social reorganization. He had a vision of a new industrial society that was to be a combination of agricultural and industrial commune and harkened back to the lost days of more primitive people. Philosophically, he viewed people as powerless, held in the grips of revolutionary forces of the new age of machinery, which destroyed moral purpose and social solidarity.

EARLY MANAGERIAL EXPERIENCES

A self-made man imbued with the self-confidence that typified the early entrepreneurs, Owen, at the age of eighteen, founded his first factory in Manchester, England, during an age of war prosperity when many were getting rich. There was a great impetus in cotton trade, and the new water frame, the weaving machines of Arkwright and Crompton, and the power sources of Watt made large factories feasible. Owen described his introduction to managing: "I looked very wisely at the men in their different departments, although I really knew nothing. But by intensely observing everything, I maintained order and regularity throughout the establishment, which proceeded under the circumstances far better than I had anticipated."[1] Owen's firm was profitable, but he decided to become a salaried manager and sold his equipment to a Mr. Drinkwater and became employed by him. Still with a modicum of experience, he applied himself to the new position:

> I looked grave, inspected everything very minutely . . . I was in with the first [workers] in the morning, and I locked up the premises at night. I continued this silent inspection and superintendence day by day for six weeks, saying merely yes or no to the questions . . . I did not give one direct order about anything. But at the end of that time I felt myself so much master of my position as to be ready to give directions in every department.[2]

Owen, left on his own by Drinkwater, made a success of the mill. He rearranged the equipment, bettered the conditions of the workers, and achieved a great deal of influence over his subordinates. He later attributed his success with the workers to his "habits of exactness" and his knowledge of human nature. He left Drinkwater in 1794 or 1795 to establish a new partnership, the New Lanark, Scotland, venture. At New Lanark, he encountered the ubiquitous problem of scarcity of labor and noted, "It was most difficult to induce any sober, well-doing family to leave their home to go into cotton mills as then conducted."[3] Perhaps this difficulty in attracting labor influenced his personnel policies, and he began forming his visions of a new society. At New Lanark, he employed between four hundred and five hundred parish apprentices, the pauper children furnished by the Poor Law Authorities to whomever would take them. The children worked thirteen hours per day including an hour and a quarter off for meals. Owen continued to employ children, but tried to improve their living and working conditions, even though he could not persuade his partners to accept all his reforms. His reform efforts aimed to reshape the whole village of New Lanark, including the streets, houses, sanitation, and educational system.

At New Lanark, Owen began to form some new ideas about the welfare of society. Industrial progress, he felt, was not adequate to support the growing population. He

---

1. Robert Owen, *The Life of Robert Owen* (London: Effingham Wilson, 1857; reissued by Augustus M. Kelley, 1967), pp. 31–32.

2. Ibid., p. 39.

3. Ibid., p. 79.

prepared a report to the citizens of Lanark County that began with "manual labor, properly directed, is the source of all wealth and national prosperity." The economic and social problem was to develop agriculture to use more intensive methods of cultivation to feed more people. He therefore prepared a plan:

1. To cultivate the soil with a spade instead of the plough.
2. To make such changes as the spade cultivation requires, to render it easy and profitable to individuals, and beneficial to the country.
3. To adopt a standard of value, by means of which, the exchange of the products of labour may proceed without check or limit, until wealth shall become abundant, that any further increase to it will be useless, and will not be desired.[4]

Owen's spade husbandry plan of 1821 would create jobs, enabling more people to be employed, thereby increasing their ability to consume the products of industry. This plan of creating more arduous, menial jobs flew in the face of the mechanical progress that was being made at that time. It was a preface, however, to his plans that would lead to his formula for a communal society.

At New Lanark, Owen faced the same disciplinary problems faced by other manufacturers. Like others who had attempted to create a new factory ethos, he tried to use moral suasion rather than corporal punishment. He developed one particularly unique device, the silent monitor, to aid discipline. Under this system, Owen awarded four types of marks to his superintendents, and they in turn rated their subordinates. These marks were translated into color codes of black, blue, yellow, and white in ascending order of merit. A block of wood was mounted on each machine and the four sides painted according to the code. At the end of each day, the marks were recorded, translated, and the appropriate color side of the block turned to face the aisle. Owen reported that he "passed daily through all the rooms and the workers observed me always to look at these telegraphs—when black I merely looked at the person and then at the colour."[5] This wooden albatross motivated laggards to overcome their deficiency and supposedly induced the white block good guys to maintain theirs. It was most certainly a precursor of modern management's public posting of sales and production data to instill departmental pride or to encourage competition.

---

4. Robert Owen, *Report to the County of Lanark of a Plan for Relieving Public Distress* (Glasgow: Wardlaw and Cunninghame, 1821), p. 131.

5. Owen, *Life of Robert Owen*, p. 80. The electric telegraph of Robert Morse had not been invented; Owen used "telegraph" to mean viewing a record of performance from a distance.

Robert Owen. Courtesy of the
Warren J. Samuels Portrait
Collection at Duke University.

THE CALL FOR REFORM

Predating Mayo, Roethlisberger, Likert, and others who have urged concern for the human resource assets of a firm, Owen set forth his rationale for a new philosophy:

> You will find that from the commencement of my management I viewed the population [the labor force] ... as a system composed of many parts, and which it was my duty and interest so to combine, as that every hand, as well as every spring, lever, and wheel, should effectually cooperate to produce the greatest pecuniary gain to the proprietors. ... Experience has also shown you the difference of the results between a mechanism which is neat, clean, well-arranged, and always in a high state of repair; and that which is allowed to be dirty, in disorder, without the means of preventing unnecessary friction, and which therefore becomes, and works, much out of repair. ... If, then, due care as to the state of your inanimate machines can produce such beneficial results, what may not be expected if you devote equal attention to your vital machines [the human resource], which are far more wonderfully constructed?[6]

Owen chided his fellow manufacturers for not understanding the human element. He charged that they would spend thousands on the best machines, yet buy the cheapest labor. They would spend time improving machines, specializing labor, and cutting costs, yet make no investment in the human resource. He appealed to their pecuniary instincts, claiming that money spent on improving labor "would return you, not five, ten, or fifteen per cent for your capital so expended, but often fifty, and in many cases a hundred per cent."[7] He claimed a 50 percent return at New Lanark and said it would shortly reach 100 percent. He claimed that it was more profitable to show such concern for people and that it also served to relieve the "accumulation of human misery."

Accounting records from the New Lanark venture indicate that Owen's estimates of return on investment and profits were only slightly exaggerated. At New Lanark the partners each took 5 percent of their investment as a return to capital, and then prorated the share of each partners' profits based on their investment. During Owen's involvement at New Lanark (1799–1828), his approximate share of gross

---

6. Ibid., app. B, p. 260.

7. Ibid., p. 261.

profits was £128,500 (British pounds sterling) plus 5 percent of his £130,000 capital (£6,500 per year). His annual return on investment typically exceeded 15 percent and, from 1811 to 1814, some 46 percent.[8]

Owen's venture at New Lanark was profitable, but at least one person doubted whether this was due to his personnel policies. One biographer noted that profits in the cotton-spinning industry at that time were so large, averaging 20 percent or more on capital invested, that any personnel policy could have been profitable. "In fact the margin of profit was so wide that we need scarcely look for any other explanation of Owen's success as a manufacturer."[9] Whatever the reasons for his own success, Owen deplored the commercialism of life. He declared an intellectual war on capitalism and also attacked the church because it condoned the evils of the new industrial age. These views branded him as a radical and made it more difficult for him to persuade others of the need for reform. Owen felt that the crucial error of all established religions was the preaching of the doctrine of human responsibility. He held that humans were creatures of their environment, relatively incapable of escaping it without a moral rearmament through education. Contrary to the church view that good character was promoted by the promise of rewards and punishment, especially in the hereafter, Owen felt that character developed solely if the material and moral environment was proper. To these ends, he became more active politically about 1813 and proposed a factory bill to prohibit the employment of any child under the age of ten and to limit work to ten hours per day with no night work for children. His proposal was too radical for other manufacturers and politicians of that time. After many political intrigues, the bill became law in 1819, but instead of applying to all factories, it applied only to cotton mills and set the age limit at nine and not ten.

A biographer suggested that, frustrated in his attempts to reform society, Owen became slightly mad in 1817.[10] Failing to achieve his goals in Great Britain, he read an ad in the *London Times* that offered for sale some thirty thousand acres in Posey County, Indiana, in the United States of America. The sellers were a religious society, the Harmonians, followers of George Rapp; the asking price was £30,000, and the land was situated along the Wabash River. In the decade or so that the Harmonians had been there, some two thousand acres had been cleared for vineyards, orchards, and gardens; a sawmill, machine shops, and cotton and woolen mills had been erected; and numerous brick and log dwellings had been completed.

Owen acquired the property, renamed it New Harmony, and set out to achieve his social reforms. The primary goal of Owen's new moral society was to provide for the happiness of its members. A new currency would be created based on the labor credits, there would be no division of labor, everyone would receive a general education, and although people would be trained for jobs, they would be able to

---

8. John Butt, "Robert Owen as a Businessman," in *Robert Owen, Prince of Cotton Spinners*, ed. John Butt (Bristol: David & Charles, 1971), pp. 199–201, 211–13.

9. Frank Podmore, *Robert Owen, a Biography* (New York: Appleton, 1924), p. 642.

10. G. D. H. Cole, *The Life of Robert Owen*, 3rd ed. (Hamden, CT: Archon Books, 1966), p. 197.

work in other jobs as they wished. Freedom of speech was guaranteed, and women were guaranteed the same rights and privileges as men. Owen promised to give the property to the community.

News of New Harmony spread quickly, and by the time it opened, eight hundred people were ready to move onto the property formerly occupied by seven hundred Harmonians. Although the quantity of people that came to live in New Harmony was a problem, the greatest difficulty arose from the quality of the settlers. There were a few dedicated people who were aware of Owen's beliefs and took them as their own, but there were also those who had heard that New Harmony was a place where you could work a little, or not at all, and the society would still feed, clothe, and house you. For a few months the excitement of the new adventure kept everyone's morale high, but steadily the excitement and newness began to wear off. For lack of brewers, the brewery was idle. Because there were no millers the grain mill was not in use. With only a few dozen farmers, the task of feeding a population swollen to nearly one thousand was a difficult one. Although the communal society was by no means ready to collapse, its problems seriously lowered the general morale. Owen assumed the position of governor, and many felt that in reassuming his previous position of complete authority, he was abandoning his promise to turn all property over to the community. Owen tried to reorganize the society, but gave up, leaving in 1827.[11]

After New Harmony, Owen found himself both financially and emotionally broken. Owen had thought that what he had learned and applied in his cotton mills could be applied to the whole society, but he was unable to persuade others that his new moral order was realistic and not Utopian. As a reformer, Owen devised laws for relief of the poor and proposed solutions to unemployment problems. He proposed Villages of Cooperation, like New Harmony, which would have a communal sharing of surplus and be based on agriculture. He fought against the Malthusian doctrine of overpopulation, saying that if all shared, none would hunger. He deplored the evils of the division of labor; in his ideal system, each person would do a number of different jobs, switching easily from one to another. For him, it was the evils of the wage system and capitalism that maintained life at a subsistence level. In 1834, Owen led the British Trade Union movement, a working-class movement based on the idea of collective action to control the means of production. He failed. Nevertheless, Robert Owen, a Utopian socialist, sowed the first seeds of concern for the human element in industry.

CHARLES BABBAGE: THE IRASCIBLE GENIUS

To call Charles Babbage (1792–1871) an irascible genius is to pay him the greatest compliment, for he fitted both qualities and emerged as a significant figure in management thought well before Frederick W. Taylor. Largely technique oriented

11. More detailed accounts of the New Harmony experiment may be found in Podmore, *Robert Owen*, ch. 13; and George B. Lockwood, *The New Harmony Movement* (New York: Appleton, 1905), pp. 59–68.

like his contemporaries, Babbage, through his application of technological aids to human effort, earned a place in history as the patron saint of operations research and management science. He theorized and applied a scientific approach to management long before the scientific management era began in the United States. Born in Devonshire, England, the son of a wealthy banker, Babbage used his inheritance in a lifelong quest "into the causes of all those little things and events which astonish the childish mind."[12] He remarked that his first question after receiving a new toy was invariably, "Mamma, what is inside of it?" and he also invariably broke open the toy if the answer did not appear satisfactory. The value of his work was recognized by few of his contemporaries, and he was generally considered a crackpot by his neighbors. His personal traits were not endearing to those who disturbed his cogitations. In retaliation against the ubiquitous English organ-grinders, he blew bugles and created a commotion outside his house to scare them away. One contemporary, perhaps a neighbor, wrote, "He spoke as if he hated mankind in general, Englishmen in particular, and the English Government and organ grinders most of all."[13]

THE FIRST COMPUTER

Babbage's scientific output was phenomenal. He demonstrated the world's first practical mechanical calculator, his difference engine, in 1822. Ninety-one years later, its basic principles were being employed in Burroughs's accounting machines. Babbage had governmental support in his work on the difference engine, but his irascibility cost him the support of government bureaucrats for his analytical engine, a versatile computer that would follow instructions automatically. As early as 1833 he conceived his analytical engine that could, in effect, scan a stream of instructions and put them into operation. Touring textile mills in France, he saw looms weaving very complicated patterns from instructions cut into cards. A silk weaver, Joseph Marie Jacquard, had developed punched cards strung together to make a chain and to fall at the appropriate time with a hole signaling the loom to lift a thread and become part of the design, or a blank that stopped a thread. The Jacquard loom anticipated the binary zero/one, off/on system of George Boole's algebra that formed the principle for modern computer operations. Babbage borrowed Jacquard's concept, but demonstrated foresight in his use of punch cards for the storage of information as well as the guidance of machine operations. Half a century later, Herman Hollerith invented the earliest practical punched-card tabulating machine, probably building on the ideas of Jacquard and Babbage.

---

12. Charles Babbage, *Passages from the Life of a Philosopher* (London: Longman Green, 1864), p. 7.

13. "The Cranky Grandfather of the Computer," *Fortune*, March 1964, pp. 112–113. See also an excellent biography by Maboth Moseley, *Irascible Genius: A Life of Charles Babbage, Inventor* (London: Hutchinson & Co. Publishers, 1964).

In concept, Babbage's computer had all the basic elements of a more modern version. It had a store (or memory device), a mill (or arithmetic unit), a punch-card input system, external memory storage, and conditional transfer.[14] In retrospect, "Babbage's genius was not in the calculating power of his engine but in the mechanization of the organizing and logical control of the arithmetic function."[15] Babbage also conceived an "apparatus for printing on paper, one, or if required, two copies of the results" of the output—a Victorian version of a modern printer.[16] Babbage was so fascinated with designing his analytical engine that he never built one. One design would suggest an improvement, then another, and another because he could never stop short of perfection. Shortly before his death in 1871 he wrote: "If I survive some few years longer, the Analytical Engine will exist, and its works will afterwards be spread over the world."[17] For more than a century his work would lie dormant, waiting other times and other people to advance his seminal ideas.

One of the few bright spots in Babbage's life was his friendship with Augusta Ada (1816–1852), countess of Lovelace and daughter of the poet Lord Byron. The countess had a gift for mathematics and engineering and was one of the few who really understood Babbage's work. She wrote treatises on his work, expressed his ideas better than he could, and wrote programs for the computer. She warned people against becoming dependent on the computer, which "has no pretentions [sic] whatever to originate anything . . . [and would] do whatever we know how to order it to perform."[18] Together with Babbage, she developed a surefire system for betting on horses; unfortunately, the horses did not follow the system, and the countess had to pawn her jewels. Undaunted by the countess's loss of the family jewels (though the count of Lovelace was upset), Babbage continued his work and developed for his computer gaming programs that were a forerunner of modern business gaming techniques. He limited his research to developing a computer program to play tick-tack-toe and chess, but he saw that the machine (he called it an automaton) could be programmed to make the best possible combinations of positions and moves, including anticipation as far as three moves in advance. Development of this automaton to play chess and tick-tack-toe certainly must have brought him to the fringe of probability theory in programming for player positions and decision alternatives.

---

14. In computer terminology, conditional transfer refers to the "if" statement: that is, instructing the computer "if such and such occurs, follow this path; if not, proceed in the normal sequence of control."

15. Daniel A. Wren, "A Calculating Genius," *Knowledge Management* 2 (May 1999), p. 104.

16. Details of Babbage's printing apparatus are provided in Harry W. Buxton, *Memoir of the Life and Labours of the Late Charles Babbage, Esq. F.R.S.*, ed. Anthony Hyman (Cambridge, MA: The MIT Press, 1988), p. 182.

17. Babbage, *Passages from the Life of a Philosopher*, p. 449.

18. Margot Strickland, *The Byron Women* (London: Peter Owen Ltd., 1974), pp. 206–207.

ANALYZING INDUSTRIAL OPERATIONS

Inevitably, Babbage's inquisitive mind and wide interests led him to write of management. His most successful book was *On the Economy of Machinery and Manufactures*, published in 1832. Babbage became interested in manufacturing and management as a result of his problems supervising construction of his own engine, and he visited a wide variety of British and French factories. He described in great detail the tools and machines, discussed the "economical principles of manufacturing," and, in the true spirit of inquiry for a researcher, analyzed operations, the kinds of skills involved, and the expense of each process and suggested directions for improving the then-current practices.[19]

As a management scientist, Babbage was interested in machinery, tools, the efficient use of power, developing counting machines to check quantity of work, and economy in the use of raw materials; these he called the mechanical principles of manufacturing. He developed a "method of observing manufactories," which was closely akin to a scientific, systematic approach to the study of operations. The observer prepared a list of questions about the materials used, normal waste, expenses, tools, prices, the final market, workers, their wages, skill required, length of work cycle, and so on. In essence it was the same procedure that an operations analyst or a consultant would use in approaching an assignment. Babbage emphasized the difference between "making" products (which could be done in small workshops) and "manufacturing," operating on a larger scale, which necessitated the careful arrangement of the "whole system of [the] factory" to reduce the cost of production. In this early concept of economies of scale, Babbage also recognized that a competitive market called for "ingenuity," innovation and improvement, if a firm was to remain viable.

On the human side, he recalled the Luddite movement and pleaded with workers to recognize that the factory system worked for their betterment: "It is of great importance that the more intelligent amongst the class of workmen should examine the correctness of these views; because . . . the whole class may . . . be led by designing persons to pursue a course, which . . . is in reality at variance with their own best interests."[20]

His attempts to show the mutuality of interests between the worker and the factory owner were somewhat similar to what Frederick Taylor said seventy-five years later. According to Babbage,

> the prosperity and success of the master manufacturer is essential
> to the welfare of the workman . . . whilst it is perfectly true that

19. Charles Babbage, *On the Economy of Machinery and Manufactures* (London: Charles Knight, 1832), pp. 94–96. It should be noted that Babbage's discussion of expenses has the appearance of an early form of cost accounting. However, it differed from modern cost accounting in that it described costs rather than providing for an analysis of what costs ought to be, as under a standard cost system.

20. Ibid., p. 192.

workmen, as a class, derive advantage from the prosperity of their employers, I do not think that each individual partakes of that advantage exactly in proportion to the extent to which he contributes to it ... it would be of great importance, if ... the mode of payment could be so arranged, that every person employed should derive advantage from the success of the whole; and that the profits of each individual should advance, as the factory itself produced profit, without the necessity of making any change in wages.[21]

Babbage's profit-sharing scheme had two facets: that a portion of wages would depend on factory profits, and that the worker "should derive more advantage from applying any improvement he might discover," that is, a bonus for suggestions. Workers would receive a fixed salary based on the nature of their task plus a share in the profits, and the suggestion system would use a committee to determine the proper bonus for production savings. Babbage saw a number of advantages in his proposal: (1) each worker would have a direct interest in the firm's prosperity, (2) each would be stimulated to prevent waste and mismanagement, (3) every department would be improved, and (4) "it would be the common interest of all to admit [hire] only the most respectable and skillful [workers]." In effect, the work group, operating under a profit-sharing plan, would act to screen out undesirables who would reduce its share. Finally, Babbage saw his scheme as removing the necessity for combinations of workers because their interests would be the same as those of the employers. With this mutuality of interests between worker and manager, neither would oppress the other, and all would prosper.

Beyond his significant scientific contributions, Charles Babbage made significant advancements in understanding the problems of the emerging factory system. His analytic, scientific approach to the study of manufacturing, his recognition of the need for new incentives to enlist the cooperation of the worker, and his search for new harmonies between manager and worker placed him as a person of vision in management.

ANDREW URE: PIONEERING IN MANAGEMENT EDUCATION

It was the task of Andrew Ure (1778–1857) to provide academic training for fledgling managers in the early factory system. Ure studied at Edinburgh and Glasgow universities, receiving his MD from the latter in 1801. In 1804, Ure became professor of chemistry and natural philosophy at Anderson's College in Glasgow, where he was to remain until 1839. Dr. John Anderson, the founder of the college, had lectured on science and through his will founded an institution to educate

---

21. Babbage, *On the Economy of Machinery and Manufactures*, 3rd ed. (1833), p. 253.

adult workers in science.[22] Educational pressures for technically trained white-collar workers and managers soon shifted the composition of Ure's classes from workers to clerks, warehouse workers, artisans, and shopkeepers; from these classes managers for the ever-growing factory system were to be recruited. Ure knew the French engineer and management writer Charles Dupin, and when Dupin visited Great Britain in 1816–1818, Ure escorted him around the Glasgow factories. Dupin commented that many of the managers of these factories were Ure's own students. This fact was acknowledged by Ure, who said that his students were "spread over the [United] Kingdom as proprietors and managers of factories."[23] Dupin's work was influenced by Ure and, in turn, as suggested later, influenced Henri Fayol, another pioneer whose ideas helped lead to modern management theory.

PRINCIPLES OF MANUFACTURING

Ure, deeply concerned with industrial education, set out to prepare for publication a systematic account of the principles and processes of manufacturing. The essential principle of the factory system was the substitution of "mechanical science for hand skill ... [and to provide] for the graduation of labor among artisans."[24] Although Ure devoted a large portion of his book to the technical problems of manufacturing in the silk, cotton, woolen, and flax industries, he eventually dealt with the problems of managing. Obviously pro-management in his analysis, Ure sought an automatic plan to prevent individual intractable workers from stopping work as they pleased and thereby throwing a whole factory into disorder. According to Ure, workers had to recognize the benefits of mechanization and not resist its introduction. To establish this automatic plan, management had to "arrange and connect" manufactures to achieve a harmony of the whole. In every establishment there were "three principles of action, or three organic systems: the mechanical, the moral and the commercial."[25]

Although these formed no clear-cut notions of organizing work, Ure did seek to place them in the harmony of a "self-governing agency." "Mechanical" referred to the techniques and processes of production, "moral" to the condition of personnel, and "commercial" to sustaining the organization through selling and financing. The mechanical part of manufactures was treated extensively by the scientist Ure; the

---

22. We know relatively little about Dr. John Anderson. At the University of Glasgow, Anderson gave James Watt a model of Thomas Newcomen's engine to repair. Watt recognized the deficiencies and began to work on the ideas that led to his engine. Anderson also had Andrew Ure as a student at the University of Glasgow and hired him to teach when Anderson started his college for working people, which was the beginning of Britain's mechanics institutes.

23. Andrew Ure, *The Philosophy of Manufactures: Or an Exposition of the Scientific, Moral and Commercial Economy of the Factory System of Great Britain* (London: Charles Knight, 1835), p. viii.

24. Ibid., p. 20.

25. Ibid., p. 55.

moral aspect brought out the pro-management side of the educator. The factory system of Ure's day was under attack from a number of sources, and Ure set out to defend industrial practices. He argued that factory operatives were better treated "as to personal comforts" than artisans or other workers in nonindustrial establishments. They ate better, enjoyed more leisurely labor because of the machines provided by the factory owner, and were better paid. Instead of appreciating this largess, factory workers engaged in strikes, sabotaged equipment, and caused capital losses for their employers, thus working against their own continued employment. Rebutting the investigations into child labor, Ure noted that most of the witnesses had never visited the factories; he also engaged in some character assassination, charging that one witness was an atheist, one a tavern keeper, and one an assaulter of women. For positive evidence, Ure noted that children lived in well-kept cottages, received both practical and religious education, and were better fed and enjoyed better health than children in the general community. Children employed in agriculture were paid half the factory wages and kept in ignorance. Citing medical investigations sponsored by the Factory Commission, Ure concluded that the incidence of disease, the dietary habits, and the general state of health of all factory workers were better than in the general population.

To illustrate worker nonappreciation of employers' concern for their health, Ure cited an instance in which large ventilating fans had been installed in one factory to reduce the foulness of the air. Instead of thanking the employer, the workers complained that the fresh air had increased their appetites, and therefore they were entitled to a corresponding wage increase! The factory owner reached a compromise with his workers by running the fan only half the day, thereafter hearing no more complaints about foul air or appetites. In terms of the evidence presented in Chapter 3, Ure was probably more right than wrong concerning the condition of labor. He was a defender of the factory system, seeing more benefits accruing to society than disadvantages.

Ure based his conclusions on an 1833 survey of cotton mills in England, primarily those in the Lancashire district, the heart of the textile industry.[26] The survey covered 1,070 mills owned by 157 firms of all sizes, ranging from 19 to 1,692 employees. Of these one thousand plus mills, 332 were still using water to power their looms, some fifty plus years after the Industrial Revolution was triggered by the steam engine. The estimated amount of capital needed for twelve thousand throstles and twenty-four thousand mule spinning machines, plus building, land, and other equipment, was £47,134. Capital intensity was increasing due to the cost of steam power and the mule spinner of Samuel Crompton. Female employees exceeded the number of males (51.6 to 49.4 percent); adults, those age eighteen and above, comprised 59 percent of the workforce, with those under age eighteen forming 41 percent.

---

26. Andrew Ure, *The Cotton Manufactures of Great Britain*, 2 vols. (London: Charles Knight, 1836), vol. 1, pp. 334–42. For a map of the Lancashire Cotton District, see Michael Huberman, *Escape from the Market: Negotiating Work in Lancashire* (Cambridge: Cambridge University Press, 1996), p. 4.

Ure drew some comparisons of the cotton industry with the year 1804 and found that the average work week had declined from seventy-four to sixty-nine hours; the average annual wage had increased from sixty to sixty-five shillings in 1833; and the purchasing power (real wages) of the sixty-five shillings was greater in 1833 than the sixty in 1804. For example, in 1804 sixty shillings would buy 117 pounds of flour and 62.5 pounds of meat; in 1833 sixty-five shillings would buy 267 pounds of flour and 85 pounds of meat. From these data, Ure formed his conclusions about the progress in the cotton industry compared with agricultural workers who were still laboring at subsistence income levels. Child and female labor was widely used in the cotton mills, but no more than previously in the domestic system or in agriculture. Rising real wages, a trend toward shorter and more regular hours, and advancing mechanization were the hallmarks of Ure's cotton industry study. Ure's focus on the cotton industry precluded any generalization about management, but saw progress in the advance of mechanization and the condition of labor.

CHARLES DUPIN: INDUSTRIAL EDUCATION IN FRANCE

A second individual who pioneered in industrial education was the French engineer Baron Charles Dupin (1784–1873). As noted earlier, Dupin had visited Great Britain (1816–1818) and observed the results Andrew Ure was obtaining in preparing individuals for factory management. In 1819, Dupin was named professor of mathematics and economics at the Conservatory of Arts and Professions in Paris.[27] He must have immediately initiated his own curriculum, for in 1831 he wrote, "For 12 years I have had the honor of teaching geometry and mechanics applied to the arts, in favor of the industrial class . . . on the most important questions to the well-being, education, and morality of the workers, to the progress of national industry, to the development of all means of prosperity that work can produce for the splendor and happiness of our country."[28] One of Dupin's colleagues at the conservatory was Jean Baptiste Say, a professor of industrial economy. Say was the person who brought Adam Smith's ideas to France and added to them by identifying management as a fourth factor of production. Because Say and Dupin taught the evening classes "beginning at 8:30 p.m. to artisans and working mechanics [who] have completed the labours of the day," it is reasonable to assume that both Say and Ure influenced Dupin's view of management.[29] Dupin's contribution lay in the influence he had on the course of industrial education and perhaps, though there is no direct historical support, on the later work of Henri Fayol. Fayol is generally

---

27. *La Grande Encyclopaedie*, vol. 15, p. 81.

28. Charles Dupin, *Discours sur le Sort des Ouvriers* [*Discourse on the Condition of the Workers*] (Paris: Bachelier Librairie, 1831), p. 1.

29. "The Conservatory of Arts," *American Mechanics Magazine* 1 (July 2, 1825) p. 343.

credited with being the first to distinguish between technical and managerial skills and the possibility and necessity of teaching management. Yet examine this passage from Dupin, eight decades or so earlier:

> It is to the director of workshops and factories that it is suitable to make, by means of geometry and applied mechanics, *a special study* of all the ways to economize the efforts of workers. . . . For a man to be a director of others, manual work has only a secondary importance; it is his intellectual ability (*force intellectuelle*) that must put him in the top position, and it is in instruction such as that of the Conservatory of the Arts and Professions, that he must develop it.[30]

The special study would be the classes Say, Dupin, and Ure were teaching, and Dupin clearly distinguished this type of program from manual or technical instruction. Fayol, himself educated as an engineer in France, could possibly have read Dupin and gleaned his own notions of teaching management.

Hoaglund reported that by 1826 Dupin's materials on management had been presented in ninety-eight French cities to five thousand or more workers and supervisors.[31] Because his *Discours* was not published until 1831, the number of people he influenced must be greatly expanded. Dupin also demonstrated a rudimentary grasp of the concept of time study and the need to balance workloads after labor was divided: "When [the] division of work is put into operation the most scrupulous attention must be exercised to calculate the duration of each type of operation, in order to proportion the work to the particular number of workers that are assigned to it."[32] He wrote of the need for clear, concise instructions to workers, for producing the desired level of work with the least expenditure of worker energy, and for studying each type of industry in order to find and publish the best results of industrial practice.

The *Discours* was not so much an examination of management as it was an exhortation to remove industrial strife. Dupin also recognized worker uneasiness over the introduction of mechanization into French industry, discussed the work of James Watt, and encouraged workers and managers to recognize the benefits of mechanization to them and to society. Regarding the dangers of technological displacement, he noted that before Watt's engine, British industry employed fewer than one million workers; by 1830, over three million were employed in industry and combined with machinery were equivalent to the power of seven million workers. For Dupin, this was ample proof that mechanization created jobs rather than destroyed them. Evidently the French had their Luddites, and Dupin indicated that

---

30. Ibid., pp. 12–13. Emphasis added. (Author's translation.)

31. John H. Hoaglund, "Management before Frederick Taylor," *Proceedings of the Academy of Management*, ed. Billy Goetz, December 1955, pp. 15–24.

32. Charles Dupin, *Geometrie et Mechanique des Arts et Metiers et des Beaux Arts* (Paris: Bachelier, 1826). Cited and translated by Hoaglund, "Frederick Taylor," p. 30.

such resistance to mechanization was futile. As a solution, he called for widespread industrial training to permit the agrarian and unskilled worker to share in the prosperity of industrialization: "He who perfects the machines tends to give them the advantage over the worker; he who perfects the worker, gives him the same fighting chance, and makes the machine serve his well-being, instead of having to suffer from their competition. Let us concern ourselves with man involved with the difficulties of the work and of the industry."[33] These were insights applicable not only to early nineteenth-century France but also to the world of the twentieth and the twenty-first centuries.

THE PIONEERS: A FINAL NOTE

The four pioneers discussed here were formulating the seeds of a management discipline. But, at their best, these were sparse and rudimentary. What prevented the formalization of a body of management thought during this early stage rather than some three-quarters of a century later? Why did Frederick Taylor, and not Charles Babbage, receive credit for founding scientific management? In retrospect, the reasons are manifold. First, early writings emphasized the techniques and not managing per se. In an age of expanding technology, it was difficult for early writers to separate the managerial function from the technical and commercial aspects of running a firm. Management was more concerned with finance, production processes, selling, and acquiring labor, all of which were indeed critical at the time, rather than with developing principles or generalizations about management. An analogy might be that of young children learning to walk: the motor urge is so great and consumes so much of their energy and attention that the development of speech is retarded. As the skill of walking is perfected, speech develops. The early entrepreneurs were just learning to walk in the new factory system; the technical and human problems consumed so much of their time that they had little left over for articulating generalizations about management.

Second, the period was dominated by the technical genius, the inventor–pioneer, and the owner–founder. Success or failure was more likely to be attributed to their individual characteristics rather than to any generalized ideas about what skills managers needed. Each industry and its problems were considered unique, and hence the principles derived by one entrepreneur were not considered applicable to different situations. Finally, the state of the art of disseminating knowledge must be considered. Few were literate, books were expensive, and schools were either classically oriented toward developing scholars or technique oriented toward the artisan. Scholars read the books of other scholars; it is not likely that Babbage, Dupin, and Ure were widely read by the practicing manager. The classes of Say, Ure, and Dupin undoubtedly reached into some factories but this was probably only a minor fraction of the total management market.

---

33. Dupin, *Discours*, p. 9.

Summary

In Great Britain, and France to a lesser extent, can be found the genesis of modern management thought. Robert Owen appealed to the heart as well as to the pocketbook in his search for a New Harmony between the human factor and the age of machines. Charles Babbage appealed to the mind, became the grandfather of scientific management, and applied a scientific approach to management before Taylor. Andrew Ure taught his experiences and observations and developed managers for the new factories. Dupin learned from Ure and worked with Say to start management classes in France. With the genesis of management thought in Great Britain, the exodus of our story will be the study of management in the United States before the scientific management era.

5

The Industrial Revolution in the United States

T he nineteenth century in the United States was an age of dynamic growth and expansion of the factory system. A colony of mighty Great Britain twenty-four years before the beginning of this age and torn by half a decade of internecine strife in midcentury, the United States was to become the world's leading political and industrial force by the close of the century. This chapter focuses on the Industrial Revolution in the United States, the industries it spawned, and the work of some pre–Civil War management pioneers.

ANTEBELLUM INDUSTRY AND MANAGEMENT

America was a colony for almost as many years as it has been a nation. For its settlers, the lure was manifold: social betterment, economic opportunity, religious freedom, and political separation. No element explains the whole, for the nation that was to emerge was a conglomerate of parts defying a separate identification and explanation. The newcomers to these alien and, often, hostile shores were aristocrats as well as felons, tramps, and petty criminals as well as budding tycoons. Efforts to develop colonial manufactures were frowned on by Great Britain, for they posed the possibility of dangerous competition for Great Britain's early factories. Two documents of 1776 tolled the death of mercantilism: the Declaration of Independence and Adam Smith's *Wealth of Nations*. America's economic heritage was largely mercantile, but the pressures for an escape from the policies of Great Britain were strong. Coincident with the Declaration of Independence in America, Smith's book appeared in Great Britain. It was a declaration of economic independence.

In the years between 1776 and 1787, the ideas of Adam Smith were widely read and discussed by U.S. business and political leaders. Smith's writings fitted into the philosophical concept of the new nation held by those who protested the strong role of government in economic matters. Smith's laissez-faire inclinations were acceptable to the framers of the Constitution. Article I, Section 8, gave Congress the power to impose and collect taxes, borrow money, coin money, fix standards of weights and measures, punish counterfeiters, issue patents, and "regulate commerce with foreign nations and among the several states." Except for those powers, government was to have a relatively hands-off approach to economic affairs and to act primarily to maintain uniformity and order among the states. In addition to a favorable political climate, economic and social conditions were ripe. The United States was a land rich in natural resources, with a growing labor supply. Many colonial merchants had made their fortunes in trade. These funds, aided by the dicta of thrift of early Puritanism, made increasing amounts of capital available for manufacturing. Three of these prosperous merchants, William Almy, Smith Brown, and Moses Brown, of Providence, Rhode Island, provided the capital that opened the industrial age of the United States.

EARLY INDUSTRIAL DEVELOPMENT

Great Britain sought to prevent industrial development by prohibiting the sale of manufacturing equipment and the emigration of skilled labor to the United States. Samuel Slater (1768–1835), an experienced builder and mechanic for the machinery of Richard Arkwright, the British textile pioneer, called himself a farmer on his emigration papers and gained passage to the United States. At this time, cloth was made in the home for home use, put out by various merchants under the domestic system, and occasionally made in small manufactories with hand looms. The firm of Almy and Brown had a small textile operation, but Moses Brown foresaw tremendous possibilities in the more advanced Arkwright machinery. Dangling the lure of a partnership, Brown induced Samuel Slater to bring his technical knowledge to their operations. The result was the country's first technologically advanced textile mill of seventy-two spindles at Pawtucket, Rhode Island, in 1790. Although the Almy, Brown, and Slater partnership did not last, this became known as the Rhode Island System, and it followed closely the managerial practices found in Great Britain. The Rhode Island System relied on a sole proprietorship or a partnership as the form of ownership and spun fine yarn in the mill, but put out weaving to be done by families in the homes. Slater exercised supervision of operations, assisted by his sons, his brother, and other relatives.

By 1808 the United States could boast of fifteen mills, over half of them connected with Slater and his assorted associates. Another conflict with Great Britain, the War of 1812, was to lead to another surge in U.S. textiles. Francis Cabot Lowell, a prominent merchant, had visited Great Britain and observed textile manufacturing by a new power loom driven by waterwheels, rather than by hand-driven looms. Lowell copied these designs and founded the Boston Manufacturing Company of Waltham, Massachusetts. Rather than emulating Slater's management methods, the Waltham System used joint-stock companies and the corporate form of ownership; did not put out work but integrated spinning and weaving to manufacture goods in large quantities; hired nonfamily supervisors and managers for their mills; and relied on adult female labor.

By 1816 the Waltham System became the dominant method of textile manufacturing. Slow to change, Slater and his colleagues waited almost a decade before they changed their strategy.[1] In 1827, Slater became one of the few to use steam-driven power looms at his Steam Cotton Manufacturing Company in Providence, Rhode Island. Whereas other manufacturers depended on the level of water flowing in rivers and streams, Slater was able to regularize production and employment. Slater also began to integrate the manufacturing operations to spin, weave, and finish cloth, ending the putting-out activities. As Slater's mills became more successful, numbering some fifteen separate locations by 1835, he ran out of relatives and began to hire professional managers to whom he delegated the authority and responsibility of running the various mills. Slater also pioneered the use of a factory ledger to accumulate data to determine the cost of producing a yard of cloth. Finally, Slater moved to vertically integrate his operations: moving forward to establish a sales operation in New York and backward by employing individuals to go to sources and purchase the raw materials needed. In brief, the Slater story provides an excellent example of the dynamics of early U.S. enterprise and its strategic response to technological as well as foreign and domestic competitive pressures.

The textile mills also provide some early ideas on organization and management as well as personnel policies. Although the firms were relatively small, a managerial hierarchy did develop when those who owned gradually had to relinquish personal supervision because of the growth of the firm. Thus Slater, Lowell, and others employed salaried managers and created an intermediate level of management. There is also evidence that some rudimentary staff duties were evolving. A mill manager was often "assisted by a superintendent, a technically trained man, and there were overseers with technical responsibilities that cut across the operations of the mill: overseers of repairs . . . or of belting."[2] Thus machinists, woodworkers, and other technically competent persons were hired to oversee the repairs, for example, whereas still other supervisors were responsible for managing the workforce as well as the technical overseers. Supervisors did not need both technical and managerial ability (remember Charles Dupin?) but could rely on specialists. In these early mills, we may have found the antecedents of Frederick Taylor's "functional foremen."

Personnel policies, like managerial strategies, also differed between Slater's Rhode Island System and the Waltham System of Lowell and his associates. The early workforce was largely unskilled because Great Britain attempted to prevent skilled workers from emigrating to the United States.[3] To attract workers,

---

1. Barbara M. Tucker, *Samuel Slater and the Origins of the American Textile Industry, 1790–1860* (Ithaca, NY: Cornell University Press, 1984), especially pp. 99–124.

2. Steven Lubar, "Managerial Structure and Technological Style: The Lowell Mills, 1821–1880," in Jeremy Atack, ed., *Business and Economic History* 12 (March 1984), p. 21.

3. Theodore Marburg, "Aspects of Labor Administration in the Early Nineteenth Century," *Business History Review* 15, no. 1 (February 1941), pp. 1–10.

Slater's Rhode Island System was patterned after the British practice of employing the whole family if possible, and it therefore resulted in more child labor. In contrast, the Waltham System was designed to attract female labor to the factory by establishing company boarding houses. Workers in the Waltham System textile factories were mainly young Yankee females, and they were brought to the factories from neighboring farms by agents who toured the countryside and emphasized the moral and educational advantages of factory work.[4] The females had to be in at 10:00 p.m., and their moral conduct was carefully watched by a housemother.

Even that vocal critic of the British factory system, Charles Dickens, praised the Waltham System factories for their treatment of labor. He reported that the female factory workers were clean, healthy, and of sound moral deportment. He felt the British could learn a great deal by the U.S. example.[5] However, it appears that the Waltham plan was less successful in keeping a labor force; Ware estimated that the females working in New England cotton mills stayed, on the average, one year.[6] The introduction of steam-powered looms, however, had a dramatic effect on the employment of child labor: "with the mechanization of picking and weaving in the early 1820s, Pawtucket's factory system had reached maturity and as a consequence had come to rely increasingly on adult factory labor."[7] Consequently, the U.S. factory did not demonstrate evils in the same depth as did the British factory. Employers were paying high wages to attract and hold their labor, child labor was not as prevalent, and abuses were less frequent and less severe.[8]

The U.S. worker was less resistant to the introduction of machinery, and the Luddites found few followers, except in Pittsburgh, where some hand-loom weavers rioted and destroyed their machines. Americans also took a different stance with respect to organized labor. A legacy from laws concerning guilds in Great Britain was the view that combinations of workers were conspiracies in restraint of trade and therefore illegal. Local craft unions made some headway in the United States, but often ran into court-ordered injunctions when they sought to strike. In a landmark case in 1842 (*Commonwealth v. Hunt*), the Supreme Court of Massachusetts held that a combination of workers was not illegal per se, though if the object of the combination were criminal, then it could be prohibited. The court held that seeking a closed shop (workers must be union members) and striking were not illegal goals and

---

4. Thomas C. Cochran and William Miller, *The Age of Enterprise* (New York: Harper and Row, 1961), p. 19.

5. Charles Dickens, *American Notes for General Circulation*, vol. 1 (London: Chapman and Hall, 1842), pp. 156, 163–164. Corroborating evidence for Dickens's observations may be found in William Scoresby, *American Factories and Their Female Operatives* (Boston: W. D. Ticknor Co., 1845).

6. Norman Ware, *The Industrial Worker: 1840–1860* (Gloucester, MA: Peter Smith Co., 1959), p. 149.

7. Gary B. Kulik, "The Beginnings of the Industrial Revolution in America: Pawtucket, Rhode Island, 1672–1829," Ph.D. dissertation, Brown University, 1980, p. 341.

8. Ross M. Robertson, *History of the American Economy* (New York: Harcourt Brace Jovanovich, 1955), p. 184. Based on his own research, Ware also found fewer evils in the U.S. factory system.

that worker alliances for those purposes were proper. Although the decision applied only to Massachusetts, it discouraged attempts in other states to prosecute worker organizations on conspiracy grounds. In brief, early U.S. industrial development was fostered by the economic, social, and political conditions that encouraged work, thrift, innovation, and competition. The U.S. Industrial Revolution began in textiles but would soon evolve into more far-reaching effects.

THE AMERICAN SYSTEM OF MANUFACTURES

In 1851, the Great Exhibition of the Industry of All Nations was staged in London in the Crystal Palace. What amazed the visitors most was the U.S. exhibit of the unpickable locks of Alfred Hobbs, the sewing machine of Isaac Singer, the repeating pistol of Samuel Colt, and the mechanical reaper of Cyrus McCormick. Not only were these products superior to those of other nations, but also they were all made in a unique fashion—the parts were built to such exacting standards that they were interchangeable, so a person could pick up the parts at random and assemble a complete product. This emergent production technique became known as the American System of Manufactures.

To conclude that manufacture by interchangeable parts was solely the work of the U.S. industry would be inaccurate. As early as 1436, the Arsenal of Venice (Italy) was manufacturing warships by means of standard parts. For example, all bows were built to fit any arrow, all stern posts fit all rudders, and the deck furnishings and riggings were all uniform.[9] Weapons makers in Switzerland, France, and other countries had followed this principle in their work; however, no one had moved the principle of interchangeable parts from weaponry to industry until the Americans did so. What could have happened in the United States to lead to this advance?

In the United States, as elsewhere, it began in the manufacture of arms. Early private contractors, such as Eli Whitney and Simeon North, had made small batches of arms using interchangeable parts, but with limited success.[10] The Springfield (Massachusetts) Armory was established in 1795 as a central workshop to bring weapons makers together to produce armaments, but it really did not begin to develop improved management techniques until Colonel Roswell Lee became superintendent in 1815. Under Lee, a reorganization of centralized authority established definite areas of responsibilities. An early piece-rate accounting system was developed for wage payments and later used to control the time spent by workers and the materials used. The specialization of labor also increased: in 1815, there

---

9. Claude George, *The History of Management Thought*, 2nd ed. (Englewood Cliffs, NJ: Prentice Hall, 1972), p. 39.

10. More information about Eli Whitney and the American system of manufacturers can be found in Robert S. Woodbury, "The Legend of Eli Whitney and Interchangeable Parts," *Technology and Culture*, vol. 1 (1960), pp. 235–253; see also Robert C. Ford, "The Springfield Armory's Role in Developing Interchangeable Parts," *Management Decision*, vol. 43 (2005), pp. 265–278.

were thirty-six different occupational specialties; in 1820, eighty-six; and by 1825, one hundred.[11] Arms were made by specialists rather than by craft workers in metals and wood. New developments in metalworking machines and tools and improved gauges to measure the accuracy of parts came into use. Thus the parts could be manufactured to closer tolerances, which increased their interchangeability. Colonel Lee also tightened discipline with a new policy in 1816 that prohibited "scuffling or playing in the shops, wanton destruction of government property, noise, gambling ... [and] the grazing of cattle or swine on public property."[12] The Springfield Armory was not a profit-making organization, but it provided us with a better prototype for the development of a modern factory than the early textile mills. The division of labor, the clearly defined organization, the use of accounting techniques for wage payments and control of time and material costs, the uniform standards, the measurement techniques for inspection and control, and the advanced methods of metalworking were all crucial to what came to be called the American System of Manufactures.

The developments at the Springfield Armory were not typical of what was happening in the private sector. In 1832, a report was submitted to the secretary of the treasury, Louis McLane, which provided a partial census of U.S. manufactures of that time. In the ten states surveyed, there were 106 manufacturing establishments with $100,000 or more in assets; eighty-eight of these were in textiles, twelve in iron making, and a scattering of others in the production of nails, axes, glass, and so on. Only thirty-six of the companies in the ten states employed 250 or more workers; thirty-one of these were textile firms, three were in iron, and the others were in nails and axes.[13] In 1832, the Springfield Armory employed 246 workers, so it must be ranked among the largest organizations of this period. Other than the textile companies and a few iron makers, most organizations were relatively small, employing an average of ten to twelve persons. The McLane report also indicated that most firms were family owned and managed as sole proprietorships or partnerships and that corporations were few. Finally, steam power was rarely used, as the firms relied primarily on water power. Recalling Andrew Ure's study of the Lancashire cotton mills during this same period, there are remarkable similarities in the size of the firms and how they were managed, but the British were ahead on the use of steam power.

In short, U.S. manufacturing before 1835 was characterized by small, family-run, water-powered organizations. In the 1840s and 1850s, however, U.S. entrepreneurs unleashed a host of products and implements that would revolutionize industry.

---

11. Alfred D. Chandler, Jr., *The Visible Hand: The Managerial Revolution in American Business* (Cambridge, MA: Harvard University Press, 1977), p. 73.

12. Russell I. Fries, "Springfield Armory, 1794–1820; An Early Industrial Organization," unpublished paper, Orono, Maine, 1967, p. 29.

13. Chandler, *Visible Hand*, pp. 60–62.

The principles of manufacturing pioneered at the Springfield Armory and elsewhere provided the basis for the later manufacture of axes, shovels, sewing machines, clocks, locks, watches, steam engines, reapers, and other products. What visitors admired at the Crystal Palace exhibit of 1851 was the product of a long chain of developments—beginning with early experimentation and transferring to private industry. Mass production had not yet been perfected, but its antecedents were present.

THE RAILROADS: PIONEERING IN U.S. MANAGEMENT

Although textiles represented the largest private enterprises of this period in the United States, a transportation and communication revolution was on the horizon. Development of the iron rail, flanged wheel, and puffing locomotive began around 1830. Opposed initially by the canal supporters, who were fearful of its competition, the rail industry by 1850 had brought a new dimension to U.S. life. It started with Colonel John Stevens of Hoboken, New Jersey, who obtained from the New Jersey legislature the country's first railroad charter in 1815.[14] Deemed eccentric, he could not obtain financial backing until 1830, when he built the twenty-three-mile-long Camden and Amboy Railroad. Stevens made numerous other technical contributions and earned the title Father of American Engineering. After the Camden and Amboy, other lines, such as the Chesapeake and Ohio and the Baltimore and Ohio, were built and expanded, until by 1850, nine thousand miles of track extended all the way into Ohio. The railroad would provide a revolution in transportation and, as we shall see, an emphasis on managing in a systematic fashion. First, however, let us examine a concurrent revolution in communication, the telegraph.

THE COMMUNICATION REVOLUTION

Tom Standage reminds us that humans are chronocentric; that is, we have

> the egotism that one's own generation is poised on the cusp of history. Today, we are repeatedly told that we are in the midst of a communication revolution. But the electric telegraph was in many ways, far more disconcerting for the inhabitants of that time [the 1800s] than today's advances are for us. . . . Heavier than air flying

---

14. An interesting account of John Stevens's various activities, including his anticipation by three years of Fulton's steamboat, may be found in Dorothy Gregg, "John Stevens: General Entrepreneur," in William Miller, ed., *Men in Business* (New York: Harper & Row, 1957), pp. 120–152.

machines were, after all, thought by the Victorians to be totally impossible. But for the Internet—well, they [the Victorians] had one of their own.[15]

This "Victorian Internet" that Standage refers to was the telegraph, the invention of Samuel F. B. Morse, who built on a long line of scientific discoveries about electricity and magnetism. The possibilities of "distance signaling" through metal wires were developed by Morse in 1832, but not patented until 1837, the same year that William Cooke and Charles Wheatstone obtained a British patent and installed thirteen miles of wires on poles along Britain's Great Western Railroad. Morse gained a competitive advantage by developing a code, consisting of dots and dashes, which became the standard format for transmitting messages.

The telegraph provided the beginnings of a nationwide communication system. An experimental line was completed between New York and Washington, D.C., in 1844, and by 1860 about fifty thousand miles of wires and poles crisscrossed the eastern half of the country. Usually built along railroad rights of way, the telegraph facilitated the transportation system as well as handling commercial and personal messages. The impact on business communication was dramatic—where it might take days, weeks, or months for messages to be sent and received, the telegraph shrank the world of words. News items could be sent by telegraph, enabling daily newspapers to keep their readers informed; stock prices were sent from trade exchanges via ticker tape for investors; money could be sent by wire; a submarine cable under the Atlantic Ocean connected America to Great Britain and the European continent; and credit for the first electronic commerce belongs to Richard Sears, who used his skills at telegraphy to sell a shipment of gold-filled watches through other station agents along the Minneapolis and Saint Louis Railroad.

These technological revolutions, the railroad and the telegraph, in transportation and communication would sweep away local trade barriers, open new lands for settlement, extend markets and reshape distribution strategies, and provide an inexpensive, rapid, year-round means for travel and commerce.

THE AGE OF RAILS

The railroads were truly the United States' first big business. The textile industry, though growing and dominating the Northeast, never developed into companies of the size and scope of the railroads. Textile firms remained relatively small, the Springfield Armory rarely employed more than 250 people, and capital investment in industry was relatively low. The railroads, however, grew to such a size and complexity that means had to be developed of coping with massive financial requirements,

---

15. Tom Standage, *The Victorian Internet: The Remarkable Story of the Telegraph and the Nineteenth Century's On-Line Pioneers* (New York: Walker and Company, 1998), p. 213. Standage cites instances of romance blossoming and marriages made via the telegraph, as well as a familiar contemporary problem, a concern for privacy.

developing integrated systems of trackage and station agents, spreading large fixed costs, and handling a labor force dispersed over a wide geographical area. These factors required managers to develop ways of managing the first U.S. industry of larger than local scope. Unlike textile and other plants, railroad operations were spread out and could not be controlled by personal inspection of the hundreds of stations and thousands of miles of track, thus making communications a significant problem. The investments in track and rolling stock were immense, and extensive long-range planning was required to prevent large fixed capital outlays from being placed in the wrong market area. Passenger safety and the prevention of damage to or loss of cargo were critical to successful operations. Scheduling service required planning and coordination, and standing rules and policies had to be developed to guide the decisions of lower organizational elements.[16]

The twenty-three-mile track of John Stevens's Camden and Amboy line required little in the way of organization and management. Other lines, however, grew in scope and distance. In 1841, after a series of accidents, the Western Railroad of Massachusetts established certain areas of responsibility and a clear hierarchy of authority to ensure performance. Another large line, the Baltimore and Ohio (B&O), was reorganized in 1847 by Benjamin Latrobe to separate operations from finance and to establish departments for functions, such as machine shops, road maintenance departments, and so on. Although the Western and the B&O responded to growth with more definitive organizational structures, it was the New York and Erie Railroad that pioneered systematic management in the first big business in the United States.

DANIEL McCALLUM: SYSTEM AND ORGANIZATION

Daniel Craig McCallum (1815–1878) was born in Scotland but came to the United States in 1822.[17] He received some elementary schooling in Rochester, New York, but decided not to enter his father's occupation of tailor. He left home and school, became an accomplished carpenter and architect, and designed and built numerous buildings. He left this field to join the New York and Erie Railroad Company in 1848. He showed a talent for management as well as engineering and became superintendent of the Susquehanna Division, where he developed an early set of procedures to govern that division's operations. Faced with growing problems of rail integration and a high accident rate, the Erie management made McCallum general superintendent of the Erie line in May 1854. In June of 1854, the workers went on strike for ten days, not for shorter hours or more pay, but in defiance of McCallum's institution of his system.

---

16. Alfred D. Chandler, Jr., ed., *The Railroads: The Nation's First Big Business, Sources and Readings* (New York: Harcourt Brace Jovanovich, 1965), pp. 9–10.

17. Personal data on McCallum are from W. Jerome Arnold, "Big Business Takes the Management Track," *Business Week*, April 30, 1966, pp. 104–106, and Dumas Malone, ed., *Dictionary of American Biography*, vol. 6 (New York: Charles Scribners' Sons, 1965), p. 565.

Daniel C. McCallum, circa 1865.

To McCallum, good management was based on good discipline, specific and detailed job descriptions, frequent and accurate reporting of performance, pay and promotion based on merit, a clearly defined hierarchy of authority of superiors over subordinates, and the enforcement of personal responsibility and accountability throughout the organization. He stated his principles of management as:

1. A proper division of responsibilities
2. Sufficient authority conferred to enable such responsibilities to be fully carried out
3. The means of knowing whether such responsibilities are faithfully executed
4. Great promptness in the report of all derelictions of duty, so that evils may be corrected quickly
5. Such information to be obtained through a system of daily reports and checks that will not embarrass principal officers nor lessen their influence with their subordinates
6. The adoption of a system, as a whole, that will not only enable the general superintendent to detect errors immediately, but will also point out the delinquent[18]

McCallum developed a high degree of organizational specificity to carry out these principles. First, he separated and identified each grade of worker as to task and required all workers to wear a prescribed uniform with the insignia of their grade. Second, he developed comprehensive rules to limit the ability of individuals to do their tasks as they pleased. Rule 6, for example, mandated that the engineer was responsible if the train ran off a switch, even if the switch operator had not done a proper job. Engineers were expected to slow down at all switches, whether they were stopping or not, to check the switches personally.[19]

Finally, McCallum developed a formal organizational chart (which his advocate Henry Varnum Poor had lithographed and put on sale to the general public for a price of $1). The chart took the form of a tree and depicted the lines of authority and responsibility, the division of labor among operating units, and the communication lines for reporting and control. The roots of the tree represented the board of directors and the president; the branches were the five operating divisions plus

18. Daniel C. McCallum, "Superintendents' Report," in *American Railroad Journal*, ed. H. V. Poor, vol. 29 (April 12, 1856), pp. 225–226. Reprinted in Daniel A. Wren, ed., *Early Management Thought* (Brookfield, VT: Dartmouth Publishing Company, 1997), p. 9.

19. Walter Licht, *Working for the Railroad* (Princeton, NJ: Princeton University Press, 1983), pp. 246–247.

the staff service departments of engine repairs, car, bridge, telegraph, painting, treasurer's, and secretary's offices; the leaves were the various local freight and ticket forwarding offices, subordinate supervisors, crews, and so on to the lowest element. Adherence to the formal lines of authority was to be absolute:

> The enforcement of a rigid system of discipline . . . is indispensable to success. All subordinates should be accountable to, and be directed by their immediate superiors only; as obedience cannot be enforced where the foreman in immediate charge is interfered with by a superior officer giving orders directly to his subordinates.[20]

McCallum saw no exceptions to this unity of command principle; to do otherwise would break down his control system, which was based on personal accountability.

McCallum also developed information management to probably the highest state of the art for the times. He used the telegraph to make operations safer as well as to facilitate administration by requiring hourly reports to show the position of every train in the system, daily reports on passengers and cargo, and monthly reports to give management statistical accounts for planning, rate making, and control. He designed a clever cross-check control system by requiring both freight and passenger conductors to report on train movements, loadings, damaged freight, and so on; by comparing the reports, he could readily spot discrepancies and dishonesty.

McCallum's system was successful from management's point of view, but trouble was brewing over Rule 6. The engineers had never forgiven McCallum; twenty-nine engineers had been dismissed for breaking Rule 6 and for avoiding various other safety rules McCallum had devised. A six-month strike ensued, and McCallum was unable to replace the striking engineers. He resigned, along with the company president, in 1857. However, McCallum had earned the highest praise of Henry Varnum Poor, the eminent editor of the *American Railroad Journal* and spokesperson for the industry. Poor later had some doubts about the system, but thought that it was a step in the right direction.

McCallum's managerial days were not over, however. While on the Erie, he had invented and patented (1851) an inflexible arched truss bridge. In 1857 he established the McCallum Bridge Company and built bridges throughout the country, earning an income of $75,000 per year. In 1862 he was asked by Secretary of War Stanton to manage the nation's railways, with the power to seize and operate any railroad necessary to the Union's war effort. By the end of the war he was a major general, and his main feat was supplying General Sherman's two-hundred-day Atlanta campaign.[21] After the war, McCallum served as a consultant for the Atlantic

---

20. McCallum, in Chandler, *Railroads*, p. 104.

21. An extensive account of McCallum's managerial feats in running the Northern railroads during the Civil War may be found throughout Thomas Weber, *The Northern Railroads in the Civil War* (New York: Columbia University Press, 1952).

and Great Western Railroad and the Union Pacific. Failing health prompted an early retirement to Brooklyn, where he did not get into the bridge business but wrote poetry. His best-known poem was "The Water-Mill," which concluded:

> *Possessions, Power, and blooming health,*
> *must all be lost at last,*
> *The mill will never grind with water*
> *that is past*

McCallum's approach to management was not lost, despite his setbacks at the Erie. Henry Poor publicized his work widely, and numerous others followed McCallum's style in systematizing the country's first big business. Albert Fink developed a cost accounting system that used information flows, classification of costs, and statistical control devices and became a model for modern corporate control.[22] Auditing as a separate staff function from accounting also began on the railroads. As early as 1847 the B&O used an internal auditor to check on the handling of receipts and disbursements. External auditing by independent public accounting firms also began as early as 1854, as stockholders, separate from management, wanted to verify management's reports.[23]

Organizational growth, geographical separation of activities, and the separation of ownership and management were the driving forces for systematizing railroad management. The most faithful adoption of McCallum's system, however, came on the Pennsylvania Railroad. J. Edgar Thomson and Thomas A. Scott applied McCallum's ideas for geographical departmentation, formal lines of authority and responsibility, communications, line and staff duties, measuring performance, and cost accounting. The Pennsylvania tree bore the fruit of systematic management, not the Erie. On the Pennsylvania was a young manager who learned McCallum's system from Thomson and Scott; his name was Andrew Carnegie, and he will enter our story again shortly.

HENRY V. POOR: A BROADER VIEW OF MANAGEMENT

Henry Varnum Poor (1812–1905), through his position as editor of the *American Railroad Journal*, essayed to become the conscience of the first large business. Whereas McCallum spoke of internal operating problems, Poor looked for broader principles of railroad operations, including financing, regulation, and the role of the railroad in U.S. life. Poor was well educated and came from a more select background than McCallum; his biographer tells us that Poor was thoroughly imbued with the

---

22. Albert Fink, "Classification of Operating Expenses," in *Annual Report of the Louisville and Nashville Railroad Company* (1874), in Chandler, *Railroads*, pp. 108–117.

23. James L. Boockholdt, "A Historical Perspective on the Auditor's Role: The Early Experiences of the American Railroads," *The Accounting Historians Journal* 10 (Spring 1983), pp. 69–86.

romance and optimism of the nineteenth-century United States.[24] As editor of the *Journal* in the pre–Civil War years, Poor made it the leading business periodical of the day and a reliable source of information for the railroad investor as well as the manager. His editorials discussed railroad developments, problems, and needed reforms in operating practices and presented detailed financial and operating data. After the war, his *Manual of Railroads in the United States* continued his efforts to further the dissemination of financial and operating information.[25] His life was marked throughout by the critical age of railroads coming from infancy to maturity and by their amazing impact on opening the West and tying the United States together with a web of steel.

In its early years, the Erie was one of Poor's favorite targets, for it was poorly managed and financed. The advent of McCallum's reforms soon made Poor the biggest booster of the Erie as an example of proper management. Poor saw a need for managerial reform through development of a group of professional managers rather than speculators and promoters to build the nation's transportation system. Poor looked for a science, or system, of management, and from McCallum's work Poor gleaned three fundamental principles: organization, communication, and information.[26] Organization was basic to all management: There had to be a careful division of labor from the president down to the common laborer, each with specific duties and responsibilities. Workers should be directly accountable to their immediate superiors; Poor repeatedly used the terms *responsibility* and *accountability* in his editorials. Communication meant devising a method of reporting throughout the organization to give top management a continuous and accurate accounting of operations. Finally, information was "recorded communication"; Poor saw the need for a set of operating reports to be compiled for costs, revenues, and rate making. This third principle was an early appearance of a database concept in management literature in the sense that management would build up a fund of data on operations to analyze the present system and to provide a basis for changes to improve service. The influence of McCallum on Poor's writing is readily apparent, and the development of the third principle can be traced to Albert Fink's efforts to install statistical control systems in the corporate structure.

Just as McCallum's work was becoming widely known, in large part due to Poor's editorials, Poor began having doubts about whether organization, communication, and information were adequate principles to encompass the task of management. Poor visited Great Britain in 1858 to view its railway system, and on his return he wrote about "the grave difficulties of adapting human capabilities and current

---

24. Alfred D. Chandler, Jr., *Henry Varnum Poor: Business Editor, Analyst, and Reformer* (Cambridge, MA: Harvard University Press, 1956). An interesting sidelight is that Chandler was the great-grandson of Henry Varnum Poor.

25. Henry V. Poor established *Poor's Publishing* in 1860 to provide financial information about other industries; in 1941, a merger with *Standard Statistics* created the *Standard and Poor's* of today.

26. Chandler, *Poor*, pp. 146–147. Chandler's work is based on Poor's editorials and will be cited here without referring to specific dates and issues of the *Journal*.

business practices and institutions to the severe requirements demanded by the efficient operation of such large administrative units." Both in Great Britain and on the Erie, Poor saw worker resistance developing to the discipline required by systematic management. The tighter control required to bring order from chaos, the limiting of individual discretion in the performance of tasks, and the rigid hierarchical specifications of a formal organization were all leading to worker protests against the system. This protest was not new in the annals of management history, nor has the issue ever been fully resolved. Poor, however, thought these protests were too extreme and defended the need for systematization: "We can see no other way in which such a vast machine can be safely and successfully conducted," that is, except through order, system, and discipline.

Accordingly, Poor began to look for some broader principles to overcome the dangers of "regarding man as a mere machine, out of which all the qualities necessary to be a good servant can be enforced by the mere payment of wages. But duties cannot always be prescribed, and the most valuable are often voluntary ones."[27] Close prescription of duties and the bureaucratization of management reduced incentives and would inevitably lead the railroads, in Poor's view, to the problems inherent in the rigid managerial structures such as those of the military and the government. Poor's solution was a leadership that would overcome dullness and routine by infusing the organization with an esprit de corps. Top management should become "the soul of the enterprise, reaching and infusing life, intelligence and obedience into every portion of it. This soul must not be a fragmentary or disjointed one giving one direction to the head, another to the hands, and another to the feet. Wherever there is lack of unity there will be a lack of energy—of intelligence—of life—of accountability and subordination."[28]

In anticipating Fayol's unity of direction principle by sixty years, Poor regarded the problems of top management as those of assuming and of getting subordinates to assume a total systems view of the organization. Leaders not only had to know all aspects of railroad operation and administration but also needed to be able to handle people, to know the total system, and to prevent interdepartmental conflicts that could destroy unity of purpose. The breakdown in leadership came from two sources: selection on some basis other than ability or training, and lack of an information system to pinpoint weak managers. Poor's pleas for professional managers to manage well the property of others were not dissimilar to the problems Adam Smith had pointed out nearly a century before.

EMERGING GOVERNANCE ISSUES

Early textile mills were largely owned and managed by partnerships and sole proprietorships. The money was "all in the family," and requirements for accounting and financial reporting were reduced. Adam Smith cautioned of the dangers of joint-stock, limited-liability firms, where ownership and management were typically

---

27. Ibid., p. 155.

28. Ibid., p. 157

separated and rarely did anyone watch over other people's money as they would exercise vigilance over their own. Smith was deceased, however, by the time the earliest incident of this problem appeared when the British railroad system was developing. The railroads required capital, both debt and equity financing, on a scale unknown to any previous business ventures.

George Hudson, a friend of the British railway pioneer and innovator George Stephenson, envisioned a network of rails for the whole of England, Scotland, and Wales. In 1844, Hudson began promoting assorted ventures to raise capital for new lines and to acquire existing ones. Under British law, each joint-stock company was authorized by a separate Act of Parliament, leading to different charters and requirements for each. At this time, there were no general rules for accounting and financial reporting, and corporate law was in its infancy. The railways held a romantic fascination for investors, leading to waves of rampant speculation in railway shares, or, in more modern terms, "irrational exuberance." It has been estimated that by 1845, £71 million British pounds sterling had been invested in railroads, and another 620 new railway schemes amounted to £563 million pounds sterling, equivalent to over two-thirds of the national debt of Great Britain.[29]

Hudson took advantage of these speculative impulses, and by 1849, nearly one-third of Great Britain's five thousand miles of lines were under his management or control. In addition, he had raised money to buy land, build docks, and form canal ventures. He was, as all Britain knew, the "Railway King."[30] His operations extended from Brighton and Southampton, in the southeast of that island nation, to Edinburgh in the northeast.

An early, if not the earliest, example of top management malfeasance exists in the deeds of George Hudson. He paid dividends out of capital, both existing and borrowed; altered accounts of railway traffic and revenue to indicate more profitability than existed; published false statements to investors; and, in one instance, bought iron rails from one of his lines for £9 each and sold them to another of his interests for £11, pocketing a £6,000 profit.

Parliament passed a Companies Clauses Consolidation Act in 1845 to bring some uniformity to corporate charters, to require "full and true" accounts to be maintained and to mandate that three directors and the chief executive sign and verify the firm's balance sheet. It was not legislation, however, that stopped Hudson's chicanery; his actions led to shareholder investigations and lawsuits. His estimated ill-gotten gains amounted to £598,785.[31] Hudson went into exile, and his creditors were never fully satisfied.

How does the brief account of George Hudson fit into America's economic development and the efforts of Henry Varnum Poor? Poor kept abreast of railroad developments abroad and addressed governance issues in his editorials. For example,

---

29. J. J. Glynn, "The Development of British Railway Accounting, 1800–1911," in R. H. Parker and B. S. Yamey, eds., *Accounting History: Some British Contributions* (Oxford: Clarendon Press, 1994), pp. 327–342.

30. Richard S. Lambert, *The Railway King, 1800–1871* (London: George Allen and Unwin, 1934).

31. Ibid., p. 273.

he complained that railroads did not separate construction from operating costs, thus screening the cost of operations from the investor. It was not an uncommon practice to put operating expenses in the construction account, thus showing higher profits from operations. This practice enabled the declaration of higher dividends that otherwise would have been unwarranted. (Does history provide explanations for why we have rules for accounting practice?)

What was the path to reform? According to Poor:

> Now the germ of all improvement is *knowledge* ... the only way to introduce honesty into the management of railroads is to expose every thing in or about it, to the public gaze. Concealment in either case is certain to breed disease. Instances are very rare in which integrity is preserved unless strict accountability is exacted. Such accountability to the public should be exacted from directors of railroads. ... For the dishonesty and incapacity in the management of railroads the holders of their securities have in a great measure to thank themselves. They put them in charge of a body of men, responsible to no authority, who soon come to practice concealment, either to escape the consequences of mistake or dishonesty. The perpetuation of their power is an easy matter, so long as they can sustain themselves by the various modes resorted to for borrowing.[32]

Poor lashed out against the promoters and speculators and reflected the laissez-faire spirit by calling for unrestricted competition. Rates should not be regulated by government, and the only legislation necessary was that to protect "honest rational men" from the dishonest promoters. He insisted that the rapid development of the U.S. railroad system was "proof that reliance on the self-interest of individuals operating under conditions of unrestricted competition resulted in the greatest good for the greatest number."[33] Through publicity to inform stockholders and the public, through professionalization of management, and through protection of the rational from the irrational, the railroads could achieve their proper role in the economy.

Henry Varnum Poor articulated issues that face management today and will be present tomorrow. His position that the role of government was to protect, not to control, illustrates a recurring problem of management vis-à-vis government. His search for order out of chaos without destroying individual incentive and dignity also is a recurring problem. He was one of our most outstanding early contributors to management thought.

---

32. Henry V. Poor, "How to Improve the Management of Railroads," *American Railroad Journal* 30 (June 20, 1857), p. 392. For a concise history of the law and American railroads before the Civil War, see Charles W. Wootton and Christie L. Roszkowski, "Legal Aspects of Corporate Governance in Early American Railroads," *Business and Economic History* 28 (Winter 1999), pp. 325–336.

33. Chandler, *Poor*, p. 260.

Summary

In 1790, the largest city in the United States of America was New York City, with a population of 33,131; next came Philadelphia, with a population of 28,522; and then Boston, with 18,300 persons. Even the largest city was smaller than the student body at some of today's state universities. In 1790, an estimated 90 percent of the estimated total population of 3,231,533 was engaged in agriculture. From the time of gaining independence from Great Britain up to 1860, the United States made marvelous progress. Textile factories provided inexpensive clothing to a national market, replacing the domestic system of production; railroads spread westward, opening new lands and opportunities; the telegraph sent messages tapping across vast distances; and mechanical devices such as the sewing machine and the reaper caused others to praise the American System of manufacturing.

When we think of modern enterprise, it is essential that we think of this period as critical. The domestic system of putting out work into homes was disappearing, to be replaced by family- and partner-owned and managed small-scale firms in a central workplace powered by the steam engine. Capital requirements increased with the railroads, the telegraph enabled the growth of the firm for economies of scale and scope, and this growth created the need for a hierarchy of nonowning managers. If one views the enterprise as an input-throughput-output system, the inputs come from external markets in the form of human, capital, technology, and other resources. Through a hierarchy of managers, the firm became a means of transforming these inputs and coordinating and monitoring their use. For the outputs of the firm, the market came into play through consumer demand. In this way, we can see how events in the early nineteenth century helped shape the nature of the business firm.

If you were a male and born in Massachusetts in 1789, you could expect to live 34.5 years, and if you were a female, 36.5 years. By 1855, these expectancies had risen to 38.7 and 40.9 years, respectively. Not only were people living longer, but they were living better: real wages (purchasing power) rose from an index number of 41 in 1820 to 57 in 1860 (1913 = 100).[34] By 1860, there were an estimated 1,385,000 people employed in manufacturing; 20 percent of these were females, and child labor in factories had all but disappeared. Times were better, and this was only the beginning of the Industrial Revolution in the United States.

---

34. Edgar W. Martin, *The Standard of Living in 1860* (Chicago: University of Chicago Press, 1942), pp. 220, 415.

6

Industrial Growth and Systematic Management

T he years of internecine strife from 1861 to 1865 were a tragic pause in the move of the United States toward world industrial leadership. When the Industrial Revolution reached the United States, it spawned the textile industry, opened new vistas in manufacturing techniques at the Springfield Armory, and created our first big business on the railroads. This chapter will describe how the revolution resumed in the growth of enterprise, discuss the renaissance of systematic management, and examine the economic, social, political, and technological situations in the United States on the eve of the scientific management era.

THE GROWTH OF U.S. ENTERPRISE

The Industrial Revolution in the United States began in textiles, but textile firms made relatively few advancements over earlier British management methods. The Waltham System and Samuel Slater, in his later years, exemplified integrated firms, employed professional managers, and adopted steam power. Most firms in the United States prior to the Civil War, however, were family owned and managed, small, and technologically underdeveloped. The Springfield Armory used more advanced management techniques, but systematic management really began on the railroads. The railroads, powered by steam, led a transportation revolution; the telegraph and the transatlantic cable created a communication revolution. Together, these forces combined to create the growth of large-scale organizations.

THE ACCUMULATION OF RESOURCES

No student of U.S. business history has a keener eye for the growth of large organizations than Alfred D. Chandler,

Jr. (1918–2007).[1] In some early work, Chandler traced the history of various firms and delineated four phases in the history of the large U.S. enterprise: (1) "the initial expansion and accumulation of resources"; (2) "the rationalization of the use of resources"; (3) "the expansion into new markets and lines to help assure the continuing full use of resources"; and (4) "the development of a new structure" that rationalized the renewal of growth. For various companies, the phases started and ended at different times, depending on the state of technology and the firm's ability to react to and capitalize on market opportunities. During the latter part of the nineteenth century, many major industries were forming and would fit into Chandler's phase 1 or resource accumulation stage.

Chandler further noted two facets of industrial growth and their time periods: (1) horizontal growth from 1879 to 1893 and (2) vertical growth from 1898 to 1904. Horizontal growth occurred when producers in similar fields combined through mergers, pools, or trusts to gain economies of scale in manufacturing. Examples include firms in oil, beef, sugar, tobacco, rubber, liquors, and so on. Mergers into larger units enabled the firm or firms to control their market, gain financial leverage, and cut production costs. Vertical growth occurred when firms moved backward or forward in terms of the production process. Moving backward meant the acquisition of raw material sources or suppliers; moving forward meant establishing marketing outlets for the firm's own products. For example, a petroleum-refining company would move backward to explore, acquire oil leases, drill, and build pipelines to its refinery; it would move forward to acquire wholesale agents and perhaps its own retail stations.

Chandler found a close connection between advancements in transportation and communication and the accumulation of resources that led to industrial growth. When transport was crude and slow, markets for products were largely localized, so there was little or no need to enlarge the volume of goods manufactured. Thus the domestic system was entirely appropriate to its time because it served limited markets with little capital investment. When the Industrial Revolution provided steam power for locomotives and steamboats, markets were extended, and a larger scale of production with more advanced mechanization became desirable. Communication techniques, such as the telegraph, provided a network to connect suppliers, producers, distributors, and consumers over a larger geographical area. With improved transportation and communication, it became possible to produce and market in volume; thus production could be done in large batches or in continuous processing, and firms could seek volume distribution in a mass market. A greater capital intensity was required for this enlarged scale of output and distribution. As the capital investment rose, for example, with large blast furnaces for steel production, costs could be reduced only if these expensive pieces of equipment could be used at some optimal output level. In Chandler's terms, these

---

1. The subsequent discussion relies heavily on Alfred D. Chandler, Jr., *Strategy and Structure: Chapters in the History of the Industrial Enterprise* (Cambridge, MA: MIT Press, 1962); idem, *The Visible Hand: The Managerial Revolution in American Business* (Cambridge, MA: Harvard University Press, 1977); idem, *Scale and Scope: The Dynamics of Industrial Capitalism* (Cambridge, MA: Harvard University Press, 1990).

capital-intensive industries had to operate at a "minimum efficient scale" (i.e., at the level that resulted in the lowest unit costs) to attain a cost advantage. With a cost advantage, prices could be lowered and markets extended, and eventually the whole cycle of mechanization, greater output, increased distribution volume, and so on, would be repeated.

There are limits, of course, to the cost advantages of large-scale production and volume marketing. In Chandler's thesis, however, this explanation of mass production illustrates the growth of enterprise and the need for a managerial hierarchy. The key to organizational success is not in capacity (the potential to produce or sell) but in how well the throughput is managed. There must be a smooth flow of inputs in terms of employees, materials, supplies, and so on into the factory where the production is done (throughput). Then a well-coordinated system is needed for the outputs (finished products) to flow through the distribution channels to the customers. Chandler's analysis of organizational growth and the need for a managerial hierarchy to coordinate organizational work is of far-reaching importance. As we view the latter half of the nineteenth century in the United States, we can see how advances such as new production processes for making steel, refining sugar and corn products, milling grains, canning, and packaging led to the growth of enterprise, as Chandler's thesis would predict. One of the best examples of organizational growth and the throughput notion is found in the story of Andrew Carnegie.

CARNEGIE AND THE GROWTH OF ENTERPRISE

The name of Andrew Carnegie (1835–1919) conjures a portrait of an entrepreneur who built an empire in steel and left a fortune in the millions. But where did Carnegie learn his management skills? Carnegie, an immigrant like so many other entrepreneurs of this age, early learned the trade of a telegrapher. Thomas A. Scott, superintendent of the Western Division of the Pennsylvania Railroad, hired Carnegie as his personal telegrapher for dispatching trains over the mountainous divisional lines. Carnegie learned fast and made his mark one day when he untangled a traffic tie-up after a derailment. Scott was absent at the time, and Carnegie sent out orders using Scott's initials. He was rewarded for this usurpation of authority, and his initiative led to a change in the organization by providing for a delegation of dispatching authority (formerly, only the superintendent had the authority). Carnegie learned of railroad management from Scott and J. Edgar Thomson, who, as mentioned earlier, had applied McCallum's ideas to the Pennsylvania Railroad. It was McCallum's system of organization, reporting, accounting, and control that Carnegie learned at the railroad. At age twenty-four, Carnegie became superintendent of the Western Division, which at the time was the largest division of the nation's largest railroad. Under his supervision, divisional traffic quadrupled, track mileage doubled, and the division had the lowest ton-per-mile costs of any railroad in the United States. Carnegie was offered the post of general superintendent in 1865, but declined because he wanted to become an entrepreneur rather than a salaried manager.

Andrew Carnegie, circa 1878.

To understand Carnegie and his influence, it is necessary to examine the development of the steel industry. Steel is the sinew of any industrial economy. Iron, because of its impurities, caused many problems for early machine designers and factory owners. The race to improve iron production proceeded, as is often the history of invention, on separate concurrent paths in Great Britain and the United States. William Kelly of Kentucky began his experiments in 1847 and perfected a system of refining iron by subjecting it to a blast of hot air in a specially built furnace. Unfortunately, Kelly did not apply for a patent until 1857, two years after Sir Henry Bessemer had obtained his patent in Great Britain. The Bessemer process, based on the same idea, was quite an improvement over the very slow process of puddling iron (the removing of carbon and other impurities by passing heated gases over the molten iron).

In 1865, the steel industry in the United States was not integrated. Some firms owned the furnaces that smelted the ore into pig iron; others had the rolling mills and forges that converted the pig iron into bars or slabs; and still others took the bars or slabs and rolled them into rails, sheets, nails, wire, or whatever. Between each of these independent operations, an intermediary took the output of one and sold it to the next producer, also taking a profit for providing this service. After Carnegie saw the Bessemer process in operation, he had a vision of how this improved technology could be used. In 1872, he decided to concentrate on steel because "Every dollar of capital or credit, every business thought, should be concentrated upon the one business upon which a man has embarked. He should never scatter his shot. . . . Put all your eggs in one basket, and then watch that basket, is the true doctrine—the most valuable rule of all."[2]

Using the Bessemer converters, Carnegie began to integrate operations, cutting out the intermediaries' profits, speeding up the volume of throughput, and selling aggressively to extend the market for steel products. He used cost accounting to assist in setting prices to undersell his competitors, who did not know their costs. He integrated vertically into iron and coal mines and other steel-related operations to ensure a flow of materials into the furnaces to use their capacity more fully. By coordinating the flow of materials, the furnaces, forges, rolling mills, and so forth, he could move the process faster from its beginning, as ore, into finished steel products. By combining the Bessemer technology with the management methods of Daniel McCallum, Carnegie became a success.

---

2. Andrew Carnegie, *The Empire of Business* (New York: Doubleday, Doran, 1933), p. 100.

It was on the Pennsylvania Railroad that Carnegie learned how to measure performance, control costs, and assign authority and responsibility; it was in the steel industry that he applied these lessons.[3] Until 1908 and the perfection of the open hearth method of making steel, the Bessemer process was the basis for the world's steel industry. When Carnegie started, iron rails cost $100 per ton; when he sold his steel interests in 1900, one ton of steel rails cost $12. Perhaps that was Carnegie's greatest philanthropy, or as Jonathan Swift expressed it in *Gulliver's Travels:* "Whoever could make two ears of corn or two blades of grass to grow upon a spot of ground where only one grew before would deserve better of mankind and do more essential service to his country than the whole race of politicians put together."[4] To unscramble the metaphor, Carnegie found a way to combine technology and management to create more jobs, reduce prices, expand markets, and advance industrial development. In 1868 the United States produced 8,500 tons of steel and Great Britain, 110,000; in 1879, the countries' outputs were nearly equal; but by 1902, the United States produced 9,138,000 tons and Great Britain produced 1,826,000. U.S. industry was showing its mettle.

THE RENAISSANCE OF SYSTEMATIC MANAGEMENT

The steel industry has provided an illustration of the growth of business after the Civil War. Steel was not the only industry, however, to thrust the United States into the world limelight and reinforce British and European beliefs in the superiority of the American System of Manufactures. As technology advanced in transportation, communication, machine making, and power sources, old industries were revitalized, and new ones emerged to grow into large-scale enterprises. Chandler saw this phase as the accumulation of resources and noted the relationship between velocity of throughput in capital-intensive industries and the growth of a managerial hierarchy to coordinate the activities necessary to achieve the minimally efficient scale of production. In summary, management was the key to the efficient use of an organization's resources.

Daniel McCallum brought systematic management to some of the railroads, and Andrew Carnegie learned his lessons well and created a steel colossus. As other firms and other industries began to grow, they, too, faced the problems of managing large-scale organizations. They needed to plan for the acquisition of people, materials, equipment, and capital; to organize these resources by dividing labor, delegating authority, assigning responsibility, and grouping activities into

---

3. Numerous parallels between McCallum and Carnegie may be found in Harold C. Livesay, *Andrew Carnegie and the Rise of Big Business* (Boston: Little, Brown, 1975).

4. Jonathan Swift, *Gulliver's Travels*, Great Books of the Western World, vol. 36 (Chicago: Encyclopaedia Britannica, Inc., 1952), p. 78. Originally published in 1726.

departments; to lead and coordinate human efforts by providing incentives, handling interpersonal relations, and providing a means of communication within the organization; and to control by measuring performance, comparing actual to planned performance, and taking corrective action when necessary. With growth came the need to formalize communications for purposes of coordination and control, especially in written memos and reports (with coordinating copies to all concerned).[5] At this time, however, there was very little understanding of the job of the manager; a great deal of emphasis was placed on technical or financial ability, but very little on management itself. Faced with the accumulation of resources in large-scale enterprises, how could managers learn to manage better?

ENGINEERS AND ECONOMISTS

Engineers played a large role in building canals and railroads and in designing and installing industrial equipment. Thus they frequently became the managers of enterprises; examples include Samuel Slater, Daniel McCallum, and others. The professionalization of engineering began with the formation of the American Society of Civil Engineers in 1852, followed by the American Institute of Mining Engineers in 1871. Neither of the groups, however, was interested in the problems of the factory, power sources, machine belting, or the operations of a machine shop or other type of factory. The first forum for those interested in factory problems appears to have been the *American Machinist*, an "illustrated journal of practical mechanics and engineering" that began in 1877. In 1878, James Waring See, writing under the name of Chordal, began a series of letters to the editor of the *American Machinist*. See was a veteran of working in and supervising machine shops.[6] He established a successful practice as a consulting engineer and used his letters to the editor to describe machine shop practices and management. He advocated systems of work that resulted from two principles: "a place for everything and everything in its place" and "specific lines of duty for each man."[7] See noted that good workers rarely made good supervisors and that good supervisors should not bully their workers but should be tactful and understanding.

Soldiering, or a worker's deliberate slowing of output, existed and could be handled best if the supervisor had an "understanding with [the worker] that he is to work for you five days a week for pay, and soldier one day at his own expense . . . one week-day idle in a man's life will make him feel glad to get into the shop for five days of occupation."[8] See also advocated paying high wages to attract better workers, the

---

5. Jo Anne Yates, *Control Through Communication: The Rise of System in American Management* (Baltimore: Johns Hopkins University Press, 1989).

6. William F. Muhs, Charles Wrege, and Arthur Murtuza, "Extracts from Chordal's Letters: Pre-Taylor Shop Management," in K. H. Chung, ed., *Proceedings of the Academy of Management* (San Diego, 1981), pp. 96–100.

7. James W. See, *Extracts from Chordal's Letters* (New York: American Machinist Publishing, 1880), p. 242.

8. Ibid., p. 139.

standardization of tools, and other techniques for better shop management. Except to readers of the *American Machinist*, See's writings remained relatively obscure for a century. It would appear, however, that his experiences and advice may have influenced later writers, even though his work was not cited explicitly.

The *American Machinist* also had a hand in another signal event of this period, the formation of the American Society of Mechanical Engineers (ASME) in 1880. The ASME first met at the Stevens Institute of Technology, Hoboken, New Jersey, and its purpose was to address those issues of factory operation and management neglected by the other engineering groups. A landmark meeting of the ASME was held in Chicago in May 1886. Henry R. Towne (1844–1924), an engineer, cofounder of the Yale Lock Company, and president of the Yale and Towne Manufacturing Company, presented a paper entitled, "The Engineer as an Economist." Towne observed that

> there are many good mechanical engineers; there are also many good "businessmen"; but the two are rarely combined in one person. But this combination of qualities . . . is essential to the management of industrial works, and has its highest effectiveness if united in one person . . . the matter of shop management is of equal importance with that of engineering . . . and the *management of works* has become a matter of such great and far-reaching importance as perhaps to justify its classification also as one of the modern arts.[9]

Because no group appeared to be concerned with management, Towne proposed that the ASME create an economic section to act as a clearinghouse and forum for shop management and shop accounting. Shop management would deal with the subjects of organization, responsibility, reports, and all that pertained to the executive management of works, mills, and factories. Shop accounting would treat the questions of time and wage systems, determination and allocation of costs, methods of bookkeeping, and all matters that pertained to manufacturing accounts.

A second significant paper at the 1886 ASME meeting was presented by Captain Henry Metcalfe, an intellectual heir of the pioneering work of Roswell Lee of the Springfield Armory. In 1881, at the Frankford Arsenal (near Philadelphia) and the Watervliet Arsenal (Troy, New York), Metcalfe had a shop-order system of accounts that used cards to facilitate the coordination and control of various batches of work as they flowed through the shop.[10] These cards accompanied the work, and the amount of labor spent and materials used were recorded on the cards. When the order was finished, management could determine direct costs (such as labor and materials) as well as indirect costs (administrative overhead). In the discussion that

---

9. Henry R. Towne, "The Engineer as an Economist," *Transactions, ASME* 7 (1886), pp. 428–429. Italics are Towne's.

10. Henry Metcalfe, "The Shop-Order System of Accounts," *Transactions, ASME* 7 (1886), pp. 440–468. This paper was a summary of Metcalfe's pioneering book in cost accounting, *The Cost of Manufactures and the Administration of Workshops, Public and Private* (New York: John Wiley and Sons, 1885).

followed, Frederick W. Taylor of Midvale Steel said they had been using a similar system for the past ten years, except that Midvale used a central office and clerks, rather than the supervisors, to handle much of the paperwork. Taylor had joined the ASME in 1886. We shall learn more about Taylor later.

Almost all the discussion of the Towne and Metcalfe papers focused on the shop-order system of accounts, and the creation of an economic section of the ASME received scant notice. Despite evidence that business leaders were coming from technical schools, such as the Stevens Institute of Technology, and that their duties were managerial rather than technical,[11] only four other papers on management subjects were presented at the ASME meetings from 1887 to 1895.[12] This lack of attention was probably due to a lack of clarity about the skills and abilities a manager needed. A manager, at that time, was part engineer, part business leader, and part accountant. The emphasis was on the shop, that is, manufacturing, and not on the whole organization. Shop management focused on the machine shops, where the trend had been to move from small batch production to a larger scale of output based on the American System of Manufactures. The problem was how to handle the increased throughput volume.

One early writer noted that large-scale manufacture required the "utmost system ... necessary in every detail [for] the economy and uniformity of production."[13] Thus *system* referred to the development of rules, standards, and procedures to handle the increased volume of activity in the production shop. Included in systematic management would be topics such as setting standards for tools, quality and quantity of work, coordination of work flow through routing and scheduling, wage incentives, accounting for costs, assigning responsibility, and handling labor problems such as soldiering.[14]

In other circles there was a resurgence of interest by economists in management as a factor of production. Jean Baptiste Say had made this observation earlier, and it was reborn in the 1880s and 1890s. An economist of this period, Edward Atkinson,

---

11. The Stevens Institute of Technology had 600 graduates between 1872 and 1896; of these, 230 (38 percent) were in executive positions by 1900. William D. Ennis, "The Engineering Management of Industrial Works," *Engineering Magazine* 22 (November 1901), pp. 241–246.

12. Hirose noted, however, that some mechanical engineers favored scientific management; only in 1920 did the majority of ASME members agree to a separate division of management. Mikiyoshi Hirose, "The Attitude of the American Society of Mechanical Engineers toward Management: Suggestions for a Revised Interpretation," *Kansai University Review of Economics and Business* 25 (September 1996), pp. 125–148.

13. Oberlin Smith, "System in Machine Shops," *American Machinist* 8 (October 31, 1885), p. 1.

14. Joseph A. Litterer, "The Emergence of Systematic Management as Shown by the Literature of Management from 1870 to 1900," Ph.D. dissertation, University of Illinois, Urbana, 1959. From this came two excellent articles: Joseph A. Litterer, "Systematic Management: The Search for Order and Integration," *Business History Review* 35 (Winter 1961), pp. 461–476; and idem, "Systematic Management: Design for Organizational Recoupling in American Manufacturing Firms," *Business History Review* 37 (Winter 1963), pp. 369–391.

noted that a "difference in management will alter results, in the same place, at the same time, in the use of similar machinery."[15] Alfred Marshall (1842–1924) and his wife, Mary Paley Marshall, wrote of the economics of industry, noting earnings of management as separate from the profit returned to shareholders, a clear distinction between shareowners and employed managers. The manager of large capital

> Always requires rarer natural abilities and a more expensive training than the management of small capital requires ... [those] who conduct a large business must look far ahead, and wide around him; and he must be continually on the look out for improved methods of carrying on his business ... [and] devotes all his energies to planning and organizing, to forecasting the future and preparing for it.[16]

As the Marshalls noted, management required special, rarer abilities and performed certain actions to manage the business firm, such as forecasting, planning, and organizing. These functions of management were not discussed in detail, but the Marshalls noted the work of management long before it would be recognized in the writings of Henri Fayol. The Marshalls also noted the division of labor in the firm, but this did not lead to monotonous jobs "when the work is light, and the hours of work not excessive." They noted the economies of scale for large firms and the internal economies that could be attained by more efficient management. In this latter sense, the Marshallian view of the firm would make it superior to the market in allocating resources and anticipated by more than a half-century the work of Nobel Prize winner Ronald Coase (see Chapter 16).

The writing of the Marshalls about the economics of industry was a prelude to Alfred Marshall's fame as the founder of the Cambridge (England) or neoclassical school of economic thought. His long-enduring principles of economic texts provided a basis for business management with the inclusion of "organization" as an "agent" of production, following the style of Jean Baptiste Say. Marshall indicated the differential advantage that management could provide:

> A manufacturer of exceptional ability and energy will apply better methods, and perhaps better machinery than his rivals: he will organize better the manufacturing and the marketing sides of his business; and he will bring them into better relation to one another. By these means he will extend his business; and therefore he will be able to take greater advantage from the specialization both of labour and of plant. Thus he will obtain increasing return and also increasing profit.[17]

---

15. Edward Atkinson, *The Distribution of Products* (New York: G. P. Putnam's Sons, 1885), p. 62.

16. Alfred Marshall and Mary Paley Marshall, *The Economics of Industry* (London: Macmillan, 1884), p. 139.

17. Alfred Marshall, *Principles of Economics*, 8th ed. (New York: Macmillan, 1920), p. 614.

Economists, such as the Marshalls, had less impact than the mechanical engineers at this stage in developing management thought. The perceived problem resided in factory management, not the firm as an enterprise. Thus methods and systems were deemed critical in achieving internal economies of scale. Another, much broader, issue concerned the relations between labor and capital and was referred to as the labor question or the labor problem.

THE LABOR QUESTION

Earlier we reviewed criticisms of the factory system in Great Britain and the Victorian sense of conscience with respect to the employment of women and children and other issues and determined that, although problems did exist, the factory system was not the cause. Women and children had worked before, under the domestic system, and if anything, the Industrial Revolution enabled a social and economic uplift. Reformers, however, tend to have short memories and a small regard for hard facts. Speaking from their heart and conscience, U.S. reformers also attacked the factory system as the cause of numerous problems. One of the most outspoken critics was Washington Gladden, a Columbus, Ohio, minister, who articulated the major problems of the times as labor unrest, intemperance, poverty, slums, and child and female labor.[18] According to Gladden, solutions for labor unrest resided largely in organizing workers into strong unions to resist employers, providing profit sharing for workers, and requiring arbitration of labor-management disputes. Temperance was essential: The greatest evil for workers was alcohol because of its contribution to poverty and an ever-widening circle of effects such as slums, family disintegration, and other social evils. As Richard T. Ely, one of the early proponents of the Social Gospel, put it, "drink [is] the poor man's curse so often, and so often the rich man's shame."[19] Some social problems, such as child and female labor, could be dealt with only through legislation. Above all, society must be Christianized and the Golden Rule applied by both labor and management. Similar appeals were made by others for profit sharing, the right to organize trade unions, arbitration of industrial disputes, cooperative stores for workers, and national legislation to govern the hiring and firing of employees, the employment of women and children, and sanitation in workplaces.[20]

Whereas reformers defined the labor question as a broad one, engineers and economists saw the answers as residing in a more limited sphere. Methods and

---

18. Washington Gladden, *Working People and Their Employers* (New York: Arno Press, 1969). Originally published in 1876. See also Jacob H. Dorn, *Washington Gladden: Prophet of the Social Gospel* (Columbus: Ohio State University Press, 1966).

19. Richard T. Ely, *The Labor Movement in America* (New York: T. Y. Crowell, 1886), p. ix.

20. For an example, see William E. Barns, ed., *The Labor Problem* (New York: Harper and Brothers, 1886); for a contrary view, see Simon Newcomb, *A Plain Man's Talk on the Labor Question* (New York: Harper and Brothers, 1886).

systems would improve factory operations, but there had to be some incentive provided to obtain worker cooperation and stimulate their response to the need to improve output. Many managers of that period, such as James W. See, noted the common problem of low productivity, which was due to soldiering, or the deliberate restriction of output. Workers tended to work in spurts, take it easy when the supervisor was not present, and do less than their abilities would allow. The one thing that engineers and economists felt they could do to solve this problem was create some payment system based on performance, that is, wage incentives or piecework payments.

In Chapter 3 we noted that Adam Smith broke with the mercantilist position that the hungriest worker was the best. Smith advocated high wages to make workers more "active, diligent, and expeditious," but noted that some employees would overwork themselves if employers did not moderate those impulses. Smith's writing also suggested a backward bending supply curve of labor; that is, workers would work in spurts, then be absent from work once their income reached the desired level to engage in leisure activities, or perhaps rest.

Another English economist, David Schloss, reported that workers disliked piecework because "the difficulty of fixing a piece wage [rate] is very great" and often depended on the employers' idea of how quickly the work should be done.[21] Employers also were prone to "nibble" at the rate, that is, gradually increase the amount of work expected for the same wage payment. Schloss also reported a "lump of labor" phenomenon, that is, in the worker's mind there was a fixed amount of work to be done and, by working more slowly, this amount of work could be spread more thinly over the workforce. Schloss attributed the fallacy of lump of labor perception to how work standards were set at that time, that is, 1894.[22] Essentially, an individual's day's work was determined by an uneasy balance between what the supervisor expected and the pressures from coworkers. If the worker did too little, the ire of the supervisor was incurred, with possible dismissal from the job. If the worker did too much, group pressures to hold back production would increase, based on the assumption of a lump of labor. Thus, a day's work was an informally bargained compromise between contending forces.

Although there were doubts about the efficacy of payment for results rather than time-work, there appeared to be a connection between higher pay, lower per unit costs, and greater productivity. A U.S. economist, Edward Atkinson, observed that "the cheapest labor is the best-paid labor; it is the best-paid labor applied to machinery that assures the largest product in ratio to the capital invested."[23] If an employer paid low wages, the output would also be low; but if workers were paid well and combined with machinery, the output would be high. Schoenhof, for example,

---

21. David F. Schloss, "Why Working-Men Dislike Piece Work," *Economic Review* 1 (1891), pp. 313, 320. Reprinted in Wren, *Early Management Thought*, pp. 229–244.

22. David F. Schloss, *Methods of Industrial Remuneration* (London: Williams and Norgate, 1894).

23. Atkinson, *Distribution of Products*, p. 63.

compared various countries and found that those that paid the highest wages had the lowest costs.[24] Thus nail makers in Pittsburgh were paid ten times as much as those in Great Britain, yet their nails cost one-half as much. This paradox of high wages and low costs resurfaces in the scientific management movement, which is presented in the next section.

If high wages led to increased productivity and to lower costs per unit, then the solution resided in linking pay with performance. One set of proposals involved profit sharing, which was recognized as early as 1775 by the French economist A. R. J. Turgot, practiced by the Parisian housepainting firm of *Maison Leclaire*, and advocated by Charles Babbage. Profit sharing would encourage workers to produce more at less cost because they would share in the benefits. By 1887, over thirty U.S. firms had adopted some form of profit sharing, including John Wanamaker Dry Goods, Pillsbury Flour, Procter & Gamble, and Yale and Towne.[25] Yale and Towne, however, dropped profit sharing after a brief period when its chief executive, Henry R. Towne, contended that profit sharing was not an appropriate solution to the problem of greater worker productivity. In profit sharing, savings from worker efforts in one department could be offset by a lack of diligence in others. Instead, Towne proposed to determine costs and productivity for each work unit or department and to return to them the gains according to their own performance. Towne's plan guaranteed a wage rate to each employee, plus a fifty–fifty split of the gain in the worker's department.[26]

Another proposal was Frederick A. Halsey's "Premium Plan of Paying for Labor," in which he attacked the evils of both profit sharing and individual piecework systems.[27] He saw a lack of motivation in profit sharing and abuses in the piece-rate system. Halsey proposed that incentives be based on past production records, plus a guaranteed minimum wage, plus a premium for doing more work. The premium would amount to about one-third more than the daily or hourly rate and leave two-thirds of the added value to accrue to the employer, who would be therefore less inclined to cut the rate.

In 1895, Frederick W. Taylor proposed a method or rate-setting and a piece-rate system as a "step toward partial solution of the labor problem." From that point forward, the systematic management movement was in firmer hands and had a more coherent direction. But the foundations had been prepared: Organizations had grown, resources accumulated, the labor question debated, and the need for resource rationalization became apparent. Systematic management was a prelude and a cohort of what came to be known as scientific management. We will return to this story later.

---

24. J. Schoenhof, *The Economy of High Wages* (1893), cited in Litterer, "Systematic Management: The Search for Order and Integration," p. 463. Litterer notes other studies that yielded similar findings.

25. Nicholas P. Gilman, *Profit Sharing between Employer and Employee* (Boston: Houghton Mifflin, 1889); and Mary W. Calkins, *Sharing the Profits* (Boston: Ginn, 1888).

26. Henry R. Towne, "Gain Sharing," *Transactions, ASME* 10 (1889), pp. 600–625.

27. *Transactions, ASME* 12 (1891), pp. 755–764.

BIG BUSINESS AND ITS CHANGING ENVIRONMENT

No nation can undergo a transformation as the United States did in the last half of the nineteenth century without substantial repercussions. An examination of the U.S. response to industrialization is necessary to understand the forces that would shape the twentieth century. We have seen the accumulation of resources and systematic management as an emerging response to the growth of large-scale organization. Let us look beyond these developments to examine evolving notions of business and society, the beginnings of a national labor movement, the new technologies that transformed how people lived, and the changing relationship between government and business.

BUSINESS AND SOCIETY: BARONS OR BENEFACTORS?

Virtuous conduct seldom makes news. Historians and journalists are awed by the extraordinary and more frequently than not overemphasize it to the detriment of those quiet, sturdy, responsible people who, unheralded, are the true productive builders. Criticism of business leaders and their practices began to appear primarily in the latter third of the nineteenth century. Although the origins are obscure, one early reference described Cornelius Vanderbilt as a medieval baron, drawing an analogy to the feudal lords who built castles along the Rhine River to exact tolls from those who passed by. The phrase *robber barons* appeared later, and Matthew Josephson popularized this phrase to such a point that the public often equated any business leader with this value system. It would be impossible to examine all those deemed to be robber barons, but some thumbnail sketches will reveal why Josephson felt that some business leaders were behaving in socially irresponsible ways.

Commodore Cornelius Vanderbilt gained control of the New York and Harlem railroad line by bribing the New York state legislature and manipulating stock. Daniel Drew had the dubious honor of being the first to engage in the practice that came to be called watering stock. He had purchased a herd of cattle with an enlistment bonus from his Civil War army days. In transporting the herd to market, he fed them salt to make them thirsty, and then offered them all the water they could drink and sold at a very large profit some temporarily overweight cattle. Together with Jay Gould and Jim Fisk, Drew turned to railroading and soon gave the Erie line its reputation for mismanagement in the days following Daniel McCallum. The Western railroaders, led by Collis P. Huntington and aided by Leland Stanford, Sr., purchased the favors of legislators who could grant them free government land, award franchises, and pass enabling legislation. One year Huntington paid $200,000 to get a bill through Congress; he later complained that Congress was costing up to a half million dollars a session and moaned, "I am afraid this damnation Congress will kill us."[28]

28. Matthew Josephson, *The Robber Barons* (New York: Harcourt Brace Jovanovich, 1934), p. 357.

Not all of the barons were railroad men. John D. Rockefeller combined audacity and cunning in building his South Improvement Company and the Standard Oil colossus. By conspiring with the railroads, he was able to extract rebates on his freight and receive rebates on oil shipped by his rivals. Andrew Carnegie at one point owned or controlled two-thirds of the nation's young steel industry. The Homestead strike earned Carnegie poor press when union efforts were met with a force of Pinkerton detectives (hired to protect the plant), who were brutally stoned and beaten by the striking workers. State troops moved in and secured the plant for a wholly nonunion crew; in the process four Pinkerton men were killed and 300 wounded.[29] These men represented, at least for Josephson, the most unsavory practices in U.S. business leadership.

What motivated the robber barons? For some social historians, it was the publication in 1859 of Charles Darwin's book, *On the Origin of Species by Means of Natural Selection, or the Preservation of Favored Races in the Struggle for Life.* This book set forth his theories concerning evolution and natural selection through the struggle for existence. Social scientists seized Darwin's theories in an attempt to apply them to human society, and the result was "social Darwinism."[30] The most striking phrases of Darwinism, "struggle for existence" and "survival of the fittest," suggested that nature would provide that the most fit in a competitive situation would win. Thus, through unrestricted competition, the most fit would survive and move up the social ladder of success and the unfit would occupy the lower class structures and eventually be eliminated through evolution.

Are these allegations true? One historian claimed that businesspeople were pragmatic doers who worked out the rules as they met them; they read or heard little of Darwin or Adam Smith and cared little for abstract social and economic theories.[31] Another agreed: "It is not true that this commitment [to competition] was grounded on Darwinian premises." Few businesspeople knew enough of Darwin "to turn biology to the uses of self-justification."[32] What can be concluded about the effect of social Darwinism on the thought and practices of those in business? The economics of the period led to mergers rather than to cutthroat competition as social Darwinism would predict. For example, Chandler saw Rockefeller's efforts as attempts to gain economies of scale rather than as an effort to monopolize the industry. Under Rockefeller, the cost of a gallon of kerosene went from 1.5 cents before the Standard Oil trust to less than one-half of 1 cent by 1885.[33] Before the

---

29. Joseph F. Wall, *Andrew Carnegie* (New York: Oxford University Press, 1970), p. 559.

30. Richard Hofstadter, *Social Darwinism in American Thought* (Boston: Beacon Press, 1945), p. 4.

31. Edward C. Kirkland, *Dream and Thought in the Business Community, 1860–1900* (Ithaca, NY: Cornell University Press, 1956), p. 14. Another who shares this pragmatic view is Peter D. A. Jones, ed., *The Robber Barons Revisited* (Boston: D. C. Heath, 1968), pp. v–xi.

32. Raymond J. Wilson, ed., *Darwinism and the American Intellectual: A Book of Readings* (Homewood, IL: Dorsey Press, 1967), p. 93.

33. Alfred D. Chandler, Jr., "The Emergence of Managerial Capitalism," *Business History Review* 5 (Winter 1984), pp. 473–503.

discovery and refining of oil, animal fat was used for lubricating wheels and gears, and before kerosene, whale oil was used for lighting. Perhaps saving the whales was not Rockefeller's intention, but kerosene kept them from extinction. Earlier we saw that Carnegie drove the price of steel downward constantly, which may have been his greatest philanthropy. Business leaders gave bribes when politicians forced them to do so; for example, when Ezra Cornell sought a charter from the New York State legislature to found a college at Ithaca, he had to strike a "bargain" with the "friends of Geneseo College," who, in return for a $25,000 gift to that college, would ensure him the needed votes. As Cornell noted in his "cipher" book, "Such is the influence of corrupt legislation."[34]

It is highly doubtful that business leaders found much in social Darwinism. Rather, it appears that the period was one of change, and business leaders were highly visible targets for the critics:

> The creation of the Robber Baron stereotype seems to have been the product of an impulsive popular attempt to explain the shift in the structure of American society ... most critics appeared to slip into the easy vulgarizations of the "devil-view" of history which ingenuously assumes that all misfortunes can be traced to the machinations of an easily located set of villains—in this case, the big businessmen of America.[35]

Rising in counterpoint to social Darwinism was another set of ideas that came closer to grasping the policies and practices of the nineteenth-century business leader. This new consciousness was described earlier as the Social Gospel, and it was seen as Christianity in action by people such as Washington Gladden. We will return to the Social Gospel and how it led to improved personnel practices and to an interest in the problems of industry.

Another set of developments also suggests that business leaders were far more generous than typically assumed. Were there any benefactions by business to society during this period? The philanthropy of business people is as ancient as business itself, including patrons of arts and letters, providers of funds for community projects, donors to churches, and endowers of educational institutions. No one questioned the right of successful persons to give away some or all of their fortunes; after all, it was their money to do with as they pleased. But what of this new phenomenon, the corporation? Could its managers and directors give away a portion of its profits to non-business-related endeavors?

Two legal principles, the notion of limited charter powers and that of management as trustee of the stockholders' property, combined to form the nineteenth-century legal basis regarding corporate philanthropy. A case precedent

---

34. Carl L. Becker, *Cornell University: Founders and Founding* (Ithaca, NY: Cornell University Press, 1943), pp. 103–107, 154.

35. John Tipple, "The Anatomy of Prejudice: Origins of the Robber Baron Legend," *Business History Review* 33 (Winter 1959), p. 521.

in 1881 involved the Old Colony Railway Company of Massachusetts, which had subscribed to underwrite the financial loss suffered by a "world's peace jubilee and international music festival." Despite the fact that the railroad had increased passenger traffic because of the jubilee, the court ruled in favor of the shareholders that this subscription was ultra vires (i.e., outside its chartered powers).[36] In Great Britain in 1883, the West Cork Railroad Company attempted to compensate its employees for the loss of their jobs occasioned by the dissolution of the corporation. In ruling against the company, Lord Justice Bowden stated the guiding rule: "Charity has no business sitting at the board of directors qua charity . . . [the board of directors] can only spend money which is not their's [sic], but the company's, if they are spending it for purposes which are reasonably incidental to the carrying on of the business of the company."[37] What might or might not be reasonably incidental would receive some clarification in the Steinway case. The court allowed piano manufacturers Steinway and Sons to buy an adjoining tract of land to be used for a church, library, and school for their employees. The court's reasoning was that the employees would benefit, so there was a definite quid pro quo accruing to the corporation's benefit in better employee relations.[38] In short, the law was fairly clear in the position that corporations were chartered to do specific things, that managers and directors were trustees of the property of the shareholders, and that directors could give away assets only if it was of measurable benefit to the corporation. Each of the legal points sorely constrained corporate philanthropy, and it would be almost three-quarters of a century before corporations could engage in philanthropic endeavors of general benefit.

Although corporate philanthropy might be questioned, it would be unlikely that the hand of individual charity would be nipped. Individual philanthropy would be the vehicle for expressing the social conscience of the nineteenth-century entrepreneur. Only a few of the great philanthropist–business leaders can be mentioned here.[39] Ezra Cornell pioneered in telegraphy, made a fortune from the Western Union Company, and provided the money to found a college (in Ithaca, New York), which would naturally be named for him; William Colgate helped people get closer to godliness with the manufacture of soap, and he and his heirs gave so much to a college that it changed its name to his; Moses Brown, Samuel Slater's partner, founded Rhode Island College in Providence (1770), which became Brown University in 1804; Johns Hopkins, founder of the Baltimore and Ohio Railroad, also founded the eminent university in Baltimore that bears his name; and

---

36. *Davis v. Old Colony Railway Company*, 131 Mass. 258 (1881).

37. *Hutton v. West Cork Railroad Company*, 23 Chancery Division Reports 654 (1883).

38. *Steinway v. Steinway and Sons*, 40 N.Y.S. 718 (1896).

39. For an extensive list, see Daniel A. Wren, "American Business Philanthropy and Higher Education in the Nineteenth Century," *Business History Review* 57 (Autumn 1983), pp. 321–346. See also Mark Sharfman, "Changing Institutional Rules: The Evolution of Corporate Philanthropy, 1883–1953," *Business and Society* 33 (December 1994), pp. 236–269.

Cornelius Vanderbilt made a large bequest in 1873 that converted a small Methodist seminary in Nashville into a well-known university that received its name from him.

There were more: Joseph Wharton, whose $100,000 grant enabled the nation's first school of business, at the University of Pennsylvania; Edward Tuck, who honored his father with a gift of $300,000 to Dartmouth College to start the Amos Tuck School of Administration and Finance (1899); Leland Stanford, who honored his son with a university (1891); John Stevens, who provided for an institute of technology (1870); and James B. Duke, who established the trust fund to create Trinity College (later renamed for the Duke family). Good fortune did not smile on all colleges who hoped for a philanthropist. Daniel Drew gave a $250,000 promissory note to endow a Methodist theological seminary in Madison, New Jersey. The seminary started its work, but Daniel Drew went bankrupt and was never able to deliver the promised money. Nonetheless, the seminary was named Drew University.

Other philanthropists are better known. Rockefeller endowed the University of Chicago in 1896, gave millions through a general education fund to educate southern African Americans, and by the time of his death in 1937 had given away half a billion dollars as well as provided for the future of the foundation that bears the family name. Carnegie had given away $350 million by the time of his death (1919), and his libraries, university, and foundation are enduring monuments to his expressed stewardship of wealth philosophy. Despite such generosity, both Rockefeller and Carnegie were denounced by the Congressional Committee on Industrial Relations in 1915 as "menaces to society."[40] Their efforts were seen as intrusions into the province of government and reflected the fear that business charity had the potential of increasing the control of the business community over society.

Times have changed: income and inheritance taxes make it difficult to accumulate as much wealth as did the entrepreneurs of the nineteenth century, the legal question of corporate philanthropy has been clarified (as we shall see later), and public expectations about the role of business in society have changed. But we are the recipients today of the benefactions of the nineteenth-century builders of the United States.

BUSINESS AND LABOR: THE CONDITION OF THE WORKER

Earlier we saw that the *Commonwealth v. Hunt* decision (1842) removed combinations of workers from the conspiracy doctrine that had prevailed in Great Britain. In the United States, labor organizations were found among craft workers, such as in the building trades, and among so-called brotherhoods of railway employees. Attempts by other workers to form unions were generally less successful. The National Labor

---

40. Cited by Clarence C. Walton, *Corporate Social Responsibilities* (Belmont, CA: Wadsworth, 1967), pp. 41–42.

Union, headed by William H. Sylvis, sought to supplant the wage system with cooperative production in which the workers would pool their resources, supply their own labor, and manage the factories. The Noble Order of the Knights of Labor, organized in 1867, sought an eight-hour day, the establishment of a bureau of labor statistics, protection of child labor, a graduated income tax, government ownership of railroads and telegraph lines, the abolition of national banks, and a system of cooperation to take the place of wages. Neither of these organizations survived.

Labor violence in the 1880s and 1890s fueled public fears of unions. The Molly Maguires terrorized the populace with murders and other atrocities in the Pennsylvania coalfields. The Haymarket Affair (1886), in which the Knights of Labor tried to enforce a general strike in Chicago, led to several deaths. The Homestead strike (1892) and the Pullman strike (1894) were other examples of violence brought about by confrontations between labor and management. Public fear of radicals and anarchists, who were often equated with legitimate union organizers, kept the union movement at a relative standstill in terms of growth as a percentage of the labor force. Total union membership grew from 300,000 members in 1870 to 868,000 in 1900; however, in 1870, only 5 percent of the total labor force was organized; this percentage declined in the 1880s and 1890s, but recovered and rose to 4.8 by 1900.

One successful union was the American Federation of Labor, organized in 1886 as a federation of craft unions that concentrated on the pursuit of immediate economic gains for the worker on the job rather than on distant political reforms. Under the leadership of Samuel Gompers, membership increased from fewer than 200,000 in 1886 to more than 2,865,000 at the time of Gompers's death in 1924.[41] Industrial workers, however, had to await other times and a changing public opinion to legitimize their attempts at organization.

Immigration provided a growing workforce for this period of rapid industrial growth: Chinese were brought in to build the railroads, and Irish, Germans, and Swedes populated the coalfields and steel mills of the United States. After 1880, another flow of Slavs, Poles, and Italians added to the swelling workforce. The increased supply of labor did not result in lower wages for the U.S. worker. Daily wages and annual earnings in manufacturing increased 50 percent between 1860 and 1890, and real wages (the purchasing power of the workers' incomes) increased 60 percent from 1860 to 1890 (1.6 percent compounded annually).[42] In summary, the U.S. worker benefited from the growth of industry in terms of employment and real income.

INVENTIVE AND INNOVATIVE IMPULSES

Earlier we saw the influence of the railroads in creating a national market, probing the interior of lands where nature had furnished no natural pathways. When the

---

41. Philip A. Taft, *The A.F.L. in the Time of Gompers* (New York: Harper and Row, 1957), ch. 3.

42. Ross M. Robertson, *History of the American Economy*, 3rd ed. (New York: Harcourt Brace Jovanovich, 1973), pp. 379–380.

Union Pacific and the Central Pacific railroads met at Promontory, Utah, in 1869, a golden spike commemorated the spanning of the nation, connecting east and west, the beginning of a network of rails that would increase from 35,000 miles in 1865 to 193,000 by 1900. Technological advancements made rail travel more pleasurable: steel rails replaced iron ones; George Pullman introduced the sleeping car in 1865; and George Westinghouse developed the air brake in 1868, making rail travel safer. The railroads fostered a retailing revolution, as we shall see, by creating greater time and place utility through mass distribution. With the railroads, interstate commerce was facilitated, but also made more complicated because there were no standard times from one area to the next. It could be noon in Chicago, 12:30 p.m. in Pittsburgh, and 11:45 a.m. in St. Louis, a most confusing situation for the shipper or the traveler. The solution was four time zones, based on the 75th, 90th, 105th, and 120th meridians. Standard times became effective on the railways in 1883, but the U.S. Congress did not accept this until 1918.

The railroads were only one technological advancement in America's last half of the nineteenth century. The remarkable spirit of inventive and innovative impulses that shaped America's technological advances were due to a number of prime movers, individuals whose ideas created the wealth of the nation. As Locke expressed it, "for wealth to be created, individuals must create it ... *prime movers* ... moved society forward by the force of their own creative imagination, their own energy, and their own productive capacity."[43] We find these individuals during this time pushing forward the nation's capacity to produce more, to create jobs, and to devise means of making, moving and packaging a cornucopia of consumer products that had few, if any, precedents.

The telegraph was the companion of railroads in this revolution in commerce. Chandler expressed these revolutions of communication and transportation and the growth of enterprise in terms of scale and scope: *scale* referred to the increased size of a single operating unit making a single product, and *scope* was used to describe the processes within a single operating unit to distribute more than one product.[44] Carnegie's vertical integration in the steel industry indicated the economies of scale, and using his facilities for different types of steel products would illustrate economies of scope. As scale and scope expanded, the need for a team of managers to plan, coordinate, and monitor the functions of the firm increased. With the rail system, the telegraph, and Alexander Graham Bell's telephone, it became possible to produce, transport, and sell in both national and international markets.

The business firm of the last half of the nineteenth century was an entirely different creation from the localized, family-owned and managed, and labor-intensive firms of the pre–Civil War period. To mention all the prime movers in the creation of the emerging capital-intensive, large-scale, professionally managed firms is beyond our present task. Some, such as Thomas Edison and George Westinghouse, enabled

43. Edwin A. Locke, *Prime Movers: Traits of the Great Wealth Creators* (New York: American Management Association, 2000), p. 7.

44. Chandler, *Scale and Scope*, pp. 17–28.

the natural force of electricity to be transformed, transmitted, and controlled by humans. John D. Rockefeller's domination of the kerosene market for lighting would be replaced with electricity. Bell's telephone did not need to follow the railroad tracks and marked the beginning of the American Telephone and Telegraph Company. Elisha Gray invented the first fax machine, his "telautograph" for facsimile writing and drawing for transmission over the telegraph.

With improvements in communication and transportation came the mass marketers, the chain-retailers, mail-order houses, and food merchants such as the Great Atlantic and Pacific Tea Company. Refrigerated rail cars transformed the meatpacking industry and brought numerous perishable products to distant markets. The American System of Manufacturers enabled mass production of Isaac Singer's sewing machine and Cyrus McCormick's grain harvester. Christopher Sholes licensed his typewriter to Eliphalet Remington for production by the Remington Arms Company. Andrew Carnegie's stronger, lighter, structural steel enabled high-rise buildings, but Elisha Otis's elevator made travel to the top less taxing. These were a few of the prime movers whose ideas were the basis of emerging large-scale enterprise in manufacturing, communications, marketing, distilling, refining, transporting, and food processing.

Corporate research and development did not begin until the twentieth century with Bell Labs, General Electric, Du Pont, and others who followed. The latter part of America's nineteenth century was the age of the individualistic inventors and innovators, the wealth creators of a new material abundance in the history of humankind.

BUSINESS AND GOVERNMENT: THE SEEDS OF REFORM

U.S. government of the nineteenth century was not noted for its progressiveness. The spoils system prevailed (that is, to the winner belong the spoils), and various attempts at reform had failed. Finally, shortly after the assassination of President James Garfield by a disappointed office seeker, the Civil Service Act of 1883 (better known as the Pendleton Act after its senatorial sponsor) was passed. The intent of the civil service reform was to bring qualified employees, rather than political favorites, to government and to provide some stability in the governmental infrastructure. Thus the seeds of systematic management and rationalization appear to have been operational in the public as well as the private sector.

Credit for attempting to bring system to governmental service must be given to Woodrow Wilson, then a young professor at Bryn Mawr College. In 1887, Wilson recognized that civil service reform must extend beyond personnel matters into the organization and methods of governmental offices. To accomplish this, Wilson recommended "administrative study to discover, first, what government can properly and successfully do, and secondly, how it can do these proper things with the utmost possible efficiency and the least possible cost either of money or energy." The study of government, according to Wilson, had focused too long on politics and not enough on how to manage the public's business. After all, "the field of administration is a field of business ... removed from the hurry and strife of politics. ... The object of administrative study is to rescue executive methods from the confusion and costliness of empirical experience and set them on foundations laid deep in stable principle."[45] Wilson would move on to higher office, but his thinking was clear in terms of bringing improved systems and methods to government.

In terms of national policy there were few effective efforts at the regulation of business, as government held true to a narrowly construed commerce clause. The first attempts to reform business practices came very logically with the railroads. In 1869, Massachusetts passed the first statutes regulating railroads; the Granger laws of the seventies brought regulation to others, and the Interstate Commerce Act of 1887, though it proved generally ineffective in practice, became the first national regulation. Beyond the railroads, the Sherman Antitrust Act of 1890 sought to check corporate trusts and monopoly practices "in restraint of trade." Poorly defined and narrowly construed, it was generally ineffectual. To illustrate further the hands-off policy, even taxpayers benefited. The first peacetime federal income tax was imposed by the Wilson-Gorman Tax Act of 1894. It levied a 2 percent personal tax on all incomes above $4,000 and a 2 percent tax on all corporate net income. In 1895, the Supreme Court declared the act unconstitutional. Taxpayers could rest easy for a few more years. In brief, the nineteenth-century political environment remained relatively laissez-faire, true to the precepts of Adam Smith; the twentieth century would bring a host of changes in this philosophy.

SUMMARY OF PART I

Part I of this study has been an examination of management thought prior to the scientific management era in the United States and may be visually conceptualized as Figure 6-1. People, a fundamental focus of our study, have manifold needs and wants, which they seek to satisfy through organized endeavors. In organizations, management is an activity that performs certain functions to obtain the effective acquisition, allocation, and utilization of human efforts and physical resources to meet the organization's objectives and yield positive benefits to organizational members. The cultural environment, characterized as having economic, social, technological, and political facets, shapes values and forms institutional arrangements that have a significant bearing on people, organizations, and management as an activity.

Early civilizations reflected some attempts to relate individuals to organizations, but generally placed a low value on economic activity and held a parochial view of the management function. The cultural rebirth brought new views of people, economic

---

45. Woodrow Wilson, "The Study of Administration," *Political Science Quarterly* 2 (June 1887), pp. 197, 210.

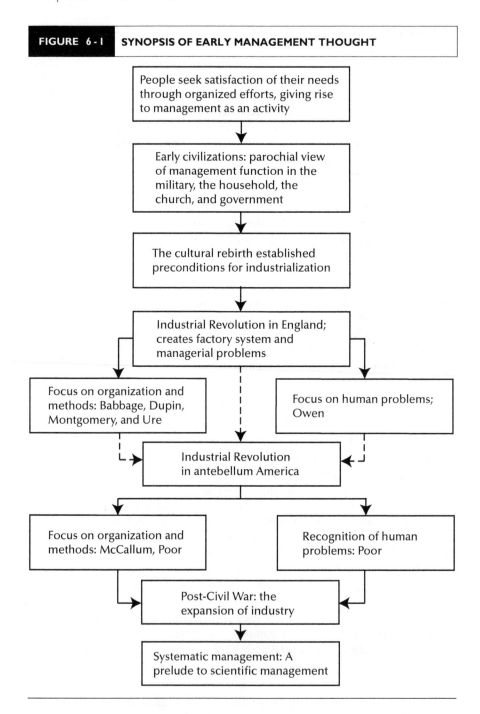

FIGURE 6-1 SYNOPSIS OF EARLY MANAGEMENT THOUGHT

People seek satisfaction of their needs through organized efforts, giving rise to management as an activity

Early civilizations: parochial view of management function in the military, the household, the church, and government

The cultural rebirth established preconditions for industrialization

Industrial Revolution in England; creates factory system and managerial problems

Focus on organization and methods: Babbage, Dupin, Montgomery, and Ure

Focus on human problems; Owen

Industrial Revolution in antebellum America

Focus on organization and methods: McCallum, Poor

Recognition of human problems: Poor

Post-Civil War: the expansion of industry

Systematic management: A prelude to scientific management

activity, social values, and political arrangements and established the preconditions for the Industrial Revolution. This technological and cultural revolution created the factory system to replace the domestic system and posed managerial problems on a scale never before encountered. Broadly viewed, these problems may be grouped in three categories: (1) the organizational and methods problems of melding technology, materials, organizational functions, and productive processes in an efficient manner; (2) the human problems of acquiring, developing, stimulating, and controlling human behavior toward preconceived ends; and (3) the managerial problem of fusing both these facets to accomplish objectives.

Throughout this study of management thought, we will see that various writers shift their relative emphasis on the importance of the organization and methods facets vis-à-vis the human facet. This does not mean that these two facets are mutually exclusive, but that it is a matter of relative focus, and this focus to a large degree is influenced by the cultural environment. For example, Charles Babbage was concerned with the human problems of the factory, but his primary interest was the analysis of production techniques. Robert Owen, on the other hand, was more concerned with the impact of industrialization on people. Likewise, Henry Varnum Poor was concerned with the systematization of the railroads but recognized the interaction of the organization and methods facets with the human facet.

Figure 6-1 illustrates in summary form management thought before scientific management. It shows early ideas about management activity, depicts the relative emphases of management pioneers, and provides the basis for the beginnings of the scientific management era in the United States.

The Scientific Management Era

P art II begins with the work of Frederick W. Taylor and examines management thought in Europe, the United States, and elsewhere up to the early 1930s. Taylor provided the major thrust for an era characterized by a search for workplace efficiency and systematization. Those who rallied around Taylor, such as Carl G. Barth, Henry L. Gantt, the Gilbreths, Morris L. Cooke, and Harrington Emerson, spread the gospel of efficiency worldwide. Though the work of Taylor and his followers dominated this era, the contributions of selected psychologists and sociologists are also reviewed as a prelude to the emergence of the human-relations movement in industry. The works of Henri Fayol and Max Weber, who wrote during the scientific management era but whose contributions to the development of management thought were not recognized much later, are examined next. Finally, this part concludes with a conceptual view of the economic, social, and political conditions that comprised the cultural environment of scientific management.

CHAPTER 7

The Advent of Scientific Management

arlier chapters reviewed the transformation of American industry in the post–Civil War period. The Industrial Revolution in Great Britain initially spread to North America with the mechanization of textile manufacturing. Given the westward advance of the U.S. frontier, the Industrial Revolution was most evident in the railroad industry. People needed an inexpensive mode of transportation, and the railroads also provided a cost-effective means for transporting manufactured goods, raw materials, and food. The seeds of the modern industrial corporation—the forerunner of today's *Fortune* 500 company—were sown. As noted in Chapter 5, in the United Sates, the railroad industry was to feel the resulting need for improved management. Daniel McCallum introduced systematic management on the Erie Railroad, and his ideas moved onward to influence other railways and Carnegie in steel. Railroads opened new markets, and the telegraph connected the nation for financial, production, marketing, and other transactions.

Another stage of the Industrial Revolution began in the latter half of the nineteenth century. It was a complex, uneven, and interacting outcome of technological advances, changing power sources, evolving labor-management relations, and a desperate need to bring all these factors into some concordance by improving managerial practices. As engineers were vital to developing and installing advances in technology and power, it was natural that they became a prime source of ideas for meeting new managerial challenges. Henry Towne, for example, called for engineers to look beyond the technical side of manufacturing and become involved in increasing the managerial efficiency of industrial operations. One of the engineers who responded to Towne's appeal was Frederick W. Taylor, and he is the focal point of this chapter.

FREDERICK WINSLOW TAYLOR: THE EARLY YEARS

Frederick Winslow Taylor (1856–1915) was born in Germantown, Pennsylvania. His father was a fairly prosperous lawyer of Quaker stock, and his mother traced her Puritan roots to a Plymouth, Massachusetts, ancestor, who arrived in America in 1629.[1] Taylor's early education was liberally sprinkled with the classics, the study of French and German, and three and a half years' schooling and travel in Europe. His parents intended that he should follow his father's profession of law and in 1872 duly enrolled him at Phillips Exeter Academy in Exeter, New Hampshire, to prepare for Harvard University. The competition was stiff, and Taylor's zeal and restless energy led to late nights and long hours, eventually impairing his eyesight and causing headaches. Although he graduated at the head of his class and passed the Harvard entrance exams with honors, and eyeglasses would ultimately solve the vision and headache problems, Taylor decided to turn away from further study. His parents suggested that he consider becoming an engineer. So, at the age of 18, he began an apprenticeship as a patternmaker for the Enterprise Hydraulic Works (Philadelphia), a pump-manufacturing company owned by family acquaintances.[2] Patternmakers were skilled workers who crafted wooden molds that were used to make hollows in hard pressed sand to shape molten metal into iron and brass castings. Taylor's decision to enter an apprenticeship was not unusual. Upper-class Philadelphians had long been educated in this manner. It was an accepted means of developing elite mechanical engineers. As was customary, Taylor started his four-year apprenticeship at no wage. During his second year, he earned $1.50 a week. By his fourth year he was pocketing the princely sum of $3.00 a week. At Enterprise, Taylor developed empathy for the workers' point of view; he could swear with the best of them and admired the pride they took in their craftsmanship. He, however, saw about him what he called "bad industrial conditions," worker restriction of output, poor management, and lack of harmony between labor and management.

---

1. The life of Taylor is a popular subject for biographies. A much-cited source is Frank Barkley Copley's authorized autobiography, *Frederick W. Taylor: Father of Scientific Management*, 2 vols. (New York: Harper & Brothers, 1923). Other useful sources are Charles D. Wrege and Ronald G. Greenwood, *Frederick W. Taylor, the Father of Scientific Management: Myth and Reality* (Homewood, IL: Business One Irwin, 1991); Daniel Nelson, *Frederick W. Taylor and the Rise of Scientific Management* (Madison: University of Wisconsin Press, 1980); and Robert Kanigel, *The One Best Way: Frederick Winslow Taylor and the Enigma of Efficiency* (New York: Viking, 1997).

2. Robert Kanigel, "Frederick Taylor's Apprenticeship," *Wilson Quarterly* 20 (1996), pp. 44–51.

TAYLOR AT MIDVALE

Having completed his apprenticeship, Taylor joined the Midvale Steel Company (Philadelphia) in 1878.[3] Midvale specialized in the manufacture of locomotive wheels and railway axles. The economic consequences of the financial panic of 1873 lingered, and jobs were scarce. Taylor consequently took a job as a laborer. Midvale, under the presidency of William Sellers, one of the nineteenth century's most prominent inventors of machine tools, was one of the leading steel firms of the era. There Taylor rose from common laborer to clerk, to machinist, to gang boss of machinists, to machine-shop supervisor, to master mechanic in charge of all repairs and maintenance, and to chief engineer—all in six years.

Taylor's twelve years at Midvale (1878–1890) were years of experimentation, during which he gained invaluable insights that would be the basis for his later ideas about proper management. Realizing that he lacked a "scientific education," he took a home-study course in mathematics and physics at Harvard University. He then enrolled in a home-study course from Stevens Institute of Technology (Hoboken, New Jersey). Without ever having been on campus, except to take his entrance examination and each of his required course examinations, Taylor graduated with a degree in mechanical engineering in 1883. Given that Taylor was able to immediately pass many of his exams in French, German, history, and so on, due to his experience abroad and to general reading, he was able to graduate in about two and a half years, all the while fulfilling his duties at Midvale.

Taylor had no formal training in management and relied solely on his own experiences to determine what should be done to improve Midvale's production. The company had established a piecework incentive system that Taylor knew to be ineffective from his days as a laborer. Midvale's management felt that the workers would produce more if they were paid a fixed "piece rate" for each unit produced than if they received a flat day rate. When Taylor became gang boss, he learned otherwise. He quickly realized that output was unnecessarily low due to a practice called "soldiering," whereby workers deliberately worked as slowly as they dared, while at the same time trying to make their bosses believe they were working fast. Indeed, he estimated that worker output was only one-third of what was possible.

Taylor distinguished between two types of soldiering. "Natural soldiering" proceeded from "the natural instinct and tendency of men to take it easy"; "systematic soldiering" came from the workers' "more intricate second thought and reasoning caused by their relations with other men."[4] Natural soldiering could

---

3. Charles D. Wrege and Ronald G. Greenwood, "The Early History of Midvale Steel and the Work of Frederick W. Taylor: 1865–1890," *Canal History and Technology Proceedings* 11 (1992), pp. 145–176.

4. Frederick W. Taylor, *Shop Management* (New York: Harper & Brothers, 1903), p. 30.

Frederick W. Taylor from his Midvale days, circa 1886. Courtesy Frederick Winslow Taylor Collection, Samuel C. Williams Library, Stevens Institute of Technology, Hoboken NJ.

be overcome by inspiring or forcing workers to come up to the mark. Systematic soldiering posed a different problem, and managers for years had been attempting to cope with the tendency of workers to deliberately "underwork." Taylor understood that workers soldiered for several reasons. First, they feared that if they worked faster, they would complete their jobs and be laid off; second, based on their experience of being paid by the piece, if they produced more, management would likely cut the piece rate governing their wages and they would end up doing more work for the same take-home pay; and third, they adhered to rule-of-thumb work methods handed down from generation to generation.[5] Taylor placed the blame on management, not on the workers, for he thought that it was management's responsibility to design jobs properly and offer appropriate incentives to overcome worker soldiering.

In no small part, soldiering arose out of a "lump of labor" theory, which held that there was a fixed amount of work to be done in the world, so any increase in the amount each worker produces reduces the number of available jobs.[6] A flat daily or hourly wage rate encouraged soldiering, because workers had no incentive to produce more today than yesterday. Pay was based on attendance and position, not effort. Working harder brought no reward and, thus, workers were actually encouraged to be lazy. Piece-rate systems, old long before Taylor's time, sought to encourage individual productivity by paying workers on the basis of their output, but such systems had generally been failures; standards were often poorly set, employers cut pay rates as the increased output became the norm, and workers hid their shortcut methods to keep management ignorant of how fast work could be done. Not surprisingly, workers developed a consensus about how much each should produce and earn, not only to protect themselves but also to avoid sanctions being placed on the less capable. Management was seemingly unaware of the resulting inefficiencies.

Taylor's initial experiences as a machine-shop supervisor resulted in a bitter encounter with Midvale's machinists. He told the machinists that he knew they could do more and that he was going to see that they did. Taylor started by showing them how to use metalworking lathes to get more output with little additional effort. The machinists refused to follow his instructions. Taylor then turned to training

5. Frederick W. Taylor, *The Principles of Scientific Management* (New York: Harper & Brothers, 1911), pp. 15–16.

6. John Wilson, "Economic Fallacies and Labour Utopias." *Quarterly Review* 131 (1871), pp. 229–263.

apprentice laborers. Facing established output norms, however, they promptly disavowed Taylor's methods. Taylor admitted, "I was up against a stone wall. I did not blame these laborers in my heart; my sympathy was with them all of the time."[7] In an effort to force the machinists to work faster to earn the same daily pay, Taylor cut the prevailing piece-rate. The machinists retaliated by breaking and jamming their machines. Taylor countered by imposing a system of fines (the proceeds going to a worker benefit fund) for damaged equipment. After three years, the machinists finally gave in and adopted Taylor's methods. This bitter experience taught Taylor a valuable lesson. He saw that a business is a system of human cooperation that will be successful only if all concerned work toward a common goal. Never again would he impose fines, and he would later establish strict rules against rate cutting. More important, Taylor realized that a new industrial system was essential for preventing such bitter labor–management encounters. Taylor set out to develop such a system.

THE SEARCH FOR SCIENCE IN MANAGEMENT

Taylor thought he could overcome soldiering by determining how each job could be done most efficiently and then establishing performance standards. He believed that once workers saw that performance standards had been set "scientifically," rather than on tradition, there could be no appeal and their motivation to soldier would be eliminated. The problem was in defining a fair day's work for each job. Taylor set out to determine what the workers *ought* to be able to do with their equipment and materials. This was the beginning of what was to be called "scientific management," that is, the application of the scientific method to empirically establish the most efficient way to perform each worker's job. Taylor had concluded that labor–management conflict was due to ignorance on both sides. Management expected and workers were ready to provide "a fair day's work" for "a fair day's pay." Neither side, however, knew what constituted a day's work. Both relied on vague impressions that led to continuing disputes.

Time study became the foundation of Taylor's work. With a stopwatch, weight scale, and tape, he literally measured the distances that workers and materials traveled. Gradually, he determined that a large share of both effort and materials was needlessly wasted because of improper management. Some critics would question the originality of Taylor's work. Charles Babbage had previously used a watch to record the labor operations and times necessary for manufacturing pins. In 1912, a subcommittee of the American Society of Mechanical Engineers issued a report on time study that made no mention of Taylor's work but referenced Babbage and Adam Smith. Taylor contributed to a discussion of this report in an effort to clarify his concept of time study and answer those who doubted the originality of his work.

> Time study was begun in the machine shop of the Midvale Steel Company in 1881.... It is true that the form of Tables 1 and 2

---

7. Copley, *Taylor*, vol. 1, p. 162.

[from Babbage's 1835 book *Economy of Machinery and Manufacture*] is similar to that of the blanks recording time study, but here the resemblance ceases. Each line in Table 2, for instance, gives statistics regarding the average of the entire work of an operative who works day in and day out, in running a machine engaged in the manufacture of pins. This table involves no study whatever of the movements of the man, nor of the time in which the movements *should* have been made. Mere statistics as to the time which a man takes to do a given piece of work do not constitute "time study." "Time study," as its name implies, involves a careful study of the time in which work *ought* to be done . . . [rather than] the time in which the work actually was done.[8]

Unlike Babbage, Taylor used time study for inferential rather than descriptive purposes. Rather than simply describe "what is," Taylor used time study to discover "what was possible" in improving job performance. Taylor's time study had two phases: *analysis* and *synthesis*. In analysis, each job was broken into its elementary movements. Nonessential movements were discarded and the remainder carefully examined to determine the quickest and least wasteful means of performing a job. These elementary motions were then described, recorded, and indexed, along with the amount of time required to cover unavoidable delays, minor accidents, and rest. In the second stage, synthesis, the elementary movements were combined in the correct sequence to determine the time and the exact method for performing a job. This phase also led to improvements in tools, machines, materials, methods, and the ultimate standardization of all elements surrounding and accompanying a job.[9]

THE QUEST FOR IMPROVED INCENTIVES

The search for effective piece-rate incentive plans for increasing output is probably as old as humankind.[10] Payment based on individual performance was the basis of the "putting out" or domestic system of production, and piece-rate incentives were used before and during the Industrial Revolution. As American industry developed after the Civil War, numerous schemes were proposed for paying labor. These included Henry Towne's gain sharing and Frederick Halsey's premium plan. Taylor's first paper, presented to the ASME in 1895, criticized both the Towne and Halsey plans and proposed a new alternative.[11] In Taylor's opinion, a weakness

---

8. Ibid., p. 226.

9. Taylor, *Shop Management*, pp. 149–176.

10. E. Brian Peach and Daniel A. Wren, "Pay for Performance from Antiquity to the 1950s," *Journal of Organizational Behavior Management* 12 (1992), 5–26.

11. Frederick W. Taylor, "A Piece-Rate System, Being a Step Toward Partial Solution of the Labor Problem," *Transactions, ASME* 16 (1895), pp. 856–883. This paper is reprinted in Sasaki Tsuneo and

in the Towne and Halsey plans was that they took current worker output as their performance standard. In contrast, Taylor proposed a new three-part plan that extended an earlier piecework system developed by Charles A. Brinley at Midvale Steel: (1) observation and analysis through time study to set output standards and pay rates; (2) a differential piecework system in which a higher rate per piece is paid if work is done in less time than specified and a lower rate is paid if it is done in more time than allowed; and (3) "paying men and not positions."

In Taylor's opinion, profit sharing failed because it discouraged personal ambition by allowing all to share in profits regardless of their contribution and because of the "remoteness of the reward." In recognizing this shortcoming, Taylor showed an appreciation of what is now known as the *principle of temporal contiguity*, that is, the importance of the timing between a stimulus and a response in conditioning behavior, and reflected Taylor's view that sharing profits at the end of a year gave little incentive for improved daily performance.

In his 1895 paper, Taylor had clearly put the onus on management to establish daily output standards rather than following the established practice of allowing workers to determine how jobs should be performed. In commenting on the audience remarks that followed his presentation, Taylor said he was "much surprised and disappointed that elementary rate-fixing has not received more attention during the discussion."[12] In Taylor's view, those present evidently did not realize that proper performance standards had to be determined before establishing a fair piece rate. Under Taylor's plan, a special department analyzed each job and then set a performance standard and pay scale instead of relying on guesswork and tradition.

Taylor's notion of paying men rather than positions was designed to partially address soldiering, but primarily intended to reward the initiative of individual workers. Taylor also understood he was dealing with humans as well as material and machines. He readily acknowledged, "There is another type of scientific investigation . . . which should receive special attention, namely, the accurate study of the motives which influence men."[13]

Taylor's 1895 ASME paper also outlined his view of unions, especially with respect to regulating wages and conditions of employment:

> The [author] is far from taking the view held by many manufacturers that labor unions are an almost unmitigated detriment to those who join them, as well as to employers and the general public. The labor unions . . . have rendered a great service not only to their members,

Daniel A. Wren (editors), *Intellectual Legacy of Management Theory*, ser. 2, pt 1, vol. 2 (London: Pickering and Chatto, 2002), pp. 59–108. See also Charles D. Wrege and Ronald G. Greenwood, *Frederick W. Taylor, the Father of Scientific Management: Myth and Reality* (Homewood, IL: Business One Irwin, 1991), p. 20.

12. Taylor, Piece-Rate System," pp. 903–904.

13. Taylor, *Principles of Scientific Management*, p. 119.

but to the world, in shortening the hours of labor and in modifying the hardships and improving the conditions of wage-workers.... When employers herd their men together in classes, pay all of each class the same wages, and offer them no inducements to work harder or do better than the average, the only remedy for the men lies in combination; and frequently the only possible answer to encroachments on the part of their employers is a strike.... This state of affairs is far from satisfactory and the writer believes the system of regulating wages and conditions of employment of whole classes of men by conference and agreement between the leaders, unions and manufacturers to be vastly inferior... to the plan of stimulating each workman's ambition by paying him according to his individual worth, and without limiting him to the rate of work or pay of the average of his class.[14]

Taylor saw no need for unions under his piece-rate incentive plan. Unions, to foster class solidarity, insisted that their members all be treated the same. For Taylor, this prevented union members from fulfilling their personal ambitions. Rather than being encouraged to better themselves, in Taylor's mind, unions stifled individual initiative.

Taylor's comments on properly setting performance standards, appropriate piece-rate incentives, and relations between labor and management anticipated his belief that the concerns of employee and employer should be based on a "mutuality of interests." Countering the assumption that if workers earned more, they did so at their employer's expense, Taylor advocated a system that would benefit both employer and employee. In doing so, he addressed the contradiction inherent in the "paradox of high wages and low costs," which on the surface appear to be diametrically opposed concepts. Rather than employers' attempting to buy the cheapest labor and paying the lowest wages possible, in the belief that high wage rates were accompanied by high per-unit costs, Taylor showed that high wages could be associated with low costs. Taylor advocated paying first-class workers a high wage, thereby inducing them to produce more under standard, efficient conditions with no greater expenditure of effort. The result would be greater productivity and, hence, lower per unit costs, making higher wages possible. High wages and low costs were possible by using scientific principles to empirically establish the most efficient way to perform each worker's job. Throughout history, it had been taken as self-evident that workers could produce more only by working harder or longer. Taylor showed that the real potential for increased output was not "working harder" but "working smarter." Toward this end, Taylor said the aim of management should be that each workman

1. ... be given as far as possible the highest grade of work for which his ability and physique fit him.

---

14. Taylor, "Piece-Rate System," p. 882; also in Taylor, *Shop Management*, pp. 185–186.

2. ... be called upon to turn out the maximum amount of work which a first-rate man of his class can do and thrive.

3. ... when he works at the best pace of a first-class man, ... be paid from 30 percent to 100 percent according to the nature of the work which he does, beyond the average of his class.[15]

The notion of a "first-class man" indicated that Taylor was aware of the need to match people's abilities to job requirements. In this respect, scientific management anticipated the importance of what is known today as "person–job fit" in employee selection.[16] His use of the term "first-class man," however, caused him much grief, especially when explaining it to others. In testimony before a special committee of the U. S. House of Representative charged with investigating "the Taylor and other systems of shop management," Taylor defined what he meant by a "first-class man" by describing a man who did not meet his definition:

> I believe the only man who does not come under "first-class" as I have defined it, is the man who can work and will not work. I have tried to make it clear that for each type of workman some job can be found at which he is first class, with the exception of those men who are perfectly well able to do the job but won't do it.[17]

Under these terms, non-first-class workers would be those who were physically or mentally unsuited for the work to which they had been assigned (in which case they should be retrained or transferred to another job for which they were suited) or who were unwilling to give their best. In setting pay rates for each job, Taylor wrote that performance standards should be set at the pace a first-class worker "can keep up for a long term of years without injury to his health. It is a pace under which men become happier and thrive."[18] Taylor anticipated what today is considered sound human-resource management; that is, matching workers' abilities to assigned jobs.

It was management's task to identify the work for which employees were best suited, to assist workers in becoming "first-class," and to provide them with an incentive to give their best. Taylor's views on the first-class worker were closely intertwined with his personal philosophy of "the will to get there," the success drive that was the basis of his own life. It was his observation that individuals differ not so much in brains, but in their will to achieve.[19] First-class workers were people with

---

15. Taylor, *Shop Management*, pp. 28–29.

16. Jeffrey R. Edwards, "Person-Job Fit: A Conceptual Integration, Literature Review, and Methodological Critique," *International Review of Industrial and Organizational Psychology* 6 (1991), pp. 283–357.

17. Hearings before Special Committee of the House of Representatives to Investigate the Taylor and Other Systems of Shop Management under Authority of House Resolution 90 (Washington, DC: U.S. Government Printing Office, 1912), p. 1451.

18. Taylor, *Shop Management*, p. 25.

19. Copley, *Taylor*, vol. 1, p. 183.

ambition and who were suited to their work. They were not super humans, as the term later came to connote.

THE TASK-MANAGEMENT SYSTEM

At Midvale, Taylor was laying the foundations of what he preferred to call the "task-management system." An essential ingredient in this system was time study and the development of performance standards; a second ingredient was the selection of workers who could meet those standards when motivated by a differential pay plan. The system, however, was still incomplete. Taylor began to build further. He defined management as "knowing exactly what you want men to do, and then seeing that they do it in the best and cheapest way." Taylor added that no concise definition could fully describe the art of management but that "the relations between employers and men form without question the most important part of this art."[20] He saw unevenness in the quality of management and challenged the assumption that if the right person was hired such considerations would take care of themselves.

Taylor's task-management system depended on careful planning. Each day workers were to be assigned tasks and given detailed written instructions and a time allowance for their completion. Time study was used to determine the amount of time each task required. Methods, tools, and materials were standardized. Following Taylor's differential pay plan, workers who performed assigned tasks in the time allotted received extraordinarily high wages, whereas ordinary wages went to those who did not.

An immediate demand faced by managers under Taylor's system was how best to organize and guide work toward completion. To assist managers, Taylor developed a unique form of supervision called "functional foremanship." Taylor specified the qualities that he felt made up a well-rounded foreman: "brains; education; special or technical knowledge; manual dexterity or strength; tact; energy; grit; honesty; judgment or common sense; and good health."[21]

Taylor thought that it would be almost impossible to find enough managers with all these qualities. By assigning specialists to each component part, Taylor believed the physical and mental demands on individual managers could be reduced.[22] Initially, as a foreman, Taylor employed assistants to prepare instruction cards and perform other associated duties. As his thinking evolved, he gave more

---

20. Taylor, *Shop Management*, p. 21.

21. Ibid., p. 96.

22. Richard Whiting found that Taylor's concept of functional foremen was also used as early as 1884 by John Richards, owner and manager of the San Francisco Tool Company. Richards, apparently also having difficulty in finding well-rounded foremen, created five separate functional areas in the shop with one person in charge of each. Richard J. Whiting, "John Richards—California Pioneer of Management Thought," *California Management Review* 6, no. 2 (Winter 1963), p. 37.

and more responsibility to these assistants by assigning different duties to different assistants. The typical manager of the period was not much of a planner; workplace layout largely dictated how tasks were performed. No one yet had developed task planning to the same degree as Taylor. His new style began with a distinction between the planning of work and its performance, a notable advance for the times.

Taylor advocated the use of "functional foremen," each in charge of a different responsibility (i.e., function). These foremen would operate out of a central "planning department." An "order of work route clerk" determined work flow and the most efficient assignment of workers and machines; an "instruction card clerk" furnished written information on necessary tools and materials, the prevailing piece rate and performance premium, and other operating directions; a "time and cost clerk" maintained time tickets and recorded the costs associated with each work order; and a "shop disciplinarian" kept a record of each worker's "virtues and defects," served as a "peacemaker," and selected and discharged employees as necessary. A "gang boss" was in charge of all work up to the time that it was machined; a "speed boss" took over while work was being machined, determining the tools, the required cutting operations, and appropriate machine speeds; an "inspector" was responsible for output quality; and a "repair boss" was in charge of machinery care and maintenance.

The functional foremanship (Figure 7-1) made specialized skills available relatively quickly rather than require additional time to either recruit or train well-rounded managers. Taylor saw no conflict between his system and the unity-of-command principle, which held that no subordinate should report to more than one superior, thereby eliminating the possibility that a subordinate might receive conflicting orders from different supervisors. To Taylor, *knowledge* must prevail; orders should be issued on the basis of specialized knowledge rather than on the basis of title or position. Hence, there was no conflict, because each worker had only one boss on any one aspect of a task. Emphasizing his general objectives of harmony and mutuality of interests among workers and managers, Taylor believed that a spirit of cooperation would further prevent conflicts under functional foremanship.

Taylor had little difficulty in selling functional foremanship to the Midvale workers; their immediate supervisors, however, resisted because it restricted the range of their authority and activities.[23] Taylor did not specify that a separate foreman had to be in charge of each planning department function; in smaller units, one person might fill multiple roles. Taylor's purpose was to focus specialized management knowledge on the work at hand. As functional foremanship has evolved to the present, specialized knowledge is exercised through *functional authority* over a task, not over individual workers, and without circumventing their supervisor. Taylor's functional foremanship never became widespread in practice. Its lack of widespread adoption was not a result of worker confusion or a violation of unity of

---

23. Copley, *Taylor*, vol. 1, p. 292.

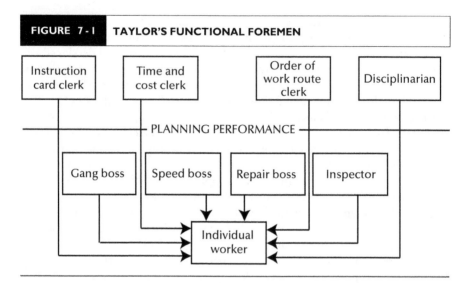

| FIGURE 7-1 | **TAYLOR'S FUNCTIONAL FOREMEN** |

Adapted from Frank B. and Lillian M. Gilbreth, *Applied Motion Study*, New York: Sturgis & Walton Co., 1917.

command, but rather the recognition that it failed to develop managers capable of performing their jobs without being overly dependent on staff specialists.

The value of specialists would be recognized, but primarily in assisting general managers juggle the many demands of a large organization. This would especially be the case when it came to dealing with either particular areas of expertise (such as legal matters) or significant exceptions from planned performance. In this way, those activities requiring specialized knowledge or immediate attention (the "exceptions") could be promptly and knowledgeably addressed. The "exception principle" was one of Taylor's more important contributions:

> Under it the manager should receive only condensed, summarized, and *invariably* comparative reports, covering . . . all of the exceptions to past averages or to the standards . . . both the especially good and especially bad exceptions . . . leaving him free to consider broader lines of policy and to study the character and fitness of the important men under him.[24]

For Taylor, all authority was to be based on knowledge, not position, and the exception principle improved efficiency by allowing managers time to attend to their most pressing and important concerns.

---

24. Taylor, *Shop Management*, p. 126.

TAYLOR: THE MANAGER AND THE CONSULTANT

Taylor's years at Midvale Steel had been full: increasing responsibilities and numerous promotions; teaming with his brother-in-law, Clarence M. Clark, to win the first U.S. Lawn Tennis Association's amateur double lawn tennis championship in 1881; a mechanical engineering degree from Stevens Institute in 1883; marriage to Louise M. Spooner in 1884; experiments on cutting metals and machine belting; and developing the essentials of his task-management system all made for a busy twelve years. In 1890, he left Midvale to become general manager of the Manufacturing Investment Company (MIC), a converter of wood products into paper fiber. His experiences at MIC were not wholly rewarding. Taylor felt that the company's operational difficulties were due to a new papermaking process it had installed, whereas its owners believed that Taylor lacked the broad executive experience necessary to bring the process online. In 1893, Taylor resigned from MIC, expressing a contempt for financiers who were interested only in "making money quickly" and had "absolutely no pride of manufacture."[25] Taylor's experience at MIC would not be his last encounter with owners who, in Taylor's opinion, were resistant to change and the improvements engineers could provide.

Although Taylor developed contempt for financiers, he did realize his shortcomings in accounting. At MIC, R. D. Hayes, a former railroad manager, revamped the bookkeeping system and hired William D. Basley, an experienced railroad accountant, to operate the system. Basley had worked for the Newark and Hudson Railroad, which was controlled by the Erie Railroad, where Daniel McCallum had developed accounting and reporting systems in the 1850s.[26] Taylor was impressed by Hayes's and Basley's methods, which would later form the basis of his own bookkeeping system, so the years at MIC had not been a total loss. With his newly acquired knowledge of accounting and his engineering background, Taylor decided to become a consulting engineer for management.

One of Taylor's clients was the Steel Motor Works (Johnstown, Pennsylvania). Asked to increase the company's efficiency, in 1896, Taylor developed a system of cost accounts for purchasing materials, as well as tracking and issuing inventory. Taylor also devised a routing chart showing how all the parts comprising the company's principal product, an electrical car motor, were assembled.[27] While at Steel Motor Works, Taylor worked closely with Tom L. Johnson, the company's founder; A. J. Moxham, who later became an executive with the Du Pont Company;

---

25. Taylor, quoted in Nelson, *Taylor*, p. 53.

26. Charles D. Wrege, "Nineteenth Century Origins of 'Bookkeeping under the Taylor System,'" in Kae H. Chung, ed., *Proceedings of the Annual Meeting of the Academy of Management* (1983), pp. 106–110; see also Nelson, *Taylor*, pp. 54–55.

27. Michael Massouh, "Technological and Managerial Innovation: The Johnson Company, 1883–1889," *Business History Review* 50, no. 1 (Spring 1976), pp. 66–67.

and Coleman du Pont. Moxham later adopted Taylor's cost-accounting system at the Du Pont Powder Company, then under the direction of Pierre du Pont.[28]

Another of Taylor's clients was Simonds Rolling Machine Company (Fitchburg, Massachusetts), where (in 1897) he conducted experiments in the manufacture of bicycle ball bearings. In the final stage of the manufacturing process 120 women inspected the ball bearings for flaws. Over a period of time, Taylor gradually shortened the work day from ten and a half hours to eight and a half hours a day, introduced morning and afternoon rest periods, identified the best inspectors, and put the women on a piecework pay schedule. The interaction of these changes was complex, and it would be difficult to fix causes and results. The outcome, however, was that thirty-five women were able to do the work of 120, as output increased from five million to seventeen million bearings per month, accuracy improved by two-thirds, wages were averaging 80 to 100 percent higher, and "each girl was made to feel that she was the object of especial care and interest on the part of management."[29] While at Simonds, Taylor also introduced the Hayes and Basley accounting system to set up expense classifications, distribute overhead expenses, and improve materials handling and control.

Taylor's most challenging and controversial consulting assignment was for the Bethlehem Iron Company (South Bethlehem, Pennsylvania). Taylor came to Bethlehem (later Bethlehem Steel Company) in 1898, at the request of the company's largest stockholder, Joseph Wharton. The founder of America's first school of business at the University of Pennsylvania, Wharton sought Taylor's assistance in decreasing operating costs and improving Bethlehem's overall efficiency. At that time, Bethlehem's management was under federal investigation for overcharging and price colluding on defense contracts. From his initial hiring, the company's top managers resented Taylor's assertiveness. Taylor felt that many of the top managers were unqualified, having gained their position due to family connections rather than their ability. After much opposition, Taylor was finally able to convince Bethlehem's owners to reorganize the company, but as a result further alienated the company's top managers. These managers, in turn, sought every opportunity to subvert Taylor's efforts.

Taylor established a central planning department, organized a tool crib and storeroom, and implemented the cost-accounting system he had developed for Steel Motor Works. To assist in his work, Taylor brought in Sanford Thompson, who had probably conducted more time studies than Taylor ever dreamed of doing; Henry Gantt, who had worked with Taylor at Midvale; Carl Barth, a mathematics whiz; Dwight Merrick, who became a leading authority on time study; James Gillespie,

---

28. H. Thomas Johnson, "Management Accounting in an Early Integrated Industrial: E. I. Du Pont de Nemours Powder Company, 1903–1912," *Business History Review* 49, no. 2 (Summer 1975), p. 194.

29. Taylor, *Principles of Scientific Management*, pp. 95–96. Nyland used Taylor's work at Simonds to illustrate the contribution of Taylor to reducing hours of work in industry. See Chris Nyland, "Taylorism and Hours of Work," *Journal of Management History* 1, no. 2 (1995), pp. 8–25.

who had been involved with time studies at Simonds; and Maunsell White, who had earlier helped Taylor with a series of metal-cutting experiments.

In 1899, the price of pig-iron rose sharply, and Bethlehem promptly sold 10,000 tons from its inventory. Shipping the iron by rail required that it be manually loaded onto gondola cars. The iron had been cast as ninety-two pound ingots or "pigs." At the time, Taylor and Thompson were preparing a handbook on the elements of work. The required loading provided an opportunity for them to gather information for the handbook on the time required to perform this type of work. Taylor assigned James Gillespie and Hartley C. Wolle the task of conducting a study to collect the desired information. The workers who loaded the pig-iron were known as "pig-iron handlers." They were paid a fixed "piece rate" for each ton loaded. Gillespie and Wolle selected ten of the "very best men" and ordered them to work at "maximum speed." During the first 10-hour day, the workers loaded seventy-five long tons each, filling one railway car. Because the tons loaded per day had previously averaged about twelve and a half tons per worker, the pig-iron handlers were exhausted. Based on these figures, Gillespie and Wolle, factoring in time for unavoidable delays and rest, set a new output standard at forty-five long tons (2,240 pounds = a long ton) per worker per day. Taylor then set the piece rate at $.0375 per ton, which meant that the first-class worker who met the new forty-five standard would earn $1.85 per day. Because the average flat day rate for a common laborer at Bethlehem was $1.15 per 10-hour day, the new piece rate represented a more than 60 percent increase in pay.

Taylor used the pig-iron-handling story in his writings after 1899 and in his later talks to those who gathered at his home, Boxly, in Chestnut Hill (Pennsylvania), to illustrate the savings that could come from carefully examining even menial jobs. On June 4, 1907, a stenographer was hired to record Taylor's "Boxly" talk. A relatively standardized presentation, Taylor described how he selected one of the pig-handlers, a "Pennsylvania Dutchman" by the name of "Schmidt," for the Gillespie and Wolle study.[30] Schmidt, whose real name was Henry Noll (Knolle), became the focal point of Taylor's comments on how to secure higher performance by using piece-rate incentives. Noll was then 27 years old, 5 feet 7 inches tall, and weighed 135 pounds. He was singled out because he had been observed trotting "back home for a mile or so after his work in the evening, about as fresh as he was when he came trotting down to work in the morning."[31] Noll was also building a home for himself at the time and was known as someone who placed "very high value on a dollar."

---

30. Charles D. Wrege, "F. W. Taylor's Lecture on Management, 4 June 1907, an Introduction," *Journal of Management History* 1 (1995), pp. 4–7; the stenographer's transcript follows on pp. 8–32.

31. Taylor, *Principles of Scientific Management*, pp. 43–44. Also see James Gillespie and H. C. Wolle, "Report on the Establishment of Piecework in Connection with the Loading of Pig Iron, at the Works of the Bethlehem Iron Co., South Bethlehem, PA," June 17, 1899, Taylor Collection, Stevens Institute of Technology, Hoboken, NJ, Files 32A and 32J. We are indebted to Jill Hough for a copy of this report.

Although the story of Schmidt has entered the management literature as an example of Taylor's scientific study of work, its veracity has been challenged. Wrege and Perroni have examined various versions of the story as told by Taylor, as well as a report prepared by Gillespie and Wolle, and noted numerous discrepancies. Among these discrepancies were the reasons for Bethlehem selling pig-iron from its inventory, the amount to be loaded, the method of loading, the number of pig-iron handlers, and so on. Wrege and Perroni reached the conclusion that the Schmidt story was, to borrow their phrase, a "pig-tale," an embellishment by Taylor of the truth.[32]

Working from a film that portrays Frank Gilbreth studying pig-iron handling, Hough and White, however, have concluded that Taylor's figures were basically accurate. They maintained that the story of Schmidt was more important as an "object lesson" for Taylor's audiences:

> The story was not intended as a precise, scientific account of the pig-iron loading experiments. Rather, Taylor used the tale in an effort to persuade listeners that systematic management could be applied to even the most basic work processes and still yield substantial improvement.[33]

Support for the position that the pig-tale story was an object lesson comes from an unpublished address Taylor delivered in 1915 to the Cleveland Advertising Club. In the address, Taylor refers to what became known as the "four principles of scientific management." These principles will be discussed shortly. Once again, a stenographer recorded Taylor's words:

> Most people think scientific management is chiefly handling pig-iron. I do not know why (laughter). I do not know how they have gotten that impression, but a large part of the community has that impression. The reason I chose pig-iron for the first illustration is that, if you can prove to any one that the strength, the effort of these four principles

---

32. Originally, Wrege and Perroni stated that Taylor had embellished the pig-iron report. See Charles D. Wrege and Amadeo G. Perroni, "Taylor's Pig-Tale: A Historical Analysis of Frederick W. Taylor's Pig-Iron Experiment," *Academy of Management Journal* 17 (March 1974), pp. 6–26. Later, Wrege and Greenwood, in *Taylor*, p. 102, wrote that the "pig-tale" was "prepared by Taylor's assistant, Morris L. Cooke." The mystery remains: the penmanship was Cooke's, but were the words Cooke's or Taylor's?

33. Jill Hough and Margaret A. White, "Using Stories to Create Change: The Object Lesson of Frederick Taylor's 'pig-tale,'" *Journal of Management* 27 (2001), pp. 585–601. In *The Quest of the Best Way: Original Films of Frank B. Gilbreth* (Harry W. Bass Business History Collection, University of Oklahoma), one of the narrators (James S. Perkins) states, "Gilbreth agreed with Taylor's findings" with respect to the pig-iron study. Gilbreth's replication, however, raises numerous questions about how closely it paralleled the Gillespie and Wolle study. Hough and White's conclusions have been vigorously challenged in Charles D. Wrege and Regina Greenwood, "Frederick W. Taylor's Pig Iron Loading Observations" at Bethlehem, March 10, 1899–May 31, 1899: The Real Story," *Canal History and Technology Proceedings* 17 (1998), pp. 159–201.

when applied to such rudimentary work as that, the presumption is that it can be applied to something better. The only way to prove it is to start at the bottom and show these four principles all along the line.[34]

Taylor's intent was to illustrate, but he was inconsistent in retelling the Schmidt story and omitted facts that more fully convey what actually occurred as reported by Gillespie and Wolle. For the record, there were three "first-class" workers, not one. Noll was joined in this elite group by Joseph Auer and Simon Conrad. At times, Conrad loaded more tons than Noll: on June 1, 1899, 70.7 tons for Conrad, 48 tons for Noll; on June 2, 1899, 55.7 tons for Conrad, 68.3 for Noll; and on June 3, 1899, 70.9 tons for Conrad, 39.7 for Noll, and 30.1 tons for Auer. The story of Schmidt, as told and retold by Taylor, oversimplified what actually occurred at Bethlehem, but made the power of Taylor's methods more memorable to the audiences gathered at Boxly to learn more about his revolutionary work.

Further, for those who may think that the pig-iron handlers were exploited, working day in and day out to achieve the incentive rate, the fact is that they never worked more than three days without going back to a flat day rate. Moreover, it should be noted that $1.69 in 1899 is equivalent to $43.58 in "purchasing power" in 2007 dollars. For the time span of the pig-iron study, March 10 to May 31, 1899, Noll and Conrad worked a total of thirty-six days on incentive and forty-one on a flat day rate, thus, less than one-half of their work time was on the incentive rate. Further, for all 75 of Bethlehem's pig-iron handlers, Wrege and Hodgetts have concluded that only 27 percent of their work time was on a piece-rate schedule.[35]

Although Taylor referred frequently to the pig-iron loading observations at Bethlehem as a success, they were actually less then ideal. Gillespie and Wolle arbitrarily set a 40 percent time allowance for rests and delays; Taylor likewise did so for the per ton piece rate; and Noll and the other pig-iron handlers studied were not scientifically selected. Even so, the results were impressive: yard labor costs fell from $.072 per ton under day-work wages to $.033 per ton under a piecework schedule; and the pig-iron handlers averaged a 60 percent increase in wages.

Taylor's implementation of the cost-accounting system he had developed for Steel Motor Works earned him further animosity among Bethlehem's top managers. Taylor referred to the system as "in general the modern railroad system of accounting adapted and modified to suit the manufacturing business."[36] This was the Hayes-Basley accounting system that Taylor had learned at MIC and adapted

34. Frederick W. Taylor, "The Principles of Scientific Management," address before the Cleveland Advertising Club, 3 March 1915. Manuscript from the Taylor Collection, Stevens Institute of Technology, reprinted in Sasaki Tsuneo and Daniel A. Wren, *Intellectual Legacy of Management Theory*, ser. 2, pt. 2, vol. 2 (London; Pickering and Chatto, 2002), pp. 387–441.

35. Charles D. Wrege and Richard M. Hodgetts, "Frederick W. Taylor's 1899 Pig Iron Observations: Examining Fact, Fiction and Lessons for the New Millennium," *Academy of Management Journal* 43 (2000), p. 1287.

36. Copley, *Taylor*, vol. 1, p. 364.

and applied in various companies. Taylor's system of accounts called for a rigorous classification of costs, and the required reporting procedures clearly reflected his exception principle. Taylor abhorred the futility of postmortem accounting that provided annual, semiannual, or monthly reports that were received too late for managerial action. At Bethlehem, he moved the cost-accounting function to the newly established planning department and, thereby, generated cost figures coincident with daily operations reports. Costs then became an integral part of daily planning and control, not a subject for analysis long after they had been incurred. The system was effective, in fact, so much so that Bethlehem's top managers tried to check its implementation. Apparently they did not care for an accurate and timely appraisal of their performance. Taylor eventually lost in his struggle to introduce improved managerial methods at Bethlehem and his consulting contract was terminated in 1901.

TAYLOR:
THE PERIPATETIC PHILOSOPHER

Frederick and Louise Taylor were unable to have children of their own. In 1901, seventeen years after their marriage, and when Fred was forty-five years old, a tragedy left four children of the Aiken family without parents. The Aikens were relatives of Mrs. Taylor's, and she and Fred adopted three of the children: Kempton, Robert, and Elizabeth. A fourth child, Conrad, was older and did not join the Taylor family—he later became a Pulitzer Prize–winning poet and a literary critic.[37] The Taylors and their new family moved from South Bethlehem to Germantown (Pennsylvania), while they awaited the construction of Boxly, where another stage in Taylor's career would begin.

At Midvale and Bethlehem, Taylor demonstrated his talents as an inventor and mechanical engineer. He developed and patented a steel hammer (for forging steel plates), numerous machine tools such as grinders and boring and turning mills (lathes), and, with Maunsel White, a process for cutting metal with high speed, "self-hardening" steel-cutting tools. The Taylor-White process was patented in 1900, and Taylor's share of the royalties amounted to some $50,000 before the patent was nullified in 1909.[38]

37. John A. Bromer, J. Myron Johnson, and Richard P. Widdicombe, "A Conversation with Robert P. A. Taylor" (October 14 and 15, 1976), Ch. 2, pp. 1–3, Taylor Collection. *Business Week* (May 15, 1995, p. 34) reported that Frederick W. Taylor was "micromanaging from the grave" with a gift of $10 million to the Stevens Institute of Technology. Rather than coming from Taylor, the gift came from his son, Robert P. A. Taylor, and was given in the name of his father.

38. Thomas J. Misa, *A Nation of Steel* (Baltimore: Johns Hopkins University Press, 1995), pp. 197–198, 204–205. For White's typically unsung contribution to the Taylor-White process, see Christopher P. Neck and Arthur G. Bedeian, "Frederick W. Taylor, J. Maunsell White III, and the Matthew Effect: The Rest of the Story," *Journal of Management History* 2 (1996), pp. 20–25. Also see Charles D. Wrege, Ronald

As Taylor's notoriety spread, he gained disciples, and his task-management system was installed at other companies. These included James Mapes Dodge at the Link-Belt Engineering Company and Wilfred Lewis at the Tabor Manufacturing Company, a manufacturer of molding machines. In his spare time, Taylor landscaped and renovated Boxly; developed new mixtures for soils to improve golf greens, was one of the first to develop turf to be specifically used in constructing putting greens, and designed golf clubs. He received a patent for a putter with a Y shaft, experimented with lengths and thicknesses of golf-club shafts, and spent a great deal of time on the links, or more euphemistically, in experimentation. He had taken up golf at the age of forty (in 1896), and his skills developed rapidly; he played to an eight handicap and won the men's championship at the Philadelphia Country Club in 1902, 1903, and 1905.[39]

In 1906, Taylor was elected president of the American Society of Mechanical Engineers. His fame was growing, and those who were to spread Taylor's message were growing in numbers. Henri Le Chatelier, Horace King Hathaway, Morris L. Cooke, Sanford E. Thompson, Frank B. Gilbreth, and others were joining the earlier apostles, Gantt and Barth.

Asked to teach a course at Harvard University at what was to become the Graduate School of Business Administration, Taylor refused, saying that his task-management system could be learned only in practice. Professor Edwin Gay, soon to be dean of the school, told Taylor that the course on scientific management would be taught with or without him, period. Taylor succumbed, although he was never entirely happy about teaching his system in a classroom. Taylor was not against business education, but felt that experience was the only way to learn his methods. Taylor's Harvard lectures began in 1909 and were given each winter through 1914.[40] For all his lectures, Taylor never accepted a penny of reimbursement, not even for traveling expenses. Likewise, he refused payment for the years of consulting at the Brooklyn Navy Yard and the U.S. Army Ordnance Department.

———

G. Greenwood, and Ti Hsu, "Frederick W. Taylor's Early Work at Bethlehem Steel Company: First Phase; 1898–1899—Some Insights," *Canal History and Technology Proceedings*, 12 (1993), pp. 102–138; *idem*, "Frederick W. Taylor's Work at Bethlehem Steel, Phase II, The Discovery of High-Speed Tool Steel, 1898, Was It An Accident?" *Canal History and Technology Proceedings*, 13 (1994), pp. 115–161; *idem*, "Frederick W. Taylor's at Bethlehem Steel, Phase III: Sale of the 'Taylor-White' Patent and the Initiation of the High Speed Steel Patent Suit: 1902–1905," *Canal History and Technology Proceedings*, 14 (1995), pp. 105–127; *idem*, "Frederick W. Taylor at Bethlehem Steel Company, Phase IV: The High-Speed Steel Patent Suit, 1906–1908," *Canal History and Technology Proceedings*, 15 (1993), pp. 125–164.

39. Shannon G. Taylor and Arthur G. Bedeian, "From Boardroom to Bunker: How Fred Taylor Changed the Game of Golf Forever," *Management & Organizational History*, 2 (2007), pp. 195–218.

40. Frederick W. Taylor, "An Outline of the Organization of a Manufacturing Establishment under Modern Scientific or Task Management," one of Taylor's lectures at Harvard. The typescript from the Taylor Collection is reprinted in Sasaki and Wren, *Intellectual Legacy of Management Theory*, ser. 2, pt. 2, vol. 2, pp. 259–303.

THE EASTERN RATE CASE

Taylor also found his task-management system getting some extraordinary free publicity. The Boston lawyer Louis D. Brandeis, later Associate U. S. Supreme Court Justice, was becoming known in the early twentieth century as the people's lawyer.[41] In 1910, when a group of railways operating north of the Ohio and Potomac rivers and east of the Mississippi (known collectively as the Eastern railroads) asked the Interstate Commerce Commission for a hike in freight rates, Brandeis took up the cause of the shippers (banded together as the Commercial Organizations of the Atlantic Seaboard) who would be affected by the proposed increase. In doing so, he brought about an unusual series of hearings that thrust Taylor's task-management system into the public eye. At a loss for what to call the Taylor system, Brandeis, Gilbreth, Gantt, and several other engineers met in the Great Northern Hotel in New York City to discuss the matter.[42] Brandeis noted that Taylor frequently used the word "scientific" in his work, and all agreed to the use of the term "scientific management" to designate the emerging efficiency movement. Brandeis's argument before the Interstate Commerce Commission was based on the inefficiency of railroad management, and he contended that no rate increase would be necessary if the railroads applied scientific management. To prove his case, a parade of witnesses testified about the efficiencies to be gained; James M. Dodge, H. K. Hathaway, Henry R. Towne, and Harrington Emerson were some of the proponents of adopting more efficient management methods based on Taylor's work.

Hathaway testified about how scientific management had increased workers' wages at the Tabor Manufacturing Company; Dodge gave evidence of progress at the Link-Belt Company; and Gilbreth said that scientific management could be used in a union shop. It was Emerson's testimony, however, that sensationalized the hearings. Emerson had developed "standard unit costs" for the Atchison, Topeka & Santa Fe Railroad; comparing the costs of other railroads with these standards, he estimated that by adopting Taylor's methods the railroads could annually eliminate $240 million in labor costs and cut $60 million in materials and maintenance expenses.[43] His calculations were complex, overlooked differences among various railroads, never examined the question of whether Taylor's methods could be applied to the transportation industry, and may have been presented for effect. Regardless of

---

41. Oscar Kraines, "Brandeis and Scientific Management," *Publication of the American Jewish Historical Society*, 1951, 41(1), pp. 41–60.

42. Horace B. Drury, *Scientific Management: A History and Criticism* (New York: Columbia University Press, 1922), p. 38; Henry Van Riper Scheel, "Some Recollections of Henry Laurence Gantt," *Journal of Industrial Engineering* 12 (May–June, 1961), p. 221.

43. *Evidence Taken by the Interstate Commerce Commission in the Matter of Proposal Advances in Freight Rates by Carriers*, Senate Document 725, 61st Cong., 3rd sess. (Washington, DC: U.S. Government Printing Office, 1911), pp. 3540–3551 and 3563–3564.

these potential limitations, Emerson's testimony stunned the popular press and was reported in the next morning's papers. When Taylor was asked about Emerson's $300 million annual savings, he replied:

> I believe we can save a million dollars a day, just as he said we can, but the reports of these hearings in Washington were not quite fair enough to say that it can't be done all at once. It would take four or five years.[44]

Taylor accepted the Brandeis-coined phrase "scientific management," but with reluctance, however, fearing that it sounded too academic. The phrase caught on with the press, however, and Taylor gained a place in the public spotlight. The hearings, with the decision going against the railroads, concluded that it was too early to judge the merits of scientific management. Nevertheless, the resulting widespread publicity popularized Taylor's ideas, with both desirable and undesirable consequences. Within twenty-four hours, scientific management, previously an obscure technology developed by a relatively unknown engineer, became international news. Although Taylor had not testified, most of Brandeis's witnesses acknowledged him as their teacher. Taylor became a national hero overnight. Newspaper and magazines published dozens of articles about his work. This publicity and the publication of Taylor's book, *The Principles of Scientific Management,* in 1911, gave a new impetus to the campaign for efficiency. Within two years of publication, Taylor's book was translated into French, German, Dutch, Swedish, Russian, Italian, Spanish, and Japanese. Conferences were held and societies formed to study Taylor's work.

On the other hand, collective-bargaining labor unions, especially the machinists union and various railway brotherhoods, opposed all aspects of Taylor's methods, especially time study. Labor leaders characterized Taylor's piece-rate pay plan as a return to "sweat shop" exploitation. Because Taylor's more efficient methods often led to layoffs of unnecessary workers, labor feared that adaption of his methods would lead to loss of jobs. Organized labor had struggled long and hard to achieve status, and it instinctively assumed that anything new originating in management was for ownership's advantage and labor's disadvantage. Because Taylor firmly believed that his methods were objective, or scientific, he never fully comprehended organized labor's hostility. He tried to counter labor's opposition by stating his support of unions and pointed out that efficient methods such as those he proposed had historically increased employment, not reduced it. Nevertheless, for a company to introduce scientific management was to invite labor trouble.

---

44. Frederick W. Taylor, "The Conservation of Human Effort," address to the Philadelphia Club, January 14, 1911. Taylor Collection. Reprinted in Sasaki and Wren, ser. 2, pt. 2, vol. 2, pp. 256–257.

WATERTOWN AND THE CONGRESSIONAL INVESTIGATION

The 1910 Interstate Commerce Commission railroad rate-increase hearings brought publicity, but as suggested, there were also unanticipated repercussions. At the time, Taylor was introducing his methods at the Brooklyn Navy Yard and the U.S. Army Ordnance Department. Despite repeated attempts, his efforts at the Navy Yard were largely unsuccessful, as his methods were rejected by the naval bureaucracy.[45] In contrast, General William Crozier, head of the Ordnance Department, had read Taylor's work and saw its applicability to army arsenals. Crozier selected the army's arsenals at Watertown, Massachusetts, and Rock Island, Illinois, as sites to test Taylor's methods. At Rock Island, a representative of the International Association of Machinists (IAM) railed against time studies, saying it reduced workers to virtual slavery and low wages. The IAM opposed Taylor's methods in both governmental and nongovernmental applications.

Taylor advised Crozier to install scientific management at Watertown despite the resistance at Rock Island, but cautioned him to do so carefully, step-by-step, including first sounding out worker sentiments in each department. Carl G. Barth attempted to follow Taylor's advice, but trouble started when Dwight V. Merrick, who was assisting Barth, began to use a stopwatch to time the procedures used by the arsenal's molders. One of the molders refused to allow Merrick to time his work, citing "the organization" (the union) as the reason for his refusal. Lt. Colonel Charles B. Wheeler, the arsenal's commanding officer, explained to the worker why the stopwatch timing was necessary. The worker again refused and was discharged for "refusal to obey orders."[46] In sympathy, the arsenal's other molders likewise refused. In August 1911, the first strike under Taylor's task-management system occurred at the Watertown Arsenal. Taylor attributed the whole problem to a mistake in tactics: the sentiments of the molders had not been examined nor had they been briefed on the purposes of the time study. Taylor did not fault the union, but blamed a premature attempt to time various jobs without following his recommended technique of consulting the workers first. Moreover, as was Taylor's practice before conducting any time studies, the arsenal had not yet been reorganized following his methods. The strike lasted one week before the workers returned and offered no further resistance.

After the strike, however, union leaders petitioned Congress to investigate the arsenal workers' complaints of unsatisfactory working conditions and humiliating

---

45. Peter B. Petersen, "Fighting for a Better Navy: An Attempt at Scientific Management (1905–1912)," *Journal of Management* 16 (March 1990), pp. 151–166.

46. Copley, *Taylor*, vol. 2, p. 344.

treatment.[47] As a consequence, the House of Representatives appointed a special committee to investigate what it called "the Taylor system." The committee consisted of William B. Wilson, a former official of the United Mine Workers, then chair of the House Labor Committee and later Secretary of Labor under President Woodrow Wilson; William C. Redfield, a manufacturer who later became Secretary of Commerce under Wilson; and John Q. Tilson, the only Republican member, as an umpire.

The hearings began in October 1911 and ended in February 1912. Taylor spent twelve hours scattered over four days testifying. As Copley stated, "terrorism was in the air," as the unions set out to harass Taylor. The hearing transcripts illustrate the hostility and sharpness in both questions and answers. For example, following a series of questions and discussion about the effect of scientific management on worker displacement, the following clash erupted over Taylor's definition of a "first-class man."

> The Chairman [Mr. Wilson]. Is it not true that a man who is not a good workman and who may not be responsible for the fact that he is not a good workman has to live as well as the man who is a good workman?

> Mr. Taylor. Not as well as the other workman; otherwise, that would imply that all those in the world were entitled to live equally well whether they worked or whether they were idle, and that certainly is not the case. Not as well.

> The Chairman. Under scientific management, then, you propose that because a man is not in the first class as a workman that there is no place in the world for him—if he is not in the first class in some particular line that this must be destroyed and removed?

> Mr. Taylor. Mr. Chairman, would it not be well for me to describe what I mean by a "first-class" workman. I have written a good deal about "first-class" workmen in my books, and I find there is quite a general misapprehension as to the use of that term "first-class."

> The Chairman. Before you come to a definition of what you consider a "first-class" workman I would like to have your concept of how you are going to take care, under your scientific management, of a man who is not a "first-class" workman in some particular line?

---

47. Hugh G. J. Aitken, *Scientific Management in Action: Taylorism at Watertown Arsenal, 1908–15* (Princeton, NJ: Princeton University Press, 1985).

Mr. Taylor. I cannot answer that question until I define what I mean by "first-class." You and I may have a totally different idea as to the meaning of these words, and therefore I suggest that you allow me to state what I mean.

The Chairman. The very fact that you specify "first-class" would indicate that in your mind you would have some other class than "first-class."

Mr. Taylor. If you will allow me to define it I think I can make it clear.

The Chairman. You said a "first-class" workman can be taken care of under normal conditions. That is what you have already said. Now, the other class that is in your mind, other than "first-class," how does your system propose to take care of them?

Mr. Taylor. Mr. Chairman, I cannot answer that question. I cannot answer any question relating to "first-class" workmen until you know my definition of that term, because I have used these words technically throughout my paper, and I am not willing to answer a question you put about "first-class" workmen with the assumption that my answer applies to all I have said in my book.

The Chairman. You yourself injected the term "first-class" by saying that you did not know of a condition in normal times when a "first-class" workman could not find employment.

Mr. Taylor. I do not think I used that term "first-class."

Mr. Redfield. Mr. Chairman, the witness has now four times, I think, said that until he is allowed to define what he means by "first-class" no answer can be given, because he means one thing by the words "first-class" and he thinks that you mean another thing.

The Chairman. My question has nothing whatever to do with the definition of the words "first-class." It has to do with the other class than "first-class" not with "first-class." A definition of "first-class" will in no manner contribute to a proper reply to my question, because I am not asking about "first-class," but the other than "first-class" workmen.

Mr. Taylor. I cannot describe the others until I have described what I mean by "first-class."

Mr. Redfield. As I was saying when I was interrupted, the witness had stated that he cannot answer the question for the reason that the language that the chairman uses, namely, the words "first-class" do not mean the same thing in the Chairman's mind that they mean in the witness's mind, and he asks the privilege of defining what they do mean, so that the language shall be mutually intelligible. Now, it seems to me, and I think it is good law and entirely proper, that the witness ought to be permitted to define his meaning and then if, after his definition is made, there is any misunderstanding, we can proceed.[48]

Then the chair, Redfield, and Tilson engaged in a spirited discussion of whether or not Taylor should be allowed to define his terms; Redfield and Tilson prevailed, and Taylor proceeded to explain his use of the term "first-class" and concluded:

> . . . among every class of workmen we have some balky workmen—I do not mean men who are unable to work, but men who, physically well able to work, are simply lazy, and who through no amount of teaching and instructing and through no amount of kindly treatment, can be brought into the "first-class." That is the man whom I call "second-class." They have the physical possibility of being "first-class," but they obstinately refuse to do so.
>
> Now, Mr. Chairman, I am ready to answer your question, having clearly in mind that I have these two types of "second-class" men in view; the one which is physically able to do the work, but who refused to do it—and the other who is not physically or mentally fitted to do that particular job. These are the two types of "second-class" men.
>
> The Chairman. Then, how does scientific management propose to take care of men who are not "first-class" men in any particular line of work?
>
> Mr. Taylor. I give it up.
>
> The Chairman. Scientific management has no place for such men?
>
> Mr. Taylor. Scientific management has no use for a bird that can sing and won't sing.
>
> The Chairman. I am not speaking about birds at all.
>
> Mr. Taylor. No man who can work and won't work has any place under scientific management.
>
> The Chairman. It is not a question of a man "who can work and won't work"; it is a question of a man who is not a "first-class" man in any one particular line, according to your own definition.

---

48. *Hearings to Investigate the Taylor System*, pp. 1452–1453.

> Mr. Taylor. I do not know of any such line of work. For each man some line [of work] can be found in which he is first-class.[49]

In another instance, Taylor was being questioned by John R. O'Leary (third vice-president of the International Molder's Unions of North America) on fines that had been levied on workers at Midvale Steel:

> Mr. O'Leary. Did I understand you to say that you had the permission and cooperation of the men in putting in that system?
>
> Mr. Taylor. Yes . . . they ran it, invested the funds, took care of the sick; they furnished the doctor and nurse. . . .
>
> Mr. O'Leary. What did they charge the men who were injured, for the Doctor?
>
> Mr. Taylor. Not a cent. The services were all free.
>
> Mr. O'Leary. Are you aware that there have been many suits instituted against the Midvale Steel Co. to recover those fines, and that they were recovered?
>
> Mr. Taylor. No; I am not aware of it.
>
> Mr. O'Leary. Are you aware that men are fined a dollar for going to the urinal?
>
> Mr. Taylor. I have not the slightest idea that is true. Who ever said that told an untruth. Nothing of that kind was done while I was there.[50]

No support for O'Leary's charges ever appeared in any other testimony. As Ida M. Tarbell, one of the leading "muckrakers" of her day, declared:

> One of the most sportsmanlike exhibits the country ever saw was Mr. Taylor's willingness to subject himself to the heckling and the badgering of labour leaders, congressmen, and investigators of all degrees of misunderstanding, suspicion and ill will. To a man of his temperament and highly trained intellect, who had given a quarter of a century of the hardest kind of toil to develop useful truths, the kind of questioning to which he was sometimes subjected must have been maddening.[51]

---

49. Ibid., pp. 1455–1456.

50. Ibid., pp. 745–746.

51. Ida M. Tarbell, *New Ideals in Business: An Account of Their Practice and Their Effects Upon Men and Profits.* (New York: Macmillan, 1916), p. 315.

Coming from Tarbell, this was quite a compliment. Baited, insulted, and made to appear a beast, Taylor staggered from the stand at the close of his testimony. Taylor's pride was sorely wounded, his lifework reviled before a congressional committee. At one point, it appeared as if blows would be struck between Taylor and his labor-leader opponents. The ensuing exchange was so heated that it was struck from the record.[52] There was no victory for anyone in the committee's final report. Phrased in good political double-talk, the report said that it was too early "to determine with accuracy their [Taylor's and other scientific management systems'] effect on the health and pay of employees and their effect on wages and labor cost."[53] The committee found no evidence to support abuses of workers or any need for remedial legislation. It did refer to possible abuses, perhaps as a bone for opponents, but presented no evidence that they had occurred.

Despite recommending that no legislation was needed, the congressional representatives from the Watertown and Rock Island districts succeeded in passing a House resolution to prevent the use of time-measuring devices and incentive payments in any military agency of the government.[54] In considering the 1914–15 military appropriation bill, however, a heated debate occurred in the Senate. Among the pro-rider anti-Taylor advocates was Henry Cabot Lodge, a descendant of the early Massachusetts textile tycoons, who spoke of ending "the days of slavery" brought about by men such as Taylor who thought it "profitable to work the slaves to the last possible point and let them die."[55] Such demagoguery clearly indicated his ignorance of what Taylor was attempting. The rider failed in the Senate, but was restored in conference between the two chambers. Legislation prohibiting the use of federal funds for "time-study with a stopwatch or other time-measuring device" stayed in effect until 1949.[56] It should be noted that there was never a strike at any company at which Taylor personally was in charge nor had any workers operating under his system found it desirable to unionize. Nevertheless, it would be many years before labor and management would share the "mental revolution" that Taylor regarded as the essence of scientific management.

52. Copley, *Taylor*, vol. 2, p. 348.

53. Hearings to Investigate the Taylor System, p. 1930.

54. U.S. House of Representatives, Labor Committee, Hearings on House Resolution 8662, A Bill to Prevent the Use of Stop Watch or Other Time-Measuring Devices on Government Work and the Payment of Premiums or Bonuses to Government Employees (Washington, DC: Government Printing Office, 1914).

55. Copley, *Taylor*, vol. 2, p. 351. Mary Barnett Gilson, an early employment counselor and later lecturer at the University of Chicago, called Senator Lodge an "exhibitionist" who tilted at windmills. M. B. Gilson, *What's Past Is Prologue* (New York: Harper & Brothers, 1940), p. 55.

56. Milton J. Nadworny, *Scientific Management and the Unions: 1900–1923* (Cambridge, MA: Harvard University Press, 1955), p. 103.

THE MENTAL REVOLUTION

In the first decade of the twentieth century, concern over the depletion of America's resources was voiced by President Theodore Roosevelt and others. This concern was seen as preliminary to a larger question of national efficiency. Taylor, who had fought against the misuse of both physical and human resources for almost thirty years, wrote about the conservation of the nation's resources in his 1911 book *The Principles of Scientific Management*. He stated the book's objectives as:

> *First.* To point out, through a series of simple illustrations, the great loss which the whole country is suffering through inefficiency in almost all of our daily acts.
>
> *Second.* To try to convince the reader that the remedy for this inefficiency lies in systematic management, rather than in searching for some unusual or extraordinary man.
>
> *Third.* To prove that the best management is a true science, resting upon clearly defined laws, rules, and principles, as a foundation. And further to show that the fundamental principles of scientific management are applicable to all kinds of human activities, from our simplest individual acts to the work of our great corporations, which call for the most elaborate cooperation.[57]

"The principal object of management," said Taylor, "should be to secure the maximum prosperity for the employer, coupled with the maximum prosperity for each employee."[58] Taylor called for a "mental revolution" where "both sides take their eyes off the division of surplus... and together turn their attention toward increasing the size of the surplus."[59] Thus, as envisioned by Taylor, the concerns of labor and management should be based on a "mutuality of interest." In brief, he advocated a congruency between the goals of employee and employer. In his words: "It is safe to say no system or scheme of management should be considered which does not in the long run give satisfaction to both employer and employee, which does not make it apparent that their best interest are mutual, and which does not bring about such thorough and hearty cooperation that they can pull together instead of apart."[60] Taylor recognized that self-proclaimed "efficiency experts" were giving scientific management a black eye. He warned that "the mechanism of management

---

57. Taylor, *Principles of Scientific Management*, p. 7.

58. Ibid., p. 9.

59. *Hearings to Investigate the Taylor System*, p. 1388.

60. Taylor, *Shop Management*, p. 21.

must not be mistaken for its essence, or underlying philosophy."[61] This philosophy, based on a mutuality of interests, had four basic principles:

> *First:* The development of a true science.
>
> *Second:* The scientific selection of the workman.
>
> *Third:* His scientific education and development.
>
> *Fourth:* Intimate friendly cooperation between the management and the men.[62]

For Taylor, no single element constituted scientific management. Rather it was a combination of elements, which could be summarized as:

> Science, not rule of thumb.
>
> Harmony, not discord.
>
> Cooperation, not individualism.
>
> Maximum output, in place of restricted output.
>
> The development of each man to his greatest efficiency and prosperity.[63]

Taylor's ideas aroused much interest, and unfortunately, many imitators used his name but short-circuited his methods. Taylor deplored these fakers, properly fearing that they promised quick panaceas without grasping the fundamental attitudes that had to be changed and the necessity of gaining workers' acceptance of his methods. Taylor made a marked distinction between "true" scientific management and the efficiency craze that had suddenly emerged. True scientific management required a "mental revolution" on the part of employers and employees, which came about from mutual respect over a period of time and not from the mechanical adoption of purported efficiency devices. At the Congressional hearings following the Watertown Arsenal strike, Taylor tried to clarify first what scientific management was by explaining what it was not:

> Scientific management is not any efficiency device, not a device of any kind for securing efficiency; nor is it any bunch or group of efficiency devices. It is not a new system of figuring costs; it is not a

---

61. Taylor, *Principles of Scientific Management*, p. 128.

62. Ibid., p. 130n.

63. Ibid., p. 140.

new scheme of paying men; it is not a piecework system; it is not a bonus system; it is not a premium system; it is no scheme for paying men; it is not holding a stop watch on a man and writing things down about him; it is not time study; it is not motion study nor an analysis of the movements of men; it is not the printing and ruling and unloading of a ton of blanks on a set of men and saying, "Here's your system; go use it." It is not divided foremanship or functional foremanship; it is not any of the devices which the average man calls to mind when scientific management is spoken of. The average man thinks of one or more of these things when he hears the words "scientific management" mentioned, but scientific management is not any of these devices. I am not sneering at cost-keeping systems, at time study, at functional foremanship, nor at any new and improved scheme of paying men, nor at any efficiency devices, if they are really devices that make for efficiency. I believe in them; but what I am emphasizing is that these devices in whole or in part are not scientific management, they are useful adjuncts to scientific management, so are they also useful adjuncts of other systems of management.

Now, in its essence, scientific management involves a complete mental revolution on the part of the workingman engaged in any particular establishment or industry—a complete mental revolution on the part of these men as to their duties toward their work, toward their fellow men, and toward their employers. And it involves the equally complete mental revolution on the part of those on the management's side—the foreman, the superintendent, the owner of the business, the board of directors—a complete mental revolution on their part as to their duties toward their fellow workers in the management, toward their workmen, and toward all of their daily problems. And without this complete mental revolution on both sides scientific management does not exist. That is the essence of scientific management, this great mental revolution.[64]

Taylor believed that labor-union leaders were the principal opponents of his methods, not the unions' rank-and-file members. He was convinced that there was a conspiracy among union leaders to oppose scientific management. In a discussion with Nels P. Alifas, representing the Metal Trades Department of the American Federation of Labor, Taylor presented the case for time study, improving work methods, and rewarding workers based on output. Alifas stated the position of the Metal Trades workers:

---

64. *Hearings to Investigate the Taylor System*, p. 1387.

Some people may wonder why we should object to a time study.... The objection is that in the past one of the means by which an employee has been able to keep his head above water and prevent being oppressed by the employer has been that the employer didn't know just exactly what the employee could do. The only way that the workman has been able to retain time enough in which to do the work with the speed with which he thinks he ought to do it, has been to keep the employer somewhat in ignorance of exactly the time needed. The people of the United States have a right to say we want to work only so fast. We don't want to work as fast as we are able to. We want to work as fast as we think it's comfortable for us to work.... We are trying to regulate our work so as to make it an auxiliary to our lives and be benefited thereby.[65]

Taylor made repeated offers to Samuel Gompers, president of the American Federation of Labor, to visit plants using scientific management and to get the facts for himself; Gompers refused.[66]

In Taylor's view, the unionists' philosophy and that of scientific management were in direct opposition. Whereas labor unions stood "for war, for enmity," scientific management encouraged a "mutuality of interests."[67] To Gompers, "more, more, more" meant labor's gains came from employers' pockets; for Taylor, "more" came to everyone through improved productivity.[68] True, by searching for technological breakthroughs, scientific management made it possible to get more output for the same amount of input and, thus, higher profits. At the same time, working with better technology and work methods, scientifically selected and trained workers naturally produce more output per hour. In a competitive labor market, the demand for these more productive workers increases, driving up their wages. Clearly, both employers and employees have a mutuality of interests in increasing a company's efficiency so it will pay one of them wages and the other one profits. If

---

65. "Scientific Shop Management," from a publication of the Milwaukee Federation of Labor, 1914, reprinted in John R. Commons, ed., *Trade Unionism and Labor Problems*, 2nd ser. (Boston: Ginn, 1921), pp. 148–149.

66. Copley, *Taylor*, vol. 2, pp. 403–404. In his testimony before the committee to investigate the Taylor System, Gompers categorically denied the existence of soldiering and labor resistance. *Hearings to Investigate the Taylor System*, p. 27. Gompers's biographer, Philip Taft, has suggested that Gompers himself was not unalterably opposed to scientific management. According to Taft, Gompers yielded to the influence of the socialist president of the International Association of Machinists, William H. Johnson, because the machinists were the largest and most powerful affiliate in the American Federation of Labor. Philip Taft, *The A. F. of L. in the Time of Gompers* (New York: Harper, 1957), pp. 299–300.

67. Copley, *Taylor*, vol. 2, p. 407.

68. Robert F. Hoxie, "President Gompers and the Labor Vote," *Journal of Political Economy* 16(10), (1909), p. 694.

the company fails, they both lose. Taylor considered his inability to convince labor to accept scientific management to be his greatest failure.[69]

TAYLOR AND THE HUMAN FACTOR

In response to the charges that scientific management was cold and impersonal and disregarded the human factor, Taylor wrote about systems and people: "No system can do away with the need of real men. Both system and good men are needed, and after introducing the best system, success will be in proportion to the ability, consistency, and respected authority of the management."[70] Taylor well understood he was dealing with human needs as well as materials and machines. Writing in his book *Shop Management*, he quoted from his first 1895 ASME paper:

> No system of management, however good, should be applied in a wooden way. The proper personal relations should always be maintained between the employers and men; and even the prejudices of the workmen should be considered in dealing with them.

> The employer who goes through his works with kid gloves on, and is never known to dirty his hands or clothes, and who either talks to his men in a condescending or patronizing way, or else not at all, has no chance whatever of ascertaining their real thoughts or feelings.

> Above all it is desirable that men should be talked to on their own level by those who are over them. Each man should be encouraged to discuss any trouble which he may have, either in the works or outside, with those over him. Men would far rather even be blamed by their bosses, especially if the "tearing out" has a touch of human nature and feeling in it, than to be passed by day after day without a word, and with no more notice than if they were part of the machinery.

> The opportunity which each man should have of airing his mind freely, and having it out with his employers, is a safety-valve; and if the superintendents are reasonable men, and listen to and treat with respect what their men have to say, there is absolutely no reason for labor unions and strikes.

> It is not the large charities (however generous they may be) that are needed or appreciated by workmen so much as small acts of personal kindness and sympathy, which establish a bond of friendly feeling between them and their employers.

---

69. Kenneth E. Trombley, *The Life and Times of a Happy Liberal: A Biography of Morris Llewellyn Cooke* (New York: Harper & Brothers, 1954), p. 258.

70. Taylor, *Shop Management*, p. 148.

The moral effect of this system on the men is marked. The feeling that substantial justice is being done them renders them on the whole much more manly, straightforward, and truthful. They work more cheerfully, and are more obliging to one another and their employers. They are not soured, as under the old system, by brooding over the injustice done them; and their spare minutes are not spent to the same extent in criticising their employers.[71]

On resistance to change:

Through generations of bitter experiences working men as a class have learned to look upon all change as antagonistic to their best interests. They do not ask the object of the change, but oppose it simply as *change*. The first changes, therefore, should be such as to allay the suspicions of the men and convince them by actual contact that the reforms are after all rather harmless and are only such as will ultimately be of benefit to all concerned.[72]

Taylor believed that it took two to five years to fully install his task-management system; thus explaining his reaction to Emerson's testimony promising quick savings. Scientific management was not an overnight panacea. Its implementation required diligence and understanding of his philosophy of management to be successful. Even then, there was never only "one best way":

Scientific management fundamentally consists of certain broad principles, a certain philosophy, which can be applied in many ways.... It is not here claimed that any single panacea exists for all of the troubles of the working people or of employers.... No system of management, no single expedient within the control of any man or any set of men can insure continuous prosperity to either workmen or employers.[73]

In 1915, three weeks before his death, Taylor spoke to the Cleveland Advertising Club:

Scientific management at every step has been an evolution, not a theory. In all cases the practice has preceded the theory...all the men that I know of who are connected with scientific management

---

71. Ibid., pp. 184–185.

72. Ibid., p. 137.

73. Ibid., pp. 28–29. Taylor made a similar statement in his presentation at the first conference on scientific management: Frederick W. Taylor, "The Principles of Scientific Management," in *Scientific Management: First Conference at the Amos Tuck School, Dartmouth College* (Hanover, NH: Plimpton Press, 1912), p. 54.

are ready to abandon any scheme, any theory, in favor of anything else that can be found which is better. There is nothing in scientific management that is fixed.[74]

In recognizing that there was never only "one best way," Taylor realized that management should continually strive to improve managerial practices through scientific investigation. Worried by the declining health of his wife, bedeviled by the antagonism of organized labor, and frustrated by imitators who used his name but short-circuited his methods and forgot his philosophy, Taylor's last days were nigh. In a drafty railcar drawing room, while returning from a speaking trip, he caught pneumonia. He died one day after his fifty-ninth birthday. His headstone at the West Laurel Hill Cemetery, Philadelphia, bears this inscription: "Frederick W. Taylor, 1856–1915, Father of Scientific Management."

SUMMARY

Frederick W. Taylor was a central figure in the development of management thought. Entering the American industrial scene at a time of transition from entrepreneurial, manager–owner firms to large-scale, fully integrated corporations, Taylor gave a push and provided credibility to the idea of management as an independent science and discipline. The engineers of the day, having opened the door to efficient resource utilization, turned to technical subjects and left the way open for Taylor and others to promote what would come to be known as scientific management. Characterized by advancing technology, market growth, labor unrest, and a lack of managerial knowledge, U.S. companies of all sizes and in all industries were eager to learn better methods to manufacture and market products. To meet this need, Taylor provided a voice, a spirit that captured the imagination of the public, business leaders, and academics.

Although Taylor died almost a hundred years ago, he is still considered by historians to be "the most influential business guru of the 20th century."[75] In a contemporary review of Taylor's ideas, Locke concluded that "Taylor's track record is remarkable...*most of his insights are still valid today.*"[76] Undeniably, Taylor was sometimes dogmatic and expressed himself in terms that made him an easy target for contemporary social critics. He once remarked, for example, that the first

---

74. Copley, *Taylor*, vol. 2, p. 348.

75. Geoffrey Colvin, "Managing the End of an Era," *Fortune* (March 6, 2000), p. F-8. See also: Arthur G. Bedeian and Daniel A. Wren, "Most Influential Management Books of the 20th Century," *Organizational Dynamics* 29 (2001), pp. 221–225 and Daniel A. Wren and Robert D. Hay, "Management Historians and Business Historians: Differing Perceptions of Pioneering Contributions," *Academy of Management Journal* 20 (1977), pp. 470–475.

76. Edwin A. Locke, "The Ideas of Frederick W. Taylor: An Evaluation," *Academy of Management Review* 7 (1982), pp. 22–23. Italics in the original.

requirement of a pig-iron handler is that he be so dull that he resemble an ox, and that an "intelligent gorilla," if properly trained, would be better suited to the job.[77] Arguably, his point was intended to illustrate the application of scientific management to menial jobs requiring only physical labor, and to emphasize that there was nothing special about the fact that some workers were suited to this kind of job and others were not.[78] His choice of analogies, however, was less than diplomatic, and such references, understandably, were ill received. All the same, as Nelson has observed, social scientists of every stripe have set up Taylor as a "straw man," emblematic of a hierarchical, authoritarian style of management that caused decades of labor strife, forgetting that his "commitment [was] to knowledge, reason and continuous attention to detail that was equally antithetical to old-fashioned empiricism and to new-fashioned panaceas."[79]

Taylor's work was, and still remains, revolutionary. The original seed he sowed has spread and multiplied a millionfold. It has spread from the mechanical operations on which he focused at the beginning of his career into activities such as employee selection and training, job design, inventory control, and wage and salary administration. Further, Taylor's efforts began a revolution that enabled industrial workers to earn middle-class wages and achieve middle-class status. Moreover, it is precisely the application of scientific management to the study of work that has enabled many of the world's underdeveloped and poverty-stricken countries to become world-class competitors within a single generation.

Just as important, Taylor's work produced a change in the way managers regarded themselves. The old "rule-of-thumb" and "seat-of-the-pants" images were replaced by "an attitude of questioning, of research, of careful investigation . . . of seeking exact knowledge and then shaping action on the discovered facts."[80] Scientific management was to be a tool for greater productivity, greater purchasing power, and a higher standard of living.

On balance, Taylor left an indelible mark on his age and ours. His emphasis on efficiency remains a prevailing value of contemporary management. He was not alone, but was joined by numerous others who would apply, adapt, refine, and fly the scientific management banner. Taylor, however, was the polestar that guided all those who have since followed in his footsteps to bring professional management to the workplace and replace opinion with fact.

---

77. Taylor, *Principles of Scientific Management*, p. 40 and p. 59.

78. Lyndall F. Urwick, "The Truth about 'Schmidt': Reflections of Col. Lyndall F. Urwick," *Working Paper Series*, 3, No. 1., Management History Division, Academy of Management, 1978, pp. 8–9, 12.

79. Daniel Nelson, ed., *A Mental Revolution: Scientific Management Since Taylor* (Columbus: Ohio State University Press, 1992), p. 239.

80. Majority Report of Sub-Committee on Administration, "The Present State of the Art of Industrial Management," *Transactions, ASME* 34 (1912), p. 1137.

CHAPTER

8

Spreading the Gospel of Efficiency

S pace and time rarely allow the full measure of a person and that person's work. This is true of Frederick W. Taylor and also applies to those who joined with and followed Taylor in propagating scientific management. This chapter focuses on six individuals who rallied around Taylor and were prominent in the embryonic days of the scientific-management movement: Carl G. Barth, Henry L. Gantt, Frank B. and Lillian M. Gilbreth, Harrington Emerson, and Morris L. Cooke. These people were at the vanguard in spreading the gospel of efficiency.

THE MOST ORTHODOX: CARL BARTH

Of all the disciples in the vanguard of the scientific management movement, Carl G. Barth (1860–1939) was the most orthodox. Barth was born in Norway and educated at the Horten Technical School (1875–1877), which provided training for Norwegian naval engineers. He began his apprenticeship as a machinist in 1877 at the Horten Navy Yard, earning less than three cents per hour. In 1881 he emigrated to the United States in hope of better wages. His first job was with the William Sellers Company (Philadelphia), a leading machine-tool manufacturer, where he began as a draftsman earning two dollars a day. As his talents were quickly recognized, his salary was soon raised to twenty dollars a week. Barth worked at Sellers for fourteen years and rose to the position of chief-machine designer. He subsequently taught mathematics and manual trades.[1]

Barth was an instructor at the Ethical Culture Day School in New York City when a friend recommended him to Fred Taylor, who was searching for someone to handle complex mathematical problems in his metal-cutting experiments at Bethlehem Steel. Barth joined Taylor at Bethlehem in 1899,

---

1. Kenneth Bjork, *Saga in Steel and Concrete: Norwegian Engineers in America* (Northfield, MN: Norwegian- American Historical Association, 1947), pp. 278–312.

and his first assignment was to help Henry L. Gantt with machine feed and speed problems that had plagued Taylor since his early days at Midvale Steel. Barth's solution was a logarithmic slide rule in circular form that gave near instantaneous solutions.[2] Taylor credited Barth's extraordinary analytic ability with eliminating rule-of-thumb procedures in determining the one best combination of machines, tools, feeds, and speeds for cutting metals.

During the remainder of his life, Taylor relied on Barth more than anyone for assistance in developing new engineering methods. Barth assisted Taylor in the pioneering installations of scientific management at the Tabor Manufacturing Company, the Link-Belt Engineering Company, Fairbanks Scale, Yale & Towne Manufacturing Company, and later at the Watertown Arsenal. He also assisted George D. Babcock in installing scientific management in the Franklin Motor Car Company (1908–1912) and thus was a pioneer in the rationalization of the automobile industry. In the days before the moving assembly line, component parts were brought to stationary work areas for assembly. Franklin made three models of cars—touring, runabout, and sedan—and relied on a sales forecast to determine which models to produce, when, and in what quantities. One hundred cars were produced per month in lots, or batches. Franklin was unprofitable due to high manufacturing costs and rampant labor turnover (425 percent). After Barth finished installing scientific management, Franklin was producing forty-five cars per day, wages were up 90 percent, labor turnover was less than 50 percent, and it was profitable.[3] Between 1908 and 1913, the Ford Motor Company would perfect the moving assembly line for the mass production of automobiles to replace the small-batch assembly methods of the past.

Barth lectured on scientific management at the University of Chicago (1914–1916) and at Harvard University (1911–1916 and 1919–1922) and was "exceedingly proud of being accused of being Mr. Taylor's most orthodox disciple."[4] He resisted any tampering with Taylor's methods and later maintained that only those who had worked directly with Taylor fully understood the task-management system. Barth's contribution to management thought was confined to his faithful execution of Taylor's methods. He was patient and accurate in his experiments and analyses. Whereas he may not have possessed Taylor's imagination, Barth performed a bulk of the technical work necessary for developing scientific management. In this respect, Taylor and Barth complemented one another in temperament and skills. Barth conducted his later consulting management work in conjunction with his son, J. Christian Barth, under the firm name of Carl G. Barth & Son.

———

2. Carl G. Barth, "Supplement to Frederick W. Taylor's 'On the Art of Cutting Metals'—I," *Industrial Management* 58 (September 1919), pp. 169-175.

3. George D. Babcock, *The Taylor System in Franklin Management: Application and Results* (New York: Engineering Magazine, 1917).

4. Carl G. Barth, "Discussion," *Transactions, ASME* 34 (1912), p. 1204.

THE MOST UNORTHODOX: H. L. GANTT

Henry Laurence Gantt (1861–1919) was born into a prosperous Maryland farm family. When the Civil War left the family destitute, Gantt learned at an early age the demands of hard work, frugal living, and the self-discipline required to make one's way in the world.[5] Graduating with distinction from Johns Hopkins University in 1880, Gantt taught natural science and mechanics at the McDonagh School (Owings Mills, Maryland) for three years. McDonagh had been founded in 1872 as a "school farm" for "poor boys of good character." Gantt subsequently returned to college at the Stevens Institute of Technology, earned a mechanical engineering degree in 1884, became a draftsman for an engineering firm, and in 1886 returned to his teaching post at McDonagh. He joined the Midvale Steel Company in 1887 as an assistant in the engineering department. Here the twenty-six-year-old Gantt met and began to work with a man who would have a significant influence on his future career, Fred Taylor.

Taylor and Gantt were an unusual team: they shared a common interest in science as a means of improving management methods and developed a deep mutual admiration for each other's work. Gantt grasped the essence of Taylor's work and, though they clashed at times, became one of his leading disciples. He worked closely with Taylor at Midvale, followed him to the Simonds Rolling Machine Company to become superintendent, and joined him again at Bethlehem Steel. In 1901, Gantt became a "consulting industrial engineer" on his own, and although he espoused the tenets of scientific management throughout his life, he later expanded his concern to the nation's economic environment. During his lifetime he published over 150 titles, including three major books; made numerous presentations before the ASME (becoming vice president in 1914); patented more than a dozen inventions; lectured at universities, including Stevens, Columbia, Harvard, and Yale; and became one of the first successful management consultants.

THE TASK AND BONUS SYSTEM

Gantt's initial ideas on machines, tools, and methods were a direct outgrowth of his association with Fred Taylor. Taylor's ideas on recognizing a mutuality of interests between labor and management, scientifically selecting workers, incentive rates to stimulate performance, detailed task instructions, and more are reflected in Gantt's early work. Gantt recognized that the workingman, "a human unit in a living organization," was the most important element in management. He believed that if management was to reflect social values and serve social purposes, exploitation of

---

5. Biographical data are from Leon P. Alford, *Henry L. Gantt: Leader in Industry*, prepared originally as a memorial volume for the ASME and later published by Harper & Brothers, New York, 1934. See also Alex W. Rathe, *Gantt on Management* (New York: American Management Association, 1961); and Peter B. Petersen, "A Further Insight into the Life of Henry L. Gantt: The Papers of Duncan Lyle," in Dennis F. Ray, ed., *Proceedings of the Southern Management Association*, New Orleans, 1984, pp. 198–200.

Henry L. Gantt as a student at the Johns Hopkins University, circa 1880. Courtesy of Peter B. Petersen.

workers could not be tolerated. In his words, "the only healthy industrial condition is that in which the employer has the best men obtainable for his work, and the workman feels that his labor is being sold at the highest market price."[6]

On this road to high wages and low costs, Gantt developed a task and bonus system of wage payments that was simpler than Taylor's differential piece-rate incentive plan. His view on unions paralleled that of Taylor, but he was more persuasive and philosophical in stating the issue:

> If the amount of wealth in the world were fixed, the struggle for the possession of that wealth would necessarily cause antagonism; but, [because] . . . the amount of wealth is not fixed, but constantly increasing, the fact that one man has become wealthy does not necessarily mean that someone else has become poorer, but may mean quite the reverse, especially if the first is a producer of wealth. . . . As long . . . as one party—no matter which—tries to get all it can of the new wealth, regardless of the rights of the other, conflicts will continue.[7]

The "more, more, more" of organized labor hence became an antagonistic force unless it cooperated in producing more for the mutual benefit of both labor and management—and vice versa. Gantt was not convinced that a differential piece-rate incentive plan favored by Taylor would secure worker cooperation.[8] Gantt's "task work with a bonus" system guaranteed a day wage and paid a daily bonus of fifty cents if workers completed all their assigned tasks. Gantt later discovered that this arrangement offered little incentive for additional effort beyond the required standard. To overcome this defect, he modified his task and bonus system to pay workers if a task was completed in less than standard time. A worker could thus receive four hours' pay for doing a three-hour job in less than three hours.[9]

Further, Gantt adapted the idea of a colleague, E. P. Earle, to give first-line supervisors a bonus for each of their workers who reached the standard set for their job, plus an extra bonus based on the bonuses earned by the workers

---

6. Henry L. Gantt, *Work, Wages, and Profits,* 2nd ed. (New York: Engineering Magazine, 1916), p. 33.

7. Ibid., p. 55.

8. Alford, *Gantt,* p. 85.

9. Ibid., p. 165. For a detailed explanation and the computations necessary to Gantt's task and bonus plan, see Charles W. Lytle, *Wage Incentive Methods* (New York: Ronald Press, 1942), pp. 185–200.

being supervised. Thus, if nine of ten workers in a department achieved standard production, their supervisor would receive ten cents per worker, or $0.90; if all ten met the standard, the first-line supervisor would receive fifteen cents per worker, or $1.50. Gantt viewed this extra bonus as a way to encourage supervisors to teach and help workers improve their performance. He knew the importance of education from his days as a teacher and felt that "task work with a bonus" would shift first-line supervisors from drivers to workplace leaders.[10] Gantt was convinced that force could not be the basis for leadership. Increased productivity could only be achieved through knowledge. Like Taylor, Gantt encountered more resistance from first-line supervisors concerned with protecting their authority than from the workers they supervised. For Gantt, all components within an enterprise must cooperate to achieve efficient performance. Further, he felt that workplace rewards should be equitably distributed according to the contributions of each participant.

THE HABITS OF INDUSTRY

As a consulting industrial engineer, Gantt would serve some fifty clients before his death in 1919. Taylor would occasionally recommend Gantt for jobs requiring an engineer-manager. At the American Locomotive Company, Robins Conveying Belt Company, Brighton Mills, and other firms, Gantt installed Taylor's methods. Sayles Bleacheries, a textile plant located in Lincoln, Rhode Island, was one of Gantt's early clients. Despite patenting three different machines to help reduce waste and inefficiency, Gantt encountered resistance from both management and labor. Ultimately, the workers in a folding room went out on strike. The workers folded 155 pieces of cloth each day for a weekly wage of ten dollars. They objected to Gantt's work methods, asked for a ten percent increase in wages, and struck when the wage increase was refused. The strike spread, and Gantt had to hire and train replacement workers. This experience forced Gantt to rethink how to best train workers; from then on he considered intensive employee training to be an essential responsibility of management.

In training employees, Gantt felt that supervisors should do more than improve worker skills and knowledge; he added an ingredient to training called the "habits of industry." These habits were *industriousness* and *cooperation*, which would facilitate the acquisition of all other knowledge. Gantt felt that as a result of doing their work promptly and to the best of their ability, workers would experience pride that comes from quality as well as quantity of work.[11] As an example, he cited a group of women who formed a society of "bonus producers," with membership open only to those who consistently earned a daily bonus. To Gantt, this was the ideal in labor-management. Gantt believed, however, that such relations could only come about after management had created a proper atmosphere of workplace cooperation

---

10. Henry L. Gantt, *Industrial Leadership*. (New Haven, CT: Yale University Press, 1916).

11. Gantt, *Work, Wages, and Profits*, p. 154.

and trust. The result would be a win-win situation: higher wages for employees and lower costs due to greater productivity for employers. Moreover, the harmonious cooperation between labor and management would create the élan, or morale, vital to successful cooperative endeavors.

GRAPHIC AIDS TO MANAGEMENT

Gantt was less inclined toward painstaking experiments than either Taylor or Barth. Eventually he turned to graphic methods for recording and conveying operating information. One of his early graphic portrayals involved using horizontal bars to illustrate the progress of workers toward meeting performance standards. Daily records were kept of whether workers met production standards and received a bonus, recorded in black, or did not, recorded in red. The bars on the graph provided performance feedback to both management and workers, as shortfalls ("exceptions") were clearly highlighted. Gantt expanded his graphical portrayals to include charts showing daily output, production costs, output per machine and worker in comparison with original planning estimates, and losses due to idle machinery.[12] His major breakthrough in charting came, however, when serving as a dollar-a-year consultant to the Department of the Army during World War I (1914–1918).

The conversion of U.S. industry to wartime production did not come quickly or smoothly. The United States had the productive capacity, but the coordination of private industrial efforts with government agencies was haphazard. Plants were scattered all over the nation, shipments were late, warehouses were crowded or disorganized, and the military utilized its resources poorly. Gantt had had some contact with governmental work before the war. In 1911, with Charles Day and Harrington Emerson, he was commissioned to study the management of navy yards. Their efforts went for naught when, following the Interstate Commerce Commission hearings in late 1911, the Secretary of the Navy announced that he would never allow scientific management to be applied in the nation's shipyards.[13] Just prior to the war, Gantt had also served as a consultant to General William Crozier, head of the U. S. Army Ordnance Department.[14] Crozier, impressed by Gantt's graphic displays, developed a series of progress and performance charts to aid in managing army arsenals. When Gantt gave up his consulting work to aid in the war effort, he puzzled over how to track the huge amount of defense work being performed at so many different sites. Scheduling was especially crucial, and the information necessary to

---

12. Peter B. Petersen, "The Evolution of the Gantt Chart and Its Relevance Today," *Journal of Managerial Issues* 3 (Summer 1991), pp. 131–155.

13. Peter B. Petersen, "Fighting for a Better Navy: An Attempt at Scientific Management (1805–1912)," *Journal of Management* 16 (March 1990), pp. 151–166.

14. Peter B. Petersen, "The Pioneering Efforts of Major General William Crozier (1855–1942) in the Field of Management," *Journal of Management* 15 (September 1989), pp. 503–516.

plan and coordinate private contractors' efforts with those of government agencies was lacking. Gantt spent three months trying to solve this puzzle before realizing that "We have all been wrong in scheduling on a basis of *quantities*; the essential element in the situation is *time*, and this should be the basis in laying out any program."[15]

Gantt's solution was a bar chart for planning and coordinating work. Although numerous variations were developed, the essence of what came to be known as a Gantt Progress Chart is to show how work is to be routed and scheduled, through various operations, to completion. For example, a manager can see from the Gantt chart in Figure 8-1 that the project in question is behind schedule. Corrective action can now be taken to move the project ahead.

The Gantt chart was hailed as *"the most notable contribution to the art of management made in this generation."*[16] In their simplest form, Gantt charts allow managers to easily determine a project's progress and to take actions, if necessary, to ensure its timely completion. Gantt never patented his bar-chart concept, nor profited from it, but he was awarded the Distinguished Civilian Service Medal "for meritorious service to the government of the United States." A member of Gantt's consulting firm, Wallace Clark, popularized the Gantt chart in a book that was translated into eight languages. Gantt charts formed the basis for the Soviet Union's first Five-Year Plan during the 1920s and soon provided the world with a graphic means of planning and coordinating work.[17] All subsequent production project

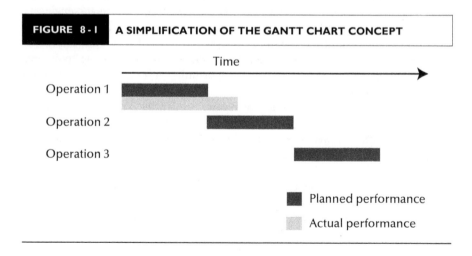

| FIGURE 8-1 | A SIMPLIFICATION OF THE GANTT CHART CONCEPT |

Time

Operation 1

Operation 2

Operation 3

■ Planned performance

▨ Actual performance

15. Alford, *Gantt*, p. 207.

16. Wallace Clark, "The Gantt Chart—I: Its Principles, Techniques, Application, and Use," *Management Engineering* 1 (August 1921), p. 77.

17. Wallace Clark, *The Gantt Chart: A Working Tool of Management* (New York: Ronald Press, 1922). For further information on Wallace Clark, see Harold Smiddy, "Wallace Clark's Contribution to International Management," *Advanced Management* 23 (March 1958), pp. 17–26.

controls drew their inspiration from Gantt's bar-chart concept; the modern variation became the Program Evaluation and Review Technique (PERT), a computerized, more intricate scheme for planning and controlling both times and costs. World War I took a measurable turn for the better as the result of Gantt's contributions. Materials flowed more smoothly, shipbuilding boomed, and the productive might of the United States was brought to fruition. Surely this must have provided some consolation for the man whose efforts to improve the management of navy shipyards had been spurned so few years before.

GANTT: THE LATER YEARS

As a result of his participation in World War I, Gantt widened his views on industry and the role of industrial engineers in serving the nation. In particular, he deplored the failure of U.S. industrial leadership, which, in his opinion, was caused by the rise of leaders to power based on favoritism or special privilege rather than ability. Gantt argued for a "new" leadership in which the industrial engineer, not the financier or the labor leader, would lead an industrial democracy based on equality of opportunity. Because only industrial engineers could cope with the complexities of creating wealth, they would be an educated elite to lead the United States, not with a concern for profits, but rather for productive efficiency. Gantt was influenced by Thorstein Veblen's criticism of laissez-faire economics and the role of big business in shaping modern society. He saw a conflict between businessmen and engineers, with businessmen defending the status quo and engineers as championing new ways of doing things.[18] Gantt was also impressed by the views of New York City writer and newspaperman Charles Ferguson, who "wanted to reconcile the traditional ideals of individualism and freewheeling opportunity with the increasing need for cooperation and social control."[19]

In late 1916, Gantt formed an organization called the New Machine, whose membership was comprised of engineers and other sympathetic reformers seeking to acquire political as well as economic power.[20] The New Machine operated on the premise that engineers would form Ferguson's "aristocracy of the capable." The leaders of the New Machine called for President Woodrow Wilson to transfer "control of the huge and delicate apparatus [i.e., industry] into the hands of those who understand its operation," to establish bureaus for better placement of employees, and to set up "public service banks" to extend credit on the basis of ability and personality rather than property.[21]

---

18. Alford, *Gantt*, p. 264.

19. Robert D. Cuff, "Woodrow Wilson's Missionary to American Business, 1914–1915: A Note," *Business History Review* 43 (Winter) 1969, pp. 545–551.

20. Peter B. Petersen, "Correspondence from Henry L. Gantt to an Old Friend Reveals New Information about Gantt," *Journal of Management* 12 (September) 1986, pp. 339–350.

21. Alford, *Gantt*, pp. 269–277.

Gantt soon lost his concern for mere factory matters and sought broader areas for reform. He attacked the profit system, and on this point he appears to have been largely influenced by the swirl of world events. In January 1917, Tzar Nicholas II was overthrown by the Bolsheviks, and violent bloodshed swept Russia. Eugene Debs, a founder of the International Labor Union and the Industrial Workers of the World (IWW), as well as five-time Socialist Party of America candidate for President of the United States, was something of a folk hero; there had been Communist uprisings in Bavaria and Hungary; the Wobblies (as IWW members were known) were provoking labor unrest; and many people were firmly convinced that the Bolsheviks were about to overturn society. In the preface to his last book, written in 1919, Gantt wrote:

> The attempt which extreme radicals all over the world are making to get control of both the political and business systems on the theory that they would make the industrial and business serve the community, is a real danger so long as our present system does not accomplish that end. ... [T]o resume our advance toward the development of an unconquerable democratic civilization, we must purge our economic system of all autocratic practices of whatever kind, and return to the democratic principle of rendering service, which was the basis of its wonderful growth.[22]

Gantt believed that to continue to profit from economic activity, businessmen must render a corresponding amount of service to the community, by which he meant the total integrated economic environment of the nation. He argued, "The business system must accept its social responsibility and devote itself primarily to service, or the community will ultimately make the attempt to take [the organization of industry] over in order to operate it in its own interest."[23] To this end, he further contended that, "the engineer, who is a man of few opinions and many facts and many deeds, should be accorded the economic leadership which is his proper place in our economic system."[24] In November 1919, Gantt was stricken with a "digestive disturbance" and died at age fifty-eight. After Gantt's death, the New Machine dissolved. The most unorthodox of Taylor's followers, Gantt did not live to see the shift in management thought that would occur in the 1920s and afterward. Rather than engineers providing the economic leadership advocated by the New Machine, U.S. industry would turn to improved human-resource practices, labor-management cooperation, improved employee representation plans, and, overall, a better understanding of the human factor at work. With his concern for the "working man," Gantt would have been pleased. In 1929, Gantt was posthumously

---

22. Henry L. Gantt, *Organizing for Work* (New York: Harcourt Brace Jovanovich, 1919), pp. iv–v.

23. Ibid., p. 15.

24. *New York Sunday World*, October 12, 1919, cited by Alford, *Gantt*, p. 298.

awarded the first Henry Laurence Gantt Medal by the Institute of Management and ASME—"For his humanizing influence upon industrial management and for invention of the Gantt chart."

PARTNERS FOR LIFE: THE GILBRETHS

Frank B. Gilbreth (1868–1924) and his wife Lillian M. (1878–1972) were contemporaries of Fred Taylor and part of the small band of original scientific-management pioneers.[25] Their accomplishments still stand out for their fervor and devotion to a single goal: the elimination of waste and the discovery of the "one best way" of doing work. It was the Gilbreths' contention that of the various ways a particular job could be performed, only one was the best, and it was their job to find it. This ideal became their credo and religion, and they did everything in their power to end the tragedy, as they saw it, of waste going on everywhere. They viewed their quest for the "one best way" as the means by which individuals' personal potential could be maximized with benefit both to themselves and to society.

Frank was the son of a Maine hardware merchant, and he learned early the virtues of frugality and thrift characteristic of New England Puritanism. When he was three years old, his father died, and his family moved to Boston. He was educated at Phillips Academy, Andover, and locally at Rice Grammar School. Although he had passed the Massachusetts Institute of Technology entrance exams, Frank was unwilling to go to college while his mother ran a boarding house to support him and his two sisters. Frank was urged to take up bricklaying by his Sunday-school teacher, Renton Whidden, who offered Frank the impressive pay of $3 a day. Frank needed the money and took the job. To learn his new job, he studied how bricklayers worked. He found they performed their task in three ways: They used one set of motions when working deliberatively but slowly, a second when working rapidly, and a third when trying to teach an apprentice. It was this simple observation that led to the first precepts of *motion study*. For, as Frank reasoned, if one set of motions was right, then the other two must be wrong.[26]

Frank was determined to learn to lay bricks the "right" way. At first he was the slowest apprentice on the job, but soon he began developing his own ideas. Designing his own scaffolds and work methods for everything from mortar consistency to trowel usage, he cut the motions required to lay a brick from 18 to 6. Within a year

---

25. Biographical information on the Gilbreths is from Edna Yost, *Frank and Lillian Gilbreth: Partners for Life* (New Brunswick, NJ: Rutgers University Press, 1949) and Jane Lancaster, *Making Time: Lillian Moller Gilbreth—A Life Beyond "Cheaper by the Dozen"* (Boston: Northeastern University Press, 2004). A treasure from the Gilbreth archives at Purdue University is Lillian M. Gilbreth, *As I Remember*, an autobiography written in 1941 but not published until 1998 (Norcross, GA: Engineering and Management Press).

26. Lillian M. Gilbreth, *The Quest for the One Best Way* (New York: Society of Industrial Engineers, 1924), p. 16.

The Gilbreth family at their summer home in Nantucket, 1923—Left to right, Frank (Sr.), Frank (Jr.), Bill, Fred, Dan, Jack, Bob, Jane, Lil, Martha, Ernestine, Anne, and Lillian Gilbreth. (Not pictured is Mary Elizabeth, who died at the age of six.) Courtesy of Ernestine Gilbreth Carey and the Gilbreth Family.

he was faster than any of his coworkers. A journeyman was expected to lay 175 bricks an hour. Frank could easily lay 350. In all, by age 20, he could draw journeyman's pay in more than 50 trades.

Several years later (1910), Frank testified before the Interstate Commerce Commission in the Eastern Rate Case. He explained his new science of bricklaying as follows:

> Bricks have been laid the same way for 4,000 years. The first thing a man does is to bend down and pick up a brick. Taylor pointed out that the average brick weighs ten pounds, the average weight of a man above his waist is 100 pounds. Instead of bending down and raising this double load, the bricklayer could have an adjustable shelf built so that the bricks would be ready to his hand. A boy could keep these shelves at the right height. When the man gets the brick in his hand, he tests it with his trowel. If anything, this is more stupid than stooping to pick up his material. If the brick is bad he discards it, but in the process it has been carried up perhaps six stories, and must be carted down again. Moreover, it consumes the time of a $5-a-day

man when a $6-a-week boy could do the testing on the ground. The next thing the bricklayer does is to turn the brick over to get its face. More waste: more work of the $6 boy. Next what does the bricklayer do? He puts his brick down on the mortar and begins to tap it down with his trowel. What does this tapping do? It gives the brick a little additional weight so it will sink into the mortar. If anything this is more stupid than any of the others. For we know the weight of the brick and it would be a simple matter in industrial physics to have the mortar mixed so that just that weight will press it down into the right layer. And the results? Instead of having eighteen motions in the laying of a brick, we have only six. And the men put on the work to try to lay 2,700 with apparently no more effort than they laid a thousand before.[27]

NOTHING SUCCEEDS LIKE . . .

By 1895 Frank had begun his own construction business in Boston with *speed work* as its motto. To ensure that cost arrangements would be satisfactory to his customers, Frank designed a Cost-Plus-A-Fixed-Sum Contract. Before long, Frank's work spread from Maine to New Mexico and from London to Berlin. At one time he employed up to 10,000 men. He even maintained an office in London, performing work for the Admiralty and War Office.

To keep track of all the work his company was doing, Frank ordered weekly photographs be taken, showing the progress of each job. These were supplemented by daily correspondence and an array of supporting forms. Dams, houses, factories, canals, skyscrapers, and even whole towns (for example, Woodland, Maine) were constructed by the Gilbreth Company. Much work was performed in San Francisco following the great earthquake and fire.

Frank's reputation for record-setting performances drew increasing attention. One of his most famous—and least conventional—practices was to start moving construction materials toward a job site even before a contract was awarded. Then, once the contract was signed, he would startle the public by beginning work within hours. Frank soon became one of the best-known building contractors in the world.

As Frank's ideas gained prominence, they also gained acceptance. Persuaded that a system that was not in writing was unworthy of the name, he set out to put his ideas into book form.[28] Working in conjunction with Lillie, he published *Field System* and *Concrete System* in 1908, and followed with *Bricklaying System* (1909), *Motion Study* (1911), *Fatigue Study* (1916), and *Applied Motion Study* (1917).

---

27. Frank B. Gilbreth quoted in Paul U. Kellogg, "A National Hearing for Scientific Management," *The Survey* (December 3, 1910), pp. 411–412.

28. Gilbreth, *Quest for the One Best Way*, p. 22.

The Field System was an accounting system without a set of books. It was designed to aid construction contractors by showing costs, costs related to estimates, and the total cost of a job each Saturday up to the previous Thursday. No bookkeepers were needed, and because original memoranda or receipts were filed, there was no general ledger. Gilbreth developed other facets of the field system and provided detailed instructions for its use, even including a rule about no smoking on the job and the admonition that whistle blasts at starting and quitting time should not be over four seconds long. He demonstrated the value of worker involvement in making improvements by establishing a suggestion program, including a $10 first prize each month for the best idea on how to improve work, give better service to customers, or secure additional construction jobs. Included in the field system were provisions for photographing working conditions at the time of any accident for use in lawsuits or other claims. Though his advice was quite detailed and largely only applicable to construction, it was indicative of Gilbreth's desire to rationalize work.

The Concrete System contained detailed advice for concrete contractors. Gilbreth wrote here too of motivating workers, including the use of athletic contests between work groups to give them a spirit of competition in completing a job. A total job was divided between equal groups of workers, who competed to finish a wall or build concrete pillars. *The Bricklaying System* was also technical but brought forth a facet of study new to Gilbreth. His original concern was with the training of apprentices, and Gilbreth saw the wastefulness of hand-me-down instruction from experienced workers. For example, he proposed first finding the best way of laying bricks through motion study, followed by instruction, and insisted that an emphasis be placed on learning the right way to lay bricks before maximum output was expected of a new bricklayer. This early work was but a prelude to his later in-depth analysis of motions and fatigue. In this connection, Frank devised a system for classifying hand motions into seventeen basic divisions called *therbligs* (*Gilbreth* spelled backwards with the *th* transposed).

As Frank's contacts grew, his interests broadened. Through membership in ASME, he met Taylor and other leaders of the new scientific-management movement—men like Barth and Gantt.

AND SO, INTO SCIENTIFIC MANAGEMENT

By 1912 Frank had completely given up the construction business and began devoting full-time efforts to management consulting. With the same single-minded attention he had given to bricklaying, he now studied the field of scientific management. More and more convinced that "the greatest waste in the world comes from needless, ill-directed, and ineffective motions,"[29] Frank sought new methods of discovering that waste and eliminating it. In 1892, he was the first person to use motion picture

---

29. Frank B. Gilbreth and Lillian M. Gilbreth, "Motion Study and Time Study Instruments of Precision," *Transactions, International Engineering Congress*, 1915, Vol. II (San Francisco, 1916), p. 473.

cameras to analyze a worker's motions. In 1915, he put roller skates on messengers in a Montgomery Ward office to reduce their fatigue and increase delivery speed. In another experiment, he observed 150 appendectomies to find the "one best way." In conjunction with Lillie, he authored papers such as "The Application of Scientific Management to the Work of the Nurse," "Motion Study in Surgery," and "Scientific Management in the Hospital." At one point, he even studied the motions of epileptics. And with the same dedication, working now with Walter Camp, he filmed and analyzed the swings of golf champions such as Gil Nichols and Francis Ouimet. Nor was the national pastime exempt from his studies after he filmed and analyzed a baseball game between the Phillies and the Giants at the Polo Grounds.[30] Frank's many industrial clients included Eastman Kodak, Lever Brothers, Pierce Arrow Motor Cars, and U.S. Rubber.

Frank's use of a motion-picture camera to study motions was a major contribution to the emerging field of scientific management. Initially he and Lillie filmed a worker going through his work cycle against a background of four-inch squares. Then they would run the film forward and backward to study the worker's motions. They called this "micromotion study." They then conceived the idea of attaching small electric lights to the worker so that by filming the worker in motion, they would be able to obtain a continuous white tracing of the worker's movements. They called this a *cyclegraph*. To reproduce the time occupied in each movement, they created a *chroncyclegraph* showing, instead of a continuous white tracing, a series of dashes, with the pattern of dashes—bunched up (where the movement had been slowest) or spread out at greater intervals elsewhere—giving an indication of the time occupied in a worker's separate movements. As a further refinement, they employed a stereoscopic camera to see a worker's movements in three dimensions. This they called a *stereochronocyclegraph*. Finally, they developed a *microchronometer* to show correct time to the thousandth of a minute.

Despite the connotations of *speed work*, Frank remained something of an idealist. It is said that "nothing ever aroused his temper more than a selfish employer who wanted to adopt all the latest things in management in his plant but wanted to hog all the savings himself and not share with his workers."[31] In contrast to the "blacklists" of the period, Frank instituted a "white list" designed to provide rewards for men who had performed well. In an effort to develop the skills of the men who worked for him, Frank developed "a three-position plan" of promotion.

---

30. Richard Lindstrom, "'They All Believe They Are Undiscovered Mary Pickfords: Workers, Photography, and Scientific Management," *Technology and Culture* 41 (October 2000), pp. 725–751; Terrie C. Reeves, W. Jack Duncan, and Peter M. Ginter, "Motion Study in Management and the Arts: A Historical Example," *Journal of Management Inquiry* 10 (June 2001), pp. 137–149. Earlier photographic studies of human and animal motions were by Etienne-Jules Marey and Eadweard Muybridge. See Sonya F. Premeaux, "The Flying Horse: Eadweard Muybridge's Contribution to Motion Study," *Journal of Applied Management and Entrepreneurship* 8 (October 2003), pp. 36–51.

31. Arthur G. Bedeian, "Finding the 'One Best Way,'" *The Conference Board Record* 13 (June 1976), pp. 38–39.

Under the plan, each man should perform his own job but also train the man below him to be his successor and to learn the next higher position to which he might be promoted. These efforts were part of his goal of developing employees to their fullest potential. As Frank put it, "We want to find the highest task a man can perform permanently, year after year, and thrive, and be happy. A man wanted to do more than get fat; he wants to be happy."[32]

Frank's efforts paralleled what Taylor was attempting, although they differed in terminology. Taylor called his work "time study," and Frank called his "motion study." In practice they were measuring the same thing, with the objective of eliminating motions to reduce fatigue and improve productivity. Frank maintained that the stopwatch was not an essential ingredient to his system, but in one of the many amusing anecdotes about the Gilbreths in *Cheaper by the Dozen*, his son, Frank, Jr., and daughter, Ernestine, wrote that Frank was fascinated with time and always the efficiency expert at home and on the job. He buttoned his vest from the bottom up, instead of top down, because the former took only three seconds and the latter took seven. He used two shaving brushes to lather his face and found that he could reduce shaving time by seventeen seconds. He tried shaving with two razors and found that he could reduce the total shaving time by forty-four seconds, but abandoned this scheme because it took two minutes per bandage applied to the cuts. His children suggested that it was the two lost minutes that bothered him and not the cuts.[33]

SUPPORT FOR THE SCIENTIFIC-MANAGEMENT MOVEMENT

Frank was one of the scientific-management movement's most fervent advocates. Taylor devoted eight pages of *Principles of Scientific Management* to Frank's motion studies of bricklayers. In 1911, Taylor asked Frank to write responses to all the letters he had received after the serialized publication of *The Principles of Scientific Management* in *The American Magazine*. Frank eagerly accepted Taylor's request. Frank's responses became the basis for his *Primer of Scientific Management*. In the 103-page *Primer*, Frank posed common questions about scientific management and provided answers in an effort to explain Taylor's workplace philosophy. The following questions and responses are illustrative examples:

Q. Does [Scientific Management] not make machines out of men?

A. Is a good boxer, or fencer, or golf player a machine? He certainly approaches closely the 100% mark of perfection from the standpoint

---

32. Frank B. Gilbreth quoted in Milton J. Nadworny, "Frank and Lillian Gilbreth and Industrial Relations," *Journal of Industrial Engineering*, Special Reprint 13 (May 1962), p. SR-16.

33. Frank B. Gilbreth, Jr., and Ernestine Gilbreth Carey, *Cheaper by the Dozen* (New York: Crowell, 1948), p. 3.

of the experts in motion study. It is not nearly so important to decide whether or not he is a machine as to decide whether or not it is desirable to have a man trained as near perfection as possible. . . .

Q. Does not the monotony of the highly specialized subdivision of work cause the men to become insane?

A. No, he will not become insane, for if his brain is of such an order that his work does not stimulate it to its highest degree, then he will be promoted, for under Scientific Management each man is specially trained to occupy that place that is the highest that he is capable. . . .

Q. Does not the "speed boss" speed up the men to a point that is injurious to their health?

A. "Speed boss," like "task," is an unfortunate name . . . the speed boss does not tell the men how fast they shall make their motions . . . [but he does] tell the men at what speeds their machines shall run. . . .

Q. If Scientific Management is a good thing for the workers, why do the labor leaders all oppose it?

A. They do not all oppose it. Some oppose it for the simple reason that they do not understand it; the others have visions that Scientific Management is something that will reduce the value of their jobs—and all are afraid, because of the bad treatment that workmen as a whole have had in the past, that Scientific Management is simply a new "confidence game," presented in a more attractive manner than ever before . . . they simply cannot imagine Dr. Taylor or any other practical man working for their interests unless there is a "comeback" somewhere. . . .[34]

Frank also observed that Taylor's ideas and scientific management should not be confused with what Henry Ford was doing with assembly-line production. He had toured a Ford assembly plant and was totally out of sympathy with how jobs were designed:

At the Ford plant he [Frank] saw men at benches too low for them, men stretching farther than their normal reach, men in uncomfortable positions as they put on rear wheels, and much other evidence of making workers adjust to the line rather than making the line conform to the best needs of human beings. Management

---

34. Frank B. Gilbreth, *Primer of Scientific Management* (New York: Van Nostrand Reinhold, 1912), pp. 49–50, 53–54, 65, 887–888. See also Carol Carlson Dean, *Primer of Scientific Management* by Frank B. Gilbreth: A Response to Publication of Taylor's *Principles* in *The American Magazine* 3(1) (1997), pp. 31–41.

claimed that people adjusted to these things and did not mind, just as contractors kept saying that bricklayers did not mind stooping for bricks.[35]

Although Frank had been one of Taylor's most devout disciples, beginning in 1912, the two became increasingly estranged.[36] This was partially due to a problem Frank encountered in applying Taylor's methods, and partially because Frank's innovations made him a competitor with Taylor in the scientific-management movement. Their final break came in 1914 when Frank incurred difficulties implementing the Taylor system at Herrman, Aukam & Company, a New Jersey handkerchief-manufacturing company. Milton C. Herrman complained to Taylor that Frank had overcharged, and that inferior assistants had been assigned in Frank's place while he was on another job in Germany. Taylor wrote Gilbreth concerning these complaints, ending his letter with "Is there anything that you wish me to do in this matter?"[37] Subsequently, Taylor dined with the Gilbreths at their home, received an autographed copy of Lillie's book *The Psychology of Management*, and the Herrmann, Aukam matter was discussed further. We do not know the course of that evening, but Horace King Hathaway took over the consulting work at Herrman, Aukam. Frank was understandably bitter. In the ensuing years, the Gilbreths went their own way, concentrating their efforts on motion, skill, and fatigue problems.

THE FIRST LADY OF MANAGEMENT

In his move away from the Taylor system, Frank was increasingly aided by Lillie, the daughter of a German-born sugar refiner, who spent her early years in Oakland, California. She had attended the University of California at Berkeley, majoring in English and modern languages. A Phi Beta Kappa graduate in 1900, she was the first woman to give the university's commencement day address. After receiving an MA degree in English literature, she began work toward a PhD degree in psychology. She interrupted her studies in mid-1903 for a trip abroad and upon arriving in Boston prior to embarking, was introduced to Frank. Shortly after her return from Europe, he proposed marriage and a dozen children, which by his calculation was the most efficient number. Lillie and Frank married in 1904. After the marriage, Lillie changed the focus of her academic interests to psychology, for she thought that this field would best complement Frank's work. Combining marriage and an ever-growing family with assisting in Frank's work, Lillie continued to do research on her thesis, "The Psychology of Management," and submitted it in 1912. The

---

35. Yost, *Frank and Lillian Gilbreth*, p. 246.

36. See Milton Nadworny, "Frederick Taylor and Frank Gilbreth—Competition in Scientific Management," *Business History Review* 21, no. 1 (Spring 1957), pp. 23–34; and Daniel Nelson, *Frederick W. Taylor and the Rise of Scientific Management* (Madison: University of Wisconsin Press, 1980), pp. 131–136.

37. F. W. Taylor to F. B. Gilbreth, March 11, 1914, Taylor Collection, file 59A.

Lillian Gilbreth, First Lady of Management, 1914. Ronald G. Greenwood Collection, courtesy of Regina A. Greenwood.

University of California informed her that the thesis was acceptable, but that she would have to return to campus for a year of residency before her PhD degree could be granted. Lillie had been led to believe that this requirement would be waived in her case, but university officials were steadfast. Frank was furious and began looking for a publisher for what was to have been Lillie's thesis, one of the first contributions of its kind. The *Industrial Engineering Magazine* published the thesis in serial form (May 1912–May 1913), and it was eventually published in book form by the firm of Sturgis & Walton, but only after she agreed that her name would appear as L. M. Gilbreth and that no publicity would be given to the fact that the author was a woman.[38] Eventually the university authorities agreed that Lillie could spend her residency in any college that granted advanced degrees in industrial psychology or management. Such institutions were scarce at that time, but Frank discovered that Brown University was planning to offer a PhD degree in applied management. At Brown, Lillian wrote a new dissertation, "Some Aspects of Eliminating Waste in Teaching," finally completing her PhD degree requirements in 1915.[39]

Although Lillie was not the originator of industrial psychology, she brought a human element into scientific management through her training, insight, and understanding. In *The Psychology of Management*, she defined her topic as "the effect of the mind that is directing work upon that work which is directed, and the effect of this undirected and directed work upon the mind of the worker."[40] Heretofore, management had been considered an area in which no one could hope to succeed who had not inherited the "knack"; with scientific management, it became possible to base management on "laws" and study it in the classroom. Successful management "lies on the man, not on the work," and scientific management provided a means to make the most of people's efforts. Lillie characterized three historical styles of management: *traditional, transitory*, and *scientific*. Traditional management was the driver, or Marquis of Queensbury, style that followed the unitary line of command and was typified by centralized authority. Lillie adapted the prizefighting term "Marquis of Queensbury" because she felt that it typified the

38. Lillian M. Gilbreth, *The Psychology of Management: The Function of the Mind in Determining, Teaching and Installing Methods of Least Waste* (New York: Sturgis & Walton, 1914).

39. Ronald G. Greenwood, Charles D. Wrege, and Regina A. Greenwood, "Newly Discovered Gilbreth Manuscript," in Kae H. Chung, ed., *Proceedings of the Academy of Management* (August 1983), p. 111.

40. Gilbreth, *The Psychology of Management*, p. 1.

physical and mental contest waged between workers and managers "according to the rules of the game." Transitory management referred to all forms in the interim stage between the traditional and the installation of scientific management. Scientific management, or the Taylor plan of management, described the goal toward which all firms should strive.

Gilbreth compared and contrasted these three styles of management according to how they affected individuality, functionalization, measurement, analysis and synthesis, standardization, records and programs, teaching, incentives, and welfare. On individuality, she noted that psychologists up to that time had been largely concerned with the psychology of crowds. Comparatively little work had been done on the psychology of individuals. Under traditional management, individuality was stifled by the power of the central figure; under scientific management, it became a fundamental principle in selection, incentives, and overall consideration of worker welfare, that is, "general well-being, mental, physical, moral, and financial."[41] The object of scientific management was to develop each worker to the fullest potential by strengthening personal traits, special abilities, and skills. The focus was on how management could develop workers for their mutual benefit, not on workers' use and exploitation, as under the Marquis of Queensbury type of management.

Functionalization promoted worker welfare by improving skills through special-ization, enabling greater pride in output and higher wages; measurement ensured that the workers received the product of their labors; standardization improved morale and prevented workers from becoming a machine; and teaching overcame fear and instilled pride and confidence in the worker. Traditional management relied solely on rewards and punishment, whereas scientific management attempted to enlist worker cooperation. The rewards under scientific management differed because they were predetermined (ensuring against fear of rate cutting), prompt (rather than delayed under profit sharing), and personal (in the sense that workers were rewarded for their efforts and not by their class of work). Under scientific management, workers gained "mental poise and security," rather than the anxiety created by traditional management. Concerning welfare, scientific management promoted regular work, encouraged good personal habits, and fostered the physical, mental, moral, and financial development of workers.

Lillie fully intended to become a practicing psychologist. She soon found, however, that she was devoting most of her time to the rearing of the twelve Gilbreth children. The scientific management of the Gilbreth family and their Montclair, New Jersey, home was immortalized in the best-selling books and movies, *Cheaper by the Dozen* and *Belles on Their Toes*, as well as in the later novel, *Time Out for Happiness*.[42]

———

41. Ibid., p. 30.

42. Frank B. Gilbreth, Jr., and Ernestine Gilbreth Carey, *Cheaper by the Dozen* (New York: Crowell, 1948); Frank B. Gilbreth, Jr. and Ernestine Gilbreth Carey, *Belles on Their Toes* (New York: Crowell, 1950; Frank B. Gilbreth, Jr., *Time Out for Happiness* (New York: Crowell, 1970).

In 1924, tragedy struck the Gilbreths. Shortly before Frank was to leave to attend the First International Management Congress in Prague, Czechoslovakia, he suffered a heart attack and died while talking to Lillie from a telephone booth at the Montclair railroad station. A family meeting was held, and Lillie decided to fulfill Frank's commitments. She sailed five days later and in Prague read the paper he was to have presented, presided at the session he was to have chaired, and was made a member of the Czechoslovakian Masaryk Academy.

Returning to Montclair, Lillie was determined to continue Frank's work. She became president of Gilbreth, Inc., and in the fall of 1924 joined the faculty at Purdue University as a lecturer. In 1935 she was made a professor of management in the Purdue School of Mechanical Engineering, the first woman to hold such an appointment.

A strong psychological thread ran through all of Lillie's work, and she made contributions in several areas, such as the application of management and motion study techniques to the home, rehabilitation of the handicapped,[43] elimination of fatigue, and the use of leisure time to create "happiness minutes." As a result of Frank's service as an Army Major during World War I, he and Lillie became interested in how to use motion study to design jobs to retrain soldiers, especially amputees, so they could resume a productive life after the war. They developed devices to assist the disabled, such as a typewriter for a one-armed person, and Lillie worked with the General Electric Company to redesign home appliances for disabled homemakers.[44] The Gilbreths were among those who lobbied Congress to pass the War Risk Insurance Act for disabled soldiers. Later, this act served to pioneer legislation for those who were not war casualties, but needed vocational rehabilitation.[45]

Lillie also contributed to healing the rift between Frank's motion study and Taylor's time study. In 1921, years after Taylor's death, the Gilbreths issued an "indictment" of time study in the *Bulletin of the Taylor Society*. They attacked Taylor's followers (Carl G. Barth, Dwight V. Merrick, and Sanford E. Thompson) for continuing to promote stopwatch study because of their interest in selling time devices, forms, and books about time study. Further, time study was less precise, therefore less scientific, whereas motion study provided absolutely accurate times

43. See J. Michael Gotcher, "Assisting the Handicapped: The Pioneering Efforts of Frank and Lillian Gilbreth," *Journal of Management* 18 (1992), pp. 5–13; and Franz T. Lohrke, "Motion Study for the Blinded: A Review of the Gilbreths' Work with the Visually Handicapped," *International Journal of Public Administration*, 16(5), pp. 667–682.

44. See Lillian M. Gilbreth, *The Home-Maker and Her Job* (New York: Appleton-Century-Crofts, 1927); and *idem, Management in the Home: Happier Living through Saving Time and Energy* (New York: Dodd, Mead, 1955).

45. Daniel A. Wren and Ronald G. Greenwood, *Management Innovators: The People and Ideas That Have Shaped Modern Business* (New York: Oxford University Press, 1998), p. 146.

and the "one best way."[46] The attack was probably unnecessary. After Taylor's death, his followers began to recognize that to overcome union resistance, they needed to address the widespread belief that time study was synonymous with "speed work."

The Gilbreths' indictment of time study nonetheless led to a rift in relations with Taylor's remaining followers.[47] After Frank's death, however, Lillie wrote in the *Bulletin of the Taylor Society* that time study and motion study were complementary, that the stopwatch was used by Gilbreth's protégés when it was appropriate, but filmed studies were more accurate and useful.[48]

Moving out further from under Frank's shadow, Lillie went on to pioneer in the field now known as human-resource management. She was keenly interested in the scientific selection, placement, and training of workers. Always progressive in her thinking, she displayed a deep appreciation of the human factor in industry. Whereas much of her work is now taken for granted, it was far in advance of its time. More than 50 years ago, she publicly urged an end to discrimination in both hiring and retention of workers over 40.[49] Convinced that programs to hire and train "older" workers were simply "good business," she called for research to measure comparative job performance by age. In the larger public arena, Lillie served under Presidents Hoover, Roosevelt, Eisenhower, Kennedy, and Johnson on committees dealing with civil defense, war production, aging, and rehabilitation of the physically handicapped.

In addition to lecturing throughout the world, Lillie taught at the University of Wisconsin at Madison; Rutgers University at New Brunswick, New Jersey; and Newark College of Engineering. The Gilbreth Medal, named for both Frank and Lillian, was awarded to Lillie in 1931—the only female recipient to date; she was also the only woman to receive the coveted Gantt Gold Medal and the only woman to be awarded the prestigious Comite Internationale de l'Organisation Scientifique (CIOS) Gold Medal. In 1985 she was selected as one of the 100 most important American women of the past 100 years. The recipient of 24 honorary degrees, she was the first woman to be named an honorary member of the ASME, as well as the first elected to the National Academy of Engineering. In 1987, she was honored when the U.S. Postal Service issued a stamp to commemorate her achievements. Is there any doubt about why she has been called the First Lady of Management?

---

46. Frank B. and Lillian M. Gilbreth, "An Indictment of Stop-Watch Time Study," *Bulletin of the Taylor Society* 6 (June 1921), pp. 99–108.

47. See the comments that followed the Gilbreth paper in the *Bulletin of the Taylor Society*, cited above, pp. 109–135.

48. Lillian M. Gilbreth, "The Relations of Time and Motion Study," *Bulletin of the Taylor Society* 13 (June 1928), pp. 126–128.

49. Lillian M. Gilbreth, "Scrapped at Forty," *The Survey* 62 (July 1, 1929), pp. 402–403; Lillian M Gilbreth, "Hiring and Firing: Shall the Calendar Measure Length of Service?" *Factory and Industrial Management* 79 (February 1930), pp. 310–311.

The Gilbreths were a formidable team. He an engineer and she a psychologist, they pooled their talents in search of the "one best way." Their interests ranged widely. They made contributions to materials handling and work methods, to the study of motions and fatigue, to the theory of skill transfer, and to modern human-resource management. The impact of their contributions continues today. Indeed, the configurations for the crew compartment, crew seats, and instrument panel of the National Aeronautical and Space Administration's Apollo command and service modules were designed using techniques pioneered by Frank and Lillian Gilbreth.[50]

EFFICIENCY THROUGH ORGANIZATION: HARRINGTON EMERSON

Harrington Emerson (1853–1931) was a Presbyterian minister's son who believed in the Protestant virtues of thrift and the efficient use of resources. Educated in Europe, he was symbolic of the new breed of "efficiency engineers" (a term he invented) who were bringing new methods of time and cost savings to U.S. industry. Emerson began as a troubleshooter for the general manager of the Burlington Railroad and went on from there to become a consultant to the Atchison, Topeka, & Santa Fe Railroad. Beginning in 1904, Emerson improved methods and equipment, centralized the manufacture of material and tools, and installed an individual reward system. After two years, output was up 57 percent, costs were down 36 percent, and the average pay of Santa Fe workers was up 14.5 percent. Although there was a conflict with unionized shop workers (who lost the struggle), Emerson's methods were praised as an example of what scientific management could do for the nation's railroads.[51] With his success at Santa Fe, Emerson sought to apply his efficiency concepts in other areas. Emerson largely worked on his own. Although he and Fred Taylor corresponded, Emerson was never part of the small group sanctioned to represent Taylor's methods.

Like the Gilbreths, waste and inefficiency were the twin evils that Emerson saw pervading the entire U.S. industrial system. His experience had shown that railroad repair shops averaged 50 percent efficiency and that preventable labor and material wastes were costing the railroad industry $300 million annually (hence his well-publicized Eastern Rate Case testimony of savings of $1 million a day). According to Emerson, inefficiency was not, however, confined to the railroads, but could be found in manufacturing, agriculture, and education. National prosperity was not a function of abundance or lack of natural resources in different countries,

---

50. N. J. Ryker, "Man-Equipment Task System for Apollo," in *The Frank Gilbreth Centennial* (New York: ASME, 1969), pp. 4–36.

51. Carl Graves, "Applying Scientific Management Principles to Railroad Repair Shops—The Santa Fe Experience, 1904–1918," in Jeremy Atack, ed., *Business and Economic History*, 2nd ser., vol. 10 (1981), pp. 124–136.

but rather the "ambition, the desire for success and wealth" of a nation's workers.[52] In Emerson's view, the United States possessed abundant resources and an ambitious workforce, which had led to its rise as a world industrial power, yet it was losing its advantage as a result of inefficiencies in using its resources. To Emerson, one of the greatest problems was the lack of organization. He was convinced that waste could only be reduced by the proper organization of men, machines, and materials.

LINE AND STAFF ORGANIZATION

Taylor's "functional foremanship" did not appeal to Emerson. He agreed with Taylor that the specialized knowledge of staff members was necessary, but differed in how best to use this knowledge. Influenced by his European education, Emerson admired the organizational efforts of Count Helmuth Karl Bernhard Graf von Moltke, who from 1857 to 1888 had developed the modern general staff concept while chief of the Prussian army.[53] The logic behind the general staff concept was straightforward. Each subject vital to military efforts was to be studied to perfection by a separate staff specialist who, with other specialists, formed a supreme general staff to advise a commander.

Emerson sought to apply Moltke's staff concept to industrial practice to bring about "complete parallelism between line and staff, so that every member of the line can at any time have the benefit of staff knowledge and staff assistance."[54] As outlined by Emerson, each firm was to have a chief-of-staff serving over four major subdivisions: one to plan, direct, and advise on the well-being of employees; a second to plan, direct, and advise on structures, machines, tools, and other equipment; a third to plan, direct, and advise on materials, including their purchase, custody, issue, and handling; and the fourth to plan, direct, and advise on methods and conditions, including standards, records, and accounting. Staff knowledge and advice were to be available to every member of the line: "It is the business of staff, not to accomplish work, but to set up standards and ideals, so that the line may work more efficiently."[55] The distinction between Emerson's system of organization and Taylor's functional foremanship is thus apparent: Instead of giving one person the responsibility and authority over each workplace function, Emerson left supervision and authority to line managers, who then accessed staff for specialized knowledge and advice. This shift maintained the advantages of specialized knowledge and facilitated coordination without the disadvantages associated with violating the unity of command principle.

---

52. Harrington Emerson, *Efficiency as a Basis for Operations and Wages* (New York: Engineering Magazine, 1911), p. 37.

53. Ibid., pp. 64–66. Karl von Clausewitz noted the use of the general staff concept in the Prussian Army as early as 1793. Karl von Clausewitz, *On War* (New York: Random House, 1943), p. 489. Originally published in 1832.

54. Emerson, *Efficiency as a Basis for Operations and Wages*, p. 69.

55. Ibid., p. 112.

PRINCIPLES OF EFFICIENCY

Emerson made other contributions in cost accounting, in using Hollerith tabulating machines for accounting records, and in setting standards for judging worker and shop efficiency. In cost accounting, Emerson made a clear distinction between historical cost accounting (descriptive) and "the new cost accounting," which estimated what costs should be before work commenced. Although others had written about cost-accounting standards, Emerson appears to have been the first to develop a system of standardized costs for more accurately assessing relative efficiencies in materials and services.[56] Emerson also devised an incentive system that paid workers a 20 percent bonus for 100 percent efficiency; above 100 percent efficiency, workers received their standard wages for time saved plus a 20 percent bonus for the time worked. For example, at 100 percent efficiency, the bonus was 20 cents per one dollar of wages; at 120 percent efficiency, the bonus was 40 cents per one dollar of wages (i.e., 40 cents = 20 cents for bonus and 20 cents for working 20 percent more efficiently).[57]

Ironically, Emerson's efficiency work was somewhat overshadowed by the notoriety given to Taylor's task-management system in the Eastern Rate Case hearings. Subsequent to the hearings, Emerson published *Twelve Principles of Efficiency*, which became another landmark in the history of management thought. A chapter was devoted to each of the eponymous principles; broadly conceived, the first five concerned relations with people, and the remainder concerned methods, institutions, and systems. The principles were considered to be interdependent and to be coordinated to form a structure for building a management system. In the book's preface, Emerson stated his basic premise: "It is not labor, not capital, not land, which has created modern wealth or is creating it today. It is ideas that create wealth, and what is wanted is more ideas—more uncovering of natural reservoirs, and less labor and capital and land per unit of production."[58]

No modern author could state the contemporary challenges facing today's global organizations more cogently. For Emerson, ideas were the dominant force for eliminating waste and creating a more efficient industrial system. Principles were the instruments to reach this goal, and the basis of all principles was the line-staff form of organization. To Emerson "defective organization" was the "the industrial hookworm disease."[59] With respect to Emerson's twelve principles of efficiency:

---

56. Ibid., p. 102ff; and Harrington Emerson, "Standardization and Labor Efficiency in Railroad Shops," *Engineering Magazine* 42 (1911), pp. 10–16. See also Paul Sutcliffe, "The Role of Labor Variances in Harrington Emerson's 'New Gospel of Efficiency' (1908)," *Accounting and Business Research* 12 (Spring 1982), pp. 115–123; and Nathan Kranoski, "The Historical Development of Standard Costing Systems until 1920," in E. N. Coffman, ed., *The Academy of Accounting Historians Working Paper Series* 2 (1979), pp. 206–218.

57. Emerson, *Efficiency as a Basis for Operations and Wages*, pp. 193–196.

58. Harrington Emerson, *The Twelve Principles of Efficiency* (New York: Engineering Magazine, 1913), p. x.

59. Ibid., p. 29.

The first principle was "clearly defined ideals." This principle made explicit the need for agreement among employees and employers on workplace goals ("ideals") and the importance of everyone pulling in a "straight line." Emerson hoped to reduce intraorganizational conflict, vagueness, uncertainty, and the aimlessness that arose when people did not understand or share a common purpose. The second principle, common sense, exhorted managers to take a larger view of problems and to seek special knowledge and advice wherever they may be found. Employees at all levels who had something of value to contribute were encouraged to participate in problem solving.[60] The third principle, competent counsel, was related to the second principle, in that it pertained to assembling an experienced and knowledgeable staff. Discipline became the fourth principle and provided for obedience and adherence to workplace rules. It was a foundation for the other eleven principles and prevented anarchy. The fifth and final principle pertaining to people was the fair deal. Peace, harmony, and high performance were dependent on fairness in all employee–employer relations. Rather than be patronizing or altruistic, the employee–employer relationship was to be based on mutual advantage.

The seven principles pertaining to workplace methods were more mechanistic and largely self-explanatory: "reliable, immediate, accurate, and permanent records" (information and accounting systems); "dispatching" (planning and routing of work); "standards and schedules" (methods and time for tasks); "standardized conditions"; "standardized operations"; "written standard practice instructions"; and "efficiency reward" (rewards proportionate to efficiency). Each principle was liberally sprinkled with examples from Emerson's consulting experience and formed a thorough, though often redundant, statement of his workplace philosophy.

Emerson achieved renown in his own time, and his consulting firm was a seedbed for others who became distinguished consultants and executives. These included Earl K. Wennerlund, later a vice president of production at General Motors; Charles E. Knoeppel, who would form his own consulting firm and develop the "profitgraph," a forerunner to the breakeven chart; and Herbert N. Casson, who would take efficiency methods and scientific management to Great Britain.[61] Originally called Emerson Engineers, even though none of the members of the association were engineers, the firm later took the name Emerson Consultants.

Emerson testified before the special committee of the House of Representatives (1911–1912) to investigate the Taylor and other efficiency systems; helped found the Efficiency Society (1912); served on the Federated American Engineering Societies' Committee on the Elimination of Waste in Industry (1921); and was instrumental in the founding of the Association of Management Consulting Firms (1929).

---

60. William F. Muhs, "Worker Participation in the Progressive Era: An Assessment by Harrington Emerson," *Academy of Management Review* 7 (January 1982), pp. 99–102.

61. William F. Muhs, "The Emerson Engineers: A Look at One of the First Management Consulting Firms in the U.S.," in John A. Pearce II and Richard B. Robinson, Jr., eds., *Proceedings of the Annual Meeting of the Academy of Management* (1986), pp. 123–127. For extensive insights into the life and work of Herbert N. Casson, see Morgan Witzel, ed., *The Biographical Dictionary of Management* (Bristol, England: Thoemmes Press, 2001), pp. 137–144.

Emerson has been called the "high priest of efficiency" for his efforts to eliminate waste in industry.[62] His contributions were unique in advocating a line–staff form of organization and developing standards for use in cost accounting. His testimony at the Eastern Rate Case hearings brought the Brandeis-coined "scientific management" phrase and the work of Fred Taylor to the world's attention. An early management consultant, he recognized the need for ethical standards of practice and, when consulting engineers primarily focused on technical problems, he focused equal attention on managerial problems.

The Gospel in Public-Sector Organizations: Morris L. Cooke

While Taylor, Barth, the Gilbreths, Gantt, and Emerson were eliminating waste in industrial enterprises, Morris Llewellyn Cooke (1872–1960) was extending the gospel of efficiency to public-sector organizations. Cooke attended Lehigh Preparatory School and Lehigh University, graduating in 1895 with a degree in mechanical engineering. After an apprenticeship at Cramp's Shipyard (Philadelphia), he went to work in various companies and long before he had met or heard of Fred Taylor, he was applying a "questioning method" to the waste he saw all around him. As Taylor's work became more widely known, Cooke became an avid defender of Taylor's methods. He eventually met Taylor and evidently impressed him, because Taylor asked Cooke to become a member of a committee attempting to apply scientific management to the administration of ASME. Taylor personally financed the study and paid Cooke's salary; during the year-and-a-half study, their friendship grew, and Cooke soon became an insider in the scientific-management movement.

Distrustful of the so-called new breed of efficiency engineers, Taylor designated only four men as qualified enough to be considered "scientific management experts": Barth, Gantt, Horace King Hathaway, and Cooke.[63] Known as a friend of labor, Cooke once saw a sign at a factory gate reading, "Hands Entrance"; he asked the owner, "Where do the heads and hearts enter?"—the sign was promptly removed.[64] Perhaps he was being flippant, but he made his point—scientific management called for more than hands.

In 1909, the president of the Carnegie Foundation for the Advancement of Teaching asked Taylor to help determine if the best use was being made of university faculty and facilities. At Taylor's suggestion, the Foundation sent Cooke to visit nine

---

62. [W. Jerome Arnold] "Famous Firsts: High Priest of Efficiency," *Business Week*, June 22, 1963, pp. 100, 104.

63. Frank B. Copley, *Frederick W. Taylor: Father of Scientific Management* (New York: Harper & Brothers, 1923), vol. 2, p. 357.

64. Kenneth E. Trombley, *The Life and Times of a Happy Liberal: A Biography of Morris Llewellyn Cooke* (New York: Harper & Brothers, 1954), p. 10.

universities and report on their organization from a businessman's viewpoint. The resulting report was a bombshell in the academic world.[65] Although only physics departments were studied, because they were believed representative of the existing level of teaching and research, Cooke included nothing in his final report that he did not feel applied to other departments as well. The report was quite lengthy and detailed, and Cooke attempted something that few were then, or are today, eager to do—that is, measure the cost of inputs relative to outputs in teaching and research.

His findings were quite upsetting: inbreeding (an institution hiring its own graduates) was widespread; managerial practices in education were even worse than the acknowledged poor state of industrial practice; committee management was a curse; departments enjoyed excessive autonomy, which worked against universitywide coordination of course offerings and scheduling; pay was based on longevity not merit; and life tenure for professors should be scrapped and unfit teachers retired. Cooke believed that professors should spend more time in teaching and research, leaving administration to specialists rather than faculty committees. Assistants should be used more widely, allowing higher-priced talent to take more complex jobs, and the costs of teaching and research should be more closely controlled by a university's central administration. Cooke concluded that "there are very few, if any, of the broader principles of management which obtain generally in the industrial and commercial world which are not more or less applicable to the college field, and so far as he discovered no one of them is now generally observed."[66] Initial reactions to the report were predictable: Richard Cockburn Maclaurin, president of the Massachusetts Institute of Technology, said it read "as if the author received his training in a soap factory."[67]

BOXLY TALKS

Throughout this period Taylor continued to give his "Boxly talks." Taylor requested that Cooke analyze his standard talk with an eye to improving its flow and content. A stenographer was hired to transcribe Taylor's June 4, 1907, presentation. It was also suggested that a transcription of Taylor's remarks might provide a basis for Cooke to write a book about the Taylor system. In the preface to his talk, Taylor assured his audience that task management (his preferred term before the popularized label of scientific management) was superior to previous ideas:

> I ought to say at the start that what I am going to say will sound extremely conceited. It will sound as though we were very much stuck on ourselves, but we are not so much stuck on ourselves as we

---

65. Morris L. Cooke, *Academic and Industrial Efficiency* (New York: Carnegie Foundation for the Advancement of Teaching Bulletin No. 5, 1910).

66. Cooke quoted in "Scores Management of Our Universities," *New York Times*, (December 19, 1910), p. 1.

67. Trombley, *Cooke*, p. 11.

are on the idea. I am very much stuck on the idea and not particularly on ourselves, although the general impression will be that we have a wonderfully high opinion of ourselves and of everything we are doing.

I want to try to convince you that the task idea, because that is what is back of everything we do, is overwhelmingly better than the other idea in its practical results.[68]

Taylor's two-hour talk, plus a question-and-answer period, was strongly worded and included his well-worn pig-iron-handling anecdote. When Taylor read the stenographic transcription, he was surprised at what he had actually said and responded, "Did I say that?"[69] He vowed to be more careful in the future about what he said and how he spoke about task management.

After Cooke acquired a copy of the Boxly talk transcription, he told Taylor that he did, indeed, intend to write a book about the Taylor system, tentatively titled *Industrial Management*, to enable people to more fully understand Taylor's methods. In the course of events, Cooke's intended book was not published but, according to Wrege and Stotka, became Taylor's *The Principles of Scientific Management*. Taylor "attached his name to someone else's work," and Cooke "created a classic."[70] Was the "Father of Scientific Management" a plagiarist? Or, was this a mutual agreement between Taylor and Cooke to promote Taylor's ideas? The story is convoluted, but it merits examination.

The basis for Cooke's *Industrial Management* was Taylor's Boxly talk, which Cooke was to improve. In 1907, Cooke wrote Taylor that he intended "to edit 'Industrial Management' ... because I think to write a popular exposition of the Taylor System will be a thing worthwhile."[71] At one point, while Cooke was "boiling down the Boxly talks," he and Taylor were to be coauthors. Cooke edited an initial manuscript that had been prepared, rewrote thirty-one pages of Taylor's sixty-two page Boxly talk, and added forty-three pages from other sources. The resulting Cooke manuscript was never published, but sixty-nine pages of *Industrial Management* (which began with the stenographer's transcription of Taylor's talk) were incorporated into Taylor's *The Principles of Scientific Management*.[72] On this basis, Wrege and Stotka concluded that Cooke "created the classic" and that "Taylor's use of Cooke's manuscript is merely an example of [Taylor's] tendency to publish, under his own name, material written by others."[73]

---

68. "Report of a Lecture by and Questions put to Mr. F. W. Taylor: A Transcript," *Journal of Management History* 1 (1995), pp. 8–32. The introduction is by Charles D. Wrege, pp. 4–7.

69. Copley, *Taylor*, vol. 2, p. 284.

70. Charles D. Wrege and Anne Marie Stotka, "Cooke Creates a Classic: The Story Behind F. W. Taylor's *Principles of Scientific Management*," *Academy of Management Review* 3 (October, 1978), pp. 736–749.

71. Ibid., p. 738.

72. Wrege and Greenwood, *Taylor*, p. 182.

73. Wrege and Stotka, p. 749.

Is there another side to this story? On the *Industrial Management* manuscript he was preparing, Cooke printed this comment:

> ... this chapter [Chapter 2] is very largely a recital of Mr. Taylor's personal experiences in the development of scientific management, and as such has been written by himself in the first person.[74]

Cooke told Taylor that he would forgo any profits from *Industrial Management*, but Taylor responded that he would assign all royalties from *The Principles of Scientific Management* to Cooke. The archives of Harper & Brothers, Taylor's publisher, indicate that $3,207.05 in royalties was paid to Cooke from June 1911 (the month *The Principles of Scientific Management* was published) until the last quarter of 1913.[75] According to Dean:

> ... the royalty money was likely a minor matter to both Taylor and Cooke. Neither of them needed the royalty money, as suggested by the fact that Cooke was making nearly $50,000 a year through Taylor [from consulting referrals]—a considerable sum considering the time. The royalty payment to Cooke was likely a mere gesture on Taylor's part for Cooke's contribution to Taylor's "principles."[76]

A reasonable conclusion is that Cooke contributed to, but did not write, *The Principles of Scientific Management*. He edited and enriched Taylor's talks at his home and duly received royalties for his efforts. It was an arrangement agreed on and fulfilled, indicating the solid relationship that existed between Taylor and Cooke.

PUBLIC ADMINISTRATION

In addition to working closely with Taylor and consulting with various businesses, Cooke also became involved in public administration. In 1911, Rudolph Blankenburg, a reform candidate, was elected Mayor of Philadelphia. He asked Taylor to assist with municipal administration. Once more, Taylor sent Cooke into the breach. Cooke had been itching for reform ever since, as a poll watcher, he had been bullied by a machine politician. Cooke served (1911–1915) as Director of Public Works in the Blankenburg administration. He found the Department of Public Works honeycombed with corruption. Cooke insisted that government be nonpolitical and use science and technology for the public good. In four years he saved the city over 1 million in garbage–collection costs, achieved a $1.25 million reduction in utility

---

74. Ibid., pp. 746-747.

75. *Archives of Harper & Brothers (1817–1914)*. Reels 31 and 32 of microfilm published by permission of Harper and Row and the Butler Library, Columbia University. Index compiled by Christopher Feeney, University Press, Cambridge, 1982. We are indebted to Carol Carlson (Dean) Gunn for a photocopy.

76. Carol Carlson Dean, "The Principles of Scientific Management by Fred Taylor: Exposures in Print beyond the Private Printing," *Journal of Management History* 3 (1997), pp. 11–12.

rates, fired 1,000 inefficient workers, established pension and benefit funds, opened channels of communication for workers and managers, and moved municipal administration from smoke-filled rooms into the sunshine. In his book, *Our Cities Awake*, Cooke argued for the use of scientific management to improve municipal administration. As Public Works Director, Cooke successfully established a functional management organization patterned after Taylor's ideas, revamped budgeting procedures, hired numerous experts to replace political favorites, advocated hiring a professional city manager, and sought to replace committees by individuals who had responsibility and authority. He called for cooperation and full workplace participation by employees at all levels:

> Here then is a work in which we can all have a hand, a work which will always be ineffectually done if it is confined to well-educated and highly trained men at the top . . . administrative leadership will in the future more and more consist in getting the largest possible number "into the play" in having the great body of employees increasingly critical in their judgments about both their own work and the work which is going on around them.[77]

Cooke saw that it was not the system, but the public's confidence in the system that made scientific management effective.

After serving in the Blankenburg administration, Cooke opened his own consulting firm in 1916. Like other scientific-management pioneers, he contributed his knowledge to the War Department during World War I, serving as executive assistant to the United States Shipping Board. Always concerned with gaining the cooperation of labor, he became increasingly interested in the growing national labor movement. He became a friend and advisor to Samuel Gompers, president of the American Federation of Labor. Cooke saw a need to bring labor and management together in a time of mutual antagonism. He held that labor was just as responsible for production as management and stressed that improved production was an effective barrier against unemployment and low wages. In this last book, coauthored with Philip Murray, Cooke advised management to "tap labor's brains," so as to benefit from the ideas of those closest to the work being done.[78] As the first president of the Steel Workers Organizing Committee (SWOC), the first president of the United Steelworkers of America (USWA), and the longest-serving president of the Congress of Industrial Organizations (CIO), Murray was one of the most important labor leaders of the era.

---

77. Morris L. Cooke, *Our Cities Awake* (New York: Doubleday, 1918), p. 98.

78. Morris L. Cooke and Philip Murray, *Organized Labor and Production* (New York: Harper & Brothers, 1940).

During the administration of Franklin D. Roosevelt, Cooke held numerous positions, chief among them being Director of the Rural Electrification Administration (1935–1937). In 1950, President Harry S. Truman appointed Cooke chairman of the President's Water Resources Policy Commission. When Cooke was asked by his biographer to list his lifetime accomplishments, he replied, "Rural electrification, inexpensive electricity in our homes, progress in labor-management relations, conservation of our land and water, and scientific management in industry."[79] Cooke sought to apply the tenets of scientific management to public administration. He worked to further cooperation between labor and management and favored increased worker participation in workplace decision making. If scientific management was to make headway in the twentieth century, it required someone like Cooke to open new vistas in nonindustrial organizations and to gain the support of the U.S. labor movement.

SUMMARY

The adolescence of a movement is analogous to life's teenage years in growth, rebellion, and the search for the mellowing of adulthood. From Taylor's notion of science in management at Midvale and Bethlehem to the maturity of the movement in the 1920s, the diversity of scientific management's adolescence is reflected in the life stories of the individuals examined in this chapter. Carl G. Barth was the true believer who remained a faithful adherent to Taylor's orthodoxy. Henry L. Gantt began under Taylor's guidance, contributed significantly, and then developed his own unique ideas. The Gilbreths combined motion study with Taylor's time study, studied fatigue, and emphasized the psychology of scientific management. Harrington Emerson embraced Taylor's notion of efficiency while rejecting his "functional foremanship" concept and differential piece-rate wage incentive plan. Morris L. Cooke, nurtured by Taylor, introduced scientific management to the public sector and sought a rapprochement between management and organized labor. These pioneers were at the vanguard in spreading the gospel of efficiency in the embryonic days of scientific management. As we will see, however, changing times would bring new challenges.

---

79. Trombley, *Cooke*, p. 249.

CHAPTER 9

The Human Factor: Preparing the Way

S cientific management was born and nurtured in an era that emphasized science as a way of life and living. As noted in Chapter 7, in the first decade of the twentieth century, concern over the depletion of America's resources was voiced by President Theodore Roosevelt and others. This concern was seen as preliminary to a larger question of national efficiency and the misuse of both physical and human resources. One manifestation of this concern was an apprehension regarding the efficiency of "industrial and manufacturing establishments" in general and, in particular, the "men...working in these establishments." For Fred Taylor and the band of scientific-management pioneers that had gathered around him, the "blundering" methods used by management were "ill-directed" and responsible for an untold waste in human effort.[1] Their solution to eliminating this waste was the careful selection and development of "first-class" workers. Simply stated, their goal was to put "The Right Man in the Right Place." This chapter examines how modern personnel management (or as we know it today, "human-resource management") grew from "welfare work," on the one hand, and scientific management on the other.[2] Even more broadly inspired social forces were also at work during the same period, and these are examined as they affected industrial psychology, industrial sociology, and industrial relations. Together, these forces set the stage for later developments in labor-management relations, the human relations school of management, and eventually, the field of organizational behavior.

---

1. Frederick W. Taylor, *The Principles of Scientific Management* (New York: Harper & Brothers, 1911), pp. 5–8.

2. Henry Eilbirt, "The Development of Personnel Management in the United States," *Business History Review* 33 (Autumn 1959), pp. 345–364.

Personnel Management: A Dual Heritage

Modern personnel management, or as it is also known, personnel administration, has a dual heritage. This heritage may be traced to the early 1880s and the near simultaneous emergence of the scientific-management and "welfare work" movements. Scientific management was essentially an engineering approach that focused on the need for the "strictest economy in the use of workers."[3] By contrast, the roots of welfare work lie in religion and philanthropy and the desire to improve "the general tenor of American living and the standards of the poor and unfortunate."[4]

PERSONNEL AS WELFARE WORK

Paternalism, whether by state, church, or business, is as old as civilization. The feudal system of the Middle Ages was based on paternalistic ideals, and many early factory owners, such as Robert Owen, sought to ameliorate the anguish of working life and to "elevate" their employees by providing recreational activities, dancing lessons, meals, housing, education, sanitation, and so on. The Waltham System of textile manufacturing, popular in the early 1800s, had paternalistic overtones as management looked after the education, housing, and morals of employees (see Chapter 5). The McLane Report of 1832 depicted the typical manufacturing establishment as family owned and with relatively few employees. At this stage of our nation's industrial growth, that is, when firms were smaller, those who owned the firms also managed them. The rapid growth of the U.S. economy in the latter third of the nineteenth century, however, created unprecedented accumulations of physical and human resources in industrial and manufacturing establishments. This rapid growth moved the means of production from small workshops and homes to factories, where it was possible to manufacture products on a grand scale. It also changed relations between owner–managers and their employees. The Social Gospel movement emerged as a counterpoint to social Darwinism. Social Gospel activists felt that they had a duty to reform social and economic conditions. Rather than waiting for a gradual improvement in the poverty level and the quality of life found in slum neighborhoods, one place where immediate reform action could be taken was in improving personnel and industrial relations practices. In large measure, the responses of the era's managers built on the familial traditions of the past as expressed through "industrial betterment" or "welfare work."[5]

---

3. Ordway Tead and Henry C. Metcalf, *Personnel Administration: Its Principles and Practices.* (New York: McGraw-Hill, 1920), p. 27.

4. Eilbirt, "Development of Personnel Management," p. 348.

5. Edwin E. Witte, *The Evolution of Managerial Ideas in Industrial Relations*, Bulletin 27. (Ithaca, NY: New York State School of Industrial and Labor Relations, Cornell University), 1954.

The first recorded attempt to establish a "welfare work office" was at the National Cash Register Company in 1897. The company's founder and president, John H. Patterson, appointed Lena H. Tracy as the firm's first welfare director.[6] Joseph Bancroft and Sons appointed a welfare secretary in 1899, the H. J. Heinz Company employed a social secretary in 1902, the Colorado Fuel and Iron Company named a social secretary in 1901, and the International Harvester Company followed in 1903. Other cases include Filene's Department Stores, the Natural Food Company, Plymouth Cordage, John B. Stetson Company, and Westinghouse Electric.

Although employee welfare programs were, in part, motivated by a desire to counter a growing union movement, they also resulted from the realization that "employees' productivity depended quite as much upon their environment and lives in the fourteen hours away from work as the ten hours while at work."[7] As a consequence, many welfare programs extended beyond the workplace into employees' homes and included their spouses and children. Thus, "welfare secretaries" were tasked with improving the lives of employees, both off and on the job. The secretaries handled employee grievances, operated dispensaries, provided recreation and education activities, arranged job transfers, administered dining facilities, prepared nutritious menus, and oversaw the moral behavior of employees, especially unmarried females.[8] Many of the era's welfare secretaries were women with backgrounds in vocational guidance and social work. In addition to Lena H. Tracy at National Cash Register, other women welfare secretaries included Gertrude B. Beeks at International Harvester Company, Elizabeth Briscoe at Bancroft and Sons, Florence Hughes at New Jersey Zinc, Laura Ray at Greenhut-Siegel, Aggie Dunn at H. J. Heinz, Lucy Bannister at Westinghouse, and Diana Hirschler at Filene's.[9]

The exact role of welfare secretaries, however, was not always clearly defined, as the experience of Henry L. Gantt at Bancroft Mills illustrates. Bancroft's first welfare secretary, Elizabeth Briscoe, was appointed in 1902. In 1903, Bancroft experienced

---

6. See Lena Harvey Tracy, *How My Heart Sang: The Story of Pioneer Industrial Welfare Work* (New York: R. R. Smith Publisher, 1950); and John H. Patterson, "Altruism and Sympathy as Factors in Works Administration," *Engineering Magazine* 20 (1900) pp. 577–602; reprinted with photographs of NCR's activities in Wren, *Early Management Thought* (Aldershot, England; Dartmouth, 1997), pp. 403–428. Company bands and singing groups were also popular for morale building. See Kenneth S. Clark, *Music in Industry* (New York: National Bureau for the Advancement of Music, 1929).

7. Witte, *Evolution of Managerial Ideas*, p. 8.

8. For more on the duties of social secretaries, see William H. Tolman, *Social Engineering* (New York: McGraw, 1909), pp. 48–59. See also Stuart D. Brandes, *American Welfare Capitalism: 1880–1940* (Chicago: University of Chicago Press, 1976); and Nick Mandell, *The Corporation as Family: The Gendering of Corporate Welfare, 1890–1930* (Chapel Hill: University of North Carolina Press, 2002).

9. Lee Anne G. Kryder, "Transforming Industrial Welfare Work into Modern Personnel Management: The Contributions of Gertrude B. Beeks," Paper presented at the Annual Academy of Management meeting, Dallas, August 16, 1983; and Charles D. Wrege and Bernice M. Lattanzio, "Pioneers in Personnel Management: A Historical Study of the Neglected Accomplishment of Women in Personnel Management," *Working Paper Series*, Management History Division, Academy of Management, 1977.

severe productivity problems, and its owner, John Bancroft, employed Gantt as a consultant. Gantt's recommendations soon ran counter to Briscoe's welfare efforts. When Gantt, for instance, suggested dismissing inefficient employees, Briscoe objected. She insisted that all workers, inefficient or not, should be retained. Gantt argued that poor personnel selection and assignments were contributing to the productivity problem that he had been hired to solve. Although Gantt was able to improve work methods, upgrade training, and install a bonus system in one department and, thus, increase productivity, he was unable to fully implement his recommendations. When Gantt completed his consultancy, in 1909, it appeared that welfare work had won out over scientific management.[10] In later years (1911–1927), however, Bancroft melded "welfarism" and scientific management to fit its owner's Quaker beliefs about how employees should be treated and still improve efficiency. Thus, Gantt may have "lost" initially, but in the long run it was seen that welfare work and scientific management could complement one another by enhancing both employee relations and productivity.

Nonetheless, during the years 1900 to 1915, "welfare work and even the term became increasingly discredited," as a result of being associated with "hysterical elements" and "charity."[11] Moreover, as welfare work reached further into employees' personal lives, it became resented, with employees objecting to being told what they could or could not do on their own time and in their own homes. Although welfare secretaries and welfare work offices are no longer part of the modern workplace, their legacy survives in the "fringe benefits" and industrial relations polices of contemporary human-resource programs.

SCIENTIFIC MANAGEMENT AND PERSONNEL

Implicit in Taylor's functional foremanship is the notion that the job of most foremen is "simply too big for one man."[12] At the turn of the twentieth century, at the gates of many factories across the country, unskilled workers would line up each morning, and a foreman would appear to hire the day's labor. This often, however, amounted to little more than hiring friends or the well-connected, or even in some

---

10. Daniel Nelson and Stuart Campbell, "Taylorism versus Welfare Work in American Industry: H. L. Gantt and the Bancrofts," *Business History Review* 46, no. 1 (Spring 1972), pp. 1–16. Nelson and Campbell concluded that Gantt lost this battle at Bancroft; however, there is other evidence that Gantt introduced Bancroft's senior management to options they would pursue later. For this latter viewpoint, see Peter B. Petersen, "Henry Gantt's Work at Bancroft: The Option of Scientific Management," in John A. Pearce II and Richard B. Robinson, eds., *Proceedings of the Annual Meeting of the Academy of Management* (1985), pp. 134–138. For more on Briscoe's contributions, see Peter B. Petersen, "A Pioneer in Personnel," *Personnel Administrator* 33 (June 1988), pp. 60–64.

11. Eilbirt, "Development of Personnel Management," p. 351. See also Meyer Bloomfield, "Man Management: A New Profession in the Making," in Daniel Bloomfield, ed., *Problems in Personnel Management* (New York: H. W. Wilson, 1923), p. 13.

12. Ibid., p. 359.

cases, selling jobs. As foremen had the power to hire, they also had the right to fire. Although Taylor did not provide for a personnel department per se, he did suggest that an Employment Bureau should be part of a central Planning Department, and one of the specialized functions he identified was "shop-disciplinarian." Taylor listed the duties of the shop-disciplinarian as selecting and discharging employees, keeping performance records, handling disciplinary problems, administering wage payments, and serving as a peacemaker. As Eilbirt notes, "by this route, Scientific Management arrived at the borders of personnel administration."[13] Several of the earliest "employment departments" were founded by Taylor disciples, including Henry P. Kendall at Plimpton Press and Richard A. Feiss and Mary B. Gilson at Joseph & Feiss Company.[14]

Created in 1910, the Employment Department at Plimpton Press was managed by Jane C. Williams. Succinctly stated, its purpose was to achieve savings by minimizing human costs. Williams's duties included determining the suitability of job applicants, training and orienting workers, maintaining performance records, interviewing employees monthly, reviewing efficiency ratings every six months to determine pay increases, hearing grievances, providing a nurse in case of accident or illness, maintaining a library of popular and technical magazines and books, helping families with financial counseling, and operating a lunchroom. This was undoubtedly the most advanced employment department of its day.[15]

Ordway Tead dated the appearance of the modern personnel department at "about 1912," when some dozen companies had established distinct functions devoted to personnel work.[16] The first national association to deal with personnel matters was the National Association of Corporation Schools (NACS), founded in 1913. Its goal was to advance the training and education of industrial employees. By 1917, the NACS had expanded its reach to include "human relations" (meaning, employee relations). The second national personnel manager association was founded in 1918. The National Association of Employment Managers (NAEM) grew out of a local Employment Managers Association started in Boston in 1912 by Meyer Bloomfield. In 1922, the NACS and the NAEM merged to form the National Personnel Association.

In 1915, Harlow Person introduced the first training program for employment managers at Dartmouth College's Amos Tuck School of Administration and Finance.

---

13. Ibid., p. 348.

14. See Mary B. Gilson, *What's Past Is Prologue* (New York: Harper and Brothers, 1940), pp. ix–x; see also Charles D. Wrege and Ronald G. Greenwood, "Mary B. Gilson—A Historical Study of the Neglected Accomplishments of a Woman Who Pioneered in Personnel Management," in Jeremy Atack, ed., *Business and Economic History*, 2nd ser., vol. 11 (Urbana, Ill.: College of Commerce, University of Illinois, April 1982), pp. 35–42.

15. Jane C. Williams, "The Reduction of Labor Turnover in the Plimpton Press," *The Annals of the American Academy* 71 (May 1917), pp. 71–81.

16. Ordway Tead, "Personnel Administration," in Edwin R. A. Seligman (Ed.), *Encyclopedia of the Social Sciences*, vol. 12 (New York: 1934), p. 88.

The program required preparing "a thesis which is the solution of a specific problem of management in a specific plant."[17] Through his role in the Society for the Promotion of the Science of Management (SPSM), later renamed The Taylor Society, Person was able to promote employment management, or as it was called by the 1920s, "personnel administration," as a means for treating workers with the fairness and dignity to which they were entitled.[18]

Despite rising professionalism, personnel practices of the era commonly reflected earlier welfare programs. For example, in March 1913, Ford Motor Company, faced with a tight labor market and 10 percent annual employee turnover in its factories, created a Sociological Department to improve employees' standard of living. On January 5, 1914, Ford cut the length of its workday from nine to eight hours, raised the minimum wage it paid from $2.50 to $5.00 per day, and announced a plan to share $10,000,000 of profits with employees. Over 15,000 would-be employees besieged Ford's Detroit plant seeking some 3,000 available jobs. Fire hoses had to be used to disperse the crowd. Company founder Henry Ford saw the $5.00 a day wage as "neither charity nor wages [but] simply profit sharing."[19] Of the $5.00, $2.34 was earned for working and $2.66 *could* be earned if employees led a moral life. Ford feared that a doubling in pay would lead the company's employees astray, so he hired one hundred "advisers" to visit the employees' homes to ensure that the homes were neat and clean and to verify that the employees did not drink too much, that their sex lives were without tarnish, and that they used their leisure time wisely. Ford's concern for his employees' private lives, however, lasted less than two years. It ended in November 1915, when Ford engaged his Episcopalian pastor, the Very Reverend Samuel S. Marquis, to head the Sociological Department. Ford told Marquis, "There is too much of this snooping around in private affairs. We'll change this from a Sociology department to an Education department."[20] Thereafter, the home visits stopped, and the Ford Company turned its attention to advising and educating its employees.

It has been estimated that from 1915 to 1920 at least 200 personnel departments were established in the United States.[21] "Present development," Tead and Metcalf wrote, in 1920, "is in the direction of a new science and a newly appreciated art—the science and art of personnel administration."[22] A Bureau of Labor Statistics study for the years 1913 to 1919 determined that modern employment practices reduced labor

---

17. Harlow S. Person, "University Schools of Business and the Training of Employment Executives," *Annals of the American Academy of Political and Social Science* 65 (May 1916), p. 126.

18. Witte, *Evolution of Managerial Ideas*, p. 9.

19. Henry Ford quoted in "Ford Gives Reasons for Profit Sharing," *New York Times* (January 9, 1914), p. 1.

20. John R. Commons, "Henry Ford, Miracle Maker," *The Independent* 102 (May 1, 1920), p. 160.

21. Daniel Nelson, "'A Newly Appreciated Art': The Development of Personnel Work at Leeds & Northrup, 1915–1923," *Business History Review*, 44 (Winter 1970), pp. 520–535.

22. Tead and Metcalf, *Personnel Administration*, p. 1.

turnover, thus decreasing training and other costs, while also providing workers with more stable employment, especially in larger firms. The study found that the larger the firm, the lower the turnover rate. Larger firms could pay higher wages, provide better working conditions, and guarantee stable employment. They were also more likely to have a central department devoted to employee welfare.[23] Interest in improved employment practices was not confined to the United States. In Great Britain, for example, during the 1920s, B. Seebohm Rowntree, owner of the Cocoa Works at York, employed a sociologist in a psychological department to supervise employee education, health, canteens, housing, and recreation. Rowntree has been called the "Father of British Management."[24]

Interest in the potential of personnel management to increase employee productivity led to significant changes in assumptions about human behavior. For instance, Tead partially backed away from an earlier "instinct" theory of behavior he had developed to coauthor an early personnel administration text with Henry C. Metcalf.[25] They concluded that instincts (inborn tendencies) still had a great deal to do with human conduct, but that advances in personnel research were opening new vistas that enabled the scientific selection, placement, and training of employees. Writing yet later, Tead argued that managers should adopt a "psychological point of view" to seek "the cause and effect relations in behavior." He believed that such relations could be studied for the purpose of guiding human conduct.[26] Moreover, he contended that an understanding of such relations would encourage proper work habits.

In brief, the dual origins of personnel management led to a common meeting ground in the 1920s. Although the employee welfare movement realized that productivity depended, in part, on employee attitudes and loyalty, it lacked the rigor and professionalism necessary to sustain the growth of modern organizations. Scientific management provided some of this rigor by being coupled with industrial psychology (which will be discussed next), by actuating national interest in professional associations, and by inspiring the first college-level preparation for personnel specialists. Welfarism was not dead, but would continue in a less-emphatic fashion

---

23. Paul F. Brissenden and Emil Frankel, *Labor Turnover in Industry* (New York: Macmillan, 1922), especially pp. 54–79.

24. Lyndall F. Urwick, "The Father of British Management," *The Manager* 30 (February 1962), pp. 42–43; Morgen L. Witzel, "Benjamin Seebohn Rowntree," in M. L. Witzel, ed., *The Biographical Dictionary of Management* (Bristol, England: Thoemmes Press, 2001), vol. 2, pp. 863–865.

25. Tead and Metcalf, *Personnel Administration*. See also *idem, Instincts in Industry: A Study of Working-Class Psychology* (London: Constable, 1919). Tead's thinking on instincts "stemmed indirectly" from Thomson J. Hudon's *The Law of Psychic Phenomena: A Systematic Study of Hypnotism, Spiritism, and Mental Therapeutics, Etc.* (Chicago: A. C. McClurg, 1893), among other influences. See Ordway Tead, "Ordway Tead," in Louis Finkelstein, ed., *Thirteen Americans: Their Spiritual Autobiographies* (New York: Institute of Religious and Social Studies, 1953), pp. 17–30.

26. Ordway Tead, *Human Nature and Management: The Applications of Psychology to Executive Leadership* (New York: McGraw-Hill, 1929), p. 9.

in the years ahead. Scientific management, on the other hand, would find its goals and methods reshaped by the behavioral and social sciences. Together, the scientific management and "welfare work" movements paved the way for modern personnel management.

Psychology and the Individual

In Greek mythology, Plutus was the god of wealth; from this foundation came plutology, a branch of economic theory that dealt with how humans attempted to satisfy their wants. Near the middle of the nineteenth century, Australian economist William E. Hearn advanced a theory that more closely resembles modern thinking about human needs:

> Food, drink, air and warmth are the most urgent of [our] necessities [which] . . . man shares with all other animals. . . . The satisfaction, therefore, of his primary appetites is imperative upon man . . . first in the degree of their intensity . . . and the first which he attempts to satisfy. . . . Man is able not merely to satisfy his primary wants, but to devise means for their better and more complete gratification. . . . Thus the comparative range of human wants is rapidly increased . . . as the attempt to satisfy the primary appetites thus gives rise to new desires . . . [and] when they have acquired such comforts they are pained at their loss, but their acquisition does not prevent them from continuing to desire a further increase. [27]

This anticipation (by some four score years) of a hierarchy of human needs and the premise that once a lower level need is satisfied further needs are pursued was not a result of empirical investigation, but rather observation and logical deduction. Before the advent of scientific management, psychology was based on such introspective, armchair, or deductive bases. Pseudosciences, such as astrology, physiognomy, phrenology, and graphology, were commonly used by managers seeking to select employees based on the movement and position of the stars in the heavens, the employees' physical characteristics, bumps on their skulls, and their handwriting.[28] Even in reputable consulting firms such as Emerson Engineers, Katherine M. H. Blackford, a physician, emphasized the study of physiognomy and graphology as an aid in selecting employees. She also advocated the study of physical

---

27. William E. Hearn, *Plutology, or the Theory of the Efforts to Satisfy Human Wants* (Melbourne, Australia: G. Robertson, 1863), pp. 12–15.

28. See Mary H. Booth, *How to Read Character in Handwriting* (Philadelphia: John C. Winston, 1910); Katherine M. H. Blackford and Arthur Newcomb, *Analyzing Character: The New Science of Judging Men; Misfits in Business, the Home and Social Life* (New York: Blackford, 1916); and Gerald E. Fosbroke, *Character Reading Through Analysis of the Features* (New York: G. P. Putnam's Sons, 1914).

characteristics such as hair coloring, the curvature of noses, facial features, and head proportions in evaluating potential employees.[29]

TOWARD SCIENTIFIC PSYCHOLOGY

Elsewhere, psychology was escaping its introspective, pseudoscience beginnings. When Wilhelm Wundt opened the world's first psychological laboratory in 1879 at the University of Leipzig (Germany), scientific methods took hold in psychology. Wundt did not entirely abandon introspection, but began to examine human behavior through controlled experiments. As the founder of experimental psychology, he opened the way for applied and, eventually, through his students, the nascent field of industrial or, as it is called today, "industrial-organizational psychology." Wundt sought to understand "psychological man" by identifying the constituent parts of human consciousness. His own observations of human behavior, combined with the emergence of the psychoanalytical theories of Sigmund Freud, soon led Wundt to an instinct-based explanation for behavior and thought. Concluding that people are not rational, but controlled by innate (i.e., inborn) instincts, Wundt believed that by understanding "instinctive actions," the secrets of the hitherto unexplored mind could be revealed. In ensuing years, economist Thorstein B. Veblen would identify two major instincts: workmanship and predation; William James, the "Father of American Psychology," identified twenty-eight: including fear, jealousy, curiosity, and Ordway Tead identified ten: including sex, self-assertion, and submissiveness.[30]

The disparities and disagreements among these competing lists of instincts soon proved that this approach was futile, and instinct theory was dismissed as an oversimplified basis for explaining behavior. The variability noted in attempts to identify a set of universal human instincts, however, led to recognition of the sizable psychological differences between individuals. In the same way that Taylor had recognized the importance of employee selection, psychologists came to understand that a science of human behavior required the study of individuals and not innate instincts. It is here that applied psychologists formed an alliance with scientific management.

THE BIRTH OF INDUSTRIAL PSYCHOLOGY

Scientific management gave industrial psychology its scope and direction. Echoing the scientific-management ethos, the earliest objective of industrial psychology was to promote "the maximum *efficiency* of the individual in industry" and "his

---

29. Katherine M. H. Blackford and Arthur Newcomb, *The Job, The Man, The Boss* (New York: Doubleday, 1916), ch. 7, pp. 176, 184.

30. Thorstein Veblen, *The Instinct of Workmanship, and the State of the Industrial Arts* (New York: B. W. Huebsch, 1914); William James, *The Principles of Psychology* (New York: H. Holt, 1890); Tead, *Instincts in Industry*.

optimum *adjustment* . . . in the industrial situation."[31] Whereas the engineer studied mechanical efficiency and the industrial psychologist studied human efficiency, their goal was the same—the elimination of waste and the securing of the greatest personal employee satisfaction.

Hugo Münsterberg (1863–1916) is generally credited with creating the field of industrial psychology. Münsterberg recognized Fred Taylor as "the brilliant originator of the scientific management movement," saying that Taylor had "introduced most valuable suggestions which the industrial world cannot ignore."[32] In promoting industrial psychology, Münsterberg drew on Taylor's work and stressed the importance of efficiently using workers to achieve economic production. He, however, did not fail to appreciate the social implications of his work and, industrial psychology, in general. As he explained,

> We must not forget that the increase of industrial efficiency by future psychological adaption and the improvement of the psychophysical conditions is not only in the interest of the employers, but still more of the employees; their working time can be reduced, their wages increased, their level of life raised. And above all, still more important than naked commercial profit on both sides, is the cultural gain which will come to the total economic life of the nation, as soon as every one can be brought to the place where his best energies may be unfolded and his greatest personal satisfaction secured. The economic experimental psychology offers no more inspiring idea than this adjustment of work and psyche by which mental dissatisfaction in the work, mental depression and discouragement, may be replaced in our social community by overflowing joy and perfect inner harmony.[33]

Born in Danzig (Germany) and educated in Wundt's University of Leipzig laboratory, Münsterberg was enticed to join the Harvard University faculty by William James. His interests were far-ranging, including the application of psychological principles to crime detection, education, morality, and philosophy. To lay a broader foundation for scientific management, he met with President Woodrow Wilson, Secretary of Commerce William C. Redfield, and Secretary of Labor William B. Wilson to encourage them to create a government bureau dedicated to applying scientific research to the psychological problems of industry. Interest in scientific management was high, and Münsterberg sought to place the study of workplace behavior in the hands of qualified scientists and at the forefront of the nation's

---

31. Morris S. Viteles, *Industrial Psychology* (New York: W. W. Norton, 1932), p. 4.

32. Hugo Münsterberg, *Psychology and Industrial Efficiency* (Boston: Houghton Mifflin, 1913), pp. 166, 50. Originally published 1912.

33. Ibid., pp. 308–309.

consciousness. According to Münsterberg, "While today the greatest care is devoted to the problems of material and equipment, all questions of the mind . . . like fatigue, monotony, interest, learning . . . joy in work . . . reward . . . and many similar mental states are dealt with by laymen without any scientific understanding."[34]

Even though the government bureau Münsterberg sought never materialized, his applied research interests grew. In attempting to understand "business life," he once again echoed Taylor in seeking answers to three primary questions:

> We ask how we can find the men whose mental qualities make them best fitted for the work which they have to do; secondly, under what psychological conditions we can secure the greatest and most satisfactory output from every man; and finally how we can produce most completely the influences on human minds which are desired in the interests of business. In other words, we ask how to find the best possible work, and how to secure the best possible effects.[35]

The direction of Münsterberg's work was directly linked to Taylor's vision for scientific management and contained three broad parts: (1) "The Best Possible Man"; (2) "The Best Possible Work"; and (3) "The Best Possible Effect." Part 1 was a study of the demands jobs place on people and the necessity of identifying those people whose mental qualities made them best fit for the work they had to do. Part 2 sought to determine psychological conditions under which the greatest and most satisfactory output could be obtained from every person. Part 3 examined the necessity of producing the influences on human needs that were desirable for the interests of business. For each of these objectives, Münsterberg outlined definite proposals relating to the use of tests in worker selection, the application of research on learning in employee training, and the study of psychological techniques to increase workers' ethical and aesthetic motives. To illustrate his proposals, Münsterberg drew on evidence gathered from studies he had conducted on trolley-car motormen, telephone operators, and merchant marine officers.

Taylor had called for studies that would provide insights into the "motives that influence men."[36] Münsterberg answered that call. The spirit of scientific management was readily apparent in his focus on the individual, his emphasis on efficiency, and his awareness of the social benefits to be derived from applying

---

34. Margaret Münsterberg, *Hugo Münsterberg: His Life and Work* (New York: Appleton-Century-Crofts, 1922), p. 250. See also Merle J. Moskowitz, "Hugo Münsterberg: A Study in the History of Applied Psychology," *American Psychologist* 32 (October 1977), pp. 824–842; Frank J. Landy, "Hugo Münsterberg: Victim or Visionary?" *Journal of Applied Psychology* 77 (1992), pp. 787–802; and Jutta Spillman and Lothar Spillman, "The Rise and Fall of Hugo Münsterberg," *Journal of the History of the Behavioral Sciences* 29 (1993), pp. 322–338.

35. Münsterberg, Psychology and Industrial Efficiency, pp. 23–24.

36. Frederick W. Taylor, *The Principles of Scientific Management* (New York: Harper & Brothers, 1911), p. 119.

the scientific method to investigate human behavior in the workplace. Moreover, Münsterberg's notoriety stimulated an increasing interest in workplace behavior. Among those who followed Münsterberg were Charles S. Myers, who pioneered industrial psychology in Great Britain; Walter D. Scott, who devised personnel classification tests for the U.S. Army during World War I; Cecil A. Mace, who performed the first experiments in goal setting as a motivational technique; Walter Van Dyke Bingham, whose Division of Applied Psychology at the Carnegie Institute of Technology led to the creation of the Bureau of Personnel Research; Morris S. Viteles, whose textbook became the "bible of industrial psychology"; and more.[37] It was Münsterberg, though, who blazed the way by defining the goals and terrain of industrial psychology.

FOUNDATIONS OF THE SOCIAL PERSON: THEORY, RESEARCH, AND PRACTICE

Scientific management shaped its times and in turn was shaped by them. It provided the rationale for personnel management and for industrial psychology. The course of history is such that one idea typically leads to a better idea, and this was the fate of scientific management. Another set of forces, related to scientific management only in terms of time, would apply Christian principles to society as a whole. From this beginning, the road was opened for the era of the "social human being."

THE ANTECEDENTS OF INDUSTRIAL SOCIOLOGY

As described earlier, the Social Gospel movement emerged as a counterpoint to social Darwinism. Social Gospel activists (predominantly Protestant but also Catholic and Jewish), felt that they had a duty to reform social and economic conditions. One proponent of the Social Gospel movement was C. Whiting Williams (1878–1975). Born into a relatively prosperous family, Williams was educated at Oberlin College, graduating in 1899. He held various positions before being named vice president and director of personnel for the Hydraulic Pressed Steel Company (Cleveland,

---

37. See F. C. Bartlett, "Remembering Dr. Myers," *Bulletin of the British Psychological Society* 58 (January 1965), 1–10; Edmund C. Lynch, "Walter Dill Scott: Pioneer Industrial Psychologist," *Business History Review* 42, no. 2 (Summer 1968), pp. 147–170; Paula L. Phillips (Carson), "Cecil Alec Mace: The Life and Times of the Original Goal-Setting Experimenter," in Jerry L. Wall and Lawrence R. Jauch, eds., *Proceedings of the Annual Meeting of the Academy of Management* (August 1991), pp. 142–146; Michelle P. Kraus, *Walter Van Dyke Bingham and the Bureau of Personnel Research* (New York: Garland, 1986); Morris S. Viteles, "Morris S. Viteles," in E. G. Boring and Gardner Lindzey, eds., *The History of Psychology in Autobiography*, vol. 5 (New York: Appleton-Century-Crofts, 1967), pp. 417–449; and *idem*, "Industrial Psychology: Reminiscences of an Academic Moonlighter," in Theophile S. Krawiec (ed.), *The Psychologists: Autobiographies of Distinguished Living Psychologists* (New York: Oxford University Press, 1974), pp. 440–500.

Ohio) in 1918. He resigned from this position after only a year because he felt he did not know enough about workers and their lives to be a personnel director. As the Social Gospel movement was based on direct involvement in social and political action, Williams shed his white collar and headed out disguised as a worker to study industrial conditions first-hand.[38] He felt the only way to gain an intimate familiarity with workers' daily lives was to participate and observe at the same time. He explained, "Men's actions spring rather from their feelings than their thoughts, and people cannot be interviewed for their feelings."[39] His first job was in a steel mill, cleaning out open-hearth furnaces so they could be rebricked and refired. It was hot, dirty work; the daily shifts were twelve hours long; and the pay was forty-five cents per hour, with

Whiting Williams, working on the railroad, 1922. The Western Reserve Historical Society, Cleveland, Ohio.

time-and-a-half for work over eight hours a day. This was Williams's introduction to workers' lives on the job. Over a period of seven months, he labored in coal mines, a railroad roundhouse, a shipyard, and an oil refinery, as well as various steel mills.

According to Williams, the workers' prayer was, "Give us this day our daily job," because a job meant "bread," sustenance for the workers and their families. He discovered that all workers—including managers—measured their individual worth and their value to society in terms of their jobs. Jobs influenced workers' social standing, and how they earned their living determined where and how they and their families lived. Without jobs, people were isolated not only economically, but also from their community and society-at-large: "[the worker's] vision of himself, his friends, his employer, and the whole of this world to come is circumscribed by his job."[40] Work was thus central to workers' lifestyles, friends, where they lived, how they spent their leisure time, and how they felt about themselves. "This vital connection between job status and social status means that the problem of effective relations with the worker inside the factory cannot be successfully separated from the whole problem of general social relations outside [the factory]."[41] Williams's appreciation of work as important not only for economic support, but also for social

---

38. Daniel A. Wren, *White Collar Hobo: The Travels of Whiting Williams* (Ames: Iowa State University Press, 1987).

39. Whiting Williams, *What's on the Worker's Mind? By One Who Put on Overalls to Find Out* (New York: Charles Scribner's Sons, 1920), p. vi.

40. Ibid., p. 299.

41. Whiting Williams, "Theory of Industrial Conduct and Leadership," *Harvard Business Review* 1 (April (1923), p. 326.

and psychological well-being, placed him in advance of other theorists who were just beginning to view the workplace as part of a broader social system in which work provides a sense of fulfillment and happiness, as well as a source of identity and self-worth.

Within factories, Williams observed the operations of a job hierarchy that had little or nothing to do with pay, but rather emphasized the nature of an individual's work. While working in a steel mill, he was promoted to millwright's helper. His pay was now two cents per hour more, but his former fellow shovelers envied him, not because of the pay increase, but because the nature of his job had changed from the dirty, hot work of a shoveler to the cleaner, more pleasant work of an assistant to a skilled worker. This made Williams skeptical about the notion that people would necessarily work harder if they are given more money. He recognized that social status is conferred by one's occupation or the type of work one performs:

> We give the dollar altogether too great an importance when we consider it the cause . . . of men's industry. . . . The dollar is merely an especially convenient and simple means for facilitating the measurement of a man's distance from the cipher of insignificance among his fellows. . . . Beyond a certain point . . . the increase of wages is . . . quite likely to lessen as to increase effort.[42]

Williams's view was unique in that he established earnings as a means of social comparison—that is, the pay a worker received was considered not in absolute terms, but relative to what others received. A person's "distance from the cipher of insignificance" was facilitated by using the dollar as a unit of self-evaluation. This did not mean that money was unimportant, but that it was a carrier of social value that might enhance or deflate how people viewed themselves relative to others. Hence, incentive plans that ignored this fact were less than effective as motivators. The mainspring of workers was the "wish to enjoy the feeling of [their] worth as persons among other persons."[43] Togetherness in thinking, feeling, and being part of a group was important to workers. From their peers workers drew their social sustenance, security, and concept of self-worth. Workers chose to get along with one another not because they could not always find another job, but because they could not always move from their respective communities. From their employer, and especially their supervisor, they expected recognition and treatment conducive to preserving self-worth. It was not the paternalistic clubs, cafeterias, and recreation activities that won worker loyalty, but successful relations with their supervisors as representatives of management. Williams recommended an Eleventh Commandment, "Thou Shalt Not Take Thy Neighbor for Granted," and urged management to change from appeals to fear to appeals to "hope and

---

42. Williams, *What's on the Worker's Mind?* p. 323.

43. Whiting Williams, *Mainsprings of Men* (New York: Charles Scribner's Sons, 1925), p. 147.

surety of reward." Latent in Williams's study of workers' daily lives was Charles H. Cooley's "looking-glass self" (the idea that the self arises reflectively in reaction to the opinions of others) and the realization that one's self is embedded in one's work group as a primary social unit of importance.[44]

Other findings from Williams's "shirt-sleeve empiricism" included: (1) workers restricted output ("stringing out the job") because they perceived scarce job opportunities, and employers tended to hire and lay off indiscriminately; (2) unions arose out of workers' desire for job security, and the unions would not have made much progress if employers had evidenced concern for this worker need; (3) long factory hours (e.g., twelve-hour shifts in steel mills) made both workers and supervisors grouchy and tired, causing interpersonal conflict; and (4) workers listened to radical agitators because employers failed to speak "of the plans and purposes, the aims and ideals—the character of the company." Williams made a career of lecturing, consulting, and writing of his experiences as a worker. Over the years, he resumed his worker's disguise to also study strikers and strikebreakers, unemployment, and labor–management relations in Great Britain and continental Europe.[45] Despite his pioneering work in the field that today is called industrial sociology, Williams's efforts were not widely recognized. The roots of industrial sociology are traditionally traced to the Hawthorne studies, to be discussed in Chapter 13. There are, perhaps, several reasons why Williams's work was largely overlooked. One reason appears to be the academic distaste and disregard for any theory advanced by nonacademicians. According to Keller, the personal and institutional academic prestige of those who propose a theory contributes to the influence and acceptance of that theory.[46] Williams was never affiliated with an academic institution; in contrast, the Hawthorne studies bore the seal of approval of several universities, including Harvard and the Massachusetts Institute of Technology. Further, Williams's works were rarely reviewed in the scholarly journals of the period. Last, as a relatively young field, sociology was striving to become more scientific. The prestige of academic sociologists associated with leading universities provided a mantle of legitimacy that Williams's work lacked. Nevertheless, the roots of industrial sociology—as was the work of Whiting Williams—are deeply embedded in the Social Gospel movement that emerged in the late nineteenth century.[47]

———

44. Charles H. Cooley, *Human Nature and the Social Order* (New York: Charles Scribner's Sons, 1902).

45. Williams's study of British workers is found in *Full Up and Fed Up: The Worker's Mind in Crowded Britain* (New York: Charles Scribner's Sons, 1921); his experiences in France, Germany, Italy, and Spain are reported in *Horny Hands and Hampered Elbows: The Worker's Mind in Western Europe* (New York: Charles Scribner's Sons, 1922).

46. Robert T. Keller, "The Harvard 'Pareto Circle' and the Historical Development of Organization Theory," *Journal of Management* 10 (Summer 1984), p. 193.

47. Daniel A. Wren, "Industrial Sociology: A Revised View of Its Antecedents," *Journal of the History of the Behavioral Sciences* 21 (October 1985), pp. 311–320. See also Mark Pittenger "'What's on the Worker's Mind': Class Passing and the Study of the Industrial Workplace in the 1920s," *Journal of the History of the Behavioral Sciences* 39 (Spring 2003), pp. 143–161.

SOME EARLY EMPIRICAL INVESTIGATIONS

Before Whiting Williams undertook his own brand of "shirt-sleeve empiricism," other studies had been done on workers' daily lives. Two of these studies merit brief mention because of their unique insights and international perspectives. Anticipating Williams by some 25 years, in 1891, Paul Göehre, General Secretary of the Evangelical Congress, worked for three months in a Chemitz (Germany) machine-making factory to see why workers were attracted to Social Democracy, an ideology that advocated a peaceful transition from capitalism to socialism.[48] Göehre observed that workers took more pride in producing a complete unit of work rather than an unidentifiable fragment, that higher productivity occurred when supervisors instilled a feeling of group interdependence and teamwork, and that there were informal group pressures for adherence to norms. Lower morale and lower efficiency resulted when workers were isolated and felt a lack of "community of labour." Göehre's findings presaged research on the relationship between job-design and productivity that first appeared in the 1940s (see Chapter 15).

In an equally prescient effort, in 1924 and 1926, Belgian psychologist Hendrik de Man asked seventy-eight "wage earners and salaried workers of both sexes from various parts of Germany" who were attending lectures he gave at the University of Frankfurt-on-Main to provide, in conjunction with completing a detailed questionnaire, "written reports concerning their own feelings about their daily work."[49] Based on these autobiographical reports, he concluded that there was a natural impulse in people to find "joy in work." As explained by De Man, this impulse reflected a desire for activity, play, constructiveness, curiosity, self-assertion, and a longing for "mastery" (power). Inhibitive factors that contributed to "distaste for work" derived from job elements such as detail work, monotony, reduction of worker initiative, fatigue, and poor working conditions; and in "social hindrances," such as a sense of dependency, unjust wage systems, speedups, insecurity of livelihood, and lack of social solidarity. De Man's main conclusion that a worker's mental attitude toward work is a mix of "pleasurable and unpleasurable elements" is remarkably similar to Frederick A. Herzberg's later two-factor theory of work motivation (see Chapter 20), published some thirty years later. Much like Herzberg, De Man felt that work itself was a motivator and that management's job was to remove the "hindrances" that prevented finding joy in work.

---

48. Paul Göehre, *Three Months in a Workshop: A Practical Study*, trans. A. B. Carr (London: Swan Sonnenschein, 1895). Originally published in 1891. See also Richard J. Whiting, "Historical Search in Human Relations," *Academy of Management Journal* 7 (March 1964), pp. 45–53.

49. Hendrik de Man, *Joy in Work*, trans. Eden and Cedar Paul (London: G. Allen & Unwin, 1929), p. 9. Originally published in 1927.

THE "DEMOCRATIZATION OF THE WORKPLACE"

Theory and research into various aspects of industrial life steadily advanced during the first two decades of the twentieth century. Inspired by the spirit of democracy enshrined in Abraham Lincoln's immortal words, "A government of the people, by the people, for the people," there were also advances directly involving labor–management relations. These advances were most evident in the trade union movement and the changing nature of union–management cooperation.

THE TRADE UNION MOVEMENT

The year 1886 was marked by several momentous events. While Henry R. Towne was encouraging engineers to think in economic terms, the American Federation of Labor (AFL) was being formed under the presidency of Samuel T. B. Gompers. The AFL was a federation of craft unions that would succeed where the Knights of Labor and the National Labor Union had failed (see Chapter 6). A third event in 1886 was the publication of economist Richard T. Ely's *The Labor Movement in America*. As Ely explained, this volume was meant to be a clarion call "designed to protect and advance the interest of the great mass of working classes" by uniting in associations to bargain collectively with employers.[50]

Although at one time associated with the Social Gospel movement, Ely's ideas regarding the role of labor incorporated both Christian and socialist elements. He advocated independent worker associations and public ownership of the nation's railway, gas, electric, telephone, and telegraph industries. He would later reverse his views regarding converting private property to public use and operation, but continued to see capitalist employers as a separate social class.[51] He insisted, however, that neither socialism nor communism could advance the cause of labor more than workers forming voluntary associations to negotiate with employers.

Prior to the publicity given scientific management in the 1910 Eastern Rate Case, organized labor had paid scant attention to Fred Taylor and his followers. In 1912, following on the heels of the 1911 House of Representatives investigation into the Taylor system, Congress created a Commission on Industrial Relations to "inquire into the general condition of labor in the principal industries of the United States."[52] One member of the commission was Ely's former pupil and University of Wisconsin colleague, John R. Commons. As an advocate for social justice and someone who

---

50. Richard T. Ely, *The Labor Movement in America* (New York: T. Y. Crowell, 1886), p. 92.

51. Richard T. Ely, *Social Aspects of Christianity, and Other Essays* (New York: T. Y. Crowell, 1889), pp. 72–78; and *idem*, *Ground Under Our Feet: An Autobiography* (New York: Macmillan, 1938), pp. 251–252.

52. *Final Report of the Commission on Industrial Relations*, Senate Document no. 415, 64th Cong., 1st sess. (Washington, DC: U.S. Government Printing Office, 1916), vol. 1, p. 6.

believed that carefully crafted legislation could create social change, Commons had taken an early position that the "clever devices of compensation," formulated by Taylor, Gantt, Emerson, and others, divided workers and forced job negotiations between an employer and individual employees.[53] He felt strongly that workers needed to organize and bargain collectively to offset employers' economic strength.

As a member of the Commission on Industrial Relations, Commons had the opportunity to meet with Taylor and "came to realize that improved methods of management and personnel administration were yet another valuable approach to solving labor problems and improving industrial relations."[54] After visiting various factories that had implemented Taylor's methods, Commons concluded that scientific management and labor could cooperate, but only under certain circumstances. Plimpton Press, one of the most scientifically managed companies Commons visited, was unionized, but experienced little labor–management conflict. Similarly, the Clothcraft Shop of Joseph and Feiss Company, another model Taylor installation, was not unionized, but was managed so well that Commons felt a union was unnecessary. In Commons's judgment, however, such companies were rare. Indeed, he believed that some 75 to 90 percent of the nation's companies were so "inefficient or greedy . . . that only the big stick of a union or government" could ensure worker interests were protected.[55]

In his book, *Industrial Goodwill*, Commons wrote of the need for workers to unionize so that they would have a "voice" in workplace governance. He called on employers to view workers as "human resources," in which parents, taxpayers, and the nation had made a significant investment.[56] Although Commons openly admired Taylor, he felt that scientific management cut across "the solidarity of labor," placed job knowledge in the hands of employers rather than workers, and had the "defects of autocracy."[57] In his autobiography, Commons explained, "I was trying to save capitalism by making it good . . . as good as the best instead of negligent. . . . I wanted also to make trade unions as good as the best of them that I knew."[58]

Based on his work with the Commission on Industrial Relations and his contact with Taylor, Commons took a broad view of labor-management relations. He was concerned with the greater strength of employers relative to employees. In response to the inadequacies of individual workers bargaining alone, he sought to strengthen labor by advocating industrial goodwill, sound managerial practices, and government legislation and oversight. In time, Commons would come to be

53. John R. Commons, "Organized Labor's Attitude Toward Industrial Efficiency," *American Economic Review* 1 (September 1911), pp. 463–472.

54. Bruce E. Kaufman, "The Role of Economics and Industrial Relations in the Development of the Field of Personnel/Human Resource Management," *Management Decision* 40 (10) (2002), p. 970

55. John R. Commons, *Industrial Government* (New York: Macmillan, 1921), p. 263.

56. John R. Commons, *Industrial Goodwill* (New York: McGraw-Hill, 1919), pp. 129–130.

57. Ibid., pp. 13–16, 18–19.

58. John R. Commons, *Myself* (New York: Macmillan, 1934), p. 143.

considered the "Father of Industrial Relations."[59] Other prominent economists who also played a role in expanding personnel management to include industrial relations included such luminaries as Senator Paul H. Douglas (Illinois) and Harvard University professor Sumner H. Slichter.[60]

Practitioners and consultants were also influential in reshaping industrial relations, especially in the post–World War I period. The philosophy of the American Federation of Labor, as represented by Samuel Gompers, was to achieve gains for labor through power rather than cooperation.[61] Organized labor during this period viewed scientific management as autocratic, because it forced employees to depend on an employer's conception of fairness. Employees had no voice in setting standards, determining rates, or deciding other work-related issues. When asked what organized labor wanted, Gompers simply replied: "more, more, and then more."[62]

THE CHANGING NATURE OF UNION–MANAGEMENT COOPERATION

To understand the eventual union–management cooperation that was achieved following Fred Taylor's death in 1915 and in subsequent periods, it is necessary to reach back to the Social Gospel movement, which espoused industrial betterment and sought to resolve labor unrest through associations such as the National Civic Federation (NCF), formed in 1900.[63] The NCF sought to mediate disputes, educate the public about labor–management relations, improve industrial relations, and demonstrate that labor and management had mutual interests. The era's most prominent call for improved labor–management relations came from President Woodrow Wilson, who declared that "there must be a genuine democratization of industry based upon a full recognition of the right of those who work . . . to participate in some organized way in every decision which directly affects [the

---

59. Bruce E. Kaufman, *The Origins and Evolution of the Field of Industrial Relations in the United States* (Ithaca, NY: ILR Press, 1993): *idem*, "John R. Commons: His Contributions to the Founding and Early Development of the Field of Personnel/HRM," *Proceedings of the 50th Annual Meeting Industrial Relations Research Association.* (Madison, WI: IRRA, 1998), pp. 328–341.

60. Bruce E. Kaufman, "Personnel/Human Resource Management: Its Roots as Applied Economics," in Roger E. Backhouse and Jeff Biddle, eds., *Toward a History of Applied Economics.* (Durham, NC: Duke University Press, 2000), pp. 229–256; *idem*, "Human Resources and Industrial Relations: Commonalities and Differences," *Human Resource Management Review* 11 (Winter 2001), pp. 339–374; and *idem*, "The Theory and Practice of Strategic HRM and Participative Management: Antecedents in Early Industrial Relations," *Human Resource Management Review* 11 (Winter 2001), pp. 505–533.

61. Jean Trepp McKelvey, *AFL Attitudes toward Production: 1900–1932* (Ithaca, NY: New York State School of Industrial and Labor Relations, Cornell University, 1952), pp. 6–11.

62. Samuel Gompers, quoted by Florence Thorne, *Samuel Gompers: American Statesman* (New York: Greenwood, 1969), p. 41.

63. Marguerite Green, *The National Civic Federation and the American Labor Movement, 1900–1925* (Washington, DC: Catholic University Press, 1956).

workers'] welfare."[64] During World War I, President Wilson's National War Labor Board, established in 1918, also furthered many of organized labor's goals: for example, it prohibited employers from engaging in antiunion activities, required time-and-one-half pay for work over eight hours per day, established the principle of shop committees elected by employees to confer with management regarding grievances, proposed the principle of a "living wage" for all workers (in practice, this became an early minimum wage), acknowledged the right of women to receive equal pay for equal work, and provided mediation and conciliation services to settle unresolved disputes.[65]

Under the Wilson administration (1912–1920) almost one and a half million workers were added to union rolls. The economic, social, and political tides, however, soon began to shift. A short, steep depression in 1921 weakened unions; further, companies were becoming increasingly benevolent; management was waging intense drives for "open shops," in which workers were not required to join or financially support a labor union as a condition of hiring or continued employment; and government and the courts were growing hostile to union organizers' aggressive tactics. There was also a concern that "radicals" and Bolsheviks, who had seized power in Russia during 1917, were gaining a foothold in the union movement. The general public reacted with alarm.[66] Union membership suffered, declining from around five million in 1920 to three and a half million in 1921. In response to the resulting loss in bargaining power, unions had little choice but to become less confrontational and more cooperative.

Under the leadership of Daniel Willard, president of the Baltimore and Ohio Railroad, and Bert M. Jewell, president of the AFL's Railway Employees' Department, a model plan for labor–management cooperation was developed following what came to be known as the Great Railroad Strike of 1922. The strike prompted an anguished outcry as nationwide rail travel was halted. In the strike's aftermath, some firms moved to in-house unions, thus ousting the AFL. Recognizing that the momentum of the pro-union Wilson years had been lost, the AFL called for an end to waste in industry, gave its support to several joint labor-management initiatives to improve productivity and, departing from earlier policies, agreed to the linking of wages to productivity increases.[67]

---

64. Quoted in Ray Stannard Baker, *The New Industrial Unrest: Reasons and Remedies* (Garden City, NY: Doubleday, Page, 1920), p. 52. Wilson had been a student of Richard Ely's at Johns Hopkins University. See Ely, *Ground Under Our Feet*, pp. 108–119.

65. Valerie Jean Conner, *The National War Labor Board* (Chapel Hill: University of North Carolina Press, 1983). The seeds planted by the National War Labor Board would bear fruit for more than half a century through legislation such as the National Labor Relations Act, the Fair Labor Standards Act (FLSA), and the Equal Pay Amendment to FLSA.

66. Sanford M. Jacoby, "Union-Management Cooperation in the United States: Lessons from the 1920s," *Industrial and Labor Relations Review* 37 (October 1983), pp. 18–33.

67. Ibid., p. 24.

In coming years, successful union–management cooperation could be found in the clothing trades and the railroads. The clothing unions, under the stewardship of Sidney Hillman, were among the first segments of organized labor to agree to cooperation and implementation of scientific management techniques. Hillman was head of the Amalgamated Clothing Workers of America and a key figure in the founding of the Congress of Industrial Organizations. The railroads also developed extensive plans for cooperation, first on the Baltimore and Ohio and then later on the Chesapeake & Ohio, the Chicago and North Western, the Canadian National Railways, and others.[68] In each instance, the railway unions implicitly accepted scientific management and participated through joint union–management shop committees in improving work routing and scheduling, hiring practices, and job analysis.

When William F. Green was elected AFL president in 1924, scientific management gained even greater acceptance. At its 1925 convention, the AFL "declared unreservedly for a policy of cooperation with progressive management in the elimination of industrial waste." Scientific management was to be supported to the extent that it, "first, recognizes the right of workers to organize into responsible trade unions; second, is just as much concerned with the welfare of the human being engaged in manufacture as with the increased production of material goods; third, recognizes the potential value of trade unions as a constructive factor in production, and fourth, is willing to participate in the setting up of joint union–management cooperative machinery directed to increase productivity with these conditions." It soon thereafter began articulating a set of what was to grow to be sixteen principles of "progressive management." These were published in 1930 under the title "Labor's Principles of Scientific Management".[69] In an effort to further cooperation between labor and management, the AFL maintained an engineering service and an educational department that were available to employers.[70] The goal of both units was to demonstrate how union–management cooperation could lead to increased employer profits as well as improved employee benefits. This "new unionism," with its recognition of what Fred Taylor had earlier termed a "mutuality of interests," completed a cycle in labor–management relations. Scientific management was now accepted by both labor and management.

---

68. Otto S. Beyer, Jr., "Experiences with Cooperation between Labor and Management in the Railway Industry," in *Wertheim Lectures on Industrial Relations, 1928* by Otto S. Beyer, Jr., Joseph H. Willits, John P. Frey, William M. Leiserson, John R. Commons, Elton Mayo, and Frank W. Taussig. Cambridge, MA: Harvard University Press, 1929, pp. 3–31.

69. Geoffrey C. Brown, "Labor's Principles of Scientific Management," *The American Federationist* 37 (February 1930), pp. 194–195.

70. Geoffrey C. Brown, "What the Union Offers the South," *The American Federationist* 37 (September 1930), 1068–1073. See also Rexford Guy Tugwell, *Industry's Coming of Age* (New York: Harcourt, Brace, 1927), p. 41; and Tom Tippett, *When Southern Labor Stirs*. New York: Jonathan Cape & Harrison Smith, 1931), p. 183.

SUMMARY

The dual heritage of modern personnel management may be traced to the early 1880s and the near simultaneous emergence of the scientific management and "welfare work" movements. Whereas scientific management was essentially an engineering approach that focused on the economic use of workers, welfare work proponents strived to improve the lives of the poor and unfortunate. Scientific management inspired psychologists and sociologists to become involved in the study of workplace dynamics. With advances in understanding the relationship between work and workers' lives on and off the job, there were also advances involving labor–management relations. These advances were most evident in the trade union movement and the changing nature of union–management cooperation. The path was made ready for further progress in understanding people at work.

10

The Emergence of the Management Process and Organization Theory

H istory rarely provides a full measure of people during their lifetimes. Epitaphs are often prematurely written, and succeeding events bring newfound appreciation to previously unrecognized accomplishments. Such is the case with the two individuals whose contributions are the focus of this chapter. Both lived during the late nineteenth and the early twentieth centuries, both wrote during the scientific management era, both were Europeans, and both made lasting contributions to the evolution of management thought. One was a practicing manager and one an academician; one was trained in the physical sciences, the other in the social sciences; and neither was accorded the full measure of his contributions until some decades after his death. Henri Fayol, a French manager–engineer, was the first writer to advance a formal statement of management elements and principles. Max Weber, a German economist–sociologist, addressed the more fundamental issue of how organizations should be structured. Both Fayol and Weber sought to combine theory with practice. Their ideas have influenced succeeding generations of managers and scholars and, even today, continue to significantly influence managerial thinking.

HENRI FAYOL: THE MAN AND HIS CAREER

Jules Henri Fayol (1841–1925) was born in Constantinople (now Istanbul, Turkey). His father was an engineer fulfilling his military service obligation by supervising construction projects under an agreement between France and Turkey.[1]

---

1. Tsuneo Sasaki, "Henri Fayol's Family Relationships," *Journal of Management History* 1 (1995), pp. 14–15; and Tsuneo Sasaki, "The Comambault Company Revisited," *Journal of Economics* (College of Economics, Nihon University, Tokyo, Japan) 68 (January 1999), pp. 113–128. Reprinted in Sasaki and Wren, *Henri Fayol and the Process School*, series 3 of the *Intellectual Legacy of Management Theory* (London: Pickering and Chatto, 2004).

Henri Fayol, circa 1872.
Source: La Societe de Commentry-
Fourchambault et Decazeville,
1854–1954, Paris: Brodard et
Taupin, 1954, p. 160.

Henri's parents, André and Eugénie Cantin Fayol, returned to France after André completed his military service. The family lived in La Voulte, where Henri received his elementary education. André worked as a superintendent at iron foundries in Le Pouzin and Le Teil, near La Voulte. Henri attended a polytechnic school in Valence, where he graduated from the *Lycée Impérial* (Imperial High School) in 1858. Henri followed in his father's footsteps, entering the National School of Mines at Saint Étienne at age seventeen to become a mining engineer. He graduated in 1860 and went to work at the Commentry coalfield in central France. The coalfield was owned by the Société Boigues, Rambourg and Company, a limited partnership (*société en commandité*) that also owned steel mills at Fourchambault and Torteron, a forge at d'Imphy, foundries at Fourchambault and Montlucon, and an iron mine at Berry. Following the death of several partners in 1874, Boigues, Rambourg and Cie was reorganized as Commentry-Fourchambault (Comambault), a joint-stock company (*société ànonyme*).[2]

From 1860 until 1866, Fayol worked as an engineer and made notable advances in the technique of fighting underground coal fires. His efforts were rewarded with a promotion to manager of the Commentry coalfield at age twenty-five; six years later, he was placed in charge of several colliers.[3] In 1888, Comambault was in dire financial straits: no dividends had been paid since 1885, its Fourchambault and Montlucon facilities were losing money, and the coal deposits at Commentry and Montvicq were nearing depletion. This same year, Fayol was named Comambault's managing director (chief executive officer) and charged with revitalizing its operations. He closed the foundry at Fourchambault and centralized production at Montlucon to gain economies of scale. He acquired new coal deposits at Brassac and Decazeville and iron reserves at Joudreville. With the assistance of Joseph Carlioz, who was in charge of Comambault's commercial department, Fayol integrated Comambault backward to mine coal and iron ore and forward to smelt the iron into steel and to sell both the mined coal and raw steel.[4] Fayol established research facilities

———

2. Ibid.

3. John D. Breeze, "Harvest from the Archives: The Search for Fayol and Carlioz," *Journal of Management* 11 (Spring 1985), pp. 43–47. See also John D. Breeze and Arthur G. Bedeian, *The Administrative Writings of Henri Fayol: A Bibliographic Investigation*, 2nd ed. (Monticello, IL: Vance, 1988).

4. John D. Breeze, "Administration and Organization of the Commercial Function by J. Carlioz," in Kae H. Chung, ed., *Proceedings of the Annual Meeting of the Academy of Management* (August, 1982), pp. 112–116.

to advance Comambault's technological capacity; entered into alliances with or acquired other firms; opened new mills to expand Comambault's geographical base; hired staff specialists in research, manufacturing, and selling; and, to gain a competitive advantage, repositioned Comambault as a supplier of specialty steels.

Although his training was in engineering, Fayol realized that managing a geographically dispersed company with ten thousand employees required skills other than those he had studied. He viewed management as more than devising systems and methods for increasing throughput (as it had been for scientific management). For Fayol, management involved all the activities associated with producing, distributing, and selling a product. A manager needed to be able to formulate plans, organize plant and equipment, deal with people, and much more. Engineering school had never taught such skills.[5]

From his experiences as a general manager, Fayol began to develop his own ideas about managing.[6] Beginning in his early days as a mining engineer at the Commentry coalfields, Fayol had kept notes on events that had affected mine output. For example, as early as 1861 he observed that all work had to be stopped because a horse working in the St. Edmund mine fell and broke its leg. A replacement draft horse could not be secured in the absence of the mine's manager, and the livery stable-keeper had no authority to act on his own.[7] Fayol's resolution of this impasse was not a result of his technical training, but the managerial insight that responsibility and authority must be coequal or delays and disorder would result.

Foreshadowing modern thinking on work groups, Fayol organized miners into self-selected teams. This increased group cohesiveness and, in turn, reduced employee turnover. Moreover, work-group output increased as the teams refused to accept inferior members. Anticipating the job-redesign movement by some fifty years (see Chapter 15), Fayol also recognized that some jobs could be enlarged to relieve monotony and enhance skill levels. When managing at Commentry, he returned the responsibility for reinforcing mine tunnels (so that a tunnel's walls and roof would not collapse) to the miners rather than use timbering crews.[8]

Speaking at the 1900 International Mining and Metallurgical Congress, Fayol expressed the belief that: "All employees in an enterprise participate to a greater or lesser degree in the administrative function . . . [and] have occasion to exercise their administrative faculties and be noticed for them. [Those] who are particularly

---

5. Norman M. Pearson, "Fayolism as the Necessary Complement to Taylorism," *American Political Sciences Review* 39 (February 1945), p. 73.

6. Daniel A. Wren, "Henri Fayol: Learning from Experience," *Journal of Management History* 1 (1995), pp. 5–12.

7. Henri Fayol, diary entry of 29 July 1898. In Frédéric Blancpain, ed., "Les Cahiers Inédits d'Henri Fayol," *Bulletin de l'Institute International d'Administration Publique* 28 (1973), p. 23.

8. Donald Reid, "Fayol: From Experience to Theory," *Journal of Management History* 1 (1995), pp. 21–36.

talented can climb from the lowest rung to the highest levels of the hierarchy of an organization."[9] In this simple statement, Fayol was beginning to distinguish between managerial ability and technical knowledge. By 1908, Fayol's thinking had evolved further. Addressing the Society of the Mineral Industry, he noted that the effect of management on business activities was not fully understood and that technical expertise "can be completely destroyed by defective administrative procedures." Building on his 1900 theme, he further observed that "a leader who is a good administrator but technically mediocre is generally much more useful to the enterprise than if he were a brilliant technician but a mediocre administrator." Thus, according to Fayol, a firm's performance depended more on its leaders' managerial ability than technical abilities. In this same address, Fayol also presented an early list of management principles, including: unity of command, hierarchical transmission of orders, separation of powers among distinct departments, and centralization/decentralization. In addition to these and other principles, Fayol spoke of *prévoyance* ("foresight"), the act of forecasting, planning, and budgeting. He also stressed the value of organization charts, meetings and reports, and an accurate and rapid accounting system.[10] Although Fayol's 1908 address revealed advances in his thinking, it lacked the depth and conceptual clarity of his yet-to-come *magnum opus*.

Fayol's masterpiece, *Administration Industrielle et Générale*, was first published in the *Bulletin de la Societe de l'Industrie Minerale* in 1916.[11] Republished in book form the next year by Librairie H. Dunod and E. Pinat, it was known throughout France as "a catechism for the chief executive's education."[12] Fayolisme became as firmly entrenched in French management thinking as Taylorism had become in the United States. From 1918 to his death in 1925, Fayol presided over the meetings of the Centre d'Etudes Administratives, a group he formed to promote the advancement of Fayolisme. Shortly after Fayol's death, the Centre merged with the Henri le Chatelier's Conference de l'Organisation Française to form the still active Comité National de l'Organisation Française.[13] This merger brought together France's two main professional management associations.

Dissemination of Fayol's ideas beyond France was initially slowed by World War I, and it was almost four decades before his originality was appreciated outside a small

---

9. Daniel A. Wren, Arthur G. Bedeian, and John D. Breeze, "The Foundations of Henri Fayol's Administrative Theory," *Management Decision* 40 (2002), p. 908.

10. Ibid., p. 910, pp. 912–916.

11. Henri Fayol, "Administration Industrielle et Generale," *Bulletin de la Societe de l'Industrie Minerale,* 5th series, 10(3) (1916), pp. 5–162.

12. Charles de Fréminvillé, "Henri Fayol: A Great Engineer, a Great Scientist, and a Great Management Leader," *Bulletin of the Taylor Society* 12 (February 1927), p. 304.

13. John D. Breeze, "Henri Fayol's Centre for Administrative Studies," *Journal of Management History* 1 (1995), pp. 37–62.

circle of scholars in Europe and Great Britain.[14] Early interpretations contrasted Fayol's and Taylor's work. Whereas Taylor approached the study of management from the workshop or technical level, Fayol approached it from the viewpoint of upper-level administration. Fayol's emphasis on administrative management reflected his more than fifty years' experience as an industrial mining executive. Be that as it may, Fayol insisted that his work complemented Taylor's thinking, in that both he and Taylor sought to improve managerial practice.

THE NEED FOR MANAGEMENT THEORY

In earlier writings, Fayol noted managerial ability was essential for organizational success. If managerial ability was important, however, then why did schools and universities neglect managerial training to focus exclusively on teaching technical skills? The answer, according to Fayol, was the absence of management theory. Fayol defined theory as "a collection of principles, rules, methods, and procedures tried and checked by general experience."[15] Writing from his years of experience, he noted that many managers theorized, but that in practice there existed many managerial contradictions and little systematic reflection. Fayol believed that a lack of a management theory made it more difficult to teach and practice management because managers' experiences were localized and not easily understood by other managers or students of management.

Every firm required management: "Be it a case of commerce, industry, politics, religion, war, or philanthropy, in every concern there is a management function to be performed."[16] Thus, like Charles Dupin (see Chapter 4), Fayol felt that management required special study apart from technical matters and could be taught in schools and universities as theory was developed and codified.

Managerial ability, according to Fayol, depended on certain qualities and knowledge:

- Physical qualities: health, vigor, address [literally, manner of behaving]
- Mental qualities: ability to understand and learn, judgment, mental vigor, and adaptability
- Moral qualities: energy, firmness, willingness to accept responsibility, initiative, loyalty, tact, dignity

---

14. See Henri Fayol, *Industrial and General Administration*, trans. J. A. Coubrough (Geneva: International Management Institute, 1930); Henri Fayol, "The Administrative Theory of the State," trans. Sarah Greer, in Luther Gulick and Lyndall Urwick, eds., *Papers on the Science of Administration* (New York: Institute of Public Administration, Columbia University, 1937), pp. 99–114; and Henri Fayol, *General and Industrial Management*, trans. Constance Storrs (London: Sir Isaac Pitman and Sons, 1949).

15. Fayol, *General and Industrial Management*, trans. Storrs, p. 15. Except where specifically noted, the Storrs translation will be referenced, as it is more readily available than other translations.

16. Ibid., p. 41.

- General education: general acquaintance with matters not belonging exclusively to the function performed
- Special knowledge: that peculiar to the function, be it technical, commercial, financial, managerial, and so on
- Experience: knowledge arising from the work proper; the recollection of lessons a person has derived from things[17]

Fayol even diagrammed what he believed to be the relative importance of technical and managerial abilities for employees with different levels of authority. As he explained, at the worker level, technical ability was most important; but as individuals moved up the "scalar chain," the relative importance of managerial ability increases while the need for technical ability decreases. The higher the level of authority, the more dominant the need for managerial ability. Ability in commercial, financial, security, and accounting matters also diminishes in importance as a manager's authority increases. As for differences in firm size, Fayol contended that managers of small firms need relatively more technical ability than their counterparts in larger firms, whereas managerial rather than technical ability is required at higher levels in larger firms.

In summary, Fayol contended that all employees, from foremen to work superintendents, should receive some managerial training. He believed schools and universities did not teach management because it was thought that experience was the only way to acquire managerial ability. Recognizing that most higher managers have "neither the time nor inclination for writing,"[18] Fayol used his experiences and observations to propose a body of knowledge that included principles as guides to thinking and practice and elements of management as a description of the functions managers performed. His goal was to start a general discussion from which a theory of management might emanate.

THE PRINCIPLES OF MANAGEMENT

Fayol recognized that the term *principles* is often misunderstood. To some observers, it suggests an unquestioned or rigid way of doing things, on the order of laws in the physical sciences. For this reason, Fayol was careful to explain what he meant by "principles":

> For preference I shall adopt the term principles whilst dissociating it from any suggestion of rigidity, for there is nothing rigid or absolute in management affairs, it is all a question of proportion. Seldom do we have to apply the same principle twice in identical conditions; allowance must be made for different and changing circumstances. . . .

---

17. Ibid., p. 7.
18. Ibid., p. 15.

Therefore principles are flexible and capable of adaptation to every need; it is a matter of knowing how to make use of them, which is a difficult art requiring intelligence, experience, decision and proportion. Compounded of tact and experience, proportion is one of the foremost attributes of the manager.[19]

Moreover, Fayol stressed that in advancing a list of principles of management, he was not suggesting that there is a limit to the number of principles that might apply in different situations. Other principles could be identified. The principles he chose to review were simply those he had found most useful in his own career. The fourteen principles on which Fayol concentrated were:

- Division of work
- Authority
- Discipline
- Unity of command
- Unity of direction
- Subordination of individual interests to the general interest
- Remuneration
- Centralization
- Scalar chain (line of authority)
- Order
- Equity
- Stability of tenure of personnel
- Initiative
- *Esprit de corps*

Division of work is the well-known idea of assigning separate tasks to individual specialists with the intent of producing "more and better work with the same effort." Fayol recognized that division of labor leads to heightened expertise, which increases productivity. He also noted that as a result of the specialization that derives from division of work, jobs are performed more quickly because employees do not lose time shifting from one activity to another. At the same time, Fayol appreciated that benefits derived from dividing work must be balanced against obvious disadvantages associated with such negatives as boredom and monotony. As he unequivocally stated, "division of work has its limits which experience and a sense of proportion teach us may not be exceeded."[20]

Authority was defined as "the right to give orders and the power to exact obedience." Fayol distinguished between the formal authority managers held by

---

19. Ibid., p. 19.
20. Ibid., p. 20.

virtue of office or rank and personal authority, which was "compounded of intelligence, experience, moral worth, ability to lead, past services, etc."[21] Well ahead of modern-day scholars, Fayol recognized that savvy managers complement their official authority with personal authority. He further realized that authority and responsibility are corollaries in the sense that wherever authority is exercised, responsibility arises. Fayol stated the classic case for authority being commensurate with responsibility. This principle appears throughout the management literature.

Discipline is essentially respect and obedience between a firm and its employees. Fayol felt that discipline was vital for a smoothly functioning and prosperous firm. He viewed "defects in discipline" to be a result of ineptitude on the part of a firm's managers. Discipline came from placing knowledgeable managers at all levels of authority, workplace agreements that are satisfactory to both managers and employees, and the judicious use of employee sanctions.

Unity of command was expressed as: "For any action whatsoever an employee should receive orders from one superior only."[22] Just as the Biblical injunction advises: "No one can serve two masters." To Fayol, dual command was a threat to authority, discipline, and stability.

Unity of direction means "one head and one plan for a group of activities having the same objective."[23] It provides the coordination necessary for focusing a firm's efforts. Unity of direction comes from a sound organization structure and is essential to "unity of action."

Subordination of individual interests to the general interest is a plea to abolish "ignorance, ambition, selfishness, laziness, weakness and all human passions."[24] As viewed by Fayol, the placing of an individual's or group's interests over a firm's general welfare would inevitably lead to conflict among participating parties. Fayol's observations in this respect represent an early expression of what agency theory refers to as "opportunism," meaning a form of self-interested behavior (see Chapter19). Fayol recognized that individuals or groups who serve only themselves are harmful to the interests of their fellow employees and the interest of the firm in general.

Remuneration deals with day wages, piece rates, bonuses, and profit sharing. Fayol concluded that appropriate employee remuneration depends on many factors. In general, however, a firm's method of payment should be fair, should motivate by rewarding successful performance, and should not lead to excessive overpayment. Fayol also acknowledged nonfinancial incentives as a form of remuneration.

Centralization is a principle that Fayol felt was always present to a greater or lesser extent and, thus, belonged to the "natural order." His discussion of centralization as a question of proportion unique to each firm and his appreciation

———
21. Ibid., p. 21.

22. Ibid., p. 24.

23. Ibid., p. 25.

24. Ibid., p. 26.

of the distortion that occurs as information is serially transmitted along a scalar chain continues to offer valuable insights for contemporary managers:

> Centralization is not a system of management good or bad of itself, capable of being adopted or discarded at the whim of managers or of circumstances; it is always present to a greater or less extent. The question of centralization or decentralization is a simple question of proportion, it is a matter of finding the optimum degree for the particular concern. In small firms, where the manager's orders go directly to subordinates, there is absolute centralization; in large concerns, where a long scalar chain is interposed between manager and lower grades, orders and counterinformation, too, have to go through a series of intermediaries. Each employee, intentionally or unintentionally, puts something of himself into the transmission and execution of orders and of information received, too. He does not operate merely as a cog in a machine. What appropriate share of initiative may be left to intermediaries depends on the personal character of the manager, on his moral worth, on the reliability of his subordinates, and also on the condition of the business. The degree of centralization must vary according to different cases. The objective to pursue is the optimum utilization of all faculties of the personnel.[25]

Scalar chain refers to "the chain of superiors ranging from the ultimate authority to the lowest ranks."[26] As Fayol explained, this path shows a firm's line of authority and the links through which communications are transmitted from the top to the bottom of a firm and back. To counter possible communication delays caused by the unity-of-command principle, Fayol developed what is referred to as the "gang plank." The gang plank allows communications to cross lines of authority. Thus Foreman F, desiring to communicate a message to Foreman P, could do so directly without reporting upward (F through E to A) and having the message in turn transmitted downward to P. The gang plank (see Figure 10-1) permits lateral communication through the shortest path and avoids overburdening a firm's scalar chain.

Order, with regard to material things, ensures, in the words of a time-honored adage, "A place for everything and everything in its place." As Fayol noted, the same may be said for people, "The right man in the right place." The objective of *material order* is to avoid wasting resources. Fayol recognized that *social order* requires good organization and good selection and, by necessity, a need to balance a firm's human requirements with its available resources. Fayol considered ambition,

---

25. Ibid., p. 33.
26. Ibid., p. 34.

FIGURE 10-1 **FAYOL'S GANGPLANK**

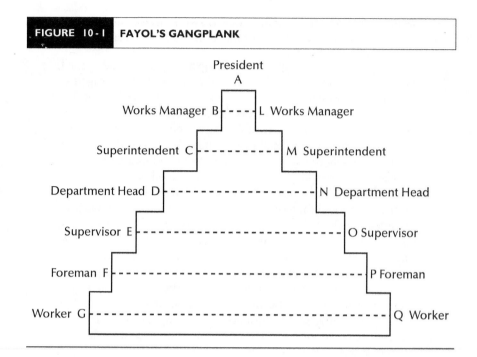

nepotism, favoritism, or merely ignorance, resulting in unnecessary positions or positions filled with incompetent employees, to be the enemies of social order.

Equity, as envisioned by Fayol, results from a combination of kindliness and justice. As such, equity provides a basis for dealing with employees and instilling devotion and loyalty. Fayol took care to distinguish between equity and equality and, in doing so, anticipated modern equity theory (see Chapter 20). Recognizing the difficulty invoked in instilling a sense of equity at all levels of a firm, Fayol—no doubt reflecting on his personal experience—observed that in dealing with employees' desire for equity, "the head of the business must frequently summon up his highest faculties."[27]

Fayol's twelfth principle, *stability of tenure of personnel*, sought to provide for orderly human-resource staffing and establishing provisions to ensure that a firm's employees possessed the requisite abilities for the work to be performed. Fayol appreciated that it took time to develop the necessary skills to perform at a superior level. He also recognized that it took time for a manager and a group of employees to develop into a high-performing team. In particular, managers must get to know their employees to inspire their confidence and, from experience, Fayol knew this can be a lengthy matter.

27. Ibid., p. 38.

Initiative, as a principle, exhorted employees to display zeal and energy in all endeavors. Fayol observed that "thinking out a plan and ensuring its success is...one of the most powerful stimulants of human endeavour...and...[this] is what is called initiative." Fayol considered the "freedom to propose and execute" to be key aspects of initiative that were essential to subordinate satisfaction. As Fayol thus realized, "The initiative of all, added to that of the manager, and supplementing it if need be, represents a great source of strength for businesses."[28]

Finally, *esprit de corps* stressed building harmony and unity within a firm. Fayol warned against sowing dissension among subordinates. Calling once again on his years of experience as a manager, he understood that "real talent is needed to co-ordinate effort, encourage keenness, use each man's abilities, and reward each one's merit without arousing jealousies and disturbing harmonious relations." Quoting the proverb, "union is strength," Fayol advised: "Dividing enemy forces to weaken them is clever, but dividing one's own team is a grave sin against the business."[29]

As Fayol explained, his principles were intended as guides to theory and practice and were not meant to be exhaustive in scope, nor were they meant to be rigidly applied. The factory system of production that developed during the Industrial Revolution (see Chapter 3) reflected many of these principles in practice. Fayol, however, was the first person to formulate them as a set of general management principles.

THE ELEMENTS OF MANAGEMENT

Fayol is also credited with being the first person to identify and describe the elements or functions that comprise a manager's job. He labeled these elements planning, organizing, command, coordination, and control. Taken together, these five elements represent what is often referred to as "the management process."

Planning

Fayol recognized that planning, by defining a firm's objectives, set the stage for the other elements of a manager's job. At various times, he used the French *prévoyance* (anticipation or foresight) instead of *préparer* (to plan) when discussing this element. To Fayol, managing meant looking ahead, and foresight was an essential element of managing. As described by Fayol, a firm's plan of action represented "the result envisaged" and should rest on (1) a firm's resources, including buildings, tools, materials, employees, sales outlets, and public relations; (2) the nature of work in process; and (3) future trends in a firm's business activities that cannot be predetermined. In modern terms, Fayol was describing a

---

28. Ibid., p. 39.
29. Ibid., p. 40.

rudimentary strategic audit that assesses a firm's present capabilities and strengths and scans the surrounding task environment to anticipate future marketplace opportunities. Fayol also understood the importance of what modern authorities call "contingency planning." He observed, "The best of plans cannot anticipate all unexpected occurrences which may arise, but it does include a place for these events and prepares the weapons which may be needed at the moment of being surprised."[30] On another occasion he observed:

> One cannot anticipate with precision everything which will happen over a longer period but one can minimize uncertainty and carry out one's program as a result. . . . any long-term program should be susceptible to being changed according to the variety, complexity and instability of events. Like any living object the industrial enterprise undergoes continuing transformations: the personnel, the tooling, the methods, even the goals of the association change; the program must without ceasing be kept, as far as possible, in harmony with the environment.[31]

In commenting on the advantages and shortcomings of the forecasting system he used at Comambault, Fayol underscored the benefit of involving a firm's managers in forecasting. In doing so, he showed an early appreciation of what would become known as "participative management":

> The study of resources, future possibilities, and means to be used for attaining the objective call for contributions from all departmental heads within the framework of their mandate, each one brings to this study the contribution of his experience together with recognition of the responsibility which will fall upon him in executing the plan.[32]

Such participation ensured that no resource was neglected and promoted managerial interest in a firm's future success. Furthermore, Fayol realized that lower-echelon managers would give increased attention to planning because they would be more committed to executing what they themselves had planned. Fayol saw that a good plan of action would facilitate the efficient use of a firm's resources and, in doing so, would possess certain characteristics: unity (one overall plan followed by specific plans for each supporting activity); continuity (incorporate both short-range and long-range plans); flexibility (be capable of adjusting to unexpected events); and precision (eliminate as many uncertainties as possible). Considering these characteristics, Fayol advised that firms establish a series of separate plans that

---

30. Ibid., p. 49.

31. Henri Fayol, "L'Exposé des Principes Généraux d'Administration," in Wren, Bedeian, and Breeze, "The Foundations of Henri Fayol's Administrative Theory," p. 915.

32. Fayol, *General and Industrial Management*, p. 48.

would together constitute one overall plan for obtaining their objectives. Thus, he recommended that daily, weekly, monthly, annual, five-year, and ten-year forecasts (or plans) be prepared and redrafted as time passed or as conditions changed.

Fayol's stress on long-range planning was a unique contribution to management thought, and his ideas are as important today as they were for his own time. He also offered innovative insights about planning on a national scale. The French government planned and budgeted on an annual basis with little or no regard for long-term development; the result was hand-to-mouth operations and a lack of fiscal responsibility on the part of government ministers. Fayol attributed the ministers' failure to develop long-term forecasts on the fact that ministers "come and go" and, thus, "have no time to acquire professional competence, business experience and managerial capacity indispensable to the drawing up of a plan."[33] For this reason, he argued for an increase in ministerial tenure to tie ministers to their work and to give them a sense of moral responsibility for the future of France.

Organizing

Organizing is the second element or function that Fayol identified as being part of a manager's job. For Fayol, organizing meant providing a firm with everything it needed to achieve its objectives. This included the classical factors of production: land, labor, and materials. Later writers divided Fayol's organizing element into two separate functions: organizing and staffing (human-resource management). According to Fayol, it was management's duty to ensure that a firm's "human and material organization is consistent with [its] objectives, resources, and require-ments."[34] In this regard, a firm should be structured to provide unity of direction, clearly defined duties, spur initiative and encourage responsibility, harmonize activ-ities and coordinate efforts, and ensure control without an "excess of regulation, red tape, and paper control."[35] Fayol appreciated that structure should not be an end in itself, ignoring the human factor:

> [T]o create a useful organization it is not enough to group people [into departments] and distribute duties; there must be knowledge of how to adapt the organic whole to requirements, how to find essential personnel and put each where he can be of most service. . . . Of two organizations similar in appearance, one may be excellent the other bad, depending on the personal qualities of those who compose them.[36]

33. Ibid., p. 52.
34. Ibid., p. 53.
35. Ibid., p. 54.
36. Ibid., p. 57.

Thus, Fayol realized it was people, not structure, that made the difference between the success of two otherwise similar firms. In retrospect, Fayol anticipated modern contingency theories of organizational design (see Chapter 20).

Fayol noted that the successive layers of authority that comprise an organization (the so-called organizational pyramid) are a product of functional and scalar growth. "Functional growth" relates to the horizontal structure of a firm, in that employees are added to perform functional duties as a firm's workload expands. In contrast, "scalar growth" is vertical, caused by the need to add layers of supervision to coordinate various activities divided among departments. Fayol described what happens to a firm's structure as its workforce increases. As an illustration he considered what happens relative to functional and scalar growth in a firm where fifteen employees report to each first-line supervisor, and in turn, each group of four supervisors is under the direction of a higher-level supervisor or manager. In such a situation, every sixty employees required four supervisors, and these four supervisors required one common manager. Fayol realized that there is a limit to the number of subordinates that a manager can effectively supervise. The number of subordinates that report directly to a manager is termed "span of control." Fayol advocated relatively narrow spans of control throughout a firm. With the exception of first-line supervisors, Fayol felt managers should typically have direct control over less than six subordinates. Where work was simple, a first-line supervisor could direct up to twenty or thirty employees.

On the subject of staff employees, Fayol visualized a group of individuals who had the "strength, knowledge, and time" to assist line managers by acting as an "extension of a manager's personality." Staff employees were to take orders only from a firm's general manager and to "subserve" line managers in dealing with daily obligations such as correspondence, interviews, and conferences, as well as to assist in harmonizing current and future plans. Based on his own experience as an executive, Fayol believed that line managers generally had neither the time nor the energy to devote to long-term considerations. Staff employees, freed of daily pressures associated with running a department, could "search for improvements" in work methods, identify developing changes in immediate business conditions, and consider longer-term trends.[37]

Fayol reviewed the differences between his recommendations for utilizing staff employees and Taylor's functional foremanship. Fayol agreed with Taylor's goal, providing specialized assistance, but disagreed with the means. Functional foremanship negated the unity-of-command principle, and to Fayol, this was treading on dangerous ground. Order must be maintained, and for Fayol this was possible only if no subordinate reported to more than one superior: "So.... let us treasure the old type of organization in which unity of command is honoured. It can, after all, be easily reconciled . . . with [staff] assistance given to superintendents

---

37. Ibid., p. 63.

and foremen."[38] In extending his comments, Fayol expressed the opinion that organization charts, showing all the positions in a firm and their relationships to one another, aided in maintaining the unity-of-command principle throughout a firm. He observed that, compared to lengthy written descriptions, organization charts enabled managers to more easily grasp a firm's "organic whole." Unfortunately, Fayol's complete thoughts on organizing were not published until many years after his passing.[39]

Focusing on what he referred to as the "body corporate," Fayol also commented on developing a firm's human resources. He especially viewed employee selection and training to be vital for determining a firm's fate. Fayol considered selecting capable employees to be among "the most important and most difficult of business activities." Noting that the consequences of poor selection are "commensurate with the rank of the employee," Fayol advised that the length of time devoted to choosing an employee should increase with the level of the position being filled. On balance, like Taylor, Fayol's treatment of evaluating a firm's employees was limited, reflecting the rudimentary practices of the day. Training, in contrast, was dealt with at length, primarily because Fayol had an ulterior motive. As previously discussed, Fayol called for less technical training of young engineers and an increase in attention to the elements of management. In Fayol's view, contemporary education in French schools was based on two illusions: "that the value of engineers and industrial leaders comprises technical ability almost exclusively [and] bears a direct relationship to the number of years devoted to the subject of mathematics."[40] Fayol believed that the latter "illusion" was just as "dire" as the former, but would likely prove harder to dispel: "Long personal experience has taught me that the use of *higher* mathematics counts for nothing in managing businesses."[41] Basic mathematics helped train the mind, but further study should be devoted to management rather than more mathematics. Fayol sought balance and advised young engineers to study workmen, "their behaviour, character, abilities, work, and even their personal interests."[42] Indeed, Fayol thought that everyone should study the elements of management, for they were necessary in the workshop as well as in the home.

Command, Coordination, and Control

Having been formed, Fayol reasoned that a firm must be set into motion. He viewed this as the "mission of command," as spread among a firm's managers. Fayol used

---

38. Ibid., p. 70.

39. What was to be a continuation of Fayol's *Administration Industrielle et Générale* appears in Jean-Louis Peaucelle, *Henri Fayol, Inventeur des Outils des Gestion: Textes Originaux et Recherches Actuelles* (Paris: Economica, 2003).

40. Fayol, *General and Industrial Management*, pp. 83–84.

41. Ibid., p. 84. By "higher mathematics" Fayol meant "special mathematics," such as differential and integral calculus.

42. Ibid., p. 91.

the French *commander* (to command) as well as *diriger* (to direct) in his writing. Because "command" has a more specific meaning in English, perhaps the most representative translation of this third element of management would be "to direct or to supervise." Fayol felt that it was every manager's duty to "get the optimum return from all employees" and that doing so required certain personal qualities and principles of management. Fayol held that managers should:

- Have a thorough knowledge of their employees
- Eliminate incompetent employees
- Be well versed in the agreements binding a firm and its employees
- Set a good example for others
- Conduct periodic audits of a firm's performance
- Confer with their assistants as a group to provide for unity of direction and the focusing of effort
- Avoid becoming engrossed in detail
- Strive at making unity, energy, initiative, and loyalty prevail among all employees[43]

In a diary entry dated July 29, 1898, Fayol wrote: "In business administration, the question of [managing] people represents more than one-half of the problem."[44] As a young manager, Fayol had built effective work teams in the Commentry mines, discontinued paternalistic practices such as monitoring employee church attendance, closed company-owned stores in areas where local merchants were present, and demonstrated other people-management skills that led to his promotions. With people representing one-half of the challenge managers faced, Fayol learned that communication skills were crucial. He saw conferring with assistants to be important for establishing and maintaining clear communications. His admonition to avoid being engrossed in detail was not antithetical to keeping informed, but rather meant to be a warning not to neglect large problems while lavishing attention on picayune matters. Further reflecting an appreciation of the human element, Fayol believed that to encourage initiative, managers should allow subordinates "the maximum share of activity consistent with their position and capability, even at the cost of some mistakes."[45] Moreover, Fayol felt that authority should be delegated downward to develop employees' abilities and to avoid "drying up initiative and loyalty."

Coordination was Fayol's fourth element or function of management. By coordination, Fayol meant "to harmonize all the activities of a concern so as to facilitate its working, and its success."[46] Later writers have stressed the necessity of coordination in all elements of management rather than treating it as a separate element. To Fayol, coordination required balancing expenses with revenues, equipment maintenance

43. Ibid., pp. 97–98.

44. Henri Fayol, in Blancpain, "Les Cahiers Inédits d'Henri Fayol," p. 24.

45. Fayol, *General and Industrial Management*, pp. 102–103.

46. Ibid., p. 103.

with meeting production goals, and sales against production. The functions of planning and organizing facilitated coordination by specifying duties, establishing schedules, and focusing responsibilities on furthering a firm's objectives. Command instilled initiative, and conferences with assistants and subordinates provided a clearinghouse for airing problems, progress, and plans. Fayol recommended that line managers use staff employees to enhance coordination, but warned that their use did not replace line managers' direct responsibility for achieving a firm's objectives.

Control, Fayol's final element of management, consisted of "verifying whether everything occurs in conformity with the plan adopted, the instructions issued, and the principles established."[47] According to Fayol, the objective of control was to identify errors so as to correct them and prevent their recurrence. Control was to be applied to people, objects, and activities. Effective control should be based on prompt action, followed by sanctions, if necessary. Fayol saw control as having an integrative effect on the other elements of management because it could be used to stimulate better planning, simplify and strengthen a firm's organization structure, enhance the directing of employees, and facilitate coordination. In effect, control completed a cycle of managerial activities that could then be improved as the management process continued.

A FINAL NOTE

Fayol's orientation was that of an upper-level administrator. He believed that "the responsibility of general management is to conduct the enterprise toward its objective by making optimum use of available resources. It is the executive authority, it draws up the plan of action, selects personnel, determines performance, ensures and controls the execution of all activities."[48]

For all intents and purposes, Fayol was a strategist before that term became popular.[49] The familiar ring of Fayol's ideas suggests how thoroughly they have penetrated current managerial thinking. Whereas many of them may seem relatively self-evident today, they were revolutionary when first advanced. They remain important not only because of Fayol's influence on succeeding generations of managers, but also because of the continuing validity of his work. As a keen observer of management practice has noted: "Whether they admit it or not, it's obvious most managers today are fundamentally Fayolists."[50] For this reason, Fayol is known as the "Father of Modern Management."

---

47. Ibid., p. 107.

48. Fayol, *General and Industrial Management*, pp. 61–62. Also see p. 6.

49. Daniel A. Wren, "Henri Fayol as Strategist: A Nineteenth Century Corporate Turnaround," *Management Decision* 39 (2001), pp. 475–487. See also Lee D. Parker and Philip A. Ritson, "Revisiting Fayol: Anticipating Contemporary Management," *British Journal of Management* 16 (2005), pp. 175–194; Daniel A. Wren, "The Influence of Henri Fayol on Management Theory and Education in North America," *Enterprises et Histoire* 34 (2003), pp. 98–107.

50. [W. Jerome Arnold], "Famous Firsts: Discoveries from Looking Inward," *Business Week* (June 6, 1964), p. 152.

BUREAUCRACY: MAX WEBER

The life and work of Max Weber (1864–1920) ran chronologically parallel to those of Henri Fayol and Frederick Taylor. Born in Germany to a life of affluence in a family with social and political connections, Weber (pronounced *Vay-ber*) was an intellectual of the first degree, with far-ranging interests in sociology, religion, economics, and political science. In 1904, while in the final stages of preparing his epochal study, *The Protestant Ethic and the Spirit of Capitalism*,[51] on why capitalism flourished in certain parts of seventeenth- and eighteenth-century Europe and not others, Weber had an opportunity to visit the United States, which he considered the most capitalistic of all nations. Weber was invited to give a lecture, "The Relations of the Rural Community to Other Branches of Social Sciences," at the International Congress of Arts and Sciences, which was being held in conjunction with the St. Louis World's Fair.[52] He

*Max Weber, circa 1896 or 1897.
© 1988 by Transaction Publishers.
Reprinted by the permission of the
publisher.*

combined attending the conference with a stop in New York City to do some further research at Columbia University and the New York Public Libraries, a short stay with relatives in Mount Airy, North Carolina, and, to see firsthand how the spirit of capitalism abounded in the United States, visits to various cities, including Philadelphia, Washington, Baltimore, Boston, Chicago, New Orleans, and Tuskegee, Alabama, and the Muskogee Indian Territory in Oklahoma.[53]

The economic developments he observed in the United States were somewhat different from those in Germany. U.S. manufacturing and marketing had grown from small stores and owner-managed businesses to large professionally managed firms that were bound together by an intercontinental network of communication and transportation. In Germany, large-scale firms had been developed only in chemicals, metals, and complex industrial machine-goods.[54] In these industries,

---

51. Max Weber, *The Protestant Ethic and the Spirit of Capitalism*, trans. Talcott Parsons (London: Allen & Unwin, 1930). (Originally published 1904.)

52. Max Weber, "The Relations of the Rural Community to Other Branches of Social Science," C. W. Seidenadel, trans., in Howard J. Rogers, ed., *Congress of Arts and Science, Universal Exposition*, St. Louis, vol. 7. (Boston: Houghton Mifflin, 1906), pp. 725–746.

53. Brann, Henry Walter, "Max Weber and the United States," *Southwestern Social Science Quarterly* 25 (June 1944), pp. 18–30. See also Larry G. Keeter, "Max Weber's Visit to North Carolina," *Journal of the History of Sociology*," 3 (1981), pp. 108–114.

54. Alfred D. Chandler, Jr., "The Emergence of Managerial Capitalism," *Business History Review* 58 (Winter 1984), pp. 498–501.

cartels had been formed to control prices and ration markets. Whereas in the United States this practice was limited by antitrust laws, German cartels could operate without fear of either government intervention or threat of competition. In contrast to Germany, in the United States a "spirit of capitalism" encouraged innovation and competition.

BUREAUCRACY AS THE IDEAL

Primarily prescriptive in nature, Weber's writings strike an interesting contrast with the practitioner-oriented recommendations offered by Taylor and Fayol. Weber's major contribution was an outline of the characteristics of what he termed "bureaucracy," that is, government by bureaus (German *Büro*).[55] In reviewing Weber's work, it is important to emphasize four points:

1. Weber did not use the term *bureaucracy* in the disparaging, emotionally tinged sense of red tape, endless lines, and rule-encumbered inefficiency. Rather, he used it as a noncritical label referring to what he regarded as the most modern and efficient method of organizing yet developed. In Weber's words,

   > Experience tends universally to show that the purely bureaucratic type of administrative organization—that is, the monocratic variety of bureaucracy—is, from a purely technical point of view, capable of attaining the highest degree of efficiency and is in this sense formally the most rational known means of carrying out imperative control over human beings. It is superior to any other form in precision, in stability, in the stringency of its discipline, and in its reliability. It thus makes possible a particularly high degree of calculability of results for the heads of the organization and for those acting in relation to it. It is finally superior both in intensive efficiency and in the scope of its operations and is formally capable of application to all kinds of administrative tasks.[56]

   What is not often understood is that bureaucracy developed as a reaction against the personal subjugation and cruelty, as well as the capricious and subjective judgments, of earlier administrative systems (such as monarchies and dictatorships) in which the lives and fortunes of all were completely dependent on the whims of a despot whose only law was his own wish. For

---

55. The word "bureaucracy" was coined by Frenchman Vincent de Gournay in 1745. See Fred Riggs, "Shifting Meanings of the Term 'Bureaucracy,'" *International Social Science Journal* 31 (1979), pp. 563–584.

56. Max Weber, *The Theory of Social and Economic Organization*, trans. A. M. Henderson and Talcott Parsons, ed. Talcott Parsons (New York: Free Press, 1947), p. 337. (Originally published 1922.)

this reason, the benefits Weber attributed to bureaucracy can perhaps best be understood when compared to the alternatives it replaced. "Thus, for example, tax farming, whereby local collectors worked for a percentage of the take, was displaced by bureaucracies staffed with full-time salaried officials; inside contracting, whereby owners of equipment and materials contracted with foremen for labor, gave way to modern hierarchies."[57] When compared to the administrative practices that preceded them, the efficiencies attributed to bureaucracies become understandable.

The world observed by Weber was decidedly unjust. It was dominated by class consciousness and nepotism. To be a military officer or a leader in government or industry presupposed an aristocratic birth. In Weber's view, this was a ridiculous waste of human resources that ran counter to his belief that the working class could produce leaders as well as followers. Bureaucracy, with its emphasis on legal authority (see point 3), was intended to put an end to the exploitation of employees and to ensure equal opportunity and treatment for all.

2. To Weber, bureaucracy was an ideal that did not exist in reality.[58] It was a standard or model to be used not only in organizing a firm, but also in assessing, through comparison, its relative performance. In this regard Weber's bureaucratic model is hypothetical rather than factual. It is not meant to be a working model, nor is it meant to correspond to reality.

3. Weber's ideal bureaucracy is based on *legal* authority as contrasted with that which rests on either *tradition* (custom) or *charisma* ("the gift of grace").[59] As developed by Weber, legal authority stems from rules and other controls that govern an undertaking in the pursuit of specific goals. Managers are given the authority to interpret and enforce these rules and other controls by virtue of their position. Obedience is not owed to a person but to the impersonal authority of an office. Thus, authority adheres to specific positions rather than to individuals. This is necessary if authority is to outlast the tenure of individual officeholders. Familiar examples of legal authority structures are the military, politically elected offices, government bureaus, colleges or universities, and business firms (especially those above a certain size).

---

57. Marshall W. Meyer, "Organizational Structure as Signaling," *Pacific Sociological Review* 22 (1979), p. 484.

58. Max Weber, *The Methodology of the Social Sciences*, ed. and trans. Edward A. Shils and Henry H. Finch (Glencoe, IL: Free Press, 1949). (Originally published 1914–1917.)

59. Weber, *The Theory of Social and Economic Organization*, p. 328. See also Max Weber, "The Three Types of Legitimate Rule," trans. Hans Gerth, *Berkeley Journal of Sociology* 4 (1958), pp. 1–11. (Originally published 1922.)

4. The need Weber identified for efficient organizing is inherently culture free. Reliance on rationality and legalism, the idea of equality of citizens and the vast services offered in a modern state, make some form of expert administration unavoidable. In addition, the increasing size of firms, advanced technology, and the global marketplace make bureaucracy inevitable. Thus, bureaucracy in government was followed by an increase in the bureaucracy of business corporations, trade unions, churches, service groups, and voluntary associations. Today, *all* undertakings of any size in any culture are bureaucratic to some degree.

THE ADVANTAGES OF BUREAUCRACY

Weber identified the essential characteristics of his "ideal" bureaucracy and believed that specific advantages would accrue to undertakings that embodied them. These characteristics and sample advantages include:

- *Division of Labor.* Labor is divided so that authority and responsibility are clearly defined.

     Advantage—*Efficiency* will increase through specialization.

- *Managerial Hierarchy.* Offices or positions are organized in a hierarchy of authority.

     Advantage—A clear chain of command will develop from the highest to the lowest level of an organization (Fayol's scalar chain principle), defining different levels of authority, and thus individual discretion, as well as enabling better communication.

- *Formal Selection.* All employees are selected on the basis of technical qualifications demonstrated by formal examination, education, or training.

     Advantage—Employees will be hired and promoted based on merit and expertise, thus, benefiting both them and their employer.

- *Career Orientation.* Although a measure of flexibility is attained by electing higher-level officials who presumably express the will of an electorate (for example, a body of citizens or a board of directors), employees are career professionals rather than "politicians." They work for fixed salaries and pursue "careers" within their respective fields.

     Advantage—The hiring of "career" professionals will ensure the performance of assigned duties without regard for extraneous pressures, as well as ensure a continuity of operations across election cycles.

- *Formal Rules and Other Controls.* All employees are subject to formal rules and other controls regarding the performance of their duties.

     Advantage—Efficiency will increase as formal rules and other controls relating to employee performance are enforced.

- *Impersonality.* Rules and other controls are impersonal and uniformly applied in all cases.

     Advantage—When rules and other controls are applied impersonally and uniformly, involvement with personalities and personal preferences is avoided. Subordinates are thereby protected from arbitrary actions of their superiors.[60]

THE DISADVANTAGES OF BUREAUCRACY

Although Weber considered bureaucracy to be the most efficient means of organizing, both his own experience and subsequent research have shown that it often results in certain disadvantages. These include:

- Rules and other controls may take on a significance of their own and, as a consequence, become ends in themselves. Employees, for example, may accuse budget personnel of being more interested in applying rules and regulations than achieving a firm's primary goals.
- Extreme devotion to rules and other controls may lead to situations in which past decisions are blindly repeated without appreciation or concern for changed conditions. Such "bureaucratic rigidity" results in managers being compensated for doing what they are told and not for thinking. The result is "rule by rules" rather than common sense.
- Whereas delegation of authority to lower levels may increase operational effectiveness, it may also encourage an emphasis on subunit rather than overall goals, thereby prompting subunit conflict and decreasing effectiveness. A typical example can be found in many universities where conflicts over which department is going to offer what courses often result in unnecessary duplication of subject offerings, as well as the unnecessary expenditure of resources.
- Although rules and other controls are intended to counter worker apathy, they may actually contribute to it by defining unacceptable behavior and, thus, specifying a minimum level of acceptable performance. That is, it is possible, once rules have been defined, for employees to *remain* apathetic, for they now know just how *little* they can do and still remain secure.

---

60. Max Weber, *From Max Weber: Essays in Sociology*, ed. and trans. Hans H. Gerth and C. Wright Mills (New York: Oxford University Press, 1946), pp. 196–294. (Originally published in 1922.)

This is commonly known as "working to the rules," because what is not covered by rules is by definition not an employee's responsibility. Within an educational setting, statements such as "all students must attend at least 50 percent of the classes during a term to pass" or "the minimum requirement for graduation is a C average on all course work undertaken" are illustrations of this phenomenon in that they clearly define *minimum* levels of acceptable behavior. Unfortunately, a typical administrative response in such circumstances is to enact additional bureaucratic rules (such as mandatory class attendance) and, in turn, further aggravate an already poor situation. Unless care is taken, however, such a situation may result in a "vicious circle of bureaucracy," because once employees discover the appeasing effect of rules, they may push for even more controls to further restrict management's power. Therefore rules maybe functional in one sense, but in another (unintended) sense, they permit employee involvement without requiring emotional commitment.

Despite these and other criticisms, bureaucratic management is a central feature in modern societies. It is thus important to realize that the disadvantages just outlined are not necessarily inherent in bureaucracy per se. As envisioned by Weber, the bureaucratic model is both rational and efficient. Gaining its benefits, however, requires learning enough about its characteristics to avoid being controlled by them.

Though many of us may feel that we live in a bureaucratic world of baffling rules and other controls, we should not forget that bureaucracy also makes it possible for us to get potable water instantly, place an international telephone call in seconds, and have a package delivered a continent away overnight. Indeed, almost all the benefits we take for granted in today's society—modern medicine, modern science, modern industry—rest on a bureaucratic foundation. In this respect, Weber's ideas have stood the test of time remarkably well. His pioneering work, like that of Fayol, has stimulated a wealth of research into the management process and remains a landmark in the evolution of management thought. In recognition of his contributions in developing the tenets of bureaucracy, Weber is known as the "Father of Organization Theory." Weber's goal was not perfection, but systematization—moving managerial practice and organizational design toward more logical ways of operating. Weber's work on bureaucracy remained largely unknown to English-speaking audiences until it began to be translated in the late 1920s. Like Fayol, Weber had to wait until cultural conditions created the need to think in theoretical terms. As firms grew in size and complexity, the search for a theory of organizations led researchers and practitioners to Max Weber and his bureaucratic model.

SUMMARY

The emergence of the management process and organization theory took place in two forms: Fayol's identification of the principles and elements of management and Weber's search for an ideal way of organizing. From different backgrounds and perspectives, both Fayol and Weber attempted to develop methods for managing large-scale organizations. Fayol stressed education for management rather than technical training, the importance of planning, organizing, command, coordination, and control. Weber sought to replace authority based on tradition and charisma with legal authority and to prescribe an impersonal and merit basis for selecting, hiring, and promoting employees. Both Weber and Fayol had history's misfortune of being overshadowed by others and having to wait until after their deaths to receive proper credit for their roles in the ongoing evolution of management thought.

11 Scientific Management in Theory and Practice

Whereas Taylor and his contemporaries provided the early impetus for the scientific-management movement, several other individuals helped shepherd the movement to maturity. Their efforts took place along various dimensions. First, following the urging of Towne and Fayol, there was an increased recognition of the need to introduce college curricula to formalize the study of management, as well as to undertake efforts to educate practicing managers in properly applying the principles of scientific management. Second, as the scientific management movement grew in the United States, it sparked attention in other parts of the world, including Great Britain, continental Europe, the Soviet Union, and Japan. Finally, moving beyond the shop floor, an interest in scientific management led to a broader conception of general management and the need to examine and refine a wide range of organizational practices related to large-scale enterprises.

THE STUDY AND PRACTICE OF SCIENTIFIC MANAGEMENT

The Wharton School of Finance and Economy, established at the University of Pennsylvania in 1881, was the world's first successful undergraduate school of business. The Wharton School was founded by Joseph Wharton, a philanthropist and industrialist in Philadelphia, who had built an industrial empire focusing on metallurgy, running both the Bethlehem Steel Corporation and the American Nickel Company. It was not until seventeen years later (1898) that the second and third schools of business were begun at the University of Chicago and the University of California at Berkeley. The Amos Tuck School of Administration and Finance at Dartmouth College, founded in 1900, was the first graduate school of business administration; the second graduate school of business was founded in 1908 at Harvard University. Tuck was the first institution to offer the Master of Business Administration (MBA) degree. Despite Taylor's belief that aspiring managers had to live their calling and learn through years of shop-floor experience, the benefits of studying management as a formal discipline were quickly recognized.

EDUCATION FOR INDUSTRIAL MANAGEMENT

Exactly when management first became an academic subject per se is impossible to determine. Towne's 1886 American Society of Mechanical Engineering (ASME) paper, in which he observed that the study of management was wholly unorganized, had no medium for the exchange of experience, and was without professional associations, was clearly a landmark in calling for a remedy to what he recognized as an untenable situation. In October 1895, John Richards (1834–1917) presented a series of ten lectures on works administration at Stanford University.[1] Dexter Kimball (1865–1952), dean of Cornell University's Sibley College of Engineering, credited Taylor's 1903 ASME paper on shop management with inspiring his own course in works administration.[2] Starting in the spring term of the 1904–1905 academic year, the course addressed the economic basis of "modern" production. His 1913 textbook, *Principles of Industrial Organization,* grew from his course notes.[3] The course applied scientific management to plant location, equipment policies, production control, labor compensation, and much more. Kimball stressed the need for scientific management, noting that "as industrial enterprises have grown in magnitude, as processes have become more refined and competition more keen the problems of organization have steadily grown in importance."[4]

With a growing appreciation and emphasis on scientific management among engineers, in particular, and the general public, more widely, ASME experienced an identity crisis: Was its purpose to further mechanical engineering, or was it to become an outlet for ideas about incentives, cost accounting, and other facets of sound management? ASME refused to publish Taylor's *The Principles of Scientific Management* in its official journal due to disagreements within the society about its appropriateness and interest to the membership. As a result, Taylor had the book privately printed and distributed.[5] By 1919, however, four years after Taylor's

———

1. Richard J. Whiting, "John Richards—California Pioneer of Management Thought," *California Management Review* 6, no. 2 (Winter 1963), pp. 35–38.

2. Dexter S. Kimball, *I Remember* (New York: McGraw-Hill, 1953), p. 85.

3. *Idem, Principles of Industrial Organization* (New York: McGraw-Hill, 1913).

4. Ibid., p. vii.

5. Carol Carlson Dean, *The Principles of Scientific Management* by Frederick W. Taylor: The Private Printing," *Journal of Management History*, 3 no. 1 (1997), pp. 18–30.

death, ASME recognized industrial engineering as a legitimate subject for study. It created a Management Division in 1920.[6] By 1922, this was AMSE's largest division. Industrial engineering and industrial management became continuing threads in collegiate education, as the work of Taylor, Gilbreth, Gantt, and others led to research in ergonomics, or the study of human factors related to the design of jobs to maximize the efficiency and quality of employees' work.

For those pursuing graduate-level studies, Dartmouth's Tuck school led the way; by 1910 the Dartmouth catalog listed a course in business management. As dean of the Tuck School, Harlow S. Person (1875–1955) hosted the first scientific management conference in the United States.[7] As president of the Taylor Society (successor to the Society to Promote the Science of Management), Person's efforts broadened interest in scientific management. He extended the society's membership and range of interests and took an expansive view of business education. Person worked to dissipate the notion that scientific management was merely the use of a stopwatch. In Person's view, educators should emphasize the philosophy underlying scientific management and focus on developing creative leadership in industry.

Person also recognized the value of involving social scientists in the study of management. He believed that management and labor were so closely entwined in daily activities that they failed to see larger relationships; however, social scientists would be able to take a larger, more objective view of workplace dynamics to chart a future course of action for research and practice.[8]

C. Bertrand Thompson (1882–1969) was "an educator, a missionary of the gospel," who taught at Harvard from 1908 to 1917. Thompson was instrumental in inducing Taylor to give his Harvard lectures. Thompson compiled the most extensive bibliography of scientific management for that period, became a consultant (getting his start from Taylor), and did much to further the scientific-management movement in both academia and industry.[9] Thompson's Harvard affiliation and the notion

---

6. Mikiyoshi Hirose, "The Attitude of the American Society of Mechanical Engineers Toward Management: Suggestions for a Revised Interpretation," *Kansai University Review of Economics and Business* 25 (September 1996), pp. 125–148.

7. *Addresses and Discussions at the Conference on Scientific Management held October 12, 13, 14, Nineteen Hundred and Eleven* (Hanover, NH: Amos Tuck School of Administration and Finance, Dartmouth College, 1912).

8. H. S. Person, "The Manager, the Workman and the Social Scientist," *Bulletin of the Taylor Society* 3 (February 1917), pp. 1–7.

9. Ronald G. Greenwood and Regina A. Greenwood, "C. Bertrand Thompson—Pioneer Management Bibliographer," in Robert L. Taylor, Michael J. O'Donnell, Robert A. Zawacki, and Donald D. Warwick, eds., *Proceedings of the Annual Meeting of the Academy of Management* (August 1976), pp. 3–6. See also C. Bertrand Thompson, ed., *Scientific Management: A Collection of the More Significant Articles Describing the Taylor System of Management* (Cambridge, MA: Harvard University Press, 1914) and *idem, The Theory and Practice of Scientific Management* (Boston: Houghton Mifflin, 1917).

of management as a "science" gave credibility to the study of management among those who opposed business education as too vocational.[10]

Leon P. Alford (1877–1942) was another among the early group contributing to management education.[11] Alford was trained as an electrical engineer, worked in industry, became editor-in-chief of the influential journals *American Machinist, Industrial Engineering, Management Engineering,* and *Manufacturing Industries.* He also edited a number of early management handbooks. His role in management education has not been generally acknowledged by management historians; nevertheless, his influence as a journal editor, on various professional committees, and through his books was substantial.[12] Among Alford's early writings was an attempt to provide a correct interpretation of science in management. Writing with Englishman A. Hamilton Church, he deplored the term "scientific management" because it was interpreted to mean that there was "a science rather than an art of management."[13]

The weakness of the Taylor approach, in Alford and Church's view, was that it superseded the art of leadership by substituting an "elaborate mechanism," or system. They did not mean that the mechanism was useless, but rather that it overlooked the dynamic possibilities of effective leadership. Alford thought that Taylor's so-called principles were too mechanical. To remedy this problem, he (and Church) proposed three broad principles: (1) the systematic use of experience, (2) the economic control of effort, and (3) the promotion of personal effectiveness. The first emphasized both personal experiences of executives and scientific studies; the second was based on the subprinciples of division of labor, coordination, conservation (least effort expended to a given end), and remuneration; and the third stressed personal rewards, developing contented workers, and promoting the workers' physical and mental health. From these three broad, regulative principles, Alford and Church believed a truly scientific basis for the art of management could be discovered.

Alford's call for art plus science in management was a reflection of his admiration for Henry L. Gantt, about whom he prepared an excellent biography. In the style of Gantt, Alford pleaded for industrial engineers to become involved in community

---

10. Daniel Nelson, "Scientific Management and the Transformation of University Business Education," in Daniel Nelson, ed., *A Mental Revolution: Scientific Management since Taylor* (Columbus: Ohio State University Press, 1992), pp. 77–101.

11. William J. Jaffe, *L. P. Alford and the Evolution of Modern Industrial Management* (New York: New York University Press, 1957).

12. Leon P. Alford, ed., *Management's Handbook* (New York: Ronald Press, 1924); and later, *Cost and Production Handbook* (New York: Ronald Press, 1934) and *Production Handbook* with John R. Bangs, eds. (New York: Ronald Press: 1944). See also L. P. Alford, *Laws of Management Applied to Manufacturing* (New York: Ronald Press, 1928), and *Principles of Industrial Management* (New York: Ronald Press, 1940).

13. Alexander H. Church and Leon P. Alford, "The Principles of Management," *American Machinist* 36, no. 22 (May 30, 1912), pp. 857–861.

service and foster improved relations between employers and employees. Alford continued to stress these themes as a member of the American Engineering Council and contributed to the better known reports of this group, including *The Elimination of Waste in Industry, The Twelve Hour Shift,* and *Safety and Production.*

THE INTERNATIONAL
SCIENTIFIC-MANAGEMENT MOVEMENT

Europe

Whereas the Industrial Revolution began in Great Britain and spread to the United States, the scientific-management movement began in the United States and spread abroad. As early as 1907, Taylor was in touch with French scientist Henri Le Chatelier (1850–1936) regarding metal cutting, time study, and Le Chatelier's efforts to introduce scientific management in France.[14] When Fred and Louise Taylor visited Europe in 1912, and again in 1913, Le Chatelier introduced Taylor to industrialist Louis Renault and Edouard and André Michelin, founders of the Michelin Tyre Company (*Compagnie Générale des Établissements Michelin*). Before World War I, various scientific-management methods had been adapted by the Michelins and Renault and were also used in government-operated arsenals. The initial French experience with scientific management, however, was less than positive: managers seized the methods and forgot the "mental revolution." In general, as had happened to Taylor's disgust in the United States, managers perverted what Taylor had described as scientific management.[15] After a strike at the Renault automobile plant in 1913, Taylor wrote Le Chatelier: "If a man [Renault] deliberately goes against the experience of men who know what they are talking about, and refuses to follow advice given in a kind but unmistakable way, it seems to me that he deserves to get into trouble."[16] Although the French used the term *Taylorisme* to refer to *l'organisation scientifique du travail*, in reality the application of Taylor's ideas fell far short of their scientific ideal.

Another Frenchman, Charles de Fréminville (1856–1936), learned of scientific management through Le Chatelier's translations of Taylor's writings.[17] Fréminville became a second-leading French proponent of *Taylorisme*. Le Chatelier attempted to apply the principles of scientific management to the French manufacturer *Panhard et Levassor*, a pioneer in the automobile industry. Panhard and Levassor's managers resisted Le Chatelier's efforts, or simply took those parts of scientific management

---

14. Lyndall Urwick and E. F. L. Brech, *The Making of Scientific Management: Thirteen Pioneers*, vol. 1 (London: Sir Isaac Pitman and Sons, 1951), pp. 93–104.

15. George G. Humphreys, *Taylorism in France, 1904–1920: The Impact of Scientific Management on Factory Relations and Society* (New York: Garland, 1986).

16. Cited in Daniel Nelson, *Frederick W. Taylor and the Rise of Scientific Management* (Madison: University of Wisconsin Press, 1980), p. 179.

17. Urwick and Brech, pp. 105–111.

they felt would lead to quick returns at little cost. Fréminville did not lose interest, however; as noted in Chapter 10, he and Le Chatelier helped merge Fayol's *Centre d'Etudes Administratives* with the *Conference de l'Organisation Française* to form the still active *Comité National de l'Organisation Française.*

International interest widened scientific management's frontiers along separate, yet related, paths. In 1924, the First International Congress on Scientific Management was held in Prague; among those attending from the United States were Harlow Person, representing the Taylor Society, and Lillian M. Gilbreth, representing her husband, Frank. An International Committee of Scientific Management (*Le Comité International de l'Organisation Scientifique,* known as CIOS) was formed to continue meeting to exchange ideas about management. Subsequent meetings were held in Brussels (1925), Rome (1927), Paris (1929), Amsterdam (1932), London (1935), and Washington, DC (1938). The 1941 meeting, to be held in Berlin, was cancelled due to World War II. CIOS would not continue its work until after the end of hostilities.

Beginning in the 1920s, the Twentieth Century Fund, endowed by the Boston department-store owner Edward A. Filene (1860–1939) and the Rockefeller Foundation, sought to promote improved management, particularly scientific management, in European industry, which was rebuilding following World War I. The International Management Institute (IMI), a spin-off from the Geneva-based International Labor Organization, was formed in 1927 to gather research about better management practices. Frenchman Paul Devinat (1890–1980), formerly chief of the IMI Employers' Organisation Service, was appointed the IMI's first director.[18] He was succeeded in 1928 by Englishman Lt. Colonel Lyndall F. Urwick, whom we will discuss later. The IMI, however, continued to have problems with contending national employer groups, the threat of war, the rise of fascism in Europe, and a subsequent worldwide economic depression that undercut its funding. The IMI ceased its activities in January 1934, when the Twentieth Century Fund withdrew its financial support.[19]

By the close of World War I, Europe had become familiar with the principles of management as developed in the United States. This was particularly true in France. A large measure of France's success in rebuilding its industrial base following World War I was credited to the use of scientific-management methods.[20] In contrast to the French, authorities disagree on the British experience with scientific management. According to Urwick and Brech, "the Taylor doctrine" was not well received in Great Britain. Taylor had engendered a measure of bitterness with British manufacturers

18. Charles D. Wrege, Ronald G. Greenwood, and Sakae Hata, "The International Management Institute and Political Opposition to its Efforts in Europe, 1925–1934," *Business and Economic History* 16 (1987), pp. 249–265.

19. Trevor Boyns, "Lyndall Urwick at the International Management Institute, Geneva, 1928–1934: Right Job, Wrong Man?" Paper presented at the European Business History Association, 11th Annual Conference, Geneva, 13–15 September 2007.

20. Harry A. Hopf, *The Management Movement at the Cross-Roads* (New York: H. A. Hopf and Company, 1932), p. 14.

over patent rights for the manufacture of high-speed steel, and organized labor also opposed Taylor's methods.[21] Whitson, however, found that British engineering journals referred to Taylor's work fairly frequently and, often, positively.[22] The management movement in Britain did, however, take on a more conservative stance than in the United States. Evidence suggests that Hans Renold Co., a chain-making firm, was the first company to introduce scientific management as Taylor would have desired.[23] Hans Renold (1852–1943) met with Taylor in the United States on three occasions and was impressed with the application of Taylor's methods at the Link-Belt Company. Renold and his son, Charles, were able to implement scientific management successfully, but one authority has suggested that their example "did not appear to make scientific management any more widely accepted [in Great Britain]."[24]

In Germany, Taylor's work was well known, and any number of consultants claimed to apply Taylor's principles. Gilbreth's work was well known, as he spent much time in Germany. Bertrand Thompson applied Taylor's principles at AEG (General Electric Company) and a tool manufacturer. Georg Schlesinger gave lectures on the Taylor System at Charlottenburg Higher Technical School.[25]

In other countries, the scientific-management movement passed through various stages: first, propagandizing and translations by individuals such as Le Chatelier; second, adaptation by individual firms to meet their own needs; and finally, adjustment through various committees, conferences, and international organizations.[26] Varying political and economic structures across nations made it difficult to apply pure scientific management as Taylor would have advocated. Consequently, managers often grasped the mechanics of time study, incentive schemes, and so on, without applying Taylor's philosophy. Europe, which had a long history of organized labor, with an often radical nature, also encountered more resistance from unions than was encountered in the United States. Further, an anti-American sentiment in some countries led to a less-than-favorable reception before and during World War I. The 1920s were marked, however, by a widespread recognition of the need for better management. One researcher compared and contrasted U.S., British, French, German, and Italian management practices and found a widespread acceptance of scientific management.[27] Bertrand Thompson, however, provided an

21. Urwick and Brech, The Making of Scientific Management, p. 111.

22. Kevin Whitson, "The Reception of Scientific Management by British Engineers, 1890–1914," *Business History Review* 71 (1997), pp. 207–229.

23. Trevor Boyns, "Hans and Charles Renold: Entrepreneurs in the Introduction of Scientific Management Techniques in Britain," *Management Decision* 39 (2001), pp. 719–728.

24. E. F. L. Brech, *The Evolution of Modern Management*, vol. 2, *Productivity in Perspective, 1914–1974* (Bristol: Thoemmes Press, 2002), p. 30.

25. C. Bertrand Thompson, "The Taylor System in Europe," *Advanced Management* 5, no. 4 (1940), pp. 172–176.

26. Paul Devinat, *Scientific Management in Europe* (Geneva: International Labor Office, 1927).

27. Dwight T. Farnham, *America vs. Europe in Industry* (New York: Ronald Press, 1921).

assessment that was much less reassuring, noting "a large group of shameless fakers, mostly unemployed bookkeepers, who solicited clients from house to house and got quite a number of them at bargain rates." Thompson stated that he had even "seen the installation of an adding machine, or even of a telephone, referred to as 'Taylorization.'"[28]

In Poland, Karol Adamiecki (1866–1933) developed a "harmonogram," which was a graphical device for simultaneously charting several complicated operations, thus enabling their systematic arrangement. According to Mee, the harmonogram was similar to a program evaluation and review technique (PERT) network.[29] The harmonogram, developed in 1896, received some acceptance and use in Polish and Russian rolling mills, but with very few exceptions, Adamiecki's work was never translated into English during his lifetime. Whereas Adamiecki's work languished, European interest in Gantt's charts was stimulated by the work of Wallace Clark, who popularized their use as a basis for the European productivity movement (see Chapter 8).

Following the 1917 Russian revolution, Bolshevik leader Vladimir I. Lenin advocated the use of scientific management to systematize industry. In Lenin's view, scientific management was the most progressive means to achieve economic advancement.[30] His goal was to show how society would benefit if workers controlled the means of production. Although numerous conferences were held, institutes established, and attempts made to implement "the Taylor system," few improvements were made because of the Communist Party's distrust of capitalism.[31] Instead, the idea of "super-workmen" arose. Alexei Stakhanov, in particular, became nationally known for his extraordinary performance in mining coal. Stakhanov's daily production was, indeed, extraordinary—purportedly fifteen times the normal output—and he was hailed as an example for others.[32] Higher productivity for

---

28. Thompson, "The Taylor System in Europe," p. 173; p. 172.

29. John Mee, "History of Management," *Advanced Management-Office Executive*, 1 (October 1962), pp. 28–29. See also Theodore Limperg and Lyndall F. Urwick, "Charles Adamiecki (1866–1933)," *Bulletin of the International Management Institute* 3 (January, 1929), pp. 102–103; Arthur G. Bedeian, "The Writings of Karol Adamiecki: A Reflection," Paper presented at the Annual Academy of Management meeting, Minneapolis, August 20, 1974; Edward R. Marsh, "The Harmonogram of Karol Adamiecki," *Academy of Management Journal* 18, no. 2 (June 1975), pp. 358–364; Zdzislaw P. Weslolowski, "The Polish Contribution to the Development of Scientific management," in Jeffrey C. Susbauber (ed.), *Proceedings of the Annual Meeting of the Academy of Management* (1978), pp. 12–16.

30. Vladimir I. Lenin, "The Urgent Problems of the Soviet Union," *Pravada* (April 28, 1918), pp. 3–5. (Abstracted in "What Lenin Said About the Taylor Society," *Bulletin of the Taylor Society*, 1919, 4 (June), 35–38.)

31. Daniel A. Wren and Arthur G. Bedeian, "The Taylorization of Lenin: Rhetoric or Reality?" *International Journal of Social Economics* 31 (2004), pp. 287–299.

32. Arthur G. Bedeian and Carl R. Phillips, "Scientific Management and Stakhanovism in the Soviet Union: A Historical Perspective," *International Journal of Social Economics* 17 (1990), pp. 28–35.

Russian engineers came not from job analysis and improved work methods, but from the selflessness of hard work and devotion to the Soviet state.

After Lenin's death in 1924, his successor, Joseph Stalin, sought to undertake a program of national economic planning. To assist in this effort, Stalin hired one of Gantt's disciples, Marxist Walter N. Polakov (1879–1937), as a consultant. Born in the Soviet Union, Polakov became a U.S. citizen and worked with Gantt and Clark. Polakov's job was to plan and control industrial productivity so that the goals of the Soviet Union's five-year plans could be achieved. Polakov's work was widely praised, and the Gantt chart was widely accepted in the USSR.[33]

Japan

The Meiji Restoration, in 1868, marked the transition of Japan from a feudal society to a capitalist economy. Industrialization came slowly, however; in 1870, more than 80 percent of the Japanese population was employed in agriculture and less than 5 percent in manufacturing. Industry was dominated by family firms and entrepreneurs who employed few workers, was generally backward in production technology, and lacked modern management methods.[34]

Japan's first introduction to the principles of scientific management appears to have occurred in 1911. Yukinori Hoshino, director of Japan's Kajima Bank, was in the United States when Taylor's *The Principles of Scientific Management* was published. Hoshino obtained permission to translate Taylor's book, which was published in Japan in 1912. Landing in fertile soil, the seed of scientific management grew rapidly and led to a managerial revolution, replacing the entrepreneur-dominated age that had previously prevailed. Also, in 1912, Yoichi Ueno (1883–1957), a leading Japanese teacher, author, and consultant, published a paper titled, "On the Efficiency," which described the work of Taylor, Frank Gilbreth, and Bertrand Thompson. Ueno is known as the "Father of Japanese Administrative Science." Carl G. Barth visited Japan in 1924, and a chapter of the Taylor Society was formed in 1925. Ueno translated all of Taylor's writings, attended international conferences, and was the most articulate spokesperson for scientific management in Japan.[35]

In Japanese industry, the most advanced scientific-management application occurred at the Hyōgo Factory of the Kanegafuchi (Kanebō) Cotton Textile

---

33. Daniel A. Wren, "Scientific Management in the U.S.S.R., with Particular Reference to the Contribution of Walter N. Polakov," *Academy of Management Review* 5 (January 1980), pp. 1–11. See also, Diana J. Kelly, "Marxist Manager amidst the Progressives: Walter N. Polakov and the Taylor Society," *Journal of Industrial History* 6, No. 2 (November 2004), pp. 61–75.

34. Koji Taira, "Factory Legislation and Management Modernization during Japan's Industrialization, 1886–1916," *Business History Review* 44 (Spring 1970), pp. 84–109.

35. Ronald G. Greenwood, Regina A. Greenwood, and Robert H. Ross, "Yoichi Ueno: A Brief History of Japanese Management 1911 to World War II," in Kae H. Chung, (Ed.), *Proceedings of the Annual Meeting of the Academy of Management* (August 1981), pp. 107–110.

Company. Kanebō manager Sanji Mutō had studied in the United States and saw no inherent conflict between a firm paying high wages and earning high profits.[36] Like Taylor and Gantt, Mutō not only began paying more to attract better workers, but also to train workers and improve factory supervision and organization. Mutō eventually became president of Kanebō, now one of Japan's leading textile firms. He and other scientific management adherents understood that productivity is the link between high wages and high profits, and that productivity is achieved through technology, capital, and improved work methods. What many popular writers call "Japanese-style management" is not a recent phenomenon, but a direct result of scientific management's introduction into Japan during the late Meiji period.[37] Under the influence of scholars such as Ueno and practitioners such as Mutō, scientific management provided the basis for the modernization of Japanese industry.

SCIENTIFIC MANAGEMENT IN INDUSTRIAL PRACTICE

As noted in Chapter 9, companies such as the Plimpton Press, Link-Belt, Clothcraft, and Tabor Manufacturing were considered model scientific management installations. Henry P. Kendall (1878–1959), manager of the Plimpton Press (Norwood, Massachusetts), was an early promoter of scientific management in the printing industry. He thought that industrial plants could become efficient by being viewed as systems composed of interacting parts, but (like Person) that a greater long-run effect could be achieved only if the philosophy of scientific management was fully accepted by all parties.[38] Plimpton Press also developed an advanced employment department, which centralized hiring, disciplining, and discharging. Plimpton Press's employment manager, Jane C. Williams, credited scientific management with reducing labor turnover from 186 percent in 1912 to 13 percent in 1916.[39] James Mapes Dodge (1852–1915) pioneered the link-belt conveyor, which became the basis for later belt assembly line operations, and the Link-Belt Company (Philadelphia) was a showcase installation for Taylor's methods.[40]

Wilfred Lewis, president of the Tabor Manufacturing Company (Philadelphia), a machine-tool producer, was an authority on gearing and an advocate of metric reform. At Tabor, Taylor's methods were credited with increasing output

---

36. Taira, "Factory Legislation," pp. 103–105.

37. William M. Tsutsui, *Manufacturing Ideology: Scientific Management in Modern Japan* (Princeton, NJ: Princeton University Press, 1998).

38. Henry P. Kendall, "Unsystematized, Systematized, and Scientific Management," in Thompson, ed., *Scientific Management*, pp. 103–131.

39. Jane C. Williams, "The Reduction of Labor Turnover in the Plimpton Press," *Annals of the American Academy of Political and Social Science* 71 (May 1917), pp. 71–81.

40. See George P. Torrence, *James Mapes Dodge* (New York: Newcomen Society of North America, 1950); and James M. Dodge, "A History of the Introduction of a System of Shop Management" in Thompson, ed., *Scientific Management*, pp. 226–231.

250 percent.[41] Horace King Hathaway (1878–1944), general manager of the Tabor Company, advocated careful planning before installing Taylor's methods, including an extensive program of educating workers and supervisors as to the principles and purposes of scientific management. At the Clothcraft Shop of Joseph and Feiss Company (Cleveland, Ohio), Richard A. Feiss and Mary Barnett Gilson recognized the merits of scientific management in the labor-intensive clothing industry. Feiss implemented time-and-motion study, bonuses for performance and attendance, installed a planning department to smooth work flows, and employed an orthopedic surgeon to design chairs and tables for worker comfort, reduced fatigue, and efficiency. Gilson headed the Employment and Service Department (she disliked the phrase "welfare department"). She championed employment testing, proper selection and placement, promoting women to supervisory positions, and other advanced practices that made her the era's best-known and most influential personnel manager.[42] At Clothcraft, Taylor's methods were combined with the best ideas emerging in the nascent personnel management movement.

Thompson noted that an increase in the "stability of payroll" was one of the many benefits of scientific management in practice.[43] He was referring to employment stabilization through improved production planning, employee selection and placement, and job training. Scientific management sought to reduce waste, and one major contribution to increased costs was labor turnover. The first reported statistical analysis of labor turnover was conducted by General Electric's Magnus Alexander.[44] He found that, in 1912, for twelve GE factories, 22,031 employees were new unnecessary hires, amounting to a turnover rate of over 55 percent. The cost of this attrition was estimated at $831,030, which included the expense of hiring and training, as well as reduced production while new hires were learning their jobs. Joseph Willits, an instructor at the Wharton School of Finance and Commerce, replicated Alexander's study in a group of Philadelphia textile mills. He found turnover rates ranging from 50 to 100 percent, and occasionally, rates that even reached 500 percent.[45] Willits recommended improvements in selection and placement, training, and wage incentives to bolster employee retention. In brief, Taylor's

41. Wilfred Lewis, "An Object Lesson in Efficiency," in Thompson, ed., *Scientific Management*, pp. 232–241; see also H. K. Hathaway, "Wilfred Lewis," *Bulletin of the Taylor Society* 15 (February 1930), pp. 45–46.

42. David J. Goldberg, "Richard A. Feiss, Mary Barnett Gilson, and Scientific Management at Joseph and Feiss, 1909–1925," in Daniel Nelson, ed., *A Mental Revolution: Scientific Management since Taylor* (Columbus: Ohio State University Press, 1992), pp. 40–57.

43. C. Bertrand Thompson, *The Taylor System of Scientific Management* (New York: A. W. Shaw, 1917), p. 27.

44. Magnus W. Alexander, "Hiring and Firing: Its Economic Waste and How to Avoid It," *Annals of the American Academy of Political and Social Science* 65 (1916), pp. 128–144. See also Kyle Bruce, "Magnus Alexander, The Economists and Labour Turnover," *Business History* 47 (2005), pp. 493–510.

45. Joseph H. Willits, "The Labor Turn-Over and the Humanizing of Industry," *Annals of the American Academy of Political and Social Science* 61 (1915), pp. 127–137.

search for "first-class workers" and Münsterberg's search for the "best possible worker for the best possible effect" both contributed to lower labor turnover and stabilized employment. Labor turnover carried a high cost, both for employees and employers, and scientific management sought to eliminate such wastefulness.

THE HOXIE REPORT

The early opposition of organized labor to scientific management found further voice in a U.S. Commission on Industrial Relations investigation conducted under the direction of Robert F. Hoxie (1866–1916). Hoxie was a professor of political economy at the University of Chicago. He was assisted by Robert G. Valentine, an investigator and consultant in labor problems, who was to represent management's viewpoint,[46] and John P. Frey, editor of the *International Molder's Journal*, representing labor. The purpose of the study was to investigate all systems of shop management, including Taylor's, Gantt's, and Emerson's. Over the period from January to April 1915, the investigators examined thirty industrial plants employing, in whole or part, scientific management.[47]

An early inkling of controversy occurred when Hoxie insisted on making no distinction between the theory and the practice of scientific management. To Hoxie, scientific management was what was practiced by any firm if that firm called it "scientific"; to Taylor, scientific management ceased to exist if the principles and philosophy he had established were violated in practice. Hoxie's logic did not impress Taylor, and this undoubtedly led to Taylor's unfavorable opinion of the Hoxie report and a separate statement detailing his position in the report's appendix.[48]

The Hoxie report found a marked degree of diversity among the various industrial plants studied. First, Hoxie found the precepts of scientific management were often violated in practice. He discovered that many so-called efficiency experts that promised quick returns did not have "the ability or the willingness to install scientific management in accordance with the Taylor formula and ideals."[49] Second, it was revealed that functional foremanship had few adherents in practice. Some firms tried using functional foremen, but soon returned to the old-style, line type

---

46. Though calling himself a consultant to management on labor relations, Valentine had only brief experience in industry and in banking. He taught English at the Massachusetts Institute of Technology and was at one time Commissioner of Indian Affairs. Lyndall F. Urwick, *The Golden Book of Management* (London: Newman Neame, 1956), p. 3. See also Charles D. Wrege, Ronald G. Greenwoood, and Racquel A. Frederiks, "New Insights into the Contributions of the First Industrial Counselor: The Private Papers of Robert G. Valentine 1912–1916," in Kelly A. Vaverek (ed.), *Proceedings of the Southwest Division Academy of management* (1992), pp. 69–73.

47. Robert F. Hoxie, *Scientific Management and Labor* (New York: Appleton-Century-Crofts, 1915), p. 4.

48. Ibid.; Appendix II, pp. 140–149. Gantt, in Appendix III (pp. 150–151), and Emerson, in Appendix IV (pp. 152–168), also filed statements regarding Hoxie's claims. The three statements do not present a unified theory of the scientific management movement, but do agree on its fundamental aims.

49. Ibid., p. 29.

of organization. In a third area of inquiry, Hoxie found that little or no progress was being made with respect to scientifically selecting workers. "Labor heads," an early designation for employment or personnel managers, were poorly trained and of "doubtful experience and capacity."[50]

Instruction and training of workers was another area in which practice fell far short of theory. Learning proceeded by trial and error, as trained instructors were scarce, and instruction more often than not focused on attaining a level of output rather than teaching employees how to do quality work. Despite these faults, Hoxie concluded that training practices in scientific management plants were generally better than those that could be found elsewhere in industry. A fifth area of concern, and of greater criticism, was the use of time study and task setting. Standards and incentive rates were often established after only a cursory inquiry. This led to inaccuracies and injustices. In general, time-study men were poorly trained and inexperienced and often set rates based on management's desires rather than true scientific inquiry and observation. Incentive schemes also came under close scrutiny. Hoxie found no pure adoptions of the Taylor, Gantt, or Emerson payment plans. The Midvale differential piece-rate plan, used briefly by Taylor, was infrequently encountered, and most plans were modifications of the Gantt and Emerson plans.

On a broader plane, Hoxie tried to reconcile Taylor's view with that of unions regarding industrial democracy. Taylor maintained that scientific management was the essence of industrial democracy. His argument hinged on harmony and a mutuality of interest between labor and management. Employees were rewarded on the basis of their effort; discipline fell under scientifically derived laws and not under autocratic, driving management; and protests were to be handled by reliance on scientific inquiry and mutual resolution. According to the union view, however, scientific management monopolized knowledge and power in the hands of management by denying workers a voice in setting work standards, determining wage rates, and establishing conditions of employment. It introduced a spirit of mutual suspicion among employees and destroyed the solidarity and cooperative spirit of labor by emphasizing individual employees. Moreover, it destroyed unions, the protection that unions gave employees, and in turn, stymied the labor movement.

Siding with labor, Hoxie concluded that industrial democracy could come only through the collective bargaining process. He saw no other avenue, included no possibility for an educated, enlightened management, and seemed dedicated to the proposition that the interests of labor and management were inalterably opposed for all times and in all places. He brought no true bill against union officials or union members for resisting workplace improvements. On this count, his examination was less than equitable. Hoxie, however, did accuse management of seeking shortcuts to efficiency, faulted Taylor for trying to generalize his machine-shop experience to all types and sizes of firms, and denounced "efficiency experts" that were guilty of selling patent medicine panaceas to employers eager to improve employee performance.

---

50. Ibid., p. 32.

Those who criticize are also open to criticism. What can be said about the methods Hoxie used to reach his conclusions? Hoxie and his associates made numerous attempts to be fair to Taylor by noting that practice fell far short of theory. The predilections of Hoxie, Frey, and Valentine toward organized labor, however, resulted in a demonstrable research bias. There is also evidence that the investigators' methods were less than meticulous. Mary Barnett Gilson, employment manager at Clothcraft, one of the plants included in the study, wrote that when Hoxie and Frey visited Clothcraft, they held a short interview with the president, Richard Feiss, and some of his managers, took some notes, but never visited the plant's factory area. They promised to return to see working conditions in the plant, but never did.[51] If this encounter at Clothcraft was characteristic of the researchers' conduct at the other plants they visited, one must conclude that the Hoxie investigators were less than forthright. It is unfortunate that those charged with conducting a thorough study of scientific management in its early days did so with closed minds and hasty feet.

Nyland noted that the Hoxie report was "heavily skewed" toward organized labor's position, and as a consequence, "the Taylorists were charged publicly with a great many crimes, found innocent of none and guilty of many."[52] A pro-labor bias was evident in the selection of Robert Valentine to represent management. Taylor's objection, based on Valentine's lack of experience in business and familiarity with scientific management, was disregarded. Asked to give testimony before the commission, Valentine admitted his only experience with efficiency systems was, "I have run into it on the slant in a number of places . . . a half dozen cases." When asked if employees should participate if "any efficiency system" was introduced, he responded, "I not only think the individual should participate, but I think he should participate as a part of a union."[53] Valentine was appointed to represent management, but he revealed his bias for unionism.

When John Frey reminisced for a Columbia University oral history project, he "admitted that when he and Hoxie came across evidence that did not support the claims of the AFL [American Federation of Labor], he reworked the data until it confirmed his preconceived ideas."[54] Frey also had unfavorable memories of Valentine, who "didn't care to come" to their meetings, and of Hoxie, who Frey viewed as someone who knew little of practical matters and even less about work, workers, and industry.

John R. Commons (1862–1945), a University of Wisconsin labor economist and member of the Industrial Relations Commission, recalled two other events that shaped the commission's findings. Charles McCarthy, of the Wisconsin Legislative

---

51. Mary B. Gilson, *What is Past is Prologue* (New York: Harper and Brothers, 1940), p.93

52. Chris Nyland, "Taylorism, John R. Commons and the Hoxie Report," *Journal of Economic Issues* 30 (1996), p. 1007.

53. *Industrial Relations, Final Report and Testimony Submitted to Congress by the Commission on Industrial Relations*, Vol. 1 (Washington, DC: U.S. Government Printing Office, 1916), p. 853.

54. Frey, cited in Nyland, p. 1012.

Library, and a Taylor supporter, was appointed by Commons to oversee Hoxie's investigation into scientific management. The commission's chair, Frank Walsh, soon found reasons to disagree with McCarthy and had him dismissed. In the second instance, Commons recalled that Hoxie was "dropped by Walsh in the midst of his investigation of Scientific Management."[55] According to Commons, this explained why the Hoxie report was not included in the final report of the commission but was published later as a book. Hoxie's book was critically reviewed by a fellow economist who commented that "the effect of [Hoxie's] book as a whole will be to multiply misconceptions and misunderstandings with regard to the scientific management practice."[56] Hoxie and his colleagues had botched an unprecedented opportunity to evaluate the theory and practice of scientific management and purposefully misled generations of scholars about their findings.

THE THOMPSON AND NELSON STUDIES

The findings of two other studies—one conducted during the height of the scientific management movement and another conducted more recently—of organizations employing "the Taylor system of scientific management" contrast with the manner and method of the Hoxie report. Bertrand Thompson studied 172 "definitely known" applications of scientific management in eighty types of organizations; for example, factories, municipal governments, department stores, and publishing houses. Exactly 149 of the applications were in factories. At 113 factories, the installation of scientific management had progressed far enough to permit a summary analysis. Fifty-nine were judged complete successes, twenty partially successful, and thirty-four failures. Thompson attributed the failures to "the personality of the consulting engineers and ... the personality of the managements."[57] Failures by consulting engineers were due largely to their "inexperience and incompetence," whereas management failures were attributed to hasty installations, impatience with the initial pace of results, dissension within a factory's management group, and factors completely outside the control of management (e.g., the prevailing business cycle). No failures were attributed to employee shortcomings.

Thompson was aware of the Hoxie report and commented on the inclusion of plants that were not truly scientifically managed:

> If the system in the plant was developed by Mr. Taylor personally, or by any of his assistants or co-workers while associated with him, then the Taylor system may be held responsible for the results; otherwise not.

---

55. John R. Commons, *Myself* (New York: Macmillan, 1934), pp. 176–177.

56. *Scientific Management and Labor*, by Robert Franklin Hoxie, reviewed by Charles W. Mixter, *American Economic Review* 6 (1916), p. 376.

57. Thompson, *The Taylor System of Scientific Management*, p. 13.

When this qualification is kept in mind, an impartial investigator must admit that, from the viewpoint of the employer, the employee, or the public, the Taylor system is a demonstrated success.[58]

In a second study, Daniel Nelson investigated twenty-nine applications of scientific management, each directed by one of Taylor's closest followers. Although variations occurred, Nelson found a pattern of "general adherence to Taylor's ideas."[59] The two ideas that were least likely to have been introduced were the differential piece-rate (even Taylor moved to the Gantt plan) and functional foremanship. Nelson also noted a "strong positive correlation" between scientific management and industrial efficiency. Except for heat-using industries such as beverages, petroleum refining, and chemicals, scientific management was "associated with growth, not stagnation."[60] Scientific management was used mostly in batch-assembly (job shop) and labor-intensive nonassembly operations. In more capital-intensive industries, such as smelting primary metals, scientific management was less likely to be applied. In the automobile industry, scientific management was adopted before the acceptance of Henry Ford's assembly line, but not afterward (we will examine Ford's production technology in Chapter 12). Barth and George Babcock were successful at the Franklin Motor Car Company, for example, but once the moving assembly line and mass-production techniques came to the auto industry, scientific management methods were less useful.[61]

Nelson noted that the Taylor system was seen as a "partial solution to the labor problem," meaning a partial solution to finding a "scientific" basis for wage incentives.[62] It was organized labor's view that scientific management "tends to eliminate skilled crafts ... degrades the skilled worker ... [and] displaces skilled workers and forces them into competition with the less skilled."[63] The belief that skilled labor would be displaced by workplace improvements is as old as the Luddites who protested the introduction of water power to replace hand-loom weavers. In the case of scientific management, however, it was not machinery but improved work processes that threatened organized labor. Later writers, such as David Montgomery and Harry Braverman, have perpetuated this notion of the

---

58. Ibid., p. 25.

59. Daniel Nelson, "Scientific Management, Systematic Management, and Labor, 1880–1915," *Business History Review* 48 (Winter 1974), p. 500.

60. Daniel Nelson, "Taylorism," *Proceedings of the International Colloquium on Taylorism* (Paris: Éditions la Découverte, 1984), pp. 55–57.

61. Charles B. Gordy, "Scientific Management in the Automobile Industry," PhD dissertation (Ann Arbor: University of Michigan, 1929), pp. 5–7.

62. Nelson, "Scientific Management, Systematic Management, and Labor, 1880–1915," p. 479.

63. Hoxie, *Scientific Management and Labor*, p. 16.

"de-skilling" or systematic dumbing-down of jobs into easily mastered tasks as a means of decreasing management's dependence on skilled labor.[64]

What is the evidence for such claims? If scientific management de-skills jobs, we should expect a decline in craft workers and an increase in the number of unskilled laborers during this period. U.S. Census Bureau data indicate, however, that the number of "craftsmen and kindred workers," excluding foremen, increased 72 percent from 1900 to 1920 (2,900,000 to 4,997,000) and 96 percent from 1900 to 1930 (2,900,000 to 5,695,000). Similarly, the number of "operative and kindred workers" (semiskilled) increased 77 percent (3,720,000 to 6,587,000) from 1900 to 1920, and 107 percent (3,720,000 to 7,691,000) from 1900 to 1930. The number of unskilled laborers, excluding farmers and miners, increased at a lesser pace: 35 percent (3,620,000 to 4,905,000) from 1900 to 1920, and 47 percent from 1900 to 1930.[65]

Sociologist Douglas Eichar took a different tack, examining blue-collar workers by skill level as a percentage of the total labor force. Craft workers were 10.5 percent of the labor force in 1900, 13 percent in 1920; semiskilled operatives increased from 12.8 percent in 1900 to 15.6 percent in 1920; and unskilled nonfarm laborers decreased from 12.5 percent in 1900 to 11.6 percent in 1920.[66] Both in absolute numbers and as a percentage of the U.S. workforce the number of skilled craft and semiskilled operatives was increasing while the number of unskilled laborers was increasing at a far slower pace. The claim that scientific management de-skilled the general labor force is a myth that needs to be put to rest.

In summary, scientific management became an international movement in the first two decades of the twentieth century. In assessing the spread of the Taylor system, however, Thompson has cautioned that a distinction must be kept in mind. The distinction is that between the "Taylor system" and the "Taylor spirit." In this respect, Thompson has observed that "the System has served and should continue to be made to serve as a symbol, or if you like, an ideal and a model without which principles tend to dissipate into an ever less intense influence and 'spirit,' as has to a large extent already occurred."[67] Thompson's observation continues to ring true today, as the "spirit" of the Taylor system still influences modern industry throughout the world.

---

64. David Montgomery, *The Fall of the House of Labor: The Workplace, the State and American Labor Activism, 1865–1925* (Cambridge, England: Cambridge University Press, 1987), pp. 214–256; Harry Braverman, *Labor and Monopoly Capitalism* (New York: Monthly Review Press, 1974), pp. 85–168.

65. *Historical Statistics of the United States: Colonial Times to 1970*, pt. I (Washington, DC: Bureau of the Census, 1975), pp. 139–142.

66. Douglas M. Eichar, *Occupation and Class Consciousness in America* (New York: Greenwood, 1989), p. 47.

67. Thompson, "The Taylor System in Europe," p. 172.

EMERGING GENERAL MANAGEMENT

Although scientific management as a way of thinking dominated the last part of the nineteenth and the early part of the twentieth century, there were early indications of a broader concept of management emerging. In large part, this broadening was grounded in scientific management and was an extension of the need to systematize and rationalize industrial operations. It is important to remember that scientific management was a response to the growth of large-scale enterprises and the need to examine and refine managerial practices. In this response, scientific management inspired other disciplines, such as public administration, office management, marketing, and accounting; encouraged an interest in the theory and practice of organization design; provided a basis for the study of business policy; and spawned a philosophy of management.

THE IMPACT OF SCIENTIFIC MANAGEMENT ON OTHER DISCIPLINES

Stimulated by scientific management, other disciplines began to search for efficiency through science. William H. Leffingwell applied the principles of scientific management to office management.[68] The University of Chicago's Leonard D. White picked up where Morris L. Cooke left off and made numerous contributions to public administration. White was the first to teach public administration in the classroom and also pioneered in personnel management for governmental offices.[69] Arch W. Shaw, Ralph Starr Butler, Louis D. H. Weld, Paul T. Cherington, and Paul D. Converse expanded scientific management to marketing.[70]

Accounting saw the development of standard costing in Emerson and Taylor's use of the railroad system of accounts. Through the combination of ideas associated with economy in engineering and accounting techniques, managers were first exposed to contingencies in financial planning and control. The relationships among the volume of production, fixed costs, variable costs, sales, and profits has long been a vexing managerial problem. An engineer, Henry Hess, developed a "crossover" chart in 1903, which showed these variables and their relationships.[71]

---

68. William Henry Leffingwell, *Scientific Office Management* (Chicago: A. W. Shaw, 1917).

69. Leonard D. White, *Introduction to the Study of Public Administration* (New York: Macmillan, 1926); idem, *The City Manager* (Chicago: University of Chicago Press, 1927).

70. For the extent of the influence of scientific management on these pioneers, see Joseph C. Seibert, "Marketing's Role in Scientific Management," in Robert L. Clewett, ed., *Marketing's Role in Scientific Management* (Chicago: American Marketing Association, 1957), pp. 1–3; Robert Bartels, *The Development of Marketing Thought* (Homewood, IL: Richard D. Irwin, 1962), and 2nd ed., published as *The History of Marketing Thought* (Columbus, OH: Grid, Inc., 1976); and Paul D. Converse, *The Beginnings of Marketing Thought in the United States* (Austin: Bureau of Business Research, University of Texas, 1959).

71. Henry Hess, "Manufacturing: Capital, Costs, Profits, and Dividends," *Engineering Magazine* 26 (December 1903), pp. 367–379.

The position on the graph where total costs equaled total revenues was the crossover point, that is, the point where losses turned to profits. Walter Rautenstrauch, a professor at Columbia University, coined the phrase "break-even point" in 1922 to describe this same phenomenon.[72] In the same year, John H. Williams, an accountant, popularized the idea of a "flexible budget," showing how management could plan and control at various levels of output.[73] Taken together, these tools provided means for management to forecast, control, and account for unforeseen developments.

James O. McKinsey (1889–1937) also sought to expand on traditional notions of accounting and pioneered in using budgets as planning and controlling aids. McKinsey, like Taylor, deplored traditional postmortem uses of accounting. Rather than treating accounting as an end in itself, he viewed accounting information as an aid in managing operational decisions. Thus, for McKinsey, a budget was not a set of figures, but a way of assigning responsibility and measuring performance.[74] As a former professor at the University of Chicago, and later as a senior partner of McKinsey and Co., McKinsey was also influential in the early days of the American Management Association (AMA). The AMA was founded in 1923 as a somewhat adult extension university for practicing managers. Its objective was to broaden the study of management to encompass not only production control and personnel administration, but also to include sales, financial, and other facets of management. Slowly, but undeniably, management education was beginning to shift from an emphasis on shop-floor routines toward a broader view that covered all areas of business.

EARLY ORGANIZATION THEORY

During the 1920s, the study of organizations primarily focused on designing formal authority-activity relationships among individuals and departments. The early factory system, based on the division of labor, required the coordination of effort, and the grouping of activities into departments satisfied that need. Most firms were family owned and managed and had but a few employees. They thus relied on personal supervision to coordinate efforts. The first large-scale enterprises in the United States (and the world) were the railroads, for which Daniel McCallum, superintendent of the New York and Erie Railroad Company, developed the first known organization chart in the form of a tree (see Chapter 5). Almost a half century later, Joseph Slater Lewis (1852–1901) authored a "handbook for the use

---

72. Walter Rautenstrauch, "The Budget as a Means of Industrial Control," *Chemical & Metallurgical Engineering* 27 (1922), pp. 411–416.

73. John Howell Williams, *The Flexible Budget* (New York: McGraw-Hill, 1934).

74. James O. McKinsey, *Budgeting* (New York: Ronald Press, 1922); *Organization* (New York: Ronald Press, 1922); *Budgetary Control* (New York: Ronald Press, 1922); and *Managerial Accounting* (Chicago: University of Chicago Press, 1924). See also: William B. Wolf, *Management and Consulting: An Introduction to James O. McKinsey* (Ithaca, NY: Cornell University Press, 1978).

of manufacturers, directors, auditors, engineers, managers, secretaries, accountants, cashiers, estimate clerks, prime cost clerks, bookkeepers, draughtsmen, students, pupils, etc." interested in guidance for organizing their firms on "sound commercial lines."[75] Emerson followed the military line-staff tradition, but Taylor sought modification through functional foremanship. Although functional foremanship did not become widely accepted, there was a growing recognition among others that new organization forms were necessary to fulfill the requirements of large-scale enterprises of unprecedented size and scope.

In 1909, Russell Robb (1864–1927) gave a series of lectures on organization at the newly formed Harvard Business School. In the lectures, Robb argued that rather than uniformly applying a traditional military command-and-control style of organizing, firms should be individually organized given their goals and the unique demands of their specific industries. Robb anticipated modern contingency theorists when he noted that "all organizations will differ somewhat from each other, because the objects, the results that are sought, and the way these results must be attained, are different . . . there is no 'royal road,' no formula that, once learned, may be applied in all cases with the assurance that the result will be perfect harmony, efficiency, and economy, and a sure path to the main purpose in view."[76] Thus the goals sought differed, as did the means (today we might say "strategy") to attain those goals, resulting in different organization structures and no one way to organize. From this premise Robb developed his thesis that the objectives of business differed from those of the military and, therefore, their organizational emphases had to differ. Much could be learned from the military style of organizing as related to fixing responsibility and authority, clearly defining duties and channels of communication, and providing for order and discipline. The military, however, stressed a degree of control unnecessary in industry. As judged by Robb, industrial firms, built on an extensive division of labor, required greater coordination among their constituent elements than did their military counterparts. Success in industry was not based on obedience, but on economy of effort; therefore, the organization of industrial firms had to be different. More emphasis had to be placed on employee selection and training, workplace processes had to be arranged to achieve maximum efficiency, and managers had to be aware that a "great factor in organization is 'system,' the mechanism of the whole."[77]

Robb's lectures were truly remarkable for the times. He was heavily influenced by scientific management and the need for systematization. Robb, however, looked

---

75. Joseph Slater Lewis, *The Commercial Organisation of Factories: A Handbook for the Use of Manufacturers, Directors, Auditors, Engineers, Managers, Secretaries, Accountants, Cashiers, Estimate Clerks, Prime Cost Clerks, Bookkeepers, Draughtsmen, Students, Pupils, etc.* (London: E. & F. N. Spon Books, 1896).

76. Russell Robb, *Lectures on Organization* (privately printed, 1910), pp. 3, 14. Further insights into Robb's life and writings may be found in Edmund R. Gray and Hyler I. Bracey, "Russell Robb: Management Pioneer," *SAM Advanced Management Journal* 35 (April 1970), pp. 71–76.

77. Robb, *Lectures on Organization*, p. 173.

beyond both influences to see the importance of viewing organizations as a whole. While Robb's thoughts were developing, another set of ideas emerged that would lead to multidivisional organizations.

SCIENTIFIC MANAGEMENT AT DU PONT AND GENERAL MOTORS

No story is more fascinating to business historians than the emergence of large-scale enterprises. Scientific management played a part in the development of two industrial giants—Du Pont and General Motors. Two of Fred Taylor's strongest suits were cost accounting and manufacturing control techniques. He installed a cost-accounting system at the Steel Motor Works (Johnstown, Pennsylvania). As noted in Chapter 7, while at the Steel Motor Works, Taylor worked closely with A. J. Moxham and Coleman du Pont. Moxham later adopted Taylor's cost-accounting system at the Du Pont Powder Company.

In 1902, Coleman, Pierre, and Alfred I. du Pont bought control of the Du Pont Powder Company from their cousins for $12 million in thirty-year notes—no cash—and subsequently molded the company into an industrial behemoth. The du Ponts, and especially Pierre as president, sought to broaden Taylor's system of cost accounts to include a measure of overall company performance rather than just manufacturing productivity. As early as 1903, the Du Pont Powder Company used "return on investment" (ROI; the ratio between its net profit and total capital investment) to measure its efficiency in generating profit. This was apparently the initial use of this ratio for assessing an organization's profitability.[78] Pierre is credited with implementing the financial, operational, and managerial techniques necessary to turn the Du Pont Company into an effective multidivisional organization. Pierre learned the ins and outs of cost-accounting from Taylor, as well as Andrew Carnegie (who had learned McCallum's system of accounting while working on the Pennsylvania Railroad).[79] One of Pierre's key assistants was Hamilton McFarland Barksdale (1862–1918), Du Pont's general manager. Barksdale pioneered in separating the line and staff functions, in developing uniform objectives and policies for Du Pont's divisions, and in decentralizing authority to the division level.[80]

Another key figure at Du Pont was Barksdale's cousin, Donaldson Brown (1885–1965). Brown's contribution was to refine the ROI ratio into a metric for measuring and comparing the performance of various departments (rather than just

---

78. H. Thomas Johnson, "Management Accounting in an Early Integrated Industry: E. I. Du Pont de Nemours Powder Company, 1903–1912," *Business History Review* 49 (Summer 1975), p. 189.

79. Alfred D. Chandler, Jr., and Stephen Salisbury, *Pierre S. du Pont and the Making of the Modern Corporation* (New York: Harper and Row, 1971), p. xxi.

80. Ernest Dale, *The Great Organizers* (New York: McGraw-Hill, 1960). See also Ernest Dale and Charles Meloy, "Hamilton McFarland Barksdale and the Du Pont Contributions to Scientific Management," *Business History Review* 36 (Summer 1962), pp. 127–152.

measuring overall return on investment for a firm). Brown developed the formula $R = T \times P$, where R represented the rate of return on capital invested in each department, T stood for the rate of turnover of a department's invested capital, and P for the percentage of profit on a department's sales.[81] Brown also developed the famous Du Pont Chart System, which endures yet today and is used to forecast, measure, and report the financial results of Du Pont's operations.[82]

The multidivisional structure developed at Du Pont was adapted by the nascent General Motors Corporation, founded in 1908. William C. Durant conceived the idea of creating General Motors (GM) from a collection of motorcar and parts producers. The union was unwieldy, and in 1920, General Motors was plucked from the brink of financial disaster by an infusion of du Pont family money. Durant resigned, and Pierre du Pont came out of semiretirement to become GM president. Pierre made at least two key personnel decisions: one was to bring Donaldson Brown to General Motors; the other was to handpick Alfred P. Sloan, Jr. (1875–1966) as his successor. Sloan took over the GM reins in 1923. He created the concept of decentralized administration and operations, with centralized control and review. By decentralizing operations and centrally coordinating control, GM's various divisions (e.g., Chevrolet, Buick, Pontiac, and Cadillac) could more quickly respond to their competition and more efficiently integrate an increasing number of specialized skills by grouping together all the employees necessary to produce an individual product. A multidivisional ("M-form") structure enabled GM divisions to grow larger without the need to organize their activities into separate departments, each of which undertakes a distinctive function—production, marketing, finance/accounting, engineering, and so on.[83] With an M-form structure, each major product line is administered through a separate and semiautonomous division. Each division operates as a minicompany, with its own departments for production, marketing, finance, and so on. Decentralizing into product divisions also made it possible to use Brown's $R = T \times P$ formula for measuring and comparing performance across divisions.

From Taylor, Pierre du Pont learned the importance of a rational basis for controlling and assessing an organization's performance. He used this knowledge to build both Du Pont and General Motors into two of the world's largest and

---

81. Donaldson Brown, *Some Reminiscences of an Industrialist* (privately printed, 1958), pp. 26–28. See also: Ernest Dale, Regina S. Greenwood, and Ronald G. Greenwood, "Donaldson Brown: GM's Pioneer Management Theorist and Practioner," in Richard C. Huseman, (Ed.), *Proceedings of the Annual Meeting of the Academy of Management* (August 1980), pp. 119–123.

82. American Management Association, *How the Du Pont Organization Appraises Its Performance: A Chart System for Forecasting, Measuring and Reporting the Financial Results of Operations* (New York: American Management Association, 1950).

83. The General Motors story is a classic and is examined by, to name only a few: Alfred D. Chandler, Jr., ed., *Giant Enterprise* (New York: Harcourt Brace Jovanovich, 1964); Peter Drucker, *The Concept of the Corporation* (New York: John Day, 1946); and Alfred P. Sloan, Jr., *My Years with General Motors* (New York: Doubleday, 1963).

most successful corporations. Scientific management thus played a part in the development of both corporations. Pierre du Pont, Barksdale, Brown, and Sloan were major figures in creating what is today known as the modern corporation.

BUSINESS POLICY AND PHILOSOPHY

As the notion of general management was emerging during the 1920s, the idea of collegiate schools of business began to spread rapidly. Economics, once called moral philosophy and later political economy, was the womb that nurtured the emerging business subjects. Thus Henry Towne's call for the "engineer as an economist" found fulfillment not in ASME, but in schools of business that were founded throughout the United States. Their rapid growth resulted in the formation of the Association of Collegiate Schools of Business (ACSB; the present-day American Assembly of Collegiate Schools of Business) in 1916. By 1925, ACSB had thirty-eight members offering courses in accounting, economics, finance, marketing, commercial law, transportation, statistics, physical environment, social control and ethics, production, personnel, and labor.[84]

Although education for business grew rapidly in the first quarter of the twentieth century, there was little appreciation among educators of the need to integrate course offerings to provide a general management overview. Arch W. Shaw, a prominent Chicago business leader and editor and publisher of *System*, a leading periodical devoted to "output and profit increasing methods put to use in leading factories" was a notable exception. In 1908, Shaw lectured at Northwestern University's new School of Commerce, and in 1910 he spoke at Harvard University's Graduate School of Business Administration. While at Harvard, he became familiar with the problem method of instruction, which had grown out of the case method of teaching law developed in the 1870s by Christopher Langdell at the Harvard Law School. For the academic year 1911–1912, Shaw taught a course in business policy at the Harvard Business School based on the problem, or case, method. The purpose of the course was "to deal with top management problems, and it aimed also at integrating subjects that the students had studied in their first year."[85] Shaw invited business executives to attend his classes and describe a problem confronting their companies; his students were then required to discuss, analyze, and prepare reports, which were then presented to the executives. Despite Shaw's unique approach to integrating course knowledge, only two schools (Harvard and the University of Michigan) required the study of business policy in 1925, and not until 1959 did a capstone course become a requirement in. AACSB-accredited schools.

---

84. Leon C. Marshall, ed., *The Collegiate School of Business* (Chicago: University of Chicago Press, 1928), especially ch. 3.

85. Melvin T. Copeland, "The Genesis of the Case Method in Business Instruction," in M. P. McNair, ed., *The Case Method at the Harvard Business School* (New York: McGraw-Hill, 1954), p. 26.

More in the mainstream of management thought during the scientific management era was the work of A. Hamilton Church (1866–1936), who we previously discussed in connection with Leon P. Alford. Church began his career in Great Britain, became a consultant on cost accounting systems, and moved to the United States at the turn of the century. Tutored by Joseph Slater Lewis (mentioned earlier), Church sought a broader approach to the study of management than that offered by Taylor.[86] He became interested in a broadened view of management after studying the allocation of overhead costs, that is, those costs (such as management salaries) that are difficult to attribute to any one product or activity. For Church, every industrial undertaking consisted of two elements: (1) the determinative element, which fixed a firm's manufacturing and distribution policies; and (2) the administrative element, which took a firm's policies as determined and gave them practical expression through buying, manufacturing, and selling.[87] In modern parlance, Church was describing *policy formulation* (the determinative element) and *implementation* (the administrative element).[88] As Church explained, in making these two elements operational, managers used two fundamental "instruments": *analysis*, consisting of cost accounting, time and motion study, routing, machine layout, and planning; and *synthesis*, combining workers, functions, machines, and all activities effectively to achieve some useful result. In brief, managers *analyzed* to find better ways and then *coordinated* (synthesized) activities.

In Church's mind, Taylor's ideas formed a restricted view of a manager's job. Church believed that management should be concerned with a firm's total efficiency. He incorporated an executive viewpoint in his books and articles and emphasized the challenge of managing a firm's departments in relation to one another and to the firm as a whole. Writing in his book *The Making of an Executive,* Church stopped short of formulating a general management process as had Fayol, but nevertheless broadened the views of Taylor and his contemporaries, providing early insights into policy formulation and implementation.[89]

Scientific management also inspired an early philosophy of management. Whereas the work of Taylor and his contemporaries reflected a set of values or beliefs, an Englishman, Oliver Sheldon (1894–1951), was the first to lay claim to developing an explicit philosophy of management. Sheldon began and ended his business career at the Cocoa Works at York, a British chocolate-manufacturing company headed by B. Seebohm Rowntree (see Chapter 9). Sheldon was undoubtedly

---

86. Joseph A. Litterer, "Alexander Hamilton Church and the Development of Modern Management," *Business History Review* 35 (Summer 1961), p. 214.

87. Alexander H. Church, *The Science and Practice of Management* (New York: Engineering Magazine, 1914), pp. 1–2.

88. Mariann Jelinek, "Toward Systematic Management: Alexander Hamilton Church," *Business History Review* 54 (Spring 1980), p. 72.

89. Alexander H. Church, *The Making of an Executive* (Scranton, PA: International Textbook Company, 1923).

familiar with Gantt's belief that business had a larger social responsibility to serve society. Sheldon stated his own rationale for a philosophy: "We should devise a philosophy of management, a code of principles, scientifically determined and generally accepted, to act as a guide, by reason of its foundation upon ultimate things, for the daily practice of the profession."[90]

Sheldon encouraged managers to develop common motives, common ends, a common creed, and a common fund of knowledge. The basic premise of his philosophy of management, like that of Gantt, was community service:

> Industry exists to provide the commodities and services which are necessary for the good life of the community, in whatever volume they are required. These commodities and services must be furnished at the lowest prices compatible with an adequate standard of quality, and distributed in such a way as directly or indirectly to promote the highest ends of the community.[91]

In Sheldon's view, combining scientific management's emphasis on efficiency with service to the community was the responsibility of all managers. Toward this end, Sheldon held that managers must adopt three principles: (1) "the policies, conditions, and methods of industry shall conduce to communal well-being"; (2) "management shall endeavor to interpret the highest moral sanction of the community as a whole" in applying social justice to industrial practice; and (3) "management shall take the initiative . . . in raising the general ethical standard and conception of social justice."[92] In applying these principles, Sheldon believed that managers must consider both human *and* technical efficiency. He endorsed scientific methods of work analysis, but with due consideration being given to developing human potential to the greatest extent possible. In Sheldon's philosophy, the economic basis of service, the dual emphasis on human and technical efficiency, and the responsibility of management to provide social justice would all lead to a mutually beneficial "science of industrial management."

SUMMARY

Scientific management was a significant force influencing (1) the formal study of management; (2) the practice of management in the United States, Great Britain, continental Europe, Japan, and the Soviet Union; (3) applications in other disciplines; (4) the study of organizations; and (5) the integration of separate business courses to create a general business policy course and a philosophy of management. The original seed planted by Taylor provided the early impetus, but it took the

---

90. Oliver Sheldon, *The Philosophy of Management* (London: Sir Isaac Pitman and Sons, 1923), p. 283.

91. Ibid., p. 284.

92. Ibid.

efforts of many to spread the scientific management message. In practice, scientific management did not always run true to its founder's ideals: organized labor resisted it as a threat to its autonomy; its methods were adapted in different countries, but not without perverting its spirit; and much too often, U.S. firms of all types grasped its techniques and forgot its philosophy. Yet scientific management was not a failure. Growing from the need to systematize business practices, it gave a voice to efficiency and rationality, purpose to practice, and content to theory. Its youth was robust, its maturity was fruitful, and it spawned intellectual descendants throughout the world who still write about, study, and practice its teachings. Scientific management reflected the spirit of its times and prepared the way for subsequent developments.

CHAPTER 12

Scientific Management in Retrospect

S cientific management must be understood within the context of its times by examining the forces that created it as an extension of systematic management and made it the spirit of that era. After Taylor's death, scientific management continued to evolve as individuals and ideas came forth in an ever-changing cultural environment. Interacting to form a giant web of currents and eddies of change, very substantial external forces shaped the emergence, course, and progress of the scientific-management movement. In examining the cultural environment of scientific management, these economic, technological, social, and political forces are separated for expository purposes, although in reality they were interactive and mutually reinforcing. Within this framework, the whys and wherefores of Frederick W. Taylor and his intellectual heirs form a more coherent picture.

THE ECONOMIC ENVIRONMENT: FROM THE FARM TO THE FACTORY

In 1800, 90 percent of the U.S. population drew its sustenance from agriculture; by 1900, the proportion was 33 percent, and by 1929, 20 percent. The transformation from an agrarian to an industrial nation placed the United States at the world's helm in output of products and services, in wages, and in the standard of living of its citizens. The typical citizen who awakened on the morning of January 1, 1900, saw little change between the old and the new centuries. Yet the change was there, and the United States had moved into a new era. The accumulation of resources, though moving at varying speeds in various industries, was culminating in a new phase.

THE RATIONALIZATION OF RESOURCE UTILIZATION

Chandler noted that phase I (the resource accumulation phase of industrial growth) was complete in the United States by the beginning of World War I. Industrial growth in the latter part of the nineteenth century had created the giant enterprise, and in the first two decades of the twentieth century it was the task of the salaried managers to design and implement the appropriate managerial and organizational structures. Large corporations needed a formal structure of relationships between the firm's activities and personnel and also required a formalization of administrative procedures. Culmination of the resource accumulation phase meant that the typical corporation of the early twentieth century was faced with basically two problems: the need to reduce unit costs by improving production techniques and processes, and the need to facilitate planning, coordination, and appraisal of performance.[1]

This set the stage for phase II, the rationalization of resource utilization in industry. The work of Taylor and other scientific management writers was focused on meeting the industrial needs of the economic environment with respect to rationalizing resource utilization. The rational, scientific approach to problem solving was the foundation of scientific management. Time and motion study set standards, intended to reduce fatigue, and sought to eliminate wasted motions; it provided a logical approach to the design of work rather than using whimsical or rule-of-thumb methods. The "first-class man" and the scientific selection of personnel were attempts to provide a better match between people's abilities and job requirements. Piece-rate incentives sought to boost production and reduce per-unit labor costs while paying higher wages. The functional foremen were to bring specialized, expert advice and leadership; the separation of planning and doing was a concept designed to improve the planning of work; and the exception principle sought to focus managerial attention on critical performance problems. Even Taylor's philosophy of a mental revolution was an attempt to reduce friction and rationally bring together the interests of labor and management into a mutually rewarding whole. This mutuality of interests was in tune with the U.S. economic climate. A leading economist, Henry C. Carey (1793–1879), brought the optimism of Adam Smith to U.S. economic thought. Where David Ricardo, Karl Marx, and Thomas Malthus saw gloom and despair, Carey felt that the free development of a capitalistic society led to reconciliation and a harmony of interests.[2] Carey's reasoning antedated and may have influenced Taylor's mental revolution.

Those who came in Taylor's wake also followed the rationalization-of-resource-utilization theme. The Gilbreths sought economy of motion and waste reduction, and their systems books were detailed how-to-do-it procedures manuals. Gantt's work provided visual aids for scheduling, routing, dispatching, and controlling work. Carl Barth, Morris Cooke, and the others who espoused the gospel of efficiency

---

1. Alfred D. Chandler, Jr., *Strategy and Structure* (Cambridge, MA: MIT Press, 1962), pp. 386–390.

2. John Fred Bell, *A History of Economic Thought* (New York: Ronald Press, 1967), pp. 316–320.

all focused on basically this same problem of efficiency in production. Harrington Emerson, among others, wrote of efficiency through organization, a matter of some consequence to industrialists of that period. Stated succinctly, the economic milieu of the era created and accounted for the appeal of Taylor and scientific management. In summary, scientific management was a product of its environment in the sense that it grew from the pressing needs of industry for efficiency. Resources were accumulated, phase I completed, and rationalization of resource utilization (phase II) became important.

MANAGEMENT AND THE WORKER

America was a very diverse nation during this period, in contrast with the ethnically homogenous industrial nations of Britain, France, Germany, Italy, and Japan. One exception was London, where 6 percent of its population in 1890 came from outside the British Isles. In contrast, however, immigrants or children of immigrants comprised 80 percent of New York's citizenry, 87 percent of Chicago's, and 84 percent of Milwaukee's and Detroit's. By 1900 there were more people of Italian ancestry in New York than in any Italian city except Rome; more of Polish descent in Chicago than in Warsaw; and by 1920 more Irish people had immigrated to the United States than the total remaining in Ireland at that time.[3] These individuals and families were responding to the message inscribed on the Statute of Liberty in New York harbor: "Give me your tired, your poor, your huddled masses yearning to breathe free . . . I lift my lamp beside the golden door."[4]

In 1910, 48 percent of the workers in mining, 31.9 percent in manufacturing, and 26.3 percent in transportation were foreign born.[5] In 1913, Ford Motor's Highland Park (Michigan) plant had a workforce of 71 percent foreign-born workers from twenty-two different national groups. Southern and eastern Europeans were the majority and included (in rank order from high to low percentages) Poles, Russians, Romanians, Italians and Sicilians, Austro-Hungarians, and Germans.[6] Few of these spoke English, making communication difficult for supervisors and coworkers. To lessen the problem, Ford Motor started an "English School" to find a common ground for diverse work group members to be able to communicate. The population and the workforce during this time was a heterogeneous one, perhaps with limited English skills, and with relatively little education. Recruiting, selecting, training, and monitoring the performance of these individuals presented a challenge to

---

3. Thomas K. McCraw, "American Capitalism," in Thomas K. McCraw, ed., *Creating Modern Capitalism* (Cambridge, MA: Harvard University Press, 1997), p. 307.

4. Inscription by Emma Lazarus, November 2, 1883.

5. Sumner H. Slichter, "The Current Labor Policies of American Industries," *The Quarterly Journal of Economics* 3 (May 1929), p. 394.

6. Daniel A. Wren and Ronald G. Greenwood, *Management Innovators: The People and Ideas That Have Shaped Modern Business* (New York: Oxford University Press, 1998), p. 46.

management. The nature of this workforce suggests why so much emphasis was placed on developing systems and procedures, standardizing tools and work methods, and the increased reliance on personnel departments as staff to assist managers.

Contrary to what might be expected in economic theory, this largely immigrant influx of labor did not drive down wages. As noted earlier, real wages (that is, purchasing power) doubled between 1865 and 1890; from 1890 to 1921, the annual compound increase in real wages was 1.6 percent, enabling another doubling. In addition to gaining in terms of real wages, the hours of labor were starting to decrease: in 1890 the average industrial workweek was sixty hours; in 1910, fifty-five hours, and in 1920, fifty hours.[7] Life expectancy also increased during this period of industrial growth. For a male born in Massachusetts in 1855, the life expectancy was 38.7 years, 40.9 years for a female. By 1929, a male's life expectancy had increased to 58.1 and a female's to 61.4 years.[8] Taylor's hope of a mental revolution, a mutuality of interests between labor and management, found new life in modern times as a mutual gains strategy:

> Taylor's claim that his system of management would benefit both worker and employer was accompanied by a call for the partners in production to work together to enhance the output of the firm. The pursuit of mutual benefits and cooperation as regards the enhancement of production amounts to a mutual-gains approach to industrial relations as the notion understood by analysts such as . . . Kochan and Osterman. That Taylor advanced a mutual-gains program is seldom recognized. . . .[9]

The scientific management era improved the condition of workers through higher real wages, increased longevity, and the opportunity to improve their skill levels. The "lamp beside the golden door" fulfilled its promises.

The new economics of mass production demanded an even sharper focus on the development of management. Large accumulations of resources were requisite to meet the demands of mass markets and mass distribution. As the industrial giants grew, the individuals who built the empires were passing from the helm and being replaced by a new breed of salaried managers. The personalized, informal structures of the family business yielded to the logic of size in industrial administration. No longer could owner–entrepreneurs depend on their own personal supervision. Technology demanded specialized knowledge, and staff departments were added to handle personnel, engineering, production, purchasing, legal affairs, and other

---

7. Ross M. Robertson, *History of the American Economy*, 3rd ed. (New York: Harcourt Brace Jovanovich, 1973), pp. 379–380.

8. Edgar W. Martin, *The Standard of Living in 1860* (Chicago: Chicago University Press, 1942), p. 220.

9. Chris Nyland, "Taylorism and the Mutual-Gains Strategy," *Industrial Relations* 37 (October 1998), p. 521. See also Thomas A. Kochan and Paul Osterman, *The Mutual Gains Enterprise* (Boston: Harvard Business School Press, 1994).

functional activities. Melman found that between 1899 and 1929, the percent of employees in management relative to those in production almost doubled (9.9 percent in 1899 to 18.5 percent in 1929), and between 1929 and 1947 the increase was from 18.5 percent to 22.2 percent. According to Melman, the only significant factor related to this growth of managerial vis-à-vis production employees was "the addition of new functions carried out by the [managerial] personnel... [because of] the addition of specially designated persons or departments."[10] In short, this growth of staff specialists and other managers in the hierarchy reflected the need to perform the tasks required in the emerging large-scale enterprise of the twentieth century. The growth of a managerial hierarchy was necessary to plan, organize, lead, coordinate, and control the organizations' input-throughput-output system. The economics of mass production and mass distribution required a fund of managerial talent, and one familiar with the latest methods and the most current thinking in the management of organizations.

As previously indicated, scientific management was associated with growth and efficiency and was more likely to be used in labor- rather than capital-intensive industries. Improved work methods, reduced fatigue, accurate work standards, better personnel selection, incentive payment plans, and other scientific management techniques would have less impact in a capital-intensive industry, where the most advanced technology leads to the greatest gains. One set of statistics indicates that manufacturing output per worker hour went from an index number of 21.2 in 1890 to 52.0 in 1929 (1958 = 100).[11] Another study, taking sort of a reverse view, found that the number of worker hours input per unit of output fell from an index number of 74 in 1919 to 42 in 1929 (1899 = 100), for a gain in efficiency of 43 percent.[12] Regardless of the approach, the result was still increased productivity. One historian attributed this increase in productivity during this period to "(1) the methods of mass production, (2) Taylorism, and (3) better and cheaper sources of power."[13]

President Calvin Coolidge, in a frequently misquoted speech, capsulized the era:

> After all, the chief business of the American people is business. They are concerned with producing, buying, selling, investing, and prospering in the world ... wealth is a product of industry, ambition,

---

10. Seymour Melman, "The Rise of Administrative Overhead in the Manufacturing Industries of the United States, 1899–1947," *Oxford Economic Papers* 3 (January 1951), pp. 66–68, 91. Melman used the U.S. Census of Manufactures' definition of management as salaried employees (i.e., line and staff) and production as wage earners.

11. U.S. Dept. of Commerce, Bureau of the Census, *Historical Statistics of the United States: Colonial Times to 1970* (Washington, DC: U.S. Government Printing Office, 1975), pt. 1, p. 162.

12. Solomon Fabricant, *Labor Savings in American Industry: 1899–1939* (New York: National Bureau for Economic Research, 1945), pp. 43–46, 50.

13. George Soule, *Prosperity Decade: From War to Depression* (New York: Holt, Rinehart and Winston, 1947), pp. 127–128. Soule did not rank nor assign any weights to the influence of these three factors.

character, and untiring effort. ... So long as wealth is made the means and not the end, we need not greatly fear it.[14]

Economically, the United States came of age in this period. More complex organizational and hierarchical managerial structures were required to cope with the economics of mass production and mass distribution. Resource usage had to be rationalized, and scientific management was the conventional wisdom that could handle the task. It was an age of concern for economic efficiency.

TECHNOLOGY: OPENING NEW HORIZONS

In Chapter 6 we saw how developments in transportation and communication spurred the growth of enterprise. New firms and industries were forming, and their growth and development led to a managerial hierarchy and for the need to improve the technologies of manufacturing and distributing their products. A survey of *Fortune* 500 companies in 1994 found that 247 of them had their beginnings during this period we are studying, roughly 1880 to 1929.[15] Although their original names might have been different, these were the start-ups for such modern firms as Eastman Kodak, Coca-Cola, Sears, General Electric, Pepsico, Goodyear, Ford Motor, General Motors, IBM, Boeing, Walt Disney, Delta Airlines, and so on. Many of these represented new industries, such as photographic film, automobiles, and aircraft.

New technologies enabled both old and new firms to compete more successfully. In steel, the Bessemer process would yield to the open hearth; in petroleum, developments in "cracking" oil molecules during refining enabled richer fuels for automobiles and aircraft. Orville Wright would never have flown at Kitty Hawk, North Carolina, in 1903 if the internal combustion engine had not been developed. Du Pont's research led to discoveries in synthetic materials, such as rayon. Charles F. Kettering removed the dangerous task of starting an internal combustion engine by a hand crank when he developed an electric self-starter for automobiles. Lee De Forest and Guglielmo Marconi pioneered the vacuum tube and wireless telephony, such as the radio. In some cases, the improvements came by creating paths between the seas: the Suez Canal (1869) sped trade between Europe and Asia; the Panama Canal (1914) connected the Atlantic and Pacific Oceans. The developments of this time period were as astounding to our ancestors as those of today are to us.

Energy developments of the period also deserve mention. Coal was the primary source of energy for the steam-driven wheels of industry. Although coal continued to dominate, new discoveries of petroleum deposits were soon to reshape the energy

---

14. Calvin Coolidge, "The Press under a Free Government," address before the American Society of Newspaper Editors, Washington, DC, January 17, 1925; reprinted in Calvin Coolidge, *Foundations of the Republic: Speeches and Addresses* (New York: Charles Scribner's Sons, 1926), pp. 187–188.

15. Harris Corporation, "Founding Dates of the 1994 *Fortune* 500 U.S. Companies," *Business History Review* 70 (Spring 1996), pp. 77–84.

base. Electrical energy also entered the scene. Although not invented in the usual sense, the principles of electricity were applied to generate a new power source for factory gears and home lights and appliances. Edison's central power plant in New York City was built in 1882. By 1920 one-third of the nation's industrial power came from electricity and half the urban homes had electricity. In the rural areas 98 percent of the homes still relied on kerosene lamps and candles, but not for long.

The automobile was another technological advancement that brought about substantial economic and social change during this period. A four-cycle, internal combustion engine perfected by the German mechanic Nicholas August Otto was first shown at the Paris Exposition in 1869, patented in 1877, and soon became part of a vehicle originally called the horseless carriage. The automobile gave people a new mobility, a freedom of movement that led to decentralization of the cities into suburban living and posed a threat to older, established forms of transportation. Automobile manufacturing began in small shops, and experiments were made with electric (battery), steam, and internal combustion engines. In 1900, for example, the automobile industry produced 4,192 cars; of these, 1,681 were steam powered, 1,575 were electric, and 936 were gasoline powered. Previously, we saw how Carl Barth used scientific management to improve production at the Franklin Motor Car Company. In that case, and others, the parts were brought to an assembly platform where the automobile would be assembled. This process was labor intensive and relatively slow. Henry Ford, like other manufacturers, used this stationary assembly process, and Ford Motor historians have suggested that Ford's engineers "had doubtlessly caught some of Taylor's ideas... [and] kept in touch with the ideas of men like Taylor."[16] Nelson's study of the twenty-nine installations of scientific management from 1901 to 1917 by Taylor and his followers, however, does not include Ford Motor Company (but does include Barth's work at Franklin).[17] This suggests that Ford engineers may have been familiar with scientific management, but no work at Ford Motor Company was by Taylor, nor Gilbreth, nor Barth, nor anyone closely connected to scientific management. When interviewed by contemporaries, Henry Ford denied "any systematic theory or organization or administration, or any dependence on scientific management."[18] It would be difficult to make a connection between the practices at Ford Motor and scientific management.

The idea of bringing the chassis to the worker, not vice versa, was an idea that evolved slowly. The initial effort was the fly-wheel magneto, assembled as it moved on a conveyor by the workers. Previously, an employee did the entire assembly, averaging about twenty minutes per assembly, or thirty-five to forty magnetos in nine hours by one worker. After changeover to a moving belt, the assembly was

---

16. Allan Nevins and Frank E. Hill, *Ford* (New York: Scribner's, 1954), pp. 468, 474.

17. Daniel Nelson, "Scientific Management, Systematic Management, and Labor, 1880–1915," *Business History Review* 48 (Winter 1974), pp. 489–490.

18. Horace L. Arnold and Fay L. Faurote, *Ford Methods and Ford Shops* (New York: Engineering Magazine, 1915), p. 20.

divided into twenty-nine operations performed by twenty-nine workers spaced along the belt. The average assembly time dropped to thirteen minutes per magneto, then to seven minutes, and finally to five minutes.

Ford was initially skeptical, but the results were proof that the conveyor line worked. Next came the motor, and then the transmission, all with successful results. By 1913, three feeder lines (magneto, motor, transmission) could produce more subassemblies than the final assembly could tolerate. The solution was a motorized capstan that dragged a line of chassis along the floor, and parts were added as it flowed. Ford, Charles Sorenson, and their associates in the shop, W. C. Klann, Clarence W. Avery, James O'Connor, and P. E. Martin, created the moving assembly line for mass production.[19]

The results were impressive: in 1910 (pre–assembly line), 2,773 workers produced 18,664 autos (6.73 per worker); in 1914 (post–assembly line), 248,307 autos were produced by 12,880 workers (19.28 per worker). Prices were driven downward as productivity increased: in 1910 a fully equipped Model T touring car was priced at $950; in 1914, $490; and in 1916, $360; a Model T roadster was priced at $900 in 1910, $269 in 1924.

Scientific management was not applied on the assembly line at Ford. Jobs were timed to match the speed of the conveyor, and Frank Gilbreth complained about the poor job design (see Chapter 8). Scientific management and Henry Ford and his associates approached work design quite differently. For example, a film of Frank Gilbreth's work shows an employee trimming the edges of a bar of soap that was formed in a mold, polishing the soap, wrapping, and placing the soap bars in a box,[20] a very labor-intensive task that later manufacturers would seek to automate. Further, Taylor's pig-iron loading and shoveling studies would not have impressed Henry Ford. Ford's engineers developed conveyor belts for moving materials, such as sand and coal, and hoists for lifting heavy objects and relocating them. Scientific management focused on the workshop and labor-intensive activities; beyond this manufacturing stage, technology would use various power sources and machinery to replace the laborious monotonous tasks.

Henry Ford and his associates divided labor and standardized parts and transformed these old ideas into a logic of mass production on an assembly-line basis, which could be called the Second Industrial Revolution. Mass production yielded cost savings that in turn were passed on to the consumer via lower prices. Using lowered product prices to expand the market and the expanded market to achieve production savings, Ford personified Adam Smith's idea that the market was the only force limiting the division of labor. Ford's startling announcement in

---

19. Jay H. Heizer, "Determining Responsibility for Development of the Moving Assembly Line," *Journal of Management History* 4 (1998), pp. 94–103. See also David A. Hounshell, *From the American System to Mass Production, 1800–1932* (Baltimore: Johns Hopkins University Press, 1984), pp. 249–253.

20. *The Quest of the Best Way: The Original Films of Frank B. Gilbreth,* Harry W. Bass Business History Collection, University of Oklahoma.

1914 of a $5 a day minimum wage operated on two premises: that the best workers could be attracted and retained, and that workers needed the wherewithal to buy industry's output. Although Ford lost his domination of the automobile industry as consumer preferences changed and General Motors recognized that different product lines would fit different market segments, his introduction of the logic of mass production had a lasting impact on U.S. thought.

Information technology in the spirit of Henry Poor's definition of information as "recorded communication" was also evolving. Partnerships and sole proprietorships could rely on informal communication, account books, and face-to-face exchanges to keep track of their business affairs. As the managerial hierarchy was extended with the growth of enterprise, this became more difficult, and we see a revolution in the ways organizations gathered, recorded, and maintained information about business activities.[21] Decision making, coordination, and monitoring performance required more formally developed systems.

Christopher Latham Sholes' typewriter provided a means of communication in a more legible fashion than handwriting. Sholes also left us with the standard QWERTY keyboard when he de-engineered it to prevent speedy typing that often jammed the typeface bars. In 1936, August Dvorak used time-and-motion study to rearrange the keyboard for greater efficiency. Alas, his innovative change met enduring resistance. Carbon paper was developed for copies made during typing; this was a lot less expensive than photocopying, which was accomplished with a camera and light-sensitive paper at a cost of ninety-eight cents per copy in 1911.[22] Vertical file cabinets facilitated arranging correspondence and records. The A. B. Dick Company bought the rights to Thomas Edison's "multiplying letters" device and turned it into a mimeograph machine that could print many copies from a typed stencil. Sir Isaac Pitman's method of taking "shorthand" notes enabled secretaries to take dictation and then polish it by typing. Pneumatic tubes were designed and installed in factories and retail stores to send money, receipts, and other papers from floor to floor and between departments. Long before Nike, the first "whoosh" was the sound of information transmitted via the pneumatic tube.

Another advancement was developing graphical means of displaying data. Gantt's chart and the Du Pont chart system were mentioned previously. Brinton collected and published numerous graphic methods for illustrating statistical facts.[23] He published two of Gantt's earliest charts; portrayed Hollerith's punched-card machine for recording, tabulating, and printing data; and criticized corporate annual reports for their poor job of informing shareholders. Brinton, and others such as Gantt, recognized the importance of information as firms grew beyond

---

21. For developments in the Illinois Central Railroad, Scoville Manufacturing Company, and Du Pont, see JoAnne Yates, *Control through Communication: The Rise of System in American Management* (Baltimore: Johns Hopkins University Press, 1989).

22. Yates, p. 54.

23. Willard C. Brinton, *Graphic Methods for Presenting Facts* (New York: Engineering Magazine, 1914).

informal means of communicating. This revolution in information technology had an unintended effect: it shifted clerical work from males to females and created office work as an alternative to the factory for females.[24]

In brief, advancing technology was reshaping the nature of work by increasing number of skilled and semiskilled workers, creating alternative career paths for females, substituting machinery and capital intensity for labor intensity, and providing improved means for material handling. The new horizons were at work and in transport by air and auto.

THE SOCIAL ENVIRONMENT: FROM ACHIEVEMENT TO AFFILIATION

Between the Civil War and 1900, Horatio Alger, Jr., wrote more than one hundred books for boys with such piquant titles as *Bound to Rise, Luck and Pluck, Sink or Swim*, and *Tom, the Bootblack*. At least twenty million copies were sold, and "Horatio Alger" became synonymous with a success story.[25] The typical plot involved a young but poor hero, beset by the unscrupulous people on all sides, who worked his way to wealth by the virtues of diligence, honesty, perseverance, and thrift. Quite often he was befriended by a benevolent benefactor who recognized his latent talent for capital accumulation and aided him in the climb to the pinnacle of the financial world. The hero of Alger's books was a personification of McClelland's "high achiever" and Riesman's "inner-directed" individual, who had a personal gyroscope that enabled unerring progress on the path to success.[26] The hero exhibited the self-control, hard work, and frugality of the Protestant ethic and of Ben Franklin's Poor Richard. He learned in the school of hard knocks; no formal schooling could prepare him for success in business. Charles M. Schwab, a protégé of Andrew Carnegie, stated the case:

> If the college man thinks that his education gives him a higher social status, he is riding for a fall. Some college men ... have pride in their mental attainments that is almost arrogance. Employers find

24. Elyce J. Rotella, "The Transformation of the American Office: Changes in Employment and Technology," *Journal of Economic History* 41 (March 1981), pp. 51–57.

25. The life of Horatio Alger, Jr. (1832–1899), formed an interesting paradox to the type of novels he wrote. He wrote rags-to-riches success stories, yet he neither was born poor nor died rich. About fifteen million of the twenty million copies of his books were sold after his death. Frederick Lewis Allen, "Horatio Alger, Jr.," *The Saturday Review of Literature* 18 (September 17, 1938), pp. 3–17.

26. McClelland, in *The Achieving Society*, found that the need for achievement increased regularly from 1800 to 1890, peaked, and declined thereafter. See also David Riesman, Nathan Glazer, and Reuel Denney, *The Lonely Crowd* (Garden City, NY: Doubleday, 1950), pp. 29–32.

it difficult to control, guide, and train such men. Their spirit of superiority bars the path of progress.[27]

Early scientific management theory was consonant with the social values of reward for individual effort and the classical virtues of the rational person directed by self-interest. Utilitarian economics, then in vogue, held that individuals rationally calculated what was to their own advantage based on the seeking of pleasure and the avoidance of pain. Workers, like all human beings, were motivated by their own self-interest. In the classical period of economics, this self-interest was largely the monetary reward that came from work, giving rise to the idea of the economic person. Before Taylor, management by incentives had failed largely because management had not cleared the obstacles to gain from the workers' paths and had indulged in rate cutting when earnings became too high. Taylor's conception of a management that facilitated worker effort by study and proper job design was supposed to open the door and free the workers' basic drive for economic rewards. Rate cutting was not in management's self-interest because it only served to force workers to return to their former habits of soldiering. The mental revolution between labor and management was the recognition of mutual self-interest. From management's vantage point, a rational system of work, proper incentives, no cutting of rates, and leadership by knowledge and not by drive would lead to lower costs and higher profits. For their part, workers would recognize that standards had been properly established by scientific study and that by following instructions and procedures, they would be able to calculate rationally that they could best serve their own self-interest by following Taylor's system. In brief, the ideals of scientific management were compatible with the prevailing views of people's needs and aspirations.

THE COLLISION EFFECT

Cultural change, that third eternal inevitability, like death and taxes, is always difficult to pinpoint historically. But times were changing, and the milieu of scientific management slowly assumed new dimensions that affected the course of management thought. Two disparate yet strangely congenial forces were forming to mark a new era in U.S. cultural thought: the closing of the frontier and the Social Gospel and its successor, progressivism. The United States of the early twentieth century was in the turmoil of urbanization and industrialization. The noted historian Frederick Jackson Turner identified four forces that were reshaping U.S. economic, social, and political ideals: (1) the exhaustion of the supply of free land and the closing of the West; (2) the concentration of wealth and power in the hands of a few fundamental industries; (3) the political expansion by the United States into

---

27. Charles M. Schwab, "The College Man in Business," in Alta G. Saunders, ed., *The Literature of Business*, rev. ed. (New York: Harper and Row, 1923), p. 5.

territories beyond its own borders; and (4) the rise of populism.[28] The West in the United States typified the ideals of individualism, economic equality, freedom to rise on one's own initiative, and democracy. Whenever social conditions became too oppressive, capital pressed on labor, or political restraints became too great, the West provided an avenue of escape. When the safety valve offered by the West closed, new institutional arrangements were necessary to attain the U.S. ideal of democracy for which the West had long provided.

William G. Scott built on Turner's thesis and called the culmination of these cultural forces the "period of collision" (Figure 12-1). The collision effect was characterized by conflict and resulted from forces that had drawn people into an inescapable proximity and interdependency. Unmitigated, the collision effect would have led eventually to social and psychological degeneration. However, Scott's thesis

FIGURE 12-1	MANAGEMENT THOUGHT IN A CHANGING CULTURE

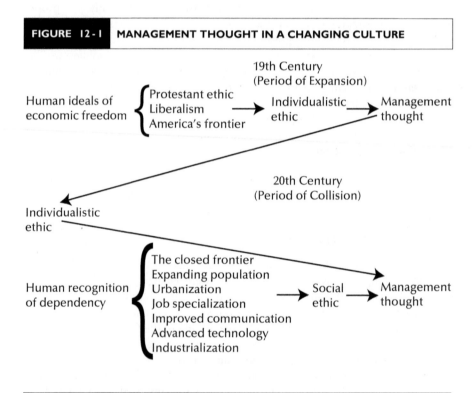

Adapted from William G. Scott, *The Social Ethic in Management Literature*, Atlanta: Georgia State College of Business Administration, 1959, p. 10

---

28. Frederick Jackson Turner, *The Frontier in American History* (New York: Holt, Rinehart and Winston, 1921), pp. 244–247.

was that the decline of the "individualistic ethic" of the period of expansion was slowly being replaced by a "social ethic," which substituted human collaboration for human competition "with a prayer that a social philosophy would lead to industrial harmony."[29] Basic to this search were Taylor's notions of "harmony, not discord," "cooperation, not individualism," and the "mental revolution" on the part of both labor and management.

There were elements of both the individualistic and the social ethics in Taylor's philosophy. In Scott's analysis, the social ethic began with the group as a source of value and the individualistic ethic started with the person as the primary value. Taylor's "cooperation, not individualism" would suggest that he accepted the social ethic. However, people are neither purely individualistic because they normally desire social intercourse, nor are they purely group-oriented because of their own ego needs. Taylor's philosophy bridged the gap between the two ethics by stressing the mutuality of interests and collaboration at work (the social ethic) coupled with individually based economic incentives and the selection and development of each person to the highest extent possible (the individualistic ethic). Taylor was clearly in touch with the problems of the industrialized society of the period. Though not known nor regarded as a social philosopher, he perceived the industrial dilemma and proposed one means of alleviating the detrimental effects of the disharmonies of urbanization and industrialization.

THE SOCIAL GOSPEL

Emerging in the late nineteenth century as a counterpoint to social Darwinism, the Social Gospel shaped the field of personnel management, formed an antecedent for industrial sociology, and was a social precursor to the politics of progressivism. Whiting Williams imbibed the Social Gospel and used his shirtsleeve empiricism to study industrial conditions. The industrial betterment/welfare work movement stimulated the formation of employment departments and groups, such as the National Civic Federation, which sought remedies for industrial unrest.

To those of the Social Gospel persuasion, unions were instruments of social and economic reform, and such individuals as Robert G. Valentine envisioned the eventual replacement of trade unions by enlightened consumer unions in their evolution toward true industrial democracy.[30] The transition period was to be marked by a rapprochement between scientific management and organized labor based on efficiency and consent. Worker participation plans evolved; some involved union consent and cooperation, whereas others gave employees a voice and a choice

---

29. W. G. Scott, *The Social Ethic in Management Literature* (Atlanta: Georgia State College of Business Administration, 1959), p. 9.

30. R. G. Valentine, "Scientific Management and Organized Labor," *Bulletin of the Society to Promote the Science of Management* 1 (January 1915), pp. 3–9.

through various types of employee representation plans. The industrial better-ment/welfare movement was an uneven mixture of philanthropy, humanitarianism, and business acumen. Industrialists such as John H. Patterson of National Cash Register set the pattern for the industrial welfare movement.[31]

Welfare schemes had the objectives of preventing labor problems and improving performance by providing hospital clinics, lunchrooms, bathhouses, profit sharing, recreational facilities, and a host of other devices to woo worker loyalty. To this group, human happiness was a business asset, and it was the wise, profit-minded employer who nurtured worker loyalty to the firm through various employee welfare schemes. The efficiency engineers, especially Taylor, complemented the work of the betterment or welfare proponents by linking efficiency and morality. For Taylor, hard work led to morality and well-being; for the industrial betterment advocates, morality and well-being yielded hard work. This reciprocal work–welfare equation was the core of the romance between the progressives and scientific management. Societal uplift through efficiency was in vogue.

In retrospect it is clear that social forces were generating and sanctioning an efficiency craze during the Taylor era. A proliferation of popular and technical literature appeared on efficiency in the home, in education, in conservation of natural resources, in the church, and in industry. The noted psychologist H. H. Goddard thought that the efficiency of group endeavors was not a function so much of intelligence but of the proper assignment of workers to a grade of work that met their mental capacity.[32] This psychological notion of the "first-class man" reflected the grip of Taylor's ideas on the academic community. U.S. educational institutions, seeking reform and a broader base for their efforts, seized on Taylor's system and discovered the efficiency expert.[33] Conservationists, spurred by presidents T. R. Roosevelt and William Howard Taft, also found comfort in the gospel of efficiency.[34] Feminists saw a saving grace in efficiency that would release women from the drudgery of housework and free them to assume an equal role in society. Reverend Billy Sunday recommended functional foremanship for the church so that each department could obtain expert advice and lasting results.[35]

---

31. Samuel Crowther, *John H. Patterson: Pioneer in Industrial Welfare* (Garden City, NY: Doubleday, 1923).

32. Henry Herbert Goddard, *Human Efficiency and Levels of Intelligence* (Princeton, NJ: Princeton University Press, 1920).

33. See Raymond E. Callahan, *Education and the Cult of Efficiency* (Chicago: University of Chicago Press, 1962); and J. M. Rice, *Scientific Management and Education* (New York: Hinds, Noble and Eldredge, 1914).

34. Samuel P. Hays, *Conservation and the Gospel of Efficiency* (Cambridge, MA: Harvard University Press, 1959).

35. Samuel Haber, *Efficiency and Uplift: Scientific Management in the Progressive Era 1890–1920* (Chicago: University of Chicago Press, 1964), p. 63. See also Ernest J. Dennen, *The Sunday School under Scientific Management* (Milwaukee: Young Churchman, 1914); and Eugene M. Camp, *Christ's Economy: Scientific Management of Men and Things in Relation to God and His Cause* (New York: Seabury Society, 1916).

This cultural fetish for efficiency was soon to wane. By the 1920s, a marked shift had occurred from the individualistic ideal of Horatio Alger. The gospel of production efficiency was dying as factories poured forth an abundance of goods. Prosperity reigned, and a new gospel of consumption emerged with a heavy stress on sales and selling all people on the importance of being middle class. Such individuals as Whiting Williams, Elton Mayo, and Mary Parker Follett were beginning to play down the emphasis on the individual and stress the importance of the group in industry. The burgeoning discipline of personnel management emphasized industrial welfare, better worker selection, improved morale, and worker happiness as both social and business assets. The need for affiliation was rising, there was security in conformity, and people were becoming more conscious of social relations and less aspiring in maximizing individual gain. The frontier was closed, and new social values were replacing the Western ideal of rugged individualism. The seeds were sown for the social person.

THE POLITICAL ENVIRONMENT: FROM ONE ROOSEVELT TO ANOTHER

The task of government and political institutions throughout time has always revolved around balancing two basic themes: (1) the need to establish equity and order to protect one person from another, and (2) the need to limit governmental power to protect a person from the state. Political theorists, such as Machiavelli and Hobbes, saw a central role for the state over the individual; Rousseau and Locke sought a system of balances through which individuals could check the excess of governmental power. Constitutional or representative government, the philosophy of Locke and Rousseau made manifest in the United States, makes consent of the governed the proper source of all legislative authority. The United States of the late nineteenth century was seeking to perfect democracy, and dissatisfied groups and individuals were responding to the collision effect with an outpouring of legislation to change the relations between individuals and the state and between business and government. Founded on the premises of limited government, private property, freedom of economic opportunity, stress on individual initiative, and a government that should keep its hands off business, the United States encountered imbalances and imperfections between the ideals and practice of economic democracy.

SCIENTIFIC MANAGEMENT AND THE PROGRESSIVES

The political articulation of the Social Gospel was found in the Populist-Progressive movement that attempted to provide a broader base for democracy to mitigate the perils of the collision effect. It is a strange quirk of history that Taylor would never have been considered progressive by modern critics, yet his work and philosophy eventually became embedded in Progressive thought. Progressivism had its roots in the populist movement of the 1870s and 1880s. Whereas populism was overwhelmingly rural and provincial, progressivism was urban, middle class, and nationwide.[36] Both were reform movements, and progressivism picked up where the populism of William Jennings Bryan left off. For both movements, the central problem was to restore equality of opportunity by removing the interventions of government that benefited large-scale capital and by replacing those interventions with ones that favored persons of little or no capital.[37] Populism waned because it was based on support from the declining segment of the population in the rural areas. Progressivism succeeded because it was concerned with labor, small business, and the urban population. The Progressives sought to enfranchise women, elect U.S. senators by direct popular vote, aid lower-income groups, establish a minimum wage, enact workers' compensation laws, encourage trade unions, and enact a federal income tax.

There was probably little in the Progressive platform that would have appealed to F. W. Taylor, but reform movements have a facility for making a union of odd couples. Scientific management caught the Progressives' eye at the Eastern rate hearings. Brandeis, a leading Progressive, helped coin the catchy title "scientific management" that made efficiency synonymous with morality and social order. The public could be saved from a rate increase if efficiency was introduced and labor and management were denied unwarranted gains. Everyone would benefit from lower costs and higher wages if industrial leaders would accept Taylor's precepts. It was here that the Progressives' romance with scientific management began. The reformers did not wish to root out capitalism, but sought orderly change in the structure of industry vis-à-vis the public. Some reformers, like the Socialist Eugene Debs, wanted to replace the whole system. More moderate individuals, like Louis Brandeis, Herbert Croly, and Walter Lippman, thought that efficiency through science and leadership by professional experts would bring social order and harmony. Each envisioned a professionalization of business leadership that would remove management from the "cesspool of commercialism" and turn the manager into an "industrial statesman."[38] The appeal of scientific management was that it offered leadership by expertise and knowledge and hence would rise above class prejudice and rule by drive and whim. The high wages and low costs promised by efficiency systems would check the greed of the employer and the laziness of the employee. Finally, scientific management showed that the interests of the employer and the employee were identical and the wastes of class conflict were therefore unnecessary.[39]

---

36. Richard Hofstadter, *The Age of Reform* (New York: Vintage Books, 1955), p. 131.

37. Eric F. Goldman, *Rendezvous with Destiny* (New York: Vintage Books, 1952), p. 59.

38. Walter Lippman, *Drift and Mastery* (New York: Mitchell Kennerly, 1914), pp. 10–11. See also Louis Brandeis, *Business—A Profession* (Boston: Small, Baynard, 1914).

39. Haber, *Efficiency and Uplift*, pp. 58–59, 89–90.

BUSINESS AND THE PROGRESSIVES

The big change in the relations between government and business came in 1901 after the assassination of President McKinley and the succession of Theodore Roosevelt. At first, the new president gave business leaders and the financial interests no cause for alarm. His well-phrased first message to Congress did well to balance his own Progressive inclinations with a probusiness stance

The honeymoon was brief. In 1902, President Roosevelt brought suit to dissolve the Northern Securities Company by invoking the Sherman Act. This direct blow at Northern Securities, a holding company set up by J. P. Morgan and Edward H. Harriman to control three major railroads, opened a new era in government–business relations. Known as a prime proponent of conservation of natural resources as well as a trustbuster, the first Roosevelt placed government in a new role as a regulator of business activity. Antitrust suits were filed against the Beef Trust (1905), the Standard Oil Company of New Jersey (1906), and the American Tobacco Company (1907); and new legislation regulated the railroads (Elkins Act, 1903, and Hepburn Act, 1906) the telephone, telegraph, and wireless industries (Mann-Elkins Act, 1910). Other state and federal legislative enactments sought to limit hours of work and regulate female and child labor. The Clayton Act and the Federal Trade Commission Act (1914) strengthened the Sherman Act and made more explicit other discriminatory business practices. The Federal Reserve Act (1913) created a more elastic currency and weakened the hold of big New York City banks over cash and reserves.

To illustrate further the decline of laissez-faire economics, taxpayers lost their earlier reprieve with the passage of the Underwood-Simmons Tariff Act of 1913. The act provided for a 1 percent tax on personal incomes over $3,000, and a surtax was added progressively on incomes up to $20,000; the maximum rate was 7 percent on incomes in excess of $500,000. Taxpayers reported their income on Form 1040. The Supreme Court let this act stand; only the rates have changed. In retrospect, the political environment of the early scientific-management era sought to bring a new balance between the power of business vis-à-vis the public. Though Taylor did not concern himself with the political environment to any large extent, his own battles with entrenched, resistant business leadership, for example, that of Bethlehem Steel, indicate that he sought to replace management by privilege with management by science based on expertise. The mental revolution was to de-emphasize the division of the surplus and stress production for lower prices and higher wages. The romance of Taylor and the Progressives had political as well as social ramifications. After the war the United States witnessed the decline of the progressivism of Roosevelt and Wilson and welcomed the return to normalcy of Warren Harding. The United States withdrew from the world arena of politics and turned inward to enjoy a decade of prosperity.

SUMMARY OF PART II

Figure 12-2 provides a visual summary of the emergence, growth, and evolution of the scientific-management era. Scientific management was not an invention; it was a synthesis, a stage in evolving management thought. Charles Babbage could lay a valid claim to the formation of a rational, systematic approach to management, but it was Frederick W. Taylor who gave systematic management a voice.

Taylor was the deus ex machina who became the focal point for an idea. Scientific management was more than methods and time study; it was a much deeper philosophy of managing human and physical resources in a technologically advanced world where people had gained greater control over their environment than ever before. The Industrial Revolution had provided the impetus; Taylor provided the synthesis. As people gained greater power over the physical world, they sought to direct and guide the products of that greater prosperity to more rational ends. Taylor had an idea, a great idea, on how that might be done—by a mental revolution for all parties, founded on science and not whim, and leading to harmony and cooperation. Perhaps he was idealistic, even Utopian, but it would be wrong to criticize him for holding forth the promise of joining industrial harmony, individual betterment, and greater productivity.

Those who followed Taylor represented divergence from his orthodoxy. Some were major figures, leaving larger footprints in the sands of time, whereas others left merely tracings. But each in some way provided for industrial education, academic awareness of management, and improved productivity and service to society by industry. Two of Taylor's contemporaries, Fayol and Weber, were to achieve acclaim only in more modern times; but all those examined during this era reflected the imprint of Taylor's search for rationality in a world of large enterprise.

The historical question of whether the person makes the times or vice versa cannot be begged. Certainly it is a mutually reciprocating force, an action-reaction throughout history. Taylor and his followers were the products of an era that in economic terms sought a rationalization of resource utilization, in social terms sanctioned individual reward and effort, and in political terms encouraged uplift through efficiency. In return, the individuals affected the times by giving voice to a movement toward material prosperity and industrial harmony to retard the collision effect and making the United States into the world's economic and political leader. Scientific management was the child of its culture and in turn made its culture an adult of industrial, social, and political vigor.

FIGURE 12-2   SYNOPSIS OF THE SCIENTIFIC MANAGEMENT ERA

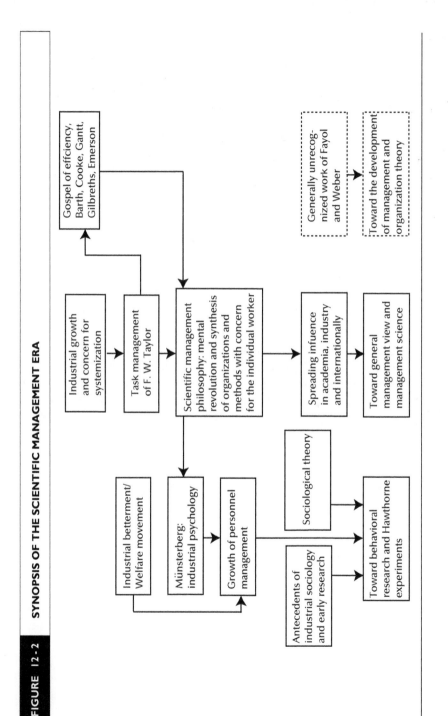

The Social Person Era

E ras in management thought never begin and end neatly in any particular year. Just as in a musical performance, there is a blending of movements as themes shift among major and minor keys. The notion of a "social person era" reflects more of an emerging philosophy than a criterion for managerial action. Although born late in the scientific-management era, it did not achieve any large degree of recognition until the 1930s. It was dominated by the belief that employee satisfaction and productivity were dependent on favorable social interactions among employees and between employees and their supervisors and, therefore, the key to efficiency and workplace harmony was supportive human relations. Part III begins by examining the Hawthorne studies, which served to give academic credence to the human-relations movement. The work of Mary P. Follett and Chester I. Barnard is then introduced and their unique views on authority and organizational integration are discussed. Next, two streams of management thought that developed from about 1930 into the early 1950s are reviewed. Part III concludes with a look at human relations in theory and practice and a discussion of the economic, social, and political environment of the social person era.

CHAPTER

13

The Hawthorne Studies

N
o studies in the history of management thought have received as much publicity, been subjected to so many different interpretations, and been as widely praised and thoroughly criticized as those begun in 1924 at the former Hawthorne (Cicero, Illinois) Works of the Western Electric Company, the manufacturing arm of AT&T. The studies spanned an eight-year period and dramatically revealed previously unappreciated patterns of employee behavior. Perhaps the most significant feature of the studies was that, for the first time, resources comparable to those normally devoted to research in the physical sciences were devoted to the human side of management, thereby counterbalancing the largely technical engineering emphasis of the scientific-management era. Referred to as the "Hawthorne studies," this research had a profound effect on the so-called human relations movement.

At the time of the studies, the Hawthorne Works employed some 40,000 people in nearly every trade and profession. It was noted for its enlightened human-resource policies and generous employee benefits. It sponsored athletic, recreational, and social programs for its employees, operated a store where employees could purchase a wide variety of merchandise at discount, and sponsored an evening school. It maintained an employee building and loan association, a noncontributory benefit plan, a savings plan, and an employee stock purchase program. It also operated a company restaurant, several cafeterias, and numerous lunch counters where employees could purchase meals at cost. Employee morale was thought to be high, and there had been no labor unrest. As Hawthorne was virtually AT&T's sole supplier of telephone apparatus, there was intense pressure to meet production schedules and, thus, to avoid any form of work stoppage.[1]

---

1. Joseph M. Juran, "Early SQC: A Historical Supplement," *Quality Progress* 30 (September 1997), p. 74.

THE HAWTHORNE STUDIES BEGIN
ILLUMINATION STUDY (1924–1927)

Initiated in collaboration with the Council on Industrial Lighting, an element of the National Research Council of the National Academy of Sciences, what was to become known as the Illumination Study was conducted under the direction of Dugald C. Jackson, a professor of electrical engineering at the Massachusetts Institute of Technology (MIT). The original intent of the study was to investigate the relationship between variations in workplace lighting and employee productivity. Based on prior research, it had been hypothesized that as workplace illumination was increased, employee productivity would increase. In the winter of 1924, the MIT researchers investigated existing lighting conditions and performance in Western Electric's punch press, coil winding, and relay-assembly departments to establish a baseline against which to measure employee productivity. The level of illumination was then varied in each department, with the result that "output bobbed up and down without direct relation to illumination."[2]

In the summer of 1925, the researchers selected two groups of coil-winding operators, equal in experience and performance, and designated one the variable group (that is, the level of lighting was to be varied) and the other a control group (no changes in lighting were to be made). The groups were placed in two different buildings away from their regular department. The researchers systematically modified the level of illumination in the building housing the variable group, fully anticipating employee output to vary directly with light intensity. The results, however, showed no such effect. Regardless of whether the lighting was brighter, dimmer, or constant, output in general increased. Other study variations yielded similarly unanticipated and seemingly contradictory results. In one instance, Homer Hibarger, a Western Electric employee, studied two operators and gradually reduced the light intensity to the equivalent of ordinary moonlight (0.06 footcandles) and output still increased. Wanda Beilfus, one of the operators, recalled:

> Geri [Geraldine Sirchio] . . . was with me. We were taken to a small room. Mr. Hibarger was there with us, but it wasn't that bad. The lighting was a little darker but we could see what we were doing. . . . They found out even with the bad lighting we did just as well.[3]

In April 1927, the illumination study was abandoned. Two conclusions seemed obvious: (1) illumination was only one of many factors affecting employee output,

---

2. Charles E. Snow, "Research on Industrial Illumination: A Discussion of the Relation of Illumination Intensity to Productive Efficiency." *Tech Engineering News* 8 (November 1927), p. 272.

3. Wanda Beilfus (née Blazejak) quoted in Alfred A. Bolton, "Relay Assembly Testroom Participants Remember: Hawthorne a Half Century Later," *International Journal of Public Administration* 17 (1994), p. 377.

and (2) no simple cause-and-effect relationship existed between illumination and employee productivity. It was thus recognized that other factors would have to be investigated and that better experimental controls would be necessary. In preparing a report on the study's findings, Charles E. Snow, an MIT electrical engineering instructor, concluded that there were too many factors at play to definitely establish that illumination was directly related to employee productivity. Snow acknowledged that whereas many of these factors could be controlled or eliminated, the "one great stumbling block remaining is the problem of the psychology of the human individual."[4] At this juncture, it would have been easy to move on to other pursuits. Hibarger, however, intrigued by the unanticipated and seemingly contradictory results, felt the study should be continued, and George Pennock, Assistant Works Manager, and Clarence Stoll, Works Manager, agreed. With their support, Hibarger designed and conducted a second study.

RELAY-ASSEMBLY TEST ROOM STUDY (1927–1932)

In early 1927, a second study was begun in an effort to solve the puzzle presented by the contradictory results of the Illumination Study. The goal of this second study was to determine the effects of working conditions, such as rest breaks, workday length, company-provided midmorning lunches, and method of payment, on employee productivity. This phase of the Hawthorne studies, known as the Relay-Assembly Test Room studies, lasted five years. The original study participants were five relay assemblers (Adeline Bogotowicz, Irene Rybacki, Theresa Layman, Ladialas "Wanda" Blazejak-Beilfus, and Anna Haug), one layout operator (Bea Stedry), who supplied the assemblers with parts, and Hibarger, who served as the test room's initial observer. The number of assemblers who participated in the study was limited by the capability of a recording device that would punch a hole in a telegraph tape each time an assembler would complete and drop a relay down a collection chute. The telegraph tape had only five channels. The function of the observer was to keep daily records of significant events, employee conversations, and his own impressions. The work consisted of repetitively assembling telephone relays. The relays weighed a few ounces, consisted of a coil, armature, contact-springs, and insulators held in position by several machine screws. They required approximately one minute to assemble. How the study participants were selected offers a glimpse of work life in the late 1920s. Frank Platenka, the regular relay-assembly department supervisor, told Wanda Beilfus there was going to be a study and asked her to "pick out girls who I felt would not be married soon" and who would like to work on a special room to be used for the study.[5] The assemblers were invited to Pennock's office

---

4. Snow, "Research on Industrial Illumination," p. 282.

5. Wanda Beilfus (née Blazejak) quoted in Bolton, "Relay Assembly Testroom Participants Remember," p. 361.

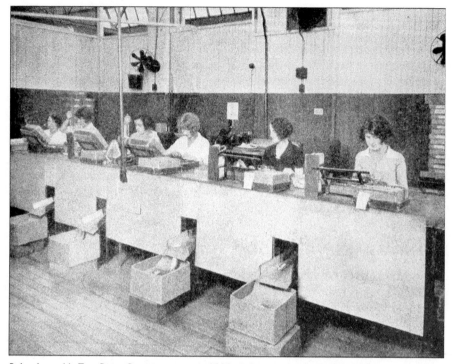

Relay Assembly Test Room Participants, circa 1928: (left to right) Beatrice Stedry (layout operator), Anna Haug (operator #5), Wanda "Lottie" Beilfus (operator #4), Theresa Layman (operator #3), Geraldine Sirchio (operator #2), and Mary Volango (operator #1). Ronald G. Greenwood Collection, courtesy of Regina A. Greenwood.

"where the plan and objectives of the study were explained ... [and] they readily consented to take part in the study."[6]

The assemblers were observed in their regular department (without their knowledge) for two weeks prior to moving to a special test room, where work conditions could be more closely controlled.[7] Additionally, careful measurements were made of factors such as pulse rate, blood pressure, blood condition ratings, and

---

6. Claire E. Turner, "Test Room Studies in Employee Effectiveness," *American Journal of Public Health* 23 (June 1933), pp. 577–584.

7. Much of the following section is based on the seminal research of Charles D. Wrege, "Facts and Fallacies of Hawthorne: A Historical Study of the Origins, Procedures, and Results of the Hawthorne Illumination Tests and Their Influence on the Hawthorne Studies" (Ph.D. dissertation, New York University, 3 vols., 1961); and on Ronald G. Greenwood, Alfred A. Bolton, and Regina A. Greenwood, "Hawthorne a Half Century Later: Relay Assembly Participants Remember," *Journal of Management* 9 (Fall 1983), pp. 217–231. The Wrege dissertation was reprinted under the same title in 1986 by Garland Press (New York).

vascular skin reactions, as well as general weather conditions and test room temperature and humidity. Every six weeks the assemblers were given a complete medical examination to track their health and menstrual cycles. Records were kept of the amount of sleep each assembler had had the previous night, what food she had eaten, recreations, home conditions, and other outside influences. Hibarger's role as observer was to record the principal events in the room hour by hour and to create and maintain a friendly atmosphere. Unlike their regular department, the assemblers were allowed to talk and to leave their workbenches whenever they wished. The assemblers had no supervisor, as they would have had in a regular department. At most, Hibarger exercised a quasi-supervisory function. After about six weeks, the assemblers were placed on an incentive plan that tied their pay to the performance of their small group rather than staying on the payment plan that applied to assemblers in their regular department. The assemblers were told to work at a "comfortable pace" and that they would not suffer financially but had the chance to make more money than possible under their former payment plan. Thus the researchers reported that "we were able to easily convince the operators that any gains in output would be returned entirely to them and we were thus reasonably assured of their cooperation."[8]

During the first seven periods of the study (April 25, 1927 to January 21, 1928), various working conditions were changed to determine the effect, if any, on output. Two five-minute rest periods were introduced, followed by two ten-minute rests, then six five-minute rests, and later a lunch was provided in Western Electric's employee restaurant. Whenever a change was planned, its purpose was explained to the assemblers and their comments solicited. Changes that did not meet their approval were abandoned. The most surprising finding during this time was that the assemblers' productivity "tended in general to increase no matter what changes in working conditions were introduced."[9] There was an emerging concern, however, about the behavior and production of Adeline Bogotowicz and Irene Rybacki. Hibarger had evidence that Bogotowicz was restricting output (she and Rybacki were consistently the lowest producers); and Theresa Layman, who sat at a workbench closest to Bogotowicz, said that Bogotowicz and Rybacki talked only to each other and refused to talk with others. Rybacki and Bogotowicz were dismissed from the test room and returned to the regular relay-assembly department. The reasons offered for their dismissal were "lack of co-operation" and "poor output"

---

8. Western Electric Company, "An Investigation of Rest Pauses, Working Conditions, and Industrial Efficiency," supplementary program report as of May 11, 1929, p. 144; also reproduced on Reel 1, Box 1, Folder 6, of the microfilmed Records of the Industrial Relations Experiment Carried Out by the Western Electric Company at the Hawthorne Works, Hawthorne, Illinois. Hawthorne Studies Collection, Baker Library, Harvard University Business School, Boston, Mass.

9. George A. Pennock, "Industrial Research at Hawthorne: An Experimental Investigation of Rest Periods, Working Conditions and other Influences," *Personnel Journal*, 8 (1930), p. 297.

by employees who had a "talking problem."[10] An undated Hawthorne report, however, noted that Rybacki had been cooperative when the study began and became antagonistic only after her health declined. Medical tests disclosed that Irene was severely anemic: she received medical treatment and a two-week paid leave, and was able to recover her health and return to work in the regular relay-assembly department.[11]

Bogotowicz's and Rybacki's positions in the test room were assigned to Mary Volango and Geraldine Sirchio, two experienced relay-assemblers. Output in period eight went up as soon as Sirchio and Volango arrived, exceeding any previous level by the original five assemblers. Sirchio became the work group's informal leader, and although output would vary from one period to the next, the trend continued upward, exceeding previous peak performances. Then, in period twelve, over a year after the study started, rest periods were removed, the workday and workweek were returned to their original length, and the assemblers once again had to furnish their own lunches. Total output went up as the workweek increased to $5\frac{1}{2}$ days (48 hours), but hourly output declined. Rest periods were reinstated in period thirteen and weekly and hourly output reached an all-time high.

It was clear to Pennock, Hibarger, and others that something unusual was happening. Pennock visited MIT, his alma mater, in the winter of 1927 to seek professional advice. MIT's President Stratton recommended that Pennock seek out Clair E. Turner (1890–1974), an MIT professor of biology and public health. Turner soon joined the study as a consultant. At Turner's suggestion, fatigue, health habits, and mental attitudes were explored as potential explanations of the assemblers' enhanced productivity.[12] Turner was able to establish that reduced fatigue as a result of rest periods was not the cause of the assemblers' increased output. The rest periods, however, gave the assemblers more opportunities for social interaction, and mental attitudes, more than anything else, seemed to explain their performance increases. In order of importance, Turner attributed the assemblers' increase in output to (1) working in a small group, (2) a less restrictive and friendlier supervisory style,

---

10. T. North Whitehead, *The Industrial Worker: A Statistical Study of Human Relations in a Group of Manual Workers*, Vol. 1 (Cambridge, MA: Harvard University Press, 1938), p. 117; and Fritz J. Roethlisberger and William J. Dickson (with the assistance and collaboration of Harold A. Wright). *Management and the Worker: An Account of a Research Program Conducted by the Western Electric Company, Hawthorne Works, Chicago* (Cambridge: MA: Harvard University Press, 1939), p. 53.

11. "Explanation of Removal of Two Operators," no date, reproduced on Reel 3, Box 5, Folder 2, of the microfilmed Records of the Industrial Relations Experiment Carried Out by the Western Electric Company at the Hawthorne Works, Hawthorne, Illinois. Hawthorne Studies Collection, Baker Library, Harvard University Business School, Boston, Mass.

12. Claire E. Turner, *I Remember*. (New York: Vantage Press, 1974), pp. 83–87; and Charles D. Wrege, "Solving Mayo's Mystery: The First Complete Account of the Origin of the Hawthorne Studies—The Forgotten Contributions of C. E. Snow and H. Hibarger," in Robert L Taylor, Michael J. O'Donnell, Robert A. Zawacki, and Donald D. Warwick (eds.), *Proceedings of the Annual Meeting of the Academy of Management* (1976), pp. 12–16.

(3) increased earnings, (4) the novelty of being a study participant, and (5) the attention given to the assemblers by company officials and the researchers.[13]

Pennock was the first to note the influence of supervisory style on the assemblers' productivity. The assemblers were aware they were producing more in the test room than they had in their regular department, and they said the increase had occurred without any conscious effort on their part. They offered two explanations. First, "it was fun" working in the test room. They enjoyed being the center of attention. Second, the new supervisory style, or more accurately, the absence of the old supervisory style, allowed them to work freely without anxiety. For example, in the test room, the women were allowed to talk with one another, whereas in their regular department, conversation was not allowed. Hibarger's efforts to create a friendly atmosphere in the test room resulted in the women receiving a great deal of considerate and personal attention. In short, the test room supervision was more thoughtful and less authoritarian than the assemblers had previously experienced, and the atmosphere was freer and less anxiety-provoking. This was in dramatic contrast to the atmosphere created by the regular relay-assembly room supervisor, Frank Platenka. As one of the operators, Theresa Layman, explained, "We were more relaxed. We didn't see the boss [Platenka], didn't hear him ... he was mean. He died; I didn't even go to see him." Another operator, Wanda Beilfus added, "It [the test room] was just family, you know, real friendly."[14] Turner summed up the results: "[There was] a fundamental change in supervision ... no group chief ... but instead a 'friendly observer'. .... Discipline was secured through leadership and understanding. .... An esprit de corps grew up within the group."[15]

At this point, style of supervision and the formation of small groups to build esprit de corps or morale were believed to explain the increases in productivity. One other factor, the assemblers' wage incentive plan, was thought to contribute but had not yet been examined empirically. Because the assemblers were paid on the output of six rather than one hundred or more assemblers, their pay was tied more closely to their own individual effort. The average wage of the assemblers before going into the test room was $16 per week; in the test room, however, their average weekly earnings ranged from $28 to $50. Could this boost in wages possibly explain the increase in output?

To test this possibility, two new study groups were formed: a group of five relay-assemblers and a group of five operators splitting mica, which was used as an insulator (Figure 13-1). The relay-assemblers had been on a group incentive plan in the regular relay-assembly department, and for their first nine weeks together were placed on the small-group incentive plan. Initially, total output went up, leveled off (for all but one assembler whose output decreased), and then remained constant at the new higher level (112.6 percent over an established output base of 100 percent).

---

13. Turner, "Test Room Studies," p. 583.

14. Greenwood, Bolton, and Greenwood, "Hawthorne," pp. 222, 224.

15. Turner, "Test Room Studies," p. 579.

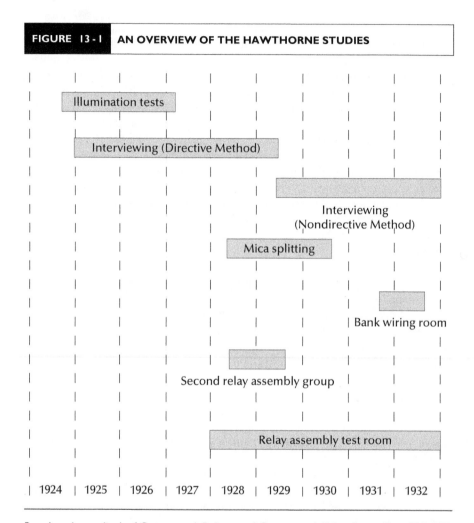

FIGURE 13-1 AN OVERVIEW OF THE HAWTHORNE STUDIES

- Illumination tests
- Interviewing (Directive Method)
- Interviewing (Nondirective Method)
- Mica splitting
- Bank wiring room
- Second relay assembly group
- Relay assembly test room

| 1924 | 1925 | 1926 | 1927 | 1928 | 1929 | 1930 | 1931 | 1932 |

Based on Appendix A of Greenwood, Bolton, and Greenwood, "Hawthorne," pp. 229–230. One experiment involving a typewriting group has been omitted because no report was issued.

After returning to the original group incentive plan for a period of seven weeks, the relay-assemblers' performance dropped to 96.2 percent of the established output base. The mica splitters had always been on an individual incentive system. After being moved to a special observation room, the mica splitters' rest periods and length of workday were varied, as had been done earlier in the relay-assembly test room. Changes in the mica splitters' output were similarly recorded. The mica splitters were studied for fourteen months, and their average hourly output rose 15 percent.

Although output had gone up in both new groups, except when the relay-assemblers were returned to the same group incentive plan used in the regular relay-assembly department, Turner was hesitant to attribute the increase to the differing payment scheme: "[The] changed pay incentive may have been one factor in increasing output but it certainly was not the only factor."[16] An interim report dated May 1929 summarized the results of all three studies: output of the assemblers was up from 35 to 50 percent; fatigue reduction was not a factor in this increased output; payment in the small group "was a factor of the appreciable importance in increasing output"; and the workers were more "content" owing to the "pleasanter, freer, and happier working conditions" caused by the "considerate supervision."[17]

THE INTERVIEWING PROGRAM (1925–1932)

During the Illumination Study, Charles Snow and Homer Hibarger had begun interviewing Western Electric employees to gain insights into employee–supervisor relations.[18] They used a set list of questions, such as: How is your general health? Are you happy on the job? Are you influenced by any pressure from your working associates? Because these items could be answered "yes" or "no," they only learned a limited amount of additional information. Clearly, another approach was needed if the desired insights into work life at Western Electric were to be achieved. To backtrack briefly, when George Pennock recruited Clair Turner from MIT to help explain the puzzling results of the relay-assembly room study, he crossed the Charles River to enlist the aid of Harvard University professor George Elton Mayo (1880–1949).[19] Mayo was an Australian who had received his MA degree in logic and philosophy from the University of Adelaide in 1899. He had taught logic and philosophy at Queensland University and later studied medicine in Edinburgh.[20] While in Scotland, he participated as a research associate in a study of psychopathology, the scientific study of mental disorders; this experience served as a basis for his work as an industrial researcher. Under a grant from the Laura Spelman Rockefeller Fund, Mayo immigrated to the United States, where he was associated

---

16. Ibid, p. 582.

17. Western Electric Company, "Investigation," pp. 126–128.

18. Scott Highhouse, "The Brief History of Personnel Counseling in Industrial-Organizational Psychology," *Journal of Vocational Behavior* 55 (1999), pp. 318–336.

19. George Pennock to Elton Mayo, March 15, 1928. Reproduced on Reel 7, Box 17, Folder 2, of the microfilmed Records of the Industrial Relations Experiment Carried Out by the Western Electric Company at the Hawthorne Works, Hawthorne, Illinois. Hawthorne Studies Collection, Baker Library, Harvard University Business School, Boston, Mass.

20. An excellent biography is Richard C. S. Trahair, *The Humanist Temper: The Life and Work of Elton Mayo* (New Brunswick, NJ: Transaction Books, 1984). Also see Lyndall F. Urwick, "Elton Mayo—His Life and Work," in *Papers and Proceedings XIIth International Congress of Scientific Management* (Melbourne: CIOS, 1960), n.p.

with the University of Pennsylvania's Wharton School of Finance and Commerce. In earlier research Mayo had found that employee workplace difficulties could not be explained by any one factor, but had to be dealt with in what he called "the psychology of the total situation."[21] This was a Gestalt concept that formed the basis for Mayo's view of organizations as social systems. In a study remarkably similar to the original goal of the Hawthorne researchers, Mayo had followed the conventional wisdom of the time and sought a relationship between working conditions and employee output at Continental Mills, a woolen mill near Philadelphia.[22] By introducing rest periods, Mayo was able to reduce employee turnover in the mule-spinning department from 250 to 5 percent and to improve man-hour efficiency. The rest periods, in Mayo's terms, reduced employees' "pessimistic reveries," hence improving their morale and productivity. By "pessimistic reveries" Mayo meant a specific state of consciousness in which melancholic preoccupations or thoughts are uppermost in an individual's mind and completely overshadow everything else.[23] Mayo considered employee reveries to be a form of mild mental illness or psychopathology encouraged by industrial society.[24]

Mayo first visited the Hawthorne plant for two days in 1928, then for four days in 1929, and then began a deeper involvement in 1930. The 1929 visit, however, was critical for the interviewing program. Mayo felt that "a remarkable change of mental attitude in the group" was the key factor in explaining the Hawthorne puzzle. In his opinion, the relay-assemblers had become a social unit, had liked the increased attention they had received, and had developed a great deal of pride in being associated with the study. According to Mayo, "The most significant change that the Western Electric Company introduced into its 'test room' bore only a casual relation to the experimental changes. What the Company actually did for the group was to reconstruct entirely its whole industrial situation."[25]

To understand an employee's "total situation," Mayo felt that a conversational, or nondirective, approach should be used when interviewing employees. The basic premise of this approach was that a "new" supervisory role was necessary. This role would be one of openness, concern, and willingness to listen. The Hawthorne researchers had noted that the relay-assemblers were "apprehensive of authority,"

---

21. Elton Mayo, "The Basis of Industrial Psychology: The Psychology of the Total Situation Is Basic to a Psychology of Management," *Bulletin of the Taylor Society* 9 (December 1924), pp. 249–259. See also Elton Mayo, "The Irrational Factor in Human Behavior: The Night Mind in Industry," *Annals of the American Academy of Political and Social Science* 110 (November 1923), pp. 117–130.

22. Elton Mayo, "Revery and Industrial Fatigue," *Personnel Journal* 8 (December 1924), pp. 273–281.

23. George C. Homans, "Report of the Committee," in National Research Council, Committee on Work in Industry, *Fatigue of Workers: Its Relation to Industrial Production* (New York: Reinhold, 1941), p. 71.

24. Mark A. Griffin, Frank J. Landy, and Lisa Mayocchi, "Australian Influences on Elton Mayo: The Construct of Revery in Industrial Society," *History of Psychology* 5 (2002), pp. 356–375.

25. Elton Mayo, *The Human Problems of an Industrial Civilization* (New York: Macmillian, 1933), p. 73.

but that once the researchers had shown more concern with the assemblers' personal needs, the assemblers lost their shyness and fear and talked more freely to company officials and observers. Moreover, the assemblers developed a greater zest for work and formed personal friendships, both on and off the job. The assemblers began seeing one another socially after working hours, attending parties in one another's homes and going to the theater together. In sum, the women became a cohesive group that stressed loyalty and cooperation. This seemed to improve their morale and to be closely associated with a friendlier supervisory style and, in turn, increased productivity. This presumed link between supervision, morale, and productivity became the foundation of the so-called human relations movement.

Using the nondirective technique Mayo recommended, the Hawthorne interview program allowed employees to express their feelings more freely. An interviewer's job was to keep employees talking, and the average length of employee interviews increased from thirty to ninety minutes. After this modification, employees expressed the opinion in follow-up interviews that working conditions had improved (although they had not changed) and that wages were better (even though the wage scale was the same). In short, the opportunity to let off steam made the workers feel better about their total work situation even though it remained the same.

The complaints gathered in the interviews were thoroughly investigated and found generally to be irrelevant to actual facts. This separation of fact and sentiment led the researchers to distinguish between the *manifest* (material) and *latent* (psychological) content of a complaint. For example, one interviewee was preoccupied with the noise, temperature, and fumes in his department. Further examination revealed that his latent concern was the fact that his brother had recently died of pneumonia, and the interviewee feared that his own health might be impaired. In another case, complaints about a low piece-rate were traced to an interviewee's concern for medical bills arising from his wife's illness. In essence, *"Certain complaints were no longer treated as facts in themselves but as symptoms or indicators of personal or social situations which needed to be explored."*[26] From the researchers' viewpoint, workers' preoccupation with personal concerns inhibited their performance, a conclusion that, as noted, Mayo had called "pessimistic reveries" in his early research. The outcome of the interviewing program was supervisory training in the need to listen and understand employees' personal problems. Supervisors were trained to be interviewers, to listen rather than to talk, and "to exclude from their personal contacts with employees any moral admonition, advice, or emotion."[27]

Use of this nondirective interviewing technique enabled supervisors to handle employees' personal problems more intelligently, to locate factors adversely affecting employee performance, and to remove the events or factors in the employees' social or physical environment that were adversely influencing their lives. The "new"

---

26. Roethlisberger and Dickson, *Management and the Worker*, p. 269.

27. Ibid., p. 323.

supervisor was to be more people oriented, more concerned, less aloof, and skilled in handling social and personal situations. The product of this human-relations style of management was to be better employee morale, fewer pessimistic reveries, and improved output.

BANK-WIRING OBSERVATION ROOM STUDY (1931–1932)

Clair Turner wrote Mark L. Putnam, one of Western Electric's managers, in late 1930 that the mica-splitting study was not yielding useful information and suggested that "we would do well to substitute a test room study group of men" to gain additional insights into what factors influence group output.[28] The Bank Wiring Department as a whole was subsequently chosen as a group to be studied. At this point, however, the researchers' plan took a different turn because of objections by the department's supervisor, Henry S. Wolff, and his fellow supervisors. They were concerned that the purpose of the proposed study was to increase output, as had happened in the relay-assembly test room, and that this would reflect unfavorably on the supervisors and the current output. William J. Dickson, chief of Hawthorne's employee-relations research department, summarized the supervisors' sentiments:

> They felt that those girls [in the relay-assembly test room] had been given special inducements in the form of a special gang rate, the ordinary production difficulties had been carefully eliminated, and that the operators had been petted and babied along from the start. "Of course," they said, "anybody could get production that way, only we [bank-wiring supervisors] can't get away with things like that."[29]

To overcome the bank-wiring supervisors' concerns, the researchers agreed to a number of changes in their proposed plans: A group of bank-wiring room operators would be segregated in a special area for observation, but visitors would not be allowed; employee earnings would be based on their output as a group, factored into the output of the operators remaining in the regular bank-wiring department;

---

28. Claire E. Turner to M. L. Putnam, October 13, 1930, reproduced on Reel 7, Box 17, Folder 3, of the microfilmed Records of the Industrial Relations Experiment Carried Out by the Western Electric Company at the Hawthorne Works, Hawthorne, Illinois. Hawthorne Studies Collection, Baker Library, Harvard University Business School, Boston, MA. Although Turner planned these studies, the primary investigator was W. Lloyd Warner, at the time a University of Chicago anthropologist. See: Dietrich Herzog, *Klassengesellschaft ohne Klassenkonflikt: Eine Studie über William Lloyd Warner und die Entwicklung der neuen amerikanischen Stratifikationsforschung.* (Berlin: Duncker & Humblot, 1965).

29. William J. Dickson, "Procedure in Establishing Bank Wiring Test Room," undated, but circa mid-July, 1931. Reproduced on Reel 3, Box 7, Folder 1, p. 3, of the microfilmed Records of the Industrial Relations Experiment Carried Out by the Western Electric Company at the Hawthorne Works, Hawthorne, Illinois. Hawthorne Studies Collection, Baker Library, Harvard University Business School, Boston, MA.

the operators' supervisor would remain the same, and an observer working with the researchers would be kept in the background rather than being "friendly and supportive," as Hibarger had been with the relay-assemblers; and workplace layout and procedures would remain constant. In brief, the only similarities to the relay-test room would be placing the operators in a separate area and the presence of an observer.

The operators selected for study were a group of fourteen men—nine wiremen; three solder men, and two inspectors—engaged in assembly terminal banks for use in telephone exchanges. It was clear from early findings that the men constituted a complex social group with well-established norms and a common body of sentiments beyond that formally required by their work. They had their own conception of a "fair day's work" and prevailed as a group on one another not to exceed this level of output. Operators who exceeded the agreed-on rate were known as "rate-busters." The operators feared that those who could not keep up with the pace of "rate-busters" would be "bawled out." They also were worried that if the rate-busters' output was adopted as a daily standard, the accepted *bogey* (the daily output expected of each operator) would be increased, and they would find themselves having to work harder for the same amount of pay. At the same time, the men strongly believed that an operator's output should not fall too far below the group norm. If it did, an operator was known as a "rate chiseler." In addition, the operators held that no one should ever say or do anything that would injure a fellow operator. If he did he was a "squealer." The operators engaged in several practices that violated company policies. For instance, although it was forbidden, the operators frequently traded jobs. There also was a great deal of informal helping among operators, which, too, was against company policy. Thus, it was important that no one squeal on a fellow operator. Finally, the operators felt that a person should not attempt to maintain social distance. For example, if someone was an inspector, he should not act like one.[30]

The bank-wiring room operators had developed various methods for enforcing their norms. Pressure was executed through subtle forms of ridicule, sarcasm, and *binging*, a practice whereby one operator expressed displeasure with the actions of another by hitting him as hard as possible on the upper arm. Exceeding the accepted output norm would elicit such chastisement, along with taunts of "Speed King" or "The Slave." The virtue of these practices did not lie in the resulting physical hurt experienced by an operator, but rather in the mental hurt that came from knowing that one's coworkers disapproved of one's behavior.

Discovery of the bank-wiring room operators' "informal organization" and their restriction of output surprised the Hawthorne researchers. Fred Taylor was keenly aware of systematic soldiering and group pressures; Whiting Williams had recounted his own experiences of informal relationships and attitudes toward work; and Stanley Mathewson had made an extensive study of pressures leading to

---

30. Roethlisberger and Dickson, *Management and the Worker*, p. 522.

restriction of output.[31] Despite the experiences of others, the researchers found it noteworthy that "attention had been called to the fact that social groups in shop departments were capable of exercising very strong control over the work behavior of their individual members."[32] Output restriction was news to the researchers because they claim to have been "unaware of its implications for management practice and employee satisfaction."[33] Knowledge builds on knowledge, and the failure of the researchers to learn from prior writings on informal group behavior is a fault that was roundly criticized,[34] although it should not detract from the significance of their findings.

What explained the variations in output between the relay-assemblers and the bank-wiring room operators? In the former case, the employees had increased productivity, but in the latter, output restriction was the norm. Both groups included observers working with the researchers, but their roles were different. In the relay-assembly study, the observer took the assemblers into his confidence, asked for study suggestions, and encouraged them to participate in decisions affecting their welfare. In the bank-wiring room, however, the observer merely watched while the operators engaged in the same informal behavior they had practiced in the past. The Hawthorne researchers' eventual explanation for the output differences would add ammunition to their arguments for a new style of supervision. In explaining the bank-wiring observation room findings, additional insights for understanding organizations as social systems would be forthcoming.

The researchers found that informal work groups perform two functions: (1) they protect employees from internal indiscretions of coworkers, such as rate busting or chiseling; and (2) they protect employees from managers who would attempt to raise output standards, cut pay rates, or challenge workplace norms. Informal groups are, in effect, instruments used by employees to control one another's activities and sentiments, as well as to provide protection from the actions of their employers. As discovered in the Hawthorne interview program, in studying group behavior, fact had to be separated from sentiment. To this end, the Hawthorne researchers began to explore the "facts" as perceived by employees, as contrasted with company practices as seen by company officials. In regard to output restriction, the researchers concluded that fears of an economic depression and layoffs were not the sole reasons for evading work because employees restricted output in both good and bad economic times. Restriction was actually detrimental to employees, because it increased unit costs and could therefore lead to a decrease in pay rates, an increase in required output, or the introduction of new technology to offset higher

---

31. Stanley B. Mathewson, *Restriction of Output Among Unorganized Workers* (New York: Viking Press, 1931).

32. Roethlisberger and Dickson, *Management and the Worker*, p. 379.

33. Ibid., p. 380.

34. Mary B. Gilson, [Review of the book *Management and the Worker*], *American Journal of Sociology* 46 (July 1940), pp. 98–101.

costs. Because Western Electric had a long record of enlightened workplace polices and generous employee benefits, the researchers considered the employees' belief that restricting output was in their best interests to be "nonlogical," based on a misconception of reality.

Having concluded that mismanagement or general economic conditions were not related to informal groups, the researchers sought an explanation by viewing the bank-wiring room as part of a larger social system, influenced by group sentiments and activities. The researchers reasoned that employees viewed interactions with extradepartmental personnel, such as efficiency experts and other staff members, as disturbing because their actions could impinge on the employees' welfare. Such staff members tended to follow the "logic of efficiency," according to which maximizing goods and minimizing costs is the ultimate argument for doing things. Not surprisingly, employees perceived this approach as interfering with their autonomy. Further, supervisors (as a class) represented authority and, thus, possessed power to discipline employees in an effort to ensure conformity to managerial policies. Recognizing that employees were apprehensive of such authority, the researchers reckoned that employees resisted supervisory attempts to force their behavior into an efficiency mold. Again, the researchers concluded that this was nonlogical behavior on the employees' part, but stressed that management must recognize this phenomenon and take into account employee sentiments when an efficiency is introduced. The Hawthorne researchers thus admonished managers to view every organization as a social system. As they understood, a strict logic of efficiency in administering a technical system would inevitably fail because it omitted the sentiments and nonlogical components of an organization's social system.

ORGANIZATIONS AS SOCIAL SYSTEMS

As seen earlier, Vilfredo Pareto's ideas were introduced to Mayo and others through seminars conducted by Lawrence J. Henderson. Although Mayo was never a full-fledged Paretian, he did accept many of Pareto's ideas. Mayo's student, Fritz J. Roethlisberger (1898–1974), however, was closer in his general philosophy to Paretian thinking, especially about organizations as social systems. Roethlisberger received an AB degree from Columbia University in 1921 and a BS from the Massachusetts Institute of Technology in 1922. From 1922 to 1924 he was engaged in industrial practice as a chemical engineer; he then returned to Harvard in 1925 to pursue an MA degree. He later joined Harvard's industrial research department and soon became involved in the Hawthorne research.[35]

---

35. Fritz. J. Roethlisberger, *The Elusive Phenomena*, ed. George F. F. Lombard (Cambridge, MA: Harvard University Press, 1977). A special tribute to Roethlisberger appears in George F. F. Lombard, ed., *The Contributions of F. J. Roethlisberger to Management Theory and Practice* (Cambridge, MA: Graduate School of Business, Harvard University, 1976).

Roethlisberger and William J. Dickson prepared the most widely read report of the Hawthorne studies, *Management and the Worker*. In this report, the influence of Pareto thinking is clearly evident, especially as regards the notion of organizations as social systems. According to Roethlisberger and Dickson, the technical requirements for efficiency and economic return should be viewed as interrelated with a concern for the human element found in every organization. Employees have physical needs, but they also have personal needs. These needs arise from early social conditioning and persist in relations with coworkers and other workplace participants. Roethlisberger and Dickson recognized that events and objects in an organization's physical work environment "cannot be treated as things in themselves. Instead they have to be interpreted as carriers of social value."[36] For example, a physical desk has no social significance, but if individuals who have desks supervise others, then a desk becomes a status symbol and a carrier of social value. Other items, such as type of clothing, age, gender, seniority, and so on, can also take on social significance. Roethlisberger and Dickson concluded that because individuals are not governed by facts and logic, sentiments about events and objects in an organization's physical environment must be considered when dealing with employees, as well as people in general.

As described by Roethlisberger and Dickson, the existence of a formal structure within an organization with its rules, policies, and procedures, inextricably coupled with independent groups created for their members' purposes and based on common interests that may not support an organization's goals, invariably poses managerial challenges. They stressed, however, that such informal groups should not be viewed as "bad," but as an inevitable aspect of formal organizations as social systems. Viewing an organization as a social system enables managers to balance the "logic of efficiency" demanded by formal rules, policies, and procedures and the "logic of sentiments" that is the basis for informal groups.[37] Thus, Roethlisberger and Dickson held that managers must strive to achieve equilibrium between an organization's technical and human requirements. It thus follows, that to survive, an organization must secure its economic goals in such a way that "individuals through contributing services to this common purpose obtain personal satisfaction that makes them willing to cooperate."[38]

In short, the outcome of the Hawthorne studies was a call for a different mix of managerial skills. These skills were those crucial to handling human interactions: first, diagnostic skills in understanding human behavior, and second, interpersonal skills in counseling, motivating, leading, and communicating with employees. Technical skills alone were insufficient to cope with the sentiments and behavior discovered at Hawthorne.

———

36. Roethlisberger and Dickson, *Management and the Worker*, p. 557.

37. Ibid., pp. 556–564. "Logic of sentiments" is actually a contradiction, because Roethlisberger and Dickson concluded that sentiments were nonlogical.

38. Ibid., p. 569. The authors acknowledged their indebtedness to Chester I. Barnard (who is discussed in the next chapter) for this distinction.

Human Relations, Leadership, and Motivation

Over the intervening years, interpreting what happened at Hawthorne has become part of an evolving story. In particular, a phenomenon known as the *Hawthorne effect* has long been part of social-science folklore. One of the early explanations offered for the relay-assemblers' increased output was the increased attention they received. The researchers removed the assemblers from their regular department, placed them in a test room, and assumed a new supervisory style. The use of less-stringent controls created a new social situation for the relay-assemblers. The assemblers were advised and consulted about changes, their views were listened to sympathetically, and their physical and mental health became matters of great concern to the researchers and company officials. As the Hawthorne studies progressed, they became a less controlled experiment and more inclined toward creating a social environment in which employees felt free to air their problems and in which they established new interpersonal bonds with their coworkers and supervisors.

The assemblers, in particular, felt they were part of something special and showed a great deal of pride in being associated with the relay-assembly room study. Viewed psychologically, the assemblers had become ego-involved in their work. These changes have prompted the charge that the researchers' actions—indeed, their very presence—altered the situation they hoped to investigate and, thus, tainted their findings. In particular, it has been suggested that the increase in assemblers' productivity was a result of being singled out and made to feel important. Variously defined, the central idea behind the "Hawthorne effect," a term coined by John R. P. French, is that changes in participants' behavior during the course of a study may be "related only to the special social position and social treatment they received," rather than a hypothesized cause or influence.[39] Simply put: You can seldom observe a phenomenon closely without affecting it somehow.

Was there a Hawthorne effect that biased the studies' results? Did the rise in the relay-assemblers output occur because they were being observed and had gained near-celebrity status? Theresa Layman, one of the relay-assemblers, recalled, "No, we kept working. It didn't matter who watched us or who talked with us." Donald Chipman, who succeeded Hibarger as the test room's observer, recalled, "I agree ... early in the study it had some bearing but ... that just wore off."[40] Clair Turner stated, "We at first thought that the novelty of test room conditions might be partly responsible for increased output but the continuing increase in production over a four-year period suggests it was not of great importance."[41]

---

39. J. R. P. French, "Field Experiments: Changing Group Productivity," in James G. Miller (Ed.), *Experiments in Social Process: A Symposium on Social Psychology* (New York: McGraw-Hill, 1950), p. 82.

40. Greenwood, Bolton, and Greenwood, "Hawthorne," p. 223.

41. Turner, "Test Room Studies," p. 584.

A survey of industrial/organizational and organizational behavior textbooks has concluded that "mythical beliefs among students about the Hawthorne Studies . . . [and] the Hawthorne Effect [are] probably an unfortunate tradition."[42] Although the Hawthorne effect is widely referenced, there is considerable doubt that being observed had any continuing impact on employee performance.

HUMAN RELATIONS AND HUMAN COLLABORATION

As the economic depression that followed the stock market crash of October 1929 deepened, hours-of-work at Hawthorne were reduced and the original relay-assembly test room study was discontinued. With the passage of time, Mayo changed his interpretation of what happened at Hawthorne.[43] As early as October 1931, he began to emphasize the need for "effective collaboration" and a restoration of "social solidarity" in a changing world that left people without stability, purpose, or norms. When Mayo began to elaborate on his social philosophy, he gained a wider audience. Both academics and business leaders were attracted to his view that workplace unrest and political dissidence were symptoms of psychopathology caused by unsuitable working environments. By contrast, the views of Clair Turner, who had been more involved in the Hawthorne studies, became less influential in explaining the studies' results. Thus MIT's star waned, and Harvard's waxed. As Roethlisberger recalled, "Mayo was an adventurer in the realm of ideas . . . the [Hawthorne] data were not his; the results were not his; but the interpretations of what the results meant and the new questions and hypotheses that emerged from them were his."[44]

Mayo's education and experiences suggest the basis for his emerging interpretation of human behavior. For a short time Mayo studied medicine, and though he never received a medical degree, he developed an interest in psychopathology. At that time, individuals such as Jean-Martin Charcot, a French neurologist; Carl G. Jung, a Swiss psychiatrist; Pierre M. F. Janet, a French psychologist; and Sigmund Freud, the Austrian originator of psychoanalysis, were in the vanguard of analyzing psychopathological thought. Mayo was especially intrigued by the works of Janet. His last book before retiring was devoted to a critique of Janet's theories of obsessive thinking.[45] Janet believed that obsessive thinking was the primary mental disorder

---

42. Ryan Olson, Jessica Verley, Lindsey Santos, and Coresta Salas, "What We Teach Students about the Hawthorne Studies: A Review of Content within a Sample of Introductory I-O and OB Textbooks," *The Industrial-Organizational Psychologist* 41 (January 2004), pp. 34–35.

43. Trahair, *Humanist Temper*, p. 254.

44. Roethlisberger, *Elusive Phenomena*, pp. 50–51.

45. Elton Mayo, *Some Notes on the Psychology of Pierre Janet* (Cambridge, MA: Harvard University Press, 1948). See also Yeh Hsueh, "The Hawthorne Experiments and the Introduction of Jean Piaget in American Industrial Psychology, 1929–1932." *History of Psychology* 5 (May 2002), pp. 163–189.

among trauma patents. Freudians called this compulsion. Mayo viewed Janet's theories of obsessive thinking and Freud's views on compulsive disorders to be complementary.[46] The essence of Mayo's obsession–compulsion interpretation was that individuals were incapacitated by their obsessions to such a degree that they were inflexible in their responses to life, including their personal, social, and work-place behavior. With respect to work, Mayo maintained that obsessions reduced an individual's general satisfaction with life, which then led to decreased productivity and increased turnover and absenteeism.

Although Mayo never once concluded that any large number of the employees at Hawthorne were severe trauma sufferers, he did think that the interviewing program had demonstrated that minimal levels of obsession (or preoccupation) existed in the sense that "conditions of work tended in some way to prevent rather than facilitate a satisfactory personal adaptation."[47] In Mayo's view, some employees are unable to find satisfactory outlets for expressing personal problems and dissatisfactions in their work life. This blockage leads to "pessimistic reveries" and preoccupations with personal problems at a latent level, which emerge at the manifest level as apprehension of authority, restriction of output, and a variety of other behaviors that reduce morale and output. To Mayo, industrial life caused a sense of personal futility, which leads to social maladjustment and, eventually, to obsessive, irrational behavior.

> Human collaboration in work, in primitive and developed societies, has always depended for its perpetuation upon the evolution of a non-logical social code which regulates the relations between persons and their attitudes to one another. Insistence upon a merely economic logic of production ... interferes with the development of such a code and consequently gives rise in the group to a sense of human defeat. This human defeat results in the formation of a social code at a lower level and in opposition to the economic logic. One of its symptoms is "restriction."[48]

From this psychopathological analysis of industrial life, Mayo and Roethlisberger formed the philosophical rationale for the human-relations movement.[49] The goal was effective human collaboration; the means was the restoration of a social code to facilitate adjustment to industrial life.

---

46. Mayo, *Human Problems of an Industrial Civilization*, pp. 107–110.

47. Ibid., p. 114.

48. Ibid., pp. 120–121.

49. Roethlisberger also adopted the obsession-compulsion approach of Janet and Mayo. See Fritz J. Roethlisberger, "The Nature of the Obsessive Thinking," *Man-in-Organization: Essays of F. J. Roethlisberger* (Cambridge, MA: Belknap Press of Harvard University Press, 1968), pp. 1–19. This paper was written in June 1928, but was not published until 1968.

ANOMIE AND SOCIAL DISORGANIZATION

Mayo borrowed Émile Durkheim's term *anomie* (from the Greek word meaning "without norms") as a basis for his thinking about effective human collaboration. In traditional societies individuals knew their place and their future, and there was social solidarity. The prevailing domestic system, built around family and kinship, gave individuals a workplace identity as well as an identity in their social life. The onset of the Industrial Revolution destroyed this solidarity through the division of labor, increased social and physical mobility, and the growth of large-scale organizations in which the manner of dealing with interpersonal relations shifted from a personal to an impersonal base. The result was a normless and rootless mode of life in which individual identities were lost along with the social bonds that provided continuity and purpose to human existence. This anomie led to social disorganization in personal lives and in communities and affected a general overall sense of personal futility, defeat, and disillusionment. Social inventions to cope with industrial changes had not kept pace with technological developments. This social lag was responsible for a widespread sense of futility and resultant social disorganization. The rapid economic growth experienced by the United States both before and after the turn of the century had disturbed "communal integrity."

Mayo argued that the advance of a technically oriented society placed undue emphasis on engineering and yielded a technological interpretation of the meaning of work in the sense that achievement was based on an economic-based logic of efficiency. The social needs of individuals were pushed into the background, thereby reducing their "capacity for collaboration in work."[50] Managerial emphasis on a logic of efficiency stifled individuals' desire for group approval, social satisfaction, and social purpose gained through communal life. Drawing on Pareto's notion of economic elites, composed of property owners and entrepreneurs, Mayo championed the creation of an administrative or managerial *élite* that was not only technically oriented, but who also understood human nature.[51] He hoped that an administrative *élite* would restore opportunities for human collaboration in work and in life by recognizing people's need for social solidarity. As envisioned by Mayo, managers could aid in accomplishing this goal by receiving training in the human and social aspects of industrial organization, developing listening and counseling skills, and recognizing and understanding the nonlogical side of the social code that regulates relationships between persons and their attitudes toward others. The problem, as Mayo perceived it, was that managers thought the answers to industrial problems resided in technical efficiency, when in fact the answers to such problems were both social and human.

---

50. Mayo, *Human Problems of an Industrial Civilization*, p. 166.

51. Mayo, *Human Problems*, p. 177.

DEVELOPING THE HUMAN RELATIONS LEADER

Mayo had set the stage for the social person era. He argued for creating an administrative elite, which, buttressed by social and human skills, would overcome anomie and social disorganization. In its very essence, Mayo espoused the same goal—collaboration and cooperation in industry—as Fred Taylor. The means they advocated for achieving this goal differed, but the end that both anticipated was the recognition of a mutually beneficial relationship between employees and employers. Mayo felt that the world must rethink its concepts of authority by abandoning the notion of unitary authority from a central source, be it government, church, or industrial leaders. Drawing heavily from Chester I. Barnard, Mayo concluded that authority should be based on social skills in securing cooperation rather than on technical skill or expertise. The human-relations-oriented manager would act as an investigator of social sentiments to further collaborative efforts to achieve organizational goals. Because people spent so much time in groups and because much of their satisfaction was the product of cooperative efforts, Mayo felt that managers had to focus their efforts on the maintenance of group integrity and solidarity. Groups were the universal solvent, and it was a manager's task to find the universal container.

First-line supervisors, management's first contact with labor, played a particularly crucial and often conflicting role in restoring "social solidarity." In the bank-wiring observation room, for example, the work-group supervisor did not push management's expectation that an operator wire 7,312 terminals a day (the "bogey"), but accepted the average of 6,000 to 6,600 per day. The supervisor's dilemma was explained in an interim program report:

> In such circumstances the first line supervisor finds himself in a conflict situation. He can do either of two things; uphold the system of ideas common to management and attempt by driving or other methods to enforce them, or take the side of the workmen and conceal the true situation from his superiors. In the test room the Group Chief has seen fit to side with the workmen, and perhaps rightly. It is quite likely that by opposing them he would only aggravate the situation.[52]

First-line supervisors were caught as Roethlisberger's "man-in-the-middle" and, in this instance, were ill-prepared to provide the requisite leadership. The

---

52. Arthur C. Moore and William J. Dickson, "Report on Bank Wiring Test Group for the Period November 9, 1931 to March 18, 1932," March 21, 1932, reproduced on Reel 3, Box 7, Folder 3, of the microfilmed Records of the Industrial Relations Experiment Carried Out by the Western Electric Company at the Hawthorne Works, Hawthorne, Illinois. Hawthorne Studies Collection, Baker Library, Harvard University Business School, Boston, MA. See also Fritz J. Roethlisberger, "The Foreman: Master and Victim of Double Talk," *Harvard Business Review* 23 (Spring, 1945), pp. 285–294

challenge for industrial leadership revolved around the premise that it was a rare supervisor who possessed technical and economic skills, as well as human-relations skills. The ability to meet a logic of efficiency was different from the ability to meet the nonlogic (or psychologic) of employee sentiments. Supervisors tended to confuse fact with sentiment and, as the research group found in the Hawthorne interviewing program, assumed that what the employees told them was the way things really were. Communications and listening skills hence became an important part of a supervisor's tool kit.

The answer to preparing managers for their new human-relations role was training at all levels to develop skills in understanding the logic and non-logic, employee sentiments through listening and communicating skills, and in developing the ability to maintain an equilibrium between the economic needs of a formal organization and the personal needs of employees. For Mayo, equilibrium was the keynote of organizational effectiveness. Through an organization's social structure, employees obtained recognition, security, and satisfaction that made them willing to cooperate and contribute their services toward the attainment of an organization's objectives. Disequilibrium occurred when technical change was introduced too fast or when management was out of touch with employee sentiments. This was the new leadership, one that could distinguish fact from sentiment and that balanced economic logic with the nonlogic of sentiment.

HUMAN RELATIONS AND MOTIVATION

As we will see in Chapter 17, how the human-relations-oriented leader motivated people became a controversial subject. Early reports of the Hawthorne studies gave some credence to the conclusion that changing to a small-group incentive payment plan was one factor in explaining the increased output in the relay-assembly test room. Mark Putnam told *Business Week* that pay was the number one concern expressed by Hawthorne employees during interviews in 1930.[53] When the assemblers were asked what they liked in the test room, one responded, "*We made more money in the Test Room.*"[54] Wrege quoted from a November 12, 1930, Hawthorne memo to Mayo: "Economic and financial factors are of considerable importance in the Test Room. The employees are anxious for high earnings. The Test Room has apparently removed the doubt in the employees' minds that the company would permit them to make very high earnings."[55] The evidence regarding economic

---

53. "Human Factor in Production Subject of Unique Research," *Business Week*, January 21, 1931, p. 16.

54. Greenwood, Bolton, and Greenwood, "Hawthorne," p. 220.

55. Charles D. Wrege, "Review of 'The Hawthorne Myth Dies Hard,'" unpublished manuscript, August 1, 1979; quoted in Greenwood, Bolton, and Greenwood, "Hawthorne," p. 220.

incentives and output at Hawthorne was available, but the published results took on a different interpretation.[56]

There is evidence that the official accounts of Hawthorne assumed a meaning of their own due to Mayo's influence. Mayo's writings, and his influence on those who wrote the official results, Roethlisberger and Dickson, and presented a different interpretation of what happened at Hawthorne. An early indication of Mayo's influence is in a memo written by Roethlisberger in which he reported that there appeared to be a significant relationship between physiological factors and output. According to Roethlisberger, this made Mayo very happy because "it looked as if the organization of the girls in the relay-assembly test room was more conditioned by biological factors rather than anything so naive as economic incentive. As this fits in with what Mayo has been saying for the last five years we were very pleased."[57]

In *Management and the Worker*, Roethlisberger and Dickson stated that the "efficacy of the wage incentive was so dependent on its relation to other factors that it was impossible to consider it as in itself having an independent effect on the individual."[58] That is, pay for performance was only one factor that could not be addressed separately. As time went on, Roethlisberger mentioned other factors that explained human motivation:

> Whether or not a person is going to give his services whole-heartedly to a group depends, in good part, on the way he feels about his job, his fellow workers, and supervisors ... [a person wants] ... social recognition ... tangible evidence of ... social importance ... the feeling of security that comes not so much from the amount of money we have in the bank as from being an accepted member of a group.[59]

Still later it appears that the notion of the "economic man" was discarded:

> Far from being the prime and sole mover of human activity in business, economic interest has run far behind in the list of incentives that make men willing to work ... man at work is a social creature as well as an "economic man." He has personal and social as

---

56. See, for example, Stuart Chase, "What Makes the Worker Like to Work?" *Reader's Digest* 38 (February 1941), pp. 15–20.

57. F. J. Roethlisberger to Emily Osborne, April 5, 1932, F. J. Roethlisberger Papers, Folder 1, Baker Library, Graduate School of Business Administration, Harvard University, Boston. Quoted in Richard Gillespie, *Manufacturing Knowledge: A History of the Hawthorne Experiments* (Cambridge, England: Cambridge University Press, 1991), p. 88.

58. Roethlisberger and Dickson, *Management and the Worker*, p. 160.

59. Fritz J. Roethlisberger, *Management and Morale* (Cambridge, MA: Harvard University Press, 1942), pp. 15, 24–25.

well as economic needs. Work provides him with a way of life as well as a means of livelihood ... As we discarded the notion of "economic man," we began to question the concept of business organization as merely a logical organization of operations for the efficient production of goods.[60]

What was the human-relationists' view of motivation? In early reports, employees were quoted to the effect that they worked harder because "they made more money" or that pay was their "number one" concern. As noted, however, Clair Turner felt that money was important, but not the only explanatory factor in increased employee output. As Roethlisberger and Mayo examined the Hawthorne data, the importance of financial incentives faded. In brief, the Hawthorne studies have been subjected to so much manipulation and misinterpretation that their actual results are clouded in myth and advocacy.[61] Mayo wanted to promote social collaboration at work, not pay for performance, and it would require a later generation of scholars to iterate that the social person supplemented, but did not supplant, economic man.

Summary

In addition to challenging many prevailing assumptions of the day, the Hawthorne studies immeasurably increased our knowledge and understanding of employees and their work.[62] As a result of the Hawthorne studies,

- It became clear that workers are not motivated solely by money. The importance of personal and social factors in motivation and employee attitudes (toward every aspect of their work) was revealed.
- The importance of individual attitudes in determining employee behavior became undeniable.
- The significance of effective supervision in maintaining employee job satisfaction and productivity became indisputable.
- It became evident that little was known about the character of informal work groups and their influence on employee performance.

---

60. Fritz J. Roethlisberger, "A 'New Look' for Management," *Worker Morale and Productivity*, General Management Series, no. 141 (New York: American Management Association, 1948), pp. 12–13, 16.

61. Lyle Yorks and David A. Whitsett, "Hawthorne, Topeka, and the Issue of Science versus Advocacy in Organizational Behavior," *Academy of Management Review* 10 (January 1985), pp. 21–30

62. William J. Dickson, "Hawthorne Experiments," in Carl Heyel (ed.), *The Encyclopedia of Management*, 2nd. ed., (New York: Van Nostrand Reinhold, 1941), p. 301.

Critics note that by current standards the Hawthorne studies were unscientific; that is, many of the conclusions reached do not necessarily follow from the available evidence. Nevertheless, in their day, they were an intellectual gold mine. For this reason alone the contributions of the Hawthorne studies to the growth and development of the human-relations approach can hardly be overstated. As though responding to Taylor's plea for a "study of the motives which influence men," the Hawthorne researchers systematically demonstrated the nature and content of the human element. By testing hypothetical assertions about the basis of work rather than allowing their continued acceptance, the Hawthorne researchers pioneered a course of investigation that is still being pursued today.

CHAPTER 14

The Search for Organizational Integration

I nterest in organizations as social systems was stimulated by the Hawthorne studies and would continue to grow as the social person era unfolded. This chapter examines the lives and thoughts of two individuals who, though separated in time, significantly contributed to our understanding of authority and responsibility, the need to coordinate effort, conflict resolution, and how to design organizations for maximum effectiveness and efficiency. One was a political philosopher turned business sage, who never met a payroll in her life; the other, a telephone company executive whose hobbies were classical piano and the works of Johann Sebastian Bach. Together, they were integrators who bridged the scientific management and the social person eras.

MARY P. FOLLETT: THE POLITICAL PHILOSOPHER

Born in Quincy, Massachusetts, in 1868, Mary Parker Follett had a difficult early life. Her father, an alcoholic, died young; her mother was inclined to social rather than practical matters.[1] A respectable inheritance from her maternal grandfather provided sustenance, while Follett found intellectual uplift in reading and education. She attended Thayer Academy, a preparatory school for college-bound students located in Braintree, Massachusetts. At Thayer, she found a mentor in Anna Boynton Thompson, her history teacher. Thompson introduced Follett to the German Idealist school of philosophy, including the works of Johann Fichte (1762–1814) and

---

1. The definitive biography of Follett is Joan C. Tonn, *Mary P. Follett: Creating Democracy, Transforming Management* (New Haven, CT: Yale University Press, 2003).

Mary P. Follett, 1917. Vice
President, National Community
Service Association.

Georg W. F. Hegel (1770–1831). Later Follett would tell classical scholar and friend F. Melian Stawell:

> One of these [businessmen] gave me in a nutshell the threads of a tangle he had with his employees. He wanted me to straighten it out. I answered him straight out of Fichte: he didn't know that of course, but I did, and it seemed to meet the case.[2]

After graduating from Thayer Academy in 1883, Follett continued her studies at the Harvard University Annex for woman students (renamed Radcliffe College in 1894), where she expanded her interests in philosophy and history to include psychology, especially the emerging Gestalt movement, which led her to think in patterns or wholes. Thompson encouraged Follett to interrupt her studies at the Annex to attend classes at Newnham College, Cambridge University, in England, where Follett's interests extended into law, political science, and government. While at Cambridge, she continued to do research for her first book, *The Speaker of the House of Representatives.* Still considered one of the most insightful analyses of the role of the speaker of the U.S. House of Representatives, the book established her reputation as a political philosopher and drew her into the intellectual life of Boston.[3] Two years after the book's publication in 1896, Follett received her AB degree from Radcliffe College.

With academic opportunities limited for females, she spent most of her early years working with various community service groups to provide vocational guidance, education, recreation, and job-placement assistance for the less fortunate among Boston's youth. In these largely volunteer organizations, operating with little or no formal warrant, she realized that there was a need to rethink prevailing views on authority, organization, leadership, and conflict resolution. In observing and working with different service organizations, she gained an understanding of group dynamics and the importance of teamwork. Through her work in the Boston Placement Bureau, she met an array of business leaders and became active in the Taylor Society in the period following Taylor's death. Chronologically, Follett belonged to the scientific-management era; philosophically and intellectually, she was a member of the social person era. Her work served as a link between these eras

2. F. Melian Stawell, "Mary Parker Follett," *Newnham College Roll Letter* (January 1935), p. 43.

3. Mary P. Follett, *The Speaker of the House of Representatives* (New York: Longmans, Green, 1896).

by building on the principles of scientific management while anticipating many of the ideas that would become associated with the human-relations movement.

THE GROUP PRINCIPLE

Reflecting the influence of the Gestalt movement, the basis of Follett's thinking was the "whole man" and, in particular, relations between "whole men" within groups. From her reading in philosophy, psychology, political science, and law, and her understanding of Fichte, about whom her mentor, Anna Thompson, had written a book,[4] Follett developed what she dubbed "the group principle." Fichte espoused a nationalism in which freedom of individuals was subordinated to group interests. He believed that individuals could not escape the influence of their social world and that, by extension, their ego belonged to a wider plurality or community of egos. Fichte further supposed the existence of a Great Ego that willed the common world in which we all live.[5]

In her second book, *The New State: Group Organization the Solution of Popular Government*, published in 1918, Follett indicated that the essence of what she termed the "group principle" was to bring out individual differences and integrate them into a single whole. She quoted the sixth-century BC Greek philosopher Heraclitus of Ephesus, who said, "Nature desires eagerly opposites and out of them it completes its harmony, not out of similars."[6] In Heraclitus's philosophy of "Everything is in flux," the Hegelian logic or dialectic of "thesis, antithesis, and synthesis" found expression. Follett was never a full Hegelian and felt those who interpreted Hegel's ideas to mean that the state was "above and beyond" individual citizens misunderstood his logic. As she explained,

> When we say that there is the One which comes *from* the Many, this does not mean that the One is *above* the Many. The deepest truth of life is that the interrelating by which both are at the same time a-making is constant.[7]

This vague jargon of "interrelating" and "a-making" would form Follett's notion of "circular response." Building on these and other ideas, Follett challenged the prevailing political assumptions of the period. She believed that "we find the true man only through group organization. The potentialities of the individual remain

---

4. Anna Boynton Thompson, *The Unity of Fichte's Doctrine of Knowledge* (Boston: Ginn, 1895).

5. Henry D. Aiken, *The Age of Ideology: The Nineteenth Century Philosophers.* (Boston: Houghton Mifflin, 1957), pp. 54–60. Fichte was a disciple of Immanuel Kant and in his early years followed Kantian notions of rationalism and the absolutely inalienable rights of the individual. In his later years, Fichte broke with Kant, turned to nationalism and statism, and became part of the romantic revolt against reason.

6. Mary Parker Follett, *The New State: Group Organization the Solution of Popular Government* (London: Longmans, Green, 1918), p. 34n.

7. Ibid., p. 284.

potentialities until they are released by group life. Man discovers his true nature, gains his true freedom only through the group."[8]

Follett's group principle was to be the "new" psychology and renounce the established belief that individuals thought, felt, and acted independently. She argued that groups and individuals come into existence simultaneously and believed that with "group-man appears group-rights."[9] This view demonstrated Follett's acceptance of the Gestalt movement and reflected Charles H. Cooley's "looking-glass self" (the idea that the self arises reflectively in reaction to the opinions of others) and the realization that one's self is embedded in one's work group as a primary social unit of importance (see Chapter 9).[10] Using phrases such as "togetherness," "group thinking," and "the collective will," Follett sought a new society based on groups and not particularistic individuals.

Follett's underlying premise was that only through group membership could individuals find their "true self." Based on her group principle, Follett concluded that an individual's "true self is the group-self" and that "man can have no rights apart from society or independent of society or against society."[11] In opposing the notion that the purpose of government is to protect individual rights, she proposed a new concept of democracy: "Democracy then is a great spiritual force evolving itself from men, utilizing each, completing his incompleteness by weaving together all in the many-membered community life which is the true Theophany."[12]

Follett felt that "the theory of government based on individual rights no longer had a place in modern political theory."[13] In its place, a collectivistic democracy was to be built moving in succession from small neighborhood groups to community groups, to state groups, to a national group, and eventually, to a group will, reminiscent of Fichte's Great Ego. Setting aside the issue of potential group conflicts, Follett had faith that society could grow a new "social consciousness" and that individuals could live together peaceably in what she dubbed "The World State."[14] She had little confidence in "ballot-box democracy," believing that it reflected crowd psychology and defined "right" by the sheer weight of numbers.

CONFLICT RESOLUTION

In her third book, *Creative Experience*, Follett developed the idea that through conferences, discussions, and cooperation, individuals could evoke each other's latent ideas and make manifest their unity in the pursuit of common goals. Relying

---

8. Ibid., p. 6.

9. Ibid., p. 137.

10. Charles H. Cooley, *Human Nature and the Social Order* (New York: Charles Scribner's Sons, 1902).

11. Follett, *The New State*, p. 137.

12. Ibid., p. 161. Theophany is the visible manifestation of a deity to a human person.

13. Ibid., p. 172.

14. Ibid., pp. 344–360.

heavily on Gestalt theory, which held that every psychological situation has a specific character apart from the absolute nature of its component parts, she felt that through group experiences, individuals could achieve a greater unleashing of their creative powers.[15] As viewed by Follett, the goal of group effort was an integrative unity that transcended its component parts. In essence, she was beginning to examine the issue of potential group conflicts that she had not addressed in *The New State*. Follett believed that confronting conflict would result in one of four outcomes: "(1) voluntary submission of one side; (2) struggle and the victory of one side over the other; (3) compromise; or (4) integration."[16] The first and second outcomes were clearly unacceptable because they involved the use of force or power to dominate. Compromise was likewise futile because it postponed the issue and because the "truth does not lie 'between' the two sides."[17] Integration involved finding a solution that satisfied both sides without compromise or domination. Follett gave several illustrations of what she meant by "integration." One illustration involved an exchange in the Harvard University Library:

> In the Harvard Library one day, in one of the smaller rooms, someone wanted the window open, I wanted it shut. We opened the window in the next room, where no one was sitting. This was not a compromise because there was no curtailing of desire; we both got what we really wanted. For I did not want a closed room, I simply did not want the north wind to blow directly on me; likewise the other occupant did not want that particular window open, he merely wanted more air in the room.[18]

A second illustration involved a conflict between dairy men:

> A Dairymen's Cooperative League almost went to pieces last year on the question of precedence in unloading cans at a creamery platform. The men who came down the hill (the creamery was on a downgrade) thought they should have precedence; the men who came up the hill thought they should unload first. The thinking of both sides in the controversy was thus confined within the walls of these two possibilities, and this prevented their even trying to find a way of settling the dispute which would avoid these alternatives. The solution was obviously to change the position of the platform so that both up-hillers and down-hillers could unload at the same time. But this solution was not found until they had asked the advice of a

---

15. Mary P. Follett, *Creative Experience* (London: Longmans, Green, 1924), pp. 91–116.

16. Ibid., p. 156.

17. Ibid.

18. Mary P. Follett, "The Psychological Foundations: Constructive Conflict," in Henry C. Metcalf, ed., *Scientific Foundations of Business Administration.* (Baltimore: Williams & Wilkins, 1926), p. 116.

more or less professional integrator. When, however, it was pointed out to them, they were quite ready to accept it. Integration involves invention, and the clever thing is to recognize this, and not to let one's thinking stay within the boundaries of two alternatives which are mutually exclusive.[19]

A third illustration was told by a friend and involved price competition in the paper industry:

> At a meeting of our manufacturing committee recently the following question came up. Our paper had been six cents, and the competing firm reduced their price to five and three-quarters. We then cut to five and a half and they replied with a price of five and a quarter. The question before us then was whether or not we should make a further reduction. Part were in favor; part, against. The solution came when something quite different was suggested: that we should stand for a higher quality of paper and make an appropriate price for it.[20]

Although Follett realized integration was not an option in all cases, she felt it was a viable alternative in more cases than might be assumed. As Fox explained,

> She . . . insisted that although integration is not possible in every case, it *is* possible in more cases than we realize. And perhaps if it is not possible now, it will be later. . . . The important thing is to work for something better. . . . We need not be afraid of difference, but rather should welcome it as the opportunity for new social creation. She gave us a theory of human interaction that shows how the same factors that cause change also provide the means for solving the problems presented by change, a theory that tells us that the possibilities for the healthy resolution of conflict is part of the natural process of human intercourse.[21]

Follett's single-minded search for integrative unity, for commonality of will, and for human cooperation established her reputation as a political philosopher. By 1924, however, her interest in political science had waned, replaced by a growing fascination with the results-oriented world of business. As she explained, political science "did not seem really to come to grips with our [present] problems." In turning to the world of business and business executives, Follett explained, "*There* I found hope for the future. *There* men were not theorizing or dogmatizing; they were thinking of what

---

19. Ibid.

20. Follett, *Creative Experience*, p. 158.

21. Elliot M. Fox, "Mary Parker Follett: The Enduring Contribution," *Public Administration Review* 28 (November–December 1968), p. 528.

they had actually done and they were willing to try new ways."[22] In January 1925, Follett gave the first of a series of four lectures in New York City under the auspices of the Bureau of Personnel Administration, which was dedicated to advancing sound employer–employee relations. Beginning with these lectures, Follett made the transition from being a political scientist to being a business philosopher.

THE BUSINESS PHILOSOPHER

Viewing management as a universal activity, Follett understood that the principles that apply in the political sphere necessarily apply to business, as well. The same challenges of achieving unity of effort, defining authority and responsibility, resolving conflict, exhibiting leadership, and so on exist in both politics and business. Drawing on this understanding, Follett pushed ahead into the world of business. First, from her book *Creative Experience*, she extended her thinking on "constructive conflict" and achieving unity of effort. Because domination and compromise, as methods of conflict resolution, led to strife, Follett held that integration, as a means for confronting contrasting interests, should be paramount in all business affairs. In dealing with labor, she deplored the notion of collective bargaining because it rested on a relative balance of power and inevitably ended in compromise. Bargaining meant that there were competing interests and in their efforts to gain at each other's expense the confronting sides would likely lose sight of what they had in common. In labor–management negotiations, for example, when pro-labor or pro-management positions solidified, Follett noted that the confronting parties often failed to appreciate that they were partners in a common endeavor, for which they had joint responsibilities. She felt that collective responsibility should begin with group responsibility, wherein employees are involved as partners in shaping workplace policies. Speaking to executives at the Bureau of Personnel Administration, she explained,

> When you have made your employees feel that they are in some sense partners in the business, they do not improve the quality of their work, save waste in time and material, because of the Golden Rule, but because their interests are the same as yours.[23]

In Follett's view, this was not to be a reciprocal back-scratching arrangement, but a true feeling on the part of both labor and management that they served a common purpose. She suggested that in the past an artificial line had been

---

22. Lyndall F. Urwick, "Great Names in Management: Mary Parker Follett, 1868–1933" (Unpublished speech, University of New South Wales, Kensington, Sydney, Australia, June 14, 1967), p. 3.

23. Mary P. Follett, "The Psychological Foundations: Business as an Integrative Unity," in Henry C. Metcalf, ed., *Scientific Foundations of Business Administration*. (Baltimore: Williams & Wilkins, 1926), p. 160.

drawn between those who managed and those who were managed. In reality, there was no line, and all members of an organization who accepted responsibility for work at any level contributed to what she called a "functional whole or integrative unity":

> [L]abor and capital can never be reconciled as long as labor persists in thinking that there is a capitalist point of view and capitalists that there is a labor point of view. There is not. These are imaginary wholes which must be broken up before capital and labor can cooperate.[24]

Follett's "principle of integrative unity" involved finding solutions that satisfied all parties, without domination, surrender, or compromise. It called for confronting sides to rethink their relationship and to share information openly, to avoid win–lose quick fixes, to be creative in examining differences from multiple angles, and see difficulties as "ours" and not "yours." For Follett, conflict, to be constructive, required respect, understanding, talking it through, and creating win–win solutions.

Beyond viewing a business as a working unit, Follett felt that both labor and management should recognize their interrelationships with creditors, stockholders, customers, competitors, suppliers, and society in general. This larger perspective would encourage seeing society and the larger economy as working together rather than as a "congeries of separate pieces." For Follett, integration was a principle applicable to all aspects of life.

AUTHORITY AND POWER

Follett reasoned that integration, as a principle of conduct, would be less than fully effective unless people rethought their concepts of authority and power. In this second area, Follett sought to develop "power-with" instead of "power-over," and "co-action" to replace consent and coercion. She realized that with both an "order giver" and an "order taker," integration would be difficult to achieve, as the notions of "boss" and "subordinate" created barriers to recognizing common interests. To overcome this difficulty, Follett proposed depersonalizing orders and shifting obedience to the "law of the situation, referring to the necessity of acting in accord with the unique requirements inherent in any situation": "One *person* should not give orders to another *person*, but both should agree to take their orders from the situation. If orders are simply part of the situation, the question of someone giving and someone receiving does not come up."[25] She noted that situational requirements are constantly changing, thus demanding continual efforts to maintain an effective work relationship. Thus, she observed, "different situations require different kinds of knowledge, and the man possessing the knowledge demanded by a certain situation

---

24. Follett, *Creative Experience*, pp. 167–168.

25. Mary P. Follett, "The Giving of Orders," in Henry C. Metcalf, ed., *Scientific Foundations of Business Administration*. (Baltimore: Williams & Wilkins, 1926), p. 139.

tends to be in the best managed business, and other things being equal, to become the leader of the moment."[26]

The rationale for Follett's "law of the situation" was based on scientific management, in the same sense that Taylor sought obedience to facts determined by study rather than flawed rules of thumb. In a paper for the Taylor Society, Follett put it this way: "If, then, authority is derived from function, it has little to do with hierarchy of position as such. . . . We find authority with the head of a department, with an expert . . . the dispatch clerk has more authority in dispatching work than the President . . . authority should go with knowledge and experience."[27]

Follett understood that, by shifting authority to knowledge, personal confrontations could be minimized. She explained, "If orders are simply part of the situation, the question of someone giving and someone receiving does not come up."[28] Follett admired this facet of scientific management because it divorced person and situation. To Follett, the essence of good human relations was creating the feeling of working with someone rather than working under someone. In practice, this became "power-with" versus "power-over." She believed that management should not exercise power over workers, nor should workers, through unions, exercise power over management. Jointly exercised power was "co-active," not coercive. Displaying a number of insights into the psychology of power, Follett rejected both the authoritarian's striving for power and Mohandas K. Gandhi's noncooperation as insidious uses of power. She felt that Gandhi's (1869–1948) concept of power, through humility and nonviolence, was still a desire for power-over. It was conflict, a search for bending the will of the British Colonial Authority to his own ends. Follett maintained that constructive conflict through integration could not be achieved when one or both sides to a conflict were attempting to dominate the other.

In Follett's view, in all human interactions, from interpersonal conflicts to international disputes, power-over had to be reduced, and obedience had to be shifted to the law of the situation. The basis for this shift would be what Follett called "circular response." By this, she meant a continuous reciprocal process based on the opportunity for confronting parties to influence each other, such that, through open interaction, over time, "power-with" could be obtained. For labor and management, power-with would come through full disclosure of costs, prices, and profits. Follett was an advocate of employee representation plans that were popular in the 1920s. Under these plans, employees elected representatives to shop or work councils; these representatives gave workers a voice in dealing with management. Follett found great promise in these plans because "management has seen that an enterprise can be more successfully run by securing the cooperation of the workers. . . . [Further] the aim of employee representation . . . should not be to share power, but to increase

---

26. Mary P. Follett, "Some Discrepancies in Leadership Theory and Practice," in Henry C. Metcalf, ed., *Business Leadership.* (London: Pitman, 1930), p. 213.

27. Mary Parker Follett, "The Illusion of Final Authority," *Bulletin of the Taylor Society* 2 (December 1926), p. 243.

28. Follett, "The Giving of Orders," p. 139.

power . . . in all."[29] As envisioned by Follett, employee representation plans should not be a struggle over who decided what and how profits were to be divided, but a step toward attaining integration. The National Labor Relations Act, however, outlawed such plans in 1935. Representation plans were seen as being a form of company unions, wherein representatives could not bargain as equals because they generally lacked the ability to sign legally enforceable agreements and the right of workers to strike was not recognized.

Follett thought final authority was an illusion based on a false premise of power; authority accrued to the prevailing situation, not to individuals or their position. Likewise, she held that final responsibility was also an illusion. Responsibility was inherent in each job or workplace function and was cumulative in the sense that it was the sum of all individual and group responsibilities in a system of cross-relationships. At the individual level, a person was responsible for his work, not to someone. At the departmental level, all those who contributed jointly shared responsibility for getting their jobs done. The role of a department manager was merely to interweave individual and group responsibilities. In turn, an organization's chief executive had cumulative responsibility for interweaving interdepartmental work.

In this second area of analysis, Follett advanced what were clearly iconoclastic notions of authority and responsibility. Traditional notions of authority and responsibility associated with military or other organizations held that authority was power-over and rejected the idea that responsibility accrued to a final authority. Follett was nonetheless adamant. Authority resided in the situation, not a person or position. Logically then, responsibility was inherent in the work being performed and accumulated in interweaving workplace functions. This was heady material for the executives attending Follett's Bureau of Personnel Administration presentations.

THE TASK OF LEADERSHIP

Two facets of Follett's philosophy have been explored: reduction of conflict through an integration of interests and the necessary corollary of obeying the law of the situation. A third facet of Follett's philosophy concerned building the underlying psychological processes necessary to achieve goals through coordinating and controlling effort. Follett's view of control reflected her Gestalt-psychology orientation of dealing with a functional whole or total situation to achieve unity. Follett saw that control was impossible to achieve unless there was unity and cooperation among all elements (material and people) in a given situation. In this sense, a situation was out of control when contrasting interests were not reconciled. For Follett, the basis for control resided in self-regulating and self-directing individuals and groups who recognized common interests and controlled their actions to meet agreed-on objectives.

---

29. Mary P. Follett, "How Is the Employee Representation Movement Remolding the Accepted Type of Business Manager?" in Henry C. Metcalf, ed., *Business Management as a Profession.* (Chicago: A. W. Shaw, 1927), pp. 344, 353.

Follett recognized that managers controlled not single elements, but complex interrelationships; not persons, but situations; with the desired outcome being unity and cooperation across the full range of a prevailing situation. How was this unity and cooperation to be achieved? Follett called for a new philosophy of control that was "fact-control rather than man-control" and "correlated control" rather than "super-imposed control." She argued that each situation generated its own control because the facts of the situation and the interweaving of the many groups in the situation were what determined appropriate behavior. As most situations were too complex for central control from the top to function effectively, controls were to be gathered, or correlated, at many points in an organization. This interweaving and correlation was to be based on four fundamental principles of organization:

1. Coordination as the reciprocal relating of all the factors in a situation
2. Coordination by direct contact of all the responsible people concerned
3. Coordination in the early stages
4. Coordination as a continuing process[30]

Follett concluded that organization *was* control, because the purpose of organizing and coordination was to ensure controlled performance; coordination achieved unity, and unity was control. As an illustration, Follett cited a conflict between a purchasing agent and a production manager. The purchasing agent suggested acquiring somewhat inferior materials that he said would serve the purpose for which they were intended, but because they were lower in price, they would save money. The production manager, however, maintained that he could not obtain satisfactory results with this material. According to Follett, if they had followed the principles of early and continuous coordination, each could have seen their reciprocal concerns and have turned their attention to finding quality materials at a lower cost. An integration of their goals could, thus, have been achieved to their mutual satisfaction. This synthesis of interests was self-regulation through coordination to achieve integration.[31]

Follett held that leadership should not be based on power, but instead on the reciprocal influence of leader on follower and follower on leader in the context of the prevailing situation. A leader's primary task was defining the *purpose* of an organization; the leader "should make his co-workers see that it is not *his* purpose which is to be achieved, but a common purpose, born of the desires and the activities of the group. The best leader does not ask people to serve him, but the common

---

30. Mary P. Follett, "The Process of Control," in Luther H. Gulick and Lyndall F. Urwick, eds., *Papers on the Science of Administration* (New York: Institute of Public Administration, Columbia University, 1937), p. 161.

31. Ibid., p. 167. See also Mary P. Follett, "The Psychology of Control," in Henry C. Metcalf, ed., *Psychological Foundations of Business Management* (Chicago: A. W. Shaw, 1927), p. 172.

end. The best leader has not followers, but men and women working with him."[32] Further, Follett maintained that,

> The leader then is one who can organize the experience of the group . . . and thus get the full power of the group. The leader makes the team. This is pre-eminently the leadership quality—the ability to organize all the forces there are in an enterprise and make them serve a common purpose. Men with this ability create a group power rather than a personal power. . . . When leadership rises to genius it has the power of transforming . . . experience into power. And that is what experience is for, to be made into power. The great leader creates as well as directs power. . . . Leaders and followers are both following the invisible leader—the common purpose. The best executives put this common purpose clearly before their group.[33]

Follett reasoned that an organization's goals should be integrated with individual and group purposes, and this integration called for the highest caliber leaders. Such leaders did not depend on commands and obedience, but on skills in coordinating, defining purposes, and in evoking responses to the law of the situation. Recognizing that mere exhortation would not bring about such leadership, Follett called for the training of executives in what she called the "capacity for organized thinking." Such thinking eschews dominating or manipulating others and recognizes a broader range of obligations leading to a profession of management that enlists knowledge for the service of others. To those who aspired to be managers, she advised:

> [M]en must prepare themselves as seriously for this profession as for any other. They must realize that they, as all professional men, are assuming grave responsibilities, that they are to take a creative part in one of the large functions of society, a part which, I believe, only trained and disciplined men can in the future hope to take with success.[34]

Follett felt that the notion of substituting a service motive for a profit motive was an oversimplification. Instead, she argued that these motives should be integrated into a larger professional motive:

> We work for profit, for service, for our own development, for the love of creating something. At any one moment, indeed, most of us

---

32. Mary P. Follett, "Leader and Expert," in Henry C. Metcalf, ed., *Psychological Foundations of Business Management* (Chicago: A. W. Shaw, 1927), p. 235.

33. Mary P. Follett, *Freedom and Coordination: Lectures in Business Organization*, ed. by Lyndall F. Urwick (London: Management Publications Trust, 1949), pp. 52, 55.

34. Mary P. Follett, "How Must Business Management Develop in Order to Possess the Essentials of a Profession?" in Henry C. Metcalf, ed., *Business Management as a Profession* (Chicago: A. W. Shaw, 1927), p. 87.

are not working directly or immediately for any of these things, but to put through the job in hand in the best possible manner. ... To come back to the professions: can we not learn a lesson from them on this very point? The professions have not given up the money motive. I do not care how often you see it stated that they have. Professional men are eager enough for large incomes; but they have other motives as well, and they are often willing to sacrifice a good slice of income for the sake of these other things. We all want the richness of life in the terms of our deepest desire. We can purify and elevate our desires, we can add to them, but there is no individual or social progress in curtailment of desires.[35]

A FINAL NOTE

Mary Follett passed away December 18, 1933. Tonn has remarked, "Although Mary Follett's name may be obscure, her ideas are not."[36] In this respect, Sir Peter Parker has quipped, "People often puzzle about who is the father of management. I don't know who the father was, but I have no doubt about who was the mother."[37] Follett uncannily presaged many of today's management thinkers in advocating participative management, the benefits of teams (i.e., groups), cooperative conflict resolution, and that authority should go with knowledge.

Critics might maintain, however, that elements of Follett's business philosophy are idyllic notions of a political philosopher. The simplicity of people living and working together without the use of coercion and compromise is nonetheless appealing. Integration, moving to a broader plane for problem solutions, would call for more creativity and imagination than are commonly witnessed in daily industrial, academic, political, and social life. Moreover, depersonalization of authority and obedience to the law of the situation would certainly sound the death knell for tyranny and autocracy. Further, control based on a perceived unity of purposes would make the modern workplace more palatable to both labor and management.

A call for knowledgeable leaders, dedicated to improving business practices through science and service, is a recurrent plea throughout the evolution of management thought. As one of her contemporaries recalled, "Mary Follett was a gentle person, not an impressive or aggressive spellbinder, but of all the pioneers she, more than others, approached management through human values, psychology

---

35. Mary P. Follett, "How Must Business Develop in Order to Become a Profession?" in Henry C. Metcalf, ed., *Business Management As a Profession* (Chicago: A. W. Shaw, 1927), pp. 101–102.

36. Tonn, *Mary P. Follett*, p. 492.

37. Sir Peter Parker quoted in Dana Wechsler Linden, "The Mother of Them All," *Forbes* (January 16, 1995), p. 76.

and the laboratory of collaborative work experience. The significance and originality of her contribution cannot be overrated."[38]

CHESTER I. BARNARD: THE ERUDITE EXECUTIVE

Chester Irving Barnard was a sociologist of organizations without a portfolio. Born in Malden, Massachusetts, in 1886, he personified the Horatio Alger ideal of the farm boy who made good.[39] On a scholarship at Harvard University, he supplemented his income by tuning pianos and conducting a small dance band. He studied economics at Harvard, completing all but one degree requirement in three years (1906–1909). Lacking a laboratory science, he was not allowed to graduate. Even without a bachelor's degree, he did well enough to earn seven honorary doctorates for his lifelong efforts to understand the nature and purpose of organizations.

Chester I. Barnard as he entered Harvard University, 1906.

Courtesy of William B. Wolf.

Barnard joined the statistical department of the American Telephone and Telegraph (AT&T) system in 1909 and in 1927 was named president of the New Jersey Bell Telephone Company. His unbounded enthusiasm for public service was reflected in his volunteer work for many organizations. He assisted David E. Lilienthal in developing operational policies for the Atomic Energy Commission; he served the New Jersey Emergency Relief Administration, the New Jersey Reformatory, the United Service Organization (president for three years), the Rockefeller Foundation (president for four years); and he was president of the Bach Society of New Jersey. Barnard was a self-made scholar who applied the theories of Vilfredo Pareto (whom he read in French), Kurt Lewin, and Max Weber (whom he read in German) and the philosophy of Alfred North Whitehead in the first in-depth analysis of organizations as cooperative systems. By the time of his death in 1961, this Harvard dropout had earned a place in history as a management scholar.

---

38. Luther H. Gulick, "Looking Backward to 1915" (paper presented at the Eastern Academy of Management, Hartford, Conn., May 13, 1977), pp. 5–6.

39. Biographical data and an excellent discussion of Barnard's ideas are found in William B. Wolf, *The Basic Barnard: An Introduction to Chester I. Barnard and His Theories of Organization and Management* (Ithaca: New York State School of Industrial and Labor Relations, 1974). Originally published 1968. Also see *Idem*, "Understanding Chester I. Barnard," *International Journal of Public Administration*, 17(6), 1994, pp. 1035–1069.

THE NATURE OF COOPERATIVE SYSTEMS

Barnard's best-known work, *The Functions of the Executive*, was an expansion of eight lectures given at the Lowell Institute (Boston) in November and December of 1937. His explicit purpose in presenting the lectures was to develop a theory of organizations and to stimulate others to examine the nature of cooperative systems. To Barnard, the search for universals in organizations had been hampered by too much emphasis on the nature of religious and government institutions and their differing views on the origin and nature of authority. He complained that most research focused on social unrest and reform and included "practically no reference to formal organization as the concrete social process by which social action is largely accomplished." In Barnard's opinion, social failures throughout history were due to the failure to provide for human cooperation in formal organizations. Barnard said that the "formal organization is that kind of cooperation among men that is conscious, deliberate, and purposeful."[40]

Barnard believed that by examining formal organizations, it was possible to enhance the effectiveness and efficiency of such cooperation. He sought to understand how to (1) ensure the survival of an organization by the "maintenance of an *equilibrium* of complex character in a continuously fluctuating environment of physical, biological, and social materials, elements, and forces" within an organization; (2) examine the external forces to which an organization must adjust to achieve such equilibrium; and (3) to analyze the functions performed by executives at all levels in an organization.[41] Barnard's focus on maintaining internal equilibrium while confronting external environmental forces was seen as novel as compared to more conventional thinking. He rejected the traditional view of organizations having fixed boundaries and as being comprised of a defined set of employees. In considering the larger environment in which an organization was situated, Barnard's analyses went beyond earlier thinking to also include investors, suppliers, customers, and others whose actions contributed to an organization, although technically they were not employees of the organization.[42]

Barnard's view of organizations as cooperative systems began with individuals as discrete beings; however, he noted that humans did not function except in interacting with other humans in social relationships. As individuals, people could choose whether or not they would enter into a specific cooperative system. They made this choice based on their motives (meaning purposes, desires, and impulses of the moment) or by considering whatever action alternatives were available. As described by Barnard, organizations, through their executive function, seek to

---

40. Chester I. Barnard, *The Functions of the Executive*. (Cambridge, MA. Harvard University Press, 1938), pp. 3–4.

41. Ibid., p. 6. Italics added.

42. Chester I. Barnard, "Comments on the Job of the Executive," *Harvard Business Review*, 18 (Spring 1940), pp. 295–308.

modify individuals' motives and action alternatives through influence and control. Barnard recognized that attempts at influence and control were not always successful in attaining the goals sought by both organizations and their members. The disparity between personal motives and organizational motives led Barnard to distinguish between "effectiveness" and "efficiency." A formal system of cooperation required an objective or purpose, and if cooperation was successful and the objective was attained, the system was effective. Barnard saw the matter of efficiency differently. He felt cooperative efficiency was the result of individual efficiencies, because individuals cooperated only to satisfy "individual motives." Efficiency, then, was the degree to which an individual's motives were satisfied, and only the individual could determine whether this condition had been met.[43]

As viewed by Barnard, cooperation within formal organizations afforded possibilities for expanding the power of groups beyond what individuals could accomplish alone; for example, moving a stone, producing an automobile, or constructing a bridge. Individuals cooperated to do what they could not do alone; and when their purpose for cooperating was attained, their efforts were deemed effective. Individuals, however, also had personal motives, and the degree to which individuals continued to contribute to a formal organization was a function of the satisfaction or dissatisfaction they personally derived from their membership in an organization. If members' motives were not satisfied by a formal organization, they withheld efforts or participation, and from their point of view, the organization was inefficient. Barnard contended that in the final analysis, "the only measure of the efficiency of a cooperative system is its capacity to survive."[44] For Barnard, this meant that an organization must offer inducements necessary to satisfy individual motives in the pursuit of group purposes to ensure its continued survival. Viewed in modern terms, a formal organization must renew its energy or import negative entropy by offering net satisfactions to contributing members. An inefficient organization cannot be effective and, therefore, cannot survive beyond its store of negative entropy. For Barnard efficiency and effectiveness were irrevocable and universal requirements for all formal organizations.

FORMAL ORGANIZATIONS: THEORY AND STRUCTURE

Barnard defined an organization as *"a system of consciously coordinated activities or forces of two or more persons."*[45] He intended for this definition to encompass all such systems, including military, fraternal, religious, academic, business, or whatever, irrespective of variations in terms of physical or social environment, number and kinds of members, or the nature of members' activities. Barnard treated such

---

43. Barnard, Functions of the Executive, p. 44.

44. Ibid. p. 44.

45. Ibid. p. 73.

systems "as a whole because each part is related to every other part included in it in a significant way."[46] He noted that different levels of systems existed, ranging from departments (subsystems) in a commercial firm to systems forming society as a whole. Regardless of level, Barnard held that all systems contained three elements: (1) willingness of members to cooperate, (2) a common purpose, and (3) members able to communicate with each other.[47]

As for the first of these elements, Barnard reasoned that an organization could not exist without members. Further, a willingness to cooperate to accomplish a common purpose was indispensable. He recognized that the intensity and timing of this willingness would naturally fluctuate because it was based on the satisfaction or dissatisfaction experienced or anticipated by each individual member. An organization, thus, had to provide adequate inducements, both physical and social, to offset the sacrifices individuals made by forgoing membership in alternative systems. Barnard further reasoned that, for individuals, willingness was the joint effect of "personal desires and reluctances" to participate; for an organization, it was the joint effect of "objective inducements offered and burdens imposed."[48] Inducing individuals to cooperate involved an "economy of incentives," which consisted of two parts: (1) offering objective incentives and (2) changing subjective attitudes through persuasion. Objective incentives were material (e.g., money), nonmaterial (e.g., prestige, power), and associational (e.g., social compatibility, participation in decision making). Persuasion involved changing attitudes by precept, example, and appeal to individual motives.

A common purpose, the second required element of a formal organization that Barnard identified, was a corollary to the third required element—a willingness of members to cooperate. Barnard contended that willingness to cooperate could not be induced unless members knew what efforts would be required of them and what incentives they would receive as a result. This thus required that an organization inculcate in its members a common purpose or objective. Barnard believed that it was not what an organization's purpose meant personally to its members, but what they perceived the purpose to mean to the organization as a whole. As noted earlier, Barnard recognized that the motives of an organization and its members logically differ, and members cooperated not because their personal motives were the same as an organization's, but because they felt that personal satisfaction would result from contributing to an organization's success in achieving its goals.

Barnard considered communication, the third required element of a formal organization, to be the process by which common purpose and willingness to cooperate become dynamic. He felt that all interpersonal activity was based on communication. He stated that (1) "channels of communication should be definitely known"; (2) "objective authority requires a definite formal channel of

---

46. Ibid. p. 77.

47. Ibid., p. 82.

48. Ibid., pp. 85–86.

communication to every member of an organization," that is, everyone must report to or be subordinate to someone; and (3) "line[s] of communication must be as direct or short as possible" to speed dissemination and reduce distortions caused by transmission through multiple channels.[49]

Having identified elements essential to formal organizations, Barnard sought to do the same for informal organizations. By informal organization, he meant "the aggregate of the personal contacts and interactions and the associated groupings of people" that were not a part of nor governed by a formal organization.[50] Without structure, and often without conscious recognition of a joint purpose, informal groupings arose from job-related contacts and, in turn, established shared attitudes, customs, and norms. Barnard noted that informal organizations often create conditions leading to formal organizations and vice versa. He identified three necessary functions served by informal organizations: (1) they are a means of communication, (2) they further cohesiveness among an organization's members, and (3) they protect informal group members' personal integrity.

THE ACCEPTANCE THEORY OF AUTHORITY

One of Barnard's most unusual ideas related to his theory of authority. He defined authority as "the character of a communication (order) in a formal organization by virtue of which it is *accepted* by a contributor to or 'member' of the organization as governing the action he contributes."[46] According to this definition, authority had two aspects: (1) "the subjective, personal *accepting* of a communication as being authoritative," and (2) "the character in [a] communication by virtue of which it is accepted."[51] According to Barnard, the source of authority did not reside in persons of authority, or those who gave the orders, but in the acceptance or nonacceptance of the authority by subordinates. In essence, Barnard held that the real "source of authority lies in the members of an organization, that they confer authority upon their superiors by deigning to accept and act upon commands, that they may, if they wish, decide to accept orders seriatim [i.e. one after another], and that they may withdraw conferred authority at any time by refusing to obey the commands of their superiors."[52]

Barnard's thinking in this regard was antithetical to all previous concepts of authority, which held that authority resides in "persons of authority" or "those who issue orders." Whereas Follett argued for depersonalizing authority and obeying the law of the situation, Barnard held that authority originated at the bottom of an organization and flowed upward. In this sense, formal authority becomes real

---

49. Ibid., pp. 175–177.

50. Ibid., p. 115.

51. Ibid., p. 163.

52. Cyril O'Donnell, The Source of Managerial Authority," *Political Science Quarterly* (December 1952), p. 575.

only when it is accepted by those who are subject to it. For Barnard, individuals needed to assent to authority and would accept a communication as authoritative if four conditions were simultaneously met: (1) they understand the communication; (2) they believe the communication is consistent with an organization's purpose; (3) they believe the communication is compatible with their personal interests; and (4) they are mentally and physically able to comply with the communication.

To explain how an organization could function according to his notion of authority, Barnard used the phrase "zone of indifference" to describe that set of communications that an individual would rarely challenge. This zone of indifference might be narrow or wide, depending on the degree to which inducements outweighed the burdens and sacrifices of complying with a communication. If an employee, for instance, felt that a communication ran counter to a personal moral code, the benefit of accepting the communication would be weighed against the discomfort created by acting immorally and whether or not the accompanying organization sanctions were sufficiently strong enough to induce compliance. Some communications are accepted without deliberation, but others may require considerable thought. Such discretion would pertain to what Barnard identified as the first or subjective aspect of authority.

The second, or objective, aspect of authority that Barnard identified, was more closely akin to traditional conceptions of authority. It rested on the presumption that communications were authoritative and had a "potentiality of assent" when they came from individuals in superordinate positions. In one case, a communication from a higher-up might be accepted because it came from a "person of authority"; this was formal authority, or the authority of position. In another instance, a communication might be accepted because a subordinate had respect for and confidence in a superior's personal ability, irrespective of the superior's rank or position; Barnard called this the "authority of leadership."

When authority of leadership was combined with authority of position, the zone of indifference became exceedingly broad. Nevertheless, Barnard stressed, "the determination of authority remains with the individual."[53] In a free society, individuals always have discretion in defining what is and is not acceptable communication. What is perhaps the most striking insight of Barnard's theory of authority is that all organizations depend on leaders that can develop the capacity and willingness of others to follow.

THE FUNCTIONS OF THE EXECUTIVE

Viewed more broadly, Barnard portrayed an executive's job as securing the coordination essential to achieve cooperative effort. Such coordination required a system of communication that could only function if staffed by executives (meaning managers at all levels). To quote Barnard, "It might be said, then, that the function

---

53. Ibid., pp. 173–174.

of executives is to serve as channels of communication so far as communications must pass through central positions."[54] Communication was a central value in all Barnard's writings, and undoubtedly, his views were influenced by his own experience in the AT&T system. To Barnard, executive work "is not *of* the organization, but the specialized work of *maintaining* the organization in operation. . . . The executive functions serve to maintain a system of cooperative effort. They are impersonal. The functions are not, as so frequently stated, to manage a group of persons."[55] To Barnard, the role of the executive function in an organization was analogous to that of the human nervous system in relation to the rest of the body: "It exists to maintain the bodily system by directing those actions which are necessary more effectively to adjust to the environment, but it can hardly be said to manage the body, a large part of whose functions are independent of it and upon which it in turn depends."[56]

Barnard postulated three executive functions that corresponded with the elements of all systems identified earlier: (1) "to provide a system of communication"; (2) "to promote the securing of essential efforts"; and (3) "to formulate and define purpose."[57] In providing a system of communication, Barnard believed that executives had to define organizational duties, clarify lines of authority and responsibility, and consider both formal and informal means of communication. Informal communication assisted in maintaining internal communication by allowing issues to be raised and discussed without forcing decisions and overloading executive positions. By "promoting the securing of essential efforts," the second executive function, Barnard was referring to the role executives play in establishing cooperative relationships among people and eliciting their contributions to an organization's goals. This included recruiting and selecting members who could work together compatibly. It also involved: (1) maintaining morale, (2) maintaining inducements, and (3) maintaining deterrents, such as supervision, control, inspection, education, and training, which would ensure the viability of a cooperative system.

The third executive function, formulation of purpose and objectives, was examined earlier in our comments on Barnard's thoughts relating to the nature of cooperative systems. Not previously mentioned is that Barnard viewed the delegation of objective authority as a critical aspect of this function. For Barnard, delegation involved making decisions about the placement of various responsibilities and authority within a cooperative system so that individuals would know how they contributed to the ends sought and the means to those ends. Decision making had two facets: analysis, or the search for the "strategic factors" that would create the

---

54. Ibid., p. 215.

55. Ibid., p. 216.

56. Ibid., p. 217.

57. Ibid.

set or system of conditions necessary to accomplish an organization's purposes; and synthesis, or the recognition of interrelationships among elements or parts that together made up a whole system.

Barnard borrowed the term *strategic factors* from labor economist John R. Commons to refer to those factors that limit making a decision. According to Barnard, "The strategic factor is, then, the center of the environment of decision. It is the point at which choice applies. To *do* or not to do *this*, that is the question."[58] Like Fayol, Barnard saw organizations as purposeful wholes functioning in a changing environment. Barnard's insights provided the foundation for developing the business-policy course at Harvard University and for much of the terminology still used in strategic management theory.[59]

Barnard's ruminations on the decision-making process were also a notable contribution to management thought. In "Mind in Everyday Affairs," an appendix to his *The Functions of the Executive*, Barnard noted there were two categories of mental processes, "logical" and "nonlogical." Logical processes were "conscious thinking which could be expressed in words, or other symbols, that is, reasoning," whereas nonlogical processes were those "not capable of being expressed in words or as reasoning, which are only made known by a judgment, decision, or action."[60] Nonlogical processes may be unconscious or may not require conscious effort. Barnard concluded, "Both kinds [of mental processes] together are much better than either alone if conditions permit."[61]

Barnard was clear in stating that the three executive functions he had identified had no separate existence, but were "aspects of a process of organization as a whole." He labeled this process and defined the essential nature of this "executive process" as "the sensing of the organization as a whole and the total situation relevant to it."[62] This was the art of managing and the integration of the whole with respect to an organization's internal equilibrium and its adjustment to external conditions. Working from the micro- to the macro-level, Barnard viewed all aspects of society as one large, cooperative system. Every organization had to secure members, money, and materials from its environment and could "survive only as it secures by exchange, transformation, and creation, a surplus of utilities in its own economy."[63]

---

58. Ibid., p. 205.

59. Dave McMahon and Jon C. Carr, "The Contributions of Chester Barnard to Strategic Management Theory," *Journal of Management History* 5 (1999), pp. 228–240; and Kenneth R. Andrews, "Introduction to the 30th Anniversary Edition" of Barnard's *The Functions of the Executive* (Cambridge, MA: Harvard University Press, 1968), pp. xix–xx.

60. Barnard, *Functions of the Executive*, p. 302. See also Milorad M. Novicevic, Thomas J. Hench, and Daniel A. Wren, "Playing by Ear ... in an Incessant Din of Reasons: Chester Barnard and the History of Intuition in Management Thought," *Management Decision* 40 (2002), pp. 992–1002.

61. Ibid., p. 306.

62. Ibid., p. 235

63. Ibid., p. 245.

An organization, for example, had to produce both physical utilities and social utilities to survive.

For Barnard, the creative force in all organizations was moral leadership. As he explained, this meant ethical behavior that was "governed by beliefs or feelings of what is right or wrong regardless of self-interest or immediate consequences of a decision to do or not to do specific things under particular conditions."[64] This included personal responsibility (an individual's character development); official responsibility (when acting "on behalf" of an organization); and corporate responsibility (internal to the interests of stockholders, creditors, and employees, and external to one's community and society in general). Barnard believed that executives should adhere to a moral code, demonstrate a high capacity for personal responsibility, and strive to create a moral faculty in others. He observed, "the endurance of organization depends upon the quality of leadership; and that quality derives from the breadth of the morality upon which it rests. . . . A low morality will not sustain leadership long, its influence quickly vanishes, it cannot produce its own succession."[65]

Chester Barnard was an erudite executive who drew on his own experiences and on sociological insights to build a theory of cooperative systems. As Fritz J. Roethlisberger recalled, "[Barnard was] the one and only executive in captivity who could not only run a successful organization but could also talk intelligently about what he was up to in the process."[66] Barnard not only impressed Roethlisberger, but also his teacher, Elton Mayo, who in his later work moved from his view of an organization as a biological organism to seeing organizations as cooperative social systems.[67] Barnard's thoughts on maintaining equilibrium within cooperative systems also influenced other Hawthorne researchers and later inspired Nobelist Herbert A. Simon's work on decision making in organizations.[68] Barnard's theory of authority, his call for moral leadership, and his identification of universal elements in both formal and informal organization continue as significant contributions to management thought.

---

64. Chester I. Barnard, "Elementary Conditions of Business Morals," *California Management Review*, 1 (Fall), 1958, p. 4.

65. Barnard, *Functions of the Executive*, pp. 282–283.

66. Fritz J. Roethlisberger, *The Elusive Phenomena: An Autobiographical Account of My Work in the Field of Organizational Behavior at the Harvard Business School*. Edited by George F. F. Lombard (Boston: Division of Research, Graduate School of Business, Harvard University, 1977), p. 67.

67. Robert T. Keller, "The Harvard 'Pareto Circle' and the Historical Development of Organization Theory," *Journal of Management* 10(2) (1984), p. 199.

68. See William B. Wolf, "The Barnard-Simon Connection," *Journal of Management History* 1(4) (1995), pp. 88–99 and Chester I. Barnard, "Foreword," in Herbert A. Simon, *Administrative Behavior: A Study of Decision-Making Processes in Administrative Organization* (New York: Macmillan, 1947), pp. ix–xii.

Summary

Mary P. Follett and Chester I. Barnard were bridges between the scientific-management and the social person eras. Follett ushered in a group view of society while living and working in the scientific-management period. Barnard was a student of formal organization, yet stressed the role of informal organization in achieving equilibrium within a cooperative system. Both operated on a theoretical plane in seeking to create a spirit of cooperation and collaboration within organizations and society. Both sought to reshape previous theories of authority. Both concluded moral leadership would enhance the effectiveness of organizations and the well-being of society.

CHAPTER 15

People and Organizations

T his chapter and the next examine two streams of management thought that developed from about 1930 into the early 1950s. This chapter focuses on the growth and refinement of the human-relations movement as it passed through micro and macro phases. The micro phase saw an outpouring of behavioral research into topics such as group dynamics, participation in decision making, leadership, and motivation. The macro phase witnessed a search for analytical tools and conceptual models to explain the interactions of the formal and informal aspects of organizations as social systems. The title of this chapter, "People and Organizations," conveys the human orientation of both phases, with the structural aspects of organizations being a secondary subject of inquiry. In contrast, Chapter 16, "Organizations and People," focuses on the structure and design of organizations, with the human element placed in a relatively subordinate role to other concerns.

PEOPLE AT WORK: THE MICRO VIEW

Whereas social scientists had studied workplace dynamics in the first three decades of the twentieth century, the 1930s and 1940s saw an unprecedented outpouring of research into "human relations at work." Unlike the scientific-management movement, which was dominated by engineers, the human-relations era incorporated contributions from sociologists, psychologists, and anthropologists. A common premise underlying their interdisciplinary research was the Gestalt notion that all behavior involves a "multiplier effect." That is, the behavior of group members is more than the simple sum of their individual actions. Individuals are unique due to their distinctive genetic makeup and family, social, and work experiences. When placed in an interaction with other one-of-a-kind individuals, predicting the resulting outcome is all the more difficult, if not impossible. Thus, because of the multiplier effect, individuals within groups cannot be studied in isolation, but must be analyzed as part of a dynamic social system.

DEVELOPING CONSTRUCTS FOR GROUP ANALYSIS

Interest in the study of groups appears to have been a product of the Social Gospel movement and its emphasis on industrial betterment. In 1921, the Federal Council of the Churches of Christ in America sponsored a national conference on the "meaning of Christianity for human relationships, with special attention to industry."[1] The conference, later called The Inquiry, led to seminal work in the study of groups. Sociologist Eduard C. Lindeman (1885–1954) joined with others to develop methods to observe and categorize group interactions, measure group participation, and classify the attitudes of a group's members. Lindeman was a friend of Mary Follett and appears to have been influenced by her thinking on conflict resolution and "power-with" rather than "power-over." Lindeman coined the phrase "participant-observer" to describe someone "planted" inside a group to corroborate the findings of an outside observer.[2] Over time, however, the role of participant-observers changed from that of a plant, or stooge, to that of a legitimate researcher who wished to study a situation and its characters from inside, such as the role assumed by Whiting Williams in his travels (see Chapter 9). Lindeman's pioneering work is now largely forgotten.

In contrast, the work of psychiatrist Jacob L. Moreno (1889–1974) has continued to stand the test of time. Moreno developed a therapeutic technique, *sociometry*, which had as its purpose "a process of classification, which is calculated, among other things, to bring individuals together who are capable of harmonious inter-personal relationships, and so creating a social group which can function at the maximum efficiency and with the minimum of disruptive tendencies and processes."[3]

Moreno felt the "sociopsychopathology" of group structure was not due to chance and that group structures could be studied using quantitative methods to determine the evolution and pattern of attitudes and interactions among a group's members. In his analyses, Moreno classified the pattern of attitudes and interactions that existed among group members based on three emotions: *attraction, repulsion,* and *indifference.* He assessed these emotions by asking group members to indicate whom from among the group they would and would not prefer to associate. Moreno

---

1. Charles D. Wrege, Sakae Hata, and Ronald G. Greenwood, "Before Bales: Pioneer Studies in Analyzing Group Behavior: 1921–1930" (paper presented at the meetings of the Academy of Management, Boston, 1984), p. 2.

2. Eduard C. Lindeman, *Social Discovery: An Approach to the Study of Functional Groups* (New York: Republic, 1936).

3. William A. White, "Foreword," in Jacob L. Moreno (with the collaboration of Helen H. Jennings), *Who Shall Survive? A New Approach to Human Interrelations* (Washington, DC: Nervous and Mental Disease Publishing, 1934), p. xii.

then paired and ranked group members' feelings for one another using a chart he called a *sociogram*. He recognized that group-member preferences were dynamic, varying as group membership and the problems facing a group changed. For example, in a study of "leadership structures" at the New York Training School for Girls, different pairing preferences were expressed, depending on whether respondents were choosing a roommate or a workmate. Other early research sought to increase work-team output by sociometrically selecting team members.[4]

Moreno also developed what is known as *psychodrama* and *sociodrama*. Both techniques involve dramatic enactments of real-life situations or conflicts. Together these techniques formed a basis for remedying problems in individual or group relationships. Psychodrama consists of placing individuals "on stage" to act out their personal problems with the aid of other "actors" and a facilitator.[5] Once an individual's manner of dealing with others is revealed, therapy or treatment is then recommended to resolve any problems that may have been disclosed. Psychodrama is intended to be a cathartic experience, enabling individuals to release and relieve their innermost doubts and anxieties.

Sociodrama, an outgrowth of psychodrama, focuses on understanding relationships within groups. It is based on the assumption that groups are organized according to social and cultural roles. Group therapy is used to understand these roles and might include role-playing exercises dealing with superior–subordinate relationships, interpersonal and team relationships, gender and race issues, and so forth. Role reversal, or enacting the roles of opposite social or cultural group members—for example, a white supervisor playing the role of an African-American worker—might be used to broaden role flexibility and create an understanding of others' views. In effect, sociodrama is group psychotherapy designed to reduce resentments, frustrations, and misunderstandings. Moreno's work supplemented the counseling and interpersonal relations aspects of the human-relations movement by providing techniques for studying and changing an individual's or group's behavior vis-à-vis other individuals or groups. Heretofore, psychology and psychoanalysis, both essentially concerned with the study of mental processes, had been inadequate for analyzing individual or group workplace behavior.

Group dynamics, as developed by Kurt T. Lewin (1890–1947), is another concept that developed during the same period that Moreno was popularizing his sociometric methods. Indeed, there is evidence that Moreno substantially influenced Lewin's work.[6] Lewin studied at the University of Berlin under Max Wertheimer and Wolfgang Kohler, two founders of the Gestalt movement. Lewin's own thinking

---

4. Raymond H. Van Zelst, "Sociometrically Selected Work Teams Increase Production," *Personnel Psychology* 5 (1952), pp. 175–185.

5. Jacob L. Moreno, *Psychodrama* (Boston: Beacon Press, 1946), vol. 1, pp. 177–222.

6. Barbara A, Wech, "The Lewin/Moreno Controversy," in Dennis R. Ray, ed., *Proceedings of the Southern Management Association* (November 1996), pp. 421–423. See also Pitirim Sorokin, *Fads and Foibles in Modern Sociology and Related Sciences* (Chicago: Henry Regnery, 1956), pp. 5–6.

falls under the heading of *field theory*, which holds that group behavior is an intricate set of symbolic interactions and forces that not only affect group structure but also modify individual behavior. From a field-theory perspective, a group is never at a steady state of equilibrium, but is in a continuous process of mutual adaptation that Lewin labeled "quasi-stationary equilibrium." An analogy might be that of a river flowing within its banks; it appears relatively stationary, but there is nevertheless continual movement and change.

Lewin viewed behavior as a function of the interaction between a person and his or her social environment, which Lewin regarded as a dynamic "field." This is expressed in his famous formula, $B = f(P, E)$, where behavior (B) is a function of the Person (P) and the Environment (E). Using terms such as "life space," "space of free movement," and "field forces," that is, tensions emanating from group pressures on an individual, Lewin investigated resistance to change and the social climate of groups. For example, Lewin and his graduate students studied groups of ten- and eleven-year-old boys to determine how democratic or authoritarian behavior by the groups' adult leaders affected the groups' social climate. They concluded that authoritarian behavior on the part of a leader impaired initiative and bred hostility and aggressiveness, whereas leader behaviors they labeled democratic and laissez-faire were more effective in maintaining group morale and satisfaction.[7] Unfortunately, history has left the incorrect interpretation that this was a study of leadership and its effect on productivity. In reality, Ralph K. White, one of the counselors (a group leader) was quite shy and had had little experience with young boys. Ralph was supposed to be a democratic leader, but when the results for his group were discussed, Ronald Lippitt remarked, "This isn't democratic leadership. That is *laissez-faire*." Typical of his approach to working with graduate students, rather than discard the observations from White's group, Lewin declared, "Okay, we'll make a third group. A *laissez-faire* group." Over the years the notion has been erroneously passed down that *laissez-faire* was intended as a style of leadership when in fact it was recognized as a lack of leadership.[8]

In research during World War II on changing family food habits, Lewin found that changes were more easily induced through group decision making than through lectures and individual appeals.[9] This was a new insight into introducing change. It suggested that changes are more readily accepted when people feel they have been involved in a decision to change rather than when they are simply asked or

---

7. Kurt T. Lewin, Ronald Lippitt, and Ralph K. White, "Patterns of Aggressive Behavior in Experimentally Created 'Social Climates,'" *Journal of Social Psychology* 10 (1939), pp. 271–299.

8. Recollections of Gertrud (Mrs. Kurt) Lewin, during discussion of the paper presented by Miriam Lewin Papanek, "Kurt Lewin and His Contributions to Modern Management Theory" (Boston: Academy of Management Meeting, August 22, 1973). See also Gertrud Lewin quoted in William B. Wolf, "Reflections on the History of Management Thought," *Journal of Management History* 2, no. 2 (1996), p. 8.

9. Kurt T. Lewin, "The Dynamics of Group Action," *Educational Leadership*," 1 (January 1944), pp. 195–200.

told to change. Lewin felt successful change required moving through three phases: "unfreezing" or recognizing the need for change, "changing" or modifying old ways so that new behavior patterns can be introduced, and "refreezing" or establishing new behavior patterns.[10] Lewin's three phases provided a foundation for future "action research" and organizational change and development techniques.

In 1945, Lewin founded the Research Center for Group Dynamics at the Massachusetts Institute of Technology; following his death, the center was moved to the University of Michigan, where Rensis Likert and others would further the study of participation in decision making and use of group techniques to achieve changes in workplace behavior. In 1947, another of Lewin's disciples, Leland P. Bradford, established the first sensitivity training (or human relations) laboratory, the National Training Laboratory, at Bethel, Maine. The goal of sensitivity training is to achieve changes in behavior through "gut-level" interactions that lead to increased interpersonal awareness.

By focusing on group interactions rather than isolated individuals, Lindeman, Moreno, and Lewin introduced a new perspective for understanding workplace behavior. This focus, reflecting a Gestalt orientation, led to further studies on introducing change, conflict resolution, and the effects of group processes on individual behavior. On the whole, these studies emphasized the dynamic nature of individual interactions within a group setting.

THE GROWTH OF HUMAN-RELATIONS RESEARCH AND TRAINING

The 1930s witnessed the emergence of a more favorable political climate for organized labor. The passage of the National Labor Relations Act (the Wagner Act) and the formation of the Congress of Industrial Organizations (CIO), both in 1935, brought a new emphasis on collective bargaining. Morris L. Cooke and CIO president Philip Murray called for management to "tap labor's brains" for ideas on how to increase workplace productivity.[11] Industrial democracy, meaning in essence the workplace application of a human-relations philosophy with organized labor's support, was a common theme.[12] Accordingly, a number of interdisciplinary university-based programs began to appear that would pave the way for further growth of human-relations research. In 1943, an interdisciplinary group at the University of Chicago formed the Committee on Human Relations in Industry. Drawing its members from business (Burleigh Gardner), sociology (William Foote

---

10. Kurt T. Lewin, "Group Decision and Social Change," in Theodore M. Newcomb and Eugene L. Hartley, eds., *Readings in Social Psychology* (New York: Henry Holt, 1947), p. 344.

11. Philip Murray and Morris L. Cooke, *Organized Labor and Production: Next Steps in Industrial Democracy* (New York: Harper, 1940), pp. 211–221.

12. For example, see Clinton S. Golden and Harold J. Ruttenberg, *The Dynamics of Industrial Democracy* (New York: Harper, 1942).

Whyte), and anthropology (W. Lloyd Warner), this committee was to characterize new style of social science research.[13]

Industrial relations centers also came into vogue. The first such center, the New York State School of Industrial and Labor Relations, was established at Cornell University (1945); others followed, such as the Institute of Labor and Industrial Relations at the University of Illinois (1946) and the Labor-Management Center at Yale University (1947). In 1947, a group of academicians, labor leaders, and others interested in advancing the state of knowledge in personnel and industrial relations formed the Industrial Relations Research Association.

Human-relations training also gained popularity during the late 1940s. Oriented toward overcoming barriers to communication and enhancing interpersonal skills, this training was largely based on the belief that the pathway to revealing hidden employee talents resided in group-oriented techniques, such as role-playing, nondirective counseling, group-discussion methods and, eventually, sensitivity training. It was also at this time that Carl R. Rogers (1902–1987), a clinical psychologist at the University of Chicago, developed his nondirective counseling approach, which involved creating a comfortable atmosphere for clients by accepting their feelings, regardless of content.[14] The University of Michigan's Norman R. F. Maier (1900–1977) was one of the foremost advocates of "group-in-action" training techniques. For Maier, group decision making was:

A way of controlling through leadership rather than force

A way of group discipline through social pressure

A way of being fair to the job and all members of a group

Permitting the group to jell on the idea it thinks will best solve a problem

Pooled thinking

Cooperative problem solving

A way of giving each person a chance to participate in things that concern him in his work situation

A method that requires skill and a respect for other people[15]

---

13. Burleigh B. Gardner and William Foote Whyte, "Methods for the Study of Human Relations in Industry," *American Sociological Review* 11 (October 1946), pp. 506–512.

14. Carl P. Rogers, *Counseling and Psychotherapy: Newer Concepts in Practice* (Boston: Houghton Mifflin, 1942). See also Kevin T. Mahoney and David B. Baker, "Elton Mayo and Carl Rogers: A Tale of Two Techniques." *Journal of Vocational Behavior* 60 (June 2002), pp. 437–450.

15. Norman R. F. Maier, *Principles of Human Relation: Applications to Management* (New York: Wiley, 1952), p. 30.

As result of growing human-relations training, managers during this period were encouraged to engage in participative decision making and adapt group-oriented techniques to enhance employee commitment. Human-relations training was also introduced in business-school classrooms. An interest in sharpening students' perceptiveness of human behavior and in developing their interpersonal skills led to a plethora of textbooks dealing with "human relations at work." World War II had placed great emphasis on the need for trained managers, teamwork and group leadership were in vogue, and universities sought to fill a call for graduates capable of managing both productive and satisfied workers. Drawing on the Hawthorne studies' emphasis on the importance of socially skilled managers, enhanced by the ideas and techniques of Moreno and Lewin, and popularized by university-based centers and union involvement, human-relations research and training reached their apogee in the 1950s.

CHANGING ASSUMPTIONS ABOUT PEOPLE AT WORK

As noted, whereas the scientific-management movement was largely dominated by engineers, the human-relations era was decidedly interdisciplinary in its focus. From this era came a different perspective on the nature of employee motivation, the role of managers in eliciting employee collaboration, and the importance of employee sentiments and informal workplace activities. This new perspective challenged prevailing assumptions about people at work. Investigations in the post-Hawthorne era led to (1) a deeper understanding of employee motivation, (2) questions about the benefits of division of labor, and (3) an interest in obtaining greater employee commitment to organizational goals through employee participation in decision making.

PEOPLE AND MOTIVATION

One line of thinking about why individuals are motivated to behave as they do is that all human beings have recurring needs they attempt to satisfy. *Need theory* is one of the oldest explanations for why individuals engage in particular behaviors. In 1938, Henry A. Murray (1893–1988) identified twenty-seven basic personality needs that individuals attempt to satisfy by their actions (i.e., behavior).[16] Three of these needs—the needs for Power, Affiliation, and Achievement—have been the focus of continuing research. Abraham H. Maslow (1908–1970) built on Murray's work to develop one of the most widely recognized need theories of motivation. According to Maslow, individuals are motivated to satisfy five categories of inborn needs:

---

16. Henry A. Murray, *Explorations in Personality: A Clinical and Experimental Study of Fifty Men of College Age.* (New York: Oxford University Press, 1938), p. 145.

physiological, safety, love, esteem, and self-actualization. Maslow held that these needs form a hierarchy of ascending importance, from low to high. He contended that a "lower" need must be relatively satisfied before the "next higher" need can motivate behavior. For example, an individual's safety needs would have to be generally satisfied before the next level of need (social) can motivate behavior. Thus, the strength of any need is determined not only by its position in the hierarchy, but also by the degree to which it and all lower needs have been satisfied. Relative satisfaction of a need, however, triggers dissatisfaction at the next highest level. This sequence of "increased satisfaction, decreased importance, and increased importance of the next higher need" repeats itself until the highest level of the hierarchy (self-actualization) is reached. Maslow suggested that an individual could progress down as well as up the various need levels. If a lower-level need (safety, for instance) were threatened at some later point in time, it again would become dominant and assume an important position in an individual's total motivation system.

Maslow borrowed the term "*self-actualization*" from Kurt Goldstein, a well-known "holistic" psychologist. Goldstein saw self-actualization as the master motive from which sprang all other motives.[17] Maslow, however, treated self-actualization in a more limited fashion as emerging only after all lower level needs are satisfied: "A musician must make music, an artist must paint, a poet must write, if he is to be ultimately happy. What a man *can* be, he must be ... to become more and more what one is, to become everything that one is capable of becoming."[18] Maslow believed the drive to self-actualize was universal, but that the need for self-actualization is only rarely reached and never completely.

Behaviorism and psychoanalysis were two other widely accepted motivation theories in the mid-1900s. As Maslow moved through his career, he became disenchanted with the behaviorist view that behavior is determined by stimuli and response contingencies. Sigmund Freud was the dominant figure in psychoanalysis. His thinking largely drew on the study of neurotics or psychotics. Maslow felt that there were shortcomings in basing our understanding of human motivation on the behavior of the emotionally disturbed. He believed that psychology, in general, should be a study of the whole person, those values and choices that individuals make that can be good, honorable, creative, heroic, and so on. Maslow's response, "humanistic psychology," was a revolt against behaviorism and psychoanalysis, creating what became known as the Third Force in psychology. The Third Force gathered momentum as other prominent psychologists agreed that previous research and thinking had largely overlooked the majority of well-adjusted individuals leading productive lives.

Maslow's later years brought a richness of insights into the motives of managers in business organizations. In the summer of 1962, he was named a visiting fellow at Non-Linear Systems (Del Mar, California). Non-Linear Systems president

---

17. Kurt Goldstein, *The Organism: A Holistic Approach to Biology, Derived from Pathological Data in Man* (New York: American Book, 1939). Originally published 1936.

18. Abraham H. Maslow, "A Theory of Human Motivation," *Psychological Review* 50 (1943), p. 380.

Andrew Kay arranged the appointment. This was Maslow's first exposure to a large business. He kept journals that summer and later published them as a book titled *Eupsychian Management*. Eupsychian was a neologism, a new word, and meant "good psychological management," or management by competent, mentally healthy, self-actualizing individuals. Maslow felt that one way to improve mental health in general would be to begin in the workplace, because most people are employed. He further believed that the best managers are individuals who were psychologically healthy.[19]

Whereas Maslow focused on the satisfaction of higher level needs, human-relations thinking emphasized employees' social needs. Contemporary motivational efforts focused on the social aspects of workplace behavior and on within-group relations. Adhering to the Mayo thesis that industry must promote collaboration and social solidarity,

Joseph N. Scanlon, 1955. Harry W. Bass Business History Collection. Courtesy of Daniel A. Wren.

individual incentive plans began to receive less prominence, whereas group plans received more. Perhaps the most well known effort along these lines was the Scanlon plan, named after Joseph N. Scanlon (1899–1956), a steelworker, later union official, and eventually a professor at the Massachusetts Institute of Technology.[20] The Scanlon plan was initially implemented at the Adamson Company (East Palestine, Ohio), a maker of steel storage tanks, and then at the La Pointe Machine Tool Company (Hudson, Massachusetts), which in 1938 was on the brink of bankruptcy. Scanlo, in consultation with union officials, brokered a labor–management productivity pl at Adamson that awarded employee bonuses for tangible savings in labor cost plan subsequently saved La Pointe from bankruptcy and soon spread to oth panies. The heart of the Scanlon plan was two-pronged: (a) a suggestion sought methods and means to reduce labor costs, and (b) joint labor committees that sought to solve production problems. As regard system, there were no individual awards. Cooperation and stressed over competition, and everyone benefited from th one individual. Awards were shared plantwide or compar cooperation in reducing costs. Traditional suggestion sys but under the Scanlon plan, all the employees at a p suggestion awards.

19. Abraham H. Maslow, *Eupsychian Management: A J* p. 75.

20. Frederick G. Lesieur, ed., *The Scanlon Plan: A Frontie* MA: Cambridge Technology Press of Massachusetts Institut

21. James F
Business (Cle
22. *Adam Sm*
and T. Cadell i

The Scanlon plan had great appeal to labor because it could save jobs in failing firms such as La Pointe, and because it explicitly required union participation in committees that sought to solve production problems. According to Scanlon, such participation was not intended to create a feeling of belonging or a sense of participation, but to recognize explicitly the role of employees and their union representatives in suggesting improvements and solving workplace problems. The Scanlon plan was not a profit-sharing scheme, as it did not establish a fixed percentage of profits to be shared with employees. In this respect, the Scanlon plan was and is unique in at least three ways: (1) group rewards for suggestions, (2) joint labor–management committees for solving production problems, and (3) employees' sharing in reduced costs, not increased profits per se.

Although the Scanlon plan was typical of the era's emphasis on human relations in the workplace, individual incentives did not pass entirely from the industrial scene. Writing in his book, *Incentive Management*, James F. Lincoln (1883–1965) appealed to individual employee ambition. Lincoln thought that people were giving up freedom for security, that they were relying on someone else (the government) to assume the responsibility for this security, and that pride in work, self-reliance, and other time-tested virtues was declining. The proper answer to this decline, in Lincoln's view, was to return to the "intelligent selfishness" of individual ambition. Lincoln believed that people were not primarily motivated by money, nor by security, but by recognition for their skills. As president of the world's largest producer of welding equipment, Lincoln Electric Company (Cleveland, Ohio), he pioneered a program that sought to develop employees to their highest ability and then to reward them with a bonus for their contributions to the company's success. Bonuses were over and above an employee's other wages and fringe benefits, which were comparable to those of other manufacturers in the Cleveland area. Writing in 1951, Lincoln reported that his company had never experienced work stoppages, labor turnover was almost nonexistent, individual productivity was five times that of other U.S. manufacturers, dividends per share were constantly rising, product prices were steadily declining, and worker bonuses remained high.[21]

B ENLARGEMENT

776, Adam Smith warned that, despite its economic advantages, division of labor lead to dysfunctional consequences for employees in terms of "intellectual, and martial virtues"[22] (see Chapter 2). Almost 175 years later, social scientists novative companies began to take Smith's admonition seriously. In 1944, at its t (New York) plant, the International Business Machines Corporation (IBM)

Lincoln, *Incentive Management: A New Approach to Human Relationships in Industry and* eland, Ohio: Lincoln Electric Co., 1951), pp. 251–289.

h, *An Inquiry Into the Nature and Causes of the Wealth of Nations* (London: W. Strahan the Strand, 1776), vol. 2, bk. V, ch. 1, pp. 366–367.

began to combine the jobs of two or more machine operators into one job. IBM called this *job enlargement* and found that doing so led to higher product quality, less idle time for employees and machines, and "enriched" jobs by introducing skill variety and individual responsibility.[23]

Soon afterward, in a study of an automobile factory, Walker and Guest found that assembly-line employees rebelled against the anonymity of their jobs, even though they were satisfied with their pay and job security.[24] Having met these more basic needs, the employees bridled at the repetitiveness and mechanical pacing of their conveyor belt-driven jobs. Discouraged over their inability to influence the nature of their jobs, and unable to interact with one another because their jobs were mechanically regulated, employees expressed dissatisfaction with the design of their jobs. Because of Walker and Guest's findings, job enlargement (and later job enrichment) assumed a new prominence in studies of workplace behavior. Job enlargement served to relieve monotony, enhance skill levels, and increase feelings of task significance among employees.

PARTICIPATION IN DECISION MAKING

A third area in which prevailing workplace assumptions were challenged concerned the nature of power relations within organizations. This led to a growing appeal to give employees a greater voice in workplace decisions. Operating on the premise that worker participation would yield a greater commitment to organizational goals and would further individual and group satisfaction, researchers sought to design work arrangements to involve employees in decision making. James C. Worthy (1910–1998), drawing on his experiences with Sears, Roebuck and Company, argued for "flatter," less-complex organizational structures that would decentralize power and authority and, thereby, lead to improved employee attitudes, encourage individual responsibility and initiative, and provide outlets for individual self-expression and creativity.[25] Sears, Roebuck also collaborated with the University of Chicago's Committee on Human Relations in a comprehensive study of the influence of organizational structure on employee morale. Worthy's analysis of "tall" versus "flat" structures, their impact on employee behavior, and the influence of managers' assumptions on employee morale remains a landmark in advancing our understanding of workplace dynamics.[26]

---

23. Charles R. Walker, "The Problem of the Repetitive Job," *Harvard Business Review* 28 (May 1950), pp. 54–58. See also Robert H. Guest, "Job Enlargement—A Revolution in Job Design," *Personnel Administration* 20 (March-April 1957), pp. 9–16.

24. Charles R. Walker and Robert H. Guest, "The Man on the Assembly Line," *Harvard Business Review* 30 (May–June 1952), pp. 71–83.

25. James C. Worthy, "Organizational Structure and Employee Morale," *American Sociological Review* 15 (April 1950), pp. 169–179.

26. James C. Worthy, *Brushes with History: Recollection of a Many Favored Life* (privately printed, 1998), pp. 84–101.

William B. Given, Jr. (1886–1968) of the American Brake Shoe Company and Charles P. McCormick (1876–1970) of the McCormick Tea and Spice Company were two other executives who sought to apply a human-relations philosophy to their companies. Using the catchphrase "bottom-up management," Given sought to develop and apply a system of participation "to release the thinking and encourage the initiative of all those down the line, so that ideas and impetus flow from the bottom up."[27] Bottom-up management involved widespread delegation of authority, considerable latitude in decision making, a free interchange of ideas at all levels, and the corollary acceptance of the fact that managers grow by having the freedom to fail. Recognizing that a "push from the top" was occasionally needed, Given tried to confine top-down management to setting policy, clarifying goals, and providing training programs for employees who needed them.

McCormick, president of the McCormick Company, introduced a unique model of employee participation that involved establishing a Junior Board of Directors. Part of what became known as The Multiple Management Plan, the McCormick Company Junior Board was used as a means of training and motivating younger managers. Junior board members were given free access to financial and other company records, encouraged to elect their own officers, and told that "every recommendation they made for the advancement of the business would have the serious consideration of the company."[28] The Junior Board met with the McCormick Company "senior board" once a month to submit its recommendations, which were generally accepted and acted on to a greater extent than McCormick himself had expected. In fact, McCormick attributed his company's success during the lean Depression years to the Junior Board's efforts. One example of a Junior Board recommendation involved the redesign of the traditional bottle for extracts, which McCormick expected his older executives would wish to retain. The Junior Board conducted a market investigation, considered homemakers' ideas, and came up with a new design that was immediately accepted by the company's senior board and the marketplace.

The success of the Junior Board led to the creation of two other boards at McCormick. A Factory Board and a Sales Board, which operated essentially as the Junior Board for the company's production and sales departments, were established in 1933 and 1935, respectively. In McCormick's opinion, The Multiple Management Plan offered a number of advantages: (1) it opened communication channels for junior managers; (2) it involved young managers in decision making; (3) it provided a means for identifying and developing future executives; (4) it relieved senior board members of a great deal of detailed planning and research; and (5) it provided for

---

27. William B. Given, Jr., *Bottom-Up Management: People Working Together* (New York: Harper, 1949), pp. 3–4.

28. Charles P. McCormick, *Multiple Management* (New York: Harper, 1938), p. 5. McCormick's sequel, *The Power of People: Multiple Management Up to Date* (New York: Harper, 1949), indicated further success and international acceptance in nearly four hundred companies.

interlocking arrangements between various departments to coordinate and follow through on company activities.

During the 1930s and 1940s, participation in decision making received greater and greater acclaim. It was viewed as democracy in action, opening communication channels, diffusing authority, and motivating employees by encouraging greater commitment to shared organizational goals.[29] Moreover, it was seen as challenging unilateral authority and as equalizing power between employees and employers.

LEADERSHIP: COMBINING PEOPLE AND PRODUCTION

Kurt Lewin's experiences as a Jew who fled Nazi Germany undoubtedly influenced his thinking about democratic and authoritarian leaders and their influence on the social climate of groups. Lewin's work exemplified the emergence of a pro-participation and antiauthoritarian literature during the 1930s and 1940s. Contributors to this literature included Theodor W. Adorno and his associates, who made a significant impact on the leadership literature in 1950 with their book, *The Authoritarian Personality*.[30] Influenced by the Nazism and fascism witnessed in World War II, Adorno and his associates tried to relate personality structure to leadership, followership, morals, prejudices, and politics. The F scale (Fascist Scale), developed as a part of the book, became an accepted instrument for analyzing leadership styles as well as followers' preferences for leaders.

Research, however, was beginning to challenge the idea that one leadership style was good and another bad. As early as 1945, at the University of Michigan, the Institute for Social Research, under the direction of Rensis Likert (1903–1981), began a series of studies in a variety of organizations to determine what principles and methods of leadership resulted in the highest employee productivity, the least absenteeism, the lowest turnover, and the greatest job satisfaction. The studies focused on the operation of small work groups. The studies' primary objective was to identify styles of leader behavior that resulted in high levels of work-group performance and satisfaction. As a result of this effort, two relatively distinct styles of leadership were uncovered: (a) *job-centered*—leader behavior oriented toward close supervision, pressure for better performance, meeting deadlines, and evaluating output, and (b) *employee-centered*—leader behaviors oriented toward human aspects of subordinate problems and development of effective work groups with high performance goals. Employee-centered leaders are concerned with employee needs, welfare, advancement, and personal growth.[31]

---

29. See Gordon W. Allport, "The Psychology of Participation," *Psychological Review* 53 (May 1945), pp. 117–132.

30. Theodor W. Adorno, Else Frenkel-Brunswick, David J. Levinson, and R. Nevitt Sanford (in collaboration with Betty Aron, Maria Hertz Levinson, and William Morrow), *The Authoritarian Personality* (New York: Harper, 1950).

31. See, e.g., Rensis Likert, *New Patterns of Management* (New York: McGraw-Hill, 1961) and *Idem, The Human Organization* (New York: McGraw-Hill, 1967).

The Michigan researchers emphasized that a hard-and-fast line could not be drawn between the two styles of leadership they had identified. Both were important to productivity. They explained their results as a matter of emphasis. Managers of high-producing groups were seen as emphasizing high productivity as *one* aspect of their jobs, but not the *only* aspect. In contrast, managers of low-producing groups were viewed as emphasizing high productivity to the exclusion of other important aspects of their jobs.

At about the same time the Michigan research was beginning, the Personnel Research Board of the Ohio State University began a series of studies that would result in the development of a "situational approach to leadership."[32] Conducted under the primary direction of Ralph M. Stogdill (1904–1978) and Carroll L. Shartle (1903–1993), the purpose of the studies was to determine the impact of leader behavior on job performance and employee satisfaction. The studies revealed that followers perceived their leaders' behaviors to be composed of two principal dimensions: (a) *consideration*—leader behavior oriented toward developing mutual trust, two-way communication, respect for followers' ideas, and concern for their feelings, and (b) *initiating structure*—leader behavior oriented toward structuring followers' activities for the purpose of goal attainment. Because consideration and initiating structure are independent dimensions, it is possible for a leader to be high in initiating structure and low in consideration, low in initiating structure and high in consideration, or high or low in both. Whereas consideration is similar to the Michigan dimension of employee-centeredness, initiating structure is analogous to the Michigan dimension of job-centeredness.

Although one might assume the most effective leaders would be those who ranked high on both consideration and initiating structure, the Ohio State researchers found this is not always the case. Both dimensions are necessary for effective leadership, but it was shown to be more important for a leader to strike a balance between the two that is appropriate for a particular situation than to exhibit a high degree of both at all times. Simply stated, a leader needs to be flexible, because the proper balance of leader behaviors varies from situation to situation.

In retrospect, the Michigan and Ohio State studies added immensely to our knowledge about effective leadership. Perhaps most significantly, they showed that no single leadership style is universally effective. Moreover, the systematic methodology they introduced and the increased awareness they generated concerning the importance of leader behavior served as a springboard for the leadership research that followed. In contrast to earlier trait theories of leadership, both the Michigan and Ohio State studies showed that leaders may be best characterized by how they behave rather than by their personal traits.

---

32. Carroll L. Shartle, "The Early Years of the Ohio State University Leadership Studies," *Journal of Management* 5 (Fall 1979), pp. 127–134, and Chester A. Schriesheim and Barbara J. Bird, "Contributions of the Ohio State Studies to the Field of Leadership," *Journal of Management* 5 (Fall 1979), pp. 135–145.

PEOPLE AT WORK: THE MACRO VIEW

On the macro side of the human-relations movement, a search was underway for analytical tools and conceptual models to explain the interactions of the formal and informal aspects of organizations. In this respect there were a number of attempts to understand the interaction of the social and technical systems operating within organizations. The results of these efforts laid the groundwork for later developments in organization theory.

THE SEARCH FOR FUSION

One of the earliest and most perceptive studies of the interaction of the social and technical systems operating within organizations was an analysis of human relations in the restaurant industry by William Foote Whyte (1914–2000). A key concept in his analysis was that of job status, or the relative prestige of a job in the jobholder's eyes or in the regard of others. Restaurants are characterized by many levels of job status, ranging from the low status of bussers who remove used dishes from tables, to the relatively high status of cooks. Whyte found that a restaurant's workflow—taking customer orders, preparing the orders, and serving the orders—posed a number of human-relations problems. In contrast to other restaurant employees, cooks, typically male, held to a higher set of culturally derived status distinctions; on the other hand, waitresses, usually female, were considered lower status, but were typically in the position of initiating work for the cooks by placing customer orders. Because those who initiate work for others are of higher status (managers initiate work for subordinates), Whyte discovered that conflicts were inevitable when someone in a lower-status job (e.g., waitresses) initiated work for someone of higher status (e.g., cooks). Whyte reported that restaurants avoided conflict between waitresses and cooks by placing a spindle on their order counters. The spindles are wheels on a shaft. The wheel has clips on it so that lower status waitresses can put customer orders on the wheel rather than call them out to higher status cooks. In this way, the cooks can remove and prepare customer orders under the pretext that they had not come from a lower status waitresses, but from the spindle.[33] The spindles thus effectively served to depersonalize authority and required all to obey the "law of the situation." Mary Follett would be quite pleased.

Another significant step on the macro side of the human-relations movement view was an empirical investigation of a New England telephone company by E. Wight Bakke (1903–1971), then director of Yale University's Labor-Management Center.[34] Bakke was interested in exploring how the company and the union

---

33. William Foote Whyte, *Human Relations in the Restaurant Industry* (New York: McGraw-Hill, 1948), pp. 69–76. Idem, "The Social Structure of the Restaurant," *American Journal of Sociology* 54 (January 1949), pp. 302–308.

34. E. Wight Bakke, *Bonds of Organization: An Appraisal of Corporate Human Relations* (New York: Harper, 1950).

representing its employees were bound together as a social system. He discussed five social-system elements or "bonds of organization." Bakke viewed these bonds (noted in parentheses) as important because they "weld men together as partners in production (Functional specifications); as directors and directed, representatives and represented (Status system); as givers and receivers of information (Communication system); as agents of reward and penalty (Reward and Penalty system); and as sharers of a conception of the organization as a whole (Organization Charter)."[35] Bakke concluded that all five bonds interacted to influence workplace behavior and that any change in any one bond would affect the other four. Other bonds Bakke mentioned, but did not discuss, included technology, services, and "thoughtways," which organize knowledge and govern its use.

In a later work, Bakke discussed what he labeled the "fusion process," by which he meant "the *interaction* between the organization as a functioning entity and the individual agent whose thought and action, added to and integrated with that of all other agents, constitutes organizational activity."[36] As explained by Bakke, the two elements of this "fusion process" are the "socializing process," by which employees "must be made an *agent* to some degree and molded into the image of the organization," and the "personalizing process," by which an organization is made an *agency* of its employees and is molded into their image. In Bakke's view, it was "the simultaneous operation of these two processes, as it were in opposite directions, from the organization to the individual, and from the individual to the organization," that underlie the fusion process.[37] Bakke was not giving answers to specific human-relations problems, but was proposing a conceptual diagnostic tool for understanding organizations as social systems. In retrospect, Bakke's work was a building block for the later analysis of organizations as social systems.

The Tavistock Institute (London) was also responsible for a number of studies concerning organizations both as social systems and as a part of their broader community. Elliott Jacques (1917–2003) conducted an extensive case study of the Glacier Metal Company (United Kingdom) based on Lewin's field theory and examined changes in technology as they moved through work groups into the company's surrounding community.[38] As part of the study, Jacques developed a theory of equitable payment and a technique for determining the time span of discretion for different jobs. Such longitudinal research into ongoing firms was (and is) rare.

Jacques's findings underscore the importance of studying organizations as interacting sociotechnical systems and are consistent with Barnard's ideas about all aspects of society being one large, cooperative system. Two of Jacques's Tavistock

---

35. Ibid., p. 8.

36. E. Wight Bakke, *Organization and the Individual* (New Haven, CT: Labor and Management Center, Yale University, 1952), p. 1. See also E. Wight Bakke, *The Fusion Process* (New Haven, CT: Labor and Management Center, Yale University, 1953).

37. Bakke, *Organization and the Individual*, p. 14.

38. Elliott Jacques, *The Changing Culture of a Factory* (London: Tavistock Publications, 1951).

colleagues, Eric L. Trist (1909–1993) and Kenneth W. Bamforth, reported a classic example of how changes in technology disrupt an organization's social system. They studied the social and technical consequences of the mechanized longwall method of mining coal as introduced in Great Britain following World War II.[39] This method of mining required breaking up established small, highly cohesiveness work groups and the substitution of specialized, larger groups working in shifts. Under the traditional shortwall method of mining, miners had organized relatively autonomous work groups that rotated job assignments and shifts among themselves with a minimum of supervision. By contrast, with the longwall method, each miner was responsible for a single specialized task. The introduction of the longwall method resulted in a de-skilling of the jobs performed by the miners and a loss of autonomy. This lead to decreased commitment, lower productivity, and an increasing sense of personal alienation among the miners. Trist and Bamforth documented how the longwall method so disrupted the miners' social organization that its advantages were essentially negated. The lesson: Technological changes will not be effective unless due consideration is given to maintaining the prevailing system of social relationships.

NEW TOOLS FOR MACRO ANALYSIS

A review of the macro side of the human-relations movement would not be complete without a discussion of the contributions of Carnegie Mellon University professor and Nobel laureate Herbert A. Simon (1916–2001). As noted in Chapter 14, Simon was greatly influenced by Chester I. Barnard's thoughts on decision making in organizations, especially on authority, inducements, and communications. Building on Barnard's analysis of how decisions are made in organizations, Simon questioned the validity of the rational model of decision making grounded in traditional economic theory.[40] Rather than portraying managers as completely rational decision makers who invariably seek to maximize expected benefits (or minimize costs), Simon advanced the view that managerial decisions are bounded by the limited mental capacity and emotions of the individuals involved, as well as by environmental factors over which they may have no control. He described this situation as being one of "bounded rationality," reflecting not only the limited capability of the human mind and emotions to grasp the full complexity of managerial decision, but also the uncertainty of future events with which organizations must cope. Given that organizations exist in highly complex environments, in which many possible alternatives and their consequences may remain unknown, all intended rational behavior is inherently bounded.

---

39. Eric L. Trist and Kenneth W. Bamforth, "Some Social and Technical Consequences of the Longwall Method of Coal-Getting: An Examination of the Psychological Situation and Defenses of a Work Group in Relation to the Social Structure and Technological Content of the Work System," *Human Relations* 4 (1) (1951), pp. 3–38.

40. Herbert A. Simon, *Administrative Behavior: A Study of Decision-Making Processes in Administrative Organization* (New York: Macmillan, 1945).

As this suggests, *optimum decisions* (meaning "best possible" decisions) are almost never made—except perhaps by chance. Even if it were possible to acquire perfect knowledge of all alternatives and their consequences (assumptions of classical economic theory), it is doubtful that, given the limitation of human beings as processors of information, an adequate evaluation could be made. In response to this dilemma, Simon believed that humans typically reduce the complexity they confront by constructing a simplified model of the real situation that encompasses only the information they feel equipped to handle. Thus, only a limited number of alternatives and limited range of consequences are considered.

Simon further believed that once managers have identified a limited set of alternatives, they typically deviate from the demands of rationality by selecting the first alternative deemed "satisfactory" or "good enough," rather than searching for the optimum choice. That is, rather than examine all possible alternatives and attempt to rank them according to a well-ordered and stable set of preferences (as described by classical economic theory), they conduct a sequential search and settle for the first that satisfies some predetermined "aspiration level"—a subjectively defined performance goal that is a product of past organization goals, past organization performance, and past performance of comparable organizations. Thus, choices are influenced more by the order in which alternatives are examined than by the preexistence of clear guidelines for ensuring that the optimum choice is selected.

As a shorthand label for this process, Simon used the Scottish word *satisficing* (satisfying). Examples of satisficing criteria include "share of market" versus "total market," "adequate profit" versus "maximum profit," and "fair price" versus "best price." Thus, satisficing is evident in a business whose managers are willing to hold to a decision alternative that results in a 25 percent rate of return on investment, even if they are aware there *may* be other alternatives that *might* raise profits still higher. For practical purposes (for example, selecting a source of raw materials), Simon stressed that it is important that satisficing not be seen as irrational. Given the limitations of human-information-processing, the cost of searching for alternatives, and the uncertainty of future events, satisficing is actually sensible.

On balance, Simon rejected the basic traditional economic notion that managers are completely rational decision makers. Whereas economists have typically focused on how managers *should* behave, Simon focused on how they *do* behave. He posited that organizations do not merely seek to maximize expected benefits and that managers are not completely rational. The Simon concept of bounded rationality replaced the idea of the so-called economic decision maker with the more realistic managerial decision maker.

With James G. March (1928–), Simon coauthored the influential book, *Organizations*.[41] The book's theme is that to understand organizations, one must study the network of decision processes that influence employee choices and behavior. March

---

41. James G. March and Herbert A. Simon (in collaboration with Harold Guetzkow), *Organizations* (New York: Wiley, 1958).

and Simon held that by studying the distribution and allocation of decision-making functions within an organization, it would be possible to identify the balance or equilibrium between the freedom afforded employees to make decisions and the need for organizations to place reasonable boundaries around employee choices and behavior. Simon's *Administrative Behavior* and March and Simon's *Organizations* were insightful links between Chester Barnard and later refinements in organization theory.

The work of George C. Homans (1910–1989) represents another step forward on the macro side of the human-relations movement. Influenced by Lawrence J. Henderson's work on Vilfredo Pareto (see Chapter 9), Homans attended Henderson's Pareto seminar (the Pareto Circle) and coauthored an early book on Pareto that formed the basis for his later view of organizations as social systems.[42] In *The Human Group*, Homans viewed groups as social systems that, in turn, are composed of an external system and an internal system.[43] Homans described a group's external system as being composed of forces that are determined by the nature of its particular environment. Conversely, he considered a group's internal system to be "the elaboration of group behavior that simultaneously arises out of the external system and reacts upon it," resulting in an interaction between both systems.[44] Carrying this reasoning further, Homans identified and discussed various mutually dependent elements that interact across a group's internal and external systems: (1) activities, behavior formally required of group members or that informally emerge; (2) interactions, organizationally prescribed or informally originated transactions between group members; and (3) sentiments, emotions having positive and negative values (such as like or dislike). Although the Homans treatment of groups as social systems was exceedingly broad, it provided a building block for further developments in organization theory.

Talcott E. F. Parsons (1902–1979), another member of Henderson's Pareto Circle, also played a major role in the early development of social-systems analysis. Parsons received his doctorate from the University of Heidelberg in sociology and economics, wrote his dissertation on Max Weber, and introduced Chester I. Barnard to Weber's views on bureaucracy. In an early work, Parsons drew together the ideas of Weber, Pareto, Alfred Marshall, and Émile Durkheim to develop a "voluntaristic theory of social action."[45] His ideas influenced Barnard's search for a theory of "cooperative systems." He is especially remembered for producing a general theoretical system for the analysis of society known as "structural functionalism."[46]

---

42. George C. Homans and Charles P. Curtis, Jr., *An Introduction to Pareto: His Sociology* (New York: Knopf, 1934).

43. George C. Homans, *The Human Group* (New York: Harcourt, Brace & World, 1950).

44. Ibid., p. 109.

45. Talcott E. F. Parsons, *The Structure of Social Action: A Study in Social Theory with Special Reference to a Group of Recent European Writers.* (New York: McGraw-Hill, 1937).

46. Talcott E. F. Parsons, *The Social System* (Glencoe, IL: Free Press, 1951).

SUMMARY

This was the first of two chapters examining twin streams of management thought that developed from about 1930 to the early 1950s. This chapter focused on the growth and refinement of the human-relations movement as it passed through micro and macro phases. The micro phase saw an outpouring of behavioral research into topics such as group dynamics, participation in decision making, leadership, and motivation. The macro phase witnessed a search for analytical tools and conceptual models to explain the interactions of the formal and informal aspects of organizations as social systems. The title of this chapter, "People and Organizations," conveys the human orientation of both phases, with the structural aspects of organizations being a secondary subject of inquiry. In contrast, Chapter 16, "Organizations and People," focuses on the structure and design of organizations, with the human element placed in a relatively subordinate role to other concerns.

CHAPTER 16

Organizations and People

C ontemporaneous with the writings of both Mary P. Follett and Chester I. Barnard, the advent of the Western Electric studies, and the outpouring of behavioral research into topics such as group dynamics, participation in decision making, leadership, and motivation that were reviewed in Chapter 15, a second stream of management thought focused on the structure and design of organizations. This stream of thought has been mistakenly accused of ignoring the human factor in organizations.[1] In actuality, it consciously distinguished between "the structure of positions and the behavior of persons temporarily occupying them." In doing so, it held that "the only way in which to study organization fruitfully is to isolate it from the personalities and 'politics' of particular undertakings at a particular moment."[2] Consequently, although the human element was not entirely omitted from this stream of thought, it was placed in a relatively subordinate role to other concerns. This chapter, which covers the period from the advent of the Great Depression to 1951, shows an evolution in the growth and refinement of the human-relations movement along three lines: (1) interest in and concern for organization structure, authority, coordination, span of control, and other issues relevant to organization design; (2) an increasing concern for a top-management viewpoint; and (3) antecedents to later thinking about the role of top managers and the nature of firms.

ORGANIZATIONS: STRUCTURE AND DESIGN

The so-called classicists of this era studied the functions and powers of organizations divorced from the performance of any single person. They recognized that organizations

---

1. T. E. Stephenson, "The Longevity of Classical Theory," *Management International Review* 8(6) (1968), pp. 77–93.

2. Lyndall F. Urwick, "Why the So-Called 'Classicists' Endure," *Management International Review* 11(1) (1971), p. 6.

incur obligations through the actions of managers who occupy relevant positions, and such obligations cannot be evaded by simply pleading that a manager, who for a time occupied a position, is no longer employed or has since moved on. In the classicists' view, the obligations were incurred by the organizations and it is the position in question that matters, not the manager who is its temporary tenant. The classicists examined here distinguished between designing and staffing an organization. In doing so, they studied the functions and powers of the different positions within an organization separately from the performance of the people temporarily occupying them.

JAMES D. MOONEY: THE AFFABLE IRISHMAN

During the solemn days of the Great Depression, the exhortation Onward Industry! reflected the belief that through increased industrial efficiency the lot of humankind could be improved. The like-titled book, *Onward Industry!*, was the joint effort of a General Motors executive, James D. Mooney (1884–1957), and a historian-turned-executive, Alan C. Reiley (1869–1947). It was an attempt "to expose the *principles of organization*, as they reveal themselves in various forms of human group movement, and to help industry to protect its own growth through a greater knowledge and more conscious use of these principles."[3] Although both men were credited as authors, it later became evident that Mooney was responsible for the conceptual model presented in the book and that Reiley assumed a lesser role, primarily contributing historical examples to support the model. Mooney was president of the General Motors Export Company and traveled all over the world as a goodwill ambassador and negotiator for the General Motors Corporation (GM). Described as "affable" and an "experienced diplomat," Mooney completed high school through correspondence, received a degree in mining engineering from the Case Institute of Technology in 1908, joined General Motors in 1920, and rose through the ranks to head its export division.[4] Mooney was selected by President Franklin D. Roosevelt to be his personal, secret emissary to German Führer Adolph Hitler when there were attempts to stop World War II, in 1939 and 1940, before the United States became involved. Failing in this, Mooney was charged with converting General Motors to defense production. He left General Motors in 1942 to head the U.S. Navy Bureau of Aeronautics and after the war became president and chairman of the board of Willys Overland Motors.

In the foreword to *Onward Industry!*, Mooney stated that industrial objectives could be justified only by the worthiness of their purpose. He observed that the purpose of industrial enterprises was usually "profit through service." This involved

3. James D. Mooney and Alan C. Reiley, *Onward Industry! The Principles of Organization and Their Significance to Modern Industry* (New York: Harper, 1931), p. xiii. This book was published in a more concise form under the title *The Principles of Organization* (New York: Harper: 1939).

4. [W. Jerome Arnold], "Drawing the Rules from History," *Business Week* (August 3, 1963), pp. 46, 51.

justifying a service and both creating and equitably dividing profits. For Mooney, the goal of industrial effort was "the alleviation of human want and misery."[5] Mere productive efficiency, though necessary, in providing a service was insufficient. Equal efficiency must be realized throughout an organization, including the distribution or supplying of material wants to those who, due to poverty, were unable to purchase them. To this end, Mooney felt that the application of the principles of organization could solve the problems of modern civilization.

As conceptualized by Mooney, efficient organization must have its formalism, which means its method for "the efficient coordination of all relationships."[6] Further, this coordination must be based on principles of organization. Mooney viewed organization as a process and defined it as follows: *"Organization is the form of every human association for the attainment of a common purpose."*[7] Mooney's notion of management was distinct from organization and was explained in the following manner:

> Management is the vital spark which actuates, directs, and controls the plans and procedure of organization. With management enters the personal factor, without which no body could be a living being with any directive toward a given purpose. The relation of management to organization is analogous to the relation of the psychic complex to the physical body. Our bodies are simply the means and the instrument through which the psychic force moves toward the attainment of its aims and desires.[8]

Using a body–mind analogy for organization and management, the conceptual model Mooney developed consisted of three principles of organization: (a) the coordinative principle, (b) the scalar principle, and (c) the functional principle. The first principle, coordination, meant *"the orderly arrangement of group effort, to provide unity of action in the pursuit of a common purpose."*[9] Coordination was a broad principle that included all the other principles of organization. The foundation for coordination was authority, "the supreme coordinating power." Authority in this sense did not imply autocracy, but as Mooney explained, "In a democracy like our own, this authority rests with the people, who exercise it through the leaders of their choice."[10] Because coordination implied a mutual aim or objective, Mooney felt every member of an organization had to understand this shared purpose. He called this *doctrine* and explained that in the "primary sense" it means the *"definition of the objective."* Doctrine was similar to the religious concept of *creed*, but for industry, it

---

5. Mooney and Reiley, *Onward Industry!* p. xiii.

6. Ibid., p. xv.

7. Ibid., p. 10.

8. Ibid., p. 13.

9. Mooney and Reiley, *The Principles of Organization* (New York: Harper, 1939), p. 5.

10. Ibid., p. 7.

meant the attainment of *"surplus through service,"* which (as noted) should be the purpose of industrial enterprises. Mooney reasoned that the more an organization's doctrine guides its members' actions, their level of teamwork will increase, as will the accomplishment of its objectives.

The scalar principle pertained to the "formal process through which [the supreme] coordinating authority operates from the top throughout the entire organized body."[11] This principle had its foundation in leadership, which was how authority entered the scalar chain. Delegation of authority allowed a superior to confer authority on a subordinate. Delegation always meant the conferring of authority, whether authority over people or authority for task performance. Conversely, authority always carried with it responsibility for accomplishing what was authorized.

The functional principle pertained to the *"distinction between different kinds of duties."* Functional differentiation exists in every organization to the extent that people perform different kinds of duties, such as production, sales, accounting, security, and so on. This principle can be seen in the division of labor, which creates a need for coordination. Another example of functional differentiation is the distinction between line and staff. According to Mooney, there should never be any confusion about line and staff because line represented "the authority of *man*; the staff, the authority of *ideas.*"[12] Line commanded, staff advised, and Mooney envisioned no potential conflict in line–staff relations as long as this dichotomy was kept in mind.

Following Mooney's section on the principles of organization, Reiley made his major contribution to *Onward Industry!* by showing how the principles of organization evolved from military and church organization. He examined Greece, Rome, and other ancient civilizations and rulers to illustrate applications of the scalar and other principles. With respect to the Catholic Church, the principle of coordination found its authority in God, who delegated it to the pope as the supreme coordinating authority. The scalar principle operated from the pope, through cardinals (who were often both line and staff), to bishops and priests by way of the delegation of authority. In the development of staff, the church operated on a *compulsory staff service* principle. Under this principle, a superior had to consult elder monks even on minor matters. On matters of major importance, everyone had to be consulted. This principle did not abridge line authority, but compelled the superior to consult with others before rendering a decision. The superior could not refuse to listen. In industry, the compulsory staff principle would not protect managers from errors in judgment, but would serve to allay errors of knowledge.

In retrospect, Mooney and Reiley's principles resembled Weber's managerial hierarchy, his legal notion of authority, and his call for formal rules and other controls (see Chapter 10). Mooney and Reiley did not refer to Weber, and because Weber's work had not been translated into English at this time, it may

---

11. Ibid., p. 14.

12. Ibid. p. 34.

be assumed that they independently developed their principles of organization. The perspective Mooney brought to his writing was grounded in his experience with mass-production at General Motors. Reiley's study of armies and the Catholic Church undoubtedly reinforced Mooney's conclusion that efficient organizations must have their formalism. Hierarchical structures, departmentation, reliance on staff, the importance of shared objectives in promoting teamwork, and the need for coordination were all found to be essential to an organization's growth. The human element was not missing entirely, but was relegated to a secondary role. For organization theory, Mooney and Reiley's major contribution was showing the interplay among principles assumed fundamental to any activity with an objective.

TEXTS, TEACHERS, AND TRENDS

Until the publication of Mooney and Reiley's *Onward Industry!* in 1931, most books on management had reflected the works administration–industrial engineering approach common to the earlier scientific-management era. For the most part, these books emphasized production layout, scheduling, materials handling, shop organization, production control, and other largely technique-oriented subjects. A growing interest in organization design, however, was emerging. This interest was evident in Henry Dennison's book, *Organization Engineering*, also published in 1931. Dennison (1877–1952) had been a pioneer in the installation of the Taylor system in his South Farmington, Massachusetts, paper-products firm, The Dennison Manufacturing Company. He advocated an approach to organization design that was diametrically opposed to that proposed by Mooney and Reiley. Dennison began with the idea that the purpose of organization engineering was "making a success of group life." He built on the belief that "all the strength of an organization comes from its members."[13] For Dennison, the first task was to form people into groups to build teamwork. Recognizing a diversity of motives, Dennison acknowledged that leadership would be required to resolve frictions among individuals. Instead of designing an organization's structure first, Dennison argued for finding like-minded people, grouping them into teams, and then developing a total organizational structure. In this sense, Dennison actually anticipated by a decade or more Moreno and others who advocated sociometrically selected work teams (see Chapter 15).

Dennison's view of motivation was also unique:

> Four general groups of tendencies which may actuate a member of any organization are: (1) regard for his own and his family's welfare and standing; (2) liking for the work itself; (3) regard for one or more members of the organization and for their good opinion, and pleasure in working with them; and (4) respect and regard for the main purposes of the organization.[14]

---

13. Henry S. Dennison, *Organization Engineering* (New York: McGraw-Hill, 1931), p. 1.

14. Ibid., pp. 63–64.

Dennison believed that a person could be "actuated" by any of these four tendencies, but "only when impelled by the four combined can all of man's power be brought into steady and permanent play."[15] To this end, he anticipated the job enlargement movement of the late 1940s by advocating the modifying of jobs so that they would provide greater employee satisfaction. He recognized the nature of informal groups and their influence on output norms and proposed nonfinancial incentives that, when properly mixed with economic incentives, built loyalty. Moreover, he realized that principles of organization were not "sacred in and of themselves," and that an organization's structure should be flexible to "strengthen its group[s], not ossify them."[16] Dennison also recognized limits to and variations in the number of persons to whom a manager could give attention without either restricting his "field of influence" or being spread too thin. The span of control, in his view, "seldom runs beyond six to twelve people."[17]

Dennison was a progressive employer. He introduced an employee profit-sharing plan, low-interest loans for employees to purchase homes, an employee representation plan, and unemployment insurance to stabilize employees' incomes.[18] Dennison quoted Mary P. Follett on coordination and the law of the situation, and she appears to have colored his view of labor–management relations.[19] Follett's influence on Dennison in this regard is evident in the following remark: "We never give an order; we sell the idea to those who must carry it out."[20]

Management textbooks popular during the 1930s largely continued to follow the works administration–industrial engineering approach that had developed during the earlier scientific management era and, thus, contributed little to the development of management thought. Writing in *Management of an Enterprise*, C. Canby Balderston, Victor S. Karabasz, and Robert P. Brecht (all from the University of Pennsylvania) defined management as "the art and science of organizing, preparing and directing human effort applied to control the forces and to utilize the materials of nature for the benefit of man."[21] They identified the "principal elements" with which all managers must deal, regardless of the type of enterprise, as men, money, machines, and material. They applied these elements to topics such as product design; provision of physical facilities; power, heat, light, and ventilation;

---

15. Ibid., p. 64.

16. Ibid., pp. 124, 126.

17. Ibid., p. 138.

18. W. Jack Duncan, "Henry Sturgis Dennison," in Morgen Witzel, ed., *Biographical Dictionary of Management*, vol. 1, pp. 233–236.

19. Dennison, *Organization Engineering*, pp. 100, 166.

20. Dennison quoted in John R. Commons, *Institutional Economics: Its Place in Political Economy* (New York: Macmillan, 1934), p. 67. See also Kyle D. Bruce "Activist Management: Henry S. Dennison's Institutionalist Economics, *Journal of Economic Issues*, 40 (December 2006), pp. 1113–1136.

21. C. Canby Balderston, Victor S. Karabasz, and Robert P. Brecht, *Management of an Enterprise* (New York: Prentice-Hall, 1935), p. 4.

controlling inventories; and planning and control of production, clerical, and sales operations. Organization was treated as a means of direction and control à la Mooney and Reiley. Together with personnel management, it was one of the few topics outside traditional works administration–industrial engineering boundaries that Balderston, Karabasz, and Brecht addressed.

In a textbook with a similar tone, but different purpose, Edward H. Anderson (University of Alabama) and Gustav T. Schwenning (University of North Carolina) outlined and described "the fundamentals underlying the process of organization for effective production."[22] Although credited as a coauthored book, the entire text was written by Anderson; Schwenning conceived and directed "the scope of the study," as well as prepared the text for publication. As a consequence, the text reflects Anderson's interest in history as a means of studying management and economics, and much like Mooney and Reiley's *Onward Industry!*, it contains examples from military history that illustrate the importance of organization and management strategies. After "appraising and synthesizing" the thoughts of other authors, Anderson and Schwenning concluded that "there is a science of organization, and that the science is the product of evolution rather than a single theory."[23] Though they introduced few new ideas, Anderson and Schwenning's analysis and synthesis, together with an extensive bibliography, made an original contribution to the development of management thought.

On December 28, 1936, Charles L. Jamison (University of Michigan) and William N. Mitchell (University of Chicago) invited a small group of management professors to the University of Chicago's Quadrangle Club to discuss the formation of a society to "advance the philosophy of management."[24] Enough interest was evidenced for Canby Balderston to invite the group to meet at Philadelphia's Lenape Club in 1937. After similar informal meetings in 1938, 1939, and 1940, a constitution was prepared by Ralph C. Davis (Ohio State University), the name "Academy of Management" was selected, officers were elected, and the Academy began formal operations in 1941. The objectives of the Academy have been stated as follows:

> The Academy is founded to foster the search for truth and the general advancement of learning through free discussion and research in the field of management. The interest of the Academy lies in the theory and practice of management . . . as it relates to the work of planning, organizing, and controlling the execution of business projects. It is also concerned with activities having to do with the forming,

---

22. Edward H. Anderson and Gustav T. Schwenning, *The Science of Production Organization* (New York: Wiley, 1938), p. v.

23. Ibid.

24. Preston P. LeBreton, "A Brief History of the Academy of Management," in Paul M. Dauten, Jr., ed., *Current Issues and Emerging Concepts in Management* (Boston: Houghton Mifflin, 1962), pp. 329–331.

directing, and co-ordinating of departments and groups which are characteristic of administrative management. . . .

The general objectives of the Academy shall be therefore to foster: (a) A philosophy of management that will make possible an accomplishment of the economic and social objectives of an industrial society with increasing economy and effectiveness. The public's interest must be paramount in any such philosophy, but adequate consideration must be given to the legitimate interests of Capital and Labor. (b) Greater understanding by Executive leadership of the requirements for a sound application of the scientific method to the solution of managerial problems, based on such a philosophy. (c) Wider acquaintance and closer co-operation among such persons as are interested in the development of a philosophy and science of management.[25]

Although inactive from 1942 to 1946 because of World War II, annual Academy meetings were resumed in 1947. Jamison served as the Academy's founding president from 1936 to 1940, Brecht was president from 1941 to 1947, and Davis became president in 1948. The Academy reflected an increased awareness of the need for management education. It continues to influence the development of management thought through the teaching and writing of its members.

A final textbook of note from this era, *Industrial Engineering and Factory Management*, was written by Arthur G. Anderson (University of Illinois) and published in 1928.[26] Like other textbooks of its type, it was largely devoted to traditional works administration–industrial engineering topics. An indication of the trend of management thought is evident in the 1942 revision of Anderson's book retitled *Industrial Management*. Joined by Merten J. Mandeville (University of Illinois) and John M. Anderson (Minneapolis Honeywell, Inc.) as coauthors, the 1942 edition introduced a larger view of management's role.[27] In its authors' view, management has a responsibility to promote both economic and social progress through productive and distributive efficiency, as well as through an emphasis on human relations in business. The authors discussed the various groups—customers, stockholders, the public at large, and employees—that play a vital role in an organization's success. In doing so, they showed an awareness of a typical organization's major stakeholders and that a manager's performance

---

25. Ibid., p. 330. See also Charles D. Wrege, "The Inception, Early Struggles, and Growth of the Academy of Management," in Daniel A. Wren and John A. Pearce II, eds., *Papers Dedicated to the Development of Modern Management* (Chicago, IL: Academy of Management, 1986), pp. 78–88.

26. Arthur G. Anderson, *Industrial Engineering and Factory Management* (New York: Ronald Press, 1928).

27. Arthur G. Anderson, Merten J. Mandeville, and John M. Anderson, *Industrial Management* (New York: Ronald Press, 1942), p. 3.

is dependent on knowing how an organization influences and is influenced by its environment.

BUILDING BLOCKS FOR ADMINISTRATIVE THEORY

In 1937, Luther H. Gulick and Lyndall F. Urwick edited a collection of papers by a number of well-known and not-so-well known authorities on management. Included were papers by James D. Mooney, Henri Fayol, Henry S. Dennison, Lawrence J. Henderson, Thomas North Whitehead, Elton Mayo, Mary P. Follett, John Lee, Vytautas A. Graicunas, and the editors themselves. The collection offered the first U.S. rendition of Henri Fayol's work, as well as a detailed demonstration by Urwick of the logical relationship between Fayol's "functions of administration" and Mooney and Reiley's principles of organization.[28] Gulick (1892–1993) was director of Columbia University's Institute of Public Administration and had served as a member of President Franklin D. Roosevelt's Committee on Administrative Management, which attempted, without much success, to reorganize the executive branch of the federal government.[29] Gulick divided the work of chief executives into seven functional elements. He used the acronym POSDCORB, representing the initials of the following activities, as shorthand for the elements:

> Planning, that is working out in broad outline the things that need to be done and the methods for doing them to accomplish the purpose set for the enterprise;

> Organizing, that is the establishment of the formal structure of authority through which work subdivisions are arranged, defined and coordinated for the defined objective;

> Staffing, that is the whole personnel function of bringing in and training the staff and maintaining favorable conditions of work;

> Directing, that is the continuous task of making decisions and embodying them in specific and general orders and instructions and serving as the leader of the enterprise;

> Coordinating, that is the all important duty of interrelating the various parts of the work;

> Reporting, that is keeping those to whom the executive is responsible informed as to what is going on, which thus includes keeping

28. Luther H. Gulick and Lyndall F. Urwick, eds., *Papers on the Science of Administration* (New York: Institute of Public Administration, Columbia University, 1937). See also, Lyndall F. Urwick, "*Papers in the Science of Administration*," *Academy of Management Journal* 13 (March 1970), pp. 361–371.

29. *Report of the President's Committee on Administrative Management* (Washington, DC: U.S. Government Printing Office, 1935).

himself and his subordinates informed through records, research, and inspection;

Budgeting, with all that goes with budgeting in the form of fiscal planning, accounting, and control.[30]

Although Gulick visualized management as a universal activity, his description of the preceding elements of a chief executive's job primarily pertained to governmental administration. Gulick went on to identify four basic systems of departmentalization: purpose, process, person or things, and place. He held that "the major purpose of organization is co-ordination."[31] In Gulick's scheme, there is no one most effective system of departmentalization. If an organization is first divided at its primary level by place (i.e., geographically), the secondary level of work might be grouped by purpose, process, clientele, or even again by place. The same would be true for the third level and so on. Any decision about how to group activities had to follow the principle of homogeneity (i.e., things grouped together must all be of the same dimension), ensure coordination, and maintain flexibility as an organization grew or as its objectives changed.

Lyndall F. Urwick (1891–1984), coeditor with Gulick of *Papers on the Science of Administration*, worked tirelessly to develop a general theory of organization and management. Educated at Oxford University, he served in Great Britain's army and government in World Wars I and II, was organizing secretary of Rowntree and Company's Cocoa Works (1920–1928), was elected and served as director of the International Management Institute in Geneva (1928–1933), and was chairman of Urwick, Orr and Partners, Ltd., management consultants, until his retirement in 1951. Greatly influenced in his thinking by B. Seebohm Rowntree and Oliver Sheldon, Urwick wrote on a wide range of subjects. He collaborated with Edward F. L. Brech in editing biographical sketches of scientific-management pioneers; with Henry C. Metcalf on editing Mary P. Follett's papers; with Gulick on compiling *Papers on the Science of Administration*; with Ernest Dale on line–staff relations; and with too many others to mention.[32]

Although Urwick wrote on numerous topics over six decades, his work in the late 1920s and 1930s was heavily oriented toward developing principles of organization. He identified eight principles applicable to all organizations: (1) the "principle of the objective," that all organizations should be an expression of a purpose; (2) the "principle of correspondence," that authority and responsibility should be coequal; (3) the "principle of responsibility," that the responsibility of

---

30. Luther H. Gulick, "Notes on the Theory of Organization," in Gulick and Urwick, *Papers on the Science of Administration*, p. 13.

31. Ibid., p. 15.

32. For further details, see Arthur G. Bedeian, "Kismet!: A Tale of Management." In Vance F. Mitchell, Richard T. Barth, and Francis H. Mitchell (eds.), *Proceedings of the Annual Meeting of the Academy of Management* (1972). 1973, pp. 134–137.

and in full agreement with Urwick's span of control principle, Gracunias concluded that the number of a manager's direct reports should be limited to a maximum of five. He conceded, however, that wider spans of control were permissible in the case of routine work at lower hierarchical levels where subordinates worked relatively independently of others, had little or no contact with others, and where supervisory responsibilities were less complex. At the same time, he advised that at upper levels, where responsibility was greater and often overlapped, a manager's span of control should be narrower. Graicunas also noted, "It is not possible to assign comparable weights to these different varieties of relationship," indicating that he was aware that not all relationships are in effect at all times. If Dick's work did not interlock with Harry's or if their jobs were routine, then the number of operative relationships would be less, and their manager's permissible span would be wider. Graicunas's formula is based on the maximum number of possible relationships, not the number that might actually exist at a given point in time.

Toward a Top-Management Viewpoint

A second facet of the focus on the structure and design of organizations involved a shift away from a shop-management, production orientation to a larger view of the managerial function. The design of organization structures and the search for principles of organization were still of concern; however, they were beginning to take a back seat to an interest in the primary responsibilities of top management. This interest was accompanied by a concern over the separation of ownership and control and the economics of business firms.

RALPH C. DAVIS: *PATER FAMILIAE ET MAGISTER*

Ralph C. Davis (1894–1986) received his mechanical engineering degree in 1916 from Cornell University. He was likely exposed to Dexter S. Kimball's *Principles of Industrial Organization* (1913), as Kimball was dean of Cornell's Sibley College of Engineering (see Chapter 11).[36] After passing the necessary licensure exam, Davis went on to work as a Registered Industrial Engineer for the Winchester Repeating Arms Company, where, as he put it, "I quickly discovered that I knew practically nothing about management."[37] He soon learned, however, by observing Carl G. Barth, Dwight V. Merrick, and staff members from A. Hamilton Church's consulting firm, who were all on assignment at Winchester. In 1923, following a stint as a labor commissioner in Cleveland, Davis was invited to Ohio State University to establish

---

36. Biographical information is based on personal correspondence from Ralph C. Davis, May 18, 1969, and on John F. Mee, *"Pater Familiae et Magister"* [father of family and teacher], *Academy of Management Journal* 8 (March 1965), pp. 14–23.

37. Davis, personal communication, May 18, 1969.

a department of management in the College of Commerce and Administration. He wrote his first book, *The Principles of Factory Organization and Management*, in 1928 for the use of his students. It followed the traditional, shop-level orientation of similar books published during this era. Davis stated that the fundamental functions and principles of factory management were universal in their application, and that certain considerations underlie good organization. As he explained,

> In developing the organization, consideration should be given to (1) the fundamental functions to be performed and their relation to one another, (2) the proper division of responsibility, (3) the definite location of responsibility, (4) the proper functioning of the system, (5) the flexibility of the organization, (6) provision for future growth, (7) personal characteristics and abilities, (8) the creation of an ideal, and (9) the quality of the leadership.[38]

In 1927, Davis was asked by General Motors to establish a department of management at the General Motors Institute (GMI; Flint, Michigan). It was at GMI, from 1928 to 1930, that he was exposed to the thinking of GM executives Donaldson Brown and Alfred P. Sloan, Jr., on what was to become the modern corporation (see Chapter 11). This exposure led Davis to move away from his previous shop-level approach to management and focus on the functions of executive leadership and the objectives of business. His focus was further influenced (in 1930 or 1931) by Coubrough's translation of Henri Fayol's *Industrial and General Administration*. By 1934 Davis had concluded that the work of the executive could be broken down into three "organic functions"—planning, organizing, and controlling.[39]

Davis's life and work illustrate the evolution of management thought over a span of more than four decades. His initial 1928 book followed a traditional, shop-level orientation; in 1934, taking a larger view of executive leadership, he introduced the concept of organic functions of management; and in 1940, reflecting a growing interest in the primary responsibilities of top management, he identified and then related the basic factors of business to these primary functions.[40] This interest was fully refined in Davis's 1951 classic, *The Fundamentals of Top Management*. His purpose in writing this book was to "present a fundamental statement of business objectives, policies, and general methods that govern the solution of basic business problems" from a top-management viewpoint.[41] Davis's original shop-level

---

38. Ralph C. Davis, *The Principles of Factory Organization and Management* (New York: Harper, 1928), p. 41.

39. Idem, *The Principles of Business Organization and Operation* (Columbus, OH: H. L. Hedrick, 1934), pp. 12–13.

40. Idem, *Industrial Organization and Management* (New York: Harper, 1940).

41. Idem, *The Fundamentals of Top Management* (New York: Harper and Row, 1951), p. xix.

orientation had completely given way to an interest in the primary responsibilities of top management.

In *The Fundamentals of Top Management,* Davis declared that management is "the function of executive leadership"; he used the terms *management* and *executive leadership* synonymously. He stressed the need for professional managers who had a sound philosophy of management with respect to the public interest. Because business organizations are economic institutions, Davis stated that their primary mission "is to supply the public with whatever goods or services it desires at the proper time and place, in the required amounts having the desired qualities, and at a price that it is willing to pay."[42] Davis added that, in pursuing their missions, businesses must necessarily adhere to accepted standards of conduct for both political and moral reasons. He considered executive leadership to be the principal force that motivates, stimulates, and coordinates an organization in accomplishing its objectives.

Davis considered the organic functions of management to be the functions of executive leadership. Planning was the "specification of the factors, forces, effects and relationships that enter into and are required for the solution of a business problem" and provided "a basis for economical and effective action in the achievement of business objectives."[43] Organizing involved the task of "bringing functions, physical factors, and personnel into proper relationships with one another" and was based on authority, which was "the right to plan, organize, and control the organization's activities."[44] This represented the traditional formal view of authority as the right to decide, which Davis found ultimately legitimated in organized society. For example, society upholds the right of private property; individuals exercise this right through stock ownership in a company and delegate the management of their property to the board of directors, who in turn delegate authority down through the scalar chain.

Davis defined control as "the function of constraining and regulating activities that enter into the accomplishment of an objective."[45] He broke control into eight subfunctions: routine planning, scheduling, preparation, dispatching, direction, supervision, comparison, and corrective action. In turn, Davis grouped these subfunctions into three phases of control: (1) *preliminary* control, which included routine planning, scheduling, preparation, and dispatching; (2) *concurrent* control, which included direction, supervision, comparison; and (3) *corrective action,* which involved correcting variations from planned performance. Preliminary control attempts to establish advance constraints and regulations that ensure proper execution of plans; on the other hand, concurrent control operates while performance is in progress. Corrective action completes the control cycle and begins

---

42. Ibid., p. 10.

43. Ibid., p. 43.

44. Ibid., pp. 238, 281.

45. Ibid., p. 663.

the preliminary phase again by identifying deviations and by replanning or taking other actions to prevent recurrence of performance shortfalls. Although many of his predecessors had written about control, Davis presented a much more insightful and comprehensive view of this function than had been previously rendered.

HARRY HOPF: TOWARD THE OPTIMUM

Harry Hopf (1882–1949) was another notable contributor to the development of management thought whose thinking, like Davis's, began with the precepts of Fred Taylor and concluded with a broader viewpoint of top management. Born in London, Hopf emigrated as a penniless youth to the United States in 1882. He would become a widely respected consultant, author, and executive.[46] Hopf began his career as a clerk in the office of a life insurance company and became acquainted with Taylor's views on eliminating workplace inefficiencies. In applying the principles of scientific management to office work, Hopf became interested in efficiency in general and, more specifically, the application of scientific management to all types of work. He studied compensation programs for office workers and wondered why so little attention had been given to typical executive-payment schemes, such as profit sharing, stock options, and deferred compensation plans. Hopf felt that such schemes did not adequately tie payment to performance, which was a conclusion Taylor had also reached about worker compensation. The conventional answer of Hopf's era was that executives did a different kind of work, which was intangible and not subject to measurement. Not satisfied with this answer, Hopf proposed principles and standards for measuring executive work in a manner that would link performance with pay.[47] He believed that all managers should be judged (and rewarded) by the results they produced.

In discussing proper organizational structure, Hopf adopted the architectural notion that form follows function; thus, structure had to follow the objectives to be sought. Otherwise, "[if] form dominates over function in organizational structure, we are bound to discover conditions of fixity and rigidity which exercise a baneful influence over accomplishment."[48] In this analogy, Hopf anticipated the dictum that "structure follows strategy," which became a guiding rule for organization theorists and business strategists in the modern era.

Hopf wrote on many other management topics: span of control, policies, coordination, and executive control, to name a few. None of his ideas were as

---

46. See Homer J. Hagedorn, "White Collar Management: Harry Arthur Hopf and the Rationalization of Business" (Ph.D. dissertation, Harvard University, Cambridge, MA, 1955), Richard J. Vahl, "A Study of the Contributions of Harry Arthur Hopf to the Field of Management" (Master of Science thesis, Louisiana State University, Baton Rouge, La., 1968), and Edmund R. Gray and Richard J. Vahl, "Harry Hopf: Management's Unheralded Giant," *Southern Journal of Business* 6 (April 1971), pp. 69–78.

47. Harry A. Hopf, "Executive Compensation and Accomplishment," *The Spectator* 147 (May 1944), pp. 34–38.

48. *Idem*, "Significant Aspects of Organization," *The Spectator* 151 (January 1944), p. 27.

far-reaching, however, as his concept of "optimology." It was this concept that would take Hopf beyond Taylor's shop management to a discussion of top-management responsibilities. Hopf defined the *optimum* as "that state of development of a business enterprise which tends to perpetuate an equilibrium between the factors of size, cost, and human capacity and thus to promote in the highest degree regular realization of the business objectives."[49] Hopf felt the typical business reversed the order of priority in fulfilling its societal role: maximize earnings and thereby serve society; whereas, in contrast, he believed that a business should serve society and thereby maximize earnings. He also felt the goal of increased size was a *faux ami* (i.e., a false friend) because it caused problems of coordination: growth in size as a goal more often than not sacrificed one part to the whole, benefiting one part at the expense of another. Instead, the optimum would balance all parts and could be achieved through carefully establishing the point (or points) of equilibrium among size, cost, and human capacity. Perhaps Hopf's most significant contribution to the development of management thought was the notion that a scientific approach can be applied to determining the proper structure for an entire organization. In doing so, he provided another step forward in developing a view of top-management responsibilities.

ANALYZING TOP MANAGEMENT

Whereas the Great Depression of the 1930s dampened economic activity worldwide, World War II mobilized vast productive capabilities, and the postwar period found managers challenged by new demands. With an unprecedented increase in international trade, executives were faced with the challenge of managing operations on a larger scale than ever before. It was toward these new responsibilities of top management that scholars turned their attention.

Searching for corporate excellence is not a new idea. One prewar study that was a model for future similar investigations attempted to find practical answers to problems of organization and control faced by top management. In this study, top management included three groups of executives: (1) boards of directors, (2) general managers responsible for a business as a whole, and (3) divisional managers responsible for major departments, divisions, or subsidiaries. The authors found that only about half their sample of thirty-one selected industrial corporations prepared detailed plans for periods up to a year in advance. Further, few had developed a system of integrated plans or developed long-range objectives. The authors reported that "one of the greatest needs observed during the course of this study is for more adequate planning and clarification of future objectives, both near-term and long-range." They traced this failing to inadequate organizational arrangements in which jurisdictions, responsibilities, and relationships were ill defined, staff departments were poorly conceived and coordinated, and committees, the bane of all

---

49. *Idem, Management and the Optimum* (New York H. A. Hopf and Company, 1935), p. 5.

organizational work, were poorly designed and used for the wrong tasks. In staffing, the authors found that "many companies" left provisions for the development and succession of key management personnel "largely to providence."[50] Control practices brought little solace; only one-half of the companies studied used budgets as a means of planning and, subsequently, for measuring "over-all results of efforts." This pioneering study was an important contribution to the development of management thought because it also empirically confirmed that managers performed the same functions (e.g., planning, organizing, and controlling) previous authors such as Fayol and Davis had identified based on personal observation and logical reasoning.

Jackson Martindell was perhaps the first person to devise a system for analyzing the quality of a company's top management. Martindell was a securities analyst who had successfully managed an investment-counseling firm in the 1920s. When the stock market crashed in 1929 and the Great Depression ensued, Martindell looked back on the investment criteria he had used as a security analyst to see if any had correctly predicted which companies were better able to weather the economic downturn. He found one answer for why some companies prevailed and others failed, "excellent management."[51] From that point forward, Martindell began a search for the factors that typified "Excellently Managed Companies." The result was a management audit that evaluated companies across ten criteria:

1. The economic function of a company
2. The organizational structure of a company
3. The health of a company's earnings growth
4. The fairness of a company's practices to stockholders
5. A company's research and development practices
6. The value contributed by a company's board of directors
7. A company's fiscal policies
8. A company's productive efficiency
9. A company's sales organization
10. The abilities of a company's executives.

Martindell's method of evaluation consisted of allocating points for performance on each of the ten criteria, summing these points for an overall evaluation, and then comparing the excellence of any particular company with the score

---

50. Paul E. Holden, Lounsbury S. Fish, and Hubert L. Smith, *Top Management Organization and Control: A Research Study of the Management Policies and Practices of Thirty-One Leading Industrial Corporations* (Stanford, CA: Stanford University Press, 1941), pp. 4–8. In a follow-up study of fifteen leading corporations, many improvements in managerial practices were noted, especially with respect to long-range planning, executive development, and management information systems. See Paul E. Holden, Carlton A. Pederson, and Gayton E. Germane, *Top Management: A Research Study of the Management Policies and Practices of Fifteen Leading Industrial Corporations* (New York: McGraw-Hill, 1968).

51. Jackson Martindell, *The Scientific Appraisal of Management: A Study of the Business Practices of Well-Managed Companies* (New York: Harper, 1950).

obtained from companies in similar industries. Whereas Martindell's approach to conducting a management audit is of doubtful validity, it contributed to the development of management by identifying criteria that could be used to judge a company's performance and, by implication, the quality of its top management in comparison to its competition.

OWNERSHIP AND CONTROL

At the outset of the Great Depression, Adolf A. Berle, Jr., a lawyer, and Gardiner A. Means, an economist, criticized top managers of large corporations for losing sight of whose interests they served: the corporations' shareholders. Citing Adam Smith's warning about those who managed "other people's money" being less vigilant than if they were managing their own funds (see Chapter 2), Berle and Means observed that the concentration of capital and power in large corporations far exceeded anything Smith could have envisioned. Smith, according to Berle and Means, felt that ownership and control should be combined; resulting in joint risk in decision making. Berle and Means found managers and directors rarely held an appreciable amount of stock in the corporations they managed. Rather, managers and directors were "economic autocrats" who formed "a controlling group [that] may hold the power to divert profit into their pockets."[52] In most instances, shareholders had little sway over the corporations they owned, having surrendered control to top management. Although Berle and Means offered no clear solution to this separation of ownership and control, they revived Smith's earlier concerns and prepared the way for later work in corporate governance and agency issues (see Chapter 19).

Berle and Means's concern found further expression in a study of 155 corporations conducted by Stanford University's Robert A. Gordon. Focusing on the direction and coordination of big business in the United States, Gordon also noted the separation of ownership and management of large corporations and that, further, many industries were dominated by a small number of competitors or, in some instances, by a single corporation. Consequently, he stressed the need for the "professionalization of management." In Gordon's view, the era of profiting by managing one's own investments had passed and had been succeeded by a new period in which salaried managers were hired by boards of directors. The result was a lessening of the profit motive in corporations, greater inflexibility, and increased bureaucracy. Gordon saw dangers in this increased insulation of managers from owners, especially with respect to the possibility that a self-perpetuating oligarchy of executives might place its own gain above the interests of a corporation's stakeholders. Gordon's answer to this dilemma was a leading role for professional executives who were responsive to the needs of a corporation's constituents.[53]

---

52. Adolf A. Berle, Jr. and Gardiner C. Means, *The Modern Corporation and Private Property* (New York: Macmillan, 1934), pp. 124, 333.

53. Robert A. Gordon, *Business Leadership in the Large Corporation* (Washington, DC: Brookings Institution, 1945).

INVISIBLE AND VISIBLE HANDS

In Chapters 3 and 6 we noted that economists Jean-Baptiste Say, Edward Atkinson, and Alfred and Mary P. Marshall considered management to be a fourth factor of production. The Marshalls, in particular, observed that the earnings of management were different from profit returned to owners. In so doing, they recognized the important role of managers in allocating resources within a business. In contrast, other economists have focused on what occurs in the broader environment or marketplace surrounding corporations, largely ignoring what happens between the acquisition of inputs (factors of production) and the sale of outputs (goods and services subsequently produced or provided). Two separate yet compatible developments in the 1930s would have a substantial impact on the evolution of management thought. Contemporary scholars, however, would only later rediscover these developments.

John R. Commons (1868–1945), the noted labor economist, noted that *transactions* were the smallest unit of analysis in the transfer of property rights. Transactions were not the exchange of commodities, but transfers of future ownership that must be negotiated "before labor can produce, or consumers can consume, or commodities be physically delivered to other persons."[54] Commons identified three types of ownership transfers: "bargaining," "managerial," and "rationing." *Bargaining transactions* derive from a market of willing buyers and sellers who negotiate the transfer, not of commodities, but of ownership rights. *Managerial transactions* occur between a superior–subordinate, such as employer–employee, where authority is used to direct the work to be accomplished. Managerial and bargaining transactions resemble one another because employees are free to negotiate regarding wages and hours of work. *Rationing transactions* involve a "collective superior," such as the budget making of a board of directors, legislators, criminal courts, or commercial arbitrators; all of which ration outcomes such as wealth or justice to subordinate others without bargaining and without managing, which is left to a superior.[55] For Commons, economics must be understood as the underlying legal and institutional relations that have evolved over time and consists of the ownership and transfer of property rights. He argued that whereas transactions involving property rights do occur outside firms, economists should not dismiss the importance of property-right transfers within firms by qualifying their findings *ceteris paribus* (other things equal) to rule out the possibility of other factors that influence cause-and-effect relationships. Commons's ideas remained relatively dormant until later writers discovered their inherent power some two decades later.

English-born and -educated Ronald H. Coase (1910–) approached the question of transactions from a different perspective. Coase had been introduced to Adam Smith's view that the "invisible hand" of the marketplace would ensure the efficient

---

54. Commons, *Institutional Economics*, p. 58.

55. Ibid., pp. 55–74.

allocation of available resources. A trip to the United States in 1931–1932 to discover why American industries were structured in so many different ways led him, however, to pose a follow-up question: If markets are so efficient, why do we have business firms? While still a 21-year-old undergraduate student at the University of London, he wrote a paper that would be published in 1937, under the title, "The Nature of the Firm." The paper would become a classic contribution to understanding the workings of business firms vis-à-vis the marketplace and be cited by the Royal Swedish Academy of Sciences in awarding Coase the 1991 Alfred Nobel Memorial Prize in Economic Sciences. In the paper, Coase asked,

> . . . in view of the fact that it is usually argued that co-ordination will be done by the price mechanism, why is such organization necessary? . . . Outside the firm, price movements direct production, which is co-ordinated through a series of exchange transactions on the market. Within a firm, these market transactions are eliminated and in place of the complicated market structure with exchange transactions is substituted the entrepreneur-co-ordinator, who directs production. It is clear that these are alternative methods of co-ordinating production.[56]

Coase realized that the "costs" associated with using a market's price mechanism might be reduced if a firm could coordinate its market transactions. With few exceptions, economists had engaged in "blackboard calculations" that failed to view firms as agents that sought to engage in exchange transactions at a cost lower than that associated with market forces. The young Coase did not pursue this line of thinking until years later. In accepting his Nobel Prize, he commented: "[I]t is a strange experience to be praised in my eighties for work I did in my twenties."[57] Later we will see how Coase's ideas re-entered management theory and were used to explain how business firms operate as "visible hands" that are typically superior to the "invisible hand" of the marketplace. Finally, we should note that, although Coase's theory of the firm is framed as a theory of a single firm, it is meant to be a theory of all firms.

SUMMARY

Whereas human-relations theorists sought greater productivity and satisfaction based on social solidarity and collaboration, the contributors to the development of management thought presented in this chapter were more concerned with the

---

56. Ronald H. Coase, "The Nature of the Firm," *Economica* 4 (1937), p. 388.

57. *Idem*, "1991 Nobel Lecture: The Institutional Structure of Production," in Oliver E. Williamson and Sidney G. Winter (eds.), *The Nature of the Firm: Origins, Evolution, and Development* (New York: Oxford University Press, 1993), p. 231.

proper structuring of activities and relationships to reach essentially the same ends. These contributors reasoned that people worked more productively and are more satisfied when they know what is expected of them. Hence, they emphasized organizational structure and organization design as means to both employee satisfaction and productivity. Their efforts were characterized by a search for principles of organization and, eventually, by a quest for broader principles of management. Mooney and Reiley deduced principles of organization for increasing efficiency and, thereby, alleviating "human want and misery"; Dennison favored forming people into groups to build teamwork; and Gulick, Urwick, Graicunas, and others also advocated formalizing relationships to make coordination easier and, thus, reduce confusion and foster predictability.

A concern with works administration and production operations persisted for much of the period from the advent of the Great Depression to 1951. The various books by Ralph C. Davis personified the shift in management thinking from a workshop perspective to a top-management viewpoint. Gulick and Urwick brought Henri Fayol to the fore, and Urwick, in turn, attempted to develop a general theory of organization and management. Hopf applied the scientific approach to designing firms, and others displayed an increasing awareness of large-scale managerial problems in the separation of ownership and control. Finally, as will be noted in Chapter 19, the roots of transaction-cost economics and the governance of contractual relations first emerged with the writings of Commons and Coase.

CHAPTER

17

Human Relations in Concept and Practice

W hat began as a study of workplace illumination and its effect on worker productivity at the Hawthorne plant of Western Electric was another step toward understanding human behavior in organizations. This chapter examines and reviews the impact of the human-relations movement on academia, industry, and organized labor and critically reviews the assumptions, methods, and results of the Hawthorne studies and other research.

THE IMPACT OF HUMAN RELATIONS ON TEACHING AND PRACTICE

The roots of concern for people in organizations may be traced historically to humanists of the Renaissance, who called for the overthrow of monolithic church authority, the participation and enlightenment of the citizenry, the breakup of rigid social structures, and the rediscovery of the human being as a unit of study. Throughout the preceding pages, varying views and assumptions about people vis-à-vis organizations have been presented. Robert Owen admonished factory owners to pay as much attention to their "vital machines," their workers, as to their physical machines. Taylor, concerned with the initiative of individual workers, understood he was dealing with humans as well as material and machines, and acknowledged that: "There is another type of scientific investigation which should receive special attention, namely, the accurate study of the motives which influence men."[1] The industrial psychology of Hugo Münsterberg was a direct response to this call for a better understanding of workplace behavior. Earlier, the antecedents of industrial sociology were traced to the Social Gospel and the contributions of Whiting Williams,

---

1. Frederick W. Taylor, *The Principles of Scientific Management* (New York: Harper, 1911), p. 119.

who extended the meaning of personnel/employee relations to include human relations and suggested that attention to people should be an organization-wide function, rather than the province of personnel managers alone. By improving human relations at every level of an organization, all parties—workers, managers, and the public—would benefit: "The coming together of factory management and factory man for the development of both will do more than humanize and justify this factory age."[2] From these varied beginnings, the human-relations movement would spread and dominate an era in management thought.

EXTENDING AND APPLYING HUMAN RELATIONS

After the Hawthorne studies, the human-relations movement took on more of an "interpersonal relations" flavor, but it still dealt with the same issues of improving labor–management relations. The human-relations movement has been tradition-ally associated with researchers from Harvard University. There were, however, many other individuals and institutions involved in the human-relations move-ment. There was the University of Chicago group that formed the Committee on Human Relations in Industry, consisting of individuals such as Burleigh Gardner, William Foote Whyte, W. Lloyd Warner, David G. Moore, and others.[3] Also at Chicago was Carl Rogers, who popularized nondirective counseling. The Chicago group focused on field-research methods, such as Whyte's study of restaurants, and studied numerous organizations, including Sears, Roebuck, where James Worthy came under the influence of Gardner, Moore, and others. Although the Chicago group disbanded in 1948, the influence of its members spread as they continued their work in numerous other places.

In London, Elliott Jacques at the Tavistock Institute used many of Lewin's ideas to study the Glacier Metal Company, as did Trist and Bamforth in their study of the social and technical consequences of the longwall method of coal-getting. The Tavistock branch of human relations emphasized longitudinal and sociotechnical systems research. At Harvard, the approach was more clinical and oriented toward case studies. Chester Barnard was closer to this Harvard group; he influenced their thinking and vice versa. A fourth branch stemmed from Lewin and flowed to the University of Michigan after Lewin's death. Here, Lewin's Center for Group Dynamics became part of the Institute for Social Research, headed by Rensis Likert. Survey research was the forte of this branch and led to studies in organizations such as Prudential Life Insurance, Detroit Edison, the Baltimore and Ohio Railroad, and the International Harvester Company.

---

2. Whiting Williams, *Human Relations in Industry* (Washington, DC: U.S. Department of Labor, 1918), pp. 9–10.

3. David G. Moore, "The Committee in Human Relations in Industry at the University of Chicago," in K. H. Chung, ed., *Proceedings of the Academy of Management* (New York, August 1982), pp. 117–121.

Like scientific management, the human-relations movement bore fruit from seeds that had been planted much earlier and nurtured in many places. As seen, human relations was also in practice in the restaurant industry, at Given's American Brake Shoe Company, and at McCormick Spice and Flavoring Company. The Scanlon plan, too, was influenced by the notions of teamwork and participation.

Although the human-relations movement was fostered by numerous individuals and groups and as a general philosophy it existed long before Elton Mayo entered the Hawthorne plant, as noted, the human-relations movement has been traditionally associated with researchers from Harvard University. Why has it been traditional to find the roots of human relations in the Hawthorne studies rather than in earlier work? As suggested in Chapter 9, one reason appears to be the academic distaste and disregard for any theory advanced by nonacademicians. O'Connor has even suggested that Hawthorne represented a sociopolitical gambit by the Harvard Business School to establish its legitimacy in academia and industry.[4] Further, the relatively young social sciences were striving to become seen as creditable. The seal of approval provided by established scholars such as Mayo from Harvard provided a legitimate cornerstone for all the social sciences, including the human-relations movement.

ORGANIZED LABOR AND HUMAN RELATIONS

Although human relations gained academic credibility and found its way into industrial practice, Mayo and his colleagues were placed under fire for a promanagement, antilabor bias. According to critics, it was not the worker but management that the Mayoists sought to save. For example, Mary Barnett Gilson noted: "In all the more than six hundred pages describing the Western Electric experiments . . . no reference is made to organized labor except a short statement, unindexed, that it was so seldom mentioned by any workers that it was not considered sufficiently important to discuss"[5] Although it is true that in *Management and the Worker*, their account of the Hawthorne studies, Roethlisberger and Dickson made no reference to the role of organized labor, it would be unfair to conclude that this constituted an antilabor bias. Until 1935, the dominant labor organizations were the American Federation of Labor, which consisted of skilled workers, and the brotherhoods that represented various groups of railroad employees. As will be seen in Chapter 18, the passage of the National Labor Relations (Wagner) Act in 1935 provided the legislative basis for a spurt in union membership from a turn-of-the-decade three and a half million to almost nine million union members by 1939.

In that the Hawthorne studies were concluded in 1932, before organized labor made its great strides, it should not be surprising to find little mention

---

4. Ellen S. O'Connor, "The Politics of Management Thought: A Case Study of the Harvard Business School and the Human Relations School," *Academy of Management Review* 24 (1999), pp. 117–131.

5. Mary B. Gilson, "Review of *Management and the Worker*," *American Journal of Sociology* (July 1940), p. 101.

of unions in the writings of Mayo and his colleagues. They did not draw any distinction between union–management relations and human relations, thus suggesting that in both union and nonunion employment there was an equal need for human-relations-oriented supervisors. This said, human-relations thought entered a revisionist period in the 1950s with an emphasis on "industrial human relations." Just as Robert Valentine and Morris Cooke tried to bring about a rapprochement between scientific management and organized labor, post-Hawthorne scholars quickly put unions into the human-relations picture. Industrial sociologists, in particular, studied the relationship between organized labor and management. Reflecting a social-systems orientation, they focused on the economic dimensions of employee–employer relations within a more encompassing societal complex.[6]

A basic assumption that appeared to prevail in this revisionist period was that there was inherent conflict between labor and management with respect to dividing surpluses created by an advanced technological society. This perception of increased industrial conflict was not a figment of someone's imagination. A comparison of work stoppages and their causes for the period 1920 to 1929 with the decade of the 1930s evidences dramatic differences. The 1920s, characterized by employee representation plans and union–management cooperation, showed a steady decline in work stoppages, whereas in the 1930s this trend was reversed. Of 14,256 work stoppages during the 1920s, 51 percent were over wages and hours of work, and 21 percent were the result of union organizing drives. From 1930 to 1934, the stoppages caused by union organizing attempts increased to 34 percent, but wages and hours still accounted for 51 percent. For the rest of the 1930s, however, and following the passage of the Wagner Act in 1935, a reversal occurred. Of the 14,290 stoppages from 1935 to 1939, 31 percent concerned wages and hours, and 53 percent were due to union organizing efforts.[7] To many scholars writing during this period, the answer to industrial conflict resided not in human-relations training per se, but in overcoming the conflicting interests and ideologies of management and labor, usually meaning organized workers. Industrial harmony would come through collective bargaining and the efforts of professional industrial-relations specialists.

In addition to bringing unions into the fold, the human-relations texts of the 1940s and early 1950s typically held that the feelings of people were more important than the logics of organizational charts, rules, and directives. Human relations were based on intangibles, not on hard, scientific investigation, and there were no final answers, that is, nothing positive or fixed in solutions to human problems. In

---

6. Examples of this way of thinking may be found in Eugene V. Schneider, *Industrial Sociology* (New York: McGraw-Hill, 1957); and Delbert C. Miller and William H. Form, *Industrial Sociology* (New York: Harper and Row, 1951). A historical perspective is provided by Bruce E. Kaufman, *The Rise and Decline of the Field of Industrial Relations in the United States* (Ithaca, NY: ILR Press, Cornell University, 1993), ch. 5.

7. U.S. Department of Commerce, Bureau of the Census, *Historical Statistics of the United States: Colonial Times to 1970* (Washington, DC: U.S. Government Printing Office, 1974), pt. 1, p. 179.

general, these early texts emphasized feelings, sentiments, and collaboration.[8] They were heuristic rather than specific or systematic, that is, the texts encouraged others to investigate and discover for themselves, rather than prescribing techniques. In brief, human relations ideas led to a revisionist period that considered organized labor. The Hawthorne findings were not antiunion per se, but reflected the limited influence of organized labor during the 1920s. Whether organized or not, it was the individual worker who was the center of attention for management's understanding and application of human-relations skills.

HAWTHORNE REVISITED

As noted in Chapter 13, no studies in the history of management thought have received so much publicity, been subjected to so many different interpretations, and been as widely praised and thoroughly criticized as those begun in 1924 at the former Hawthorne (Cicero, Illinois) Works of the Western Electric Company, the manufacturing arm of AT&T. The Hawthorne studies did not inspire any investigating commissions, congressional inquiries, or confrontations such as occurred at the Watertown Arsenal. Nevertheless, critics have had their day examining the assumptions, methods, and results of the Hawthorne studies. Among early critics, Henry A. Landsberger reviewed four separate areas of criticism: (1) the Hawthorne researchers' view of society as characterized by anomie, social disorganization, and conflict; (2) their acceptance of management's views of the worker and management's "willingness to manipulate workers for management's ends"; (3) their failure to recognize other alternatives for accommodating industrial conflict, such as collective bargaining; and (4) their specific failure to take unions into account as a method of building social solidarity.[9] Since Landsberger's review, other criticisms have been voiced. The following comments will update Landberger's review with respect to (1) the Hawthorne researchers' assumptions about an industrial civilization and (2) their methods and interpretation of study results.

THE PREMISES OF AN INDUSTRIAL CIVILIZATION

Mayo and Roethlisberger, the two principal Hawthorne researchers, both began with a view of industrial society characterized by *anomie* (from the Greek word meaning "without norms"). As noted in Chapter 13, Mayo viewed anomie as leading to social disorganization in personal lives and in communities and affected a general overall

---

8. Schuyler D. Hoslett, ed., *Human Factors in Management* (Parkville, MO: Park College Press, 1946), preface; and Burleigh B. Gardner and David G. Moore, *Human Relations in Industry* (Homewood, IL: Richard D. Irwin, 1955).

9. Henry A. Landsberger, *Hawthorne Revisited*, Cornell Studies in Industrial and Labor Relations, vol. 9 (Ithaca, NY: Cornell University, 1958), pp. 29–30.

sense of personal futility, defeat, and disillusionment. Mayo further believed that people, bound up in their "pessimistic reveries," needed identification with others and constructive outlets for their latent fears and frustrations. Industrial civilization, though making giant strides in technological progress, had created a cultural lag by diminishing the importance of collaborative social skills. Mayo's recommended response was to build from small group structures and to view people as embedded in a larger social system. Some have questioned these assumptions about the nature of industrial society and Mayo's view of society. For example, Bell charged that the Mayo and other Hawthorne researchers took the goals of production as given and viewed themselves as social engineers, who managed not people but a social system in an effort to "adjust" workers to their jobs so that the human equation matched the industrial equation. According to Bell, to think that contented workers were productive workers was to equate human behavior with "cow sociology," that is, the notion that contented cows give more milk. Counselors at Hawthorne, for which Bell used the colorful phrase "ambulatory confessors," were to be the new method of controlling humans. When employees exposed their innermost doubts and fears, they were more susceptible to managerial manipulation. The socially skilled supervisor could move from using authority to coerce desired behavior to psychological manipulation "as a means of exercising dominion."[10] Another facet of Bell's criticism was that the human-relations style of supervision was meant to replace efforts to improve workplace conditions. The social person, relieved of pessimistic reveries by the catharsis of counseling, would feel better and forget all other problems. Bell recalled a folktale to make this point:

> A peasant complains to his priest that his little hut is horribly overcrowded. The priest advises him to move his cow into the house, the next week to take in his sheep, and the next week his horse. The peasant now complains even more bitterly about his lot. Then the priest advises him to let out the cow, the next week the sheep, and the next week the horse. At the end the peasant gratefully thanks the priest for lightening his burdensome life.[11]

Another attack on premises came from those who maintained that the Hawthorne researchers presented a naive view of societal conflict. According to these critics, Mayo assumed that a commonality of interests could be found between labor and management, when in fact society was much more complex in terms of conflict between classes and interest groups. Some tensions and conflict were inevitable in every human situation, and some were even necessary. The goal should not be to eliminate conflict and tension but to provide healthy outlets for their

---

10. Daniel Bell, *Work and Its Discontents: The Cult of Efficiency in America* (Boston: Beacon Press, 1956), pp. 25–28.

11. Ibid., p. 26.

resolution.[12] Mayo's notion of a conflict-free state of equilibrium was a worthy goal, but too idealistic for the critics. The Hawthorne researchers, like Taylor and his followers, attracted faddists and saw perversions of their original intentions. These faddists often concluded that the goal of the human-relations movement was to keep everyone happy in a conflict-free state of equilibrium with resultant worker–management marital bliss. When bliss was attained, higher productivity was the corollary. As Fox put it:

> Among the guilty are the "human relationists" with an inadequate concept of human relations, who mistakenly preach participation, permissiveness, and democracy for all, and those employers who confuse popularity with managerial effectiveness and misinterpret the Golden Rule in dealing with their subordinates. . . . Many mistakenly regard it [human relations] as an "end" toward which the organization shall endeavor rather than as what it should be—a "means" for achieving the organization's primary service objectives.[13]

According to Fox, the regard for human relations as an end rather than a means misled managers to think that a conflict-free state and worker contentment would automatically lead to a company's success, when in fact the company might fail. Human relations could not be substituted for well-defined goals, policies, high standards of performance, and other managerial functions necessary for attainment of organizational goals.

Or, as McNair saw it, executives needed more than listening and human-relations skills to be effective in accomplishing organizational goals. In teaching human relations as a separate skill, McNair saw the dangers of compartmentalizing knowledge when it should be an integral part of all managerial development, whether in marketing, management, or whatever. In essence, McNair concluded, "It is not that the human relations concept is wrong; it is simply that we have blown it up too big and have placed too much emphasis on teaching human relations as such at the collegiate and early graduate level. . . . Let's treat people like people, but let's not make a big production of it."[14]

Knowles also called for a better mix of managerial skills but one that would avoid the evangelism and mysticism that so often characterized human-relations training. Evangelism represented a thesis that only human relations could "save Western Civilization from impending doom."[15] The doom theme was an old one, with roots in

12. Landsberger, *Hawthorne Revisited*, pp. 30–35.

13. William M. Fox, "When Human Relations May Succeed and the Company Fail," *California Management Review* 8 (Spring 1966), p. 19.

14. Malcolm P. McNair, "Thinking Ahead: What Price Human Relations?" *Harvard Business Review* 35 (March–April 1957), p. 39.

15. William H. Knowles, "Human Relations in Industry: Research and Concepts," *California Management Review* 1 (Fall 1958), p. 99.

the revulsion of the romantic philosophers at the perceived ravages of the Industrial Revolution. For social philosophers such as Durkheim (and Mayo), advancing technology and the specialization of labor destroyed social cohesiveness and yielded a loss of pride in work for humankind. Increased interpersonal competition and concern for material things destroyed primary groups, caused status anxiety, and created obsessive-compulsive reactions. The answer to impending doom was an evangelical zeal by human-relations advocates to downplay material acquisitiveness, rebuild primary groups, and teach people to love other people once more. The world could be saved by a sense of belonging, and people could once more find themselves by losing themselves in some larger entity. This mystical overtone, reflecting the Gestalt psychology of the totality, attributed to groups wisdom that could not be found in individuals. It was not the logic of efficiency but the illogic of sentiments that would save people from the brink. The moral uplift of scientific management had been efficiency; for the human-relations advocates, it was belonging and solidarity.

In brief, the challenges to the basic premises of Mayo and the other Hawthorne researchers were that they (1) accepted a premise that workers could be manipulated to fit into industrial equations that place production first; (2) assumed that cooperation and collaboration were natural and desirable and, thus, overlooked more complex issues in societal conflict; and (3) confused means and ends in assuming that the goals of contentment and happiness would lead to harmonious equilibrium and organizational success.

THE RESEARCH METHODS AND RESULTS

The modern management scholar is much more sophisticated in statistics and research methodology than the individuals who started the Hawthorne studies in 1924, than people like George Pennock who kept the studies alive, and than those who followed to interpret and disseminate the Hawthorne findings. Industrial research is full of cracks and crevices, and researchers are pinioned between the need for controlled laboratory experiments and the empirical reality of ongoing field studies. Seen in this light, the Hawthorne researchers were vulnerable to those critics who challenged their methods and findings. One vexing issue, seen in Chapter 13, dealt with financial incentives. A number of critics have challenged the Hawthorne findings on the question of employee motivation. Sykes contended that human-relations advocates believed that money did not motivate, when in fact the Hawthorne evidence led to just the opposite conclusion.[16]

Carey also concluded that it was completely erroneous for the Hawthorne researchers to decide that wages were not a variable and chastised them for their

---

16. A. J. M. Sykes, "Economic Interest and the Hawthorne Researchers," *Human Relations* 18 (August 1965), p. 253.

claims of "friendly supervision."[17] First, the researchers selected "cooperative" workers who were willing to participate in the studies. Second, two operators from the original relay-assembly group caused problems and "were removed for a lack of cooperation, which would have otherwise necessitated greatly increased disciplinary measures."[18] After reviewing production records, Carey concluded that output did not increase until the two operators were replaced with others that are "more cooperative." Was this friendly supervision or the use of negative sanctions to increase output? In summary, Carey maintained that the Hawthorne studies were consistent with the view of economic incentives and the use of a firm disciplinary hand to achieve higher output.

Franke and Kaul also doubted the Hawthorne results. Reanalyzing the Hawthorne data, they claimed that "three variables—managerial discipline, the economic adversity of the depression, and time set aside for rest" explained most (over 90 percent) of the variance in employee output.[19] Thus, Franke and Kaul concluded that it was not supervisory style or financial incentives, but the use of discipline, the economic milieu, and relief from fatigue that led to increased productivity.

In rebuttal, Schlaifer alleged that Franke and Kaul had improperly analyzed the Hawthorne data, that "managerial discipline" was not harsh because it involved merely sending two operators back to their original department. Schlaifer reanalyzed the Hawthorne data to show that passage of time alone was sufficient to explain increased productivity, which, according to Schlaifer, was "in all respects consistent with the conclusions reached by the original researchers."[20] Toelle confirmed Schlaifer's findings and added another criticism of Franke and Kaul's analysis—that they treated (statistically) the relay-assembly group as one group, when in fact it was two: the first group of five included the two operators who were later removed; the second group comprised the original three operators plus the two replacements. If the groups were analyzed, the passage of time alone accounted for over 91 percent of the total variance in their output.[21]

A cottage industry seems to have developed around reanalyzing the Hawthorne results. What did happen at Hawthorne? What can twenty-twenty hindsight tell

17. Alex Carey, "The Hawthorne Studies: A Radical Criticism," *American Sociological Review* 32 (June 1967), p. 410.

18. T. N. Whitehead, *The Industrial Worker*, vol. 1 (Cambridge, MA: Harvard University Press, 1938), p. 118. In *The Human Problems of an Industrial Civilization*, Mayo said they "dropped out" (p. 56); cf. Carey, p. 411.

19. Richard H. Franke and James D. Kaul, "The Hawthorne Experiments: First Statistical Interpretation," *American Sociological Review* 43 (October 1978), p. 636.

20. Robert Schlaifer, "The Relay Assembly Test Room: An Alternative Statistical Interpretation," *American Sociological Review* 45 (December 1980), p. 1005.

21. Richard Toelle, "Research Notes Concerning Franke and Kaul's Interpretation of the Hawthorne Experiments" (unpublished paper, University of Oklahoma, Norman, 1982).

about the methods and conclusions of the Hawthorne researchers? First, there is doubt that human-relations advocates, in general, neglected basic economic motives. True, the researchers did make statements that could be interpreted as a rejection of "the economic man" of classical economic theory. For example, Sykes quoted Roethlisberger and Dickson as concluding that "none of the results . . . [substantiated] the theory that the worker is primarily motivated by economic interest." Sykes did not quote the rest of that paragraph: "The evidence indicated that the efficacy of a wage incentive is so dependent on its relation to other factors that it is impossible to separate it out as a thing in itself having an independent effect."[22] Thus financial incentives should not be excluded from an explanation of increased output, but should be viewed as part of a larger, more complex situation. As Shepard commented, Roethlisberger and Dickson saw monetary incentives as "carriers of social value" rather than as absolute explanations of employee behavior and motivation.[23] In short, the "social man" supplemented, but did not supplant, "economic man."

Second, the "passage of time" interpretation suggests that trust is an important factor in building human relationships and that it took time for trust to develop between the Hawthorne researchers and study participants. Interviews with the surviving relay-group members and observer-supervisor Don Chipman indicated that this trust and friendly atmosphere did develop during the studies. In situations where the trust relationship did not develop, such as in the bank-wiring room, productivity did not increase.

Finally, there is what has become known as the "science versus advocacy" distinction.[24] It is difficult, if not impossible, for researchers to exclude personal values from their investigations. Thus Mayo, who had already formed conclusions about pessimistic reveries, found Hawthorne to be a clinical example of these industrial problems. In his view, socially skilled managers, counseling, and other appropriate manager behaviors would overcome the human problems of industry, relieve anomie, provide catharsis, and fulfill people's needs to feel important and recognized. If these conclusions went beyond the Hawthorne data, it was Mayo speaking as an advocate, not as a scientist. Gillespie claims that the Hawthorne findings were "manufactured" by Mayo and his colleagues because "in Mayo's hands, the Hawthorne experiments provided the experimental data on which he could base his political and social theory."[25] If Mayo and his colleagues became

---

22. Roethlisberger and Dickson, *Management and the Worker* (Cambridge, MA: Harvard University Press, 1939), pp. 575–576; a similar statement appears on p. 185.

23. Jon M. Shepard, "On Alex Carey's Radical Criticism of the Hawthorne Studies," *Academy of Management Journal* 14 (March 1971), pp. 23–32.

24. Lyle Yorks and David A. Whitsett, "Hawthorne, Topeka, and the Issue of Science versus Advocacy in Organizational Behavior," *Academy of Management Review* 10 (January 1985), pp. 21–30.

25. Richard Gillespie, *Manufacturing Knowledge: A History of the Hawthorne Experiments* (New York: Cambridge University Press, 1991), p. 181.

advocates, it was easy for others to follow, to perceive selectively, to tinge the intent of human relations with the flavor of a cult.

In Roethlisberger's memoirs, he noted that the Hawthorne findings "have been so often restated and misstated that it [*Management and the Worker*] has a life of its own . . . human relations was first and foremost an *investigatory and diagnostic tool*. It was not a model of what an organization should be; it was a conceptual scheme for finding out what the relations in a *particular organization at a particular place and time* were, not what they should be."[26] If Roethlisberger's plea sounds familiar, it should, because it reflects the theory-practice gap that has long plagued the management discipline. Anxious to get results or to appear up-to-date, practicing managers often grasp the straws of expediency or pick and choose the facts that are most consistent with their worldview. In a similar fashion, management theorists fall into the advocacy trap and promote interpretations that fit their preconceptions. Hawthorne, like scientific management, will be frequently revisited in our continuing attempt to disclose the past to more fully understand the present.

SUMMARY

The Hawthorne studies were an important step in advancing the idea of improving human relations in all types of organizations. An emphasis on human relations was not new, but rather a revival of humanist thinking that carried the prestige of Harvard into the classroom and the practice of management. Although Elton Mayo's name is closely connected with Hawthorne and the promotion of human relations, he was but one person in a cast of many who kept the human-relations movement going. If George Pennock, Clair Turner, and others had faltered, Mayo's efforts would have been for naught. After 1931, Mayo became more of an advocate and less of a scientific researcher, and the Hawthorne studies achieved a life of their own as expounded in Mayo's social philosophy for an industrial civilization. As the facts became clouded with ideological overtones, it became easier and easier to misperceive, misquote, and misinterpret what really happened at Hawthorne. In retrospect, certain conclusions stand out: (1) human relations was intended as a tool for understanding workplace behavior rather than as an end in itself; (2) trust was crucial in building the interpersonal relationships that provided for melding the interests of Hawthorne's management and workers; (3) financial incentives played a role in productivity gains, but these incentives could not explain all the Hawthorne results; and (4) care should be taken to avoid going beyond or selectively perceiving the Hawthorne data to advocate prior beliefs.

---

26. F. J. Roethlisberger, *The Elusive Phenomena*, ed. George F. F. Lombard (Boston: Division of Research, Graduate School of Business Administration, Harvard University, 1977), pp. 305, 311. The italics are Roethlisberger's.

CHAPTER 18

The Social Person Era in Retrospect

T he ideas of individuals in the context of their times form an interesting topic for historical discussion. Within its cultural context, scientific management as the gospel of efficiency found its basis in the economic necessities of large-scale corporate organizations, in the social sanction of individual achievement and the moral uplift of efficiency, and in political concern for national productivity and the conservation of resources. What can be said of the era from the advent of the Hawthorne experiments to the early 1950s? It has been postulated that management thought forms a more coherent picture when viewed in its changing cultural milieu of economic, technological, social, and political forces. Management is both a process in and a product of its environment. The era of the social person was an age of individual hopes dashed on the reefs of economic misfortune, of social collisions and maladies, and of political shifts heralding a transformation in traditional relationships. Though treated independently here, these cultural facets interacted to form the cultural milieu of the social person.

THE ECONOMIC ENVIRONMENT: FROM DEPRESSION TO PROSPERITY

The great crash of 1929 found the winter of its discontent in earlier days. The 1920s were prosperous, characterized by price stability, a doubling of industrial productivity, and a 55 percent rise in the real income of individuals.[1] Industrial efficiency and mass-production technology held costs down and increased the purchasing power of the dollar. But the end of this decade of prosperity came on October 29, 1929, known in U.S. economic history as Black Tuesday. On that day, the stock market crashed and wiped out $14 billion of

---

1. David N. Alloway, *Economic History of the United States* (New York: Monarch Press, 1966), p. 29.

stock values. By November 13, 1929, the stock values lost totaled $30 billion, and for more than a decade afterward life in the United States was substantially changed by that crash and the Great Depression. In 1929, 48 million persons were employed, and only about 1.5 million (3.2 percent) persons were unemployed. Using Bureau of Labor Statistics data, unemployment rose, peaking at 12,830,000 unemployed (24.9 percent) in 1933. The number of unemployed dropped below 8 million only once thereafter in that decade—in 1937, when the number was 7,700,000 (14.3 percent).[2] Using "Darby-corrected" figures, that is, following today's practice of counting government (federal and state) relief workers as employed, the late 1930s unemployment rates decline, suggesting that contracyclical work projects provided relief from unemployment. Darby-corrected unemployment rates in 1937 and 1940, for example, are more than 5 percent lower than the rates reported by the Bureau of Labor Statistics.[3] Despite federal and state attempts to create jobs, businesses failed, incomes dropped, homes were lost, family savings were wiped out, and worst of all, national morale was at an all-time low. Gone was the optimism of prosperity and promise; the old guideposts apparently had failed, as "rags to riches" became the midnight pumpkin. Recovery from the economic morass was painfully slow, but from the social and psychological viewpoint, it was even slower. Feeling inept in adjusting to economic deprivation, people turned to the government for relief.

ATTEMPTS AT ECONOMIC RECOVERY

In November 1929, President Herbert Hoover asked for labor–management cooperation in reducing the hours of work per worker per week rather than laying off workers. This work-sharing plan would reduce a worker's total weekly wages, but it was judged to be better than no work at all. To provide an example of how the hardship should be shared, Daniel Willard, president of the Baltimore and Ohio Railroad, reduced his own salary from $150,000 to $60,000 per year when the railroads were requesting a 10 percent wage reduction from the railway unions.[4]

In the early days of the Depression, labor and management responded positively to work sharing, and the workers had a better cushion against the decline. The cushion had been built out of the progressive labor policies of management during the 1920s; employer-sponsored thrift plans, for instance, gave the workers some savings to fall back on, and more workers than ever before owned their homes because they had been able to save for this investment. Employee stock ownership plans had been a mixed blessing: As stock prices soared in the late 1920s, some

---

2. U.S. Department of Commerce, Bureau of the Census, *Historical Statistics of the United States: Colonial Times to 1970* (Washington, DC: U.S. Govt. Printing Office, 1974), pt. 1, p. 135.

3. Michael R. Darby, "Three-and-a-Half Million U.S. Employees Have Been Mislaid: Or, an Explanation of Unemployment, 1934–1941," *Journal of Political Economy* 84 (1976), pp. 1–16.

4. John N. Ingham, *Biographical Dictionary of American Business Leaders*, 4 vols. (Westport, CT: Greenwood, 1983), pp. 1632–1634.

employees had sold their stock and entered into the general orgy of stock-market speculation only to regret this decision later; other employees had kept their stocks and had seen them plummet in 1929, also with regret. Intended to give the workers a share in the company, these plans proved that some modifications would have to be made in the future to protect these stocks from severe ups and downs. There was also a change in attitude about women working outside the home. From economic necessity, women were entering the labor force to try to bolster family income. Finally, evidence of the most dramatic difference between previous depressions and this one was that the workers used their automobiles to look for work. Rather than walking or hitchhiking from one employment line to another, the workers took their flivver. As the humorist Will Rogers noted: "We are the first nation in the history of the world to go to the poor house in an automobile."[5]

The new political regime of Franklin Roosevelt promised freedom from fear, from want, and from the other anxieties that bound the United States. Hoover had tried the Reconstruction Finance Corporation in 1932 as a scheme to pump government funds into private business enterprise. Roosevelt went much further with the New Economics of John Maynard Keynes. Keynesian economics was a challenge to the Protestant ethic dogma of thrift; Keynes held that savings withheld from consumption could lead to dislocation and underutilization of economic resources. Therefore, the federal government should intervene and prime the pump to stimulate consumption and provide for economic recovery. This strategy was designed to destroy the financial control of Wall Street, to link government assistance with industrial capitalism, to aid agriculture and small business in the Progressive tradition, and to increase benefits to the workers who formed the chief electorate.

Although Keynesians held that economic stimulation through government spending contributed to recovery, Friedman's supporters maintained that proper monetary action by the Federal Reserve could have prevented contraction of the money supply and allayed the Depression. Heilbroner concluded that World War II was the factor that really pulled the United States from its economic doldrums, not government pump priming.[6] Economists may fuss and fume about proper remedial actions, but in reality what might have been is a matter for other historians. The fact for management was that the government did become increasingly involved in economic life; though capitalism was preserved, with ownership and management remaining in the hands of private individuals, control and policy guidelines became more and more lodged in the hands of the dominant political party. The new concept

---

5. Will Rogers, in a radio broadcast, October 29, 1931. Cited in Richard M. Ketchum, *Will Rogers: His Life and Times* (New York: McGraw-Hill, 1973), p. 229.

6. Milton Friedman and Anna J. Schwartz, *The Great Contraction: 1929–1933* (Princeton, NJ: Princeton University Press, 1965); and Robert Heilbroner, *The Making of Economic Society* (Englewood Cliffs, NJ: Prentice Hall, 1962), p. 167. Although "Darby corrected" data indicate that federal and state projects lessened unemployment, a substantial decline in percentage of unemployed is not apparent until the onset of World War II. See Darby, p. 8.

of the corporation tied it more closely than ever before to the public interest, with concomitant calls for economic statesmanship on the part of business leaders and for public regulation of corporate concentrations of power.

THE GRASSROOTS AND BOTTOM-UP MOVEMENT

Economically it was to be the age of the farmer, the worker, the small-business owner, the unemployed, the hungry, and all others who were the waifs of economic misfortune. Somehow it was Wall Street and Big Business who were alleged to be the primary contributors to the ills of the economy. Economic policy was to come from the grass roots up to counterbalance the concentration of power in Big Business. People were concerned that there was an economic elite and sought to democratize industry, reduce power differentials, and restore the influence of those at the base of the pyramid. Boulding warned of the moral dilemma caused by the conflict between the industrial aristocracy of a hierarchy of authority and the democratic ideal of equality.[7] Following Berle and Means, James Burnham predicted that owners would delegate business operations to professional managers, who would take over the firm for their own selfish interests, dooming egalitarianism.[8] Burnham continued the long line of those who doubted the motives of those who managed other people's money.

For management scholars, this movement found its expression in bottom-up management, multiple management, and participative leadership. The Mayoists saw the root of economic problems in social problems. For them, people's anomie was made manifest in pessimistic reveries, in obsessive-compulsive behavior, in the turning inward of groups to protect themselves from management, and in the expressed needs of the workers to find social satisfaction on the job. Once social solidarity was restored, primary groups rebuilt, communications channels opened, and social and psychological needs fulfilled, people could turn their efforts to being more productive. Follett would certainly have supported this thesis in her call for depersonalizing authority, for integration, and for enlightened leadership. Barnard indicated that an organization had to be efficient in terms of satisfying individual and group needs to be effective in meeting organizational goals. Cooperation was a reciprocal process for both management and the worker. From the people's and organizations' point of view, industrial problems were to be solved by democratizing the workplace and thereby improving human relationships within the organization.

ORGANIZATION AS THE ANSWER

Whereas concern for organizational structures to rationalize resource utilization dominated the first three decades of the twentieth century, industrial attention in the

---

7. Kenneth E. Boulding, *The Organizational Revolution: A Study of the Ethics of Economic Organization* (New York: Harper and Row, 1953).

8. James Burnham, *The Managerial Revolution* (New York: John Day, 1941).

1930s was focused primarily on survival. For Mooney and Reiley, Gulick, Urwick, and others of the organizational bent, the solution resided in the proper, orderly arrangement of formal relationships. People, preferring order and certainty, would function better within a well-structured system, and management could better ensure economic survival through the practice of sound organizational principles. In their cultural context, those who focused on people and those who focused on the organization were attempting to cope with the massive social and industrial dislocations presented by the Depression.

Whereas the Depression delayed industrial growth, mobilization for the war effort created both technological and managerial advancements. Vast productive resources had been gathered, training within industry had created a deeper pool of employee talent, consumer products had been rationed, worker earnings were high, and the postwar era found the United States with a pent-up demand for products and services. With demand outrunning productive ability, the United States did not experience the anticipated postwar business slumps. The war had created new products, new technologies, new markets, and a more highly skilled, broader-based labor force. Management thought was in transition in this era, shifting from a production orientation to a top-management viewpoint that called for a changed executive role in balancing and coping with larger-scale enterprises and markets. Managers sought a broader, more flexible conceptual framework, a process of action on which they could build for a more dynamic interplay of inputs and outputs. The work of R. C. Davis was cited previously to show this transition in thought; Henri Fayol was awaiting rediscovery, and others were writing with more emphasis on top management.

The postwar period promised a new era of prosperity, expansion, and diversification. The regained prosperity and the further growth of industry were to create a new focus in evolving management thought.

SEEDS OF CHANGE: THE NEW TECHNOLOGIES

Writing in gloomy times, Joseph Schumpeter was pessimistic about the future of capitalism. Schumpeter saw the door to economic development in innovation and the entrepreneur. Economic development, according to Schumpeter, came from new products, new methods of production, new markets, using new raw materials, or a reorganization of a sector of the economy. Innovation "incessantly revolutionizes the economic structure *from within*, incessantly destroying the old one, incessantly creating a new [economic structure]."[9] "Creative Destruction," as he called this process, sometimes occurred in rushes with intervening quiet periods, but nevertheless was incessant. Contrary to John Maynard Keynes, who advocated

---

9. Joseph A. Schumpeter, *Capitalism, Socialism, and Democracy* (New York: Harper and Brothers, 1942), p. 83. Italics are Schumpeter's. See also Tim Kiessling, "Entrepreneurship and Innovation: Austrian School of Economics to Schumpeter to Drucker to Now," *Journal of Applied Management and Entrepreneurship* 9 (2004), pp. 80–92.

stimulating the demand side of the economic equation, Schumpeter favored the supply side to create the new technological forces for development. Schumpeter would have been less pessimistic if he had observed the new technologies, which were emerging in the late 1920s until the mid-1930s.

In transportation, automobiles were miraculous inventions, but were limited in their scope of travel by the lack of paved roads. Enabling legislation in 1926 provided for a "national" highway, Route 66, which began on the shores of Lake Michigan in Chicago, sloped westward across Illinois and Missouri, crossed the great plains and deserts of the southwest, and culminated on the shores of the Pacific Ocean at Santa Monica, California. All two thousand miles were paved by 1938, beginning the construction of a truly national highway system.

Only forty years since Orville Wright's inaugural machine powered flight, test pilot Chuck Yeager broke the sound barrier in a jet powered test plane, the X-1, at the speed of 640 miles per hour. Charles Lindbergh soloed the Atlantic Ocean in 1927; Igor Sikorsky perfected the first helicopter in 1943; German rockets were built for World War II but became useful in later years for exploring space and launching communication satellites; and radar was invented for air defense, then became vital for air traffic control and in the kitchen for microwave ovens. Travel was expedited by the emergence of aircraft manufacturers such as Boeing, Lockheed, and McDonnell Douglas, who supplied new airlines such as Delta, American, Pan American, and others. Piston-driven craft, then jet-powered ones, essentially removed long-distance passenger travel from the railroads.

In communication and entertainment, the radio was becoming a household staple. The first Rose Bowl football game was broadcast in 1927; by 1930, twelve million homes had a radio. RCA provided the first glimpse of television at the 1939 World's Fair in New York City; fifteen years later, one-half of the American homes wired for electricity had television sets; and someday, it was hoped, Ed Sullivan could be seen in color. Ampex invented the first video tape recorder, a three-quarter-inch band of ribbon to preserve television images, and reel-to-reel magnetic tape recorders could preserve voices and music. General Electric invented the first practical device for recording sound on film in 1926 for the movies, a growing industry. True to Schumpeter's notion, however, Western Electric made technological advances to replace GE as the leading provider of sound recording and reproducing equipment.

Alan Turing knew of Charles Babbage's calculating engines and turned this knowledge to developing a special-purpose computer that broke the German signal code during World War II. This was only the beginning of a revival of interest in computing machinery. Remington-Rand, IBM, Minneapolis-Honeywell, RCA, and others began making monster computers. The ENIAC, for example, had eighteen thousand vacuum tubes, weighed thirty tons, performed five thousand calculations per second, and required an air-conditioned room to avoid meltdowns. If anyone had suggested in 1950 that a computer could be held on one's lap, that person would have been considered daft. The miracle that transformed the computer industry was Bell Lab's transistor, invented in 1947, that would make vacuum tubes a relic, only to be replaced by later technological advances.

Another advance in the office was dry-copying, developed in 1937 by Chester Carlson, whose request for financing the venture was spurned by Western Union and IBM. It would be a decade before the Haloid Company took over the company that became Xerox. Some medical advances during this period from the mid-1920s to the 1950s were noteworthy: Jonas Salk developed the first polio vaccine; the World Health Organization announced that smallpox had been eradicated; and Alexander Fleming's serendipitous discovery of penicillin touched off research in antibiotics. Even further in the future, Rosalind Franklin and Maurice Wilkins' X-ray of the deoxyribonucleic acid (DNA) helix became relevant when James Watson and Francis Crick realized it had to be a double helix and a clue in understanding the building blocks of life.

We must not neglect the role the public sector, both state and federal, played in projects that provided employment and public works. One federal project, the atomic bomb, was the original weapon of mass destruction, but there remained hope for peaceable uses for atomic energy. The 1930s provided a building boom that no decade has surpassed: dams for hydroelectric power, irrigation, and recreation, such as the Hoover, Bonneville, Grand Coulee, and Shasta dams; and bridges, such as the George Washington Bridge, the Golden Gate Bridge, the San Francisco–Oakland spans, and the Huey P. Long Bridge over the Mississippi River at New Orleans.

The Tennessee Valley Authority (TVA) dams along the Tennessee River provided electricity for economic expansion and household use. Morris Cooke headed the Rural Electrification Authority, which brought electricity to nonurban dwellers. As electrical supplies increased, the home appliance industry blossomed: electric vacuum sweepers, food freezers, refrigerators, stoves, washing machines, clothes dryers, and a continuing host of domestic servants.

War and depression did not quell innovations and inventions. There was a lag as these products and services came into fruition in a booming postwar economy. Automobile production resumed after the war, gas was no longer rationed, and the new roads and bridges could carry the consumers to a revived marketplace.

THE SOCIAL ENVIRONMENT: THE SOCIAL ETHIC AND THE ORGANIZATION MAN

The economic temper of the times most certainly shaped the social values that came to dominate the period under analysis. Attitudes and aspirations are the founts of human strength, and the crushing economic burden for many was a violation of the previously held precepts of abundance and success for everyone. The 1920s had brought Madison Avenue to Peoria and Dubuque, and U.S. productivity and sales ability presaged more than a car in every garage and a chicken in every pot. What happened to social relationships and the assumptions that guided people's behavior in the troubled 1930s? Broadly viewed, two fairly distinct paths were reshaping social values: (1) a decline of the tenets of the Protestant ethic and the rise of a social ethic, and (2) a decline in the level of esteem given the business leader.

SHIFTING SOCIAL VALUES

The Lynds, in their famous study of the typical U.S. city of the late 1920s, found a split in values between the working-class person and the white-collar employee. For the worker, economic motives appeared to be primary: "This dominance of the dollar appears in the apparently growing tendency among younger working class men to swap a problematic future for immediate 'big money.'"[10] Whereas the workers measured social status by financial status and tended to hold to the traditional virtues of individualism, including a declining interest in belonging to organized labor, the business leaders represented a different outlook. The Lynds noted a decline in individualism among business leaders and a rapidly increasing conformity and need to belong. In their follow-up study, conducted during the Depression, the Lynds found that "the insecurity during the depression has brought with it greater insistence upon conformity and a sharpening of latent issues."[11] Workers were turning to unions for collective action, and business leaders combined to maintain the open shop; these "latent issues" sharpened class distinctions and engendered social bitterness. The economic catastrophe had brought about a shift in social values for the worker as well as for the manager.

After the crash, of what value were the time-tested Protestant ethic virtues of thrift and hard work? Apparently nearly everyone had been affected in some way, the loss of a job here, a savings account there, or a friend who had lost everything in the stock market. The new consciousness was that the disaster had struck the virtuous as well as the prodigal, the tycoon as well as the tyro, and the energetic as well as the feckless. People found their own fortunes intertwined with those of others in a pattern not subject to reason or justice.

> As time went on: ...there was a continuing disposition among Americans young and old to look with a cynical eye upon the old Horatio Alger formula for success; to be dubious about taking chances for ambition's sake; to look with a favorable eye upon a safe if unadventurous job, social insurance plans, pension plans.... They had learned from bitter experience to crave security.[12]

---

10. Robert S. Lynd and Helen M. Lynd, *Middletown: A Study in Contemporary American Culture* (New York: Harcourt Brace Jovanovich, 1929), p. 81.

11. Robert S. Lynd and Helen M. Lynd, *Middletown in Transition: A Study in Cultural Conflicts* (New York: Harcourt Brace Jovanovich, 1937), p. 427.

12. Frederick Lewis Allen, *The Big Change* (New York: Harper and Row, 1952), p. 132.

This craving for security, this turning inward of people to others who shared the same tribulations marked that generation as well as its children, and even perhaps another generation or more. Perhaps people have a natural reaction to form groups when faced with threatening circumstances—when these circumstances assume a major cultural impact, such as a depression, then people become more and more group beings. The presence of others must offer some psychological sense of relief under threatening or frustrating conditions. Erich Fromm also noted this desire of people to escape the loneliness of standing alone. In Fascist Germany, to escape this loneliness, people turned to an authoritarian regime that made their decisions for them and gave them a sense of identity, however evil it might have been. According to Fromm, this need to belong also pervaded U.S. industrial life, and an individual more frequently than not was willing to give up self to conform to the group. Whereas the Reformation and the Industrial Revolution drove people from the security of medieval life, enabling them to find freedom in the spiritual, political, and economic spheres of life, industrialization created new threats to these newfound freedoms.[13] People felt alone in the individualism of capitalism and the Protestant ethic and needed something larger than themselves—God, the Nation, the Company, the Union, or whatever—with which to identify and in which to lose the self. .

The conditions of the troubled 1930s must have compounded this desire for group affiliation as a source of strength. McClelland found in his studies that the need for achievement increased in the United States from 1800 to 1890 but decreased regularly after that date. The trade-off between the need for achievement and the need for affiliation took a dramatic shift between 1925 and 1950. In 1925, the need for affiliation was primarily a familial concern; by 1950, affiliation had become an alternative for economic achievement. By that time, people were showing more concern for affiliation and less concern for achievement.[14]

David Riesman and his associates furnished additional evidence for this era by noting the shift from the inner-directed to the other-directed person. The inner-directed person represented the era of laissez-faire capitalism and the Protestant ethic and emphasized self-direction and control. The other-directed person was characterized by high social mobility and by emphasis on consumption rather than production and on getting along and being accepted by others as the magic key to accomplishment. Riesman called the Taylor period "job-minded" and the other-directed person of the Mayoist era "people-minded."[15]

For Riesman, the shift from "invisible hand to glad hand" actually began about 1900. Up until that time, laissez-faire and the utilitarian philosophy of individualism

13. Erich Fromm, *Escape from Freedom* (New York: Holt, Rinehart and Winston, 1941), pp. 7–10.

14. David C. McClelland, *The Achieving Society* (New York: Van Nostrand Reinhold, 1961), pp. 166–167; and David C. McClelland, "Business Drive and National Achievement," *Harvard Business Review* 40, no. 4 (July–August, 1962), p. 110.

15. David Riesman, Nathan Glazer, and Reuel Denney, *The Lonely Crowd* (New Haven, CT: Yale University Press, 1950), pp. 19–40, 151.

had been the dominant force. After 1900, the closing of the frontier and restrictions on immigration began to bring less confidence in self-interest and more confidence in "groupism." The inner-directed person persisted for a period after 1900, but individuals began to feel lonelier in the crowd. People had to live where they were and were unable to move to a new frontier and use the West as a safety valve. Most of the pressing problems of production began to disappear, and the problems of consumption became more apparent. Inner-directed individuals had to cope with a niggardly material environment; the new problems that arose following relative conquest of a hostile material environment were problems with people. Entrepreneurs could deal face-to-face with most of their employees—they knew them, their problems, their likes and dislikes. Growth made industry less personal, replacing the personal style of the entrepreneur with the bureaucratic style of the administrator. The personal touch of leadership was gone, only to be replaced with the directives from the technically trained specialists required by an advanced industrial nation. Social competence, influencing others, began to assume a new importance, and technical skills were played down.

Individual loneliness in the organizational crowd led to the rise of groupism and the social person. Progressive education began fitting the child to the group in the socialization process, and the parental socialization function was replaced by peer socialization. Small groups became the panacea for individual adjustment to the loneliness of industrialization. Getting along and being accepted was the magic key to accomplishment. People were judged by what others thought of them, not what they thought of themselves. The psychological gyroscope of the inner-directed person began to waver and needed the helping North Star of others.

THE CONFUSION OF SOULS

Industrialization had not made people less religious, but they found they could more easily segment their lives into religious and nonreligious duties. When God smiled on the division of labor, thrift, and success, people found comfort in combining secular drives with spiritual grace. For one authority, the Depression caused a "confusion of souls" and a crisis for the Protestant ethic.[16] Self-help had failed, and the notion of the self-made person was rejected as the guarantee of economic order. Charity became a public rather than a private concern, and the power for the individual of the Protestant gospel of success fell into disfavor. From this confusion of souls and the debris of laissez-faire, the moral order needed to take on new dimensions. On the one hand, there was the "mind cure" approach offered by Norman Vincent Peale in *The Power of Positive Thinking;* on the other hand, the "getting along" cure of Dale Carnegie. Peale advised seeking the inner power of Christianity to cope

---

16. Donald Meyer, *The Positive Thinkers: A Study of the American Quest for Health, Wealth and Personal Power from Mary Baker Eddy to Norman Vincent Peale* (Garden City, NY: Doubleday, 1965), pp. 233–237.

with stress and crises. This turning inward helped people escape their loneliness and malaise by drawing on the greater power of God.

Dale Carnegie established the personal magnetism ethic in 1936 with *How to Win Friends and Influence People*.[17] This book, replete with how-tos of human relations, advised that the path to success resided in (1) making others feel important through a sincere appreciation of their efforts; (2) making a good first impression; (3) winning people to one's way of thinking by letting others do the talking and being sympathetic, with the caveat, "never tell a man he is wrong"; and (4) changing people by praising good traits and giving the offender the opportunity to save face. Although *Management and the Worker* had not been published at that time, the Carnegie formula bore a striking resemblance to the rules the Hawthorne researchers laid down for the counselors in the interviewing program. For Carnegie the way to success was through winning the cooperation of others.

These positive thinkers stressed two ways out of the confusion of souls: drawing on the inward power of faith and drawing personal strength by winning the cooperation of others through personal magnetism. The social ethic of the times downplayed achievement by individual striving because the Protestant ethic had run its course. This new ethic was others-oriented, with moral uplift coming not from efficiency but from getting along with others. For the most part, the social person was conceived, born, and nurtured in these trying times. People sought belonging in the group, solace in association, and fulfillment in affiliation.

THE SOCIAL ETHIC

A second facet of this attempt to understand the era of the social person must come through an analysis of the changing societal views toward the business leader. The business leader represented in fiction may or may not be a barometer of social esteem. Kavesh warned that the fictional business executive is generally portrayed in an unrealistic manner because of the writer's need to dramatize in contrasts and gain sympathy for characters.[18] Although it would be impossible to hold the business leader to blame for the Depression era's hard times, it was evident that the executive became through fictional writings the symbol of society's ills. The 1920s had canonized the business executive as hero and symbol of prosperity and the good life; when times turned turbulent, was it not fair to heap the blame on the "bankster" who robbed people of their homes and savings? Although such charges were not entirely just, the business leader as portrayed in fiction undoubtedly became a convenient focal point for public wrath.

---

17. Dale Carnegie, *How to Win Friends and Influence People* (New York: Simon and Schuster, 1936). Dale Carnegie was founder and president of the Dale Carnegie Institute of Effective Speaking and Human Relations.

18. Robert A. Kavesh, *Businessmen in Fiction* (Hanover, NH: Amos Tuck School of Business Administration, 1955), p. 11. An exception that he noted, however, was Cameron Hawley's *Executive Suite*.

Scott noted that the novels of the 1930s and 1940s were of disillusionment with individualism. Individualism became futile, and the novelists shifted the keynote to pleas for "humanitarianism and collectivism in the form of proletarian fiction."[19] The hero vanished to be replaced by a "they" who did things without reason and were beyond the control of mere mortals. "They" represented power, machines, and forces, not individual managers who could be held responsible. The corporation was a monster of oppression in which people and their lives were ground down piece by piece. Representative of this type of fiction were John Steinbeck's *Grapes of Wrath* and Nathaniel West's *A Cool Million*. For Steinbeck, it was not individuals but "they" who gave the migrants a hard time. West's Alger-type hero was caught between the contending forces of international bankers and world revolutionists, who slowly but surely destroyed his spirit of individualism and quest for free enterprise.

As the 1940s and 1950s unfolded, the manager completed the shift from the hero image by becoming more and more of an organization person. In conformity there was security, and the manager became a hero not because of "great or daring deeds, but because he tolerates grinding mediocrity and conformity."[20] In Marquand's *The Point of No Return*, Pawel's *From the Dark Tower*, and Sloan Wilson's *The Man in the Gray Flannel Suit,* the emphasis was on conformity and the futility of rebelling against the organization as a system. In Scott's thesis, novelists portrayed the shift from the individualistic ethic to the social ethic in management literature. The reference point in the social ethic was the group and the collective nature of people, a need for collaboration and social solidarity. This occurred not only in fiction, but also in the technical literature of Follett, the Mayoists, and others who were playing down the individual and reinforcing the group or collective nature of people.

The social ethic in fiction underscored conformity and depersonalization of the individual into a "they" and portrayed the corporation as a monster machine. In technical literature, the ideas of teamwork, participation, group decision making, small rather than large groups, committee management, the interweaving of responsibilities, and democratic leadership were abundant. Scott's striking parallel between the fictional and technical writers of the social person era is food for thought. Taken together with the low esteem of the business leader as symbol of the corporate monster, it was understandable that the Mayoists and others strove to remodel organizations from the bottom up to meet people's needs.

As the Mayoists sought to reform the organization through the group, the organizational engineers sought to reform the group through the organization. In their view, *Onward Industry!* was a rallying cry for coordinating and focusing

---

19. William G. Scott, *The Social Ethic in Management Literature* (Atlanta: Bureau of Business and Economic Research, Georgia State College of Business Administration, 1959), p. 47.

20. Ibid., p. 50.

group efforts, not to subdue individuals, but to release their potential. Principles were not only organizational rules, but also guides for human conduct toward a purpose. Mooney, Gulick, and others knew of people's need to belong and sought to fulfill that need through organizational definition. To these writers, it was through structure and not catharsis that people could release their potential.

Some critics held businesspeople and industrialization responsible for the ills of modern civilization. Intellectuals maintained an uneasy truce with industrial life by idealizing agriculture and denigrating business. Jeffersonian and Jacksonian democracies were examples of the praise of an agricultural, small-unit, family-owned, ideal base of society. To be big was to be bad, and to live in the city was a sign of decline. Why did intellectuals idealize agriculture and sully business? Kavesh perceptively noted that "the growth of cities is the history of business: the big businessman is the symbol of the city, and the city became the symbol of degradation."[21]

Baritz suggested that Mayo was one of those who was committed to an "Agrarian Golden Age":

> [Mayo] believed that there was a mystical but direct relationship between farming and truth. ... An industrial society, by definition, could not be virtuous, for as men lost sight of the soil they lost sight of nature; and in so doing, they lost sight of the meaning of life and fell victim to the glossy gadgetry of modern industrialism. For Mayo, then, the problem of the modern factory was clear; how to make possible the re-creation of Agrarian Virtue, Agrarian Loyalty, and the Agrarian Sense of Community in the twentieth century's world of skyscrapers and subways, of smoke and steam?[22]

For Mayo, the answer was to rebuild social solidarity and collaboration through the small group. Once the communal integrity of agrarian life was reestablished, people could cope with the evils of the city, the de-skilling of work, and the anomic depersonalization of factory routine. Perhaps the Australian Mayo was caught up in the American Jeffersonian–Jacksonian democratic tradition. He was certainly influenced by Durkheim, who saw evils in industrial life much as Robert Owen had seen them in the early nineteenth century. While Durkheim admonished people to love one another unselfishly and Owen tried to build communal centers, Mayo accepted the parameters of industrialization and tried to rebuild people's interpersonal relations within that framework. The gloom of the Depression, World War II, and the threat of the atomic bomb would certainly cause Mayo to harken back to an Agrarian Golden Age in which people could find solace in small groups.

---

21. Kavesh, *Businessmen in Fiction*, p. 6.

22. Loren Baritz, *The Servants of Power* (New York: John Wiley and Sons, 1960), p. 111.

THE POLITICAL ENVIRONMENT: FROM FDR TO EISENHOWER

While the economic cycle went from prosperity to depression and the social environment reflected increasing needs for affiliation, the political cycle saw an increasing role for government in individual and business affairs. No other period in U.S. history has seen a political administration begin in such dire times, endure for such a long period, and cope with as many adversities as the tenure of Franklin Delano Roosevelt. Roosevelt, scion of a patrician family, cousin of former president Theodore Roosevelt, and paralyzed from the waist down by polio, brought charisma to the people in the depths of their despair. In his acceptance speech for the Democratic nomination he said, "I pledge you, I pledge myself, to a New Deal for the American people." This became the slogan of the policies of the Roosevelt administration, which promised to reshuffle the old cards of society.

THE NEW DEAL

FDR saw as his first task restoring confidence to a stricken nation. The first hundred days (March 9 to June 16, 1933), in which a special session of Congress passed a multitude of bills enabling emergency legislation and giving Roosevelt tremendous political and economic powers, served as a landmark of the lengths to which he went. With his keynote phrase, "The only thing we have to fear is fear itself," Roosevelt hoped to instill in the people feelings of confidence and hope. In those first hundred days, legislation created such agencies as the Agricultural Adjustment Administration (AAA), Civilian Conservation Corps (CCC), Securities and Exchange Commission (SEC), Tennessee Valley Authority (TVA), the Home Owners Loan Corporation (HOLC), the Federal Relief Act, the Railway Reorganization Act, the Federal Deposit Insurance Corporation (FDIC), and the National Industrial Recovery Act (NIRA). The day of alphabet-soup government had been created.

Whereas some viewed the New Deal as "creeping socialism" and prophesied the end of capitalism, others saw the reforms as a necessary adjustment of capitalism while the motor was running to save free enterprise. Private enterprise endured, but in the process a lot of socialism did creep in. The restacking of the social, political, and economic order was to bring an activist role for government. Hands-off as a policy was defunct, and the role of government increased in an effort to shift the balance of power as people perceived it from the financiers of Wall Street to the farmers and organized labor. One of FDR's brain trusters, Rexford Tugwell, wrote that the idyllic days of business doing what it willed were gone and that the new leadership of industry must recognize unions, democratize industry by encouraging participation, and keep in mind the "greatest good for the greatest number."[23] Tugwell felt that

---

23. Rexford Guy Tugwell, *The Industrial Discipline* (New York: Columbia University Press, 1933), p. 158.

industry had failed to provide security for the working class and that government had to fill this vacuum. The response to this craving for security was made manifest in a number of pioneering legislative acts: The Social Security Act of 1935 sought to provide for old-age assistance; the Fair Labor Standards Act of 1938 established a guaranteed minimum hourly wage of twenty-five cents and a maximum workweek of forty-four hours for certain workers; and the Railroad Unemployment Insurance Act of 1938 was the first national unemployment protection. These and other acts marked the shift from Adam Smith's "invisible hand" to Riesman's "glad hand," from private to public charity, and from the Protestant ethic to the social ethic.

AUGMENTING THE POSITION OF LABOR

During the Roosevelt era, the role of federal power in relations between government and business achieved a dimension that even the Progressives had not envisioned. Of all the changes in the balance of power, none had a more immediate significance for management thought than the position of organized labor. The 1930s were witness to the first real successes at organizing workers on a national scale by industry rather than by craft. Previous attempts to organize workers, regardless of their skills, had met with limited success—the National Labor Union of William Sylvis and the Noble Order of the Knights of Labor, led by Terence V. Powderly, had been colossal failures in the nineteenth century. The American Federation of Labor (AFL), a federation of craft workers formed in 1886, and numerous railroad brotherhoods, beginning as early as 1863, had demonstrated that unions could be successful when the workers held common skills. There had been some successful industrial unions, such as those of the garment workers, milliners, and mine workers, but their memberships were typically small vis-à-vis the craft workers. For example, almost 60 percent of the union members in 1929 were in the building trades (919,000), which were predominantly AFL, and in transportation (892,000 members), mostly in the rail brotherhoods. The largest noncraft unions were in mining (271,000 members) and garments and millinery (218,000).[24]

The political climate of the 1930s created the opportunity for industrial union-ism to flourish. The first significant piece of legislation, the Federal Anti-Injunction Act of 1932, more commonly known as the Norris-LaGuardia Act, was passed during the Hoover administration. This act, for all practical purposes, completely divested federal courts of injunctive powers in cases growing out of a labor dispute. In 1933, Congress passed the National Industrial Recovery Act, the first in a series of New Deal enactments designed to lift the nation out of the Depression. Section 7a of the NIRA, in similar but stronger language than that of the Norris-LaGuardia Act, specifically guaranteed that "employees shall have the right to organize and bargain collectively through representatives of their own choosing . . . free from interference, restraint, or coercion of employers."

---

24. U.S. Dept. of Commerce, Bureau of the Census, *Historical Statistics of the United States*, pt. 1, p. 178.

When the NIRA was declared unconstitutional by the U.S. Supreme Court in 1935 (*United States v. A.L.A. Schechter Poultry Corporation*), Congress quickly replaced it with a law that was even more pleasing to organized labor. The National Labor Relations Act, more commonly known as the Wagner Act, was far more definitive in what it expected of collective bargaining than was the NIRA. The Wagner Act guaranteed employees "the right to self-organization, to form, join, or assist labor organization, to bargain collectively through representatives of their own choosing, and to engage in concerted activities for the purpose of collective bargaining." In addition, it placed specific restrictions on what management could do by specifying five unfair management practices. To implement these provisions, the act established a National Labor Relations Board (NLRB) that was granted the authority not only to issue cease-and-desist orders against employers violating the restrictions, but also to determine appropriate bargaining units and to conduct representation elections.

The NLRB was also instrumental in destroying employee representation plans such as the one described earlier at the Dennison Manufacturing Company. Organized labor bitterly opposed such plans, seeing them as "company unions" that hindered their organizing efforts. In 1938 the U.S. Supreme Court ruled that these plans were employer dominated and in violation of the National Labor Relations Act (*NLRB v. Pennsylvania Greyhound Lines*). Thus ended one era in labor–management relations, while yet another began.[25]

The passage of the Wagner Act marked a critical turning point in labor–management relations. John L. Lewis, president of the United Mine Workers, led the fight for industrial unionism within the AFL. Rebuffed, Lewis formed the Committee for Industrial Organization (known after 1938 as the Congress of Industrial Organizations), whose purpose was to bring workers into unions regardless of occupation or skill level. The newly founded CIO enjoyed almost instant success and was able to claim nearly 4 million members by 1937. While the CIO prospered, the AFL did too—almost doubling its membership from 2,126,000 in 1933 to 4,000,000 in 1939. With the legal climate created by the New Deal legislation, total union membership spurted from a turn-of-the-decade 3.5 million (6.8 percent of the total labor force) to almost 9 million (15.8 percent) by 1939.[26]

In retrospect, it is clear that labor gained substantial power during the 1930s through legislation. The New Deal labor policy was part of a power-equalization drive. This new role for the worker fitted into the calls for teamwork, cooperation, and democratization of the workplace through worker participation. During the war, all shoulders were turned to the wheels of industry, and differences were temporarily laid aside. Employment regulation, such as through the War Labor Board, prevailed

---

25. An excellent analysis is C. Ray Gullett and Edmund R. Gray, "The Impact of Employee Representation Plans upon the Development of Management Worker Relations in the United States," *Marquette Business Review* 20 (Fall 1976), pp. 85–101.

26. U.S. Dept. of Commerce, Bureau of the Census, *Historical Statistics of the United States*, pt. 1, p. 178.

and in general enhanced the power of labor. After the war, numerous strikes led to the public opinion that labor had too much power and resulted in the passage of the Labor-Management Relations Act (Taft-Hartley Act) in 1947. Although this act did bring about some redress in the balance of power, the employer was no longer able to pursue unilateral actions with respect to labor policies. In general, the whole environment of management had changed, not just with respect to labor, but also in all relations with government.

The political environment brought a new focus for management thought. The manager had a new set of variables with which to contend, new relationships to be managed, and a revised set of assumptions with respect to the balance of power. After World War II, the search for general management theory would emerge as a solution to the complexities of managing in the modern era.

Summary of Part III

Figure 18-1 depicts the developments in the era of the social person. Scientific management was the dominant theme in the 1920s, but sociologists and social psychologists introduced the ideas of behavioralism in management before the advent of the Hawthorne studies. Mary Follett, though chronologically belonging to the scientific-management era, served as an intellectual bridge to the emerging group approach to management's problems. The Hawthorne studies brought the human relations movement to the forefront and led to the theme of the social person. The heirs of Taylor and scientific management found new dimensions in organizations and in the job of the manager in coping with the new Zeitgeist of this era.

The Hawthorne research, beginning before but enduring through the early days of the Depression, brought about a shift in emphasis, including (1) an increased concern for people rather than production, (2) exhortations to play down the rigidity of organizational structures to increase the fulfillment of people's needs, (3) a view of financial incentives as but one part of a motivational picture, and (4) more concern for the illogic of sentiments rather than the logic of efficiency. The human relations movement and the research that followed reflected several basic themes that were products of the cultural environment: (1) calls for social, human skills rather than technical skills; (2) emphasis on rebuilding people's sense of belonging through groups and social solidarity to overcome the confusion of souls; and (3) concern for equalizing power through unions, through participative leadership, and by fusing the formal organization with the social system of the factory.

The post-Hawthorne research assumed two separate yet congenial approaches. The micro researchers established constructs for studying people in groups, postulated a hierarchy of human needs, and viewed leadership as a group-interactive-situational phenomenon. Along the macro branch, W. F. Whyte, George Homans, and E. W. Bakke sought to understand and bring about an integration of the formal system with the informal system of sentiments, activities, and

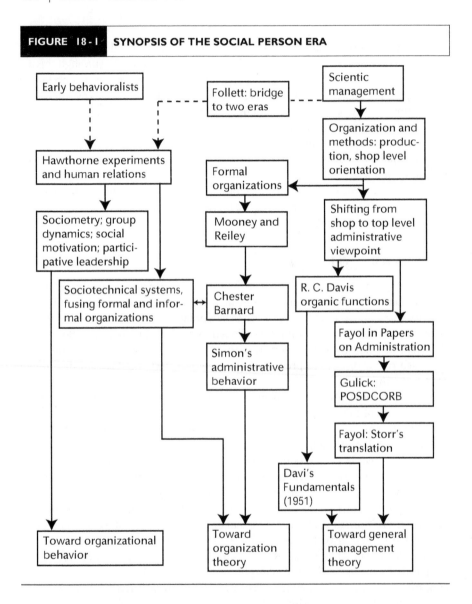

FIGURE 18-1 SYNOPSIS OF THE SOCIAL PERSON ERA

interactions. These paths would lead to organizational behavior and to organization theory in the modern era.

Chronologically parallel to these developments in the human relations movement, the descendants of scientific management offered different types of solutions to the vexing problems of the Depression. Largely shop-management oriented at the beginning, as in the case of R. C. Davis, this branch of management thought also began to assume new dimensions. On the one hand, organizational constructs were offered as one way out of the cultural impasse. Mooney and Reiley urged *Onward Industry!*, and Chester Barnard presented a sociological study of the formal organization and attempted to synthesize the formalists and the human relationists with his efficiency-effectiveness dichotomy. Alongside the organizational approach to management's problems, the elements of a top-level management viewpoint began to appear in the work of R. C. Davis, the translation of Fayol's process in the "Papers on Administration," and the efforts of Lyndall Urwick to synthesize principles of management.

Culturally, management thought was shaped by stressful times. The Great Depression, which began in 1929, was an economic, social, political, and psychological watershed. The United States was changing as the Depression brought new interpretations of the role of government in economics and in schemes to establish social floors and hedges against social maladies, such as unemployment. No longer would the virtues of self-help, thrift, and hard work be seen as the keys to success. If you were down, the government helped you up; if you lost your savings in a bank failure, the government would reimburse you; if you had saved nothing for retirement, the government would provide a pension, and so on through a host of social measures to take some of the sting out of life. Further economic growth was retarded by the Depression, and the postwar boom created a need for a top-level managerial viewpoint. The Protestant ethic and the need for achievement, though they did not disappear, declined in significance as people tried to find their identity and raison d'être through affiliation and getting along with others. People, not production, were the main concern of the manager. Politically, an increased role for government and the growth, power, and legal protection afforded organized labor introduced new variables to be considered in managerial decision making. It was out of this age of confusion, trauma, and diversity that the modern era in management thought was about to begin.

The Modern Era

N estled between the knowns of yesterday and the unknowns of tomorrow, the present is the twilight of history. It is difficult to put more recent developments in perspective; some years from now we will be able to look on this era with the aid of historical analysis, see the course of progress after it has evolved, and be better able to place this era in a clearer perspective. It is impossible to examine the full extent of modern management writings, for they are too diverse and too extensive for an in-depth analysis. Instead, it must suffice to sketch the broad outlines of evolving management thought and try to perceive major trends, shifts, and influences in the modern era.

Modern management thought is a product of past developments in four broad areas: general management theory and the study of managerial activities as extensions of the work of Henri Fayol; behavioral developments, which arose out of humanist, human relations, and other people-oriented approaches; evolving notions of the structure of organizations; and advances in quantitative and/or scientific problem-solving approaches as typified by Aristotle, Babbage, scientific management pioneers, and their heirs. In these four areas there is commonality as well as diversity. Each seeks to provide a better understanding of management, its purpose, functions, and scope; to facilitate better organizational performance and understanding of people; to balance the needs of the individual and of the organization as each seeks its objectives; and to relate the organization to its economic, technological, social, and political environment. Yet the means used by these areas of management to attain their common ends differ. This part first analyzes the search for integration in management theory for teaching, research, and practice. Next, it focuses on the organizational behavioralists and theorists to illustrate the search for harmony between the formal requirements of the organization and the informal dimensions of people in organizations. Management science and information systems are depicted as attempts to quantify variables in management decision making and to bring order from chaos through systematization and information technology. Finally, we will examine the renewed interest in business ethics, corporate social responsibility, and management thought in the cross-cultural, global arena. It is in this modern era that management thought experiences its adolescence of diversity and seeks the professional posture of maturity.

19 Management Theory and Practice

C hapter 16 described an increased concern for general management theory and postulated that this was necessitated by the further growth of organizations after World War II, the proliferation of staff specialists, increased government regulation, the spurt in the growth of unions, the need to apply the advanced technologies developed during World War II, and a greater awareness of relating management tasks to their more complex environment. If any one factor had to be chosen to explain the concern for a general theory, it would be the need for more broadly educated managers who could improve performance within the firm and understand the firm in its environmental setting. In this period management scholars turned from a shop-level management orientation to general management theory.

THE RENAISSANCE OF GENERAL MANAGEMENT

It is easy to forget just how ancient the practice of management is. Only within the last century did people begin to reflect systematically on their experiences and observations in an attempt to sort out and identify those managerial practices that seemed to work better than others. These better practices were called principles, but more closely resembled guides to managerial thought and action than scientific fact. The impetus for codifying these sound practices (principles) into a theory was the desire to transmit knowledge more coherently to those who aspired to become management practitioners. Those who tried first to describe management were primarily practitioners. The names of Owen, McCallum, Taylor, Gantt, Fayol, and Barnard are suggestive of these practitioners who tried to distill their experiences and observations for the use of others.

Henri Fayol was the first to propose a general theory of management. He defined theory as "a collection of principles, rules, methods, and procedures tried and checked by general experience."[1] Theory attempts to bring together what is known in a discipline, to explain the relationship between these knowns, and to predict likely outcomes given certain causes and relationships. Fayol's theory consisted of two parts: (1) the elements, which described what managers did—plan, organize, command, coordinate, and control; and (2) the principles, which were lighthouses, or guides, to how to manage. The purpose of theory, in Fayol's view, was to provide a body of knowledge that could be taught because managerial ability was crucial to organizational success. Fayol also noted, "There is nothing rigid or absolute in management affairs," so no theory is expected to endure for all time. As the history of management thought shows, new knowledge reshapes previously held theories. Principles and theories emerge, are tested, prove useful or not; the course of management thought is traced in this crucible of experience.

FAYOL'S INTELLECTUAL HEIRS

As seen earlier, Fayol's work received belated recognition. In the post–World War II environment, Constance Storrs's translation of Fayol's book was a timely contribution that touched off a renewal of interest in general management. Among the first efforts in the modern period was that of William H. Newman (1909–2002) of Columbia University. In 1948, Newman copyrighted materials as "Principles of Management," which were later published as *Administrative Action: The Technique of Organization and Management*.[2] Newman based his text on a study that had been conducted at the General Electric Company by Ralph Cordiner and Harold Smiddy. The GE study focused on successful company executives and what they did that made them outstanding managers. The conclusions were placed in a general management framework and used internally at GE to train younger managers. Based on this study, Newman defined administration as "the guidance, leadership, and control of the efforts of a group of individuals toward some common goal" and developed a logical process of administration as a separate intellectual activity. The elements in Newman's process were planning, organizing, assembling resources, directing, and controlling. For Newman, planning involved recognizing the need for action; investigating and analyzing; proposing action; and making a decision. The outcome of planning was the development of three broad groups of plans: (1) goals or objectives, which defined purposes of organizational effort and made integrated planning easier; (2) single-use plans, which established a course of action to "fit

---

1. Henri Fayol, *General and Industrial Management*, trans. Constance Storrs (London: Sir Isaac Pitman and Sons, 1949), p. 15.

2. William H. Newman, *Administrative Action: The Technique of Organization and Management* (Englewood Cliffs, NJ: Prentice Hall, 1951).

a specific situation and are 'used up' when the goal is reached"; and (3) standing plans, which endured over time and were changed only as the occasion warranted.

Though Newman's elements were closely akin to Fayol's, Newman recalled that he "was unacquainted" with Fayol when he wrote the book, but based it on the writings of Frederick Taylor, his Columbia colleague Luther Gulick, Chester Barnard, and Ralph C. Davis.[3] Newman also noted the importance of objectives in shaping the character of an organization. He felt that the basic objectives of the firm should define its place or niche in the industry, define its social philosophy as a business "citizen," and serve to establish the general managerial philosophy of the company.[4]

George R. Terry (1909–1979) was the first to call his book *Principles of Management*. Terry defined management as "the activity which plans, organizes, and controls the operations of the basic elements of men, materials, machines, methods, money, and markets, providing direction and coordination, and giving leadership to human efforts, so as to achieve the sought objectives of the enterprise."[5] Terry's elements included planning, organizing, directing, coordinating, controlling, and leading human efforts. Later, Terry combined the functions of directing and leading human efforts into an "actuating" function and stopped treating coordinating as a separate function. Terry defined a principle as "a fundamental statement providing a guide to action," and his principles, like Fayol's, were lighthouses to knowledge and not laws in a scientific sense.

In 1954, the Department of the Air Force prepared and distributed for training and operational purposes Air Force Manual 25-1, *The Management Process*.[6] This manual established five functions of management: planning, organizing, coordinating, directing, and controlling. Objectives, or missions in the military sense, were stressed a great deal as the foundation stone of all managerial activity. This governmental interest in the process was significant for two reasons: it signaled a further interest in the study of management as a separate activity, and it recognized the activity of management beyond the previous emphasis on the study of management in the business concern.

Harold D. Koontz (1908–1984) and Cyril O'Donnell (1900–1976) of the University of California at Los Angeles defined management as "the function of getting things done through others."[7] They furthered Fayol's ideas and sought to provide a conceptual framework for the orderly presentation of the principles

---

3. William H. Newman, "The Takeoff," in Arthur G. Bedeian, ed., *Management Laureates: A Collection of Autobiographical Essays*, vol. 2 (Greenwich, CT: JAI Press, 1993), p. 385.

4. William H. Newman, "Basic Objectives Which Shape the Character of the Company," *Journal of Business of the University of Chicago*, 26 (October 1953), pp. 211–223.

5. George R. Terry, *Principles of Management* (Homewood, IL: Richard D. Irwin, 1953), p. 3.

6. *The Management Process*, Air Force Manual 25-1 (Washington, DC: U.S. Government Printing Office, 1954).

7. Harold Koontz and Cyril O'Donnell, *Principles of Management: An Analysis of Managerial Functions* (New York: McGraw-Hill, 1955), pp. v, 3.

of management. According to Koontz and O'Donnell, managers were known by the work they performed, which was planning, organizing, staffing, directing, and controlling. These authors pointed out that, although some authorities maintained that these functions were exercised in the sequence given, in practice managers actually used all five simultaneously. They stressed that each of these functions contributed to organizational coordination. Coordination, however, was not a separate function itself but was the result of effective utilization of the five basic managerial functions. Koontz and O'Donnell offered a number of principles: in organizing, for example, "the principle of parity of authority and responsibility" and "the principle of unity of command"; in planning, "the principle of strategic factors"; and so on. The Koontz and O'Donnell text became an enduring, integral part of the search for a systematic body of management knowledge.

Fayol's heirs built on the elements and principles and saw the job of the manager as a cycle or process of functions. They attempted to identify management as a distinct intellectual activity and sought a generally accepted body of knowledge that could be distilled into principles and hence lead to a general theory of management. The applicability of planning, organizing, and controlling achieved the greatest agreement. Fayol's *diriger*, directing, was the term used by some; for others, supervising, leading, actuating, or whatever. Staffing, which Fayol had subsumed under organizing, achieved some recognition as a separate function, either explicitly for human resources or more generally under the heading of assembling resources. Coordination began and endured as a separate managerial function until 1954; afterward, it became an integral part of the entire process. As Fayol's heirs were advancing general management theory, studies of business education would lead to some changed ideas about what managers needed to know.

MANAGEMENT EDUCATION: CHALLENGES AND RESPONSES

In 1959, two reports on business education appeared that would have a significant impact on management education. Unlike Morris Cooke's study for the Carnegie Fund in 1910, these reports were taken more seriously by educators. The Ford Foundation commissioned and financed a study by Robert A. Gordon of the University of California at Berkeley and James E. Howell of Stanford University. The Carnegie Corporation sponsored a study by Frank C. Pierson of Swarthmore College.[8] Although the authors of the two reports exchanged information, they reached their conclusions independently; both reports were sharp indictments of the state of business education in the United States. Both reports noted that schools of business administration were in a state of turmoil in trying to define just what should

---

8. Robert A. Gordon and James E. Howell, *Higher Education for Business* (New York: Columbia University Press, 1959); and Frank C. Pierson, *The Education of American Businessmen: A Study of University-College Programs in Business Administration* (New York: McGraw-Hill, 1959).

be taught and how it should be done. By adhering to outworn precepts of education, the business schools were not preparing competent, imaginative, flexible managers for an ever-changing environment. Schools overemphasized vocationalism, which is training for specific jobs, rather than preparing broadly educated individuals for maximum future growth in a business career.

William H. Newman. Courtesy of Arthur G. Bedeian.

The path to preparing managers for the future resided in changing the content of the business school curriculum. More stress needed to be placed on a general education, especially in the humanities and the liberal arts; on expansion of requirements in mathematics; and on extended study in the behavioral and social sciences. For management education in particular, Gordon and Howell noted at least four different aspects of the field of organization and management: (1) managerial problem solving through the scientific method and quantitative analysis, (2) organization theory, (3) management principles, and (4) human relations.[9] Each played a part in the study of management, and the authors recommended some integration of these ideas into a sequence of courses that would better prepare future leaders, rather than leave them with a fragmented picture of the tasks of management.

To achieve this integration, Gordon and Howell recommended that business policy become a capstone course to pull together the various functions of business and provide the general management overview of the firm. The call for more mathematics and behavioral sciences led to an influx of more specialists from nonbusiness backgrounds into the business schools. What follows here is a look at how the Gordon and Howell report inspired the "management theory jungle."

THE "MANAGEMENT THEORY JUNGLE"

Although the Gordon and Howell report noted the diversity of approaches to the study of management, it was Harold Koontz who delineated the differences and applied the catchy label "management theory jungle."[10] Koontz noted six main groups, or schools, of management thought: the *management process school* "perceives management as a process of getting things done through and with people operating in organized groups." Often called the traditional or universalist approach, this school was originated by Henri Fayol and sought to identify and analyze the

---

9. Gordon and Howell, *Higher Education for Business*, pp. 179–182.

10. Based on Harold Koontz, "The Management Theory Jungle," *Journal of the Academy of Management* 4 (December 1961), pp. 182–186.

functions of the manager to form a bridge between management theory and practice. The *empirical school* identified management as the "study of experience" and used case analyses or Ernest Dale's "comparative approach" (in *The Great Organizers*) as vehicles for teaching and drawing generalizations about management. The basic premise of this school was that examining the successes and failures of managers would further the understanding of effective management techniques.

The *human behavior school*, variously called the human relations, leadership, or behavioral sciences approach, studied management as interpersonal relations because management was getting things done through people. This school used psychology and social psychology to concentrate on the people part of management. The *social system school* saw management as a system of cultural interrelationships in which various groups interacted and cooperated. The founder of this approach was Chester Barnard, and its adherents drew heavily from sociological theory. The *decision theory school* concentrated on analyzing and understanding who made decisions and how, as well as the entire process of selecting a course of action from various alternatives. Economic theory, and especially the theory of consumer choice, represented the intellectual foundations of this approach to management. The *mathematical school* viewed management as a "system of mathematical models and processes." This approach included the contributions of operations researchers, operations analysts, and management scientists, who thought that management or decision making could be "expressed in terms of mathematical symbols and relationships."

Koontz conceded that each school had something to offer to management theory, but suggested that the student of management *should not confuse content with tools*. For instance, the field of human behavior should not be judged the equivalent of the field of management, nor should a focus on decision making or mathematics be considered as encompassing the entire area of analysis. Preferably, each of these areas would provide insights and methods to aid managers in performing their tasks, and hence were tools and not schools. The causes of confusion and the "jungle warfare" between the various approaches were many: (1) "the semantics jungle" of varying uses and meanings of such terms as *organization, leadership, management, decision making*, and so on; (2) problems in defining management as a body of knowledge because the term was used under such varying circumstances and in a variety of situations; (3) the misunderstanding of principles through trying to disprove an entire framework of principles when one principle was violated in practice; and (4) the "inability or unwillingness of management theorists to understand each other" caused by professional walls of jargon between disciplines and personal and professional desires to protect one's own idea or cult. Koontz was hopeful that the jungle could be disentangled if these problems could be resolved.

In the hope of resolution, a symposium of distinguished teachers and practitioners of management met at the University of California at Los Angeles in 1962. The objective of the symposium was to convene a group of "eminent scholars with diverse research and analytical approaches to management, as well as perceptive and experienced practitioners of the managerial art from business, education, and government."[11] After much discussion and debate, Wilfred Brown capsulized much of the conference sentiment when he said, "Frankly, gentlemen, I have not been able to follow much of what's been said in the discussions."[12] As Koontz concluded, "Semantic confusion was evident throughout the discussions."[13] The UCLA symposium was indicative of the incoherent state of management theory. Perhaps the seminar topic should have been subtitled "Is Anybody Listening?" Academicians could understand only those from their own specialty, and practitioners could not understand academicians and vice versa.[14]

Some individuals remained optimistic that a general theory could be developed. William Frederick reflected this optimism in 1963 when he said: "Within perhaps five years—certainly not more than ten years hence—a general theory of management will be evolved, stated, and generally accepted in management circles."[15] Others, such as George Odiorne, posited that management situations were too complex for precise principles and propositions that would yield a sound theory. According to Odiorne: "The successful manager is too busy succeeding (existing) to spend much time on theories which would explain his success...this doesn't mean that principles aren't there [but that they]...haven't yet been uncovered nor described."[16] Thus managers had to decide and act, moving from one situation to another. Managers were action oriented, not reflective, and pragmatic, not theoretical, and the numerous and different managerial situations defied theorizing.

In brief, the pros and cons of various authors only illustrated what Koontz had said in the beginning—that a theory thicket existed. As the search continued, other ways of describing the job of the manager were offered.

OTHER VIEWS OF MANAGERIAL WORK

It was Henri Fayol who first began to reflect systematically on his experiences and observations in an attempt to sort out and identify what managers did and what managerial practices seemed to work better than others. Although Fayol's ideas provided the conceptual basis for teaching management, other researchers

---

11. Harold Koontz, ed., *Toward a Unified Theory of Management* (New York: McGraw-Hill, 1964), p. xi.

12. Ibid., p. 231. Brown was president of the Glacier Metal Co., Ltd., where a number of organizational systems studies were made.

13. Ibid., p. 238.

14. For an historical view of this problem, see Arthur G. Bedeian, "A Historical Review of Efforts in the Area of Management Semantics," *Academy of Management Journal* 17 (March 1974), pp. 101–114.

15. William C. Frederick, "The Next Development in Management Science: A General Theory," *Journal of the Academy of Management* 6 (September 1963), p. 212.

16. George S. Odiorne, "The Management Theory Jungle and the Existential Manager," *Academy of Management Journal* 9 (June 1966), p. 115.

used different methods to study the nature of managerial work. Henry Mintzberg observed five chief executives, studied their mail, and reported that their activities were sporadic, short-term copings rather than deliberative, analytical, and logical, as Fayol had suggested. Rather than engaging in the traditional functions (Fayol's elements), Mintzberg concluded that managers performed ten roles that could be described under three general categories: (1) interpersonal, (2) informational, and (3) decisional. The interpersonal role arose from the manager's formal authority and occurred when a manager dealt with others as a *figurehead, leader,* or *liaison.* The informational role involved the manager's receiving, storing, and sending information as a *monitor, disseminator,* or *spokesperson.* The decisional role involved making decisions about organizational activities as an *entrepreneur, disturbance handler, resource allocator,* or *negotiator.*[17] Although the notion of managers performing certain roles had an intuitive appeal, other investigations into Mintzberg's conclusions have not always been supportive of this approach. His findings were based on only five chief executives, and there is no reason to believe that this group represented typical managers. Further, the roles were based on observed behavior without asking the purpose of that activity.[18] Finally, there was no apparent connection between time spent in those roles and the effectiveness of task performance.[19]

Rosemary Stewart offered another view of the manager's job by examining: (1) demands—what had to be done in the job; (2) constraints—internal and external limits on what could be done; and (3) choices—areas in which different managers could do the job in different ways.[20] Using staffing as an example, the manager must find and select well-qualified people to perform the work (demands); constraints are placed on managers by company wage scales, the available supply of labor, general economic conditions, and laws with respect to employment practices; and a choice must be made about the person to select within the given constraints. Stewart's research was based on extensive interviews and observations of managers at work. Her efforts would go largely unnoticed, yet we will see that her findings could have added to upper echelons theory that will be discussed shortly.

John Kotter's study of general managers found that (1) successful managers could be very different in terms of personal characteristics and behaviors; (2) general managers thought of themselves as generalists, yet each had a very strong specialty that fitted the job demands; and (3) each had a detailed knowledge of the business

---

17. Henry Mintzberg, *The Nature of Managerial Work* (New York: Harper and Row, 1973).

18. Stephen J. Carroll and Dennis J. Gillen, "Are the Classical Management Functions Useful in Describing Managerial Work?" *Academy of Management Review* 12 (January 1987), pp. 38–51. See also Neil H. Snyder and Thomas L. Wheelen, "Managerial Roles: Mintzberg and the Management Process Theorists," in K. Chung, ed., *Academy of Management Proceedings* (San Diego, 1981), pp. 249–253.

19. Mark J. Martinko and William L. Gardner, "Beyond Structured Observation: Methodological Issues and New Directions," *Academy of Management Review* 10 (1988), pp. 676–695.

20. Rosemary Stewart, "A Model for Understanding Managerial Jobs and Behavior," *Academy of Management Review* 7 (January 1982), pp. 7–13.

and a network of relationships with other people in that business. Kotter concluded that "management at the [general manager] level looks far more like an art than a science [although] there are many regularities."[21] Kotter used the term *demands* to describe these regularities in the work of the fifteen general managers he observed in terms of setting goals, policies, and strategies; balancing the allocation of scarce resources; identifying problems and getting them under control; getting information and cooperation from others; motivating, controlling, appraising performance, and handling conflict; and overall, "getting things done (implementation) through a large and diverse group of people."[22] The activities that Kotter identified as demands and regularities bear a remarkable resemblance to the traditional management functions of planning, coordinating, staffing, controlling, and so forth. Kotter identified the differences in responsibilities and relationships that caused the job demands to vary, such as organizational size, age, performance level, culture, and product or market diversity; these irregular forces influenced the demands, but they did not eliminate them. Kotter concluded that managers developed agendas, sets of loosely connected plans, events, and tasks necessary to accomplish organizational objectives.

Kotter, but not Fayol or Stewart, would be included in another theory of general management that emerged in the mid-1980s. This theory stressed the importance of an organization's upper echelons, specifically its chief executive officer (CEO) and top management team, and how they were "reflections of the values and cognitive bases of powerful actors in the organization."[23] A firm is a reflection of its top managers, whose strategic choices and executive demands (as Stewart suggested) influence its success or failure. Understanding these forces and opportunities are key to understanding organizational strategy, strategic leadership, agency theory, executive compensation, and other important issues. This top management team, or upper echelons theory, led to extensive research in how much discretion, job demands, or both differed widely in various organizations or nations. For example, American top managers often had more discretion in their jobs than their counterparts in other nations.

Top managers do make a difference in how well a firm performs, in that their experiences and values influence their decisions, which may lead to good or not so good consequences. Hambrick stated this very succinctly: "They [top managers] matter for good or ill. They sometimes do smart things and sometimes do dumb things... but they do so as flawed human beings."[24] Hambrick and his

---

21. John P. Kotter, *The General Managers* (New York: Free Press, 1982), p. 9.

22. Ibid., p. 21.

23. Donald C. Hambrick and Phyllis A. Mason, "Upper Echelons: The Organization as a Reflection of Its Top Managers," *Academy of Management Review* 9 (April 1984), pp. 193–206. See also, Donald C. Hambrick, Sydney Finkelstein, and Ann C. Mooney, "Executive Job Demands: New Insights for Explaining Strategic Decisions and Leader Behaviors," *Academy of Management Review*, 30 (July 2005), pp. 472–491

24. Donald C. Hambrick, "Upper Echelons Theory: An Update," *Academy of Management Review* 32 (April 2007), p. 341.

colleagues did not study the elements of the managerial job or how top managers performed their roles, but established a theoretical framework for understanding top management's values, backgrounds, and personalities and how these and other factors influenced their decisions. This work prompted others to return to the study of general management theory. As Fayol intended, the stream of management theory continues to add to our understanding of organizations and people.

Carroll and Gillen concluded that Fayol's elements "still represent the most useful way of conceptualizing the manager's job, especially for management education . . . [because these elements] provide clear and discrete methods of classifying the thousands of activities that managers carry out and the techniques they use in terms of the functions they perform for the achievement of organizational goals."[25] Fells concluded that Fayol "stands the test of time," and Lamond compared Fayol and Mintzberg, concluding that Fayol's ideas are compatible with the roles approach to understanding managerial work.[26] After years of investigation, Rosemary Stewart concluded that "His [Fayol's] five-fold classification has been used, with minor modifications, to the present day."[27]

Although studies of managerial work differ in research methodology, terminology, or where these managers are in the organizational hierarchy, they are related ways of examining the same activity—that is, what managers do. To illustrate: in planning, managers receive, store, monitor, and disseminate information; they also make decisions about strategy and allocation of resources and initiate planned changes. In organizing, managers act as liaisons, establish relationships between people and activities, and make decisions about the placement and utilization of resources. The staffing job involves hiring, training, and appraising performance, as well as negotiating with labor unions. In leading, managers use their authority to accomplish goals; information and communication are two important parts of this job. Controlling is based on information about performance, decisions are made about corrective action, and coordination is essential. Stewart's work helped in understanding why some research finds managers doing similar activities (because of demands or constraints), whereas other studies find differences in managerial activity (choices). Kotter's agenda helped explain why observations of managers in action reveal behaviors that do not appear to fit some neat categories of planning and organizing—there are regularities in managerial work in terms of accomplishing goals. Upper echelon theory added an understanding of how top management's values, cognitions, and behaviors influenced decision making.

---

25. Carroll and Gillen, "Classical Management Functions," p. 48.

26. Michael J. Fells, "Fayol Stands the Test of Time," *Journal of Management History* 6 (2000), pp. 345–360; David A. Lamond, "Henry Mintzberg vs. Henri Fayol: Of Lighthouses, Cubists, and the Emperor's New Clothes," *Journal of Applied Management and Entrepreneurship* 8 (2003), pp. 5–23; and David A. Lamond, "A Matter of Style: Reconciling Henry and Henri." *Management Decision/Journal of Management History* 42 (2004), pp. 330–356.

27. Rosemary Stewart, *The Reality of Management*, 3rd ed. (Boston: Butterworth-Heineman, 1999), p. 4.

Indeed, Fayol's ideas have a remarkable longevity as a basic framework for understanding the manager's job. What often appears to be disagreement about the manager's job may in fact be only superficial and semantic. Although no general theory of management has emerged, research has enriched our understanding and has served to confirm that Fayol's ideas continue to be fundamentally sound. Although it is necessary to continue to build on Fayol's ideas to fit changing markets, technologies, and people, his work was seminal and enduring. Of course, the task of writing history is never done, for each day brings fresh ideas, new evidence, and variant ways of examining the tasks of the manager. It is difficult for modern scholars, so steeped in their own daily activities and so influenced by the current press of today's ideas, to sit back and put them in perspective. The zoom lens of history often leaves the near present slightly out of focus.

MANAGEMENT THEORY AND PRACTICE

Some two decades after first describing the management theory jungle, Harold Koontz revisited it and found it had expanded from six to eleven approaches. The operational school (a new name for the management process school) continued to study the managerial functions but had spawned two new schools, managerial roles and the contingency, or situational, approach. The empirical school remained, although its case-study approach had been influenced by both the role and situational approaches. The human behavior school had led to two new approaches: interpersonal behavior and group behavior. The social system approach had undergone the most proliferation, multiplying into the sociotechnical systems, cooperative social systems, and systems approaches. The decision theory and mathematical schools had remained the same, except for adding management science to the mathematical branch. Koontz noted, "The management theory jungle is still with us.... Perhaps the most effective way [out of the jungle] would be for leading managers to take a more active role in narrowing the widening gap . . . between professional practice and our college and university business [schools]."[28] Koontz also chastised his fellow academicians for failing to make their research more relevant to practice:

> I see too many academics forgetting what I think our job is in management, and that is to organize available knowledge; develop new knowledge, of course, but organize it in such a way that it can be useful to practicing managers to underpin management. I am surprised as I watch the literature, that some people are discovering what we've known for years. For example, some things like this: that

---

28. A discussion of each of these schools and a comparison of 1961 and 1980 views are presented in Harold Koontz, "The Management Theory Jungle Revisited," *Academy of Management Review* 5 (April 1980), pp. 175–187.

technology affects management organization. I found that out when I was in the airline industry a few years ago and I never thought it was anything very surprising. Another, that the actual managing depends on the situation.... I thought, my gosh, there must be something new there. Only to find, after spending a lot of time reading, that there wasn't anything, and I don't know any practicing manager who doesn't manage in light of the situation. I think we have to agree that management theory and science should underpin practice, otherwise why develop it?[29]

Thomas Peters and Robert Waterman, who were more closely associated with management consulting and practice, would agree with Koontz about theory and practice. They challenged academic theories, elevated the art of management over techniques and tools, and identified eight attributes that led to corporate excellence: (1) a bias for action rather than contemplation; (2) a closeness to customer needs in products and services; (3) the encouragement of autonomy and loose rather than close supervision; (4) an attitude toward employees that encouraged productivity and avoided a "we" versus "they" feeling; (5) a close touch with people in a technique called "management by walking (or wandering) around"; (6) a "sticking to knitting" philosophy by staying close to the business competencies, thus avoiding unrelated ventures; (7) a simple organizational structure and a lean staff; and (8) a control system that had simultaneous loose-tight properties of keeping on target but without stifling innovation.[30]

U.S. business responded to the Peters and Waterman book in legions, making it a best-seller. The book gave U.S. business managers a positive target, not an inferiority complex. Academicians, however, were not so enthralled. Carroll, for example, criticized Peters and Waterman's conceptual foundations and research methods as narrow, inadequate, and poorly developed.[31] Others suggested that "excellence" was too narrowly defined; that samples from *Fortune* 500 firms revealed other firms that outperformed the so-called well-managed ones; and that some of the excellence principles were contradictory (for example, was it possible to stick to the firm's "knitting" and still be innovative and entrepreneurial?).[32] The critics acknowledged,

---

29. Quoted by Ronald G. Greenwood in "Harold Koontz: A Reminiscence" (presented at the meetings of the Academy of Management, Boston, August 14, 1984).

30. Thomas J. Peters and Robert H. Waterman, Jr., *In Search of Excellence* (New York: Harper and Row, 1982). Within a decade, Tom Peters had recanted his yellow brick road to success: see Thomas J. Peters, *Liberation Management* (New York: Knopf, 1992). *Caveat lector.*

31. Daniel T. Carroll, "A Disappointing Search for Excellence," *Harvard Business Review* 61 (November–December 1983), pp. 78–88.

32. See Michael A. Hitt and R. Duane Ireland, "Peters and Waterman Revisited: The Unended Quest for Excellence," *Academy of Management Executive* 1 (May 1987), pp. 91–98; and Kenneth E. Aupperle, William Acar, and David E. Booth, "An Empirical Critique of *In Search of Excellence:* How Excellent Are the Excellent Companies?" *Journal of Management* 12 (1986), pp. 499–512.

however, that the excellence principles could be useful for improved practice but were not a magic formula for instant organizational success.

The quest for excellence in management practice is not new, as seen earlier in the work of Jackson Martindell of the American Institute of Management and Paul Holden and his Stanford colleagues. None of this pioneering work was acknowledged by Peters and Waterman, who relied solely on financial measures of success. If history provides a lesson in this case, it is that no one factor guarantees organizational success; that excellence is a composite of many things—sound strategies, action-oriented plans, clearly defined work relationships, sound leadership, motivated people, and balanced, flexible controls, to name a few of these important factors. No one technique or set of techniques will ensure successful performance; no one measure stands alone.

The American Assembly of Collegiate Schools of Business (currently the AACSB International) sponsored a three-year comprehensive study of management education that surveyed practitioners and academics. The authors of the report, Lyman Porter and Lawrence McKibbin, commented that faculty members required breadth to integrate problem finding and problem solving across various business functions. Yet many professors lacked relevant work experience and were too narrowly educated to "appreciate the complexities and subtleties of business."[33] Porter and McKibbin recommended that management educators should pay more attention to external factors, especially developments in international business; develop more ability to integrate across business functions; emphasize interpersonal and communication skills more; and develop PhDs who would have analytical sophistication as well as "the sharpened and broadened perspective of real world work experience."[34]

The Porter and McKibbin report had limited impact on management teaching and research. According to Pfeffer and Fong, management research continued to have little relevance to the practice of management, too much emphasis was placed on "hard" (quantitative) skills to the detriment of "soft" (people) skills, and "many full-time faculty have not practiced the profession or craft of management."[35] Others blamed the division of business education into disciplines, the tradition of academic freedom, and the academic reward system (publish or perish) for the intransigence of professors with respect to relevance in business education.[36] Institutional prestige and academic rewards and reputation continued to emphasize theory-based research with little or no regard for relevance to practice

---

33. Lyman Porter and Lawrence E. McKibbin, *Management Education and Development: Drift or Thrust into the 21st Century?* (New York: McGraw-Hill, 1988), p. 132.

34. Ibid., p. 327.

35. Jeffrey Pfeffer and Christina T. Fong, "The End of Business Schools? Less Success Than Meets the Eye," *Academy of Management Learning and Education* 1 (September 2002), p. 91.

36. Ben M. Oviatt and Warren D. Miller, "Irrelevance, Intransigence, and Business Professors." *Academy of Management Executive* 3 (1989), pp. 304–312.

or practicioners.[37] Longitudinal research found the theory-applications balance in management education had swings from one era to another: from applications to theory in the 1970s, theory to applications in the 1980s, with a return to an emphasis on theory in the early twenty-first century, "lending further credibility to the notion that theories are emphasized to a greater extent than the usefulness of those theories in practice at all [graduate and undergraduate] levels of our management instruction"[38]

What can be done to provide practicing managers with what they need to know and to equip students with knowledge and skills that will enhance their chances of career success? One avenue is "evidence- based learning," which means "translating principles based on the best evidence into organizational practices."[39] For example, Rousseau used Edwin Locke and Gary Latham's goal-setting theory (see Chapter 20) as an illustration of continued study and replications to find what works in motivation (i.e. the principles) and then applied this knowledge in exercises and activities that reinforce how these principles can be applied.

Another is to draw upon the work experiences of inquiring minds coupled with curious researchers to form practice-relevant knowledge and encourage more partnerships between academics and practitioners. "Management researchers must take the first step. Business firms have proven they can survive and be successful without depending on scholarly management research. Researchers must demonstrate how they can add value by offering ideas that improve organizational performance."[40] History is replete with examples of executives who, drawing on their experience, have contributed to understanding the management task. Examples would be Henri Fayol, James Worthy, Chester Barnard, William Newman, James D. Mooney and Alan C. Reiley and others who have practiced and written intelligently about management. To illustrate, James Worthy was a Vice President of Sears, Roebuck, served in the U.S. Commerce Department in both the Franklin D. Roosevelt and the Dwight D. Eisenhower administrations, worked with the Human Relations Group at the University of Chicago in some seminal studies of employee morale and organizational structure, became a Fellow of the Academy of Management, and was

---

37. Donald C. Hambrick, "The Field of Management's Devotion to Theory: Too Much of a Good Thing?" *Academy of Management Journal* 50 (December, 2006), pp. 1346–1352.

38. Daniel A. Wren, Jonathon R. B. Halbesleben, and M. Ronald Buckley, "The Theory-Applications Balance in Management Pedagogy: A Longitudinal Update, *Academy of Management Learning and Education* 6 (December 2007), p. 490.

39. Denise M. Rousseau, "Is There Such a Thing as 'Evidence-Based Management'?" *Academy of Management Review*, 31 (2) (2006), p. 256. See also Denise M. Rousseau and Sharon McCarthy, "Educating Managers from an Evidence-Based Perspective," *Academy of Management Learning and Education* 6 (April 2007), pp. 84–101.

40. Eric W. Ford, W. Jack Duncan, Arthur G. Bedeian, Peter M. Ginter, Matthew D. Rousculp, and Alice W. Adams, "Mitigating risks, visible hands, inevitable disasters: management research that matters to managers," *Academy of Management Executive* 19 (November 2005), pp. 24–37.

a professor at the Kellogg School of Management at Northwestern University.[41] James Worthy had a rare talent for combining theory and practice and provides an example of what is possible.

Theory can be a straitjacket that impedes curiosity and serendipitous encounters with possibilities that offer no previous theoretical stamp of approval. More theories are developed than tested, increasing our doubts about the relevance of theory development without a follow-through to test those propositions. Practice can be either exemplary or devoid of thought and reflection. Neither theory nor practice can stand alone, and we have much to learn to make better use of the talents and abilities that abound among those who study and those who practice management.

DRUCKER: THE GURU OF MANAGEMENT PRACTICE

Peter F. Drucker (1909–2005) titled his autobiography *Adventures of a Bystander,* which was far from describing Drucker's life and work.[42] He achieved prominence through his writings and consulting and made significant contributions to management practice. Largely influenced by the economist Joseph Schumpeter, a fellow Austrian, Drucker viewed society and business as in a constant state of creation, growth, stagnation, and decline. Abandonment of stagnating or declining ventures was also innovative, according to Drucker, because it freed resources for another innovative step. What kept an organization from failing was its ability to perform an entrepreneurial task of innovating—finding a new or better product, creating new customers or uses for old or new products, and making, pricing, or distributing the product or service in a more competitive way.

We will see Drucker's view on business strategy later in this chapter, but he stressed the need to define key areas for setting objectives and evaluating results. These were market standing (measured against the market potential); innovation (in products and services, or in improving how these products and services were made or delivered); productivity (a yardstick as a target for "constant improvement"); physical and financial resources (defining needs, planning, and acquiring); profitability (for rate of return on investment); manager performance and development (managing by objectives and self-control); worker performance and attitude (employee relations); and public responsibility (participating "responsibly in society").[43] In setting objectives, a firm had to ask the "right questions": What is our business? Who is our customer? What do our customers buy? What is the value of our business to our customers? What will our business be? And what

---

41. James C. Worthy, "From Practice to Theory: Odyssey of a Manager," in Arthur G. Bedeian (ed.), *Management Laureates,* 3 (1993), pp. 375–414. See also James C. Worthy, *Brushes with History: Recollections of a Many-Favored Life* (Evanston, IL: Thomson-Shore, 1998).

42. Peter F. Drucker, *Adventures of a Bystander* (New York: Harper Collins, 1991).

43. Peter F. Drucker, *The Practice of Management* (New York: Harper and Row, 1954), pp. 63–84.

should it be?[44] For Drucker, 90 percent of managerial work was generic, working with and through people to lead in such a manner that each individual is enabled to use his or her strengths and knowledge productively. The remaining 10 percent varied according to the mission, culture, history, and vocabulary of any specific type of organization, profit seeking as well as not for profit.[45]

Although many had written about the need for organizational objectives, Drucker was the first to publish the concept and coin the phrase "management by objectives" (MBO). According to Drucker, "A manager's job should be based on a task to be performed in order to attain the company's objectives. . . . [T]he manager should be directed and controlled by the objectives of performance rather than by his boss."[46] Management by objectives was to replace management by drive, and control was to be self-control rather than control from above. Knowing the objectives of a unit and those of an enterprise, managers could direct their own activities:

> The only principle that can do this is management by objectives and self-control. . . . It substitutes for control from outside the stricter, more exacting and more effective control from the inside. It motivates the manager to action not because somebody tells him to do something . . . but because the objective needs of his task demand it.[47]

Although Drucker got the credit for MBO, it was a General Electric Company executive, Harold Smiddy (1900–1978), who practiced the concept. Drucker was a friend of Smiddy and a consultant to GE; what Drucker did was conceptualize the label and write about it for a general audience. Drucker, with a show of intellectual modesty, maintained that MBO was not new, having been practiced earlier at GE by Smiddy, at GM by Alfred Sloan, and at Du Pont by Pierre du Pont and Donaldson Brown. Although this was an accurate analysis, Ronald Greenwood concluded, "it took Drucker to put it all together, think through the underlying philosophy, and then explain and advocate it in a form others could use."[48]

Drucker's emphasis on practice underscored the gap between academic research and the practice of management. Porter and McKibbin observed that "key managers and executives pay little or no attention to [business school] research or its findings."[49] Drucker agreed:

---

44. Ibid., pp. 49–61.

45. Peter F. Drucker, *Management Challenges for the 21st Century* (New York: Harper Business, 1999).

46. Drucker, *The Practice of Management,* p. 137.

47. Ibid.

48. Ronald G. Greenwood, "Management by Objectives: As Developed by Peter Drucker, Assisted by Harold Smiddy," *Academy of Management Review* 6 (April 1981), p. 230.

49. Porter and McKibbin, *Management Education,* p. 170.

Specialization is becoming an obstacle to the acquisition of knowledge and an even greater barrier to making it effective. Academia defines knowledge as what gets printed. But surely this is not knowledge; it is raw data. Knowledge is information that changes something or somebody—either by becoming grounds for action or by making an individual (or an institution) capable of different and more effective action.... Who or what is to blame for the obscurantism of the learned is beside the point. What matters is that the learning of the academic specialist is rapidly ceasing to be "knowledge." It is at best "erudition" and at its more common worst mere "data."[50]

As Zahra noted, Drucker's work is "grounded in management practice, [and] has also been able to communicate his ideas well to academics and leading executives."[51] Perhaps Drucker's work will help us leaven academic rigor and make it more managerially relevant; if not, knowledge will remain data and the theory-practice gap will continue.

FROM BUSINESS POLICY TO STRATEGIC MANAGEMENT

Management is an activity found in all organizations, for profit and not for profit. It seeks the optimum use of human and other resources in pursuit of objectives. Emphasis in this part of management theory and practice will be on business firms, especially on the task of top managers in integrating the functions of a firm into a coherent whole. In the late nineteenth century, Henry Towne asked engineers to think like economists; here the issue is to get economists to think like managers. This will involve recognizing once more the role of management in the firm, the notion of transaction costs, and issues within the firm such as governance and agency theory. Then we will see how early ideas of business policy evolved into strategic management. Strategic management is not the entire task of top management, but complements general management theory by helping us understand the process of management through formulating plans and policies that must be implemented by organizing, staffing, directing/monitoring, coordinating, and controlling.

MARKETS AND HIERARCHIES

As noted in previous chapters, Say, Marshall, and Atkinson viewed management as a factor of production that is capable of providing a competitive advantage in a firm's

---

50. Peter F. Drucker, *The New Realities* (New York: Harper and Row, 1989), pp. 251–252.

51. Shaker A. Zahra, "Introduction: Peter F. Drucker's *The Practice of Management*," *Academy of Management Executive* 17 (2003), p. 8.

performance. In the 1930s, Commons observed that a transaction was the smallest unit of economic analysis, and Ronald Coase asked what enables a business firm to perform better than the marketplace? (see Chapter 16). I find it surprising that we are still asking two-hundred-year-old questions about the economies to be gained by the efficient and thoughtful management of a business enterprise. Nevertheless, Coase's 1937 article marked the reemergence of this question, although his theory of the firm was occluded by Keynesian economics for many years. In his Nobel Laureate (1991) address, Coase commented on Adam Smith's example of barter being difficult because a match had to be found between the person who wanted to trade and the other person who had what the first party wanted as well as wanting what the first party had to offer.[52] Money reduced the difficulties of this transaction by exchange proceeding from a common denominator. In a similar fashion, "the operation of a market costs something and by forming an organisation and allowing some authority . . . to direct the resources, certain marketing costs are saved."[53] A firm is an alternative method of coordinating market factors and could, up to certain limits, be more efficient than the market. Coase did not try to explain why some firms were better at organizing and coordinating than others, but concluded that his point was to indicate the "dynamic factors" of a "moving equilibrium" influenced by how managers arrange the firm's factors of production. When we discuss strategic management, we will see how Coase opened the door for others to question why some firms are more competitive than others.

It would be a considerable length of time, however, before others pried open the "black box" of economics.[54] While engaged in theorizing and mathematical model building, many economists focused on the market for factors of production and the market for the sale of products to the neglect of the throughput within the firm. Oliver Williamson (1932–) inherited a great intellectual base for the development of his contributions. In his doctoral dissertation at the Carnegie Institute of Technology (today's Carnegie-Mellon University) he studied with Herbert Simon (who learned much from Chester Barnard) and Richard Cyert and James March of the so-called Carnegie School of decision making. Williamson's dissertation concerned managerial discretion in decision making, and he found that this exercise of discretionary authority often undermined the efficiency of the firm in contrast to the assumptions of classical economic theory.[55] Continuing his work, he found other flaws in classical economic theory, especially the neglect of the internal operations

---

52. Ronald H. Coase, "Prize Lecture [1991]," *Nobel Lectures, Economics,* 1991–1995 (Singapore: World Publishing, 2003).

53. R. H. Coase, "The Nature of the Firm," *Economica,* n.s., 4 (1937), pp. 386–405.

54. Kyle Bruce, "Economists' Evolving Conceptualism of Management: Opening the 'Black Box,'" in Gerard Griffin, ed., *Management Theory and Practice: Moving to a New Era* (South Yarra, Australia: Macmillan, 1998), pp. 15–36.

55. Oliver E. Williamson, "Managerial Discretion and Business Behavior," *American Economic Review* 53 (1963), pp. 1032–1057.

of the firm. By 1973 he was referring to the work of Coase and offered his initial statement of markets and hierarchies.[56]

Williamson referred to this view of the firm as the "new institutional economics" in contrast with previous work by institutionalists such as Commons. From history, Williamson saw the move from markets to "nonmarkets" based on two assumptions: one, bounded rationality; and two, opportunism, which was the "effort to realize individual gains through a lack of candor or honesty in transactions."[57] Williamson's bounded rationality evolved from Barnard's limits to "the power of choice" that was transformed in stages by Simon to factors that "bound the area of rationality" to "bounded rationality."[58] Firms were more efficient than markets because of the internalization of the costs of market transactions (Coase) and monitoring mechanisms existed to thwart (hopefully) opportunism. Williamson's interests in opportunism followed Barnard's "theory of opportunism" to a limited degree and would be deemed by Williamson as "self-interest seeking with guile," which was present in everyone because "even the less opportunistic have their price."[59] Williamson's extensions of the work of Coase and others created widespread interest in transaction-cost economics. The "visible hand" of Alfred Chandler would be found more efficient, in most cases, than the "invisible hand" of Adam Smith because of the actions of the managerial hierarchy.

GOVERNANCE AND AGENCY ISSUES

Assuming that the managerial hierarchy of a firm is more efficient, in most cases, than the market, then the actions of those who guide the conduct of the enterprise becomes a critical issue. In a corporation, the shareholders elect a group, the board of directors, who in turn are expected to employ others as managers to oversee day-to-day operations. In theory and legally, the board and these senior managers are *agents* of the shareholders and are expected to maximize the wealth of these investors. In practice, this is not always the case, raising the vital question of corporate governance.

We have discussed Adam Smith's concern about the intentions of those who managed "other peoples' money," but John Stuart Mill was not concerned, believing that the "zeal" of hired managers could be aligned by pecuniary incentives with

---

56. Oliver E. Williamson, "Markets and Hierarchies: Some Elementary Considerations," *American Economic Review* 63 (1973), pp. 316–325; and O. E. Williamson, *Markets and Hierarchies: Analysis and Antitrust Implication: A Study in the Economics of Internal Organization* (New York: Free Press, 1975).

57. Oliver E. Williamson, "Markets and Hierarchies," *American Economic Review* (1973), p. 317.

58. Chester I. Barnard, *The Functions of the Executive* (Cambridge, MA: Harvard University Press, 1938), p. 14; and Simon, *Administrative Behavior* (1945), pp. 39–41, 243–244. In the preface to the 1957 edition, Simon used "bounded rationality."

59. Oliver E. Williamson, "Transaction-Cost Economics: The Governance of Contractual Relations," *Journal of Law and Economics* 22 (1979), p. 234.

the interests of the shareholders. Others, such as Berle and Means, Burnham, and Robert Gordon, expressed concerns about the separation of ownership and control and the possibility of top managers becoming a self-perpetuating oligarchy. Peter Drucker advocated an outside board, that is, persons who had never served as full-time managers of the firm, and Myles Mace found that boards of directors were selected by the president of the firm, did what they were told, rarely evaluated the performance of a firm's president, and typically did not ask discerning questions.[60]

Michael Jensen has been a perennial critic of internal control systems as inadequate to the purposes of efficiency and value for the firm and its stakeholders. Except for external crises, Jensen judges boards as failures if they have allegiance to the president, if the board culture favors consensus and frowns on dissent, if presidents set the agendas and fail to fully disclose vital information, and if the possibility of legal liability leads board members to minimize risks and cover their backsides.[61]

The question of corporate governance is broad, touching on issues such as executive compensation, the size and inside/outside "mix" of a board, risk-taking and innovation, executive selection and development, and strategic leadership, to name a few of the vital components of effective governance. In addition, a related issue is *whose interests* are being served.

Experienced executives Chester Barnard and Henri Fayol were apparently well acquainted with opportunistic behavior among employees, managers, and workers alike. Barnard wrote of "self-abnegation" and willingness to cooperate; Fayol made the subordination of individual interest to the general interest one of his principles. In both instances, they were urging individuals to contribute their efforts to the enterprise rather than seeking personal gain. In neither case does this suggest self-sacrifice, but recognition of divergent interests. Agency theory, which may or may not be a theory, addresses opportunistic behavior, or as we saw Williamson define it, "self-interest seeking with guile." A staunch believer in agency theory would affirm that everyone, even the less opportunistic, has his or her price. This places a negative spin on what we would like to believe about our fellow human creatures, but too often we are shocked to find the price is but a few pieces of coin.

Because persons are expected to act opportunistically (except, of course, ourselves), the exercise of prudence in interpersonal and contractual relations is advised. Trust is elusive if we expect others to lie, cheat, shirk, and so on to take advantage of the situation. Means must be designed to reduce the occurrence of opportunistic behavior such as pay for performance, careful selection procedures, performance evaluation, close monitoring of behavior at work, or other methods of

60. Drucker, *The Practice of Management,* ch. 14; and Myles Mace, *Directors: Myth and Reality* (Boston: Harvard University, Graduate School of Business Administration, 1971), pp. 205–206.

61. Michael C. Jensen, "The Modern Industrial Revolution, Exit, and the Failure of Internal Control Systems," *Journal of Finance* 48 (1993), pp. 831–880.

tying the motives of individuals to the firm's goals. If errors are made in preventing opportunistic behavior, post hoc actions such as audits, random inspections, and information systems that provide some measure of effort are implemented. Hammurabi (circa 2250 B.C.E.) was no fool when he passed a law requiring receipts.

Governance and agency issues are intertwined with other management topics: organizing, human resource management, motivation, ethics, strategic leadership, interpersonal relations, communication and information systems, and control techniques, to touch the main connections. Historically, governance and agency are evergreen issues reflecting the assumptions we make about others and the actions we take.

MANAGEMENT AS AN INTEGRATING AND INNOVATING TASK

The preceding pages have provided glimpses of business policy and strategy as they evolved to provide a general management view of organizations. Wren positioned Henri Fayol as a strategist in his actions to revive Comambault as it was headed for bankruptcy.[62] Fayol stated:

> The responsibility of general management is to conduct the enterprise toward its objective by making optimum use of available resources. It [general management] is the executive authority, it draws up the plan of action, selects personnel, determines performance, ensures and controls the execution of all activities.[63]

In Britain, Alexander Hamilton Church wrote of the determination of policy and its implementation in the functions of the firm. A more recent executive's description of his job rhymes with Church: "You might ask, 'OK, you are a business person, what is it that you have to do?' I am of the school that says we have to do two things: we decide what to do, and we try to make it happen."[64] In the early twentieth century Arch Shaw (1876–1962) pioneered the study of business policy at Northwestern University and Harvard University in a course intended to integrate the business functions from a general management viewpoint. Individuals such as Edmund Learned and Roland Christensen were among those who followed in Shaw's path with Harvard's tradition of teaching by the case method.[65] Chester Barnard wrote of "strategic factors" and executive functions from his experience,

---

62. Daniel A. Wren, "Henri Fayol as Strategist: A Nineteenth Century Corporate Turnaround," *Management Decision* 39 (2001), pp. 475–487.

63. Fayol, *General and Industrial Management* (1949), pp. 60–61.

64. John A. Reed, "Citigroup's John Reed and Stanford's James March on Management Research and Practice," Anne S. Huff, ed., *Academy of Management Executive* 14 (2000), p. 57. Reed was CEO of Citigroup.

65. Edmund P. Learned, "Reflections on Leadership, Teaching, and Problem Solving Groups," in Arthur G. Bedeian, ed., *Management Laureates*, vol. 2 (Greenwich, CT: JAI Press, 1993), pp. 149–175.

and William Newman, author and coauthor of a long-lived policy text and cases, traced his roots to James O. McKinsey (1889–1937), founder of the consulting firm of that name and an advocate of budgets and planning and controlling aids. Newman focused on the role of objectives and policy as defining the character of the firm, its philosophy, and its role in society. Newman's experiences with James O. McKinsey and his approach to managing and consulting provided the framework for *Business Policies and Management*, published in 1940. Newman recalled, "This was the first textbook on business policy ever published (Richard D. Irwin did not start publishing collections of Harvard cases until after World War II)."[66] This text evolved through ten editions, the last one simply titled *Strategy*, and Newman's work bridged the years from general management as "policy" to general management as "strategy."

Peter Drucker, well known for his interest in general management, established the basic conceptual framework for business policy/strategy in 1954:

> The important decision, the decisions that really matter, are strategic. They involve either finding out what the situation is, or changing it, either finding out what the resources are or what they should be.... Anyone who is a manager has to make such strategic decisions, and the higher his level in the management hierarchy, the more of them he must make.

> Among these are all decisions on business objectives and on the means to achieve them.... The important and difficult job is never to find out the right answer, it is to find the right question.[67]

Drucker's ideas would inspire others. One possible influence appeared in the Gordon and Howell report, which proposed business policy as a capstone course to bring together the knowledge acquired in the various business functional areas. Another seminal work was Alfred Chandler's study of the influence of strategy on the organization structure of the firm. "Structure follows strategy" would become an enduring part of the literature.[68] As the study of policy and strategy evolved, it was rechristened many times. George Steiner, based on his experiences at Lockheed Aircraft, entitled his 1963 book *Managerial Long Range Planning* to describe the study of the role of management in preparing for the future.[69] Long-range planning seemed an inadequate phrase for describing the task of the general manager and the necessity of a broader view of the firm. General management was more than planning and involved integrating the parts into a whole.

---

66. William H. Newman, "The Takeoff," in Arthur G. Bedeian, ed., *Management Laureates*, vol. 2 (Greenwich, CT: JAI Press, 1993), pp. 375–397.

67. Drucker, *Practice of Management*, pp. 352–353.

68. Alfred D. Chandler, Jr., *Strategy and Structure* (Cambridge, MA: MIT Press, 1962).

69. George Steiner, "My Roads to Management Theory and Practice," in Arthur G. Bedeian, ed., *Management Laureates*, vol. 3 (Greenwich, CT: JAI Press, 1993), pp. 113–143.

H. Igor Ansoff (1918–2002) was employed by the Rand Corporation, and one of his projects involved the vulnerability of the U.S. Air Force's Strategic Air Command (SAC) to an attack from the USSR. After assisting in developing a strategy to cope with that possibility, which, incidentally, was never implemented, Ansoff joined the Corporate Planning Department of Lockheed Aircraft. Ansoff assisted in long-range planning and examining opportunities for Lockheed to diversify from the erratic defense industry business. In a later role in academia, Ansoff encountered the ideas of Peter Drucker and Alfred Chandler and formulated his notion of corporate strategy, which involved formulating objectives and strategy based on an analysis of opportunities in the environment.[70] The transition from business policy was apparent, and Dan Schendel and Charles Hofer renamed the field strategic management in 1979, calling for a "new" view of business policy and planning.[71] Thus policy was replaced (largely) by strategy, which originally was only a part of planning, which, in turn, was only part of management.

STRATEGY AND VIEWS OF THE FIRM

The format of combining industry notes with textbook cases that was developed at Harvard for business policy was in recognition of a need to place the strategy of a firm in its competitive environment. Michael Porter, a Harvard doctoral student, studied both in the business school and the economics department and recalled it as a "surreal experience" to find that both academic units were discussing industries in the study of business policy and industrial organization (I/O) economics. In Harvard's economics department, Edward Mason and Joe Bain had studied industry structure, the conduct of buyers and sellers, barriers to competition, and how these factors could affect performance and profitability.[72] "On the business school side of the [Charles] river, *ceteris paribus* [Latin for 'other things the same'] assumptions don't work. Managers must consider everything. I [Porter] concluded that we needed frameworks rather than models."[73]

The result was a frame-breaking set of ideas that would dominate the strategic management field for nearly a decade. Porter's position was that profitability of a firm was a function of "five forces" of industry structure: threat of entry of new

---

70. H. Igor Ansoff, "A Profile in Intellectual Growth," in Arthur G. Bedeian, ed., *Management Laureates*, vol. 3 (Greenwich, CT: JAI Press, 1993), pp. 1–39; see also H. Igor Ansoff, *Corporate Strategy* (New York: McGraw-Hill, 1965).

71. Dan E. Schendel and Charles W. Hofer, *Strategic Management: A New View of Business Policy and Planning* (Boston: Little, Brown, 1979).

72. Edward S. Mason, "Price and Production Policies of Large-Scale Enterprise," *American Economic Review* 29 (1939), pp. 61–74; Joe S. Bain, *Barriers to New Competition* (Cambridge, MA: Harvard University Press, 1956); and Richard E. Caves, *American Industry: Structure, Conduct, Performance* (Englewood Cliffs, NJ: Prentice Hall, 1967).

73. Nicholas Argyres and Anita M. McGahan, "An Interview with Michael Porter," *Academy of Management Executive* 16 (2002), p. 43.

competitors, the bargaining power of suppliers, the threat of product substitutes, the bargaining power of buyers, and rivalry among existing competitors. Barriers to entry and the stage of an industry's life cycle were other industry characteristics that shaped a firm's ability to compete effectively. The external factors in an industry structure shaped how firms could seek to create and sustain a competitive edge. Firms must consider their "value chain," that is, how activities were organized and linked to produce, deliver, and support products for the ultimate user. Porter suggested "generic" strategies: low cost, product differentiation, or a focus option that cut across these two where perhaps cost was less of a factor or where both cost and differentiation had to be considered.[74] Porter made a significant impact on strategic management and changed its direction from case study to industry studies regarding structure, conduct, and performance.

The next path to finding ideas about strategic management received belated recognition. Whereas Coase had asked why the firm exists, the next step was to ask why firms differ. The American-born and -educated British economist Edith Penrose (1914–1996) observed, "It is the heterogeneity, and not the homogeneity, of the productive services available or potentially available from its resources that give each firm its unique character".[75] The key words were *heterogeneity* and *resources*, and Penrose was pushing economic thinking out of its "black box" by reintroducing the role of management:

> A firm is more than an administrative unit; it is also a collection of productive resources the disposal of which between uses and over time is determined by administrative decision . . . management tries to make the best use of the resources available . . . [and] a firm is essentially a pool of resources the utilization of which is organized in an administrative framework.[76]

Penrose noted that a firm's resources were "inherited," that is, left over from prior decisions about location, special-purpose equipment, the pool of managerial talent, and "indivisible" resources, all of which posed potential limits to decisions about the future direction of the firm. "Knowledge" was also inherited, as it resided in the experience, education, and intuition of the firm's human resource. She used the word *entrepreneurs* to describe persons within the firm who could provide changes in knowledge about products, markets, technology, administrative processes, and opportunities. Rather than being closed to change, the firm could grow by "changes

---

74. Michael E. Porter, *Competitive Strategy: Techniques for Analyzing Industries and Competitors* (New York: Free Press, 1980); and Michael E. Porter, *Competitive Advantage: Creating and Sustaining Superior Performance* (New York: Free Press, 1985).

75. Edith Tilton Penrose, *The Theory of the Growth of the Firm* (New York: John Wiley and Sons, 1959), p. 75.

76. Ibid., pp. 5, 24, 149.

in the knowledge possessed."[77] Penrose's ideas would lie fallow for some years, but she had offered seminal ideas on two subsequent views of the firm.

In the 1960s, the Harvard business policy group began using SWOT analysis in the classroom. An acronym for "strengths" and "weaknesses" (within the firm) and "opportunities" and "threats" (outside the firm), SWOT was promoted by a conference held at Harvard to spread this concept in practice and academia.[78] Harvard's Kenneth Andrews credited Howard Stevenson's doctoral thesis at Harvard as "making the first formal study of management practice in defining corporate strengths and weaknesses as part of the strategic planning process."[79] Andrews added "distinctive competence" from Philip Selznick's definition as the organizational "character . . . [that] reflects the general orientation of personnel, the flexibility of the organizational forms, and the nature of the institutional environment to which the organization is committed."[80] SWOT became a neat framework for case study and discussion that incorporated specifics about the firm and information about the industry setting. For learning and teaching, the bottom line was to match strengths and distinctive competencies to opportunities while minimizing weaknesses and threats.

After a quarter century of neglect, Penrose's ideas found a home in an article by Wernerfelt in which he proposed a resource-based view (RBV) of the firm. This RBV was an extension of Andrews, Caves, and Porter's I/O economics and strategy by proposing that a firm's resources could be thought of as strengths and weaknesses. Tied to Porter's five forces framework, Wernerfelt proposed that *"what a firm wants is to create a situation where its own resource position directly or indirectly makes it more difficult for others to catch up."*[81] One example is being a "first mover" in an industry. Mergers and acquisitions, according to Wernerfelt, provided the opportunity to acquire or sell bundles of resources. Built on Harvard's policy group perspective, Penrose's work enabled the firm to think in terms of resources rather than products.

In retrospect, Wernerfelt admitted that the resource-based view did not gain credence until some years later in the work of Prahalad and Hamel and their paper on the "core competencies" of the firm.[82] For these authors, the previously used

---

77. Ibid., pp. 76–80.

78. Pankaj Ghemawat, "Competition and Business Strategy in Historical Perspective," *Business History Review* 76 (2002), pp. 41–42.

79. Kenneth R. Andrews, *The Concept of Corporate Strategy* (Homewood, IL: Dow-Jones Irwin, 1971), p. 90. See also Howard H. Stevenson, *Defining Corporate Strengths and Weaknesses* (doctoral thesis, Harvard Business School, 1969).

80. Philip Selznick, *Leadership in Administration* (Evanston, IL: Row, Peterson, 1957), pp. 42, 50–51.

81. Birger Wernerfelt, "A Resource-Based View of the Firm," *Strategic Management Journal* 5 (1984), p. 173. Italics are in the original.

82. Birger Wernerfelt, "A Resource-Based View of the Firm: Ten Years After," *Strategic Management Journal* 16 (1995), p. 171; and C. K. Prahalad and Gary Hamel, "The Core Competence of the Corporation," *Harvard Business Review* 68 (May–June 1990), pp. 79–91.

notion of the strategic business unit (SBU) focused on products rather than on the core competencies that drove current success and, in the long run, spawned new products. Rumelt had noted bundles of connected and unique resources earlier, but core competencies had a more stimulating effect.[83] Barney made competencies more specific as means to gaining a competitive advantage by suggesting the firm's resources should be rare, valuable, not easily imitated, and nonsubstitutable.[84]

In addition to stimulating numerous articles and books about the resource-based view of the firm, Penrose spawned another—the knowledge-based view: "There is no reason to assume that the new knowledge and services will be useful only in the firm's existing products; on the contrary, they may . . . provide a foundation which will give the firm an advantage in some entirely new area."[85] She cited Schumpeter on numerous occasions regarding the role of innovation through discovery. Rather than being bound by existing knowledge, the firm also has the ability to extend its capabilities through learning. Others have built on Penrose's idea and recognize the firm as a potential storehouse of knowledge.[86] At this writing, it is difficult to reach conclusions about the potency of the knowledge-based view (KBV) of the firm. For instance, how do organizations learn? Perhaps this is a property of individuals who operate at the organizational interface with customers, scientists, financiers, labor leaders, community representatives, or at conferences where communities of practice share experience. In the year before her death, Penrose said, "History matters"; where we go from here depends on the cumulative growth of knowledge from the past through the present in understanding the goal-directed firm for the future.[87]

STRATEGIC LEADERSHIP AND EVOLUTIONARY DYNAMICS

Robert Hoskisson and his colleagues have studied the swinging pendulum of strategic management theory.[88] From case studies, to I/O economics and industry studies, and to resource and knowledge-based theories of the firm, there has been an ebb and flow from specific to more encompassing theories about the firm in its quest for a competitive advantage. Whereas we can skim only a portion of a rich literature,

---

83. Richard Rumelt, "Toward a Strategic Theory of the Firm," in R. B. Lamb, ed., *Competitive Strategic Management*, (Englewood Cliffs, NJ: Prentice Hall, 1984), pp. 556–570.

84. Jay B. Barney, "Firm Resources and Sustained Competitive Advantage, *Journal of Management* 17 (1991), pp. 771–792.

85. Penrose, *Theory of the Growth of the Firm*, p. 115.

86. Bruce Kogut and Udo Zander, "Knowledge of the Firm, Combinative Capabilities, and the Replication of Technology," *Organization Science* 3 (1992) pp. 383–397.

87. Penrose, foreword to *Theory of the Growth of the Firm* (3rd ed., 1995), p. xiii.

88. Robert E. Hoskisson, Michael A. Hitt, William P. Wan, and Daphne Yiu, "Theory and Research in Strategic Management: Swings of a Pendulum," *Journal of Management* 25 (1999), pp. 417–456.

certain nagging questions continue: What roles does the general manager play in defining purpose, securing cooperation, coordinating efforts, anticipating change, and making the best possible use of the firm's resources? Once core competencies are defined and a strategy is selected, how long can these capabilities persist and sustain the firm's prosperity? Can an organization learn and change in the appropriate manner? Does a firm's past, its inheritances, lead to rigidities that narrow its discretionary scope? It has been said that history matters and management makes a difference. Those are our next topics.

In observing business practice, reading the literature of ongoing economic activity, or studying business policy/strategy cases, it is not apparent that business firms' actions can be explained by economic theories of maximizing or optimizing profits. Nelson and Winter have offered a view of "evolutionary economics" based on the writings of individuals such as Penrose and Schumpeter emphasizing a firm's ability to generate and gain competitive advantages over time through innovation.[89] A firm's inherited resources, even though they may be valuable, nonsubstitutable, and so on, may not sustain these rare capabilities over the long term. Core competencies may evaporate as new technologies emerge—for instance, the decline of Baldwin Locomotive and its advantages in steam power, which were eclipsed by General Motor's diesel-fueled locomotives. A firm's resources, both human and physical, are specific and not easily deployed to other uses, thus limiting the choices the firm has for growth. Child emphasized the role of managerial discretion in making strategic choices, but these too would be bounded by the previous paths chosen and decisions taken.[90]

The theory of evolutionary economics suggests that a firm must develop dynamic capabilities that will enable it to transform itself as competitive conditions change. This transformation comes through invention or innovation, discovering the new or finding and developing new and better ways of doing business in the Schumpeterian tradition. Transaction-cost economics, according to Lazonick, fails because it does not account for innovation and the means necessary for the enterprise to change. Transaction costs may explain why a firm is often superior to the market in allocating resources, but it does not provide for confronting change and adjusting to meet evolving circumstances.

In contrast to transaction-cost economics, Lazonick proposed organizational learning to "unbound" rationality and to provide organizational incentives to overcome "opportunism."[91] This places him in line with the work of Penrose and Chandler. For Chandler, "learned skills and knowledge [are] company-specific and

---

89. Richard R. Nelson and Sidney G. Winter, *An Evolutionary Theory of Economic Change* (Cambridge, MA: Harvard University Press, 1982).

90. John Child, "Organisational Structure, Environment and Performance: The Role of Strategic Choice," *Sociology* 6 (1972), pp. 1–22.

91. William Lazonick, "Innovative Enterprise and Historical Transformation," *Enterprise and Society* 3 (2002), pp. 13–16.

industry-specific."[92] These skills came from capabilities learned while exploiting economies of scale and capabilities developed from exploiting economies of scope. Penrose also emphasized learning, with the human resources playing a critical role in innovation. Similar to Chandler and Penrose, the dynamic capabilities position is

> ... the firm's ability to integrate, build, and reconfigure internal and external competencies to address rapidly changing environments. Dynamic capabilities thus reflect an organization's ability to achieve new and innovative forms of competitive advantage, given path dependencies and market positions.[93]

The evolutionary/dynamic capabilities theories place responsibility for change and learning squarely on the firm and its human resources. Management can make a difference in a firm's performance and particularly in the ability of its general managers to implement incentives, policies, and actions necessary to achieve change through learning.[94] The general management task has been labeled "strategic leadership" to distinguish the work of chief executives, directors, and other top level executives from leadership activities of lower-level managers. Examining what top managers do is not a recent topic: Fayol and Barnard were chief executive officers and are part of our intellectual heritage; Newman, Stewart, Kotter, Mintzberg, Drucker, and others have been keen observers of executives in action. Indeed, we may have a better understanding of top management than we have of lower levels of the hierarchy. The word *strategy* comes from the Greek verb *strategs,* meaning "to plan the destruction of one's enemies through effective use of resources."[95] Thus, from the military analogy of a general who led an army and made the necessary plans to accomplish the goal of defeating an enemy, it was not a far leap to executives who developed objectives and the plans (strategic and operational) to compete effectively in the marketplace.

Similar to Rosemary Stewart's findings regarding managerial "choices," Hambrick and Finkelstein used the phrase "managerial discretion" to refer to the latitude of action allowed the chief executive.[96] This discretionary authority may be wide or narrow, and research continues to probe this topic. That an organization is a

---

92. Alfred D. Chandler, Jr., "Organizational Capabilities and the Economic History of the Industrial Enterprise," *Journal of Economic Perspectives* 6 (1992), pp. 79–100.

93. David J. Teece, Gary Pisano, and Amy Shuen, "Dynamic Capabilities and Strategic Management," *Strategic Management Journal* 18 (1997), p. 524.

94. For example, Richard Langlois and Nicolai Foss, "Capabilities and Governance: The Rebirth of Production in the Theory of Economic Organization," *Kyklos* 52 (1999), pp. 201–218.

95. Jeffrey Bracker, "The Historical Development of the Strategic Management Concept," *Academy of Management Review* 5 (1980), pp. 219–224.

96. Donald C. Hambrick and Sydney Finkelstein, "Managerial Discretion: A Bridge Between Polar Views of Organizations," in Larry L. Cummings and Barry M. Staw, eds., *Research in Organizational Behavior* (Greenwich, Conn.: JAI Press, 1987), pp. 369–406.

"reflection of its top managers" indicates the ability of a chief executive and a top management group to establish the firm's character.[97] The historian is reminded in this case of Chester Barnard's observation that the moral tone of an organization starts at the top. In this concept of strategic leadership is found the bridge to general management theory, to the legacy of Fayol, Barnard, and others who have studied the tasks of top-level managers. *Strategos,* the art of generalship, is found in business chief executives "who must also have a strategy—a central, integrated, externally oriented concept of how the business will achieve its objectives."[98] From our understanding of dynamic capabilities, this generalship must achieve present objectives and set the stage for the learning that leads to innovation and renewal.

Viewed from the historian's position, strategic management is part of general management theory and has the potential to add to an understanding of people and organizations. Implementation is often shortchanged in the strategy literature, and the art of business policy is often estranged from the search for science in strategy. Wisdom and experience cannot be taught, but management theory provides the foundation for the practice of its application in cases, simulations, and other devices.

The factor that makes management different from other business functions, such as marketing, production, accounting, finance, and information systems, is that management pulls these functions together and aligns the firm as a whole with its economic, technological, social, and political environment. Strategic management is but one part of this model and must recognize its integrative, capstone role and how it relates to the body of management thought.

Summary

The reawakening of general management theory occurred as organizations grew and diversified and with the need for more broadly educated general managers. Fayol's heirs took his elements and formed them into the management process approach. Studies of business education led to a reformulation of curricula, identified the diversity that Koontz turned into the jungle, and brought non-business-trained specialists into the business schools. In the practice of management, managers looked to practices found in "excellent" organizations, but this did not provide the quick fix expected, nor did excellence prove so easy to measure and implement. Koontz revisited the jungle and found more schools, more diversity, in management. The Porter and McKibbin report updated the state of management education and criticized the drift that academia was experiencing. Drucker, too, emphasized the need to improve the practice of management and condemned the often sterile

---

97. Donald C. Hambrick and Phyllis A. Mason, "Upper Echelons: The Organization as a Reflection of its Top Managers," *Academy of Management Review* 9 (1984), pp. 193–206.

98. Albert A. Cannella, Jr., "Upper Echelons: Donald Hambrick on Executives and Strategy," *Academy of Management Executive* 15 (2001), p. 49.

research output of the academics. Fayol "stood the test of time," and his general management theory provided a framework for the transition to business policy and strategic management.

In accord with general management, we saw the need for economists to think like managers and a resurgence of interest in industrial/organizational economics. Firms, rather than markets, were deemed the better allocator of resources, but the visible hand of a firm's managerial hierarchy posed governance and agency issues. This view of the firm turned our attention to general management as an integrating activity in business policy as it evolved to strategic management. The literature on strategic management is vast and has its critics. Quinn, for example, argued that real-world managers developed strategies "incrementally, as a series of . . . somewhat fragmented decisions."[99] One of the greatest military strategists of all times, Von Moltke, agreed: "No plan of operations can look with any certainty beyond the first meeting with the . . . enemy [because one cannot control] the independent will of the opposing commander."[100] Mintzberg sees strategies "emerging" rather than leaping into full bloom in the mind of the strategist.[101] When the Academy of Management's membership was examined, the business policy/strategy folk clustered with those in the organization and management theory group.[102] This connection suggests a compatibility between general management theory and strategic leadership as firms are led to invent and innovate in a dynamic fashion to survive.

---

99. James Brian Quinn, *Strategies for Change: Logical Incrementalism* (Homewood, IL: Richard D. Irwin, 1980), p. 204.

100. Von Moltke, quoted in Jeffrey Record, "The Fortunes of War," *Harper's*, April 1980, p. 19.

101. Henry Mintzberg, *The Rise and Fall of Strategic Planning* (New York: Free Press, 1994), pp. 24–27.

102. Jone Pearce, "President's Message: A Bifurcated Academy?" *Academy of Management News* 34 (March, 2003), p. 1.

CHAPTER 20

Organizational Behavior and Organization Theory

P art III introduced the Hawthorne studies and their influence on the analysis of human relations; followed by the emerging ideas of Mary Follett and Chester Barnard, which paved the way for further studies of leadership, motivation, group dynamics, and early thinking about organization theory. Modern management theory makes more sense when viewed in the light of its foundations. This search for a productive and satisfactory relationship between people and organizations continues in this chapter as the modern quest to resolve the conflict between the logic of efficiency and the logic of sentiments, the search to meet human needs while fulfilling an organization's objectives.

PEOPLE AND ORGANIZATIONS

Until the 1960s, those trained in the social sciences, such as psychologists, sociologists, and anthropologists, had little impact on general management theory. True, there had been Münsterberg, Whiting Williams, Mayo, Lewin, and others, but their ideas remained in the shadow of the intellectual offspring of Fayol and Taylor. The Gordon and Howell report in 1959 on business education, however, was to change that posture with a clarion call for more social studies in business school curricula: "Of all the subjects which he might undertake formally, none is more appropriate for the businessman-to-be than human behavior. . . . The very nature of the firm and of the manager's role in the firm suggests that every person anticipating a responsible position in a modern business enterprise needs a substantial amount of knowledge about human behavior."[1] The behavioral sciences were seen as one way in which more powerful analytical and conceptual tools could be put to use in handling the problems of human behavior.

---

1. Robert Gordon and James Howell, *Higher Education for Business* (New York: Columbia University Press, 1959), p. 166.

439

The social scientists were trained differently in research methods, drew on a different body of literature, often had little experience in business practice, and gradually they found business schools receptive to their ideas and methods. By the turn of the millennium, Miner noted that almost one-half (47 percent) of those individuals in Bedeian's laureate series came from psychology, and another 32 percent came from other disciplines outside the business school.[2] The laureates were selected by Bedeian as "the management discipline's most distinguished" and influential scholars.[3] The Academy of Management, the leading international association of teachers and researchers in management, also demonstrated a split between those whose professional interests clustered around organizational behavior and those whose interests clustered around business policy and strategy.[4] Modern management theory is a bridge between these two groups, but it was clear that those from the social sciences brought substantial influence to management teaching and research in the years following the Gordon and Howell report.

HUMAN RELATIONS
AND ORGANIZATIONAL BEHAVIOR

Nowhere was the evolution in human relations thought more evident than in the work of Arizona State University professor Keith Davis (1918–2002), "Mr. Human Relations." In 1957, Davis defined human relations in the workplace as "the integration of people into a work situation in a way that motivates them to work together productively, cooperatively, and with economic, psychological, and social satisfaction."[5] This marked the beginning of a modern view of human relations that was more empirically rigorous in understanding organizational behavior and philosophically broader in understanding people's interactions in a more complex network of societal forces. Davis held that modern human relations really had two facets: one was concerned with understanding, describing, and identifying causes and effects of human behavior through empirical investigation; the other facet was the application of this knowledge to operational situations. The first could be termed *organizational behavior*, and the second facet was *human relations*. The facets were complementary in that one investigated and explained, whereas the other was a way of thinking about people at work and applying behavioral insights to operating situations. The modern human relations of Keith Davis added economic and

---

2. John B. Miner, *Organizational Behavior: Foundations, Theories, and Analyses* (New York: Oxford University Press, 2002), pp. 84, 834. Miner's analysis was based on the first five volumes of A. G. Bedeian's *Management Laureates*. Adding Bedeian's sixth volume (2002) would not have altered Miner's findings.

3. Arthur G. Bedeian, ed., *Management Laureates: A Collection of Autobiographical Essays*, vol. 1 (Greenwich, CT: JAI Press, 1992), p. vii.

4. Jone Pearce, "President's Message: A Bifurcated Academy?" *The Academy of Management News* 34 (2003), pp. 1–2.

5. Keith Davis, *Human Relations in Business* (New York: McGraw-Hill, 1957), p. 4.

psychological facets to the social nature of people. He added a broader consideration of societal forces and moved human relations from its "feelings" base toward the search for an empirical foundation associated with the study of workplace behavior.

In his early work, Chris Argyris (1923–) proposed a "personality versus organization" hypothesis, or the "immaturity-maturity" theory of human behavior, based on humanist ideas.[6] Argyris found an incongruency between the practices within formal organizations (such as a minute division of labor or closer control of individuals) and what encouraged the personality growth of healthy, mature individuals. From infancy to adulthood, there was a tendency for the healthy personality to develop along a continuum from immaturity to maturity by moving from being passive to being active, from dependence to independence, from a lack of awareness of self to awareness and control over self, and so on. An individual's degree of self-actualization could be determined by plotting one's position on the immaturity-maturity continuum.

When these incongruencies interfered with the needs of the healthy personality and the requirements of formal organizations, individuals might adopt certain defensive reactions (such as becoming aggressive or apathetic or restricting output). Management, faced with the reactions of workers, might respond by using more autocratic and directive leadership, tightening organization controls, or turning to human relations. To Argyris, managers adopted pseudohuman relations in many cases to sugarcoat the work situation rather than trying to remove the causes of employee discontent. Through Argyris's numerous books and articles, his proposals for designing organizations to reduce incongruency and achieve harmony between individuals and organizations can be traced. Like E. Wight Bakke, his erstwhile colleague at Yale University, Argyris sought to integrate "the individual and the organization."

Another important influence on Argyris was William F. Whyte, one of his professors in the doctoral program at Cornell University. We saw Whyte earlier as an advocate of "participatory action research," which became "action science" for Argyris and his longtime collaborator, Donald Schon (1930–1997). The duo of Argyris and Schon pioneered the idea of organizational learning, which grew from Argyris's early work on personality and organization. The question was, why do individuals (and groups) develop defensive reasons to interfere with organizational change? The answer, according to Argyris and Schon, echoed Kurt Lewin and resided in "unfreezing" and altering the defensive reasoning of individuals and to encourage productive reasoning that led to "double-loop" learning, that is, to learn by doing and to make corrections as needed based on the information fed back from that action.[7] This was in contrast to "single-loop" learning that did not question

---

6. Chris Argyris, *Personality and Organization: The Conflict between the System and the Individual* (New York: Harper and Row, 1957), p. 50.

7. Chris Argyris and Donald A. Schon, *Organizational Learning II* (Reading, MA: Addison-Wesley, 1996). See also Chris Argyris, "Double-Loop Learning, Teaching, and Research," *Academy of Management Learning and Education* 1 (December 2002), pp. 206–218.

the status quo, inhibiting learning from experience. Argyris and Schon's work on organizational learning stimulated further research and interest in organizational change and development and also influenced the best-selling writings of Peter Senge.[8]

THEORIES X AND Y

Douglas McGregor (1906–1964) taught in the Sloan School of Management at the Massachusetts Institute of Technology and served that institution, except for six years as president of Antioch College (1948–1954), until his death. As president of Antioch College, McGregor found that the precepts of the human-relations model were inadequate for coping with the rigors and realities of organizational life.

> It took the direct experience of becoming a line executive . . . to teach me what no amount of observation of other people could have taught.
>
> I believed, for example, that a leader could operate successfully as a kind of adviser to his organization. I thought I could avoid being a "boss." Unconsciously, I suspect, I hoped to duck the unpleasant necessity of making difficult decisions, of taking the responsibility for one course of action among many uncertain alternatives, of making mistakes and taking the consequences. I thought that maybe I could operate so that everyone would like me—that "good human relations" would eliminate all discord and disagreement.
>
> I couldn't have been more wrong. It took a couple of years, but I finally began to realize that a leader cannot avoid the exercise of authority any more than he can avoid responsibility for what happens to his organization.[9]

As early as 1953, McGregor began to formulate the ideas that would change his conception of management: "A manager who believes that people in general are lazy, untrustworthy, and antagonistic toward him will make very different decisions [from] a manager who regards people generally as cooperative and friendly."[10] In *The Human Side of Enterprise*, McGregor expanded the idea that managerial assumptions about human nature and human behavior were all-important in determining a

---

8. Peter Senge, *The Fifth Discipline: The Art and Practice of the Learning Organization* (New York: Doubleday, 1990).

9. Douglas McGregor, "On Leadership," Antioch Notes (May 1, 1954), Vol. 31, no. 9, p. 3.

10. *Causes of Industrial Peace under Collective Bargaining* (Washington, DC: National Planning Association, 1953), p. 72. This work presents cases of successful labor–management cooperation. Case number 4, "Dewey and Almy Chemical," was coauthored by McGregor and his MIT colleague, Joseph Scanlon.

manager's style of operating. Based on their assumptions about human nature, managers could organize, lead, control, and motivate people in different ways. The first set of assumptions McGregor examined was Theory X, which was to represent the "traditional view of direction and control." Theory X assumptions were:

1. The average human being has an inherent dislike of work and will avoid it if he can. . . .

2. Because of this human characteristic of dislike of work, most people must be coerced, controlled, directed, and threatened with punishment to get them to put forth adequate effort toward the achievement of organizational objectives. . . .

3. The average human being prefers to be directed, wishes to avoid responsibility, has relatively little ambition, wants security above all.[11]

McGregor thought that these X assumptions were the ones prevailing in modern industrial practice. Although he did note a shift from hard X (presumably scientific management) to soft X (human relations), McGregor maintained that no fundamental shift in assumptions or managerial philosophies had occurred. McGregor's Theory Y was put forth as a "modest beginning for new theory with respect to the management of human resources." The assumptions of Theory Y were:

1. The expenditure of physical and mental effort in work is as natural as play or rest. The average human being does not inherently dislike work.

2. External control and the threat of punishment are not the only means for bringing about effort toward organizational objectives. Man will exercise self-direction and self-control in the service of objectives to which he is committed.

3. Commitment to objectives is a function of the rewards associated with their achievement. The most significant of such rewards, such as the satisfaction of ego and self-actualization needs, can be direct products of effort directed toward organizational objectives.

4. The average human being learns, under proper conditions, not only to accept but also to seek responsibility. Avoidance of responsibility, lack of ambition, and emphasis on security are generally consequences of experience, not inherent human characteristics.

5. The capacity to exercise a relatively high degree of imagination, ingenuity, and creativity in the solution of organizational problems is widely, not narrowly, distributed in the population.

6. Under the conditions of modern industrial life, the intellectual potentialities of the average human being are only partially utilized.[12]

---

11. Douglas McGregor, *The Human Side of Enterprise* (New York: McGraw-Hill, 1960), pp. 33–34.

12. Ibid., pp. 47–48.

Using Mary Follett's terms, with a slight twist of Argyris, McGregor called Theory Y "the integration of individual and organizational goals" and held that it led to the "creation of conditions such that the members of the organization can achieve their own goals best by directing their efforts toward the success of the enterprise."[13] Managers who accepted the Y image of human nature would not structure, control, or closely supervise the work environment. Instead, they would attempt to aid the maturation of subordinates by giving them wider latitude in their work, encouraging creativity, using less external control, encouraging self-control, and motivating through the satisfaction that came from the challenge of work itself. The use of the authority of external control by managers would be replaced by getting people committed to organizational goals because they perceived that this was the best way to achieve their own goals. A perfect integration was not possible, but McGregor hoped that an adoption of Y assumptions by managers would improve existing industrial practice.

Unfortunately, many have misinterpreted McGregor, claiming that X and Y represent opposite beliefs, but he is quite clear when he says that the "cosmologies do not lie on a continuous scale. They are qualitatively different . . . *not* polar opposites; they do not lie at extremes of a scale. They are simply *different* cosmologies . . . [they] are not managerial strategies: They are underlying beliefs about the nature of man that *influence* managers to adopt one strategy rather than another."[14]

McGregor served as a bridge from the old view of human relations to the new organizational humanism. It was McGregor's fundamental belief that harmony could be achieved, not by being hard or soft, but by changing assumptions about people and believing that they could be trusted, could exercise self-motivation and control, and had the capacity to integrate their own personal goals with those of the formal organization. To McGregor, how people were treated was largely a self-fulfilling prophecy; if managers assumed that people were lazy and treated them as if they were, then they would be lazy. On the other hand, if managers assumed that people desired challenging work and exploited this premise by increasing individual discretion, workers would in fact respond by seeking more and more responsibility.

In short, Theories X and Y were sets of assumptions about human nature and represented a twentieth-century reemergence of the ideas of earlier philosophers such as Robert Owen and Jean Jacques Rousseau. Owen's "new harmony" would rebuild society to fit humanity's basic goodness. Rousseau, a French philosopher of the eighteenth century, felt that people were basically good but that their nurturing institutions (e.g., family, school) made them bad. Assumptions about human nature guide our thoughts, but no one set of assumptions is going to cover all the people all the time.

---

13. Ibid., p. 49.

14. Douglas McGregor, *The Professional Manager*, ed. Caroline McGregor and Warren G. Bennis (New York: McGraw-Hill, 1967), pp. 79–80.

PERSONNEL/HUMAN RESOURCES MANAGEMENT AND INDUSTRIAL RELATIONS

The importance of people as necessary contributors to the accomplishment of organizational objectives is not a new idea. Traditional economic theory identified land, labor, and capital as factors of production, and Robert Owen referred to his employees as "vital [i.e., living] machines." The preceding pages traced the evolution of the staffing job of the manager as recruiting, selecting, training, developing, compensating, appraising, and performing other tasks with respect to providing for the attraction, placement, reward, and retention of employees. It was customary for some period of time for this job to be done by the direct supervisor, the line manager, and this process placed a great deal of authority in the supervisor's role. Frederick Taylor replaced this practice with functional foremen, which evolved in the use of specialists to advise line managers in the employment task. For Fayol, staffing was part of the organizing job of the manager. From these beginnings personnel management gradually evolved as a standard label for this task of advising managers about recruitment, selection, and so forth. Performance of the personnel function was enhanced with the contributions of individuals, such as Hugo Münsterberg (personnel testing); disciplines, such as labor economics (for understanding labor market factors as they affected the supply of employees and prevailing wage rates); and industrial relations (for promoting better union–management relations).

Personnel management borrowed from many disciplines but did not always receive the acclaim and status that those in the field thought it deserved. In their report, Gordon and Howell made some very disparaging remarks: "Next to the course in production, perhaps more educational sins have been committed in the name of personnel management than in any other required course in the business curriculum. Personnel management is a field which has had a particularly small base of significant generalization with which to work (beyond what is important in the area of human relations), and, partly for this reason, it is an area which has not been held in high regard in the better schools."[15] One outcome of the Gordon and Howell report was to bring more social scientists into U.S. business schools. These individuals could bring their research skills and training to personnel management, and with the growth of industrial relations and labor–management research centers, personnel management could begin to build a firmer theoretical base.

The labor economist John R. Commons appears to have been the first to use the phrase "human resource" as among other factors of production. E. Wight Bakke (see Chapter 15), repeated the notion that all managers managed resources, including the human one, but that more emphasis had to be placed on the human resource to elevate its importance to be commensurate with the other resources of money, materials, and so forth. The central concern of the human resources function was not

---

15. Robert Gordon and James E. Howell, *Higher Education for Business* (New York: Columbia University Press, 1959), p. 189.

"personal happiness" but "productive work," and humans had to be integrated into the total task of every organization. Human resources work was the responsibility of all managers, not just those in personnel or labor relations departments.[16] A substantial period of time would pass before managing the human resource became every manager's job.

Wendell L. French appears to have been the first author to add "human resources" as a subtitle to a personnel management text.[17] This did not create a title wave of changes in textbooks or course names, but it was a beginning. Human-resource management carried a certain dignity with it that proposed to establish personnel management as a more legitimate field with a more rigorous basis for understanding the forces influencing decisions about employees. Beginning in the 1960s and accelerating thereafter, a series of laws about hiring practices, employment tests, compensation, pension plans, safety and health, and other facets of the staffing job of the manager made the role of the personnel specialist more important.

In the early 1900s, economists, such as Commons and others discussed in Chapter 9, were concerned with personnel activities and spearheaded the industrial relations movement. Numerous centers and institutes were established for teaching and research in industrial relations, but these centers were distanced both from economics and management. Kaufman asserted, "It is common today to view the field of personnel/human resource management . . . as distinct and largely unrelated to the discipline of economics and the field of industrial relations."[18]

George Strauss and Thomas Kochan are two notable exceptions to the drift of personnel/human-resources management from industrial relations. In graduate studies and his early career, Strauss was influenced by individuals such as Douglas McGregor, Paul Samuelson, John Dunlop, and others who provided a broad base of knowledge in economics, human relations, and industrial relations.[19] During his career, Strauss saw the transition from human relations to organizational behavior but never abandoned his belief that unions and sound labor–management relations were based on employee participation in decision making. He was a cofounder of the Organizational Behavior Teaching Society (1973) and, in collaboration with Leonard Sayles, produced an abundant body of literature that spanned personnel management, industrial relations, and organizational behavior.[20]

---

16. E. Wight Bakke, *The Human Resources Function* (New Haven, CT: Yale Labor-Management Center, 1958).

17. Wendell L. French, *The Personnel Management Process: Human Resources Administration* (Boston: Houghton Mifflin, 1964).

18. Bruce E. Kaufman, "The Role of Economics and Industrial Relations in the Development of the Field of Personnel/Human Resource Management," *Management Decision* 40 (2002), p. 962.

19. George Strauss, "Present at the Beginning: Some Personal Notes on OB's Early Days and Later," in Arthur G. Bedeian, ed., *Management Laureates*, vol. 3 (Greenwich, CT: Jai Press, 1993), pp. 145–190.

20. For examples: George Strauss and Leonard R. Sayles, *Personnel: The Human Problems of Management* (Englewood Cliffs, NJ: Prentice Hall, 1960); and Leonard R. Sayles and George Strauss, *Human Behavior in Organizations* (Englewood Cliffs, NJ: Prentice Hall, 1966).

Thomas Kochan came from a long line of the "Wisconsin School" of labor relations scholars, such as Richard Ely, John R. Commons, Selig Perlman, and others. Similar to Strauss, Kochan saw human-resources management and industrial relations as complementary: industrial relations added public policy and labor market forces in the firm's environment to intrafirm issues such as selection. Unions were legitimate and valuable components of a democratic society, enabling labor, management, and public policy to forge an agenda for mutual progress and prosperity. Reflecting Frederick Taylor's mental revolution and Mary Follett's integration, it was possible to have a "mutual gains enterprise" that promoted productivity through labor and managerial cooperation to remove barriers to efficiency and to work toward satisfaction of their mutual goals.[21]

In the resource-based, knowledge-based, and dynamic evolutionary theories of the firm, the human resource is crucial to gaining a competitive edge. The history of personnel/human resource management illustrates the need to look to industrial relations, industrial/organizational psychology, and economics for better practices and to practitioners for how well theory meets their needs. Recent reviews have noted that the field has become a research-driven rather than practice-driven study, resulting in a "scientist/practitioner gap" in which practicing managers fail to find useful implications from academic research.[22] Human-resource management has the potential to draw from multiple disciplines to discover what is of practical, if not always statistical, significance.

WORK DESIGN

How tasks should be performed is a subject of long-standing interest as well as a variety of ideas. The division of labor is an ancient practice, but as early as 1776, Adam Smith observed that this practice could be overdone and have dysfunctional effects. Taylor, Frank Gilbreth, and other scientific-management pioneers studied workers' movements and their tools and work methods with the hope of finding a better way to work to reduce fatigue and increase efficiency while rewarding the worker for improved performance. Allan Mogensen started the work simplification movement in the hope that people could learn to work smarter, not harder. Charles Walker and Robert Guest provided job enlargement to lengthen the work cycle to overcome job monotony (see Chapter 15). This brief history of work

---

21. Thomas A. Kochan and Paul Osterman, *The Mutual Gains Enterprise: Forging a Winning Partnership Among Labor, Management, and Government* (Boston: Harvard Business School Press, 1994).

22. Gerald R. Ferriss, Wayne A. Hochwarter, M. Ronald Buckley, Gloria Harnell-Cook, and Dwight D. Frink, "Human Resources Management: Some New Directions," *Journal of Management* 25 (1999), p. 407; Sara L. Rynes, Tamara L. Giluk, and Kenneth G. Brown, "The Very Separate Worlds of Academic and Practitioner Periodicals in Human Resource Management, *Academy of Management Journal* 50 (2007), pp. 987–1008; and Edward E. Lawler III, "Why HR Practices Are Not Evidence-Based," *Academy of Management Journal* 50 (2007), pp. 1033–1036.

design indicates a long-standing assumption that management has a responsibility to make jobs more meaningful as well as to improve performance.

In the modern era, Frederick Herzberg (1923–2000) and his associates began research to discover the importance of attitudes toward work and the experiences, both good and bad, that workers reported. An important influence on Herzberg's life and research was John Flanagan, a psychologist who worked with the U.S. Air Force in developing methods for crew selection. Herzberg worked in this program and learned Flanagan's "critical incidents" research technique, a way of questioning that helped isolate the behaviors of promising candidates from less-promising ones.

Recalling Flanagan's critical incident method, Herzberg asked workers to respond to this question: "Think of a time when you felt exceptionally good or exceptionally bad about your job, either your present job or any other job you have had. . . . Tell me what happened."[23] From the responses to this question and a series of follow-up questions, Herzberg set out to discover the kinds of things that made people either happy and satisfied on their jobs or unhappy and dissatisfied. From people's responses, he was able to isolate two different kinds of needs that appeared to be independent. When people reported unhappiness and job dissatisfaction, they attributed those feelings to their job environment, or the *job context*. When people reported happiness or satisfaction, they attributed the feelings to work itself or to the job *content*.

Herzberg called the factors identified in the job context "hygiene" factors, "for they act in a manner analogous to the principles of medical hygiene. Hygiene operates to remove health hazards from the environment of man. It is not curative: it is, rather, a preventive."[24] The hygiene factors included supervision, interpersonal relations, physical working conditions, salaries, company policies and administrative practices, benefits, and job security. When these factors deteriorated below what a worker considered an acceptable level, job dissatisfaction was the result. When the job context was considered optimal by a worker, dissatisfaction was removed; this did not lead to positive attitudes, however, but to some sort of a neutral state of neither satisfaction nor dissatisfaction.

The factors that led to positive attitudes, satisfaction, and motivation were called the "motivators," or things in the job content. The motivators were such factors as achievement, recognition for accomplishment, challenging work, increased job responsibility, and opportunities for growth and development. If present, these factors led to higher motivation. In this sense, Herzberg was saying that traditional assumptions of motivation about wage incentives, improving interpersonal relations, and establishing proper working conditions did not lead to higher motivation. They removed dissatisfaction and acted to prevent problems, but once these traditional motivators were optimal, they did not lead to positive motivation. According to Herzberg, management should recognize that hygiene was necessary, but that once it had neutralized dissatisfaction, it did not lead to positive results. Only the motivators led people to superior performance.

---

23. Frederick Herzberg, Bernard Mausner, and Barbara B. Snyderman, *The Motivation to Work* (New York: John Wiley and Sons, 1959), app. I, p. 141.

24. Ibid., p. 113.

Herzberg's motivation-hygiene theory has received both support and criticism. Critics have observed that when asked to do so, people take the credit when things go well, attributing satisfaction to events they can control in the job content area. They place the blame for dissatisfaction not on themselves, but on the job context—the work environment. The conclusion, then, is that Herzberg's way of asking his questions led to his results. Further, if correct, Herzberg's theory would have found that highly satisfied people were also highly motivated and high producers. The evidence so far has not found a positive relationship between worker satisfaction and productivity. Satisfied workers are not always the best producers, nor are dissatisfied workers the worst producers. To illustrate, one worker may respond to the challenge of job enrichment, whereas another may prefer to be told what to do. Work is a means for some people, not an end.

Herzberg's research stimulated interest in work design, and Turner and Lawrence studied factors that positively related to employee satisfaction and attendance and found six attributes that seemed crucial.[25] Hackman and Lawler agreed with four of these (task variety, autonomy, task identity, and feedback), defined as "core dimensions," but suggested that these tasks did not take into account an employee's desire for personal growth through satisfaction of "higher-order needs." They drew from employee need theory and expectancy theory (discussed later) as a basis for understanding employee desires for personal growth.[26] They found employees experienced "meaningfulness" in their work through skill and task variety when they were held responsible for results (autonomy, which was similar to Herzberg's "vertical loading" or job depth) and knowledge of results (feedback).

When Lawler left Yale for the University of Michigan, Hackman was joined by Greg Oldham, who suggested "task significance" be added to the earlier four factors. Hackman and Oldham were concerned with how to identify and change, if possible, specific job characteristics (i.e., task identity, task significance, skill variety, autonomy, and knowledge of results [feedback]). If these characteristics could be enhanced, for example, by increasing the variety of skills used or by providing information about how well a person was performing, then the employee would experience more "meaningfulness" on the job. Hackman and Oldham moved away from the idea of satisfying "higher-order needs," adding a situational flavor by suggesting that the degree of success of this approach depended on the individual's "growth-need strength."[27] If a person already felt sufficiently challenged and experienced the job as meaningful, growth-need strength would be low, and further efforts to enrich a job would be less effective. Some individuals seek more

25. Arthur N. Turner and Paul R. Lawrence, *Industrial Jobs and the Worker: An Investigation of Response to Task Attributes* (Boston: Harvard Graduate School of Business Administration, 1965).

26. J. Richard Hackman and Edward E. Lawler III, "Employee Reactions to Job Characteristics," *Journal of Applied Psychology* 55 (June 1971), pp. 259-286.

27. J. Richard Hackman and Greg R. Oldham, *Work Redesign* (Reading, Mass.: Addison-Wesley, 1980). Miner rates Job Characteristics Theory high in "estimated usefulness in practice and estimated scientific validity." See John B. Miner, *Organizational Behavior 3: Historical Origins, Theoretical Foundations, and the Future* (Armonk, NY: M. E. Sharpe, 2006), p. 218.

challenge, and others do not; further, some jobs can be made more meaningful, and others cannot. Job characteristics theory was not a universal solvent for all managerial problems: "the redesign of work is much more a *way of managing* than it is a prepackaged 'fix' for problems of employee motivation and satisfaction."[28] It offered, however, a way to provide a closer match between the nature of a job and employee needs.

The nature of working has changed since these theories were developed. A job may no longer be a career, and many employment arrangements have been changed by outsourcing work, using temporary employees, dual-career couples, electronic commuting, postretirement careers, and individuals needing to retool their skills/abilities at different career stages. Working is central to living, and another generation of study is needed as jobs and careers change.

MOTIVATION

Our next two topics, motivation and leadership, are closely related and separated here only to emphasize the contributions of different individuals and their theories. Individuals such as Henri Fayol and Peter Drucker have emphasized managements' responsibility for results and for effective and efficient performance. The University of Michigan's Norman Maier summarized the situation succinctly: "Performance = Ability x Motivation."[29] We have noted the influx of psychologists and other social scientists into business schools, and it is not surprising that many theories of motivation are based on the study of psychology.[30] This does not deny the evergreen topic of wondering why our fellow humans do what they do. The ancient Greek philosophy of hedonism postulated that people sought pleasure and avoided pain, opening the door to behavior modification and other schemes to change human behavior. The utilitarian movement of early economists believed that humans tried to calculate what actions would bring the most utility with the least cost, opening the way for expectancy theory. Chapter 9 described how a mid-nineteenth-century branch of economics, plutology, was able to deduce the existence of a hierarchy of human needs that changed once lower-order needs were satisfied. Abraham Maslow rediscovered this notion in the twentieth century and, along with David McClelland and John Atkinson, explained motivation in terms of needs, the "what" portion of motivation.

---

28. Hackman and Oldham, *Work Redesign*, op. cit. p. 249.

29. Norman R. F. Maier, *Psychology in Industry: A Psychological Approach to Industrial Problems* (Boston: Houghton Mifflin, 1946).

30. Gary P. Latham, *Work Motivation: History, Theory, Research, and Practice* (Thousand Oaks, CA: Sage, 2007).

Perhaps it was the shortcomings of human need theories that caused later motivation theories to change their tack. It was not the fact that need theories were completely refuted and discarded; rather, it was their incompleteness, unpredictability, and uncertainty. The response was to try to understand the *how* of motivation rather than the *what*; that is, how the motivational process worked. The focus of these how theories was understanding how human motivation might be triggered, what gave it direction, what kept it going, and how it might be extinguished if the behavior was inappropriate.

Victor Vroom. Courtesy of Victor Vroom.

One of these, expectancy theory, was developed by Victor H. Vroom and based on early psychological theories, such as Kurt Lewin's "force field" notion.[31] The premise of expectancy theory was that motivation was a process of making choices between behaviors and that people pursued the behaviors that they hoped would lead to pleasurable outcomes. According to expectancy theory, motivation was a product of valence, the value of a particular reward to an individual, and expectancy, the individual's perception of whether or not a given pattern of behavior was likely to lead to the satisfaction of unfilled needs. Valences could be positive (something highly desired) or negative (something to be avoided) and could vary in strength of the drive. Lyman Porter and Edward Lawler extended expectancy theory by adding a feedback loop from performance to the future expectancy of effort being rewarded, thus strengthening subsequent performance.[32]

Expectancy theory helped explain the choosing process involved in motivation. Motivation to perform was an interaction between the goals sought, the value placed on these goals, and the worker's expectation that a certain path would lead to those goals. Expectancy theory is a complex notion, however, and leaves numerous questions unanswered, such as: Do individuals seek to maximize their rewards, or do they "satisfice"? Do the valences remain stable over time, and if not, how much of a change must occur before a person's behavior changes?

Although equity theory is not new, management scholars have only recently paid much attention to it. Whiting Williams (see Chapter 9) put forth what was most likely the first equity theory of wages. Williams argued that pay was relative

---

31. Victor H. Vroom, *Work and Motivation* (New York: John Wiley and Sons, 1964).

32. Lyman W. Porter and Edward E. Lawler, *Management Attitudes and Performance* (Homewood, IL: Richard D. Irwin, 1968).

from a worker's point of view; that is, what was important was not the absolute pay a person received but the amount relative to what others received. Not until the 1960s did scholars begin to formulate the bases of equity theory. Although there were slight differences between the ideas of Elliott Jaques and those of J. Stacy Adams, the primary proponents of this theory, the essential rationale was that pay was a matter of distributive justice and social comparison.[33] A person's perception of salary was based on at least two ratios: (1) the person's pay relative to the pay of others; and (2) the person's "inputs" (that is, effort expended, education, skill level, training, experience) relative to the person's "outcomes" (salary). In the first case, the comparison was that of the person's pay relative to what others were getting. In the second, the comparison was that of how hard the person worked, how long the person had trained, and so on, relative to the pay received for the work. For example, a worker might be dissatisfied with his or her salary if the worker perceived that another person doing the same job was paid more; hence the cries of "equal pay for equal work" from those who feel discrimination in terms of salary. The source of dissatisfaction may not necessarily be the absolute amount of salary, but the salary in relation to others and in relation to inputs and outcomes.

Managers play an important role in deciding who and what gets rewarded. It is important for employees to feel these decisions are made on some equitable basis and are "fair" to all.[34] A manager is more likely to be trusted, to be believed, if employees feel the appropriate procedures and criteria for distributing rewards are followed. In this case, the manager as leader must be perceived as trustworthy, enhancing how his/her other decisions will be received. Certain questions remain unanswered, such as: How do people select those they consider their cohorts, and how accurate is the information on which the comparisons are based? Equity theory contributed to notions of why people might be dissatisfied, but contributed less to an understanding of how they might be motivated.

After being in eclipse, money returned to credibility as a motivational factor. To illustrate, in an extensive survey of field and experimental studies of motivation, Edwin Locke and his associates examined four widely used techniques and their impacts on employee productivity. Monetary incentives showed the greatest median increase, followed by goal setting, whereas job enrichment and participation lagged behind.[35] They did not conclude that money was the only motivator, but emphasized the "instrumentality" of money; that is, money as a medium of exchange that allowed individuals to choose how they wished to satisfy their needs.

---

33. Elliott Jaques, *Equitable Payment* (New York: John Wiley and Sons, 1961); and J. Stacy Adams, "Toward an Understanding of Inequity," *Journal of Abnormal and Social Psychology* 67 (1963), pp. 422–436.

34. Jerry Greenberg, *Managing Behavior in Organizations* (Upper Saddle River, NJ: Prentice Hall, 1999).

35. Edwin A. Locke, Dena B. Feren, Vickie M. McCaleb, Karyll N. Shaw, and Anne T. Denny, "The Relative Effectiveness of Four Methods of Motivating Employee Performance," in K. D. Duncan, M. M. Gruneberg, and D. Wallis, eds., *Changes in Working Life* (Chichester, England: John Wiley and Sons, 1980), pp. 363–388.

Goal-setting theory, with its roots in Frederick Taylor's task management, Frank Gilbreth's "three position plan" of promotion, Peter Drucker's MBO, and Cecil Mace's pioneering studies, is primarily the work of Locke and Gary Latham. Contemporary credence for goal setting was provided by Locke, who credited his mentor, Thomas Ryan, as a cocreator of this notion. Goal setting consisted of "purposefully directed action" in the process of developing and setting specific work goals or targets for employees to accomplish.[36] The more specific the goal, the better: "produce one hundred units that will pass the quality inspection" rather than "do the best you can today." Further, difficult goals were better than easy ones—the goal should challenge (but not exceed) an individual's abilities rather than ask the employees to spread a four-hour job over an eight-hour day. Employees also needed to be able to keep track of their performance by receiving regular feedback about results. Without knowledge of results, employees could not gauge the relationship between their performance and the expected performance. Incentives (both financial and nonfinancial) were also necessary to reward the meeting of the goals. Goal setting as a motivational force appeared to work equally well whether goals were assigned by management or with group participation. The assignment of goals by management worked best with people already internally motivated to do the job, such as those persons with a high need for achievement or high self-efficacy. When subordinates were familiar with and at ease with participative techniques and when their need for achievement was lower, participative goal setting was more likely to be effective. Acceptance of goals depended on a number of factors, including the extent to which employees trusted management, the fairness and difficulty of the goals, and the perceived legitimacy of management's demands.

Edwin A. Locke. Courtesy of Edwin A. Locke.

Goal-setting theory was found to be compatible with expectancy theory and social learning theory with respect to self-efficacy; for example, people with high self-efficacy chose more difficult goals, and positive performance feedback enhanced self-efficacy, creating a new cycle of high performance. Further, goal setting promoted more self-regulation of performance as individuals learned what the appropriate level of performance was. Forty years of empirical tests of Locke and Latham's goal-setting theory have been successful, and it has been rated high in estimated

---

36. Edwin A. Locke and Gary P. Latham, *A Theory of Goal Setting and Task Performance* (Englewood Cliffs, NJ: Prentice Hall, 1990); and Gary P. Latham and Edwin A. Locke, "Self-Regulation through Goal Setting," *Organizational Behavior and Human Decision Processes* 50 (1991), pp. 212–247.

scientific validity and usefulness in practice.[37] Goal-setting theory provided an integration of social science methods and findings with the practical world of the manager as it relates to general management theory. Understandable, useful research has long been the desire of practitioners, and goal-setting theory has filled this long-standing void. Theory and research are not ends in and of themselves. The goal of research is to advance teaching and practice, and teaching and practice are the crucibles in which the mettle of theory and research is tested.

LEADERSHIP

Leadership fits into general management theory because it focuses on the attainment of organizational goals by working with and through people and other resources. Various terms have been used to describe this function, such as directing, leading, actuating, and supervising, and various views of how to become a leader or what a leader does have also evolved. The earliest leadership notions were dominated by trait theory, meaning that leaders could be characterized as having different traits from nonleaders. Technical ability, intelligence, energy, initiative, honesty, and other personal qualities joined the tribal remnants of the idea that those in charge were taller, stronger, wiser, better warriors, or whatever. As these lists grew longer, and as more and more exceptions were found, the search for other explanations of leadership began. The second stage in the evolution of leadership notions sought to identify the behaviors that could be connected to those who were the leaders. Early research, such as that of Kurt Lewin, placed leadership styles on a continuum ranging from authoritarian to democratic. This clustering of leader-behavior modes reflected the idea that the authoritarian used formal authority, was production oriented, and operated unilaterally in making decisions. The democratic or participative leader, on the other hand, used formal authority sparingly, was employee centered, and involved subordinates in the decision-making process.

Participative leadership, espoused by human relationists and organizational humanists, followed the theme of power equalization, a movement to reduce the power and status differentials between the superior and the subordinate. The goal was to play down hierarchical authority, give workers a greater voice in decisions, encourage creativity, and overcome apathy by getting workers involved and committed to an organization's goals.

Rensis Likert (1903–1981), one of the foremost proponents of participative management, was trained as a psychologist and developed the widely used Likert Scale for the measurement of attitudes and values. Likert spent most of his

---

37. Edwin A. Locke and Gary P. Latham, "Building a Practically Useful Theory of Goal Setting and Task Motivation: A 35-Year Odyssey," *American Psychologist* 57 (September 2002), pp. 705–717; and John B. Miner, "The Rated Importance, Scientific Validity, and Practical Usefulness of Organizational Behavior Theories: A Quantitative Review," *Academy of Management Learning and Education* 2 (September 2003), pp. 252, 255.

life studying leadership in organizations and thought that of all the tasks of management, leading the human component was the central and most important because all else depended on how well it was done. From his earlier studies (see Chapter 15), he extended his production orientation and employee orientation to identify four types of leadership styles: "exploitive authoritative," System 1; "benevolent authoritative," System 2; "consultative," System 3; and "participative group," System 4.[38] Likert's System 4 management involved three basic concepts: (1) the principle of supportive relationships; (2) the use of group decision making and group methods of supervision; and (3) setting high performance goals for an organization. The principle of supportive relationships meant that the leader had to ensure that each member viewed the experience as supportive and one that built and maintained a sense of personal worth and importance. The second concept involved group decision making and an overlapping group form of structure, with each work group linked to the rest of an organization by means of persons who were members of more than one group (called "link pins"). The third concept was high performance goals. Superiors in System 4 organizations would have high performance aspirations, as would every work group member. Employees were involved in setting the high-level goals required for the satisfaction of their own needs.

In his last book, Likert proposed System 5, "an even more sophisticated, complex, and effective system" that would emerge as the social sciences advanced.[39] Although he never lived to advance System 5 thinking, his wife, Jane, and others continued his work. In System 5, an organization's hierarchy of authority would be replaced with a reciprocal system of participation and influence. In case of conflict, groups would work together through overlapping memberships ("link pins") until a consensus could be reached. Organization charts would look like a fishnet rather than a pyramid, as multiple linkages occurred between work units and departments. Authority would depend on the interpersonal skills of creative leaders who had the ability to get others committed and working toward organizational goals. Employees would be called "associates" (there would be no organizational titles for persons), and leadership would be a "shared sense of purpose" and a "oneness" feeling in an organization. If these ideas sound familiar, they should, because Likert was a great admirer of Mary Follett.[40] It is apparent that Likert's initial formulations of System 5 owe a bow of gratitude to her.

As ideas about leadership continued to evolve, there was dissatisfaction with prescribing any one way to lead, such as the participative style. Instead, the focus

---

38. Rensis Likert, *The Human Organization: Its Management and Value* (New York: McGraw-Hill, 1967), p. 4, passim.

39. Rensis Likert and Jane Gibson Likert, *New Ways of Managing Conflict* (New York: McGraw-Hill, 1976), p. 41.

40. Jane Gibson Likert, "The Likert Legacy: System 5 and New Organizational Forms for the Future" (paper presented at the Academy of Management meeting, Boston, August 13, 1984). See also Jane Gibson Likert and Charles T. Araki, "Managing without a Boss: System 5," *Leadership and Organizational Development Journal* 3 (1986), pp. 17–20.

shifted to contingency or situational leadership, an idea pioneered by Fred Fiedler. Fiedler proposed that a number of leadership styles might be either effective or ineffective, depending on important elements of a situation.[41] He identified leadership style by the use of the LPC (least-preferred coworker) scale. High LPC persons were concerned about interpersonal relations, felt a need for the approval of their associates, and were less distant in describing themselves and others. Low LPC persons were relatively independent of others, less concerned with feelings, and willing to reject a person who could not complete an assigned task. In essence, the high LPC leader was "consideration oriented," and the low LPC leader was "task oriented" in terms of the Ohio State studies.

Fiedler also identified three major factors in the leadership situation: (1) "leader–member relations," or the degree to which a group trusted, liked, or was willing to follow a leader; (2) the "task structure," or the degree to which the task was ill or well defined; and (3) "position power," or the formal authority as distinct from the personal power of a leader. Depending on whether the situation was very favorable or very unfavorable, Fiedler concluded that (1) task-oriented (low LPC) leaders tended to perform best in group situations that were either very favorable or very unfavorable to a leader, and (2) relationship-oriented (high LPC) leaders tended to perform best in situations that were intermediate in favorableness.

Following further research, Fiedler's theory evolved first into leader-match theory, then into cognitive resources theory. In his work, and the work of others, it was becoming obvious that it was difficult to define in more precise terms under what conditions the appropriate leadership style would be—in effect, to provide the "if" and "then" of situations. For this stage of evolving theories of leadership, there was no one best way to lead, and the question was how a leader should behave under what situations. With minute differences and with limited empirical evidence to confirm contingency theories, new opportunities were offered from a study of political leadership.

James MacGregor Burns's Pulitzer Prize–winning book, *Leadership*, coined the terms *transactional* and *transformational* to describe the types of political leaders he studied, but other leadership literature found them useful.[42] Transformational leadership theories reflected personality traits, with the exception that these leaders appeared to be more willing to share power with ("empower") their followers. These leaders also seemed to emerge at particular times, such as when an organization declined and revitalization and a renewed vision were needed. Transformational leaders are often described as those who bring a vision of the major changes needed in an organization's structure, culture, market, or whatever. This distant vision would succeed, however, only if a leader could transform the high-powered vision of the future into localized implementation in the present.

---

41. Fred E. Fiedler, *A Theory of Leadership Effectiveness* (New York: McGraw-Hill, 1967).

42. James M. Burns, *Leadership* (New York: Harper and Row, 1978).

Charisma returned to leadership theory after resting for a number of years in the ideas of Max Weber (see Chapter 10). Charismatic leaders got things done by virtue of their ability to attract followers to their cause. Followers would trust, share the vision of, often attribute mystical powers to, and offer blind obedience to a leader. As a leadership theory, charisma combined leader traits, followers, and situational variables. In House's theory, charismatic leaders seemed to emerge under certain conditions, had personal qualities that distinguished them from others, and were able to manage the impression they made on others to build and maintain their followers' confidence and trust.[43] For Bass, charisma was but one part of becoming a transformational leader by inspiring followers through setting high expectations, focusing efforts, and expressing important goals in influential ways.[44] It was not always clear in charismatic theories what would happen if a leader's intents were not socially desirable; for instance, some historical figures (Adolf Hitler comes to mind) have demonstrated this personal magnetism and led others in blind obedience but toward evil ends. Further, it is important to recall Max Weber's conclusion that charisma was an unstable situation and that after a charismatic leader departed there could be chaos.

In addition to charismatic and transformational leadership theories, transactional leadership could be found in the work of George Graen. His leader–member exchange theory (originally "vertical dyad linkage theory") suggests that, over time, leaders classify their followers as in-group or out-group members and treat the former more favorably. In exchange, these in-group members resemble informed assistants and are motivated, sometimes by participative decision making, to put forth more effort that enhances the job of the leader.[45] The exchange is reciprocal, at least for in-group followers, as the leader distributes resources (perhaps rewards) for those who give the extra effort. The quality of the exchange is associated with performance outcomes and, to some extent, with career development. Graen has been careful to emphasize that in-group and out-group categories are based on task and not friendship relationships.[46] Otherwise, there could be legal issues, as in employment discrimination, or interpersonal ones, such as playing favorites. Leader–member exchange theory has enriched previous relationship-based research, such as improved interpersonal relations at Hawthorne, and has furthered our understanding of intraorganizational connections.

---

43. Robert J. House, "A 1976 Theory of Charismatic Leadership," in J. G. Hunt and L. C. Larson, eds., *Leadership: The Cutting Edge* (Carbondale: Southern Illinois University Press, 1977), pp. 189–207.

44. Bernard M. Bass, *Leadership and Performance Beyond Expectations* (New York: Free Press, 1985). Bass is an exception among charisma theorists and notes that the charisma of Hitler led to evil consequences; see p. 20.

45. George B. Graen and Mary Uhl-Bien, "Relationship-based Approach to Leadership: Development of Leader-Member Exchange (LMX) Theory of Leadership over 25 Years: Applying a Multi-level Multi-domain Perspective," *Leadership Quarterly* 6 (1995), pp. 219–247.

46. Miner, *Organizational Behavior*, pp. 344–351.

Leadership theory presents the possibility of déjà vu to the historian. Traits such as drive, energy, initiative, honesty/integrity, self-confidence, adaptability, and others have been suggested by modern authors in a manner reminiscent of Fayol (although supported by a richer research base).[47] Hunt's application of Jaques's "stratified systems theory" to strategic leadership has "core notions of (a) increasing organizational complexity as leaders move up in the organization, and (b) a concurrent of increased required amount of leader cognitive complexity at higher organizational levels."[48] Fayol identified "intelligence and mental vigor" as becoming more important further up the hierarchical chain; "mental vigor" was defined as the ability to "deal simultaneously with many varied manifold subjects." Has the winding path of leadership theory come back to the starting point?

This winding path is characterized by a proliferation of theories, definitional issues (such as defining "management" and "leadership"), semantics problems (Is moral leadership theory the same as or different from spiritual leadership theory, authentic leadership theory, or ethical leadership theory?), reactions to contemporary "hot" topics (such as authentic leadership theory), and which level of the hierarchy is being examined (CEOs, middle managers, first-line supervisors?). Leadership theory has created its own jungle, a thicket of theories that may or may not have any historical foundation or reasoning.

Miner identified seventeen leadership theories, Hunt added eight, and a cursory review of the past five years of the eminent journal in the field, *Leadership Quarterly*, revealed others such as substitutes for leadership theory, shared leadership theory, strategic leadership theory (also referred to as executive level leadership theory), suggesting some connection to upper echelons theory.[49] This abundance of "emerging" theories has been challenged to be more precise in definition of the subject under study, measurement and validity necessities, and learning from the past: "Leadership scholars must be cognizant of the history of the field and the lessons it teaches."[50] Theory spinning stirs intellectual juices but does not add value to our understanding of leadership or provide information to those who practice management.

A scholarly exchange between Bedeian and Hunt focused on the problem of defining the terms used in the leadership literature and differentiating between management and leadership. Bedeian wrote: "It amazes me that leadership scholars

---

47. Edwin A. Locke, *The Essence of Leadership* (New York: Lexington Books, 1991). See also Henri Fayol, *General and Industrial Management* (1949), pp. 7, 76–77.

48. James G. Hunt, *Leadership: A New Synthesis* (Newbury Park, CA: Sage, 1991), p. 268. See also Fayol, op. cit., pp. 76–77. See also Elliott Jaques and Stephen D. Clement, *Executive Leadership: A Practical Guide to Managing Complexity* (Arlington, VA: Cason Hall, 1991).

49. Miner, "The Rated Importance, Scientific Validity, and Practical Usefulness..." op. cit. pp. 251–254; and James G. (Jerry) Hunt, "Explosion of the Leadership Field and *LQs* Changing of the Guard," *The Leadership Quarterly* 16 (February 2005), pp. 1–8.

50. Cecily D. Cooper, Terri A. Scandura, and Chester A. Schriesheim, "Looking Forward but Learning from Our Past: Potential Challenges to Developing Authentic Leadership Theory and Authentic Leaders," *The Leadership Quarterly* 16 (June 2005), p. 475.

continue in their research without regard to whether the individuals they are studying are, in fact, leaders. To truly understand leadership . . . requires the identification of individuals who have differentiated themselves from those around them in terms of their influence (beyond that associated with their formal position or authority), not simply the study of individuals whose names appear in a box with a title on an organization chart."[51] Articles may use leaders, managers, or supervisors as interchangeable titles as they relate to followers, subordinates, or employees without specifying precisely who is being studied. Though this may not seem to be a central interest to the researcher, a reader needs to understand what position or role a leader/manager holds in the hierarchy. Is holding a managerial position the same as being a leader? Or, can one be a leader without managerial authority and status? Or, are the two complementary? Central to progress in a discipline is a definitive use of terms that communicates to others the results of a study.

In commenting on an issue of *The Leadership Quarterly*, Hunt concluded that "none of them [authors] explicitly emphasizes their definition of leadership, it is obvious to me that it is a role definition, where anyone in a managerial role is considered a leader . . . at least some of the models and propositions need to be modified to reflect the leader/manager differences."[52] Bedeian and Hunt agreed that leadership is a part of and complements management; they also agreed that those who do leadership research need to be specific in defining their terms if what they intend to measure is truly measured. A leader and a manager may not be the same person, but both perform important roles in getting the job done.

Some progress should be noted as more scholars are recognizing the difference between leadership *of* an organization and leadership *in* an organization. According to Dubin: "The leadership *of* organizations is first and foremost leadership at a distance. Any sizable modern organization . . . [has] functionaries called leaders who are never in face-to-face contact with the vast majority of the remaining members. At best, such leaders are symbolically known to the members of the organization."[53] By more carefully defining our terms, this distinction enables a theory, such as strategic leadership theory, to be connected to upper echelons theory, for example, breaking down some academic walls and cross-pollinating the management discipline. Throughout this study of management thought, we have noted problems of overspecialization, semantics, and forgetting the lessons of the past. These are barriers to making what we learn available to students and practitioners, adding value to our work and to what we can contribute to others.

---

51. Arthur G. Bedeian and James G. Hunt, "Academic Amnesia and Vestigial Assumptions of Our Forefathers," *The Leadership Quarterly* 17 (April 2006), p. 199.

52. James G. (Jerry) Hunt, "Comments from the Yearly Review Editor—Once Again," *The Leadership Quarterly* 18 (December 2007), p. 512.

53. Robert Dubin, "Metaphors of Leadership: An Overview," in James G. Hunt and Lars L. Larson (eds.), *Crosscurrents in Leadership* (Carbondale: Southern Illinois University Press, 1979), p. 227. See also James G. Hunt, "Leadership Déjà Vu All Over Again," *Leadership Quarterly* 11 (Winter 2000), pp. 435–458.

Another promising avenue is a cross-cultural study of leadership. Project Global Leadership and Organizational Behavior Effectiveness (GLOBE) is a long-term, ambitious program to discover differences in cultural values between countries that influence leader–follower behavior and relationships. Much organizational research is a snapshot, but GLOBE's fifteen-plus-year study of 17,300 middle managers in 950 organizations in 62 participating countries in the telecommunications, food processing, and financial services industries make this project unique. Robert House is *primus inter pares* of a leadership team plus 170 researchers from the countries being studied. The study excludes military, governmental, and religious organizations to examine how culture influences organizational, societal, and leadership effectiveness.

Culture is operationalized along multiple levels and based, in the main, on the seminal work of Hofstede.[54] These orientations are Assertiveness, Future Orientation, Gender Egalitarianism, Humane Orientation, Institutional Collectivism, In-Group Collectivism, Performance Orientation, Power Distance, and Uncertainty Avoidance.[55] Definitions of each are beyond our purpose, but these were used to study different countries, and six leadership dimensions were identified and labeled: Charismatic/Value-Based Leadership (the ability to inspire, to motivate, and the expectancy of high performance outcomes); Team-Oriented Leadership (collaborative team building and implementing a common goal for the team); Participative Leadership (involving others in making and implementing decisions); Humane-Oriented Leadership (providing support, compassion, and consideration to others); Autonomous Leadership (being independent and individualistic); and Self-Protective Leadership (self-centered, covering your backside, and procedural oriented).[56]

Combining culture and leadership is not for the faint of heart. In articles plus nearly 2,000 pages of text, the GLOBE research team suggests some lessons for leadership. One, leadership is culturally dependent. This is not surprising, but confirms that we need to understand that the world is more than Anglo or English speaking. Two, there are cultural "clusters," regions that share similar cultural profiles. For example, Europe is not Europe but consists of Latin Europe, Nordic Europe, Eastern Europe, and Germanic Europe clusters. Preparing for an assignment to "Europe" would require knowing where in Europe. Third, some cultural factors are predictive of what leadership orientation might work better. Charismatic/Value-Based Leadership is typically more effective if a Performance

---

54. Geert H. Hofstede, *Culture's Consequences: International Differences in Work-Related Values* (London: Sage, 1980).

55. Robert J. House and Mansour Javidan, "Overview of GLOBE," in Robert J. House, Paul J. Hanges, Mansour Javidan, Peter W. Dorfman, and Vipin Gupta (eds.), *Leadership, Culture, and Organizations: The GLOBE Study of 62 Societies* (London: Sage, 2004), pp. 11–16.

56. Felix C. Brodbeck, Jagdeep S. Chhokar, and Robert J. House, "Culture and Leadership in 25 Societies: Integration, Conclusions, and Future Directions," in Jagdeep S. Chhokar, Felix C. Brodbeck, and Robert J. House (eds.), *Culture and Leadership Across the World: The GLOBE Book of In-Depth Studies of 25 Societies* (London: Lawrence Erlbaum, 2007), p. 1037.

Orientation is present in a culture. Or, Team-Oriented Leadership is best predicted by In-Group Collectivism and a Humane Orientation (and, unexpectedly, also in a culture that wishes to reduce uncertainty). Finally, "in all cultures, leader team orientation and the communication of vision, values, and confidence in followers are reported to be highly effective leader behaviors."[57] The GLOBE data are a rich resource to be mined as we realize that we are only beginning to understand leadership on our flat earth.

Despite the mountains of literature on leadership, much work remains to be done. Ralph Stogdill (1904–1978), a prominent researcher on leadership, reviewed some 3,000 studies in 1974 and concluded: "Four decades of research on leadership have produced a bewildering mass of findings.... The endless accumulation of empirical data has not produced an integrated understanding of leadership."[58] Some thirty-five years later it was noted: "Most leadership studies only examine events that occur during a brief time interval. Longitudinal studies are needed...leadership research seems to be biased toward easy methods and faddish topics. Too many studies are merely replications of earlier studies on a popular topic.... The primary message is the need for better balance in the design of leadership research."[59]

ORGANIZATIONS AND PEOPLE

In contrast to the social scientists who looked to leadership, motivation, and work design within organizations, organization theorists assumed a total organization or macro point of view of goals, structure, and the processes necessary to accomplish organizational goals. Mooney and Reiley found, "Organization is as old as human society itself... [and was] the form of every human association for the attainment of a common purpose."[60] These organizations carried many labels: tribe, clan, association, company, church, army, college, group, and only recently the term *corporation* emerged. All were faced with the problems of integrating human efforts to achieve expected results. They did not face the rigors of market competition, and organizational structures were designed to keep human efforts focused on an organization's purpose, to accomplish what no one person could do alone.

In ancient Greece, Aristotle wrote of centralized and decentralized authority, division of labor, and departmentation. Daniel McCallum gave the organizational structure of the Erie Railroad the appearance of a tree and developed ideas about

57. Robert J. House, "Illustrative Examples of GLOBE Findings," in House, Hanges, Javidan, et al. op. cit. p. 7.

58. Ralph M. Stogdill, *Handbook of Leadership: A Survey of Theory and Research* (New York: Free Press, 1974), p. xvii.

59. Gary A. Yukl, *Leadership in Organizations*, 6th ed. (Upper Saddle River, NJ: Pearson/Prentice Hall, 2006), p. 455.

60. James D. Mooney and Alan C. Reiley, *Onward Industry!* (New York: Harper and Brothers, 1931), pp. xiii, 10.

authority, accountability, and communication. Frederick Taylor recognized the need for expert advice with his functional foreman; and Harrington Emerson improved this scheme with a line–staff concept of organizations. In Germany, the Siemens Company introduced the idea of product divisions, an "M-form" structure, prior to its use in the United States.[61] In the United States, Du Pont organized around products in a multidivisional structure and carried this idea over to the General Motors Corporation. Henri Fayol identified organizing as an element of management, placing organizational theory squarely in the conceptual framework of general management theory.

Max Weber, a contemporary of Taylor and Fayol, whose works were translated into English much later, described bureaucracy as an ideal form of organizations based on rational-legal authority. In Chapter 16 we saw Mooney and Reiley's search for "principles" of organizations throughout history, whereas others were interested in sociotechnical systems. Barnard wrote of decision making and the formal and informal organizations, thus making a lasting impact on the Hawthorne studies and Herbert Simon. With James March, Simon saw organizations as a complex network of decision processes (see Chapter 15). From Barnard onward, the study of organizations took a new tack.

ORGANIZATIONS AS OPEN SYSTEMS

Although Chester Barnard broke with the conventional wisdom of intraorganizational analysis and viewed organizations as open systems that included investors, suppliers, customers, and others, it was not until the 1960s that systems theory made an impact on management thought. Ludwig von Bertalanffy (1901–1972), a biologist, noted the "openness" of all systems, that is, an organism was both affected by and affected its environment.[62] "Organism" has the same Greek and Latin roots as "organization" in that both deal with the function, structure, and relationship of parts to a whole. It became appropriate, then, to think in terms of an organization as an open system, taking its inputs from the environment, processing these as throughputs, resulting in outputs that are returned to a supporting environment. Organization–environment interactions became crucial to understanding organizational design.

As open systems, organizations faced an environment that might be placid and benevolent, or turbulent and harsh. Economic, social, political, and technological changes could come rapidly or slowly, and some organizational arrangements might be better able to cope with the changing environment than others. Could it be that

---

61. Alfred D. Chandler, Jr., *Scale and Scope: The Dynamics of Industrial Capitalism* (Cambridge, MA: Harvard University Press, 1990), pp. 469–471, 544.

62. Ludwig von Bertalanffy, "General Systems Theory: A New Approach to the Unity of Science," *Human Biology* 23 (December 1951), pp. 302–361.

there was no one way to structure an organization that design was influenced by environmental factors and could vary, depending on technology?

Joan Woodward (1916–1971) took this contingency view, classified organizations by the complexity of the technology used in producing goods, and found that it influenced an organization's structure. Her classification, ranging from less complex (1) to more advanced (3), consisted of (1) unit and small-batch production systems that produced made-to-order and customized products to meet consumers' needs; (2) large-batch and mass production, which involved a fairly standardized or uniform product with but few variations in its final appearance; and (3) long-run continuous-process production, which involved a standard product manufactured by moving through a predictable series of steps. Woodward's organizations in classifications 1 and 3 delegated more authority, were more permissive in leading people, and had more loosely organized work groups; so the more successful firms exhibited more organizational flexibility. Successful organizations in classification 2 tended to use the line–staff type of organization, exercised closer supervision over personnel, used more elaborate control techniques, and relied more on formal, written communications.[63] The answer to "it depends on . . ." in organizational design, according to Woodward, would be technology.

The "Aston Group," so-called because of varying teams of researchers at the University of Aston, Birmingham, England, under the primary leadership of Derek Pugh, examined technology from a broader perspective. These studies focused on how the flow of work was coordinated, operations technology, and the like, but they did not support Woodward's contention that technology was a determining factor. Rather, it seemed the size of a firm influenced the degree of formality, with larger firms being more specialized.[64] Subsequent research, however, found that neither Woodward's technological determinism nor the Aston group's work could be supported.[65] Technology might play a role, but it did not answer the "if . . . then" contingency view of organizing.

Another approach to organizational design was suggested by a number of researchers, notably Lawrence and Lorsch. They took the position that structure depended on environmental factors: (1) the rate of change in environmental conditions, (2) the certainty of information available, and (3) the time span of feedback of results on decisions made or action taken. Lawrence and Lorsch found that the more successful firms were those that adjusted to their relevant environments. Firms that faced a more stable, more certain environment were more formal and centralized. Firms that faced more unstable, less-certain environments

---

63. Joan Woodward, *Industrial Organization: Theory and Practice* (London: Oxford University Press, 1965).

64. From a vast literature, see Derek S. Pugh, David J. Hickson, and Diana Pheysey, "Operations Technology and Organization Structure: An Empirical Reappraisal," *Administrative Science Quarterly* 14 (1969), pp. 378–397.

65. Miner, *Organizational Behavior*, pp. 465, 470, 525.

were more flexible and decentralized. In both cases, success was due to organizational design consonant with the environment.[66] The work of these authors and others led to a proliferation of research on the contingency approach to organizational design. The results of these studies, however, failed to provide clear support for either approach. Technology was not an overriding factor in determining structure, nor did environmental factors provide clear guides to organizational design.

Another area of interest concerned the possibility that organizational age or size influenced an organization's structure. This notion extended the idea of a product life cycle to that of an organizational life cycle. Products appeared to go through the stages of introduction, growth, maturity, and decline. Of course, some products died young, whereas some products did not decline but were revitalized through new markets, "new and improved" versions, or other tactics devised to prevent the product's demise. Could it be that organizations also went through these stages of start-up, growth, maturity, and decline? The numerous models developed typically described the life cycle in terms of stages, such as birth, growth, and so on, with each stage leading to a point at which adjustments had to be made before another stage could be entered.[67] For instance, moving from a starting point to a growth stage could mean that the entrepreneur had to go public to raise capital, add more employees, expand production, and so on to meet the demands placed on the firm by its growth. If unsuccessful in making the necessary adjustment, the resulting crisis could mean the failure of the enterprise. Some firms expired young, others persisted, but all were vulnerable to failure at any stage of the life cycle. From the various studies of the organizational life cycle, no clear-cut, best way of organizing emerged. Creativity and innovation were necessary to successful start-up ventures, flexibility was needed for growth, stability and formality for maturity, and in the stage of decline, where flexibility was most needed, senescence too often prevailed.

Neither technology, nor environment, nor stage of the life cycle provided any best way of organizing. Although this outcome appeared discouraging, perhaps internal processes could provide answers.

BEHAVIORAL THEORIES OF THE FIRM

A turn from structure to internal processes was the theme of authors such as Richard Cyert and James March, Daniel Katz and Robert Kahn, and Karl Weick.[68]

---

66. Paul R. Lawrence and Jay W. Lorsch, *Organization and Environment* (Homewood, IL: Richard D. Irwin, 1969).

67. Larry E. Greiner, "Evolution and Growth as Organizations Grow," *Harvard Business Review* 50 (July–August 1972), pp. 37–46; and Gordon L. Lippitt and Warren H. Schmidt, "Crises in a Developing Organization," *Harvard Business Review* 45 (November–December 1967), pp. 102–112.

68. Primary works: Richard M. Cyert and James G. March, *A Behavioral Theory of the Firm* (Englewood Cliffs, NJ: Prentice Hall, 1963); Daniel Katz and Robert Kahn, *The Social Psychology of Organizations* (New York: John Wiley and Sons, 1966); and Karl E. Weick, *The Social Psychology of Organizing* (Reading, MA: Addison-Wesley, 1969).

Cyert, an economist, and March, a psychologist, emphasized internal competition for scarce resources, interest groups forming coalitions, conflict resolution, organizational learning, and among other concepts, the adaptive processes of decision making and performance feedback. Psychologists Katz and Kahn emphasized organizational roles, role conflict and ambiguity, the organization as an open input-output system, and circumstances when the hierarchy was preferable to participative styles. Weick, another psychologist, emphasized the organizing process rather than the organizational product and suggested that actions precede goals (goals are retrospective), that individual behaviors are interlocking, and so on.

All but one of those just mentioned was a psychologist by education, so it should not be surprising that their view of organization theory emphasizes internal processes and resembles the micro approach of organizational behavior. Another group of theorists, all but one educated as a sociologist, viewed organizations as a product of macro environmental forces. These behavioralists were Jeffrey Pfeffer and Gerald Salancik, Michael Hannan and John Freeman, and John Meyer and Richard Scott.[69] Pfeffer (the only nonsociologist) and Salancik presented a resource-dependent theory that postulates that organizations require support from their external environment and can only survive to the extent that this support is forthcoming. Managers form coalitions to gather support in an open system of external relationships in which there are constraints that create either a munificent or scarce resource situation. Hannan and Freeman's organizational ecology theory offers the idea that organizational survival is a process of adaptation and success, or fail to adapt and exit. The authors recognized the Darwinian nature of their theory, but have used it to study organizational populations such as labor unions and newspapers for population entries, adaptation, and mortality. The neoinstitutional theory of Meyer and Scott (and others) holds that organizational environments are shaped by societal expectations that provide legitimacy to an organization's existence. By conforming to cultural rules, such as custom or law, formal organizations are able to take on the prevailing view of society.

In the space and time permitted, the presentation of these internally and externally focused behavioral theories does not do justice to the mega-ocean of literature and the theorists extant. There are variations, refinements, added authors, and numerous critiques of these notions. The purpose has been to show how theories of organization have evolved from examining formal structures to contingency notions to emphasizing internal processes to recognizing external forces.

---

69. Primary works: Jeffrey Pfeffer and Gerald R. Salancik, *The External Control of Organizations: A Resource Dependence Perspective* (New York: Harper and Row, 1978); Michael T. Hannan and John Freeman, *Organizational Ecology* (Cambridge, MA: Harvard University Press, 1989); and John W. Meyer and W. Richard Scott, *Organizational Environments: Ritual and Rationality* (Beverly Hills, CA: Sage, 1983).

ECONOMIC AND BUSINESS THEORIES OF THE FIRM

In previous chapters we have seen how a business organization was viewed by earlier writers in business and economic literature. Adam Smith did not like the "joint-stock" company and was concerned about those who managed other peoples' money. Say's identification of management as a fourth factor of production, Ure's "organic systems" of the firm, and other presentations in the writings of John Stuart Mill and Alfred and Mary Marshall were early ideas about the functions, purpose, and scope of a firm. No grand theories developed, but a firm was seen as an entity that must be planned, organized, and monitored. The railroads, America's first big business, required organization, and McCallum and Poor wrote of those issues, whereas Carnegie put them to work in the steel and iron industry.

The Institutional Economics of John Rogers Commons and others saw the firm as part of a larger framework of economics, technology, and society. Marshall and Coase explained why a firm was more efficient than a marketplace; Penrose's writing led to resource- and knowledge-based views of firms; and Williamson built notions to explain the internal operations of firms in terms of markets and hierarchies. Few, if any, of these writers are mentioned by those who developed behavioral theories of the firm. Why? We postulate this came about because the most widely known writings of Max Weber were translated by sociologists (i.e., Gerth and Mills, and later, Henderson and Parsons).[70] Weber was trained in law and wrote of religion, the Protestant ethic, and economics, and only a portion of his work was devoted to bureaucracy. The "economy" portion of his *Wirtschaft und Gesellschaft* (*Economy and Society*) has largely been forgotten by modern scholars. The first translation of any of Weber's writings was by an economist, Frank Knight, but it remains an obscure piece of Weber's intellectual virtuosity.[71] We will leave with a final thought in the words of Barnard, educated as an economist, but a sociologist without portfolio:

> Always, it seemed to me, the social scientists—from whatever side they approached—just reached the edge of organization as I experienced it, and retreated. Rarely did they seem to me to sense the processes of coordination and decision that underlie a large part at least of the phenomena they described. More important, there was lacking much recognition of formal organization as a most important characteristic of social life, and as being the principal structural aspect of society itself.[72]

At this point, we need to examine reactions to this potpourri of theories.

---

70. Max Weber, *From Max Weber: Essays in Sociology*, trans. Hans H. Gerth and C. Wright Mills (New York: Oxford University Press, 1946); and *The Theory of Social and Economic Organization* (trans. by A.M. Henderson and Talcott Parsons), (New York: Free Press, 1947).

71. Max Weber, *General Economic History*, trans. Frank H. Knight (London: Allen and Unwin, 1927).

72. Chester I. Barnard, *The Functions of the Executive*, op. cit., p. ix.

THE PARADIGM WARS

"Paradigm" comes from the Latin and Greek words meaning to show an example, model, or pattern. As such, a paradigm is normative, informing and showing us what is a reasonable way to view situations and events, or as in this case, an organization. Van de Ven noted a "buzzing, blooming, confusing world" of organization and management theories resulting in "a tower of babbling and fragmented explanations" of differing paradigms.[73] He is not perturbed by this, although these paradigms may be confusing and lacking empirical support, but sees this as a healthy sign of the pursuit of knowledge.

Others are not so sure: Donaldson sees this theory thicket as "fragmented... [of] an anti-management quality... [and] long on assertion and short on empirical evidence."[74] Pfeffer attributes this paradigm proliferation to "journal editors and reviewers [who] seem to seek novelty, and there are great rewards for coining a new term... for formulating 'new concepts' but not for studying or rejecting concepts that are already invented."[75] Miner analyzed seventy-three theories, finding no organization theory high in "estimated scientific validity" and "estimated usefulness in application."[76] The judges of Miner's theories were past presidents of the Academy of Management and past editors and editorial reviewers from academy's research and theory journals, that is, knowledgeable academics. How these theories would have fared if practicing managers were surveyed would be interesting. In short, scholarly impulses have created a plethora of theories and an abundance of proponents and critics. Outside the halls of academe, what was happening?

STRATEGY AND STRUCTURE

"Structure follows strategy" was the thesis of Alfred Chandler, a business historian, who selected four companies from some fifty or so examples of decentralization using the multidivisional organization as their strategies unfolded in the 1920s. Whereas he built from cases, other early organization theorists were practicing executives, such as Chester Barnard and Henri Fayol. Fayol, for example, observed that an organization's structure had to be consistent with the "objectives, resources, and requirements" of the firm (see Chapter 10). Barnard's influence has been long lasting, from shaping the Hawthorne studies to Oliver Williamson and transaction

73. Andrew H. Van de Ven, "The Buzzing, Blooming, Confusing World of Organization and Management Theory: A View from Lake Wobegon University," *Journal of Management Inquiry* 8 (1999), p. 119.

74. Lex Donaldson, *American Anti-Management Theories of Organization: A Critique of Paradigm Proliferation* (Cambridge, England: Cambridge University Press, 1995), p. xi.

75. Jeffrey Pfeffer, "Barriers to the Advance of Organizational Science: Paradigm Development as a Dependent Variable," *Academy of Management Review* 18 (1993), p. 612.

76. John B. Miner, "The Rated Importance, Scientific Validity, and Practical Usefulness of Organizational Behavior Theories: A Quantitative Review," *Academy of Management Learning and Education* 2 (2003), pp. 258–259.

cost economics. Despite the experience of practicing managers (which, incidentally, is also "empirical"), academics spin theories with little or no reference to their work.

The need for economies of scale drove organizations in the late nineteenth and much of the twentieth centuries. Organizations integrated vertically to optimize their input-throughput-output operations, and they integrated horizontally to expand the scope of their distribution or production functions. The growth of a managerial hierarchy, a proliferation of staff specialists, and multidivisional structures made sense under those circumstances as Chandler observed. Examining the U.S. economy since the 1960s, a period of increasing paradigm spinning, we can see changing strategies and structures. The 1960s and early 1970s were characterized by two dominant forces—one political and one economic. Business prosperity, willing lenders, and a stock market boom encouraged firms to expand; politically, however, strict enforcement of antitrust regulations discouraged horizontal integration (acquiring firms within its industry). Firms responded with a flurry of mergers and acquisitions to diversify outside their industry.

By the late 1960s, Textron, for example, "sold zippers, pens, snowmobiles, eyeglass frames, silverware, golf carts, machine tools, helicopters, rocket engines, ball bearings, and gas meters."[77] ITT (International Telephone and Telegraph) had 150 separate divisions, each a profit center. RCA (Radio Corporation of America) produced consumer electronics, owned a broadcasting company (NBC), printed books, wove carpets, sold frozen food, leased automobiles, and built a line of computers to compete with IBM. These mergers and acquisitions led firms into unrelated fields, that is, unrelated to their primary line of business. A line–staff structure could not accommodate such diversity, so the multidivisional (M-form) structure was used to follow the strategy of unrelated product diversification.

To manage these firms, called conglomerates, the acquiring or takeover company must do a better job than the previous management—which did not always happen. These "higher levels of diversification [made] it increasingly difficult for corporate executives to use strategic controls. Their span of control is greater and, therefore, the volume of information received is increased and becomes overwhelming."[78] To cope, top management turned to financial controls, such as return on investment (ROI) and overemphasized short-term performance measures to the neglect of long-range innovation to gain technological superiority. The rate of growth of U.S. productivity had peaked near 4 percent in 1973 (the year of an international oil embargo), but then declined to about 1.5 percent per annum for the period 1973–1979. Operating costs increased, squeezing profitability, and stock prices of conglomerates declined as lower earnings were reported. Consequently, a period of divestment or leveraged

---

77. Wyatt Wells, *American Capitalism, 1945–2000: Continuity and Change from Mass Production to the Information Society* (Chicago: Ivan R. Dee, 2003), p. 64.

78. Michael A. Hitt, Robert E. Hoskisson, and Jeffrey S. Harrison, "Strategic Competitiveness in the 1990s: Challenges and Opportunities for U.S. Executives," *Academy of Management Executive* 5 (1991), pp. 7–22.

buyouts shrank the former conglomerates, moving them closer to the products and businesses they knew best. When the Reagan and Clinton administrations in the 1980s and 1990s eased up on antitrust enforcement and moved to deregulate the economy, subsequent mergers and acquisitions were horizontal integrations, such as the oil industry, banking, aluminum, and the railroads.

What lessons does history offer for understanding firm survivability over the long term? One study indicates that 39 percent (193) of the *Fortune* 500 of 1994 were over one hundred years old. Almost one-half (247) were founded between 1880 and 1920—a period characterized by increasing mass production; mass marketing; revolutions in transportation and communication; and incidentally, systematic/scientific management. These 247 companies "were often the first in their industries to make the necessary investments and create the corporate organizations essential to exploit the new technologies and markets."[79] In the last half of the twentieth century, industrial growth was fueled by science and its handmaiden, technology, in pharmaceuticals, petrochemistry, aerospace, and firms employing integrated circuitry. Some 16 percent of *Fortune's* 500 were founded in the last half of the twentieth century.

This evidence does not prove that standing among the largest five hundred companies in 1994 was due to longevity. Rather, the implication is that the firms that grew and survived were able to take advantage of changing technologies and markets, design the appropriate corporate structures to seize the opportunities offered by these developments, and foster staying power by adapting to changes over the long term. Organization theory debates will continue, but without reflecting successful practices, they will be devoid of usefulness.

SUMMARY

The influx of the social scientists into business schools had a significant impact on management thought. They brought different perspectives, research tools, and ideas to reshape human relations into organizational behavior. Argyris and McGregor called for redesigning organizations to promote individual maturity and posited that the assumptions a manager made about people determined the managerial style. Job design sought to provide greater employee involvement, and goal-setting theory provided a means of rewarding to promote self-efficacy. Personnel management evolved into human-resource management, and some connections with industrial relations were suggested. Leadership theories cycled from traits through contingency notions and back to leader styles and leader–member relations in transformational, charismatic, transactional, and leader–member exchange theories.

---

79. [Harris Corporation], "Founding Dates of the 1994 *Fortune* 500 U.S. Companies," *Business History Review* 70 (1996), p. 70.

Organization theory evolved from examining structure, hierarchy of authority, span of control, departmentation, and related ideas to possibilities of external determinants, such as technology or environment. Theories proffered by psychologists and sociologists differed—the former emphasizing internal processes, the latter external ones that shaped an organization's structure. Economists and business writers saw firms as a means of taking resource inputs, and processing them in some fashion into outputs, and Chandler stressed the influence of strategy on structure. Finally, it was suggested that better theory can be built by examining successful practices in firms over the long term.

CHAPTER

21

Science and Systems in Management

Numbers have always held a fascination for humankind; people have ascribed magical powers to some numbers, malignancy to others, and throughout history have used numbers to account for flocks of sheep as well as to reach for the stars. Numbers have no intrinsic value in themselves, but they have become symbols of the quest for knowledge because they lend a preciseness and orderliness to our environment. In observing nature, it was also noted that there was a natural rhythm of all seasons, of the solar system, and of life and death in all things. Our inquisitiveness led us to explore, to attempt to explain the inexplicable, and to search for a great force that binds the complexities observed in nature into some rational order of events. People have sought to bring order from chaos by searching for interrelationships between observed events and activities. Although we are curious and seek variety in life, we also have a need for closure, a need to bring our observations into some unity of perception. Humans are basically orderly, rational beings who desire to control their environment insofar as that is possible.

The preceding pages have described numerous attempts to rationalize and systematize the workplace and to measure and control organizational operations. Management's need for information to monitor performance and keep in touch with external events is also ancient. In earlier chapters, we saw how new technologies, such as the telegraph, enabled managers to have a systematic means of gathering, recording, and using information to make decisions. This chapter carries on from those deep roots to trace developments into the modern era.

THE QUEST FOR SCIENCE IN MANAGEMENT

The scientific method denotes a rational approach to problem solving through a statement of hypothesis, accumulation of data, identification of alternatives, and testing, verification, and selection of a path of action based on facts. In his break with the mystics who held that reality was unknowable, Aristotle established the foundations for the scientific method. After Greece and Rome fell, reason yielded to the Age of Faith during the Middle Ages, only to reemerge in the Renaissance and the Age of Reason. It was during this time that the foundations for modern mathematics and science were established. René Descartes (1596–1650) thought the world operated mechanistically and prescribed the use of mathematics to describe its movements. Isaac Newton (1642–1727) developed calculus and laws of motion and gravitation, furthering Descartes' conception of the world as a giant machine. Others also saw an orderly universe. Mathematics was the building block for bringing the parts together into one grand formula. The rediscovery of Aristotle during this time and the renewed interest in mathematics and in science led to the vast techno-logical changes in humankind's environment that became known as the Industrial Revolution.

Charles Babbage, and to some extent Andrew Ure, applied a scientific approach to the solution of the problems of the burgeoning factory system. Industrialization demanded order and predictability, and the engineers were well equipped to cope with the scientific study and systematization of work. Scientific management and the work of Taylor, Barth, Gantt, the Gilbreths, Emerson, and others constituted the Age of Reason in twentieth-century management thought. In the 1930s, scientific management declined in emphasis as society had to cope with problems beyond the production of goods. World War II and the renewed growth of large-scale enterprise, however, created a new environment for management. In the modern era, new ideas were formed to add to the tradition of Aristotle, Descartes, Babbage, and scientific management.

OPERATIONS RESEARCH

World War I gave widespread recognition and acceptance to the notion of science in management. Governmental and industrial organizations seized on the precepts of scientific management to cope with the mass assemblages of resources required to carry on the war. For more than three decades, the ideas of Gantt, Taylor, and other scientific-management thinkers were carried forward as "industrial administration" or "production management." This approach was, more often than not, a view of how to improve the production function as part of the firm's throughput, rather than as a vital ingredient of the general management of the firm. Outside events, however, soon led to added dimensions for production management.

World War II brought about a union of managers, government officials, and scientists in an attempt to bring order and rationality to the global logistics of war. The British formed the first operations research teams of various specialists in an effort to bring their knowledge to bear on the problems of radar systems, antiaircraft gunnery, antisubmarine warfare, the bombing of Germany, and civilian defense matters.[1] One of the best-known groups was under the direction of Professor P. M. S. Blackett (1897–1974), physicist, Nobel Prize winner, and codeveloper of radar. Blackett's team, called "Blackett's circus," included three physiologists, two mathematical physicists, one astrophysicist, one Army officer, one surveyor, one general physicist, and two mathematicians. It was in groups such as this one that various specialists were brought together under one tent to solve the complex problems of the war and defense efforts.

Operations research was conceived as the application of scientific knowledge and methods to the study of complex problems with the stated purpose of deriving a quantitative basis for the decisions that would accomplish an organization's objectives. The British formed the first operations research groups, but U.S. industrial organizations and private consulting firms also began to recognize that the methods of operations research were applicable to problems of a nonmilitary nature. Arthur D. Little, Inc., a private consulting firm, was one of the first to seek industrial uses for operations research. The Operations Research Society of America was founded in 1952 and began publishing a journal, *Operations Research*. In 1953, The Institute of Management Science (TIMS) stated its objectives as "to identify, extend, and unify scientific knowledge that contributes to the understanding of the practice of management" and began publishing the journal *Management Science*.

The application of operations research techniques came very naturally to production management, an area with structured kinds of problems and decisions for which decision rules could be rationally devised. There were problems with stocking the proper level of inventories, scheduling and controlling production, manufacturing in economical batches, controlling quality, and acquiring capital, as well as a host of other physical resource problems. The similarities between operations research and scientific management were striking. For his metal-cutting experiments, Frederick Taylor brought together a team of researchers that included a mathematician (Carl Barth), a metallurgist (Maunsell White), an engineer (Henry Gantt), and others to assist him in the solution of various problems. The Gilbreths spoke of the "one best way" as the objective of their scientific analysis. The modern management scientist has merely put the quest more euphemistically: "The approach of optimality analysis is to take various alternatives into account and to ask which of these possible sets of decisions will come closest to meeting the businessman's objectives (i.e., which decisions will be best or optimal)."[2] The difference between the "one best way" and an "optimal" decision is moot. The old school and the new have both sought through the scientific method to rationally evaluate alternatives

---

1. Joseph F. McClosky, "The Beginnings of Operations Research: 1934–1941," *Operations Research* 35 (1987), pp. 143–152.

2. William J. Baumol, *Economic Theory and Operations Analysis* (Englewood Cliffs, NJ: Prentice Hall, 1961), p. 4.

in an effort to find the best possible decision. In the Gilbreths' time, people had confidence that science could lead to a perfect society; today, because people are less confident in such a scheme, "optimal" sounds better than the "one best way."

Another striking similarity was that the modern researchers, like their predecessors, sought to apply the scientific method in the analysis of human behavior. The Institute of Management Science formed an interest group, the College on Management Psychology, "to investigate the processes of work and managing work by applying psychology, psychiatry, and the behavioral sciences to enhance our understanding of management." Hugo Münsterberg could not have stated the case more clearly. Modern behavioral scientists frequently viewed management science as a continuation of a mechanistic view of people and considered the behavioral and quantitative approaches to be mutually exclusive. However, it was not the wheel that was humankind's great invention, but the axle; it is important to search for how these areas complement one another and how they might be brought together in some grand scheme.

Modern management science, inverted from scientific management, was not so much the search for a science of management as a striving for the use of science *in* management. In this endeavor the tools of mathematics and science were enlisted to help solve the age-old management problem of the optimum allocation of scarce resources toward a given goal.

PRODUCTION MANAGEMENT IN TRANSITION

The Gordon and Howell report had few kind words for production management: "Production management courses are often the repository for some of the most inappropriate and intellectually stultifying materials to be found in the business curriculum . . . many faculty members have little respect for such courses . . . and students complained more strongly to us about the pointlessness of the production requirement than of any other."[3] Gordon and Howell were also particularly critical of the state of business education with respect to mathematics. The typical business school curriculum, preparing students for leadership in a computerized space age, had few if any requirements for mathematics. The modern era saw a reversal of this state of affairs, and business schools began to require more and more statistics and mathematics of their students, and a new genre of production management textbooks emerged, heavily influenced by operations research techniques. The outcome for management education was to move beyond the idea of factory/industrial/production management into an era that blended the old and the new into "production/operations management."

---

3. Robert A. Gordon and James E. Howell, *Higher Education for Business* (New York: Columbia University Press, 1959), p. 190. In a footnote, Gordon and Howell stated that statistics courses received a greater number of complaints questioning the relevance of requiring the statistics course.

The new language of production/operations management was heavily oriented toward statistics and mathematics. At its base was the scientific method of problem solving; the body was composed of specific techniques for quantifying variables and relationships; and its apex was the notion of a model representing the variables and their relationships for the purposes of prediction and control. Such techniques as statistics, linear programming, waiting line or queuing theory, game theory, decision trees, the transportation method, Monte Carlo methods, and simulation devices were part and parcel of the new language. Statistics and probability theory aided in sampling for quality control and other uses; linear programming and its special techniques facilitated the choice of a desirable course of action given certain constraints; and queuing theory helped balance the costs and the services of a machine or other service facility. Competitive strategies could be best understood by drawing on game theory; capital acquisitions could be simulated through computers and the use of probability theory; and quantitative models could be built and manipulated to test the impact of changes on one or more of the variables or the model as a whole.

Along with presenting the analytical techniques, serious attempts were made to bring the operations research tools into a conceptual framework. The "decision theorists" sought to combine the economic concepts of utility and choice with the more modern quantitative tools. One early landmark attempt was that by Miller and Starr, who stressed the executive's decision-making role in optimizing corporate goals and placed less emphasis on the techniques.[4] These more sophisticated decision-making tools reshaped notions of educating students through changes in business school curricula and also created a new variety of specialists with whom the manager had to communicate. The ideas of Henri Fayol, who had found the use of higher mathematics of no value in his managerial experience, probably would be severely shaken by today's business school.

Henry Gantt would also be surprised to find what the new quantitative methods meant to his ideas. Gantt, under pressure to handle complex industrial military interactions in World War I, had devised a graphic method of scheduling and controlling activities. In 1956 to 1957, the DuPont Company developed a computerized arrow diagram or network method for planning and controlling, which became known as the Critical Path Method (CPM). This method used only one time estimate and included only activities (arrows). In 1957 to 1958, in managing the development of the Polaris missile, the U.S. Navy encountered many of the same problems in project scheduling and evaluation as it had in Gantt's day with shipbuilding. Together with the consulting help of Booz, Allen, and Hamilton, Inc., and the Lockheed Missile System Division (the prime contractor), the U.S. Navy devised the Program Evaluation and Review Technique (PERT). This technique

4. David W. Miller and Martin K. Starr, *Executive Decisions and Operations Research* (Englewood Cliffs, NJ: Prentice Hall, 1960). See also David W. Miller and Martin K. Starr, *The Structure of Human Decisions* (Englewood Cliffs, NJ: Prentice Hall, 1967).

used statistical probability theory to furnish three time estimates (pessimistic, most probable, and optimistic) and added "events" (circles) to the graphing of activities.

Taken together, the PERT and CPM techniques served to plan a network of activities, their relationships, and their interaction along a path to a given completion date. They graphed paths for the flow of activities, provided events as checkpoints, and focused managerial attention on a critical path or paths in an effort to keep the total project on course. Although these techniques are much more complex than this brief description implies, they are really little more than the Gantt chart concept enlarged and enriched by many years of increased computing capabilities and statistical knowledge.

In brief, the earlier notions of production management were reshaped by operations researchers, statisticians, and decision theorists. The application of the scientific method and the use of mathematics in some types of managerial problems could provide better information for decision makers. Although more advanced techniques enhanced the academic credibility of production/operations management, some began to wonder whether these tools were placing too much emphasis on problem solving and not enough on problem finding. It would take a competitive challenge from abroad to move production/operations management into another stage of development.

OLD LESSONS RELEARNED

The importance of product quality is not new; in early craft guilds, for example, it was the practice to place a mark on the product (hallmark) so that customers could connect quality with the maker of the item. The manufacture of interchangeable parts increased the need to produce to close tolerances, making measurement and inspection necessary. Andrew Carnegie considered quality the bedrock of the success of his enterprise: "even in these days of fiercest competition, when everything would seem to be a matter of price, there lies still at the root of business success the much more important factor of quality.... After that, and a long way after, comes cost."[5] In his 1903 paper before the American Society of Mechanical Engineers, Frederick Taylor designated one of the functional foremen to be the first to be brought into contact with the worker, and the inspection system must be in place and understood "before any steps are taken toward stimulating the men to a larger output; otherwise an increase in quantity will probably be accompanied by a falling off of quality."[6] In the period following World War II, however, production management began to take a back seat to human relations, the financial management of corporate portfolios, and unrelated product diversification.

---

5. Andrew Carnegie, *Autobiography of Andrew Carnegie* (Boston: Houghton Mifflin, 1920), pp. 122–123.

6. Frederick W. Taylor, *Shop Management* (New York: Harper and Row, 1911), p. 144.

Hayes and Abernathy charged that U.S. industry had forgotten how to compete, produce efficiently, keep prices down, and maintain product quality.[7] As the global competitive challenge arose, especially from Japan, and U.S. productivity lagged, production management became once more a glamour stock. In contrast to the industrial engineering, shop-management approach of earlier years, the call was for improving product quality and placing production in the corporate strategy, general management mainstream. The challenge was whether the United States could relearn the lessons about quality, efficiency, and productivity that it had been teaching the rest of the world since the scientific-management period.

After World War II, as part of U.S. efforts to rebuild the Japanese economy that the war had just finished destroying, a series of events occurred that would make Japan an industrial phoenix. The Japanese productivity "miracle" was based on ideas introduced into Japan in the period immediately following World War ll. During the U.S. occupation, U.S. engineers were given the task of helping Japanese industry recover. Two engineers, Charles Protzman and Homer Sarasohn, started a series of seminars on policy, organization, operations, production controls, quality controls, and U.S. production management methods for Japanese managers. Although Protzman worked for the Hawthorne Plant of Western Electric, he felt that the Japanese needed production skills rather than human-relations skills.[8]

At Western Electric, Walter A. Shewhart (1891–1967) began working on industrial quality control problems in the early 1920s with the goal of replacing the phrase "as alike as two peas in a pod" with "as alike as two telephones." Shewhart took samples of the work done and applied statistical analysis to identify variations in performance. He devised a control chart to define the acceptable limits of random variation in any worker's task so that any output outside those limits could be detected and studied as to what caused the unacceptable variation. To illustrate his point, Shewhart used different colored chips drawn from a bowl to show that there were always differences in the number of one color of chips drawn by one person compared with the number drawn by any other person. Thus, there was always some random variation in industrial production over which the worker had no control. But over numerous trials, there would be some limits to this random variation. It was what happened outside these limits that could be examined for corrective action. Shewhart pioneered statistical quality control, but it would be one of his followers who would revive the idea of product quality in the post–World War II period.[9]

7. Robert H. Hayes and William J. Abernathy, "Managing Our Way to Economic Decline," *Harvard Business Review* 58 (July–August 1980), pp. 67–77.

8. Based on the research of Kenneth Hopper as reported in Rebecca R. Tsurumi, "American Origins of Japanese Productivity: The Hawthorne Experiment Rejected," *Pacific Basic Quarterly* (Spring–Summer 1982), pp. 14–15. See also Robert C. Wood, "A Lesson Learned and a Lesson Forgotten," *Forbes* (February 6, 1989), pp. 70–78, for Sarasohn's recollections of those events.

9. Joe Stauffer, "SQC before Deming: The Works of Walter Shewhart," *The Journal of Applied Management and Entrepreneurship* 8 (October 2003), pp. 86–94.

W. Edwards Deming. Courtesy of The W. Edwards Deming Institute®.

William Edwards Deming (1900–1993), educated as a mathematical physicist, applied Shewhart's ideas of sampling for statistical quality control in the U.S. Department of Agriculture and later as an employee of the U.S. Census Bureau. His reputation as an expert on statistical sampling led to his employment during World War II to teach engineers and technicians how to use these techniques in the production of war materials. In 1947 he went to Japan to help prepare for a 1951 census of that country. Deming was pleased when Kenichi Koyanagi, managing director of the Union of Japanese Scientists and Engineers (JUSE), invited him in 1950 to present some lectures on statistical quality control. Koyanagi and his colleagues had continued their study of U.S. manufacturing methods after Sarasohn and Protzman returned to the United States and had read Walter Shewhart's classic *Economic Control of Quality of Manufactured Product* and Shewhart's lectures, edited by Deming, on statistical quality control.[10]

Deming began his seminars in Japan in 1950 and for three decades he lectured and consulted in Japan. As a result of an NBC television program in 1980, entitled "If Japan Can...Why Can't We?" American audiences finally became aware of Deming, but they did not find a smiling face. Deming was critical of U.S. management, perhaps because he had been ignored for so long, but more likely because U.S. firms were losing market share to other, more quality oriented and more productive competitors. He blamed U.S. management: "The wealth of a nation depends on its people, management, and government, more than its natural resources. The problem is where to find good management. It would be a mistake to export American management to a friendly country."[11]

Deming identified seven deadly diseases that caused U.S. industry to go into decline:

1. Lack of constancy of purpose toward improvement of products and services
2. An emphasis on short-term profits
3. Merit rating or other evaluation of individual performance
4. Job hopping by managers
5. Managing by the numbers without considering figures that are unknown or unknowable

---

10. Walter A. Shewhart, *Economic Control of Quality of Manufactured Product* (New York: Van Nostrand, 1931).

11. W. Edwards Deming, *Out of the Crisis* (Cambridge, MA: Massachusetts Institute of Technology, Center for Advanced Engineering Study, 1986), p. 6.

6. Excessive medical costs (peculiar to the United States)

7. The litigious nature of the U.S. citizenry, causing excessive costs of liability that increased as lawyers worked on contingency fee

Deming attributed 95 percent of all errors to the systems under which people worked, not the people themselves. Quality management began at the top of the organization, not with the employee. The goal was the reduction of variation through continuous improvement (*Kaizen*), discovering what was out of control as a result of special causes. Deming's slogan was "Plan-Do-Act" in a cycle of activity that provided feedback for continuous improvement. (This carried a marked resemblance to Argyris's double-loop learning.) For a decade and a half before his death, Deming berated American managers for their faults, stimulating a new interest in quality management.[12]

Another significant person in the early quality movement was Joseph M. Juran (1904–2008). Juran worked at Western Electric, learned from Shewhart, and like Deming was inoculated with the statistical quality control ideas being implemented throughout the Bell system at this time. Juran questioned, however, whether quality was solely a matter of statistics and traced the beginning of a separate quality inspection responsibility to the writings of Frederick W. Taylor. After World War II, Juran became an independent consultant on quality control, but like Deming, found a waning interest among U.S. manufacturers. He assembled and edited a weighty handbook on quality control that became a standard reference tool on the subject and also led JUSE to invite him to Japan in 1954. Japanese managers and workers struggled trying to understand Deming's ideas on statistical quality control until Juran came and established quality control as a job for everyone. His approach asked the firm to identify and work on the most critical problems first, which he called the "vital few," before moving on to resolve the "trivial many" problems. Juran called this the "Pareto Principle," although he later admitted that this was an improper attribution to Vilfredo Pareto, a late nineteenth- and early twentieth-century economist.[13] Regardless, the Pareto effect has been passed down as an eighty-twenty rule: for example, 80 percent of the quality problems are caused by 20 percent of the manufacturing operations. By focusing on Juran's "vital few" operations first, a large number of problems could be resolved before management turned to the "trivial many."

Juran's three-part system was aimed at improving quality year after year. Firms began by setting goals, organizing into teams to work on these projects, and working with Juran and his staff through each project. This approach blended

---

12. A valuable resource on Deming is Peter B. Petersen, "Library of Congress Archives: Additional Information about W. Edwards Deming (1900–1993) Now Available," *Journal of Management History* 3 (1997), pp. 98–119.

13. Pareto quantified a nonuniform distribution of wealth in society but did not apply this to other phenomena. A U.S.-born statistician, Max Otto Lorenz, developed a "Lorenz Curve" to display the deviation of an individual's income from a perfect equality of wealth. In statistical quality control terms and in Juran's thinking, this was the deviation of a sample from the standard.

statistical analysis with traditional managerial actions of planning, organizing, and controlling. Clients admired Juran's methodical, companywide approach and the improved results as the vital few and the trivial many problems were solved.

The Japanese also pioneered the idea of forming small problem-solving groups of workers, supervisors, and specialists for the purpose of developing better ways of doing a job with higher quality. These groups, known as quality circles, enabled an industrial renaissance in Japan. As they became more competitive, their products threatened, and in some cases surpassed, U.S. products in the marketplace. As concern for quality grew, numerous others also began to write and consult about how the United States and other nations could catch up with Japan. Space does not permit a lengthy discussion of this stream of literature, so thumbnail sketches must suffice. Armand V. Feigenbaum began his career at General Electric and coined the phrase "total quality control" in the 1950s. This was a forerunner of GE's well-known "six sigma" quality program. Philip Crosby started with the Crosley Corporation but worked for other firms, consulted, and concentrated on attaining "zero defects" in manufacturing. In addition to these, numerous Japanese authorities became well known: Genichi Taguchi of Nippon Telephone and Telegraph; Taiichi Ohno and Shigeo Shingo (discussed later), who were inspired by Frederick Taylor's writings to instill quality control at Toyota; and Ichiro Ueno, son of Yoichi Ueno, who promoted scientific management in Japan. The list of contributors to the quality control movement could easily get out of control, given the confines of this historical perspective.

A long-term study of the worldwide automobile industry at the Massachusetts Institute of Technology introduced a new phrase, "lean manufacturing," to describe the integration of various quality ideas and techniques into one overall approach.[14] The study included many companies, but it was clear that Toyota of Japan was the model company for lean manufacturing. The leader of the Toyota Production System was Taiichi Ohno, assisted by Shigeo Shingo, and lean manufacturing incorporated process improvement, zero defects, just-in-time inventory management, reducing set-up and changeover times, coordination with suppliers of raw materials, and keeping in touch with the Toyota dealers. Lean manufacturing was a concept that operated across Toyota from automobile design, production and inventory management, and contacts with those in the supply chain of parts and raw materials, and the sellers and users of Toyota products. Lean management became part of the management lexicon as it influenced manufacturing, quality control, supply-chain management, and how the firm must be seen as an input-throughput-output system.

In 1980, Ohno was asked how he got his idea for the just-in-time method of handling inventories. Ohno's response was that it came from reading about Henry Ford's experiences.[15] Ford, but primarily Ernest Kanzler, one of his managers,

---

14. James P. Womack, Daniel T. Jones, and Daniel Roos, *The Machine that Changed the World* (New York: Maxwell Macmillan International, 1990).

15. Taiichi Ohno, quoted by Norman Bodek in Henry Ford (in collaboration with Samuel Crowther), *Today and Tomorrow* (1926, repr. Cambridge, MA: Productivity Press, 1988), p. vii.

developed the idea of reducing his inventory "float" by carefully planning and coordinating the input of raw materials in the factory.[16] Raw materials could be acquired and transformed into automobiles that would be on Ford's dealers' lots in fourteen instead of twenty-eight days. The savings in inventory carrying costs were substantial. Ford's inventory went from an average of $60,000,000 to $20,000,000 (in 1920 dollars). Similarly, Toyota's assembly line, designed by Ohno, *pulled* the parts to be assembled in the quantity that was needed just-in-time resulting in lower inventory carrying costs.

Improved quality and inventory management were only parts of the changing character of production/operations management. The idea that manufacturing needed to become part of a firm's strategy took longer to emerge. Gordon and Howell's characterization of production management as "intellectually stultifying" did little to promote interest in viewing manufacturing as a competitive weapon. Skinner's pioneering work indicated the need to incorporate manufacturing strategy into corporate strategy and to look beyond efficiency and production at the lowest cost to seek competitive costs, and it suggested the possibility that sound manufacturing strategy could yield a competitive advantage.[17] In product design, efficient processing technologies, and quality control, the production function could promote corporate goals.

Schonberger urged the view that the functions of the firm (e.g., marketing, engineering, and manufacturing) should be integrated to be linked in a continuous "chain of customers."[18] Every department had a customer, a user of that department's output, and human and physical resources should be organized around the flow of products or services provided. For instance, product design employees would work with process engineers, accountants, market researchers, and others in a collaborative team rather than passing a proposed new product from one department to another. The notion resembles (to this historian) Fayol's "gangplank," which was intended to provide for horizontal communication and coordination across functional boundaries. The lesson to be relearned is that a commonality of goals requires recognition of this common purpose, and in turn, there must be a willingness to break down functional barriers to provide for cooperative effort.

The old lessons came from Americans such as Ford, Taylor, Shewhart, Deming, and Juran, but the improvements in manufacturing methods and implementation came from Japan, which learned and improved on earlier ideas. As this is being written, Toyota is on the brink of passing General Motors, once the behemoth of the auto industry, as the world's number one automobile producer. There is no need for

16. Peter B. Petersen, "The Misplaced Origin of Just-in-Time Production Methods," *Management Decision* 40 (2002), pp. 82–88.

17. Wickham Skinner, "Manufacturing—Missing Link in Corporate Strategy," *Harvard Business Review* 47 (May–June 1969), pp. 136–145.

18. Richard J. Schonberger, *Building a Chain of Customers: Linking Business Functions to Create the World Class Company* (New York: Free Press, 1990).

antitrust action (as once thought) to break up General Motors; Schumpeter was right when he praised innovation and invention as the means of competitive advantage.

Systems and Information

Throughout history, people have observed orderliness in nature. They saw an ecological balance in plant and animal life; noted that the planets and stars operated predictably enough and made gods of stars and used them to chart their own life forecasts; and followed a rhythm in the coming and going of seasons to plant and harvest their crops. Primitive people built their life activities around rituals that were a part of this natural order; such ceremonies gave them the security of order and predictability.

As people designed their organizations, they sought once more the orderliness in their operations that they observed in nature. For example, early factory managers sought systematic management that would arrange the workplace, secure the proper flow of materials, and facilitate the performance of human effort to achieve some predictable result. Behavioralists spoke of social systems, studied workplaces as sociotechnical systems, and noted the need for equilibrium both within the organization and with elements outside the organization. In these notions of systems there are a number of common characteristics: (1) a goal or purpose for the organization; (2) some presumed inflow or input of materials, equipment, and human effort into the organization; (3) something done in the organization to transform these inputs into some useful product or service to meet the goals of the organization; and (4) a need to measure, control, and acquire the necessary information about performance to see whether plans were being carried out. There was a search to study the parts, to understand their interrelationships, and to arrange them to lead to the desired outcome.

GENERAL SYSTEMS THEORY

Although notions of systems existed before, the major distinction between the modern era and prior eras was in the way of thinking, or the philosophy of the systems approach. Again there are deep roots in prior thought. In the early twentieth century, psychologists and sociologists began the organismic or Gestalt approach in theories of behavior, representing a break with the previous mechanistic or fundamental unit method analysis.

Ludwig von Bertalanffy (1901–1972), a biologist, is credited with coining the phrase "general systems theory." Bertalanffy thought that it was possible to develop a systemic, theoretical framework for describing relationships in the real world and that similarities among different disciplines could enable a general systems model to be developed. Bertalanffy's objective was to search for parallelisms in disciplines that would give rise to a general theoretical framework. Bertalanffy noted certain characteristics similar in all sciences: (1) the study of a whole, or organism;

(2) the tendency of organisms to strive for a steady state or equilibrium; and (3) the "openness" of all systems, that is, an organism affects and is affected by its environment.[19] Bertalanffy's influence on management and organizational theory was described in Chapter 20.

Bertalanffy's efforts were the beginning piece in a jigsaw puzzle on which others began to build. Norbert Wiener (1894–1964) adopted the word *cybernetics* from the Greek *kubernētēs*, meaning pilot or person at the helm.[20] The study of cybernetics showed that all systems could be designed to control themselves through a communications loop, which fed information back to the organism, thus allowing it to adjust to its environment. This information feedback meant that an organization could "learn" and adapt for future situations. General systems theory and cybernetics provided the foundations for an information age of networks and systems that reshaped how we live and work.

FROM THE INVISIBLE HAND TO THE DIGITAL HAND

Suppose it is some fifty or so years ago and you are the Director of the Data Processing Department in your firm. When you arrive at work, you see numerous persons operating key punching machines to make tiny holes in eighty-column cards that carry a printed admonishment that these cards should not be folded, spindled, or mutilated; another employee is running a sorter to arrange these cards into various categories; another is operating a tabulator that reads these tiny holes and prints the results on long sheets of paper.

Assured that all is working properly, you enter your office, check your flip-the-page calendar for your appointments, and finding some spare time, you check the financial pages of the *Wall Street Journal.* You see computing machinery that includes International Business Machines (IBM), Sperry-Rand, Minneapolis-Honeywell, RCA, National Cash Register, and a few other firms, but IBM is definitely number one in the business. You decide to take a vacation and use your black, rotary-dial phone to call your local travel agent, who can make plane, hotel, and rental car arrangements and mail you some brochures describing how to find your destinations, your accommodations, and other information. Seeking information about some topic, you go to your shelves and take the appropriate encyclopedia, or wishing to spell a word properly, you also have a dictionary on your shelf.

Fast-forward to the present, and the information world you knew is quite different. You have a computer on your desk, or perhaps you brought the one that is thinner than a dictionary, and you connect with the Internet or the World Wide Web to check the stock market and now you find Dell, Microsoft, Cisco, Intel, Apple,

---

19. Ludwig von Bertalanffy, "General Systems Theory: A New Approach to the Unity of Science," *Human Biology* 23 (December 1951), pp. 302–361.

20. Norbert Wiener, *Cybernetics* (Cambridge, MA: MIT Press, 1948).

or other firms in the computing industry. You use search engines such as Yahoo or Google to seek information on such arcane subjects as the Boer War or what happened at Waterloo. For your vacation, you arrange your own transportation, compare air fares, locate sleeping accommodations, and view the dining room, sleeping area, or other facilities in the location you have chosen; you are virtually there. You have a personal digital assistant, which provides your appointments, reminds you to have your pacemaker checked via your cell phone connection to your physician, and that you will need to visit an ATM for lunch money.

What happened in those intervening fifty or so years?

You have entered an age of information enabled by advancing computer technology. Of the "ten forces that flattened the world" eight of them are related directly in some fashion to this information age: work flow software, uploading, outsourcing, offshoring, supply-chaining, insourcing, in-forming, and steroids.[21] Cortada sums up this history of evolution from the invisible hand of the market of Adam Smith, to Chandler's visible hand of management, to the digital hand of this information age that has reshaped our lives.[22] In earlier chapters we have touched on the advancements in calculating power in the work of Babbage, whose dream included a mechanical device that could be to programmed to solve all sorts of problems. The analytical engine was not built during Babbage's time because manufacturing technology was not advanced enough to build the parts to the necessary precision; besides, where could it be plugged in?

Another step in computer development was made by the British mathematician Alan Turing. In 1938, as the armies of Hitler's Germany threatened Europe, the British intelligence services became concerned with a new German message-encoding machine called Enigma. If the code could be broken, British intelligence could intercept and use the German messages to anticipate Hitler's moves. Cryptology (the devising and breaking of coded messages) was a complicated process, and the Enigma machine had defied all traditional cryptanalysis. Turing, among others, was employed by the British to break the Enigma system. Because almost all codes depend on the substitution of numbers for letters in various ways and because a huge number of combinations are possible, only a machine that could process masses of numbers could hope to break the code. Turing led the effort and developed an electrical machine, essentially a computer, to handle these calculations.[23]

Herman Hollerith developed a punch card and sorter and formed the Tabulating Machine Company (1903), which, after a period of time, became the International

---

21. Thomas L. Friedman, *The World is Flat: A Brief History of the Twenty-First Century* (updated and expanded version), (New York: Farrar, Straus, and Giroux, 2007), pp. 51–199. Friedman uses steroids to refer to increased computing power and capabilities rather than enhanced athletic performance.

22. James W. Cortada, *The Digital Hand: How Computers Changed the Work of American Manufacturing, Transportation, and Retail Industries* (New York: Oxford University Press, 2004).

23. Andrew Hodges, *Alan Turing: The Enigma* (New York: Simon and Schuster, 1983), especially pp. 166–170, 181–195.

Business Machines Corporation. During the period from 1937 to 1944, Howard Aiken designed and built an electromechanical computing machine, called the Mark I, for IBM. In Chapter 18 we saw Eckert and Mauchly's development of the gigantic ENIAC. The Eckert–Mauchly patents for ENIAC, however, were disputed in a lawsuit. John V. Atanasoff had built an electronic digital computer for Iowa State University in the 1930s. Neither Atanasoff nor Iowa State filed for a patent, but the court upheld Atanasoff's creation and stopped the royalty payments to Sperry-Rand, the holder of the Mauchly-Eckert patents.[24]

After more than a century from Charles Babbage's conception to Atanasoff's reality, the computer evolved rapidly in technological capability and in applications. The first computers were monster mainframes; expert observers thought that only a few computers would be necessary to handle the U.S. census, scientific calculations, and maybe even accounting, payroll, and inventory problems. "Electronic data processing" was the common phrase for computers, emphasizing their ability to handle masses of transactions and calculations. By 1960, IBM's revenues were twice the total of all other firms in the industry combined. Barriers to entry into the giant mainframe gave IBM a competitive advantage.

Threats to break up the alleged IBM "monopoly" were made unnecessary by advancing computer technology that moved from vacuum tubes, to transistors by Bell Labs, to integrated circuitry coinvented by Robert Noyce of Fairchild Semiconductor and Texas Instruments' Jack Kilby.[25] These microprocessors triggered a host of changes in both hardware (equipment) and software (operating systems). Originally called "microcomputers," an early, if not the first, was the Altair 8800, powered by an Intel-made chip. By 1977, some 72 percent of the microcomputer market was held by three firms: Apple, Commodore, and Tandy. Only two years earlier, Bill Gates and Paul Allen founded Microsoft. In 1980, International Business Machines (IBM) decided to enter the market, and the microcomputer began its evolution to personal computers and eventually to laptops.

Satellites would enable wireless messages across geographic boundaries, and the Internet, founded by the Department of Defense in 1960, would be privatized and provide a worldwide network for messages. Products could be bought and sold over the Internet and a borderless economy emerged, creating new opportunities as well as threats. Electronic commerce enabled customers to shop worldwide; plane reservations for U.S. travel could be made through a conversation with a person in, for example, New Delhi; and factories and operations could be monitored, regardless of the location of the firm's central office. Entertainment, such as sporting events, could be viewed internationally. As a result, this borderless market created numerous

---

24. "After Almost Half a Century, the Father of the Computer Gets a Celebration," *The Chronicle of Higher Education* 27, no. 8 (October 19, 1983), p. 17; and Clark R. Mollenhoff, *Atanasoff: Forgotten Father of the Computer* (Ames: Iowa State University Press, 1988).

25. Leslie Berlin, *The Man Behind the Microchip: Robert Noyce and the Invention of Silicon Valley* (New York: Oxford University Press, 2005), p. 3.

opportunities for entrepreneurial ventures, many originating in the Silicon Valley of California, creating a generation of dot-com billionaires.

Technology is the handmaiden of management theory and practice. Advancing computer technology also provided the *means* to advance the managerial tasks of planning, measuring, evaluating, and controlling organizational performance. From her study of organizational communications in the age before computers, Yates concluded that "technologies were adopted, not necessarily when they were invented, but when a shift or advance in managerial theory led managers to see an application for them.... The technology alone was not enough—the vision to use it in new ways was needed as well."[26] This conclusion appears to apply as well to computer technology in recent years as electronic data processing was transformed into management information systems; that is, computers became more than number crunchers and evolved toward providing information for management throughout an organization. The computer age was a time of data processing, but as technology advanced, an information age became possible. Data could be distributed through networks, interactive systems could be designed for users to access databases as decision support systems, and groups could work together to make decisions.

Information has always been necessary for managerial decision making. As transactions and interactions became more complex, information was needed for internal uses as well as for reporting to external constituents and regulatory agencies. As information-providing capabilities advanced, managers found new uses for computing machines in performing their tasks. Chandler observed that business firms need to develop competitive strengths in technical, functional, and managerial capabilities.[27] Technical capabilities develop by learning from new and existing knowledge from engineering and science. These may be firm or industry specific, but involve gathering knowledge from basic and applied research to develop or improve existing products or processes. In short, technical capabilities are the "R" in R and D (research and development) and connect the firm to our earlier discussion of innovation and dynamic capabilities for the firm. For information systems, technical capabilities involved the finding and applying of the appropriate computer hardware and software that would position a firm in a stronger competitive position.

Functional capabilities are those activities the firm must have to acquire, transform, and market its product. Production, marketing, distribution, and human resource capabilities must be developed to attain the desired volume of output and sales. Information systems are important in all functional areas: finding, developing, and rewarding the right people; planning and tracking production;

---

26. JoAnne Yates, *Control through Communications: The Rise of System in American Management* (Baltimore: Johns Hopkins University Press, 1989), pp. 274–275. A historical case study is JoAnne Yates, *Structuring the Information Age: Life Insurance and Technology in the Twentieth Century* (Baltimore: The Johns Hopkins University Press, 2005).

27. Alfred D. Chandler, Jr., *Inventing the Electronic Century: The Epic Story of the Consumer Electronics and the Computer Industries* (New York: Free Press, 2001), pp. 2–5.

maintaining contact with suppliers and customers; and engaging in electronic commerce (e-commerce) if that is appropriate or can be used to supplement traditional marketing channels.

Managerial capabilities determine strategy, formulate plans, design appropriate organizational arrangements, coordinate work flow through the value chain, and monitor performance. Huber has indicated the importance of "computer-assisted decision-making technologies (e.g., expert systems, decision support systems, online management information systems, and external information retrieval systems)" in the management process.[28] These management activities are familiar ones—the information age provided assistance for acquiring, storing, retrieving, and distributing information to be used in making decisions. Daniel McCallum's use of the telegraph to design an information system for the Erie Railroad seems trite by current practice, but perhaps what we know and how we develop, use, and transmit information today will be trite to a yet unborn generation.

Summary

This chapter has described the search for order through science and systems in management. Operations research was viewed as a modernized version of early scientific approaches to problem solving and of management's search to improve its ability to explain, predict, and control events. Operations research modified traditional production management into a broader view of production/operations management, based on more advanced statistical, computational, and mathematical techniques. Interest in production quality and lean manufacturing became an international force that leveled the competitive playing field.

Another part of this search for order and system witnessed the evolution in computing power from massive mainframes to portable computers, the development of worldwide networks of information, and a new generation of innovators and start-up ventures for microcomputing and software applications. From the invisible hand of market forces to the visible hand of management to the digital hand, which symbolized the information age, our lives were changed, and how we manage contemporary firms was revolutionized.

---

28. George P. Huber, "A Theory of the Effects of Advanced Information Technologies on Organizational Design, Intelligence, and Decision Making," *Academy of Management Review* 15 (1990), p. 47.

CHAPTER 22

Obligations and Opportunities

Management thought is both a process in and a product of its changing environment. Managers operate and make decisions in an open system of economic, social, political, and technological forces of change. Management thought is influenced by these changing forces, yet all is built on the past. From a historical perspective, this chapter examines the evolving expectations and obligations concerning business ethics and the relationship between business and society. It also examines opportunities in the global marketplace and how competing cross-culturally has influenced business decisions.

INDIVIDUALS AND ORGANIZATIONS: RELATING TO EVOLVING EXPECTATIONS

Machiavelli once said that "there is nothing more difficult to carry out nor more doubtful of success, nor more dangerous to handle, than to initiate a new order of things. For the reformer has enemies in all those who profit by the older order, and only lukewarm defenders in all those who would profit by the new order."[1] Change can come from within an individual or organization, but it is far more likely to come from without. In an open system, the economic environment can bring new opportunities as well as added competitive pressures; technology can change how we live and earn our living; the political environment may create freedom as well as limits to individual and organizational discretion; and the social environment can place more, or different, expectations on appropriate conduct. This social environment is discussed first, although it must be kept in mind that the social thread is but one part of the whole cloth.

---

1. Nicolo Machiavelli, *The Prince*, trans. Luigi Ricci (New York: New American Library, 1952), pp. 49–50.

ETHICS

The subject of ethics deals with human moral conduct, good or bad, and has occupied the thinking of theologians and philosophers since time immemorial. Ethics are the moral "oughts" that sustain a civilized society. Business transactions, so deeply embedded in trust and confidence in one's fellow human beings, have been an integral part of the search for guidelines to moral conduct beyond the question of legal boundaries. The price to charge for a product was one issue in medieval trade. Saint Thomas Aquinas stated that it should be the current market price but that, in instances of emergency or collusion, public authorities had the right to intervene and impose a fair price.[2] Sellers had a right to recover their costs, prices could vary because of supply and demand, but fraud and coercion were prohibited. We examined how the expansion of trade promoted the need for business ethics and how Friar Johannes Nider (1468) argued that business contracts for gain or profit could be spiritually acceptable as well as temporally ethical under the conditions he outlined (see Chapter 2).

Theologians and philosophers dominated ethical thinking for an extended time, but a successful business leader and founder of the world's first collegiate business school, Joseph Wharton, proposed that the curriculum of instruction

> ...should be made as to inculcate and impress upon the students... the immorality and practical inexpediency of seeking to acquire wealth by winning it from another rather than earning it through some sort of service to one's fellowmen... [and] the necessity of punishing by legal penalties and by social exclusion those persons who commit frauds, betray trusts, or steal public funds.[3]

Wharton set the ethical standards high, posing a challenge to future business schools and educators to transmit this in the classroom in the hope it would be attained in practice—a mark that would be reached with varying degrees of success.

A corporation is a legal entity, not a person, which makes the phrase "business ethics" seem incongruous. Strictly speaking, we are talking about a person's behavior as an employee or agent for a corporation. The notion of an agency relationship is not new, but interest in the topic was revived as the owners of businesses, as stockholders, became separated from a corporation's day-to-day management, and daily affairs were delegated to their agents, professional managers. Chapter 5 showed how nineteenth-century courts provided narrow interpretations of corporate charters and viewed managers as trustees of a corporation's stockholders. In the cases outlined, the courts intervened to align the interests of the principals (i.e., the

---

2. Raymond de Roover, "The Concept of Just Price: Theory and Economic Policy," *Journal of Economic History* 18 (December 1958), especially pp. 420–423.

3. Joseph Wharton to the Trustees, quoted in Stephen A. Sass, *The Pragmatic Imagination: A History of the Wharton School, 1881–1981* (Philadelphia: University of Pennsylvania Press, 1982), p. 38.

stockholders) with their agents. Still later, the separation of owners and managers became more pronounced, and with courts becoming less restrictive, there was an increase in ethical dilemmas as principal and agent interests came into conflict.

Previously we saw that agency theory involves the relationship between a principal, for example, a business owner, and an agent, for example, an employee of that business. The notion of an agency relationship is not new (Hammurabi's Code specified the need for a merchant's agent to keep records and provide receipts). Chapter 5 showed how nineteenth-century courts provided narrow interpretations of corporate charters and viewed managers as trustees representing shareholders. In the cases noted earlier, the courts intervened to align the interests of the principals with their agents. Still later, the separation of owners and managers became more pronounced, and the courts have been less restrictive, leading to more ethical dilemmas as principal and agent interests come into conflict. For instance, shareholders may want higher dividends, whereas managers may prefer to reward themselves with higher bonuses. These and other issues beg for some credo, a statement of belief about how to align the interests of all parties and prescribe the moral oughts of ethical decision making.

Understanding the what, how, and why of these conflicts of interest is always more easily seen in hindsight. The Johnson and Johnson Company's credo provides an example of explaining its purpose, providing guidance to its employees for future decision making and behavior:

> We believe our first responsibility is to the doctors, nurses, and patients, to mothers and fathers and all others who use our services... We are responsible to our employees, the men and women who work with us throughout the world... We must respect their dignity and recognize their merit... We must provide competent management, and their actions must be just and ethical.
>
> We are responsible to the communities where we live and work and the world community as well. We must be good citizens... protecting the environment and natural resources.
>
> Our final responsibility is to our stockholders. Business must make a sound profit.... Research must be carried on, innovative programs developed, and mistakes paid for... When we operate according to these principles, the stockholders should realize a fair return.[4]

Johnson and Johnson's credo became a statement of corporate beliefs that evolved as times changed and provided moral guides to be used in decision making

---

4. The entire credo may be found in Robert M. Fulmer, "Johnson & Johnson: Frameworks for Leadership," *Organizational Dynamics* 29 (Winter 2001), p. 213. The original credo is found in Robert Wood Johnson II, *Robert Johnson Talks It Over* (New Brunswick, NJ: Johnson and Johnson, 1949), p. 168.

as it faced some very perilous situations, such as the Tylenol crisis, which arose when someone purposefully contaminated bottles of these analgesic tablets. Johnson and Johnson's response was to recall all Tylenol in the interest of its customers and, as a by-product, made other firms aware of similar potential dangers, leading to new ideas about product packaging. Johnson and Johnson fulfilled its corporate credo as well as serving as a corporate role model.

When John Shad donated $23 million to the Harvard Graduate School of Business Administration for the teaching of business ethics, he commented on the decline of ethical values in the United States:

> The erosion of ethical attitudes in America since the end of World War II can be attributed to the dispersion of families, rising divorce rates, the Vietnam War, and "permissive" and "me" generations, the drug culture, the affluent society and, most important, the substitution of television for the family, church, and school as the principal purveyor of social mores...It is not enough for these [business] schools to certify that their graduates have mastered the fundamentals of their profession. The schools must hone their ability to certify that their graduates have the character and integrity to use the knowledge gained for the benefit—rather than the abuse—of society.[5]

True, business schools have an opportunity to elevate the morality of graduates by developing courses and cases to permeate their curricula and increase awareness of ethical problems as well as what might be appropriate ways of handling these situations. Less evident in Shad's comments is the responsibility of parents, schools, churches, and communities to inculcate moral dos and don'ts from the cradle onward. The expression "how the twig is bent, so grows the tree" may be trite, but it is true. Business schools, and those who employ their graduates, have a responsibility for developing ethics, but sometimes inherit a progeny shaped by earlier influences, lessening the probability of substantial change.

An early reaction to unethical business practices was legislation, such as the Interstate Commerce Act or the Sherman Anti-Trust Act. Competition from other modes of travel was more effective than legislation in limiting the strengths of the railroads, and the Clayton Anti-Trust Act (1914) closed loopholes in the Sherman Act. The Securities and Exchange Commission was established in 1934 to implement the Securities Act of 1933 and the Securities Exchange Act of 1934 to regulate securities markets, for example, full financial disclosure and independent audits of financial statements, prohibitions on "insider trading," and so forth.

Violations of these laws were rampant at the turn of the twenty-first century, and independent auditors had conflicts of interest (e.g., Arthur Andersen), top managers

---

5. John S. R. Shad, quoted in Gerald E. Cavanagh, *American Business Values*, 3rd ed. (Englewood Cliffs, NJ: Prentice Hall, 1990), p. 209.

used corporate treasuries as their personal piggy banks (e.g., Adelphia), and certain firms manipulated accounting records to conceal indebtedness (e.g., Enron) and to overstate earnings (e.g., WorldCom). So, another law, the Sarbanes-Oxley Act of 2002, was passed to create a board to oversee public auditing firms, create new disclosure requirements, provide for stronger criminal penalties for fraud, prohibit public accounting firms from serving as a consultant to firms they audit, and legislate other means to protect investors and others. Will the new act prevent future unsavory corporate and individual practices? History should teach us to be dubious about legislating to prevent unethical and illegal behavior.

Virtuous conduct is seldom newsworthy. Illegal and unethical practices splatter mistrust over all, regardless of their deeds. Machiavelli's statement about the difficulty of change is correct: Ethical behavior can be produced only by a cooperative venture among formative influences on people before they reach positions of authority and responsibility. Others, such as elected public officials, religious leaders, and educators have been known to engage in unethical behavior; thus the problem is not confined to business. Arguably, business ethics may be unable to rise above the ethics of society in general. This situation does not release managers from responsibility, but suggests that change must originate from and be implemented by multiple sources.

BUSINESS AND SOCIETY

The line between ethics and the social responsibility of business is not always clear. Johnson and Johnson's credo defined how its employees ought to behave and recognized a broader community in which it played a role. Ethics typically refers to the moral conduct of individuals, whereas social responsibility usually addresses the expectations that society has about a business firm. Ethics appears to be a broader notion, applying to expectations of personal behavior throughout life, whereas the obligations of business firms appear to be more variable and changing as social values and legal obligations change.

Business leaders have been known throughout history for their patronage and preservation of cultural heritage in literature, music, and art. Merchants as well as church officials, for instance, provided the means for artists, sculptors, and writers to become the glorifiers of the Renaissance. Businessmen, such as Robert Owen and Francis Cabot Lowell and his Waltham Associates, provided a view of the obligations of firms as the Industrial Revolution made an impact on society. Andrew Carnegie made a great deal of money and gave it all away because he believed that the acquisition of wealth imposed a duty

> to set an example of modest, unostentatious living, shunning display or extravagance; to provide moderately for the legitimate wants of those dependent upon him; and, after doing so, to consider all surplus revenues which come to him simply as trust funds, which he is called upon to administer, and strictly bound as a matter of duty to

administer in the manner which, in his judgment, is best calculated to produce the most beneficial results for the community—the man of wealth thus becoming the mere trustee and agent for his poorer brethren.[6]

Nineteenth-century court rulings placed corporations in a straitjacket, insisting that management was a trustee representing shareholders and could not do as it wished with corporate assets. Carnegie, like other business leaders of that time, engaged in individual philanthropy, as the courts did not intervene in private charity.

The legal precedents that raised doubts about whether or not a corporation could give away a portion of its profits to non-business-related endeavors were not resolved until the twentieth century. In the United States, a historic revision of the Federal Revenue Act in 1935 included a "5 percent" clause, which permitted corporations to deduct up to that amount from net income for contributions to eleemosynary institutions. Another landmark arose in 1953 with *A. P. Smith Manufacturing Company v. Barlow et al.* (13 N.J. 145). The company had donated $1,500 to Princeton University for general educational purposes. Some Smith stockholders sued, claiming that this action was outside the powers granted by the company's charter of incorporation. The New Jersey Supreme Court ruled for the company, reasoning that business support of higher education was in the best interest of a free-enterprise society. The case was not appealed, and the precedent for corporate involvement in social activities had been established.

In his study of social responsibility from 1900 to 1960, Heald wrote,

> American businessmen fully shared the social concerns and preoccupations of their fellow citizens. Although they have often been depicted—indeed, caricatured—as single-minded pursuers of profit, the facts are quite otherwise.... Like others, they were frequently troubled by the conditions they saw; and, also like others, they numbered in their ranks men who contributed both of their ideas and their resources to redress social imbalance and disorganization.[7]

Wood's study of the forces behind the passage of the Meat Inspection Act (1906) and the Pure Food and Drug Act (1906) found that business leaders were proactive, desiring laws to protect themselves as well as consumers. Passage of these laws has often been attributed to Upton Sinclair's dyspepsia-inducing book, *The Jungle*, but the facts do not support this conclusion. Individuals such as Henry J. Heinz, Frederick Pabst, Edward R. Squibb, and others from the food processing, pharmaceutical, brewing, baking, and distilling industries collaborated to support

---

6. Andrew Carnegie, *The Gospel of Wealth and Other Timely Essays* (New York: Century Co., 1901), p. 15.

7. Morrell Heald, *The Social Responsibilities of Business: Company and Community 1900–1960* (Cleveland, OH: Case Western Reserve University Press, 1970), p. 1.

this legislation.[8] These regulations protected the honest producer from the adulterer and were in the interest of business as well as being desirable public policy. This brief historical summary should provide the perspective that business firms and individuals have typically demonstrated a concern for and contributed toward the betterment of the society in which they lived, although these socially conscious efforts have been generally unpublicized.

The modern era of concern for the appropriate relationship between business and society appears to have been spearheaded by Bowen. He defined social responsibility as "the obligations of businessmen to pursue those policies, to make those decisions, or to follow those lines of action which are desirable in terms of the objectives and values of our society."[9] Synonymous with this concept are the phrases "public responsibility," "social

Keith Davis. Courtesy of Arthur G. Bedeian.

obligations," and "business morality." Bowen's book, *Social Responsibilities of the Businessman*, was sponsored by the Federal Council of the Churches of Christ in America. It focused on the ethics and human values in economic life as part of a larger society. Although Bowen sought to promote a more thoughtful attitude of businesspeople regarding their societal obligations, he recognized that business alone cannot solve the problems of economic life: "Such an assumption would be unwise and dangerous not only for society . . . but also for businesses themselves. They cannot be saddled with responsibilities which they cannot hope to discharge effectively."[10] Drawing this fine distinction between what businesses could do and should do sparked a debate that continues today.

Davis recalled that Bowen's book "crystallized" his thinking about social issues in management. "If you mess it up, you clean it up," a lesson from Davis's childhood, led him to the conclusion that because business influenced society, it had to accept the social obligations that followed.[11] In a widely cited article, Davis stated the pros and cons of social responsibility for business. Arguments in favor of social responsibility included that social responsibility served the long-run

---

8. Donna J. Wood, "The Strategic Use of Public Policy: Business Support for the 1906 Food and Drug Act," *Business History Review* 59 (Autumn 1985), pp. 403–432.

9. Howard R. Bowen, *Social Responsibilities of the Businessman* (New York: Harper and Brothers, 1953), p. 6.

10. Ibid, p. 7.

11. Keith Davis, "A Journey through Management in Transition," in Arthur G. Bedeian, ed., *Management Laureates: A Collection of Autobiographical Essays*, vol. 1 (Greenwich, CT: JAI Press, 1992), p. 285. See also Keith Davis and Robert L. Blomstrom, *Business and Its Environment* (New York: McGraw-Hill, 1966).

interest of business; that social responsibility improved the public image of business and increased its legitimacy in society; that with social responsibility, government regulation could be avoided; and that business had the resources and expertise to apply to social problems. Arguments against business acceptance of social responsibility included that as a trustee of the stockholders, management should optimize corporate return; that social involvement was costly and diluted the primary economic purpose of corporations; and that business should not be given responsibilities for which it was neither equipped to perform nor could be held accountable.[12] On balance, Davis favored social involvement on the part of business, but acknowledged Bowen's caveat that certain things should not be expected of business but should be left to others who were better able to carry out those responsibilities.

The idea that business had stakeholders became part of the domain of social responsibility. The term *stakeholder* was offered as a means of referring to the various constituencies of business who had to be considered in making decisions. Earlier writers, such as Gantt and Barnard, observed that a business firm was a part of a much larger system of investors, suppliers, employees, customers, and so on, and that the actions of these groups influenced the firm, even though they did not appear on an organizational chart. The traditional view was that management served a corporation's stockholders; in the emerging view, management had obligations toward others, its stakeholders.

Freeman noted that the word *stakeholder* entered the literature in 1963, originated by the Stanford Research Institute and defined as "those groups without whose support the organization would cease to exist."[13] Igor Ansoff, a corporate planner at Lockheed Aircraft, and his colleagues at the Stanford Research Institute intended to convey the idea that corporate objectives could not be accomplished if these stakeholder groups did not provide the necessary support. When Ansoff wrote of corporate strategy, however, he distinguished between "objectives" and "responsibilities":

> The firm has both (a) "economic" objectives aimed at optimizing the efficiency of its total resource conversion process and (b) "social" or noneconomic objectives.... In most firms the economic objectives exert the primary influence on the firm's behavior and form the main body of explicit goals used by management for guidance and control of the firm ... [while] the social objectives exert a modifying and constraining influence on management behavior.[14]

---

12. Keith Davis, "The Case for and against Business Assumptions of Social Responsibilities," *Academy of Management Journal* 16 (June 1973), pp. 312–322.

13. R. Edward Freeman, *Strategic Management: A Stakeholder Approach* (Boston: Pitman, 1984), p. 31.

14. H. Igor Ansoff, *Corporate Strategy* (New York: McGraw-Hill, 1965), pp. 37–38.

For Ansoff, the purpose of a firm was to maximize the long-term return on its assets; secondary responsibilities could not be met unless the economic objectives had been achieved. Ansoff acknowledged the earlier view of Peter Drucker that management must put economic considerations first and could justify its existence only through the economic results it produced:

> [M]anagement has failed if it fails to produce economic results. It has failed if it has not supplied goods and services desired by the consumer at a price the consumer is willing to pay. It has failed if it does not improve or at least maintain the wealth producing capacity of the economic resources entrusted to it.[15]

Drucker recognized that there could be noneconomic consequences of managerial decisions, such as improved community well-being, but that these were by-products made possible only by an emphasis on economic performance. The consensus of Drucker and Ansoff was that economic results took priority and that social or noneconomic objectives could be pursued only if the primary objectives had been attained.

Although the stakeholder concept proved useful in understanding firms in a changing economic, social, and political environment, issues remained with respect to determining who would be the primary claimants and who would be secondary. Could economic objectives override consumer safety? Or a corporate gift to education? Or the closure of an uneconomical plant that would contribute to the decline of a community or region? Carroll helped clarify these issues by describing four categories of responsibilities: economic, legal, ethical, and discretionary (later labeled philanthropic). These were "not mutually exclusive, nor . . . intended to portray a continuum with economic concerns on one end and social concerns on the other. . . . They are neither cumulative nor additive . . . [but] are simply to remind us that motives or actions can be categorized as primarily one or another of these four kinds."[16] Economic responsibilities were primary, because a business organization is a fundamental producer and seller of products and services. Legal responsibilities were those regulations and rules created by political institutions to legitimize and govern business activities. Ethical responsibilities were expectations of how a firm should conduct its business beyond what the law required. Philanthropic responsibilities were voluntary choices. The intent of this conceptual scheme was to show that corporate responsiveness was not an either-or proposition, that is, profits to the exclusion of other categories, but that each domain could interact and overlap.[17]

---

15. Peter F. Drucker, *The Practice of Management* (New York: Harper and Row, 1954), p. 8.

16. Archie B. Carroll, "A Three-Dimensional Conceptual Model of Corporate Performance," *Academy of Management Review* 4 (October 1979), pp. 499–500.

17. See Mark Schwartz and Archie B. Carroll, "Corporate Social Responsibility: A Three Domain Approach," *Business Ethics Quarterly* 13 (2003), pp. 503–530.

Business firms are part of society and depend on consumers, employees, financial institutions, and other resource suppliers from societal institutions. This is a two-way street, however; we need profitable, reputable, environmentally conscious business firms to provide the goods and services that sustain our lives and well-being. This is recognized in the writings of Ansoff, Carroll and Drucker (discussed earlier), but how this can be done is not always made explicit. The exercise of social responsibilities must be connected to the strategy of a firm and its objectives. Porter and Kramer framed the intersection in this fashion: "Strategic CSR [corporate social responsibility] unlocks shared value by investing in *social* aspects of context that strengthen company competitiveness.... A symbiotic relationship develops.... The success of the company and the success of the community becoming mutually reinforcing. Typically, the more closely tied a *social* issue is to the company's business, the greater the opportunity to leverage resources and capabilities, and benefit society."[18] Examples are offered such as Toyota's pioneering, environmentally friendly Prius; Whole Foods Market for organic, natural, and healthy products; and Nestle's Milk District in India that encourages local production, refrigeration, quality assurance, and other means to improve diets and the standard of living. Davis and Bowen noted that businesses cannot do everything, but what a firm can do within its resources and capabilities are what it *should* do. This moves the discourse about corporate social responsibility to another level with the emphasis on "doing good," rather than unfocused efforts to "look good."

Management Opportunities in a Global Arena

The history of trade among nations is more ancient than the recording of those transactions. Coins, clay tablets, and the walls of ancient forts tell the story of people engaged in economic transactions and weave the threads of civilization to bind as well as to put people of differing cultures in a competitive stance.[19] The idea of the globalization of business is not new, and this section will briefly trace the beginnings and examine the challenges and opportunities that face management.

THE GLOBALIZATION OF BUSINESS

Trade among nations has, more often than not, been initiated and carried out as a political strategy. This conclusion does not preclude those voyages motivated by

---

18. Michael E. Porter and Mark R. Kramer, "Strategy and Society: The Link Between Competitive Advantage and Corporate Social Responsibility," *Harvard Business Review* 84 (December 2006), p. 89.

19. Miriam Beard, *A History of Business*, 2 vols. (Ann Arbor: University of Michigan Press, 1938); and Karl Moore and David Lewis, *Foundations of Corporate Empire: Is History Repeating Itself?* (London: Prentice Hall, 2000).

curiosity or the desire for a more varied menu or assortment of products, but the main driving force behind the great discoveries of unknown lands and peoples was provided by the kings, queens, and potentates of various nations. National treasuries held the finances that could set on the uncharted waters the ships and explorers who would venture forth to discover new trade routes, find novel products, build empires, and strengthen the homeland in its standard of living and political clout.

The practice of mercantilism used politics to subsidize local business, tariffs to keep out products from alien lands, colonies to ensure a steady supply of raw materials, and a strong navy to keep the lanes of commerce free from pirates and interlopers. Trading companies, such as the East India Company, the Hudson Bay Company, and the Dutch East India Company, were chartered by their governments to have a monopoly over trade in the colonies of these nations. Canada, India, and the United States were colonies of Great Britain; France, Belgium, Portugal, and Germany had colonies in Africa; Indonesia was a Dutch colony, then called Dutch East India; and French Indo-China (today's Vietnam, Laos, and Cambodia) was France's colony. In each case, these colonies provided raw materials and labor and provide an early example of the globalization of business.

Mercantilism was not a particularly successful economic policy: Inefficient industries were kept alive, consumers had less variety from which to choose, colonists were bound in economic servitude, and strong defense forces had to be maintained to protect a nation's economic privileges. Adam Smith intended to sweep away mercantilism, to show that national wealth depended on trade rather than on the balance of power, and on free markets rather than on the care and feeding of uneconomical enterprise. David Ricardo, an early nineteenth-century economist, suggested that free trade provided the best of all possible worlds because all nations would concentrate on what they could best produce. What was needed was not a national economic policy, such as mercantilism, but rather a market exchange system that allowed each nation to find its comparative advantage among other trading nations.

As colonialism and mercantilism faded, trade among nations continued to thrive even though transportation was by sail or steam on the sea, by railroads on land, and by barges on the canals and rivers. In its early economic development, the United States was a debtor nation, depending on capital from abroad. The J. & W. Seligman Company, one of the first U.S. investment banking houses, had branches in London, Paris, and Frankfurt in addition to its New York headquarters. The Seligmans and representatives of other emerging U.S. banking houses went abroad to sell the securities necessary to provide the capital for the growing U.S. industrial system. Mira Wilkins observed that as late as 1914, the United States was still a debtor nation, borrowing more from abroad than it invested.[20] The United States was a lively trader in the Pacific (some eighty U.S. firms had branches in China

---

20. Mira Wilkins, *The Emergence of Multinational Enterprise: American Business Abroad from the Colonial Era to 1914* (Cambridge, MA: Harvard University Press, 1970), pp. 201–207.

alone), in South America, Africa, continental Europe, and Great Britain, but it still imported capital to fuel the fires of financing the growth of its own industry.

Technology has always been an important factor in the advancement of trade. Early trade routes hugged the shoreline because of fragile ships and poor navigational aids. Stronger masts, larger sails, and the mastery of celestial navigational techniques broadened trade horizons. Steam-powered ships, the telegraph, and transoceanic cables improved communication and reduced travel time. Faster ships, aircraft, and the wireless radio presaged the coming of jet travel and global communication by sky-based and orbiting satellites. *The Lexus and the Olive Tree* is a metaphor to illustrate the transition from the older forces of cultural identity and nationalism (the olive tree) to the Lexus announcing newer forces of economic integration and the coming of borderless business.[21] Transportation and telecommunication revolutions continue to push back trade frontiers, enabling the local markets of yesteryears to become the electronic commerce and global markets of today.

What some authors refer to as the "new" global competition is, in historical perspective, an extension of the past. The difference is primarily in the flattened world of improvements in communication and transportation that enable global exchanges of products, services, and information in a speedier fashion. If anyone had suggested in the 1960s that the U.S. automobile, electronics, tire, and other industries were in danger of losing market share to competitors from other nations, the idea would have appeared ridiculous. Seemingly safe in their market enclaves, once-dominant firms were beset by imports from nations that had cheaper labor, had found a better way to produce, or could deliver improved quality at a better price.

The tire and rubber industry provides an example of evolving multinational enterprise in the twentieth century. Natural rubber was an imported raw material for the United States, Great Britain, Germany, France, Italy, and other nations. At one stage, these nations integrated backward by starting plantations in favorable climates to cultivate the rubber tree, whereas other nations had to buy from rubber-producing nations. The tire-manufacturing nations (primarily those mentioned earlier) provided for their home markets as well as distributing and selling abroad. As markets expanded, it became economical to establish tire-manufacturing plants in other countries: for example, Great Britain's Dunlop went to Canada, where U.S. tire makers also competed; Firestone was acquired by Japan; U.S. Rubber changed its name to Uniroyal and then was acquired by France's Michelin; Goodrich exited the tire business; and General Tire was sold to a German firm. French stated that "the overall expansion of multinational investment [in the tire industry] was primarily a response to protectionism."[22] As an illustration, Michelin and Dunlop

---

21. Thomas L. Friedman, *The Lexus and the Olive Tree: Understanding Globalization* (New York: Farrar, Straus, and Giroux, 1999).

22. Michael J. French, *The U.S. Tire Industry: A History* (Boston: Twayne, 1991), p. 127.

built plants in the United States to avoid exclusion from that expanding market, while at the same time U.S. firms built factories and sales outlets in France for the same reason. Similar reasons have led automobile manufacturers, such as Honda and Toyota, to build factories in the United States.

Global rivalry has led to "outsourcing" jobs, that is, finding ways to lower costs and/or gain outside expertise by putting out work to other nations. For example, Nike and Reebok outsource most of the labor for their footwear lines and Levi Strauss for its clothing products. If the reader is in doubt, check the clothing labels in your closet to identify where those products were manufactured. Hong Kong is probably the busiest entrepôt for transshipping electronics, shoes, and clothing. Outsourcing has been one of many practices that raise issues about how workers are treated and calls for codes of ethics among nations that trade.

This more recent wave of globalization has also touched off numerous attempts at trade alliances. The North America Free Trade Agreement (commonly known as NAFTA), the European Union, and the Asia-Pacific Economic Cooperation agreement represent attempts to break down trade barriers among nations. Is this David Ricardo's law of comparative advantage coming to fruition? Will these alliances foster a new mercantilism, favoring a nation's partners but excluding free trade among all nations? Vernon warns of the tensions between national and regional trade agreements and the promise and the issues that face multinational enterprises in a world of nation-states.[23] Neomercantilism would be dangerous as a national or regional trade policy, for it could represent protectionism raised to a new level. This book focuses on history and the lessons it offers; what happens from here on depends on what lessons are learned.

MANAGING ACROSS CULTURES

As firms become more global in their outlook and operations, they find themselves working with diverse cultures. Culture is a slippery concept, but for convenience's sake, as used here, the term means a set of beliefs held in common by a group of people about economic, social, and political forms of behavior. The bottom line to globalization and culture is, how does a person behave ethically when in another culture? Is there one ethical imperative? Further, do individuals and firms follow the customs and ethics of the country in which they are doing business or are there some universal guides to conduct? What the people of a particular nation believe and how they behave is a product of their heritage as well as the present influences in their lives.

One approach has been to define "hypernorms," certain rights that should be respected across cultures: the right to freedom of movement, to freedom from

---

23. Raymond Vernon, *In the Hurricane's Eye: The Troubled Prospects of Multinational Enterprises* (Cambridge, MA: Harvard University Press, 1998).

torture, to the ownership of property, to physical security, to a fair trial, of freedom of speech and association, to subsistence, to a minimal education, to political participation, and to nondiscriminatory treatment on the basis of such traits as gender or sex.[24] A study of normative guidelines established by a variety of international groups indicated some basics were agreed on: adequate health and safety standards; the rights of all persons to life, liberty, personal security, and privacy; and environmental standards regarding pollution.[25] Some support for this is a study of Russian and American managers that suggested agreement about certain moral minimums, but differences about "local norms" in their respective counties.[26] For managers and employees, this suggests expectations about certain behaviors that exist across cultures, but vary within particular cultures.

The GLOBE research (Chapter 20) provides the most complete examination of the different dimensions existing within the cultures available to us at this time. Readers will recall leadership was culturally relative, though clusters of countries exhibited similarities. In attempts to examine ethics across cultures, these GLOBE cultural dimensions provided the measuring stick. In one study, the higher need for ethics was greater among the GLOBE dimensions of Assertiveness, Performance orientation, Power distance and Group collectivism and found in China, Poland, the United States, Hong Kong, Hungary, and South Korea. The group with a lower desire for ethics had GLOBE dimensions of Institutional collectivism, Future orientation, Gender egalitarianism, Humane orientation, and Uncertainty avoidance in the countries of Japan, France, Italy, Finland, Estonia, and Spain. In summary: "The higher scores for these practices are connected with a greater need for well-established ethical standards and values. The lower scores for these scales are connected with a lower need for ethics. People are satisfied with the current level of these practices."[27]

In Chapter 20 we addressed the question of job design and how this is an important part of an employee's life and may or may not be different in global settings. England and his colleagues studied this question and found a clear differentiation between those who defined work as something they had to do or were forced to do and those who viewed work positively and as an activity that produced something of

---

24. Thomas Donaldson, *The Ethics of International Business* (New York: Oxford University Press, 1989), p. 81.

25. William C. Frederick, "The Moral Authority of Transnational Corporate Codes," *Journal of Business Ethics*, 10 (March 1991), pp. 166–167.

26. Wendy Bailey and Andrew Spicer, "When Does National Identity Matter? Convergence and Divergence in International Business Ethics," *Academy of Management Journal* 50 (December 2007), pp. 1462–1480.

27. Ruth Alas, "Ethics in Countries with Different Cultural Dimensions" *Journal of Business Ethics* 69 (December 2006), pp. 237–247. See also Christian J. Resick, Paul J. Hanges, Marcus W. Dickson, and Jacqueline K. Mitchelson, "A Cross-Cultural Examination of the Endorsement of Ethical Leadership," *Journal of Business Ethics* 63 (February 2006), pp. 345–359.

value for society. For the former group, work had a low central value in life; these individuals placed more emphasis on the physical and economic conditions of work. The latter group placed a high centrality value on work and saw it as more of an avenue for self-expression. Of the countries studied, Japan had high work centrality; Yugoslavia (before its breakup) and Israel had moderately high work centrality; the United States and Belgium had average work centrality; the Netherlands and Germany had moderately low centrality; and Great Britain had the lowest centrality.[28] Although there were some differences by age, sex, and education, these attitudes toward working were clearly differentiated by the value attached to work as an activity. Overall, interesting work ranked number one, followed in order of importance by good pay, good interpersonal relations, job security, autonomy, and the opportunity to learn new things.

The literature on managing across cultures forms a constantly expanding universe of studies. In addition to the aforementioned summaries on the meaning of working are studies on human-resource management, organizational behavior, information and technology transfer, strategic management, and business-government relations. There are enduring questions, such as, how much do cultures vary? How does this variance influence, for example, human-resource management practices? Is this variance converging, diverging, or stable in terms of culturally held attitudes and beliefs when one country moves further along in becoming industrialized? If there is variance across cultures and, at best, a clustering of similarities among some cultures, does this mean that management theories and practices are culture bound?

Hofstede maintained that U.S. management theories are culturally constrained because management is different in every country. He characterized these cultural differences in terms of the following dimensions: power distance, defined as the degree of inequality among individuals considered by that culture as normal; individualism versus collectivism; masculinity ("tough values," such as assertiveness) versus femininity ("tender values"); uncertainty avoidance; and long-term versus short-term orientation.[29] Hofstede presented the United States as below average on uncertainty avoidance (i.e., more willing to take risks), whereas Japan was high on this dimension; Japan was high on masculinity, the Netherlands, low; France showed greater power distance (less equality) and somewhat more femininity; Asian countries appeared to be more oriented toward the long term, Americans less so. The GLOBE studies built on Hofstede and expanded our understanding of differences among and between cultures.

---

28. MOW International Research Team, *The Meaning of Working* (New York: Academic Press, 1987), especially pp. 84, 244–245.

29. Geert Hofstede, *Culture's Consequences: Comparing Values, Behavior, Institutions, and Organizations Across Nations* (Thousand Oaks, CA: Sage, 2001); Hofstede's pioneering work was a cross-cultural study of IBM, *Culture's Consequences: International Differences in Work-Related Values* (Thousand Oaks, CA: Sage, 1980).

Ethics, corporate social responsibility, and laws further complicate the issue of competing across national borders. The U.S. Foreign Corrupt Practices Act of 1977 (amended in 1988) forbade publicly traded U.S. companies from making illicit payments to officials of foreign governments or to foreign political parties, their officials, or intermediaries for the purpose of acquiring or maintaining its business. This act has been controversial and makes relatively small payments legal (called "grease"), such as expediting some activity, such as a work permit or visa; but forbids relatively large payments to political figures or their intermediaries to gain or keep a firm in business—this is considered bribery.[30] The line between grease payments and bribery may be very thin and the stuff that keeps lawyers busy.

The search for hypernorms is worthy, but ethics, like leadership, is culturally bound and contingent on where a firm expects to do business. An extensive survey by Enderle found a general belief that "good business and good ethics go hand in hand" but different nations and regions faced particular types of problems. The most common ethical issues mentioned were corruption (defined as the "misuse of power for private benefits"), the need for integrity in business and political leadership, and for greater corporate responsiveness to stakeholders and making more companies accountable.[31]

Choosing to enter the global market involves more than an understanding of cultural and ethical issues. Firms must ask whether their core competencies/strengths are appropriate to the opportunities in a particular market; will foreign investment be welcomed; can a transfer of technology benefit all; does the political system provide safeguards for employees and intellectual and physical property; is the economic system conducive to private, market-driven enterprise; is the rivalry in the intended market currently too formidable; and the list could continue. Overall, the question is a strategic one: Will competing abroad serve the long-run best interests of our stakeholders? Technologies in communication and transportation make global trading more attractive, but age-old questions of economics, politics, and social values persist.

Summary

Chapter 22 has been about obligations to behave in a legal, ethical, and socially responsible manner to compete globally across different cultures. Management thought evolves and arrives at a different, but not always a better, place. This chapter has used history as a framework to enrich an understanding of the present human condition. Ethics, codes of moral conduct, have long been of concern in history,

---

30. Archie B. Carroll and Ann K. Buchholtz, *Business and Society: Ethics and Stakeholder Management*, 6th ed. (Mason, OH: Thomson/Southwestern, 2006), pp. 312–314.

31. Georges Enderle, "A Worldwide Survey of Business Ethics in the 1990s," *Journal of Business Ethics* 16 (1997), pp. 1475–1483.

but people still struggle to make the right decisions as individuals, and this struggle is confounded as they come under the influence of others in organizations. Social responsibility, the moral conduct of business in its environment, has also undergone changes over time. Managers were previously held to be trustees of a corporation's shareholders, but their role became more complicated with the introduction of the notion of stakeholders. Economic performance is necessary for survival of the firm; compliance with legal bounds must exist; but beyond that, a firm can choose how to be responsive to the needs of its social environment.

The ancient practice of trade among nations was reviewed. Globalization has flattened the world and accelerated the pace of change because of advancements in transportation and especially in telecommunication. Global markets bring new opportunities, yet jingoism threatens the prospects of more open markets. Although people may have gained knowledge of those of other nations, it is often without a greater understanding of them.

CHAPTER
23

Epilogue

W ithin the practices of the past are relevant lessons for the future; there is a flow of events and ideas that link yesterday, today, and tomorrow in a continuous stream. We occupy but one point in this stream of time; we can see the distant past with increasing clarity as our research continues, but as we approach the present, our perspective becomes less clear. New ideas, subtle shifts in emphases and themes, and emerging environmental events all influence the evolution of contemporary management thought.

Throughout the preceding chapters, management has been viewed as an academic discipline and as an activity essential to all organized efforts. With respect to both perspectives, management finds its basis in the efficient allocation and utilization of human and physical resources necessary to attain organizational objectives. In this sense, throughout history, management thought and managerial activity have mirrored one another. Our intent in undertaking the present volume has been to reflect on these mirrored images and provide a bridge over the stream of time, uniting the past and present as they lead into the future.

Identifiable trends, forces, and philosophies have emerged in our analysis of evolving management thought and practice. Management thinking and management practice are undeniably both products of historical processes. Internally, management thought has passed through phases characterized by differing emphases on the technical aspects of production, workplace behavior and the satisfaction of innate human needs, the role of leadership in guiding goal-directed systems, and the nature of organizations as vehicles for greater good, and on the organizational and methods facets of the problems encountered in guiding goal-directed systems. Externally, management thought has been influenced by evolving technologies, by changing economic, social, and political values, and by environmental and international challenges.

FIGURE 23 - 1 **SYNOPSIS OF THE MODERN ERA**

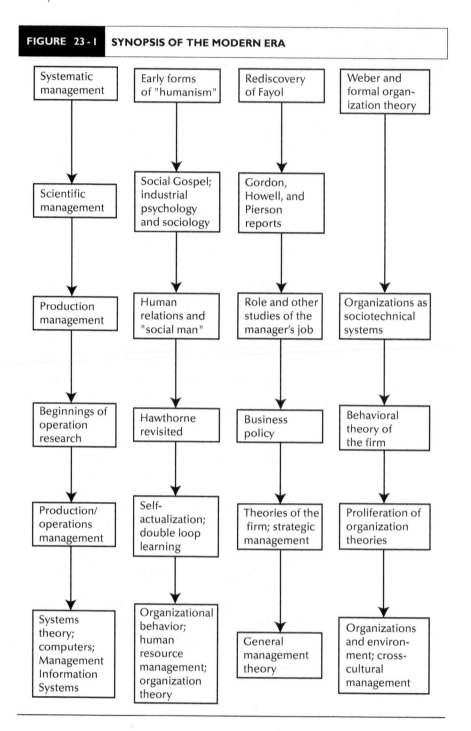

Figure 23-1 is a somewhat sketchy summary of the broad swath that has been cut through this study of management. The modern era has witnessed a proliferation of approaches, all with the same goal of meeting organizational objectives and satisfying human needs. The search continues for both better theory and improved practice, with each new approach encouraging the next. This search has made management—as an academic discipline and as an activity—the stimulating intellectual and practical exercise that it is today. Management is one of the most dynamic of all professions; as technology, institutions, and people change, management thinking has evolved to cope with humankind's oldest problem—allocating and utilizing scarce resources to meet the manifold desires of an ever-changing world. Today is not like yesterday, nor will tomorrow be like today; yet today is a synergism of all our yesterdays, and tomorrow will be the same. Not only does history tell us what has happened in the past, but it also teaches us what we must do today and tomorrow. In this sense, perhaps the most important lesson is, as Shakespeare, writing in *The Tempest* some four centuries ago, discerned, "What is past is prologue."

Name Index

Subject Index